500 SELECTED SERMONS
Volumes 1 and 2

T. De Witt Talmage

500 SELECTED SERMONS

T. DE WITT TALMAGE

IN TWENTY VOLUMES

VOLUME 1

BAKER BOOK HOUSE
Grand Rapids, Michigan

Reprinted 1978 by
Baker Book House Company

Library of Congress Catalog
Card Number: 56-10681

ISBN: 0-8010-8840-2

PHOTOLITHOPRINTED BY CUSHING - MALLOY, INC.
ANN ARBOR, MICHIGAN, UNITED STATES OF AMERICA
1978

Introduction

by

CLARENCE E. MACARTNEY

When I was a senior at the University of Wisconsin, I heard Talmage lecture at the Monona Lake Chautauqua. How clearly I can see him now after the lapse of all these years! He stood well back from the edge of the platform, above the medium height, well-proportioned, a large powerful frame, frock coat with black string tie tucked under a lie-down collar, his hair gray and his face broad, human, and kindly. He commenced speaking with his eyes closed. The voice, although not melodious like Bryan's, was powerful, arresting, and stirring. He began with a description of a man riding in a buckboard over the Illinois prairies in the springtime when the flowers were blooming. It was a vivid picture of the flowers of the field sweeping the bellies of the horses as the buckboard was driven across the plains. This went on for a minute or two. Then, opening his eyes, he leaped forward to the front of the platform, and with a mighty voice pronounced a sentence which I have not forgotten. There was something about the man that at once appealed to you. He had the air of friendliness, and also of complete command of the situation, as if there were no doubt at all that he would carry his audience with him, which, of course, he did. Many of those who formed their conceptions of Dr. Talmage from the unfriendly caricatures and criticisms in the newspapers had conceived an intense dislike for him; but that dislike generally disappeared when

Introduction

they saw the man and heard him speak. It was so with the renowned actor Joseph Jefferson. Jefferson and Talmage became intimate one winter during a stay in Florida. Jefferson recalled the famous sermon of Talmage against the theater, preached in the tabernacle at Brooklyn, and how he and other actors had gone to hear the sermon. "When I entered that church to hear your sermon, Doctor," said Jefferson, "I hated you. When I left the church I loved you."

Talmage was a unique and remarkable man. As his son expressed it in his memorial sermon for his father, no matter what it was that he did, he was sure to do it differently from anyone else. Talmage himself said: "Each life is different from every other life. God never repeats himself and he never intended two men to be alike." Certainly there was never another Talmage.

T. DeWitt Talmage was born January 7, 1832, at Middlebrook, New Jersey, where his father kept a tollgate. He was the youngest of eleven children. Four of the sons became honored ministers of the gospel, one of them, John Van Nest, a distinguished missionary in China. His father and mother, like the parents of John the Baptist, were "both righteous before God" and came of a godly line. His grandparents on the Talmage side had been converted at one of Finney's evangelistic meetings. Talmage said of his mother that when she led the family prayers she would often pray, "O Lord God, I ask not for my children wealth or honor; but I do ask that they all may be subjects of thy converting grace." When Talmage was still a very young child his parents removed to a farm near Somerville, New Jersey. This farm, with the farmhouse, and the barn and the brook, and the watering trough, and the horses

Introduction

and the carriages, frequently appears in Talmage's sermons.

At nineteen years of age Talmage entered the University of the City of New York, where he studied law. He then went to the New Brunswick Seminary of the Dutch Reformed Church. At the seminary he evinced the same extraordinary, original, and somewhat sensational style of expression in preaching as characterized him in after life. One of his instructors said to him, after he had preached his first class sermon, "DeWitt, if you don't change your style of thought and expression, you will never get a call to any church in Christendom as long as you live."

I once talked with a classmate of Dr. Talmage and asked him about his early impressions of the great preacher when he was a student in the seminary. His reply was, "Exactly the same in personality and style as he was in the days of his fame. His first sermon," he said, "was on the text, Prov. 18:24, 'There is a friend that sticketh closer than a brother.' In the sermon he described the scene in heaven when Christ set out on the mission of redemption. The astonished angels said to him, 'Shall ten thousand of us weave our wings together to make a fit chariot for thee to ride upon in thy descent to that fallen world?' This offer Christ rejected with a wave of his hand. The angels then exclaimed, 'Shall we bring together all the clouds of heaven and make a fit throne for thee to sit upon?' But this offer, too, Christ refused, saying, 'No, I cannot go in such a way.' And then he commanded them, 'Take off these royal robes,' and the angels reluctantly obeyed. And then he started away from them on his descent to earth without any of his royal insignia, alone, without a single attendant, and the

Introduction

angelic hosts, amazed, crowded out on heaven's vast balcony to see him descend, and they gazed after him, they talked so loud together about his wonderful condescension and love for men that the shepherds of Bethlehem heard them." Anyone who is familiar with the sermons of Talmage will at once recognize him in this first sermon.

On July 26, 1856, Talmage was ordained and installed as pastor of the Dutch Reformed Church at Belleville, New Jersey, near Newark. He gave an amusing account of how on the first Sabbath he had his sermon at his side as he sat on one of the great horsehair sofas which were the pulpit style in that day. To his consternation the sermon slipped down through an opening in the back of the sofa, and while the congregation were singing the hymn before the sermon he had to get down on his hands and knees and recover the manuscript. On another occasion, when gas was being introduced for the first time into the church, he planned to read an introductory part of his sermon and then launch out upon the great sea of extemporaneousness. But as he drew near the end of the written part, he became terrified and prayed that the lights would fail. His prayer was answered and the gas lamps went out, leaving the room in darkness. He then said to the congregation, "It is impossible to proceed." But when he got home he felt it to be humiliating that a man with a message from the Lord God Almighty should be dependent upon paper mills and gas meters. This made him resolve to strike out on a new line of preaching without notes. As an extemporary preacher he had few peers.

In 1859, Talmage was called to a Dutch Reformed Church in Syracuse, New York. There he attracted some little attention, and at Hudson, New

Introduction

York, delivered his first lecture, for a fee of $50. In 1862 he became the pastor of the Second Reformed Church of Philadelphia. In this same year Phillips Brooks began his notable ministry in Holy Trinity Church, Philadelphia. Nothing could have been more striking and, in a way, sensational to the Philadelphians than the pulpit style of Talmage. His preaching at once attracted great throngs. The period of the Civil War was a great age for the preacher. The times were stirring, the atmosphere was charged with electricity. A great period like that is stimulating to the intellect and imagination of the preacher. It is not strange, then, that when one calls the roll of America's famous preachers, he discovers that so many of them, Theodore Parker, Henry Ward Beecher, Matthew Simpson, Benjamin Morgan Palmer, Phillips Brooks, and DeWitt Talmage, belong to that age.

During this Philadelphia pastorate, the wife of Talmage was drowned when they were boating on the Schuylkill River.

By 1869 the fame of Talmage had gone abroad. In that year he was called to churches in Chicago, Boston, and San Francisco, and the Central Presbyterian Church of Brooklyn. He accepted the call to the depleted and faction-torn church in Brooklyn, and was installed as pastor by the Presbytery of Brooklyn, March 22, 1869. In a short time the congregations were so large that the church was not able to accommodate them. A new church, which was called the Tabernacle, was hastily built. This was destroyed by fire December 22, 1872, the first of three tabernacles to suffer such a fate. Talmage, like Beecher, held that the conventional church architecture and the pulpit arrangement were a hindrance to the preacher. Like Beecher, he had

Introduction

no pulpit, but a long platform. He made full use of his long platform and roamed to and fro over it, preaching with every inch of his body. The people were all seated near him, in front, around him, and above him. There is no doubt that for a direct appeal to an audience this is the best arrangement. The second Tabernacle was destroyed by fire in 1889, and the third in 1894. At this time Talmage had the largest congregation of any preacher in the world.

His unconventional manner and his sometimes extravagant statements made him the object of much ridicule and hostile attack. In 1879 he was accused before the Brooklyn Presbytery of falsehood and deceit, and of using improper methods of preaching which tended to bring religion into contempt. On all these charges he was aquitted. Talmage attributed much of his world-fame to the attacks that other preachers, and later, the newspapers, made upon him.

Talmage created an early sensation in Brooklyn by his explorations into the night life of New York, accompanied by elders of his church and police officers. This gave him material for some of his most graphic descriptions. They remind one of another great pictorial preacher, Thomas Guthrie, of Edinburgh, and his moving descriptions of the submerged populace of Edinburgh.

Like most great preachers, he preached to the heart. He made it the aim in his preaching always to help somebody. He said: "A preacher should start out with the idea of helping somebody. Everybody wants help except a fool."

One of the secrets of his success, undoubtedly, lay in the fact that he had a warm heart. There was a deep vein of sentiment in him. He would never

Introduction

allow the spot on the barn door at East Hampton, Long Island, where his deceased son, DeWitt, had carved his initials to be painted over or changed. He had unshaken faith in the Bible. "Science and revelation," he said, "are the bass and soprano of the same tune." Colonel Ingersoll, with his attacks on the Bible, Talmage likened to a grasshopper on a railway line when the express comes thundering along.

The preacher kept himself in physical condition by walking every day of his life; every day except Friday, Saturday, and Sunday, regardless of the weather, he covered five miles. His physical energy was inexhaustible. He said Gladstone was the only man he ever met who walked fast enough for him.

After the destruction of his third Tabernacle, Dr. Talmage became the Associate Pastor of the First Presbyterian Church of Washington. For his installation sermon he preached one of his most picturesque discourses, "All Heaven Is Looking On," from Heb. 12:1, "Compassed about with so great a cloud of witnesses."

After four years as pastor in Washington, he resigned his charge in 1899 and until his death in 1902 gave himself to lecturing, preaching, and editorial work. He was taken ill on a trip to Mexico and returned to his home in Washington, where he died April 12, 1902.

Talmage was a great traveler. He found it easy to meet distinguished men, and even the crowned heads of Europe. Through the *Christian Herald*, he loaded a ship with food supplies for the victims of a famine in Russia.

A remarkable thing about the career of Talmage is that from the time he began to draw great crowds in Philadelphia until his death in 1902, almost forty

Introduction

years, his popularity never waned. One of the secrets of his appeal undoubtedly was his invincible optimism. This radiated not only in his written and spoken sermons, but in his personal appearance, his expressive and mobile and ever smiling mouth. When he commenced his ministry he was not strong. Now and then he would overhear people say, "Ah, he is not long for this world." This made him resolve that never in meeting other people or in conversation with them would he say anything that was depressing. He was a great optimist. He believed that there was as great a number of people out of the Church as in it who followed the teachings of Christianity. It was in keeping with this invincible optimism that the last sermon that he wrote was a sermon on thanksgiving, Ps. 33:2: "Sing unto him with the psaltery."

Although not a doctrinal preacher at all, Talmage was true to the great evangelical doctrines of Christianity, and all his sermons, while they do not set forth or analyze those doctrines, are radiant with their light. He was brought to a decision for Christ by an evangelist, Truman Osborne, who was visiting the Talmage home. Osborne asked Talmage's father if all the children were Christians. His father told him that all were Christians but DeWitt. Then Osborne, looking into the fireplace, told the story of the Lost Sheep. It was this that brought Talmage into the fold.

One of the most far-reaching features of Talmage's ministry was his printed sermons. Looking one day at a pile of sermons that he had written and preached, he said to his wife, "God must have some other use for these sermons, and intend them for others than just those who heard me preach them."

Introduction

This conviction led him to make the arrangements for the weekly publication of his sermons.

A contributory cause also was the visit to Talmage of a young man, who afterward became eminent as a lawyer. He told Talmage that he was studying law in a distant city and that he must give up his studies unless he could be permitted to take down the sermons through his skill as a stenographer and arrange for their sale. At the time Talmage declined. But after some months had passed he began to reflect that it would be too bad if this brilliant young man was not able to get a legal education. He then allowed the young man to take down the sermons. Within three weeks from all over the United States requests began to come in for the sermons. They were published weekly by as many as three thousand, five hundred newspapers, and by this means Talmage spoke to a greater multitude than had any preacher of Christianity up to that time. Thousands of persons living today will remember the weekly sermons of Dr. Talmage as they appeared in the newspapers on Monday morning and in the *Christian Herald,* the weekly magazine of which he became the editor.

His style was pictorial and, like most of the great preachers, his homiletic method was topical rather than textual or expository. Illustrations came naturally to him. He said: "It has always been the question with me how to get rid of illustrations. I naturally think in metaphor." Dr. David Gregg, a contemporary in Brooklyn, thus describes his style: "He thinks in pictures and he who thinks in pictures thinks vividly. He paints with a large brush, with colors that burn and glow, and nations gather round his pictures and feel an uplift and an holy thrill." Perhaps his sermon, "All Heaven Looking On" is

Introduction

as good an example as might be quoted of his vivid imaginative style.

The thread of the atonement ran all through his preaching. Christ to him was central and the cross was central and cardinal. The future life and heaven were very real to him. Bidding good-by to an old friend who was on his deathbed, Talmage said, as if the man were going to leave for another city, "Give my love to my boy" (referring to his son DeWitt who had died years before). His emphasis on the grand particularities of the Christian faith was one of the secrets of his popularity with the masses of the people. Senator Beveridge, who heard him frequently, said: "The American people are tired of hearing learned and entertaining lectures delivered under the guise of sermons. They hunger and thirst for the preaching of the faith, unweakened by doubts, criticisms, or explanations, uncompromisingly delivered as Dr. Talmage gave it."

The desire to help and to save sounded in all his sermons. One of his famous themes on the text, "The people that do know their God shall be strong, and do exploits," Dan. 11:32, was "The Three Greatest Things to Do — Save a Man, Save a Woman, Save a Child." The contagious optimism and hopefulness of Dr. Talmage comes out in all his sermons. His last sermon, on "David's Harp," strikes this characteristic note of hope: "The greatest victories are yet to be gained; the grandest churches are yet to be built; the mightiest anthems are yet to be hoisted; the most beautiful Madonnas are yet to be painted; the most triumphant processions are yet to march. Oh, what a world this will be, when it rotates in its orbit a redeemed planet, girdled with spontaneous harvests, and enriched by orchards whose fruits are speckless and redundant;

Introduction

and the last pain will have vanished, and the last tear wept, and the last groan uttered, and there shall be nothing to hurt or destroy in all God's holy mountain!"

Most of the texts of Talmage's sermons were taken from the Old Testament. Three hundred and five of his texts are Old Testament texts and one hundred and eighty-five New Testament texts. Very often the sermons deal with some Old Testament scene or history, and this gives the preacher an opportunity to introduce his sermon with a piece of description or historical narrative. A good example of this is his well-known sermon, "The King's Wagons," on the text from Gen. 45:27, "And when he saw the wagons." The sermon commences with a description of the capital of the Pharaohs: "There were temples aflame with red sandstone, entered by gateways that were guarded by pillars bewildering with hieroglyphics, and wound with brazen serpents, and adorned with winged creatures, their eyes and beaks and pinions glittering with precious stones. There were marble columns blooming into white flower buds. There were stone pillars, the tops bursting into the shape of the lotus when in full bloom along the avenues lined with sphinx and fane and obelisk. There were princes who came in gorgeously upholstered palanquins, carried by servants in scarlet, or else drawn in vehicles with snow-white horses, golden-bitted, six abreast, dashing at full run. There were fountains from stone-wreathed vases climbing the ladder of the sun."

Thus the great word painter made the palace of Pharaoh, with all its splendor, live before his hearers. "Overdone! Too ornate!" the critic would say. But the fact is that the people enjoyed it. Talmage knew that there is a poet hidden away in the com-

Introduction

mon man, and to that man he made his appeal. In these sermons on Old Testament themes, Talmage always is able to draw simple, straightforward, and helpful lessons. For instance, in this sermon on "when he saw the wagons," his two chief points are: First, that the king's wagons bring us corn and meat and many changes of garment. By this he means God's provisions for our needs in this world. Secondly, the king's wagons bring us good news. Here he strikes the high note of immortality and union with Christ and with our departed friends. Our faith brings us word that our Joseph, Jesus, is yet alive, and that he sends messages of pardon, of peace, of life, from heaven — corn for our hunger, raiment for our nakedness. "Glorious religion!" A religion made not out of death's-heads and crossbones and an undertaker's screw driver, but one abounding with life and sympathy and gladness! The king's wagons will take us to see our lost friends." Here the great preacher has a beautiful description of a stormy Sabbath at the New Jersey farmhouse where he was brought up. On those Sabbaths the children were left at home. He tells how at twelve o'clock they would go to the window to see if their father and mother were coming, and then at half past twelve, and then at one o'clock. "After a while Mary or Daniel or DeWitt would shout, 'The wagon's coming.' And then we would see it winding out of the woods and over the brook, and through the lane and up in front of the old farmhouse, and then we would rush out, leaving the doors wide open, with many things to tell them, asking them many questions."

The clearness of Talmage's homiletic style is brought out in his sermon, "The Laughter of the Bible." The sermon has five divisions: First, Sarah's

Introduction

laugh, or the laugh of skepticism. Secondly, David's laugh, or that of spiritual exultation: "Then was our mouth filled with laughter." Thirdly, the fool's laugh, or that of sinful merriment, or "the crackling of thorns under a pot." Fourthly, God's laugh, or that of infinite condemnation: "He that sitteth in the heavens shall laugh." And fifthly, heaven's laugh, or the laugh of eternal triumph: "Blessed are ye that weep now: for ye shall laugh."

Another interesting example of Talmage's use of Old Testament incidents is his sermon on the queen of Sheba, "Behold, the half was not told," I Kings 10:7. The sermon opened with a description of Solomon's palace. Here, as we have seen, Talmage was at his best when describing the glory and splendor of some Oriental capitol or palace. At the end of this description he says, "Why, my friends, in that place they trimmed their candles with snuffers of gold, and they cut their fruits with knives of gold, and they washed their faces in basins of gold, and they scooped out the ashes with shovels of gold, and they stirred the altar fires with tongs of gold. Gold reflected in the water! Gold flashing from the apparel! Gold blazing in the crown! Gold! Gold! Gold!"

The lessons that he draws from the visit of the queen of Sheba, are, first, that it is a beautiful thing when social position and wealth surrender themselves to God; secondly, earnestness in the search of truth, how the queen of Sheba crossed mountains and deserts to get to Jerusalem; and, thirdly, that religion is a surprise to anyone that gets it. The more we have of it, the more surprised we are, and the greatest surprise of all will be heaven. Talmage always delighted to close his sermons in heaven. There is a true homiletic in that, for most of the

Introduction

great hymns close there, and there the Christian enters upon the final chapter of his life.

On occasions, Talmage took one of the great doctrines and made a serious effort to expound it. An example of this is his sermon on "Vicarious Suffering": "Without shedding of blood is no remission," Heb. 9:22. The sermon opens with an account of how John G. Whittier once asked Talmage after he had given out the hymn, "There Is a Fountain Filled with Blood," at morning devotions at a hotel in the White Mountains, "Do you really believe there is a literal application of the blood of Christ to the soul?" Talmage answered, "No," and in the sermon's introduction he properly explains how the blood stands for the life. It was Christ's life which was given for our salvation.

Then follow examples of vicarious suffering: the father toiling at his business to maintain the home; a mother watching for the sixth night with her sick child; another mother giving her life in prayer and thought and loving deeds for a prodigal son; then the soldiers of the Civil War giving life for the nation; then the doctors who gave their lives caring for the sick during a plague in the South; then William H. Seward, in 1846, sacrificing his popularity to defend an idiotic Negro who had slain a whole family.

Thus he traces through all life the scarlet thread of vicarious substitution until he comes to the substitution of Christ on the cross. "Christ gathered up all the sins of those to be redeemed under his one arm and all their sorrows under his other arm and said: 'I will atone for these under my right arm. Strike me with all thy glittering shafts, O eternal Justice! Roll over me with all thy scourges, ye ocean of sorrow!' And the thunderbolt struck him

Introduction

from above, and the seas of trouble rolled up from beneath, hurricane after hurricane, and cyclone after cyclone, and then and there, in the presence of earth and heaven and hell, yea, all worlds witnessing, the price, the bitter price, the transcendent price, the awful price, the glorious price, the infinite price, the eternal price, was paid that sets us free."

The sermon comes to a conclusion with an account of the preacher's visit to the battlefield of Waterloo, and Marshal Ney addressing his troops as he led them on the last charge. "But our great Waterloo was in Palestine. There came a day when all hell rode up, led by Apollyon, and the Captain of our salvation confronted them alone, the Rider on the White Horse of the Apocalypse going out against the Black Horse Cavalry of Death and the Battalions of the demoniacs and myrmidons of darkness. From twelve o'clock noon to three o'clock in the afternoon, the greatest battle of the universe went on. Eternal destinies were being decided. All the arrows of hell pierced our Chieftain, and the battle-axes struck him, until brow and cheek and shoulder and hand and foot were incarnadined with oozing life ; but he fought on until he gave a final stroke with a sword from Jehovah's buckler, and the Commander in Chief of hell and all his forces fell back in everlasting ruin, and the victory is ours! And on the mound that celebrates the triumph we plant this day two figures, not in bronze or ivory, or sculptured marble, but two figures of living light, the Lion of Judah's tribe and the Lamb that was slain."

Talmage's striking ability to make a Biblical scene real to his congregation is found in the introduction to his sermon, "The Wings of the Al-

Introduction

mighty": "The Lord God of Israel, under whose wings thou art come to trust," Ruth 2:12.

Scene: An Oriental harvest field, grain standing, grain in swath, grain in sheaf; at the side of the field a white tent in which to take the nooning; jars of vinegar or sour wine to quench the thirst of the hot working people; the swarthy men striking their sickles into the rustling barley, others twisting the bands for the sheaves, putting one end of the band under the arm, and with the free arm and foot collecting the sheaf; sunburned women picking up the stray straws and bringing them to the binders; Boaz, a fine-looking Oriental, gray-bearded and bright-faced, the owner of the field, looking on and estimating the value of the grain, and calculating in so many ephahs to the acre. Happy is the preacher who can make a scene as real as that to his congregation!

One of Talmage's most characteristic sermons was the first sermon he preached as pastor of the First Presbyterian Church of Washington, D. C. The subject of this sermon was "All Heaven Is Looking On," from the text Heb. 12:1, "Seeing we also are compassed about with so great a cloud of witnesses." The theme and the text gave full scope for the play of Talmage's imagination. He first describes a Roman amphitheater, with the cheering thousands, and the gladiators fighting with the beasts. The Christian fights in such an arena, surrounded by a throng of witnesses. The tigers and lions of sin come out of their dens and across the sand to attack him. One man's lion is the passion for strong drink. Every man and every woman has his or her lion or tiger. But they do not fight alone. A cloud of witnesses look down upon them.

He describes first the gallery of the angels, nam-

Introduction

ing nearly all the great angels of the Bible, from the angel that swung his sword at the gate of Eden to the angel of the incarnation, and all the seraphim and cherubim of heaven. All these angels are the friends of man in his struggle with the beast.

Then comes the gallery of the prophets and the apostles — Hosea, David, Jeremiah, Daniel, Isaiah, Peter, Paul, Moses, and Noah, all cheering the Christian on. Daniel cries out, "Thy God will deliver thee from the mouth of the lions." David, "He will not suffer thy foot to be moved." Isaiah, "Fear not: for I am with thee." Paul, "Victory through our Lord Jesus Christ." Then comes the gallery of the martyrs: Latimer, and the Theban Legion, and Felicitas, who encouraged her children while they died for the faith. Then comes the gallery of the great Christians: Martin Luther, Lyman Beecher, John Calvin, George Whitefield, and Charles Wesley, and David Brainerd, and Adoniram Judson, Isaac Watts, who sings from his gallery to the Christian struggling in the arena:

> *"Must I be carried to the skies*
> *On flowery beds of ease,*
> *While others fought to win the prize,*
> *And sailed through bloody seas?"*

Then comes the gallery of our departed friends: father, mother, children, all exhorting us to be "faithful unto death."

Talmage spoke to the average man and comforted and encouraged the average man. One of his rules for the pulpit was to remember that men need help and to try to help them. The best example of the sermon that helps is his famous, and perhaps favorite, sermon on the text I Sam. 30:24: "As his part is that goeth down to the battle, so shall his

Introduction

part be that tarrieth by the stuff." This was the last sermon preached by Dr. Talmage in an American church. The sermon opens with a graphic description of the drunken carousal of the Amalekites who had made a raid on Ziklag and had carried away the women and children, among them the wives of David. Then comes the account of David's division of the spoil; how, in spite of the men who had gone down to the battle, those who had guarded the camp received an equal portion of the spoil. The preacher relates how the earl of Kintore once said to him, "When you get back to America I want you to preach a sermon on the discharge of ordinary duty in ordinary places." It was this request which suggested to Talmage this famous and helpful sermon.

He illustrates his sermon by describing the deference paid to a distinguished merchant at a fashionable watering place. When the confidential clerk gets his week off, no one notices him, whether he comes or goes, yet without such a clerk there could be no successful merchant. Men know the names of the presidents of the great railroads, but not the names of the faithful engineers, switchmen, flagmen, brakemen. When there has been an escape from disaster at sea, the passengers thank the captain; but the captain could have done nothing without the crew, without the engineer. Then comes a moving description of how a country family deny themselves to send a promising son to college. The hired help is discharged, sugar and butter are banished from the table. Then comes Commencement Day. The brother and son receives rounds of applause as he delivers the oration of the valedictorian; but hidden away in the back of the gallery are his old-fashioned father and mother and his sis-

Introduction

ters in their plain hats and faded shawls. They made his success possible.

Then comes a passage of encouragement for the aged. The Lord will not turn off his old soldiers any more than the French did the soldiers who fought under Napoleon. The old ministers who preached on $400 a year will have their reward in heaven.

The dominant note of Dr. Talmage's preaching was that of hope and good cheer. The conclusion of the sermon strikes that note in an unforgettable way: "Cheer up, men and women of unappreciated services, you will get your reward, if not here, hereafter. When Charles Wesley comes up to Judgment and the thousands of souls which were wafted into glory through his songs shall be enumerated, he will take his throne. Then John Wesley will come up to Judgment, and after his name has been mentioned in connection with the salvation of the millions of souls brought to God through the Methodism which he founded, he will take his throne. But between the two thrones of Charles Wesley and John Wesley there will be a throne higher than either on which shall sit Susannah Wesley, who with maternal consecration, in Epworth Rectory, Lincolnshire, England, started these two souls on their triumphant mission of sermon and song through all ages. Oh, what a day that will be for many who rocked Christian cradles with weary feet, and out of a small income made the children comfortable for the winter! What a day that will be for those to whom the world gave the cold shoulder and called them nobodies and begrudged them the last recognition, and who, weary and worn and sick, fainted by the Brook Besor! Oh, that will be a mighty day, when the Son of David shall dis-

Introduction

tribute the crowns, the thrones, the scepters, the dominions! Then you and I will appreciate as never before the height, the breadth, the columned, the domed magnificence of my text, 'As his part is that goeth down to the battle, so shall his part be that tarrieth by the stuff'! Hallelujah! Amen!"

This chapter is reprinted with permission of author and publisher from: Clarence E. Macartney, *Six Kings of the American Pulpit*, The Westminster Press, 1942.

PREFACE

In opening the front door of these twenty volumes—containing over five hundred sermons which were selected from thousands of sermons, first with reference to usefulness, and next with reference to variety—an explanatory statement is appropriate.

Many of these sermons were preached during my pastorates in Philadelphia, Brooklyn, and Washington, and others in Europe and Asia and the Islands of the Sea. Chronological order has not been observed. Some of them were delivered thirty years apart, a fact that will account for certain dates and allusions. Some reference in almost every discourse will indicate the approximate time of its delivery. The publication of these volumes is partly induced by the kindness with which my previous books have been received by the press here and abroad. I am more indebted than any other man to the newspaper fraternity for the facilities they have given me for preaching the Gospel for over thirty years, without the exception of a single week, in almost every neighborhood of Christendom and in "the regions beyond;" and I gladly avail myself of every opportunity for thanking them and I thank them now.

Of the more than fifty different books published under my name in this country and in other lands,

Preface

the large majority were not authorized by me for publication, and were pirated. I knew nothing of them until I saw them advertised. I have personally corrected the proofs for these twenty volumes, and their publication is hereby sanctioned. If they shall alleviate the fatigue of some travelers on the rough road of this life, and help some to find the way to the sinless and tearless Capital, whose twelve gates stand wide open, my prayer will be answered.

T. De Witt Talmage

WASHINGTON, D. C.

CONTENTS.

ASTRONOMY OF THE BIBLE;   PAGE.

       OR, GOD AMONG THE STARS.   -   11

TEXT: *It is he that buildeth his stories in the heaven.*—Amos 9 : 6.

The starry and storied heavens as seen by Amos — God everywhere — Birth of astronomy — A great story in one verse — The stars in a postscript — The aurora borealis in the Bible — Not startled at the halting of sun and moon — Stars are inhabited worlds — Living on the ground floor — John Quincy Adams and the corner-stone — Why sin entered — A lesson for other worlds — The mirror of Pharos — A memorable November night — Meteoric wonders.

THE CONCHOLOGY OF THE BIBLE;

       OR, GOD AMONG THE SHELLS.   -   25

TEXT: *And the Lord said unto Moses, Take unto thee sweet spices, stacte and onycha.*—Exodus 30 : 34.

Shells in God's Word — Home of the onycha — A Red Sea product — Fragrant with spikenard — Voices of the sea-shells — Petrified foam of the sea — Shells saved church from extinguishment — Israelites fed on mollusks — God seen in the shells — Bewitching lessons of providence — Opulence of the world subaqueous — Divine harmonies in tinkle of the sea-shells — Bivalves and souls — God a God of emotion — Mathematics set to music — Religion is perfume — More onycha wanted — Purple of the shells — Legend of harp and lute — Climax of conchology — Pearls out of wounds.

THE ORNITHOLOGY OF THE BIBLE;

       OR, GOD AMONG THE BIRDS.   -   41

TEXT: *Behold the fowls of the air.*— Matt. 6 : 26.

Birds in the Bible — God's hand in their construction — Serenading Adam — First sound a bird's voice — Huge birds and their purpose — Moses and the birds — What a bird told Noah — Isaiah and the doves — Compared to the birds — Partridges and riches — A voice from the fir tree top — Slaughter of the hindmost — Filial affection of storks — Teaching of the speckled bird — Pens from eagles' wings — Safe nesting place of the swallows — God the architect of the birds' nests — The feathers of the Almighty.

THE ICHTHYOLOGY OF THE BIBLE;

       OR, GOD AMONG THE FISHES.   -   57

TEXT: *And God said, Let the waters bring forth abundantly the moving creature that hath life.*— Gen. 1 : 20.

A fish the monogram of Christianity — Fish from Gennesaret — Breakfast of broiled perch — An old-time breakfast recalled — Fish in Christ's time — Destruction of the fish god — Fish first living thing created — Paradisaic diet called for — Paul the phosphorescent — Ancient monsters of the deep — Old Testament similitude from the fisheries — Various

Contents

PAGE.

ways of fishing — Fishing in the night-time — Angling after rain — Fishing in the shadowed places — Right kind of bait necessary — Sorting the fish — The castaways — George W. Bethune, fisherman and preacher.

THE POMOLOGY OF THE BIBLE;

OR, GOD AMID THE ORCHARDS.   -   73

TEXT: *The fruit tree yielding fruit after his kind.*— Gen. 1 : 11.

Wednesday morning in paradise — The first orchard — Worship of Pomona — How the orchard was lost — Eden's story a frequent one — The orchard of a king — Solomonic irrigation — A religion of luxuries — Insupportable happiness — Died of joy — The musician's reward — Wellington's heroic reply — Ring before shoes — The fruit-laden table — Pilate's three-treed orchard — The tree remedial — An infinitude of fruitage — St. John's superb orchard — Pomological illustrations of heaven — Heaven both material and spiritual — Twelve-fold joy.

THE BOTANY OF THE BIBLE;

OR, GOD AMONG THE FLOWERS.   -   89

TEXT: *If then God so clothe the grass, which to-day is in the field and to-morrow is cast into the oven; how much more will he clothe you, O ye of little faith?* — Luke 12 : 28.

A volume from Palestine — The New Testament of the fields — Procession of the flowers — Christ bids us study botany — Angels of the grass — Flowers teach God's providential care — The flower that saved a life — Appropriateness of bridal wreaths — Flowers to cover death's gash — Garlands for the grave — Not unseen by the departed — Floral voices — Floral resemblances to human beings — Christ and the flowers — Preachers of the resurrection — Lord Nelson and the trumpeters — The archangel's blast — Resurrection, Resurrection !

THE GEOLOGY OF THE BIBLE;

OR, GOD AMONG THE ROCKS.   -   101

TEXT: *And when they came to Nachon's threshing floor Uzzah put forth his hand to the ark of God and took hold of it; for the oxen shook it. And the anger of the Lord was kindled against Uzzah and God smote him there for his error; and there he died by the ark of God.* — II Sam. 6 : 6-7.

A jubilant procession — A fatal touch — The Bible safe — No conflict between Moses and geology — Instruments in the same orchestra — Archæology in the witness box — Geology confirms the Bible story — Marriage of geology and theology — Geology's castaways — The Bible still entire — Attacks of the ages withstood — The Uzzahs should drop their fears — A religion of the rocks — Their lesson of patience — When God hurries — What the eagle tells the insect — Coming to the Rock of Ages.

THE SCULPTURE OF THE BIBLE;

OR, GOD AMID THE CORAL REEFS.   -   117

TEXT: *No mention shall be made of coral.* — Job 28 : 18.

Beauties of the coral — God's white palaces of the deep — Infidel surgeon's conviction — God loves the beautiful — The deep blush of the sea — Religion better than coral — Accumulative work of grace — All eternity to build up in — Patience taught by coral-builders — Hot climate produces the best coral — Prosperity stops prayers — Adversity and the catechism — Painting the look of torture — Trouble a great artist — The corallum of the soul — No homely Christian mothers — The place of two bridges — Insects building mountains — Animalcules beat back the ocean — Outlasting the coral — Beethoven's last night.

Contents

THE PRECIOUS STONES OF THE BIBLE;   PAGE.

OR, GOD AMONG THE AMETHYSTS. - 135

TEXT: *The foundations of the wall of the city were garnished with all manner of precious stones.—Rev. 21 : 19.*

Homesick for heaven — Precious stones of the Bible — The wall of Heaven — Formation of jasper — How jasper was quarried — Cameoes of jasper — Jasper on high priest's breastplate — Heaven a place of many colors — Sapphire reminiscent of blue of sky and sea — Chalcedony's pallor and purple — Emerald God's favorite among the gems — Nero's emerald glass — Among royal treasures of Tyre — The twelfth an amethyst — A violet in stone — Legendary virtue of amethyst — Amethystine chalices the cause, not the cure, of drunkenness — Amethyst and dreams.

THE CHRONOLOGY OF THE BIBLE;

OR, GOD AMONG THE CENTURIES. - 151

TEXT: *Consider the years of many generations.—Deut. 32 : 7.*

Valedictory and salutatory — Time only a piece of eternity — Bible chronology's six steps — Time calculated from Bethlehem's star — The sundial of Ahaz — Making an almanac — Marking time in old days and our days — Bible chronology and infidelity — March of the ages — A thought that encourages — A thought to startle — The world a better world — House-cleaning still in progress — Chronology's warning — Stealing other people's time — Napoleon's wish — Voltaire's regret — Value of moments — Chronology's close — A world on fire.

THE LIGHTNING OF THE SEA. - - - - 165

TEXT: *He maketh a path to shine after him.— Job. 41 : 32.*

The Bible an inexhaustible treasury of texts — What was Job's leviathan ? — Lightning of the sea — Inflorescence of the billows — Ocean in transfiguration — The bad man's wake — The skeptic's guffaw — Awful results — A crawfish's burrow and the bursting flood — The other side — Demonstrations of grace — The good man's trail — Brevity of life a misnomer — Immeasurable influences — What ordinary folks can do — *Post-mortem* influence of notable workers — In the wake of Calvary's victim — Shadow or phosphorescence — Pessimism is blasphemy — Optimism and Christianity.

THE FINGER OF GOD. - - - - - 181

TEXT: *The finger of God.—Exodus 8 : 19.*

A good text for a sermon — God's wonderful hand — Keeping worlds in motion — Only three mentions of the divine finger — Providential pointings — When lots may be cast — Things we are not responsible for — Lincoln and God's finger — Not a good week for growth in grace — Introducing rice into South Carolina — John Fletcher's life saved — Watching for God's finger — Cholera scare — God's finger points forward — Look ahead — Moscow aglow — The music of the bells — Heaven's surpassing glory.

RUBIES SURPASSED. - - - - - 197

TEXT: *Wisdom is better than rubies.—Proverbs 8 : 11.*

The ruby in the Bible — A spark from the anvil of the setting sun — Its home in Burmah — Worth more than diamonds — Wisdom better than rubies — Religion, like rubies, shines at night — Why named the White House — Worth what it will fetch — Overwhelming billows of religious joy — Ruby's color suggestive of Christ's crimson sacrifice — Only one true ruby, only one Christ — William Wallace's armed merchantman — The flag of the Cross — Contrasting death scenes — Rubies but no religion — Religion but no rubies — Richest anticipations of heaven.

Contents

PAGE.

PARENTAGE OF THE SHOWER. - - - - 211

TEXT: *Hath the rain a father ?* — Job 38 : 28.

Job the arena of theological wrangle — No trouble to accept Job or
Revelation — The rain not an orphan — Talmage's eleven stormy Sabbaths — Weather probabilities read before Bibles — Joint-stock weather
company not wanted — A lesson from Bucephalus — The everlasting
why — The rain of tears — Maniac's tearless eyes — Tears that God
fathers — The throb of God's sympathy — The infidel's surrender —
Mother and son at the foot of the Cross — Carthage receives its king —
A rain of rejoicing.

THE EAR. - - - - - - - 225

TEXT: *He that planted the ear, shall he not hear ?* — Psalm 94 : 9.

Architecture a fascinating art — Ear only made by an infinite God —
Overmastering architecture — All melody for the ear — A holy of holies —
To be guarded from blasphemies and uncleanness — Ephphatha — Restor-
ing ear of Malchus — God in our own organism — To be looked for in
the infinitesimal — Palace of the Almighty in the ear — "Shall he not
hear ?" — Jupiter of Crete without ears — God's open ears — He bends
over — Hears and holds — The ear to be consecrated to its Maker —
Rousseau's dream — Wakened by heaven's canticles.

THE EYE. - - - - - - - 239

TEXT: *He that formed the eye, shall he not see ?* — Psalm 94 : 9.

The eye in the Bible — Over five hundred references — God's two great
masterpieces — Wanted, a plain demonstration — Man's supreme optical
equipment — The world prepared for the eye — Its protection — Eight
hundred contrivances — Wonders of the eye — Its powers of expression
— Pitiableness of the blind — Bell's book on the hand — Under universal
espionage — Divine inspection — Colored man's conversion — "Thou
God seest me" — Night's stars are asterisks — Foot-notes of God — Murderer convicted by light — The miraculous kiss — Blind Katrina's
epitaph.

THE CIRCLE. - - - - - - - 253

TEXT: *It is he that sitteth upon the circle of the earth.* — Isaiah 40 : 22.

The earth's rotundity declared in Scripture — What God thinks of
mathematics — The ark the champion vessel — The world swinging in a
circle — Wheels of providence — Human events run in circles — Time
taken in pyramid building — Impatience denounced — The rebound of
the circle — Effects of forgotten deeds — Bill for martyrs' fire — The
circle of evil — Paul at his zenith — Dark vision of Voltaire — God can
break the evil circle — Shattered at the Cross — The heavenly circle —
Christ the centre.

THE SNOW. - - - - - - - 267

TEXT: *Hast thou entered into the treasures of the snow ?* — Job 38 : 22.

Maligning the winter — Father of energies — Crowns that never come
off — First snowfall of the Bible — Treasures of the snow — Job in
the crystal galleries of the snowflake — It snows! It snows! — Two
views — God's throne-room in a drop — What God has taught the lady-
bugs — Under an emperor's thumb — Mightier than the lightning —
Snow-stepped America — Tragedies of the snow — Napoleon's retreat —
Only a snowflake — Snow a means of health — Productiveness of sorrow
— Snow suggests sin covered — Gasherie DeWitt — Comfort from Mount
Blanc — The Scotch shepherds and the bell-capped crosses — A snow
song.

Contents

PAGE.

EQUIPAGE OF CLOUD. - - - - - - 285

TEXT: *Who maketh the clouds his chariot.*— Psalm 104 : 3.

Man made to look up — Glories of the clouds — Truths portrayed in clouds — Israel's illumined column of cloud — God's chariot — Ancient chariots — The king's ride — Mountains of cloud — Throwing the morning — God's evening chariot — Glories of sunset — The king's black chariot — Devastation and death — God's chariot irresistible — Justice and mercy his chariot wheels — Prayer stops the chariot — God his own driver — Ice-bound on Lake Erie — My Father drives — God's two great rides — To ride with the king.

PAGEANTRY OF THE WOODS. - - - - - 301

TEXT: *We all do fade as a leaf.*— Isaiah 64 : 6.

Truth reiterated — Schoolmaster's blackboard — Why like hind's feet — A two-thousand-mile pageant — Two strings to the harp — Fading gradually — Fading to make room for others — Elijah gives place to Elisha — Future generations not begrudged — Happy old age — Dr. Guthrie's rebuke — God's rich resources — Fading amid a myriad — Great city of silence — Outvoted by the dead — Sixteen hundred million abreast — Variety in departure — The withering black frost — Christian character attractive in dying hour — Departing in triumph.

THE GARDENS OF THE SEA. - - - - - 313

TEXT: *The weeds were wrapped about my head.*— Jonah 2: 5.

Physical science and revelation — Seaweed in a sermon — Jonah's discovery — Neptune's shorn locks — Six thousand species — Wonders of seaweeds — Subaqueous forests — Sepulchered in sea gardens — The sunken navy — Buried by God — Weed a misnomer — Street waifs not weeds but immortal flowers — A plea for the street Arabs — Pasture fields of the deep — A sunken continent — Results of science of seaweed — Particular providences demonstrated — *Post-mortem* explorations — Beauties of heaven.

SONG OF BIRDS. - - - - - - 327

TEXT: *By them shall the fowls of the heaven have their habitation, which sing among the branches.*— Psalm 104 : 12.

Indifference about bird song — Book of nature God's first bible — Bird song not haphazard — Wanted more hosannas — God launched music — When Paganini played — Singing amid a thousand perils — Songs for all moods — Bird song a family song — Slumber songs — Lasting memories of song — A "boost" over the hard places — Lost children restored by mother's song — Jenny Lind and "Home, Sweet Home" — Bird treatment affects longevity — A woodland concert — Nature's cathedral — Preaching to the birds — Life's swan song.

CHANT AT THE CORNER-STONE. - - - 343

TEXT: *Who laid the corner-stone thereof, when the morning stars sang together ?* — Job 38 : 6, 7.

Corner-stone laying — Musical preparation — An angelic choir — The universe a musical portfolio — The snapped harp string — Monsters in the world's heraldry — Turning ministers on the spit — Creation's song drowned out — Tartini's dream — The devil's sonata — Striking the wrong chord — Effect on John Sebastian Bach — Sin's pandemonium — Creation's song to be resumed — The awakening overture — The Cross the world's tuning fork — Universal chorus — Fischer Bros.' deep bass — La Bastardella's high note — Catalini's reach — Christianity's compass — Heaven's new song — Its variations — National peace jubilee — Parepa Rosa's song.

VOL. I.

Contents

PAGE.

VOICES OF NATURE. - - - - - - - 357

TEXT: *The glory of Lebanon shall come unto thee, the fir tree, the pine tree, and the box tree together, to beautify the place of my sanctuary.*— Isaiah 60 : 13.

Snow-crowned Lebanon — The earth's regeneration — The beautiful world of prophecy — Nature's testimony to truths of Christianity — Christianity and science — A verdict for religion — Buried cities and their coffin-lids — Caviglia converted by the pyramids — Dr. Jessup's skeptical friend — Truth written on the rocks — Gladstone, Talmage and the sycamore tree — Christ's fascinating "likes" — Not in technical terms — Nature's laws on the Christian's side — Earth and heavens a busy loom — Starry letters — A bird and a hymn.

THE MISSION OF THE FROST. - - - - 373

TEXT: *By the breath of God frost is given.* — Job 37 : 10.

The silent note — First Sunday of winter — King Frost's palaces — Frost as a painter — Rapid work of Weenix — Titian's first sight of Corregio's work — Wonders near at home — Frost as a physician — Talmage's brother John — Frost as a jeweler — The old testament of the fields — Penelope's amber necklace — Marie Antoinette's necklace of diamonds — The frost an evangelist — Not a lopsided book — Shelves full of balsams — Talmage's experience of abuse — Arab horses — The wild rush for the river — Compensation of heaven.

ILLUMINED CLOUDS. - - - - - - 389

TEXT: *And now men see not the bright light which is in the clouds.* — Job 37 : 21.

Light unobserved — Making the best of everything — Financial misfortune — Blessings to the soul — Saving the children — Burial-places of men who started rich — Improved spiritual prospects — Attila's three coffins — Bereavements and blessings — Taken out of trouble — Departed children gone on a May-day party — Making the best of sicknesses — Bible's most attractive characters — Physical disorders a means of grace — Jubilates of the dying — Blossom week forever — Talmage's two spring-times — Vacation is coming — The ground not cold.

The following indexes will be found at the end of volume twenty:

INDEX OF TEXTS,
INDEX OF TITLES AND TEXTS,
INDEX OF ANECDOTAL AND HISTORICAL ILLUSTRATIONS,
INDEX OF SUBJECTS.

THE ASTRONOMY OF THE BIBLE; OR, GOD AMONG THE STARS

Amos, 9: 6: "It is he that buildeth his stories in the heaven."

That is radiant poetry from Amos, the herdsman. He thrummed a lyre that has sounded through twenty-six centuries. While guarding his flocks at night, he watched the heavens. He saw stars above stars, and the universe seemed to him like a great mansion many stories high, silver room above silver room, silver pillars beside silver pillars, and windows of silver and doors of silver, and turrets and domes of silver rising into the immensities; and the prophet's sanctified imagination walks through the great silver palace of the universe, through the first story, up through the second story, up through the third story, up through the twentieth story, up through the hundredth story, up through the thousandth story, and realizing that God is the architect and carpenter and mason of all that upheaved splendor, he cries out in the words of the text: "It is he that buildeth his stories in the heaven."

It is time that we widened out and heightened our religious thoughts. In our pulpits and Sabbath classes and Christian work of all sorts we ring the changes on a few verses of Scripture until they excite no interest. Many of the best parts of the Bible have never yet been preached from or indeed even noticed. Hence, I now begin a series of sermons on God Everywhere: the Astronomy of the Bible, or God among the Stars; the Conchology of the Bible, or

God among the Shells; the Ornithology of the Bible, or God among the Birds; the Ichthyology of the Bible, or God among the Fishes; the Precious Stones of the Bible, or God among the Amethysts; the Pomology of the Bible, or God among the Orchards; the Geology of the Bible, or God among the Rocks; the Botany of the Bible, or God among the Flowers and among the Gardens of the Sea; the Sculpture of the Bible, or God among the Coral Reefs; the Chronology of the Bible, or God among the Centuries; the Lightning of the Sea, and so on, as I may think it edifying and useful.

The fact is that we have all spent too much time on one story of the great mansion of God's universe. We need occasionally to go upstairs or downstairs in this mansion; downstairs and in the cellar study the rocks, or upstairs and see God in some of the higher stories, and learn the meaning of the text when it says: "It is he that buildeth his stories in the heavens."

Astronomy was born in Chaldea. Its mother was Astrology, or the science of foretelling events by juxtaposition of stars. The Orientals, living much out of doors and in a very clear atmosphere, through which the stars shone especially lustrously, acquired the habit of studying the night heavens. In the hot seasons, caravans journeyed chiefly at night, and that gave travelers much opportunity of stellar information. On the first page of the Bible the sun and moon and stars roll in—the sun, a body nearly three million miles in circumference and more than twelve thousand times as large as our earth; the moon, more than two thousand miles in diameter. But God is so used to doing things on such an omnipotent scale that he takes only one verse to tell of this stellar and lunar manufacture. Yea, in three words all the other worlds are thrown in. The record says, "The stars also!" It takes whole pages for a man to extol the making of a telescope or microscope or a magnetic telegraph or a threshing machine, or to describe a fine painting or statue, but it was so easy for God to hang the celestial upholstery that the story is compassed in one verse: "God made two great lights, the greater light to rule the day and the lesser light to rule the night. The stars also!" Astronomers have been trying to call the roll of them ever since, and they have counted multitudes of them passing in review before the observatories built at vast expense, and the size and number of those heavenly bodies have taxed to the utmost the scientists of all ages. But God finishes all he has to say about them in three words, "The stars also!" That is, Mars with its more than fifty-five million square miles, and Venus, with its more than one hundred and ninety-one million square miles, and Saturn with its more than nineteen billion square miles, and Jupiter with its more than twenty-four billion square miles, and all the planets of our system of more than seventy-eight billion square miles; and these stars of our system, when compared with the stars of other systems, as a handful of sand compared with all the Rocky Mountains and all the Alps. "The stars also!" For brevity, for ponderosity, for splendor, for suggestiveness, for sublimity piled on sublimity, these words excel all that human speech ever uttered or human imagination ever soared after: "The stars also!" It is put in as you write a postcript— something you thought of afterwards, as hardly worth putting into the body of a letter. "The stars also!"

Read on in your Bible, and after a while the Bible flashes with the Aurora Borealis or Northern Lights, that strange illumination, as mysterious and undefined now as when, in the book of Job, it was written: "Men see not the bright light which is in the clouds. Fair weather cometh out of the North." While all the nations supposed that the earth was built on a foundation of some sort, and many supposed that it stood on a huge turtle, or some great marine creature, Job knew enough of astronomy to say it had no foundation, but was suspended on the invisible arm of the Almighty, declaring that "He hangeth the earth upon nothing." While all nations thought the earth was level, the sky spread over it like a tent over a flat surface, Isaiah declared the world to be globular—circular—saying of God: "He sitteth upon the circle of the earth." See them glitter in this scriptural sky—Arcturus, Orion, the Pleiades, and the "Bear with her young."

While running your fingers among the leaves of your Bible with the astronomical thought in your mind, you see two worlds stop—the sun and the moon. But what does that Christian know about that miracle who does not understand something of those two luminaries? Unless you watch modern astronomy put those two worlds in its steelyards and weigh them, you are as ignorant as a Hottentot about the stupendousness of that scene in the life of Joshua. The sun over three hundred thousand times as heavy as our earth and going thousands of miles the hour. Think of stopping that and starting it again without the shipwreck of the universe! But I can easily believe it. What confounds me is not that he could stop and start again those two worlds in Joshua's time, but that he could have made the wheel of worlds of which the sun and moon are only cogs, and kept that wheel rolling for thousands of years—the fly-wheel of all eternity. If an engineer can start a long train, it is not surprising that he can stop it. If God could make and move the universe, which is an express train drawn by an omnipotent engine, I am not surprised that for a part of a day he could put down the brakes on two pieces of the rotating machinery. Infidelity is hard up for ground of complaint against the Scriptures when it finds fault with that cessation of solar and lunar travel. Here is my watch. I could not make a watch if I tried, but I can stop it and start it again. My difficulty is not that God could stop two worlds and start them again, but that he could make them at all as he did make them.

What pleases and astounds me more is that each one of the millions of worlds has a God-given name. Only a comparatively small number of them have names given them by scientists. If astronomers can give a name to a whole constellation or galaxy, they think they do well, but God has a name for each star in all immensity. Inspired David declares of God: "He telleth the number of the stars, he calleth them all by their names." They are not orphans that have never been christened. They are not waifs of the night. They are not unknown ships on the high seas of immensity. They belong to a family of which God is the Father, and as you call your child Benjamin or Mary or Bertha or Addison or Josephine, so he calls all the infant worlds and all the adult worlds by their first name, and they know it as well as though there were only one child of light in all the divine family. "He calleth them all by their names," and when he calls, I warrant they come.

Oh, the stars! Those vestal fires kept burning on infinite altars. Those lighthouses on the coast of eternity. The hands and weights and pendulum of the great clock of the universe. According to Herschel, the so-called **fixed stars are not fixed** at all, but each one a sun with a mighty system of worlds rolling round it, and this whole system with all the other systems rolling on around some other great centre. Millions and millions, billions and billions, trillions and trillions, quadrillions and quadrillions!

But what gladdens me, and at the same time overwhelms me, is that those worlds are inhabited. The Bible implies it, and what a small idea you must have of God and his dominion if you think it only extends across this chip of a world which you and I now inhabit. Have you taken this idea of all the other worlds being inhabited as human guesswork? Read Isaiah, 45th chapter, 18th verse: "Thus saith the Lord that created the heavens, God himself that formed the earth, and made it; he hath established it, he created it not in vain, he formed it to be inhabited." Now, if he inhabited the earth so that it would not be created in vain, would he make worlds hundreds and thousands of times larger and not have them inhabited? Speaking of the inhabitants of this world, he says: "The nations are as the drop of a bucket." If all the inhabitants of this world are as a drop of a bucket, where are the other drops of the bucket? Again and again the Bible speaks of the host of heaven, and the word "host" means living creatures, not inert masses, and the expression "hosts of heaven" must mean inhabitants of other worlds. Again, the Bible says: "He has set thy glory above the heavens." And here my text comes in with its idea of a mansion of many stories: "It is he that buildeth his stories in the heaven." Is it possible that we who live on the ground floor of this many-storied building are the only tenants, and that the larger rooms and the more gorgeously upholstered rooms and the more brilliantly chandeliered rooms above it are uninhabited? Besides this we are positively told in the Bible that two other worlds are inhabited—the world angelic and the world diabolic. These two worlds added to our own make it positive that three worlds are inhabited. Why then stop with three worlds of living beings when there are not only millions but billions of worlds? Are they all standing like expensively furnished houses in time of financial panic marked "To Let" and no one to take them? "Waste not," God hath written all over this world of ours. And do you suppose that God would waste world-material in our solar system to the amount of what has been estimated as seven hundred trillion miles of solid contents, and that only a small part as compared with other systems which go to make up this many-storied mansion of the text, where it says: "It is he that buildeth his stories in the heaven"?

Without the use of telescope and without any observatory and without any astronomical calculation, I am convinced that the other worlds are inhabited, because my Bible and my common-sense tell me so. It has been estimated that in the worlds belonging to our solar system there is room for at least twenty-five trillion of population. And I believe it is all occupied or will be occupied by intelligent beings. God will not fill them with brutes. He would certainly put into those worlds beings intelligent enough to appreciate the architecture, the coloring, the grandeur, the beauty, the harmony of their surroundings. Yea, the inhabitants of those worlds have capacity of locomotion like ours, for they would not have had such spacious opportunity for movement if they had not powers of motion. Yea, they have sight, else why the light; and hearing, else how get on with necessary language, and how clear themselves from advancing perils. Yea, as God made our human race in his own image, he probably made the inhabitants of other worlds in his own image; in other words, it is as near demonstration as I care to have it, that while the inhabitants of other worlds have adaptations of bodily structure to the particular climate in which they dwell, there is yet similarity of mental and spiritual characteristics among all the inhabitants of the universe of God; and, made in his image, they are made wonderfully alike.

Now, what should be the practical result of this discussion founded on Scripture and common-sense? It is first of all to enlarge our ideas of God, and so intensify our admiration and worship. Under such consideration, how much more graphic the Bible question which seems to roll back the sleeve of the Almighty and say: "Hast thou an arm like God?" The contemplation also encourages us with the thought that if God made all these worlds and populated them, it will not be very much of an undertaking for him to make our little world over again, and reconstruct the character of its populations as by grace they are to be reconstructed.

What a monstrosity of criminal indifference that the majority of Christian people listen not to the voices of other worlds, although the Book says, "The heavens declare the glory of God," and, again, "The works of the Lord are great and to be sought out." How much have you sought them out? You have been satisfying yourself with some things about Christ, but have you noticed that Paul calls you to consider Christ as the Creator of other worlds, "by whom also he made the worlds?" It is time you Christians start on a world hunt. That is the chief reason why God makes the night, that you may see other worlds. Go out to-night and look up at the great clock of the heavens. Listen to the silvery chime of the midnight sky. See that your children and grandchildren mount the heavens with telescope for alpenstock, leaping from acclivity of light to acclivity of light. What a beautiful and sublime thing that John Quincy Adams, the ex-President, borne down with years, undertook at the peril of his life the journey from Washington to Cincinnati that he might lay the corner-stone of the pier of the great refracting telescope—there making his last oration! What a service for all mankind when, in 1839, Lord Rosse lifted on the lawn of his castle, eighty miles from Dublin, a telescope that revealed worlds as fast as they could roll in, and that started an enthusiasm which this moment concentres the eyes of many of the most devout in all parts of the earth on celestial discovery! Thank God that we now know where our own world is, bounded on all sides by realms of glory, instead of being where Hesiod in his poetry described it to be, namely, half-way between heaven and hell, an anvil hurled out of heaven taking ten days to strike the earth, and hurled out of earth taking ten more days to strike perdition:

> From the high heaven a brazen anvil cast,
> Nine days and nights in rapid whirls would last;
> And reach the earth the tenth; whence strongly hurled,
> The same the passage to th' infernal world.

I thank God that we have found out that our world is not half-way between heaven and hell, but it is in a sisterhood of light; and that this sisterhood joins all the other sisterhoods of worlds, moving round some great homestead, which is no doubt heaven, where God is, and our departed Christian friends are, and we ourselves, through pardoning mercy, expect to become permanent residents.

Furthermore, I get now from all this an answer to the question which every intelligent man and woman since the earth has stood has asked, receiving no answer. Why did God let sin and sorrow come into the world, when he could have prevented them from coming? I wish reverently to say I think I have found the reason. To keep the universe loyal to a holy God, it was important in some world somewhere to demonstrate the gigantic disasters that would come upon any world that allowed sin to enter. Which world should it be? Well, the smaller the world, the better; for less numbers would suffer. So our world was selected. The stage was large enough for the enactment of the tragedy. Enter on the stage Sin, followed by Murder, Pain, Theft, Fraud, Impurity, Falsehood, Massacre, War and all the abominations and horrors and agonies of centuries. Although we know comparatively little about the other worlds, lest we become completely dissatisfied with our own, no doubt the other worlds have heard and are now hearing all about this world, in the awful experiment of sin which the human race has been making. In some way interstellar communication is open and all worlds, either by wing of flying spirits or by direct communication from God, are learning that disloyalty and disobedience doom and damn everything they touch, and the spectacle practically says to all other worlds: "Obey God, keep holy and stay in the orbit where you were intended to swing, or you will suffer what that recreant world out yonder has been suffering for thousands of years." It is no longer to me a mystery why so small a world as ours was chosen for the tragedy. A chemist can demonstrate all the laws of earth and heaven in a small laboratory, ten feet by five, and our world was not too small to demonstrate to the universe the awful chemistry of unrighteousness, its explosive and riving and consuming power.

On the tower of Pharos at Alexandria, Egypt, a metallic mirror was raised which reflected all that occurred both on land and sea for a distance of three hundred miles, and so Egypt was informed of the coming of her enemies long before their arrival. By what process I know not, but in some way this ship of a struggling earth I think is mirrored to distant worlds. Surely this one experiment of a world unloosing itself from God will be enough for all worlds and all eternities.

But notice that as other worlds rolled into the first book of the Bible, the Book of Genesis, they also appear in the last book of the Bible, the Book of the Revelation. They will take part in the scenes of that occasion which shall be the earth's winding up, and a tremendous occasion for you and me personally. My father was on the turnpike road between Trenton and Bound Brook, New Jersey. He was coming through the night from the Legislative halls, where he was serving his State, to his home, where there was sickness. I often heard him tell about it. It was the night of the 12th and the morning of the 13th of November, 1833. The sky was cloudless and the air clear. Suddenly the whole heavens became a scene never to be forgotten. From the constellation Leo meteors began to shoot out in all directions. For the two hours between four and six in the morning it was estimated that a thousand meteors a minute flashed and expired. It grew lighter than noonday. Arrows of fire; balls of fire; trails of fire; showers of fire. Some of the appearances were larger than the full moon. All around the heavens explosion followed explosion. Sounds as well as sights. The air filled with uproar. All the luminaries of the sky seemed to have received marching orders. The heavens ribbed and interlaced and garlanded with meteoric display. From horizon to horizon everything in combustion and conflagration. Many a

brain that night gave way. It was an awful strain
on strongest nerves. Millions of people fell on their
knees in prayer. Was the world ending, or was there
some great event for which all heaven was illumi-
nated? For eight momentous hours the phenome-
non lasted. East, west, north, south, it looked as
though the heavens were in maniac disorder. Astronomers watching that night said that those meteors
started from 2,200 miles above the earth's surface
and moved with ten times the speed of a cannon-ball.
The owner of a plantation in South Carolina says of
that night scene: "I was suddenly awakened by the
most distressing cries that ever fell on my ears.
Shrieks of horror and cries for mercy I could hear
from most of the negroes on three plantations,
amounting in all to about six or eight hundred.
While earnestly listening for the cause, I heard a faint
voice near the door calling my name. I arose, and
taking my sword, stood at the door. At this moment
I heard the same voice still beseeching me to rise, and
saying, 'Oh, my God! the world is on fire!' I then
opened the door, and it is difficult to say which excited me the most, the awfulness of the scene or the
distressed cries of the negroes. Upward of one hundred lay prostrate on the ground; some speechless
and some uttering the bitterest cries, but most with
their hands raised, imploring God to save the world
and them. The scene was truly awful, for never did
rain fall much thicker than the meteors fell toward
the earth." But the excitement thus described by the
Southern planter ran among the whites as well as the
blacks, among the intelligent as well as the supersti-
tious. The spectacle ceased not until the rising sun
of the November morning eclipsed it, and the whole
American nation sat down exhausted with the agita-
tions of a night to be memorable until the earth itself

shall become a falling star. The Bible closes with a scene of falling lights, not only frivolous meteors, but grave old stars. St John saw it in prospect, and wrote: "The stars of heaven fell unto the earth, even as a fig tree casteth her untimely figs when she is shaken of a mighty wind." What a time that will be when worlds drop! Rain of planets. Centripetal force let loose her grip on worlds. Constellations flying apart. Galaxies dissolved. The great orchard of the universe swept by the last hurricane, letting down the stars like ripened fruit. Our old earth will go with the rest, and let it go, for it will have existed long enough to complete its tremendous experiment. But there will be enough worlds left to make a heaven out of, if any more heaven needs to be built. That day finding us in Christ, our nature regenerated, and our sins pardoned, and our hope triumphant, we will feel no more alarm than when in September passing through an orchard you hear the apples thump to the ground, or through a conservatory and you hear an untimely fig drop on the floor. You will only go upstairs into another story of the House of many mansions, a better lighted story, a better ventilated story, a better pictured story, and into a story where already many of your kindred are waiting for you, and where prophets and apostles and martyrs will pay you celestial visitation, and where, with a rapture beyond the most radiant anticipation, you shall bow before him that "buildeth his stories in the heaven."

THE CONCHOLOGY OF THE BIBLE; OR, GOD AMONG THE SHELLS

Exodus, 30: 34: "And the Lord said unto Moses, Take unto thee sweet spices, stacte, and onycha."

THE CONCHOLOGY OF THE BIBLE;
OR, GOD AMONG THE SHELLS

Exodus, 30: 34: " And the Lord said unto Moses, Take unto
thee sweet spices, stacte, and onycha."

You may not have noticed the shells of the Bible,
although in this early part of the sacred Book God
calls you to consider and employ them, as he called
Moses to consider and employ them. Behold and
wonder and worship. The onycha of my text is a
shell found on the banks of the Red Sea, and Moses
and his army must have crushed many of them under
foot as they crossed the bisected waters, onycha on
the beach and onycha in the unfolded bed of the deep.
I shall speak of this shell as a beautiful and practical
revelation of God, and as true as the first chapter of
Genesis and the last chapter of the Revelation or everything between. Not only is this shell, the onycha,
found in the Red Sea, but in the waters of India. It
not only delectates the eye with its convolutions of
beauty, white and lustrous and seriate, but blesses
the nostril with a pungent aroma. This shell-fish,
accustomed to feed on spikenard, is redolent with that
odorous plant, redolent when alive and redolent when
dead. Its shells, when burnt, bewitch the air with
fragrance. In my text, God commands Moses to mix
this onycha with the perfumes of the altar in the
ancient Tabernacle, and I propose to mix some of its
perfumes at the altar of our own tabernacle, as I now
come to speak of the Conchology of the Bible, or
God among the Shells.

Sermons by T. DeWitt Talmage

It is a secret that you may keep for me, for I have never before told it to any one, that in all the realms of the natural world there is nothing to me so fascinating, so completely absorbing, so full of suggestiveness, as a shell. What? More entertaining than a bird, which can sing, when a shell cannot sing? Well, there you have made a great mistake. Pick up the onycha from the banks of the Red Sea, or pick up a bivalve from the beach of the Atlantic Ocean, and listen, and you hear a whole choir of marine voices—bass, alto, soprano—in an unknown tongue, but seeming to chant, as I put them to my ear, "The sea is his and he made it;" others singing, "Thy way, O God, is in the sea;" others hymning, "He ruleth the raging of the sea." "What," says some one else, "does the shell impress you more than the star?" In some respects, yes, because I can handle the shell and closely study the shell, while I cannot handle the star, and if I study it I must study it at a distance of millions and millions of miles. "What," says some one else, "are you more impressed by the shell than by the flower?" Yes, for it has far greater varieties and far greater richness of color, as I could show you in thousands of specimens, and because the shell does not fade, as does the rose leaf, but maintains its beauty century after century; so that the onycha which the hoof of Pharaoh's horse knocked aside in the chase of the Israelites across the Red Sea may have kept its lustre to this hour. Yes, they are so parti-colored and multi-colored that you might pile them up until you would have a wall with all the colors of the wall of heaven, from the jasper at the bottom to the amethyst at the top. Oh, the shells! The petrified foam of the sea! The hardened bubbles of the deep! The diadems thrown by the ocean to the feet of the continent! How the shells are ribbed, grooved, cylindered, mottled, iridescent! They were used as coin by some nations, fastened in belts by others, made into handles of wooden implements by still others. Cowries are still used as coin in some parts of the world. Mollusks not only of the sea but mollusks of the land. Do you know how much they have had to do with the world's history? They saved the Church of God from extinguishment. The Israelites marched out of Egypt two million strong, besides flocks and herds. The Bible says "the people took their dough before it was leavened, their kneading troughs being bound up in the clothes on their shoulders. . . . They are thrust forth out of Egypt and could not tarry, neither had they prepared for themselves any victuals." Just think of it! Forty years in the wilderness! Infidelity triumphantly asks: "How could they live forty years in the wilderness without food? You say manna fell. Oh, that was after a long while. They would have starved long before the manna fell." The fact is they were chiefly kept alive by the mollusks of the land or shelled creatures. Mr. Fronton and Mr. Sicard took the same route from Egypt toward Canaan that the Israelites took, and they give this as their testimony:

"Although the children of Israel must have consisted of about two million of souls, with baggage and innumerable flocks and herds, they were not likely to experience any inconvenience in their march. Several thousand persons might walk abreast with the greatest ease in the very narrowest part of the valley in which they first began to file off. It soon afterwards expands to above three leagues in width. With respect to forage, they would be at no loss. The ground is covered with tamarisk, broom, clover and sainfoin, of which latter, especially, camels are passionately fond, besides almost every variety of odoriferous plant and herb proper for pasturage. The whole sides of the valley through which the children of Israel marched are still tufted with brushwood, which doubtless afforded food for their beasts, together with many drier sorts for lighting fire, on which the Israelites could with the greatest ease bake the dough they brought with them on small iron plates, which form a constant appendage to the baggage of an oriental traveller. Lastly, the herbage underneath these trees and shrubs is completely covered with snails of a prodigious size and of the best sort, and however uninviting such a repast might appear to us, they are here esteemed a great delicacy. They are so plentiful in this valley that it may be literally said that it is difficult to take one step without treading on them."

So the shelled creatures saved the host of Israelites on the march to the Promised Land, and the attack of infidelity at this point is defeated by the facts, as infidelity is always defeated by facts, since it is founded on ignorance. In writing and printing, our interrogation point has at the bottom a mark like a period and over it a flourish like the swing of a teamster's whip, and we put this interrogation point at the end of a question; but in the Spanish language, the interrogation point is twice used for each question. At the beginning of the question the interrogation point is presented upside down, and at the close of the question right side up. When infidelity puts a question about the Scriptures, as it always indicates ignorance, the question ought to be printed with two interrogation points, one at the beginning and one at the close, but both upside down.

Thank God for the wealth of mollusks all up and down the earth, whether feeding the Israelites on their way to the land flowing with milk and honey, or, as we are better acquainted with the mollusks, when flung to the beach of lake or sea. If I should ask you to name three of the great royal families of the earth, perhaps you would respond, the House of Stuart, the House of Hapsburg, the House of Bourbon, but the three royal families of mollusks are the Univalve, or shell in one part; the Bivalve, or shell in two parts, and the Multivalve, or shell in many parts; and I see God in their every hinge, in their every tooth, in their every cartilage, in their every ligament, in their every spiral ridge, and in their adaptation of thin shell for still ponds and thick coatings for boisterous seas. They all dash upon me the thought of the providential care of God. What is the use of all this architecture of the shell, and why is it pictured from the outside lip clear down into its labyrinths of construction? Why the infinity of skill and radiance in a shell? What is the use of the color and exquisite curve of a thing so insignificant as a shell-fish? Why, when the conchologist, by dredge or rake, fetches the crustaceous specimens to the shore, does he find at his feet whole Alhambras and Coliseums and Parthenons and Crystal Palaces of beauty in miniature, and these bring to light only an infinitesimal part of the opulence in the great subaqueous world. Linnæus counted twenty-five hundred species of shells, but conchology had then only begun its achievements. While exploring the bed of the Atlantic Ocean in preparation for laying the cable, shelled creatures were brought up from the depths of nineteen hundred fathoms. When lifting the telegraph wire from the Mediterranean and Red seas, shelled creatures were brought up. from depths of two thousand fathoms. The English Admiralty, exploring in behalf of science, found mollusks at a depth of twenty-four hundred and thirty-five fathoms. What a realm awful for vastness!

As the shell is only the house and the wardrobe of insignificant animals of the deep, why all that wonder and beauty of construction? God's care for them is the only reason. And if God provide so munificently for them, will he not see that you have wardrobe and shelter? Wardrobe and shelter for a periwinkle; shall there not be wardrobe and shelter for a man? Would God give a coat of mail for the defence of a Nautilus and leave you no defence against the storm? Does he build a stone house for a creature that lasts a season, and leave without home a soul that takes hold on centuries and æons? Hugh Miller found "The Footprints of the Creator" in the Old Red Sandstone, and I hear the harmonies of God in the tinkle of the sea-shells when the tide comes in.

The same Christ who drew a lesson of providential care from the fact that God clothes the grass of the field instructs me to draw the same lesson from the shells.

In almost every man's life, however well born and prosperous for years, and in almost every woman's life there comes a very dark time, at least once. A conjunction of circumstances will threaten bankruptcy and homelessness and starvation. It may be that these words will meet the ear or the eye of those who are in such a state of foreboding. Come, then, and see how God gives an ivory palace to a water creature that you could cover with a ten-cent piece, and clothes in armor against all attack a coral no bigger than a snowflake. I do not think that God will take better care of a bivalve than of one of his own children. I rake to your feet with the Gospel rake the most thorough evidences of God's care for his creatures. I pile around you great mounds of shells, that they may teach you a most comforting theology. Oh, ye of little faith, walk along these arbors of coralline, and look at these bouquets of shell fit to be handed a queen on her coronation day, and see these fallen rain-

Conchology of the Bible

bows of color, and examine these lilies in stone, these primroses in stone, these heliotropes in stone, these cowslips in stone, these geraniums in stone, these japonicas in stone. Oh, ye who have your telescopes ready, looking out on clear nights, trying to see what is occurring in Mars, Jupiter, and Mercury, know that within a few hours' walk or ride of where you now are there are whole worlds that you might explore, but of which you are unconscious; and among the most beautiful and suggestive of these worlds is the conchological world. Take this lesson of a providential care. How does that old hymn go?—

> We may, like ships, by tempest be tossed
> On perilous deeps, but cannot be lost;
> Though Satan enrages the wind and the tide,
> The promise assures us the Lord will provide.

But while you get this pointed lesson of providential care from the shelled creatures of the deep, notice in their construction that God helps them to help themselves. This house of stone in which they live is not dropped on them and is not built around them. The material for it exudes from their own bodies and is adorned with a colored fluid from the pores of their own neck. It is a most interesting thing to see these crustaceans fashion their own homes out of carbonate of lime and membrane. And all of this is a mighty lesson to those who are waiting for others to build their fortunes, when they ought to go to work and, like the mollusks, build their own fortunes out of their own brain, out of their own sweat, out of their own industries. Not a mollusk on all the beaches of all the seas would have a house of shell if it had not itself built one. Do not wait for others to shelter you or prosper you. All the crustaceous creatures of the earth, from every flake of their covering and from every ridge of their tiny castles on Atlantic and Pacific and Mediterranean coasts, say: "Help yourself, while God helps you to help yourself." Those people who are waiting for their father or rich old uncle to die and leave them a fortune are as silly as a mollusk would be to wait for some other mollusk to drop on it a shell-equipment. It would kill the mollusk, as, in most cases, it destroys a man. Not one person out of a hundred ever was strong enough to stand the possession of a large estate by inheritance dropped on him in a mass. Have great expectations from only two persons—God and yourself. Let the onycha of my text become your preceptor.

But the more I examine the shells, the more I am impressed that God is a God of emotion. Many scoff at emotion, and seem to think that God is a God of cold geometry and iron laws and eternal apathy and enthroned stoicism. No! no! The shells with overpowering emphasis deny it. While law and order reign in the universe you have but to see the lavishness of color on the crustacea, all shades of crimson from the faintest blush to blood of battlefield, all shades of blue, all shades of green, all shades of all colors from deepest black to whitest light, just poured out on the shells with no more order than a mother premeditates or calculates how many kisses and hugs she shall give her babe waking up in the morning sunlight. Yes! My God is an emotional God, and he says: "We must have colors, and let the sun paint all of them on the scroll of that shell; and we must have music, and here is a carol for the robin, and a psalm for the man, and a doxology for the seraphim, and a resurrection call for the archangel." Ay, he showed himself a God of sublime emotion when he flung himself on this world in the personality of a Christ to save it, without regard to the tears it would take or the blood it would exhaust or the agonies it would involve. When I see the Louvres and the Luxembourgs and the Vaticans of Divine painting strewn along the eight thousand miles of coast; and I hear, in a forest, on a summer morning, musical academies and Handel societies of full orchestras, I say God is a God of emotion; and if he observes mathematics, it is mathematics set to music, and his figures are written, not in white chalk on blackboards, but by a finger of sunlight on walls of jasmine and trumpet-creeper.

In my study of the conchology of the Bible, this onycha of the text also impresses me with the fact that religion is perfume. What else could God have meant when he said to Moses: "Take unto thee sweet spices, stacte and onycha"? Moses took that shell of the onycha, put it over the fire, and as it crumbled into ashes it exhaled an odor that hung in every curtain and filled the ancient Tabernacle, and its sweet smoke escaped from the sacred precincts and saturated the outside air. Perfume! That is what religion is. But, instead of that, some make it a malodor. They serve God in a rough and acerb way. They box their child's ears because he does not properly keep Sunday, instead of making Sunday so attractive the child could not help but keep it. They make him learn by heart a difficult chapter in the book of Exodus, with all the hard names, because he has been naughty. How many disagreeable good people there are! No one doubts their piety, and they will reach heaven, but they will have to get fixed up before they go there, or they will make trouble by calling out to us: "Keep off that grass!" "What do you mean by plucking that flower?" "Show your tickets!" Oh! how many Christian people need to obey my text, and take into their worship and their behavior and their consolations and presbyteries and general assemblies and conferences more onycha. I have sometimes gone in a very gale of spirit into the presence of some disagreeable Christians and in five minutes felt wretched, and at some other time I have gone depressed into the company of suave and genial souls, and in a few moments I felt exhilarant. What was the difference? It was the difference in what they burnt in their censers. The one burnt onycha; the other burnt asafœtida.

In this conchological study of the Bible I also notice that the mollusks or shelled animals furnish the purple that you see richly darkening so many Scripture chapters. The purple stuff in the ancient Tabernacle, the purple girdle of the priests, the purple mantle of Roman emperors, the apparel of Dives in purple and fine linen, ay, the purple robe which, in mockery, was thrown upon Christ, were colored by the purple of the shells on the shores of the Mediterranean. It was discovered by a shepherd's dog having stained his mouth by breaking one of the shells, and the purple aroused admiration. Costly purple! Six pounds of the purple liquor extracted from the shell-fishes was used to prepare one pound of wool. Purple was also used on the pages of books. Bibles and prayer-books appeared in purple vellum, and may still be found in some of the national libraries of Europe. Plutarch speaks of some purple which kept its beauty for one hundred and ninety years. But, after a while, the purple became easier to get, and that which had been a sign of imperial authority when worn in robes, was adopted by many people, and so an Emperor, jealous of this appropriation of the purple, made a law that any one except royalty wearing purple should be put to death. Then, as if to punish the world for that outrage of exclusiveness, God obliterated the color from the earth, as much as to say: "If all cannot have it, none shall have it." But, though God has deprived the race of that shell-fish which afforded the purple, there are shells enough to make us glad and worshipful. Oh, the entrancement of hue and shape still left all up and down the beaches of all the continents! These creatures of the sea have what roofs of enameled porcelain! They dwell under what pavilions, blue as the sky and fiery as a sunset and mysterious as an aurora! And am I not right in leading you, for a few moments, through this mighty realm of God so neglected by human eye and human footstep? It is said that the invention of the harp and lute was suggested by the fact that in Egypt the Nile overflowed its banks, and when the waters retreated, tortoises were left by the million on all the lands, and these tortoises died, and soon nothing was left but the cartilages and gristle of these creatures, which tightened under the heat into musical strings that, when swept by the wind or touched by the foot of man, vibrated, making sweet sounds, and so the world took the hint and fashioned the harp. And am I not right in trying to make music out of the shells, and lifting them as a harp, from which to thrum the jubilant praises of the Lord and the pathetic strains of human condolence?

But I find the climax of this conchology of the Bible in the pearl, which has this distinction above all other gems, that it requires no human hand to bring out its beauties. Job speaks of it; and its sheen is in Christ's sermon; and the Bible, which, opening with the onycha of my text, closes with the pearl. Of such value is this crustaceous product, I do not wonder that for the exclusive right of fishing for it on the shores of Ceylon a man paid to the English government six hundred thousand dollars for one season. So exquisite is the pearl, I do not wonder that Pliny thought it was made out of a drop of dew, the creature rising to the surface to take it, and the chemistry of nature turning the liquid into a solid. You will comprehend why the Bible makes so much of the pearl in its similitudes if you know how much it costs to get it. Boats with divers sail out from the island of Ceylon, ten divers to each boat. Thirteen men guide and manage the boat. Down into the dangerous depths, amid sharks that swirl around them, plunge the divers, while sixty thousand people anxiously gaze on. After three or four minutes' absence from the air, the diver ascends, nine-tenths strangulated and blood rushing from ears and nostrils, and, flinging his pearly treasure on the deck, falls into unconsciousness. Oh, it is an awful exposure and strain and peril to fish for pearls, and yet they do so, and is it not a wonder that to get that which the Bible calls the Pearl of Great Price, worth more than all other pearls put together, there should be so little anxiety, so little struggle, so little enthusiasm. Would to God that we were all as wise as the merchantman Christ commended, "who, when he had found one Pearl of Great Price, went and sold all that he had and bought it."

But what thrills me with suggestiveness is the material out of which all pearls are made. They are fashioned from the wound of the shell-fish. The exudation from that wound is fixed and hardened and enlarged into a pearl. The ruptured vessels of the water-animal fashioned the gem that now adorns the finger or earring or sword hilt or king's crown. So, out of the wounds of earth will come the pearls of heaven. Out of the wound of conviction, the pearl of pardon. Out of the wound of bereavement, the pearl of solace. Out of the wound of loss, the pearl of gain. Out of the deep wound of the grave, the pearl of resurrection joy. Out of the wounds of a Saviour's life and a Saviour's death, the rich, radiant, the everlasting pearl of heavenly gladness. "And the twelve gates were twelve pearls." Take the consolation, all ye who have been hurt, whether hurt in body or hurt in mind or hurt in soul. Get your trouble sanctified. If you suffer with Christ on earth, you will reign with him in glory. The tears of earth are the crystals of heaven "Every several gate was of one pearl."

THE ORNITHOLOGY OF THE BIBLE; OR, GOD AMONG THE BIRDS

Matthew, 6: 26: "Behold the fowls of the air."

THE ORNITHOLOGY OF THE BIBLE; OR, GOD AMONG THE BIRDS

Matthew, 6: 26: "Behold the fowls of the air."

There is a silence now in all our January forests, except as the winds whistle through the bare branches. The organ-lofts in the temple of nature are hymnless. Trees which were full of carol and chirp and chant are now waiting for the coming back of rich plumes and warbling voices, solos, duets, quartets, cantatas, and Te Deums. The difference between the forests in summer and the forests in winter is the difference between an academy of music with enchanted throngs listening to an inspired cantatrice and an academy of music empty. But the Bible is full of birds at all seasons, and prophets and patriarchs and apostles and evangelists and Christ himself employ them for moral and religious purposes. My text is an extract from the Sermon on the Mount, and perhaps it was at a moment when a flock of birds flew past that Christ waved his hand toward them and said: "Behold the fowls of the air." And so, in this course of sermons on God Everywhere, I preach to you this sermon concerning the Ornithology of the Bible, or God among the Birds.

Most of the other sciences you may study or not study, as you please. Use your own judgment, exercise your own taste. But about this science of ornithology we have no option. The divine command is positive when it says in my text, "Behold the fowls of the air!" That is, study their habits. Examine their colors. Notice their speed. See the hand of God in their construction. It is easy for me to obey the command of the text, for I was brought up among this race of wings, and from boyhood heard their matins at sunrise and their vespers at sunset. Their nests have to me a fascination, and my satisfaction is that I never robbed one of them, any more than I would steal a child from a cradle; for a bird is a child of the sky, and its nest is the cradle. They are almost human, for they have their loves and hates, affinities and antipathies, understand joy and grief, have conjugal and maternal instinct, wage wars and entertain jealousies, have a language of their own and powers of association. Thank God for the birds!

It is useless to expect to understand the Bible unless we study natural history. Five hundred and ninety-three times does the Bible allude to the facts of natural history, and I do not wonder that it makes so many allusions ornithological. The skies and the caverns of Palestine are friendly to the winged creatures, and so many fly and roost and nest and hatch in that region that inspired writers do not have far to go to get ornithological illustration of divine truth. There are over forty species of birds recognized in the Scriptures. Oh, what a variety of wings in Palestine! The dove, the robin, the eagle, the cormorant or plunging bird, hurling itself from sky to wave and with long beak clutching its prey; the thrush, which especially dislikes a crowd; the partridge, the hawk, bold and ruthless, hovering head to windward while watching for prey; the swan, at home among the marshes and with feet so constructed it can walk on the leaves of water-plants; the raven, the lapwing, malodorous and in the Bible denounced as inedible, though it has extraordinary head-dress; the stork, the ossifrage, that always had a habit of dropping on a stone the turtle it had lifted and so killing it for food, and on one occasion mistook the bald head of Æschylus, the Greek poet, for a white stone and dropped a turtle upon it, killing the famous Greek; the cuckoo, with crested head and crimson throat and wings snow-tipped, but too lazy to build its own nest and so having the habit of depositing its eggs in nests belonging to other birds; the blue jay, the grouse, the plover, the magpie, the kingfisher, the pelican, which is the caricature of all the feathered creation; the owl, the goldfinch, the bittern, the harrier, the bulbul, the osprey, the vulture, that king of scavengers, with neck covered with repulsive down instead of attractive feathers; the quarrelsome starling, the swallow, flying a mile a minute and sometimes ten hours in succession; the heron, the quail, the peacock, the ostrich, the lark, the crow, the kite, the bat, the blackbird, and many others; with all colors, all sounds, all styles of flight, all habits, all architecture of nests, leaving nothing wanting in suggestiveness. At the creation they took their places all around on the rocks and in the trees and on the ground to serenade Adam's arrival. They took their places on Friday, as the first man was made on Saturday. Whatever else he had or did not have, he should have music. The first sound that struck the human ear was a bird's voice.

Yea, Christian geology (for you know there is a Christian geology as well as an infidel geology), Christian geology comes in and helps the Bible show what we owe to the bird creation. Before the human race came into this world, the world was occupied by reptiles and by all styles of destructive monsters, millions of creatures loathsome and hideous. God sent huge birds to clear the earth of these creatures before Adam and Eve were created. The remains of these birds have been found imbedded in the rocks. The skeleton of one eagle has been found twenty feet in height and fifty feet from tip of wing to tip of wing. Many armies of beaks and claws were necessary to clear the earth of creatures that would have destroyed the human race with one clip. I like to find this harmony of revelation and science, and to have it demonstrated that the God who made the world made the Bible.

Moses, the greatest lawyer of all time and a great man for facts, had enough sentiment and poetry and musical taste to welcome the illumined wings and the voices divinely drilled into the first chapter of Genesis. How should Noah, the old ship carpenter, six hundred years of age, find out when the world was fit again for human residence after the universal freshet? A bird will tell, and nothing else can. No man can come from the mountain to invite Noah and his family out to *terra firma*, for the mountains were submerged. As a bird first heralded the human race into the world, now a bird will help the human race back to the world that had shipped a sea that whelmed everything. Noah stands on Sunday morning at the window of the Ark, in his hand a cooing dove, so gentle, so innocent, so affectionate, and he said: "Now, my little dove, fly away over these waters, explore, and come back and tell us whether it is safe to land." After a long flight it returned hungry and weary and wet, and by its looks and manners said to Noah and his family: "The world is not fit for you to disembark." Noah waited a week, and next Sunday morning he let the dove fly again for a second exploration, and Sunday evening it came back with a leaf that had the sign of having been plucked from a living fruit tree, and in that way the bird reported the world would do tolerably well for a bird to live in, but not yet sufficiently recovered for human residence. Noah waited another week, and next Sunday morning he sent out the dove on the third exploration, but it returned not, for it found the world so attractive now it did not want to be caged again, and then the emigrants from the antediluvian world landed. It was a bird that told them when to take possession of the resuscitated planet. So the human race was saved by a bird's wing: for attempting to land too soon they would have perished.

Ay, here come a whole flock of doves—rock-doves, ring-doves, stock-doves—and they make Isaiah think of great revivals and great awakenings when souls fly for shelter like a flock of pigeons swooping to the openings of a pigeon coop, and he cries out: "Who are these that fly as doves to their windows?" David, with Saul after him, and flying from cavern to cavern, compares himself to a desert partridge, a bird which especially haunts rocky places; and boys and hunters to this day take after it with sticks, for the partridge runs rather than flies. David, chased and clubbed and harried of pursuers, says: "I am hunted as a partridge on the mountains." Speaking of his forlorn condition, he says: "I am like a pelican of the wilderness." Describing his loneliness, he says: "I am a swallow alone on a housetop." Hezekiah, in the emaciation of his sickness, compares himself to the crane, thin and wasted. Job had so much trouble he could not sleep nights, and he describes his insomnia by saying: "I am a companion to owls." Isaiah compares the desolation of banished Israel to the owl and bittern and cormorant among a city's ruins. Jeremiah, describing the cruelty of parents toward children, compares them to the ostrich, who leaves its eggs in the sand uncared for, crying: "The daughter of my people is become like the ostriches of the wilderness." Among the provisions piled on Solomon's bountiful table, the Bible speaks of "fatted fowl." The

Israelites in the desert got tired of manna and they had quails—quails for breakfast, quails for dinner, quails for supper—and they died of quails.

The Bible refers to the migratory habits of the birds, and says: "The stork knoweth her appointed time and the turtle and the crane and the swallow the time of their going, but my people know not the judgments of the Lord." Would the prophet illustrate the fate of fraud, he points to a failure at incubation, and says: "As a partridge sitteth on eggs and hatcheth them not, so he that getteth riches and not by right shall leave them in the midst of his days and at his end shall be a fool." The partridge, the most careless of all birds in choice of its place of nest, building it on the ground and often near a frequented road, or in a slight depression of ground, without reference to safety, and soon a hoof or a scythe or a cart-wheel ends all. So, says the prophet, a man who gathers under him dishonest dollars will hatch out of them no peace, no satisfaction, no happiness, no security. What vivid similitude! The quickest way to amass a fortune is by iniquity, but the trouble is about keeping it. Every hour of every day some such partridge is driven off the nest. Panics are only a flutter of partridges. It is too tedious work to become rich in the old-fashioned way, and if a man can by one falsehood make as much as by ten years of hard labor, why not tell it? And if one counterfeit check will bring the dollars as easily as a genuine issue, why not make it? One year's fraud will be equal to half a lifetime's sweat. Why not live solely by one's wits? A fortune thus built will be firm and everlasting. Will it? Ha! build your house on a volcano's crater; go to sleep on the bosom of an avalanche. The volcano will blaze and the avalanche will thunder. There are estates which have been coming together from age to age. Many years ago that estate started in a husband's industry and a wife's economy. It grew from generation to generation by good habits and high-minded enterprise. Old-fashioned industry was the mine from which that gold was dug, and God will keep the deeds of such an estate in his buckler. Foreclose your mortgage, spring your snap judgments, plot with acutest intrigue against a family property like that, and you cannot do it a permanent damage. Better than warrantee deed, and better than fire insurance is the defence which God's own hand will give it.

But here is a man, to-day as poor as Job, after he was robbed by Satan of everything but his boils; yet, suddenly, to-morrow he is a rich man. There is no accounting for his sudden affluence. He has not yet failed often enough to become wealthy. No one pretends to account for his princely wardrobe, or the chased silver, or the full-curbed steeds that rear and neigh like Bucephalus in the grasp of his coachman. Did he come to a sudden inheritance? No. Did he make a fortune on purchase and sale? No. Everybody asks: "Where did that partridge hatch?" The devil suddenly threw him up and the devil will suddenly let him come down. That hidden scheme God saw from the first inception of the plot. That partridge, swift disaster will shoot it down, and the higher it flies the harder it falls. The prophet saw, as you and I have often seen, the awful mistake of partridges.

But from the top of a Bible fir tree I hear the shrill cry of the stork. Job, Ezekiel, Jeremiah speak of it. David cries out: "As for the stork, the fir tree is her house." This large white Bible bird is supposed, sometimes, without alighting, to wing its way from the region of the Rhine to Africa. As winter comes, all the storks fly to warmer climes, and the last one of their number that arrives at the spot to which they migrate is killed by them. What havoc it would make in our species if those men were killed who are always behind! In Oriental cities the stork is domesticated and walks about on the street, and will follow its keeper. In the city of Ephesus, I saw a long row of pillars, on the top of each pillar a stork's nest. But the word "stork" ordinarily means mercy and affection, from the fact that this bird was distinguished for its great love to its parents. It never forsakes them, and even after they become feeble, protects and provides for them. In migrating, the old storks lean their necks on the young storks, and when the old ones give out the young ones carry them on their backs. God forbid that a dumb stork should have more heart than we. Blessed is that table at which an old father and mother sit! Blessed that altar at which an old father and mother kneel! What it is to have a mother they know best who have lost her. God only knows the agony she suffered for us, the times she wept over our cradle and the anxious sighs her bosom heaved as we lay upon it, the sick nights when she watched us, long after every one was tired out but God and herself. Her life-blood beats in our heart and her image lives in our face. That man is graceless as a cannibal who ill-treats his parents, and he who begrudges them daily bread and clothes them but shabbily, may God have patience with him; I cannot. I heard a man once say: "I now have my old mother on my hands." Ye storks on your way with food to your aged parents, shame him!

But yonder in this Bible sky flies a bird that is speckled. The prophet describing the church cries out: "Mine heritage is unto me as a speckled bird, the birds round about are against her." So it was then; so it is now. Holiness picked at. Consecration picked at. Usefulness picked at. A speckled bird is a peculiar bird, and that arouses the antipathy of all the beaks of the forest. The Church of God is a peculiar institution, and that is enough to evoke attack of the world, for it is a speckled bird to be picked at. The inconsistencies of Christians are a banquet on which multitudes get fat. They ascribe everything you do to wrong motives. Put a dollar in the poor-box, and they will say that he dropped it there only that others might hear it ring. Invite them to Christ and they will call you a fanatic. Let there be contention among Christians, and they will say "Hurrah! the church is in decadence." Christ intended that his church should always remain a speckled bird. Let birds of another feather pick at her, but they cannot rob her of a single plume. Like the albatross, she can sleep on the bosom of a tempest. She has gone through the fires of Nebuchadnezzar's furnace and not got burned, through the waters of the Red Sea and not been drowned, through the shipwreck on the breakers of Melita and not been foundered. Let all earth and hell try to hunt down this speckled bird, but far above human scorn and infernal assault, she shall sing over every mountain-top and fly over every nation, and her triumphant song shall be, "The Church of God! The pillar and ground of the truth. The gates of hell shall not prevail against her."

But we cannot stop here. From a tall cliff, hanging over the sea, I hear the eagle calling unto the tempest and lifting its wing to smite the whirlwind. Moses, Jeremiah, Hosea and Habakkuk, at times in their writings, take their pen from the eagle's wing. It is a bird with fierceness in its eye, its feet armed with claws of iron, and its head with a dreadful beak. Two or three of them can fill the heavens with clangor. But generally this monster of the air is alone and unaccompanied, for the reason that its habits are so predaceous it requires five or ten miles of aerial or earthly dominion for itself. The black-brown of its back, and the white of its lower feathers, and the fire of its eye, and the long flap of its wing make one glimpse of it, as it swoops down into the valley to pick up a rabbit, or a lamb, or a child, and then sweeps back to its throne on the rock, something never to be forgotten. Scattered about its eyrie of altitudinous solitude are the bones of its conquests. But while the beak and the claws of the eagle are the terror of all the travelers of the air, the mother-eagle is most kind and gentle to her young. God compares his treatment of his people to the eagle's care of the eaglets. Deuteronomy 32:11: "As an eagle stirreth up her nest, fluttereth over her young, spreadeth abroad her wings, taketh them, beareth them on her wings, so the Lord alone did lead him." The old eagle first shoves the young one out of the nest in order to make it fly, and then takes it on her back and flies with it, and shakes it off in the air, and if it seem like falling, quickly flies under it and takes it on her wing again. So God does with us. Disaster, failure in business, disappointment, bereavement, are only God's way of shaking us out of our comfortable nest in order that we may learn how to fly. You who are complaining that you have no faith or courage or Christian zeal have had it too easy. You never will learn to fly in that comfortable nest. Like an eagle, Christ has carried us on his back. At times we have been shaken off, and when we were about to fall he came under us again and brought us out of the gloomy valley to the sunny mountain. Never an eagle brooded with such love and care over her young as God's wings have been over us. Across what oceans of trouble we have gone in safety upon the Almighty wings. From what mountains of sin have we been carried, and at times have been borne up far above the gunshot of the world and the arrow of the devil. When our time on earth is closed, on these great wings of God we shall speed with infinite quickness from earth's mountains to heaven's hills, and as from the eagle's circuit under the sun, men on the ground seem small and insignificant as lizards on a rock, so all earthly things shall dwindle into a speck and the raging river of death so far beneath will seem smooth and glassy as a Swiss lake.

It was thought in ancient times that an eagle could not only molt his feathers in old age, but that after arriving to great age he would renew his strength and become entirely young again. To this Isaiah alludes when he says: "They that wait on the Lord shall renew their strength, they shall mount up with wings as eagles." Even so the Christian in old age will renew his spiritual strength. He shall be young in ardor and enthusiasm for Christ; and as the body fails, the soul will grow in elasticity, till at death it will spring up like a gladdened child into the bosom of God. Yea, in this ornithological study, I see that Job says: "His days fly as an eagle that hasteth to its prey." The speed of a hungry eagle when it saw its prey a score of miles distant was unimaginable. It went like a thunderbolt for speed and power. So fly our days. The old earth is rent and cracked under the swift rush of days and months and years and ages. "Swift as an eagle that hasteth to its prey." Behold the fowls of the air. Have you considered that they have, as you and I have not, the power to change their eyes so that one minute they may be telescopic and the next microscopic. Now seeing something a mile away, and by telescopic eyesight, and then dropping to its food on the ground, able to see it close by, and with microscopic eyesight.

But what a senseless passage of Scripture that is,

until you know the facts, which says "The sparrow hath found a house and the swallow a nest for herself where she may lay her young, even thine altars, O Lord of hosts, my King and my God." What has the swallow to do with the altars of the Tabernacle at Jerusalem? Ah! you know that swallows are all the world over very tame, and in summer time they used to fly into the windows and doors of the Tabernacle at Jerusalem and build a nest on the altar where the priests were offering sacrifices. These swallows brought leaves and sticks and fashioned nests on the altars of the Tabernacle, and hatched the young swallows in those nests, and David had seen the young birds picking their way out of the shell while the old swallows watched, and no one in the Tabernacle was cruel enough to disturb either the old swallows or the young swallows, and David bursts out in rhapsody, saying: "The swallow hath found a nest for herself where she may lay her young, even thine altars, O Lord of hosts, my King and my God!"

In this ornithology of the Bible, I find that God is determined to impress upon us the architecture of a bird's nest and the anatomy of a bird's wing. Twenty times does the Bible refer to a bird's nest: "Where the birds make their nest," "As a bird that wandereth from her nest," "Though thou set thy nest among the stars," "The birds of the air have their nests," and so on. Nests in the trees, nests on the rocks, nests on the altars. Why does God call us so frequently to consider the bird's nest? Because it is one of the most wondrous of all styles of architecture, and a lesson of Providential care which is the most important lesson that Christ in my text conveys. Why, just look at the bird's nest, and see what is the prospect that God is going to take care of you. Here is the bluebird's nest under the eaves of the house.

Ornithology of the Bible

Here is the brown thrasher's nest in a bush. Here is the blue jay's nest in the orchard. Here is the grosbeak's nest on a tree-branch hanging over the water, so as to be free from attack. Chickadee's nest in the stump of an old tree. Oh, the goodness of God in showing the birds how to build their nest! What carpenters, what masons, what weavers, what spinners the birds are! Out of what small resources they make what an exquisite home, curved, pillared, wreathed. Out of mosses, out of sticks, out of lichens, out of horsehair, out of spiders' web, out of threads swept from the door by the housewife, out of the wool of the sheep in the pasture-field. Upholstered by leaves actually sewed together by its own sharp bill. Cushioned with feathers from its own breast. Mortared together with the gum of trees and the saliva of its own tiny bill. Such symmetry, such adaptation, such convenience, such geometry of structure.

Surely these nests were built by some plan. They did not just happen so. Who draughted the plan for the bird's nest? God! And do you not think that if he plans such a house for a chaffinch, for an oriole, for a bobolink, for a sparrow, he will see to it that you always have a home? "Ye are of more value than many sparrows." Whatever else surrounds you, you can have what the Bible calls "the feathers of the Almighty." Just think of a nest like that, the warmth of it, the softness of it, the safety of it—"the feathers of the Almighty." No flamingo outflashing the tropical sunset ever had such brilliancy of pinion; no robin redbreast ever had plumage dashed with such crimson and purple and orange and gold—"the feathers of the Almighty." Do you not feel the touch of them now on forehead and cheek and spirit, and was there ever such tenderness of brooding—"the feathers of the Almighty"? So also in this ornithology of the

Sermons by T. DeWitt Talmage

Bible God keeps impressing us with the anatomy of a bird's wing. Over fifty times does the old Book allude to the wing, "Wings of a dove," "Wings of the morning," "Wings of the wind," "Sun of righteousness with healing in his wings," "Wings of the Almighty," "All fowl of every wing." What does it all mean? It suggests uplifting. It tells you of flight upward. It means to remind you that you, yourself, have wings. David cried out, "Oh, that I had wings like a dove that I might fly away and be at rest." Thank God that you have better wings than any dove of longest or swiftest flight. Caged now in bars of flesh are those wings, but the day comes when they will be liberated. Get ready for ascension. Take the words of the old hymn, and to the tune unto which that hymn is married sing:

> Rise, my soul, and stretch thy wings,
> Thy better portion trace.

Up out of these lowlands into the heavens of higher experience and wider prospect. But how shall we rise? Only as God's Holy Spirit gives us strength. But that is coming now. Not as a condor from a Chimborazo peak, swooping upon the affrighted valley, but as a dove like that which put its soft brown wings over the wet locks of Christ at the baptism in the Jordan. Dove of gentleness! Dove of peace!

> Come, Holy Spirit, heavenly dove,
> With all thy quickening powers,
> Come shed abroad a Saviour's love,
> And that shall kindle ours.

THE ICHTHYOLOGY OF THE BIBLE; OR, GOD AMONG THE FISHES

Gen., 1: 20: "And God said, Let the waters bring forth abundantly the moving creature that hath life."

THE ICHTHYOLOGY OF THE BIBLE; OR, GOD AMONG THE FISHES

Gen., 1: 20: "And God said, Let the waters bring forth abundantly the moving creature that hath life."

What a new book the Bible is! After thirty-six years preaching from it and discussing over three thousand different subjects founded on the Word of God, much of the Book is as fresh to me as when I learned, with a stretch of infantile memory, the shortest verse in the Bible, "Jesus wept." In this course of sermons on God Everywhere I find many things I had not before noticed. To-day I speak to you concerning the Ichthyology of the Bible, or God among the Fishes. A fish was the early monogram of Christianity. It is found on the walls of the catacombs, and the Pope still wears "The Fisherman's Ring." The reason is that the Greek word for fish is composed of five letters, of which the first stands for Jesus, the second for Christ, the third for God, the fourth for Son, and the fifth for Saviour. So the word represented the initials of Jesus Christ, God's Son, the Saviour.

Our horses were lathered and tired out, and their fetlocks were red with the blood cut out by the rocks, and I could hardly get my feet out of the stirrups as, on Saturday night, we dismounted on the beach of Lake Galilee. The rather liberal supply of food with which we had started from Jerusalem was well-nigh exhausted, and the articles of diet remaining had, by oft repetition, three times a day for three weeks, ceased to appetize. I never want to see a fig again, and dates with me are all out of date. For several days the Arab caterer, who could speak but half a dozen English words, would answer our requests for some of the styles of food with which we had been delectated the first few days, by crying out, "Finished." The most piquant appetizer is abstinence, and the demand of all the party was, "Let us breakfast on Sunday morning on fresh fish from Lake Gennesaret," for you must know that that lake has four names—and it is worth a profusion of nomenclature—it is in the Bible called Chinnereth, Tiberias, Gennesaret and Galilee. To our extemporized table on Sabbath morning came broiled perch, only a few hours before lifted out of the sacred waters. It was natural that our minds should revert to the only breakfast that Christ ever prepared, and it was on those very shores where we breakfasted. Christ had, in those olden times, struck two flints together and set on fire some shavings or light brushwood, and then put on larger wood, and a pile of glowing bright coals was the consequence. Meanwhile, the disciples, fishing on the lake, had very "poor luck," and every time they drew up the net it hung dripping without a fluttering fin or squirming scale. But Christ, from the shore, shouted to them, and told them where to drop the net, and one hundred and fifty-three big fish rewarded them. Simon and Nathaniel, having cleaned some of those large fish, brought them to the coals which Christ had kindled, and the group, who had been out all night, sat down and began mastication. All that scene came back to us when on a Sabbath morning in December, 1889, just outside the ruins of ancient Tiberias, and within sound of the rippling Galilee, we breakfasted.

Now, is it not strange that the Bible imagery is so inwrought from the fisheries, when the Holy Land is,

Ichthyology of the Bible

for the most part, an inland region? Only three lakes, two besides the one already mentioned, namely, the Dead Sea, where fish cannot live at all and as soon as they touch it they die, and the birds swoop on their tiny carcases, and the third, the Pools of Heshbon, which are alternately full and dry. Only three rivers of the Holy Land—Jabbok, Kishon and Jordan. About all the fish now in the waters of the Holy Land are the perch, the carp, the bream, the minnow, the blenny, the barbel (so called because of the barb at its mouth), the chub, the dog-fish—none of them worth a Delaware shad or an Adirondack trout. Well, the world's geography has changed and the world's bill of fare has changed. Lake Galilee was larger and deeper and better stocked than now, and no doubt the rivers were deeper and the fisheries were of far more importance then than now. Besides, there was the Mediterranean Sea only thirty-five miles away, and fish were salted or dried and brought inland, and so much of that article of food was sold in Jerusalem that a fish market gave the name to one of the gates of Jerusalem near by, which was called the Fish Gate. The cities had great reservoirs, in which fish were kept alive and bred. The Pool of Gibeon was a fish-pool. Isaiah and Solomon refer to fish-pools. Large fish were kept alive and tied fast by ropes to a stake in these reservoirs, a ring having been run through their gills, and that is the meaning of the Scripture passage which says: "Canst thou put a hook into his nose, or bore his jaw through with a thorn?" So important was the fish that the god Dagon—worshiped by the Philistines—was made half fish and half man, and that is the meaning of the Lord's indignation, when in First Samuel we read that this Dagon, the fish-god, stood beside the ark of the Lord, and Dagon was by invisible hands dashed to pieces, because the Philistines had dared to make the fish a god. That explains the Scripture passage: "The head of Dagon and both the palms of his hands were cut off upon the threshold; only the stump of Dagon was left to him." Now, the stump of Dagon was the fish part. The top part, which was the figure of a man, was dashed to pieces, and the Lord, by demolishing everything but the stump or fish part of the idol, practically said, "You may keep your fish, but know from the way I have demolished the rest of the idol that it is nothing Divine."

Layard and Wilkinson found the fish an object of idolatry all through Assyria and Egypt. The Nile was full of fish, and that explains the horrors of the plague that slaughtered the finny tribe all up and down that river, which has been and is now the main artery of Egypt's life. In Job you hear the plunge of the spear into the hippopotamus, as the great dramatic poet cries out: "Canst thou fill his skin with barbed irons or his head with fish spears?" Yea, the fish began to swim in the very first book of Genesis, where my text records, "And God said, Let the waters bring forth abundantly the moving creature that hath life." Do you realize that the first living thing that God created was the fish? It preceded the bird, the quadruped, the human race. The fish has priority of residence over every living thing. The next thing done, after God had kindled for our world the golden chandelier of the sun and the silver chandelier of the moon, was to make the fish. The first motion of the principle of life, a principle that all the thousands of years since have not been able to define or analyze, the very first stir of life was in a fish. What an hour that was when, in the Euphrates, the Gihon, the Pison, and the Hiddekel, the four rivers of Paradise, the waters swirled with fins and brightened with scales. All the attributes of the Infinite God were called into action for the making of that first fish. Lanceolate and transiucent miracle! There is enough wonder in the plate of a sturgeon or in the cartilage of a shark to confound the scientists. It does not take the universe to prove a God. A fish does it. No wonder that Linnæus and Cuvier and Agassiz and the greatest minds of all the centuries sat enraptured before its anatomy. Oh, its beauty, and the adaptness of its structure to the element in which it must live: the picture gallery on the sides of the mountain trout unveiled as they spring up to snatch the flies: the grayling, called the Flower of Fishes; the salmon, ascending the Oregon and the Severn, easily leaping the falls that would stop them; the bold perch, the gudgeon, silver and black spotted; the herring, moving in squadrons five miles long; the carp, for cunning called the Fox of Fishes; the wondrous sturgeons, formerly reserved for the tables of royal families, and the isinglass made out of their membrane; the tench, called the Physician of Fishes because, when applied to human ailments, it is said to be curative; the lampreys, so tempting to the epicurean that too many of them slew Henry II.; ay, the whole world of fishes. Enough of them floating up and down the rivers to feed the hemispheres if every ear of corn and every head of wheat and every herd of quadruped, and if every other article of food in all the earth were destroyed. Universal drought, leaving not so much as a spear of grass on the round planet, would leave in the rivers and lakes and seas for the human race, a staple commodity of food, which, if brought to shore, would be enough not only to feed but fatten the entire human race. In times to come the world may be so populated that the harvests and vineyards and land animals may be insufficient to feed the human family, and the nations may be obliged to come to the rivers and ocean beaches to seek the living harvests that swim the deep, and that would mean more health and vigor and brilliancy and brain than the human race now owns.

The Lord, by placing the fish in the first course of the menu in Paradise, making it precede bird and beast, indicated to the world the importance of the fish as an article of human food. The reason that men and women lived three and four and five and nine hundred years was because they were kept on parched corn and fish. We mix up a fantastic food that kills the most of us before thirty years of age. Custards and whipped sillabubs and Roman punches and chicken salads at midnight are a gauntlet that few have strength to run. We put on many a tombstone glowing epithets saying that the person beneath died of patriotic services or from exhaustion in religious work, when nothing killed the poor fellow but lobster eaten at a party four hours after he ought to have been sound asleep in bed. There are men to-day in our streets so many walking hospitals, who might have been athletes if they had taken the hint of Genesis in my text and of our Lord's remark, and adhered to simplicity of diet. The reason that the country districts have furnished most of the men and women of our time who are doing the mightiest work in merchandise, in mechanics, in law, in medicine, in theology, in legislative and congressional halls, and all the Presidents from Washington down—at least, those who have amounted to anything—is because they were in those country districts of necessity kept on plain diet. No man or woman ever amounted to anything who was brought up on floating island or angel cake. The world must turn back to paradisaic diet, if it is to get paradisaic morals and paradisaic health. The human race to-day needs more phosphorus, and the fish is charged and surcharged with phosphorus. Phosphorus, that which shines in the dark without burning.

What made the twelve Apostles such stalwart men that they could endure anything and achieve everything? Next to Divine inspiration, it was because they were nearly all fishermen, and lived on fish and a few plain condiments. Paul, though not brought up to swing the net and throw the line, must of necessity have adopted the diet of the population among whom he lived, and you see the phosphorus in his daring plea before Felix, and the phosphorus in his boldest of all utterances before the wiseacres on Mars Hill, and the phosphorus as he went without fright to his beheading. And the phosphorus you see in the lives of all the Apostles, who moved right on, undaunted, to certain martyrdom, whether to be decapitated or flung off precipices or hung in crucifixion. Phosphorus, shining in the dark without burning! No man or woman that ever lived was independent of questions of diet. Let those who by circumstances are compelled to simplicity of diet, thank God for their rescue from the temptation of killing delicacies. The men and women who are to decide the drift of the twentieth century, which is only a short step off, are now five miles back from the rail station, and had for breakfast this morning a similar bill of fare to that which Christ provided for the fishermen-disciples on the banks of Lake Galilee. Indeed the only articles of food that Christ by miracle multiplied were bread and fish, which the boy who acted as sutler to the five thousand people of the wilderness handed over—five barley loaves and two fishes. The boy must have felt badly when he had brought out, after having caught them himself, sitting with his bare feet over the bank of the lake and expecting to sell his supply at good profit; but he felt better when by the miracle the fish were multiplied and he had more returned to him than he had surrendered.

Know, also, in order to understand the ichthyology of the Bible, that in the deepest waters, as those of the Mediterranean, there were monsters that are now extinct. The fools who became infidels because they could not understand the engulfment of the recreant Jonah in a sea monster, might have saved their souls by studying a little natural history. "Oh," says some one, "that story of Jonah was only a fable." Say others: "It was interpolated by some writer of later times." Others again say: "It was a reproduction of the story of Hercules devoured and then restored from the monster." But my reply is that history tells us that there were monsters large enough to whelm ships. The extinct ichthyosaurus of other ages was thirty feet long, and as late as the sixth century of the Christian era, up and down the Mediterranean there floated monsters compared with which a modern whale was a sardine or a herring. The shark has again and again been found to have swallowed a man entire. A fisherman on the coast of Turkey found a sea-monster which contained a woman and a purse of gold. I have seen in museums sea-monsters large enough to take down a prophet. But I have a better reason for believing, the Old Testament account, and that is that Christ said it was true, and a type of his own resurrection, and I suppose he ought to know. In Matthew, 12th chapter, 40th verse, Jesus Christ says: "For as Jonah was three days and three nights in the whale's belly, so shall the Son of Man be three days and three nights in the heart of the earth." And that settles it for me and for any man who does not believe Christ a dupe or an impostor.

Notice, also, how the Old Testament writers drew similitude from the fisheries. Jeremiah uses such im-

66

agery to prophesy destruction: "Behold I will send for many fishers, saith the Lord, and they shall fish them." Ezekiel uses fish imagery to prophesy prosperity: "It shall come to pass that the fishers shall stand upon it, from En-gedi even to En-eglaim; they shall be a place to spread forth nets; their fish shall be according to their kinds, as the fish of the great sea, exceeding many." The explanation of which is that En-gedi and En-eglaim stood on the banks of the Dead Sea, in the waters of which no fish can live; but the prophet says that the time will come when these waters will be regenerated and they will be great places for fish. Amos reproves idolatries by saying: "The days shall come upon you when he will take you away with hooks and your posterity with fish-hooks." Solomon, in Ecclesiastes, declares that those captured of temptation are as fishes taken in an evil net. Indeed, Solomon knew all about the finny tribe and wrote a treatise on Ichthyology, which has been lost.

Furthermore, in order that you may understand the ichthyology of the Bible, you must know that there were five ways of fishing. One was by a fence of reeds and canes, within which the fish were caught; but the Herodic government forbade that on Lake Galilee, lest pleasure boats be wrecked by the stakes driven. Another mode was by spearing; the waters of Galilee so clear, good aim could be taken for the transfixing. Another was by hook and line, as where Isaiah says: "The fishers also shall mourn, and they that cast angle into the brooks shall lament." Job says: "Canst thou draw out leviathan with a hook?" And Habakkuk says: "They take up all of them with the angle." Another mode was by a casting net or that which was flung from the shore. Another by a drag net, or that which was thrown from a boat and drawn through the sea, as the fishing smack sailed on. How wonderful all this is, inwrought into the Bible imagery, and it leads me to ask, In what mode are you fishing? for the Church is the boat and the Gospel is the net and the sea is the world and the fish are the souls, and God addresses us, as he did Simon and Andrew, saying: "Follow me and I will make you fishers of men." But when is the best time to fish for souls? In the night. Peter, why did you say to Christ: "We have toiled all the night and have taken nothing?" Why did you not fish in the daytime? He replies: "You ought to know that the night is the best time for fishing." At Tobyhanna Mills, among the mountains of Pennsylvania, I saw a friend with high boots and fishing-tackle starting out at nine o'clock at night, and I said, "Where are you going?" He answered, "Going to fish." "What, in the night?" He answered, "Yes, in the night." So the vast majority of souls captured for God are taken in times of revival in the night meetings. They might just as well come at twelve o'clock at noon, but most of them will not. Ask the evangelists of olden times, ask Finney, ask Nettleton, ask Osborn, ask Daniel Baker, and then ask all the modern evangelists, Which is the best time to gather souls? and they will answer, "The night; by all odds, the night." Not only the natural night, but the night of trouble. Suppose I go among this audience and ask these Christians when they were converted to God. One would answer, "It was at the time I lost my child by membraneous croup, and it was the night of bereavement," or the answer would be, "It was just after I was swindled out of my property, and it was the night of bankruptcy," or it would be, "It was during that time when I was down with that awful sickness, and it was the night of physical suffering," or it would be, "It was that time when slander took after me, and I was maligned and abused, and it was the night of persecution." Ah, that is the time for you to go after souls, when a night of trouble is on them! Miss not that opportunity to save a soul, for it is the best of all opportunities. Go up along the Mohawk or the Juniata or the Delaware or the Tombigbee or the St Lawrence right after a rain, and you will find the fishermen all up and down the banks. Why? Because a good time to angle is right after the rain, and that is a good time to catch souls—right after a shower of misfortune, right after floods of disaster. And as a pool overshadowed with trees is a grand place for making a fine haul of fish, so when the soul is under the long dark shadows of anxiety and distress, it is a good time to make a spiritual haul. People in the bright sunshine of prosperity are not so easily taken.

Be sure before you start out to the Gospel fisheries to get the right kind of bait. "But how," you say, "am I to get it?" My answer is, "Dig for it." "Where shall I dig for it?" "In the rich Bible grounds." We boys brought up in the country had to dig for bait before we started for the banks of the Raritan. We put the sharp edge of the spade against the ground, and then put our foot on the spade, and with one tremendous plunge of our strength of body and will, we drove it in up to the handle, and then turned over the sod. We had never read Walton's "Complete Angler," or Charles Cotton's "Instructions How to Angle for Grayling in a Clear Stream." We knew nothing about the modern red-hackle, or the fly of orange-colored mohair, but we got the right kind of bait. No use trying to angle for fish or angle for souls unless you have the right kind of bait, and there is plenty of it in the Promises, the Parables, the Miracles, the Crucifixion, the Heaven of the grand old Gospel. Yes, not only must you dig for bait, you must use only fresh bait. You cannot do anything down at the pond with old angleworms. New views of truth. New views of God. New views of the soul. There are all the good books to help you dig. But make up your mind as to whether you will take the hint of Habukkuk and Isaiah and Job and use hook and line, or take the hint of Matthew and Luke and Christ and fish with a net. I think many lose their time by wanting to fish with a net, and they never get a place to swing the net; in other words, they want to do Gospel work on a big scale, or they will not do it at all. I see feeble-minded Christian men going around with a Bagster's Bible under their arm, hoping to do the work of an evangelist and use the net, while they might be better content with hook and line and take one soul at a time. They are bad failures as evangelists; they would be mighty successes as private Christians. If you catch only one soul for God, that will be enough to fill your eternity with celebration. All hail the fishermen with hook and line! I have seen a man in roughest corduroy outfit come back from the woods loaded down with a string of finny treasures hung over his shoulder and his game-bag filled, and a dog with his teeth carrying a basket filled with the surplus of an afternoon's angling, and it was all the result of a hook and line; and in the Eternal World there will be many a man and many a woman who was never heard of outside of a village Sunday School or a prayer-meeting buried in a church basement, who will come before the Throne of God with a multitude of souls ransomed through his or her instrumentality, and yet the work all done through personal interview, one by one, one by one. You do not know who that one soul may be. Staupitz helped one soul into the light, but it was Martin Luther. Thomas Bailey brought salvation to one soul, but it was Hugh

Latimer. An edge-tool maker was the means of saving one soul, but it was John Summerfield. Our blessed Lord healed one blind eye at a time, one paralyzed arm at a time, one dropsical patient at a time, and raised from the dead one young girl at a time, one young man at a time. Admire the net that takes in a great many at once, but do not despise the hook and line.

God help us amid the Gospel Fisheries, whether we employ hook or net, for the day cometh when we shall see how much depended on our fidelity. Christ himself declared: "The Kingdom of Heaven is like unto a net that was cast into the sea and gathered of every kind, which, when it was full, they drew to shore, and sat down and gathered the good in the vessels, but cast the bad away: so shall it be at the end of the world, the angels shall come forth and separate the wicked from the just." Yes, the fishermen think it best to keep the useful and worthless of the haul in the same net until it is drawn upon the beach, and then the division takes place; and if it is on Long Island coast, the moss-bunkers are thrown out and the bluefish and shad preserved, or if it is on the shore of Galilee, the fish classified as siluroids are hurled back into the water or thrown upon the bank as unclean, while the perch and the carp and the barbel are put in pails to be carried home for use. So in the church on earth, the saints and the hypocrites, the generous and the mean, the chaste and the unclean are kept in the same membership, but at death the division will be made and the good will be gathered into heaven and the bad, however many holy communions they may have celebrated, and however many rhetorical prayers they may have offered, and however many years their names may have been on the church rolls, will be cast away. God forbid that any of us should be among the "cast away." But may we do our work, whether small or great, as thoroughly as did that renowned fisherman, George W Bethune, who spent his summer rest angling in the waters around The Thousand Isles, and beating at their own craft those who plied it all the year, and who the rest of his time gloriously preached Christ in a pulpit only fifteen minutes from where I formerly preached in Brooklyn, and ordering for his own obsequies: "Put on me my pulpit gown and bands, with my own pocket Bible in my right hand. Bury me with my mother, my father, and my grandmother. Sing also my own hymn—

> Jesus thou Prince of Life!
>   Thy chosen cannot die;
> Like thee, they conquer in the strife,
>   To reign with thee on high.."

THE POMOLOGY OF THE BIBLE; OR, GOD AMONG THE ORCHARDS

Gen., 1: 11: " The fruit tree yielding fruit after its kind."

THE POMOLOGY OF THE BIBLE; OR, GOD AMONG THE ORCHARDS

Gen., 1: 11: " The fruit tree yielding fruit after its kind."

It is Wednesday morning in Paradise. The birds did not sing their opening piece, nor the fish take their first swim until the following Friday. The solar and lunar lights did not break through the thick, chaotic fog of the world's manufactory until Thursday. Before that there was light, but it was electric light, or phosphorescent light, not the light of sun or moon. But the botanical and pomological productions came on Wednesday—first the flowers, and then the fruits. The veil of fog is lifted, and there stand the orchards. Watch the sudden maturing of the fruit! In our time, pear trees must have two years before they bear fruit, and peach trees three years, and apple trees five years; but here, instantly, a complete orchard springs into life, all the branches bearing fruit. The insectile forces, which have been doing their best to destroy the fruits for six thousand years, had not yet begun their invasion. The curculio had not yet stung the plum, nor the caterpillar hurt the apple, nor had the phylloxera plague, which has devastated the vineyards of America and France, assailed the grapes, nor the borer perforated the wood, nor the aphides ruined the cherry, nor the grub punctured the nectarine, nor the blight struck the pear. There stood the first orchard, with a perfection of rind, and an exquisiteness of color, and a lusciousness of taste, and an affluence of production which it may take thousands of years more of study of the science of fruits to reproduce.

Why was the orchard created two days before the fish and birds, and three days before the cattle? Among other things, to impress the world with a lesson it is too stupid to learn—that fruit diet is healthier than meat diet, and that the former must precede the latter. The reason there are in the world so many of the imbruted and sensual is that they have not improved by the mighty, unnoticed fact that the orchards of Paradise preceded the herds, the aviaries, and fishponds. Oh, those fruit-bearing trees on the banks of the Euphrates, and the Gihon, and the Hiddekel! I wonder not that the ancient Romans, ignorant of our God, adored Pomona, the Goddess of Fruits, and that all the sylvan deities were said to worship her, and that groves were set apart as her temples. You have thanked God for bread a thousand times. Have you thanked him for the fruits which he made the first course of food in the menu of the world's table—the acids of those fruits to keep the world's table from being insipid, and their sweets to keep it from being too sour?

At the autumnal season, how the orchards breathe and glow, the leaves removed, that the crimson, or pink, or saffron, or the yellow, or brown may the better appear, while the aromatics fill the air with invitation and reminiscence. As you pass through the orchard on these autumnal days and look up through the arms of the trees laden with fruit, you hear thumping on the ground that which is fully ripe, and, throwing your arms around the trunk, you give a shake that sends down a shower of gold and fire on all sides of you. Pile up in baskets and barrels and bins and on shelves and tables the divine supply. But these orchards have been under the assault of at least sixty centuries—the storm, the droughts, the winters, the insectivora. What must the first orchard have been? And yet it is the explorer's evidence that on the site of that orchard there is not an apricot, or an apple, or an olive—nothing but desert and desolation. There is not enough to forage the explorer's horse, much less to feed his own hunger. In other words, that first orchard is a lost orchard. How did the proprietor and proprietress of all that intercolumniation of fruitage let the rich splendor slip their possession? It was as now most of the orchards are lost, namely, by wanting more. Access they had to all the fig-trees, apricots, walnuts, almonds, apples—bushels on bushels—and were forbidden the use of only one tree in the orchard. Not satisfied with all but one, they reached for that, and lost the whole orchard. Go right down through the business marts of the great cities and find among the weighers and clerks and subordinates men who once commanded the commercial world. They had a whole orchard of successes, but they wanted just one more thing—one more house, or one more country seat, or one more store, or one more railroad, or one more million. They clutched for that and lost all they had gained. For one more tree they lost a whole orchard. There are business men all around us worried nearly to death. The doctor tells them they ought to stop. Insomnia or indigestion or aching at the base of the brain or ungovernable nerves tell them they ought to stop. They really have enough for themselves and their families. Talk with one of them about his overwork, and urge more prudence and longer rest, and he says: "Yes, you are right; after I have accomplished one more thing I have on my mind, I will hand over my business to my sons and go to Europe, and quit the kind of exhausting life I have been living for the last thirty years."

Sermons by T. DeWitt Talmage

Some morning you open your paper, and, looking at the death column, you find he has suddenly departed this life. In trying to win just one more tree, he lost the whole orchard.

Yonder is a man with many styles of innocent entertainment and amusement. He walks, he rides, he plays tenpins in private alleys, he has books on his table, pictures on his wall, and occasional outings, concerts, lectures, baseball tickets, and the innumerable delights of friendship. But he wants a key to the place of dissolute convocation. He wants association with some member of a high family as dissolute as he is affluent. He wants, instead of a quiet Sabbath, one of carousal. He wants the stimulus of strong drinks. He wants the fascinations of a profligate life. The one membership, the one bad habit, the one carousal robs him of all the possibilities and innocent enjoyments and noble inspirations of a lifetime. By one mouthful of forbidden fruit he loses a whole orchard of fruit unforbidden. You see what an expensive thing is sin. Sooner or later it is appalling bankruptcy. It costs a thousand times more than it is worth. As some of all kinds of quadrupeds and all kinds of winged creatures passed before our progenitor, that he might announce a name, from eagle to bat, and from lion to mole, so I suppose there were in Paradise specimens of every kind of fruit tree. And in that enormous orchard there was not only enough for the original family of two, but enough fruit fell ripe to the ground, and was never picked up, to supply whole towns and villages, if they had existed. But the infatuated couple turned away from all these other trees and faced this tree; and fruit of that they would have, though it cost them all Paradise.

This story of Eden is rejected by some as an improbability, if not an impossibility; but nothing on earth is easier for me to believe than this Edenic story, for I have seen the same thing in this year of our Lord 1899. I could call them by name, if it were politic and righteous to do so, the men who have sacrificed a paradise on earth and a paradise in heaven for one sin. Their house went. Their library went. Their good name went. Their field of usefulness went. Their health went. Their immortal soul went. My friends, there is just one sin that will turn you out of paradise if you do not quit it. You know what it is, and God knows, and you had better drop the hand and arm lifted toward that bending bough before you pluck your own ruin. When Eve stood on her tiptoe and took in her right hand that one round peach, or apricot, or apple, Satan reached up and pulled down the round, beautiful world of our present residence. Overworked artist, overwrought merchant, ambitious politician, avaricious speculator, better take that warning from Adam's orchard and stop before you are put out for that one thing alone.

But I turn from Adam's orchard to Solomon's orchard. With his own hand he writes: "I made me gardens and orchards." Not depending on the natural fall of rain, he irrigated those orchards. Pieces of the aqueduct that watered those gardens I have seen, and the reservoirs are as perfect as when, thousands of years ago, the mason's trowel smoothed the mortar over their gray surfaces. No orchard of olden or modern time, probably, ever had its thirst so well slaked. The largest of these reservoirs is five hundred and eighty-two feet long, two hundred and seven feet wide, and fifty feet deep. These reservoirs Solomon refers to when he says: "I made me pools of water, to water therewith the wood that bringeth forth trees." Solomon used to ride out to that orchard before breakfast. It gave him an appetite and something to think about all day. Josephus, the historian, represents him as going out "early in the morning from Jerusalem to the famed rocks of Etam, a fertile region, delightful with paradises and running springs. Thither the king, in robes of white, rode in his chariot, escorted by a troop of mounted archers chosen for their youth and stature, and clad in Tyrian purple, whose long hair, powdered with gold dust, sparkled in the sun." After Solomon had taken his morning ride in those luxuriant orchards he would sit down and write those wonderful things in the Bible, drawing his illustrations from the fruits he had that very morning picked or ridden under. And, wishing to praise the coming Christ, he says: "As the apple tree among the trees of the wood, so is my beloved." And wishing to describe the love of the Church for her Lord, he writes: " Comfort me with apples, for I am sick of love," and desiring to make reference to the white hair of the octogenarian, and just before having noticed that the blossoms of the almond tree were white, he says of the aged man: "The almond tree shall flourish." The walnuts and the pomegranates and the mandrakes and the figs make Solomon's writings a divinely arranged fruit-basket.

What mean Solomon's orchards and Solomon's gardens? for they seem to mingle, the two into one, flowers under foot, and pomegranates over head. To me they suggest that religion is a luxury. All along the world has looked upon religion chiefly as a dire necessity—a lifeboat from the shipwreck, a ladder from the conflagration, a soft landing-place after we have been shoved off the precipice of this planet. As a consequence, so many have said: "We will await preparation for the future until the crash of the shipwreck, until the conflagration is in full blaze, until we reach the brink of the precipice." No doubt religion is inexpressibly important for the last exigency. But what do the apples and the figs and the melons, and the pomegranates and the citron and the olives of Solomon's orchard mean? Luxury! They mean that our religion is the luscious, the aromatic, the pungent, the arborescent, the efflorescent, the foliaged, the umbrageous. They mean what Edward Payson meant when he declared: "If my happiness continues to increase, I cannot support it much longer." It means what Bapa Padmanji, a Hindoo convert, meant when he said: "I long for my bed, not that I may sleep —I lie awake often and long—but to hold communion with my God." It means what the old colored man said, when he was accosted of the colporteur: "Uncle Jack, how are you?" "I is very painful in my knee, but, thank my heavenly Master, I'm cause to be thankful. My good Master jus' gib me nuf to make me humble." "And do you enjoy religion as much now, Uncle Jack, as when you could go to church and class-meeting?" "Yes, 'joys him more. Den I truss to de people, to de meetin's, to de sarment; and when I hear de hymn sing and de pray, I feels glad. But all dis ain't like de good Lord in de heart—God's love here." It means sunrise instead of sundown. It means the Memnon statue made to sing at the stroke of the morning light. It means Jesus Christ at the wedding in Cana. It means the "time of the singing of birds is come." It means Jeremiah's "well of gladness." It means Isaiah's "bride and bridegroom." It means Luke's "bad boy come home to his father's house." Worldly joy killed Leo X when he heard that Milan was captured. Talva died of joy when the Roman senate honored him. Diagora died of joy because his three sons were crowned at the Olympian games. Sophocles died of joy over his literary successes. And religious joy has been too much for many a Christian, and his soul has sped away on the wing of hosannas.

An old and poor musician played so well one night before his king, that the next morning, when the musician awoke, he found his table covered with golden cups and plates, and a princely robe lying across the back of a chair, and richly caparisoned horses were pawing at the doorway to take him through the street in imposing equipage. It was only a touch of what comes to every man who makes the Lord his portion, for he has waiting for him, direct from his King, robes, banquets, chariots, mansions, triumphs; and it is only a question of time when he shall wear them, drink them, ride in them, live in them, and celebrate them.

You think religion is a good thing for a funeral. Yes! But Solomon's orchard means more. Religion is a good thing now, when you are in health and prosperity, and the appetite is good for citrons and apples and apricots and pomegranates. Come in without wasting any time in talking about them, and take the luxuries of religion. Happy yourself, then you can make others happy. I like what Wellington said after the battle of Waterloo, and when he was in pursuit of the French with his advance-guard, and Colonel Harvey said to him: "General, you had better not go any farther, for you may be shot by some straggler from the bushes." And Wellington replied: "Let them fire away. The battle is won, and my life is of no value now." My friends, we ought never to be reckless, but if, through the pardoning and rescuing grace of Christ, you have gained the victory over sin and death and hell, you need fear nothing on the earth or under the earth. Let all the sharpshooters of perdition blaze away; you may ride on in joy triumphant. Religion for the funeral! Yes; but religion for the wedding-breakfast; religion for the brightest spring morning and autumn's most gorgeous sunset. Religion when aspiration is easy, as well as for the last gasp; when the temperature is normal, as well as when it reaches 104. It may be a bold thing to say, but I risk it, that if all people, without respect to belief or character, at death passed into everlasting happiness, religion for this world is such a luxury that no man or woman could afford to do without it. Why was it that in the parable of the prodigal son the finger-ring was ordered to be put upon the returned wanderer's hand before the shoes were ordered for his tired feet? Are not shoes more important for our comfort than finger-rings? It was to impress the world with the fact that religion is a luxury as well as a necessity. "Put a ring on his hand and shoes on his feet." If in sermonic or exhortatory or social recommendations of religion, we put the chief emphasis on the fact that for our safety we must have it when the door of the next world is opened, poor human nature will take the risk and say: "I will wait until the door begins to open." But show them the radiant truth— that the table of God's love and pardon is now laid with all the fruits which the orchards of God's love and pardon and helpfulness can supply—and they will come in and sit down with all the other banqueters, terrestrial and celestial. Fetch on the citrons and the apples and the walnuts and the pomegranates of Solomon's orchard!

But having introduced you to Adam's orchard and carried you a while through Solomon's orchard, I want to take a walk with you through Pilate's orchard of three trees on a hill seventy feet high, ten minutes' walk from the gate of Jerusalem. After I had read that our great-grandfather and great-grandmother had been driven out of the first orchard, I made up my mind that the Lord would not be defeated in that way. I said to myself that when they had been poisoned by the fruit of one tree, somewhere, somehow, there would be provided an antidote for the poison. I said: "Where is the other tree that will undo the work of that tree? Where is the other orchard that will repair the damage received in the first orchard?" And I read on until I found the orchard, and its central tree as mighty for cure as this one had been for ruin; and as the one tree in Adam's orchard had its branches laden with the red fruit of carnage, and the pale fruit of suffering, and the spotted fruit of decay, and the bitter fruit of disappointment, I found in Pilate's orchard a tree which, though stripped of all its leaves and struck through by an iron bolt, nevertheless bore the richest fruit that was ever gathered. Like the trees of the first orchard, this was planted, blossomed, and bore fruit all in one day. Paul was impulsive and vehement of nature, and he laid hold of that tree with both arms, and shook it till the ground all around looked like the morning after an autumnal equinox, and careful lest he step on some of the fruit, he gathered up a basketful of it for the Galatians, crying out: "The fruit of the spirit is love, joy, peace, long-suffering, gentleness, goodness, faith, meekness, temperance." The other two trees of Pilate's orchard were loaded, the one with the hard fruits of obduracy, and the other with the tender fruit of repentance, but the central tree (how will I ever forget the day I sat on the exact place where it was planted!)—the central tree of that orchard yields the antidote for the poisoned nations.

There is in old England, the hollow of a tree where a king hid, and there is in New England a tree in which a document of national importance was kept inviolate; and there have been trees of great girth and immense shade and vast wealth of fruitage, but no other tree had such value of reminiscence or depth of root or spread of branch or infinitude of fruitage as the central tree of Pilate's orchard. Before I pass from under it, I would like to drop on both knees and, with both hands outspread and uplifted, cry out with all the nations of earth and the hosts of heaven: "I believe in God, the Father Almighty, Maker of heaven and earth, and in Jesus Christ, his only Son, our Lord, who was conceived by the Holy Ghost, born of the Virgin Mary, suffered under Pontius Pilate; was crucified, dead, and buried; he descended into hell; the third day he arose from the dead; he ascended into heaven, and sitteth on the right hand of God the Father Almighty; from thence he shall come to judge the quick and the dead."

Now, in this discourse on the Pomology of the Bible, or God amid the Orchards, having shown you Adam's orchard, and Pilate's orchard, and Solomon's orchard, I now take you into St. John's orchard; and I will stop there, for, having seen that, you will want to see nothing more. St. John himself, having seen that orchard, discharged a whole volley of Come! Come! Come! and then pronounced the benediction: "The grace of our Lord Jesus Christ be with you all. Amen." Then the banished evangelist closes the book, and the Bible is done. The dear old Book opened with Adam's orchard and closes with St. John's orchard. St. John went into the orchard through a stone gate, the black basalt of the Isle of Patmos, to which he had been exiled. That orchard which he saw was and is in heaven. One person will err in speaking of heaven as all material, and another person describes heaven as all figurative and spiritual, and both are wrong. Heaven is both material and spiritual. While much of the Bible account of heaven is to be taken figuratively and spiritually, it is plain to me that heaven has also a material existence. Christ said: "I go to prepare a place for you." Is not a place material? God, who has done all the world-building, the statistics of stars so vast as to be a bewilderment to telescopes, could have somewhere in his astronomy piled up a tremendous world to make the Bible heaven true, both as a material splendor and a spiritual domain. I do not believe God put all the flowers, and all the precious stones, and all the bright metals, and all the music, and all the fountains, and all the orchards in this little world of ours. How much was literal and how much was figurative, I cannot say; but St. John saw two rows of trees on each side of a river, and it differed from other orchards in the fact that the trees bore twelve manner of fruits. The learned translators of our common Bible say it means twelve different kinds of fruits in one year. Albert Barnes says it means twelve crops of the same kind of fruit in one year. Not able to decide which is the more accurate translation, I adopt both. If it mean twelve different kinds of fruit, it declares variety in heavenly joy. If it mean twelve crops of the same kind of fruit, it declares abundance in heavenly joy, and they are both true. Not an eternity with nothing but music: that oratorio would be too protracted. Not an eternity of procession on white horses; that would be too long in the stirrups. Not an eternity of plucking fruit from the tree of life: that would be too much of the heavenly orchard. But all manner of varieties, and I will tell you of at least twelve of those varieties: joy of divine worship; joy over the victories of the Lamb who was slain; joy over the repentant sinners; joy of recounting our own rescue; joy of embracing old friends; joy at recognition of patriarchs, apostles, evangelists and martyrs; joy of ringing harmonies;

joy of reknitting broken friendships; joy at the explanation of Providential mysteries; joy at walking the
boulevards of gold; joy at looking at walls green with
emerald and blue with sapphire and crimson with
jasper and aflash with amethyst, entered through
swinging gates, their posts, their hinges, and their
panels of richest pearl; joy that there is to be no subsidence, no reaction, no terminus to the felicity. All
that makes twelve different joys, twelve manner of
fruits. So much for variety. But if you take the
other interpretation, and say it means twelve crops
a year, I am with you still, for that means abundance.
That will be the first place we ever got into where
there is enough of everything. Enough of health,
enough of light, enough of supernal association,
enough of love, enough of knowledge, enough of joy.
The orchards of this lower world put out all their energies for a few days in autumn, and then, having yielded one crop, their banners of foliage are dropped out
of the air, and all their beauty is adjourned until the
blossoming of the next May-time. But twelve crops
in the heavenly orchard, during that which we on
earth call a year, means abundance perpetually.

While there is enough of the pomp of the city
about heaven for those who like the city best, I thank
God there is enough in the Bible about country scenery in heaven to please those of us who were born in
the country and never got over it. Now you may
have streets of gold in heaven: give me the orchards,
with twelve manner of fruits, and yielding their fruit
every month; and the leaves of the trees are for "the
healing of the nations; and there shall be no more
curse, but the Throne of God and of the Lamb shall
be in it; and his servants shall serve him; and they
shall see his face, and his name shall be in their foreheads; and there shall be no night there, and they need

no candle, neither light of the sun, for the Lord God giveth them light; and they shall reign for ever and ever." But just think of a place so brilliant that the noonday sun shall be removed from the mantle of the sky because it is too feeble a taper! Yet, most of all, am I impressed with the fact that I am not yet fit for that place, nor you either. By the reconstructing and sanctifying grace of Christ, we need to be made all over. And let us be getting our passports ready, if we want to get into that country. An earthly passport is a personal matter, telling our height, our girth, the color of our hair, our features, our complexion, and our age. I cannot get into a foreign port on your passport, nor can you get in on mine. Each one of us for himself needs a Divine signature, written by the wounded hand of the Son of God, to get into the heavenly orchard, under the laden branches of which, in God's good time, we may meet the Adam of the first orchard, and the Solomon of the second orchard, and the St. John of the last orchard, to sit down under the tree of which the church in the Book of Canticles speaks when it says: "As the apple tree among the trees of the wood, so is my beloved among the sons. I sat down under his shadow with great delight, and his fruit was sweet to my taste": and there it may be found that to-day we learned the danger of hankering after one thing more and that religion is a luxury and that there is a divine antidote for all poisons and that we had created in us an appetite for heaven and that it was a wholesome and saving thing for us to have discoursed on the Pomology of the Bible, or God Among the Orchards.

THE BOTANY OF THE BIBLE; OR, GOD AMONG THE FLOWERS

Luke, 12: 28: "If then God so clothe the grass, which to-day is in the field and to-morrow is cast into the oven; how much more will he clothe you, O ye of little faith?"

THE BOTANY OF THE BIBLE; OR, GOD AMONG THE FLOWERS

Luke, 12: 28: "If then God so clothe the grass, which to-day is in the field and to-morrow is cast into the oven; how much more will he clothe you, O ye of little faith?"

The Botany of the Bible, or God among the Flowers, is a fascinating subject. I hold in my hand a book which I brought from Palestine. It is bound in olive wood, and within it are pressed flowers which have not only retained their color, but their aroma; flowers from Jerusalem, flowers from Gethsemane, flowers from Mount of Olives, flowers from Bethany, flowers from Siloam, flowers from the Valley of Jehoshaphat, red anemones and wild mignonette, buttercups, daisies, cyclamens, chamomile, bluebells, ferns, mosses, grasses, and a wealth of flora that keep me fascinated by the hour, and every time I open it, it is a new revelation. It is the New Testament of the fields. But my text leads us into another realm of the botanical kingdom. Though never before visited in sermonic discourse, I think before we get through it will lead us to adoration and prayer.

The lily is the queen of Bible flowers. The rose may have disputed her throne in modern times, and won it; but the rose originally had only five petals. It was under the long-continued and intense gaze of the world that the rose blushed into its present beauty. In the Bible train, cassia and hyssop and frankincense and myrrh and spikenard and camphire and the rose follow the lily. Fourteen times in the Bible is the lily mentioned; only twice the rose. The rose may now

Sermons by T. DeWitt Talmage

have wider empire, but the lily reigned in the time
of Esther, in the time of Solomon, in the time of
Christ. Cæsar had his throne on the hills. The lily
had her throne in the valley. In the greatest sermon
that was ever preached, there was only one flower, and
that a lily. The dreamer of Bedford jail, John Bunyan, entered the House of the Interpreter, and was
shown a cluster of flowers, and was told to "consider
the lilies."

Notice the perianth and the six stamens. Steno-
graph their sermons as they preach of God and
the soul and the resurrection. We may study or
reject other sciences at our option. It is so with
astronomy, with chemistry, with jurisprudence, with
physiology, with geology; but the science of botany Christ commands us to study when he says:
"Consider the lilies." Measure them from root
to tip of petal. Inhale their breath. Notice the
gracefulness of their poise. Hear the whisper of the
white lips of the Eastern and the red lips of the American lily. Belonging to this royal family of lilies is the
lily of the Nile, the Japan lily, the Lady Washington
of the Sierras, the Golden Band lily, the Giant lily of
Nepaul, the Turk's Cap lily, the African lily from the
Cape of Good Hope. All these lilies have the royal
blood in their veins. But I take the lilies of my text
as typical of all flowers, and their voice of floral beauty
seems to address us, saying: "Consider the lilies, consider the azaleas, consider the fuchsias, consider the
geraniums, consider the ivies, consider the hyacinths,
consider the heliotropes, consider the oleanders."
With deferential and grateful and intelligent and worshipful souls, consider them. Not with insipid senti-
mentalism or with sophomoric vaporing, but for grand
and practical and every-day, and, if need be, homely
uses, consider them.

Botany of the Bible

The flowers are the angels of the grass. They all have voices. When the clouds speak, they thunder; when the whirlwinds speak, they scream; when the cataracts speak, they roar; but when the flowers speak, they always whisper. I stand here to interpret their message. What have you to say to us, O ye angels of the grass? This morning I mean to discuss what flowers are good for. That is my subject: What are flowers good for?

I remark, in the first place, they are good for lessons of God's providential care. That was Christ's first thought. All these flowers seem to address us, saying: "God will give you apparel and food. We have no wheel with which to spin, no loom with which to weave, no sickle with which to harvest, no well-sweep with which to draw water; but God slakes our thirst with the dew, and God feeds us with the bread of the sunshine, and God has appareled us with more than Solomonic regality. We are prophetesses of adequate wardrobe. "If God so clothed us, the grass of the field, will he not much more clothe you, O ye of little faith?" Men and women of worldly anxieties, take this message home with you. How long has God taken care of you? Quarter of the journey of life? Half the journey of life? Three-quarters of the journey of life? Can you not trust him the rest of the way? God does not promise you anything like that which the Roman emperor had on his table at vast expense—five hundred nightingales' tongues—but he has promised to take care of you. He has promised you the necessities, not the luxuries—bread, not cake. If God so luxuriantly clothes the grass of the field, will he not provide for you, his living and immortal children? He will.

No wonder Martin Luther always had a flower on his writing-desk for inspiration! Through the cracks of the prison floor a flower grew up to cheer Picciola. Mungo Park, the great traveler and explorer, had his life saved by a flower. He sank down in the desert to die, but, seeing a flower near-by, it suggested God's merciful care, and he got up with new courage and traveled on to safety. I said the flowers are the angels of the grass. I add now they are the evangels of the sky.

If you ask me the question, What are flowers good for? I respond, they are good for the bridal day. The bride must have them on her brow, and she must have them in her hand. The marriage altar must be covered with them. A wedding without flowers would be as inappropriate as a wedding without music. At such a time they are for congratulation and prophecies of good. So much of the pathway of life is covered up with thorns, we ought to cover the beginning with orange-blossoms. Flowers are appropriate on such occasions, for in ninety-nine out of a hundred cases it is the very best thing that could have happened. The world may criticise and pronounce it an inaptitude, and may lift its eyebrows in surprise and think it might suggest something better; but the God who sees the twenty, forty, fifty years of wedded life before they have begun, arranges for the best. So that flowers, in almost all cases, are appropriate for the marriage day. The divergences of disposition will become correspondences, recklessness will become prudence, frivolity will be turned into practicality.

There has been many an aged widowed soul who had a carefully-locked bureau, and in the bureau a box, and in the box a folded paper, and in the folded paper a half-blown rose, slightly fragrant, discolored, carefully pressed. She put it there forty or fifty years ago. On the anniversary day of her wedding she will go to the bureau, she will lift the box, she will unfold the paper, and to her eyes will be exposed the half-blown bud, and the memories of the past will rush upon her, and a tear will drop upon the flower, and suddenly it is transfigured; there is a stir in the dust of the anther, and it rounds out, and is full of life, and it begins to tremble in the procession up the church aisle, and the dead music of a half-century ago comes throbbing through the air; and vanished faces reappear, and right hands are joined, and a manly voice promises: "I will, for better or for worse," and the wedding march thunders a salvo of joy at the departing crowd—but a sigh on that anniversary day scatters the scene. Under the deep-fetched breath, the altar, the flowers, the congratulating groups are scattered, and there is nothing left but a trembling hand holding a faded rosebud, which is put into the paper, and then into the box, and the box carefully placed in the bureau, and with a sharp, sudden click of the lock the scene is over.

Let not the prophecies of the flowers, on your wedding day, be false prophecies. Be blind to each other's faults. Make the most of each other's excellences. Remember the vows, the ring on the third finger of the left hand, and the benediction of the calla lilies.

If you ask me the question, "What are flowers good for?" I answer, They are good to honor and comfort the obsequies. The worst gash ever made into the side of our poor earth is the gash of the grave. It is so deep, it is so cruel, it is so incurable, that it needs something to cover it up. Flowers for the casket, flowers for the hearse, flowers for the cemetery. What a contrast between a grave in a country churchyard, with the fence broken down, and the tombstone aslant, and the neighboring cattle browsing amid the mullein stalks and the Canada thistles, and a June morning in Greenwood, the wave of roseate bloom rolling to the top of the mounds, and then breaking into foaming crests of white flowers all around the pillows of dust. It is the difference between sleeping under rags and under an embroidered blanket. We want Old Mortality with his chisel to go through all the graveyards in Christendom, and while he carries a chisel in one hand, we want him to have some flower-seed in the palm of the other hand.

"Oh," you say, "the dead don't know; it makes no difference to them." I think you are mistaken. There are not so many steamers and trains coming to any living city as there are convoys coming from heaven to earth; and if there be instantaneous and constant communication between this world and the better world, do you not suppose your departed friends know what you do with their bodies? Why has God planted golden-rod and wild flowers in the forests and on the prairie, where no human eye ever sees them? He planted them there for invisible intelligences to look at and admire, and when invisible intelligences come to look at the wild flowers of the woods and the table-lands, will they not make excursion and see the flowers which you have planted in affectionate remembrance of them?

When I am dead, I would like to have a handful of violets—any one could pluck them out of the grass, or some one could lift from the edge of the pond a water-lily—nothing rarely expensive, no insane display, as sometimes at funeral rites, where the display takes the bread from the children's mouths and the clothes from their backs, but something from the great democracy of flowers. Rather than imperial catafalque of Russian czar, I ask some one whom I

may have helped by Gospel sermon or Christian deed
to bring a sprig of arbutus or a handful of China asters.

It was left for modern times to spell respect for
the departed and comfort for the living in letters of
floral Gospel. Pillow of flowers, meaning rest for the
pilgrim who has got to the end of his journey. Anchor of flowers, suggesting the Christian hope which
we have as an anchor of the soul, sure and steadfast.
Cross of flowers, suggesting the tree on which our
sins were slain. If I had my way, I would cover up
all the dreamless sleepers, whether in golden-handled
casket or pine box, whether in king's mausoleum or
potter's field, with radiant or aromatic arborescence.
The Bible says: "In the midst of the garden there was
a sepulchre." I wish that every sepulchre might be
in the midst of a garden.

If you ask me the question, "What are flowers good
for?" I answer, for religious symbolism. Have you
ever studied Scriptural flora? The Bible is an ar-
boretum, it is a divine conservatory, it is a herbarium
of exquisite beauty. If you want to illustrate the brevity of the brightest human life, you will quote from
Job: "Man cometh forth as a flower and is cut down."
Or you will quote from the Psalmist: "As the flower
of the field, so he perisheth; the wind passeth over it,
and it is gone." Or you will quote from Isaiah: "All
flesh is grass, and the goodliness thereof is as the flower of the field." Or you will quote from James the
Apostle: "As the flower of the grass, so he passeth
away." What graphic Bible symbolism!

All the cut flowers will soon be dead, whatever care
you take of them. Though morning and night you
baptize them in the name of the shower, the baptism
will not be a saving ordinance. They have been fatal-
ly wounded with the knife that cut them. They are
bleeding their life away: they are dying now. The

fragrance in the air is their departing and ascending spirits. Oh, yes! Flowers are almost human. Botanists tell us that flowers breathe, they take nourishment, they eat, they drink. They are sensitive. They have their likes and dislikes. They sleep, they wake. They live in families. They have their ancestors and their descendants, their birth, their burial, their cradle, their grave. The zephyr rocks the one, and the storm digs the trench for the other. The cowslip must leave its gold, the lily must leave its silver, the rose must leave its diamond necklace of morning dew. Dust to dust. So we come up, we prosper, we spread abroad, we die, as the flower—as the flower!

> Change and decay in all around I see;
> O thou who changest not, abide with me!

Flowers also afford mighty symbolism of Christ, who compared himself to the ancient queen, the lily, and the modern queen, the rose, when he said, "I am the rose of Sharon, and the lily of the valley." Redolent like the one, humble like the other. Like both, appropriate for the sad who want sympathizers, and for the rejoicing who want banqueters. Hovering over the marriage ceremony like a wedding-bell, or folded like a chaplet on the pulseless heart of the dead. O, Christ! let the perfume of thy name be wafted all around the earth—lily and rose, lily and rose—until the wilderness crimson into a garden, and the round earth turn into one great bud of immortal beauty laid against the warm heart of God. Snatch down from the world's banners eagle and lion, and put on lily and rose, lily and rose!

But flowers have no grander use than when on Easter morning we celebrate the re-animation of Christ from the catacombs. The flowers spell resurrection. There is not a nook or corner in all the building but is touched with the incense. The women carried spices to the tomb of Christ, and they dropped spices all around about the tomb, and from these spices have grown all the flowers of Easter morn: The two white-robed angels that hurled the stone away from the door of the tomb, hurled it with such violence down the hill that it crashed in the door of the world's sepulchre, and millions of dead shall come forth.

However labyrinthine the mausoleum, however costly the sarcophagus, however architecturally grand the necropolis, however beautifully parterred the family grounds, we want them all broken up by the Lord of the Resurrection. The forms that we laid away with our broken hearts must rise again. Father and mother—they must come out. Husband and wife—they must come out. Brothers and sisters—they must come out. Our darling children—they must come out. The eyes that with trembling fingers we closed, must open in the lustre of Resurrection morn. The arms that we folded in death must join ours in embrace of reunion. The beloved voice that was hushed must be retuned. The beloved form must come up without its infirmities, without its fatigues—it must come up. Oh, how long it seems for some of you! Waiting—waiting for the Resurrection! How long! how long! I make for your broken hearts to-day a cool, soft bandage of lilies. I comfort you with the thought of resurrection.

When Lord Nelson was buried in St. Paul's Cathedral in London, the heart of all England was stirred. The procession passed on amid the sobbing of a nation. There were thirty trumpeters stationed at the door of the Cathedral, with instruments of music in hand, waiting for the signal, and when the illustrious dead arrived, these thirty trumpeters gave one united blast, and then all was silent. Yet the trumpets did not wake the dead. He slept right on. But I have to tell you, what thirty trumpeters could not do for one ·man, one trumpeter will do for all nations. The ages have rolled on, and the clock of the world's destiny strikes nine, ten, eleven, twelve, and time shall be no longer! Behold the archangel hovering! He takes the trumpet, points it this way, puts its lips to his lips, and then blows one long, loud, terrific, thunderous, reverberating and resurrectionary blast! Look, look! They rise! The dead—the dead! some coming forth from the family vault; some from the city cemetery; some from the country grave-yard: and then re-clothing themselves in forms radiant for ascension.

The earth begins to burn—the bonfire of a great victory. All ready now for the procession of recon-structed humanity! Upward and away! Christ leads, and all the Christian dead follow, battalion after battalion, nation after nation. Up, up! On, on! Forward, ye ranks of God Almighty! Lift up your heads, ye everlasting gates, and let the conquerors come in! Resurrection! Resurrection!

And so I twist all the festal flowers of the chapels and cathedrals of all Christendom into one great chain, and with that chain I bind this Easter morning with the closing Easter of the world's history—resurrec-tion! May the God of peace that brought again from the dead our Lord Jesus, that great Shepherd of the sheep, through the blood of the covenant, make you perfect in every good work to do his will.

THE GEOLOGY OF THE BIBLE; OR, GOD AMONG THE ROCKS

II Samuel, 6: 6, 7: " And when they came to Nachon's threshing floor, Uzzah put forth his hand to the ark of God, and took hold of it; for the oxen shook it. And the anger of the Lord was kindled against Uzzah, and God smote him there for his error; and there he died by the ark of God."

THE GEOLOGY OF THE BIBLE; OR, GOD AMONG THE ROCKS

II Samuel, 6: 6, 7: "And when they came to Nachon's threshing floor, Uzzah put forth his hand to the ark of God, and took hold of it; for the oxen shook it. And the anger of the Lord was kindled against Uzzah, and God smote him there for his error; and there he died by the ark of God."

A band of music is coming down the road, cornets blown, timbrels struck, harps thrummed, and cymbals clapped, all led on by David, who was himself a musician. They are ahead of a wagon on which is the sacred box called the "Ark." The yoke of oxen drawing the wagon imperiled it. Some critics say that the oxen kicked, being struck with the driver's goad, but my knowledge of oxen leads me to say that if on a hot day they see a shadow of a tree or wall, they are apt to suddenly shy off to get the coolness of the shadow. I think these oxen so suddenly turned that the sacred box seemed about to be upset and thrown to the ground. Uzzah rushed forward and laid hold of the ark to keep it upright. But he had no right to do so. A special command had been given by the Lord that no one, save the priest, under any circumstances should touch that box. Nervous and excited and irreverent, Uzzah disobeyed when he took hold of the ark, and he died as a consequence.

In all ages, and never more so than in our own day, there are good people all the time afraid that the Holy Bible, which is the sacred ark of our time, will be upset, and they have been a long while afraid that science, and especially geology, would overthrow it.

Sermons by T. DeWitt Talmage

While we are not forbidden to touch the Holy Book, and, on the contrary, are urged to cherish and study it, any one who is afraid of the overthrow of the Book is greatly offending the Lord with his unbelief. The oxen have not yet been yoked which can upset that ark of the world's salvation. Written by the Lord Almighty, he is going to protect it until its mission is fulfilled and there shall be no more need of a Bible, because all its prophecies will have been fulfilled, and the human race will have exchanged worlds.

A trumpet and a violin are very different instruments, but they may be played in perfect accord. So the Bible account of the creation of the world and the geological account are different. One story written on parchment and the other on the rocks, yet in perfect and eternal accord. The word "day," repeated in the first chapter of Genesis, has thrown into paroxysms of criticism many exegetes. The Hebrew word "Yom" of the Bible means sometimes what we call a day, and sometimes, as Peter says, it may mean a thousand years (II. Peter, 3:8), and sometimes it means ages; it may mean twenty-four hours or a hundred million years. The order of creation as written in the Book of Genesis is the order of creation discovered by the geologist's crowbar. So many Uzzahs have been nervously rushing about for fear the strong oxen of scientific discovery would upset the Bible, that I went somewhat apprehensively to look into the matter, when I found that the Bible and geology agree in saying that first were built the rocks; then the plants greened the earth; then marine creatures were created, from minnow to whale; then the wings of the aerial choirs were colored, and then throats were tuned, and the quadrupeds began to bleat, and bellow, and neigh. What is all this fuss that has been filling the church and the world concerning a fight between Moses and

Geology of the Bible

Agassiz? There is no fight at all. But is not the geological impression that the world was millions of years building, antagonistic to the theory of one week's creation in Genesis? No. A great house is to be built. A man takes years to draw to the spot the foundation-stone and the heavy timbers. The house is about done, but it is not finished for comfortable residence. Suddenly the owner calls in upholsterers, gas-fitters, paper-hangers, and in one week it is ready for occupancy. Now, it requires no stretch of imagination to realize that God could have taken millions of years for the bringing of the rocks and the timbers of this world together and preparing them for their purpose, yet only one week more to make it habitable, and to furnish it for human residence. Remember, also, that all up and down the Bible the language of the times was used—common parlance—and it was not always to be taken literally. Just as we say every day that the world is round, when it is not round. It is spheroidal—flattened at the poles and protuberant at the equator. Professor Snell, with his chain of triangles, and Professor Varin, with the shortened pendulum of his clock, found it was not round; but we do not become critical of any one who says the world is round. Let us deal as fairly with Moses or Job as we do with each other.

But, for years, good people feared geology, and, without any imploration on their part, apprehended that the rocks and mountains would fall on them, until Hugh Miller, the elder of St. John's Presbyterian Church in Edinburgh, and parishioner of Dr. Guthrie, came forth and told the world that there was no contradiction between the mountains and the church, and O. M. Mitchell, a brilliant lecturer before he became brigadier-general—dying at Beaufort, S. C., during our Civil War—took the platform and spread his map of the strata of rock in the presence of great audiences, and Prof. Alexander Winchell, of Michigan University, and Prof. Taylor Lewis, of Union College, showed that the "without form and void" of the first chapter of Genesis was the very chaos out of which the world was formulated, the hands of God packing together the land, and tossing up the mountains into great heights, and flinging down the seas into their great depths. Before God gets through with this world there will hardly be a book of the Bible that will not find confirmation, either in archæology or geology. Exhumed Babylon, Nineveh, Jerusalem, Tyre, and Egyptian hyeroglyphics are crying out in the ears of the world: "The Bible is right! All right! Everlastingly right!" Geology is saying the same thing, not only confirming the truth about the original creation, but confirming so many passages of the Scriptures that I can only slightly refer to them.

But you do not really believe that story of the deluge and the sinking of the mountains under the wave? Tell us something we can believe. "Believe that," says Geology, "for how do you account for those sea-shells and sea-weeds and skeletons of sea animals found on the top of some of the highest mountains? If the waters did not sometime rise about the mountains, how did those sea-shells and sea-weeds, and skeletons of sea animals get there?"

But, now, you do not really believe that story about the storm of fire and brimstone whelming Sodom and Gomorrah, and enwrapping Lot's wife in such saline encrustations that she halted, a sack of salt? For the confirmation of that story, the geologist goes to that region, and after trying in vain to take a swim in the lake, so thick with salt he cannot swim it—the lake beneath which Sodom and Gomorrah lie buried—one drop of the water so full of sulphur and brimstone that it stings your tongue, and for hours you cannot get rid of the nauseating drop—he digs down and finds sulphur on top of sulphur, brimstone on top of brimstone, while all around there are jets, and crags, and peaks of salt, and if one of them did not become the sarcophagus of Lot's wife, they show you how a human being might in that tempest have been halted and packed into a white monument that would defy the ages.

But, now, you do not really believe that New Testament story about the earthquake at the time Christ was crucified, do you? Geology digs down into Mount Calvary and finds the rocks ruptured and aslant, showing the work of an especial earthquake for that mountain, and an earthquake which did not touch the surrounding region. Go and look for yourself, and see there a dip and cleavage of rocks as nowhere else on the planet, Geology thus announcing an especial earthquake for the greatest tragedy of all the centuries—the assassination of the Son of God.

But you do not really believe that story of the burning of our world at the last day? Geology digs down and finds that the world is already on fire, and that the centre of this globe is incandescent, molten, volcanic; a burning coal, burning out towards the surface; and the internal fires have in some places so far reached the outside rim that I do not see how the world is to keep from complete conflagration until the prophecies concerning it are fulfilled. The lava poured forth from the mouths of Vesuvius, Etna, and Cotopaxi, and Kilauea is only the regurgitation from an awful inflammation thousands of miles deep. There are mines in Pennsylvania and in several parts of the world that have been on fire for many years. These coal mines burning down and the internal fires of the earth burning up, after a while these two fires, the descending and the ascending, may meet, and then will occur the universal conflagration of which the Bible speaks when it says: "The elements shall melt with fervent heat; the earth also, and the works that are therein shall be burned up." Instead of disbelieving the Bible story about the final conflagration, since I have looked a little into geology, finding that its explorations are all in the line of confirmation of that prophecy, I wonder how this old craft of a world can keep sailing on much longer. It is like a ship on fire at sea, the fact that the hatches are kept down the only reason that it does not become one complete blaze—masts on fire, ratlins on fire, everything, from cutwater to taffrail, on fire. After Geology has told us how near the internal fires have already burnt their way toward the surface, it ought not to be a surprise to us at any time to hear the ringing of the fire-bells of a universal conflagration.

I am glad that Geology has been born! Astronomy is grand, because it tells us about other worlds; but I am more interested in our world than in any other world, and Geology tells us all about what was its cradle, and what will be its grave. And this glorious Geology is proving itself more and more the friend of Theology. Thank God for the testimony of the rocks; the Ten Commandments announced among the split rocks of Sinai; the greatest sermon of Christ preached on the basaltic rocks of the Mount of Beatitudes; the Saviour dying on the rocks of Golgotha and buried amid the limestone rocks of Joseph's sepulchre; the last day to be ushered in with a rending of rocks, and our blessed Lord suggestively entitled the "Rock of Ages." I this day proclaim the banns of a marriage between Geology and Theology, the rugged bridegroom and the fairest of brides. Let them join their hands, and "whom God hath joined together let not man put asunder."

If anything in the history or condition of the earth seems for the time contradictory of anything in Geology, you must remember that Geology is all the time correcting itself, and more and more coming into harmonization with the great Book. In the last century, the "French Scientific Association" printed a list of eighty theories of geology which had been adopted and afterward rejected. Lyell, the scientist, announced fifty theories of Geology that had been believed in and afterwards thrown overboard. Meanwhile the story of the Bible has not changed at all, and if Geology has cast out between one and two hundred theories which it once considered established, we can afford to wait until the last theory of Geology antagonizing divine revelation shall have been given up.

Now, in this discourse upon the Geology of the Bible, or God among the Rocks, I charge all agitated and affrighted Uzzahs to calm their pulses about the upsetting of the Scriptures. Let me see! For several hundred years the oxen have been jerking the ark this way and that, and pulling it over rough places and trying to stick it in the mud of derision, and kicking with all the power of their hoofs against the sharp goads, and trying to pull it into the cool shade out of the heats of retribution from a God "who will by no means clear the guilty." Yet have you not noticed that the Book has never been upset? The only changes made in it were those verbal ones in the English translation of it, by its learned friends in the Revision of the Scriptures. The Book of Genesis has been thundered against by the mightiest batteries, yet you cannot to-day find in all the earth a copy of the Bible which has not the fifty chapters of the first copy of the Book of Genesis ever printed, starting with the words, "In the beginning God," and closing with Joseph's coffin. Fierce attack on the Book of Exodus has been made because they said it was cruel to drown Pharaoh and that the story of Mount Sinai was improbable. But the Book of Exodus remains intact, and not one of us, considering the cruelties which Pharaoh would have continued among the brick-kilns of Egypt, would have thrown him a plank if we had seen him drowning. And Mount Sinai is to-day a pile of tossed and tumbled basalt, recalling the cataclysm of that mountain when the law was given. And, as to those Ten Commandments, all Roman law, all German law, all English law, all American law worth anything is squarely founded on them. So mighty assault for centuries has been made on the Book of Joshua. It was said that the story of the detained sun and moon is an insult to modern astronomy, but that Book of Joshua may be found to-day in the chapel of every university in America, in defiance of any telescope projected from the roof of that university. The Book of Jonah has been the target of ridicule for the small wit of ages; but there it stands, with its four chapters inviolate, while Geology puts up in its museums remains of sea monsters capable of doing more than the one which swallowed the recreant prophet. There stand the eleven hundred and eighty-nine chapters of the Bible, notwithstanding all the attacks of ages, and there they will stand until they shrivel up in the final fires, which geologists say are already kindled and glowing hotter than the furnaces of an ocean steamer as it puts out from New York Narrows for Hamburg or Southampton. I should not wonder if from the crypt of ancient cities the inspired manuscripts of Matthew, Mark, Luke and John, in their own chirography, may yet be taken, and the epistles which Paul dictated to his amanuensis, as well as the one in the apostle's own handwriting. At the same ratio of archæological and geological confirmation of the Scriptures, the time will come when the truth of the Bible will no more be doubted than the common almanac, which tells you the days and the months of the year, and the unbelievers will be accounted harmless lunatics. Forward the telescope and the spectroscope and the chemical batteries, and critically examine the ostracoids of the ocean depths and the bones of the great mammals on the gravely hill-tops! And the mightier and the grander and the deeper and the higher the explorations, the better for our cause. As sure as the thunderbolts of the Almighty are stronger than the steel pens of agnostics, the ark of God will ride on unhurt, and no modern Uzzah need fear any disastrous upsetting. The apocalyptic angel flying through the midst of heaven, proclaiming to all nations and kindred and people and tongues the unsearchable riches of Jesus Christ is mightier than the shying off of a yoke of oxen.

The geology of the Bible shows that our religion is not a namby-pamby, nerveless, dilettantish religion. It was projected and has been protected by the God of the Rocks. Religion a balm? Yes. Religion a soothing power? Yes. Religion a beautiful sentiment? Oh, yes! But we must have a God of the Rocks, a mighty God to defend, an omnipotent God to achieve, a force able to overcome all other forces in the universe. Rose of Sharon and Lily of the Valley is he, combination of all gentleness and tenderness and sweetness? Oh, yes! But if the mighty forces now arrayed for the destruction of the nations are to be met and conquered, we must have a God of the Rocks —the "Lion of Judah's Tribe," as well as the "Lamb who was slain." One hundred and thirty times does the Bible speak of the Rock as defense, or fortress, as refuge, as overpowering strength. David, the psalmist, lived among the rocks, and they reminded him of the Almighty, and he ejaculates: "The Lord liveth; blessed be my rock." "Lead me to the rock that is higher than I." And then, as if his prayer had been answered, he feels the strength come into his soul, and he cries out: "The Lord is my rock;" "He shall set me upon a rock." Would the Bible present a sublime picture of motherly desperation in defense of her children—it shows us Rizpah on the rock for three months, with disheveled hair and wild screams, fighting back vultures and jackals from the corpses of her sons. Would the Bible set forth the hardness of the heart and the Gospel's power to overcome it—it tells us of the "hammer that breaketh the rocks in pieces." Would our Lord represent the durability of his church against all assault—he says: "Upon this Rock will I build my church, and the gates of hell shall not prevail against it." Would he close his Sermon on the Mount with a peroration that would resound through centuries, standing on a rock so high that it overlooks Lake Galilee to the right, and on a clear day overlooks the Mediterranean to the left, I hear him stamp his foot on the rock beneath him as he cries to the surging multitudes at the base of that rock: "Whosoever heareth these sayings of mine, and doeth them, I will liken him unto a wise man, which built his house upon a rock; and the rain descended, and the floods came, and the winds blew, and beat upon that house; and it fell not; for it was founded upon a rock." We want a swarthy, a stalwart, a brawny religion. We have a great many good people who can sit and gently rock the cradle of their infantile hopes, and can faintly smile when good is accomplished, and walk softly through a sick-room, and live inoffensive lives, and manage to tread on no one's prejudices; and their religion is at

Geology of the Bible

the best when the wind is from the northwest and the thermometer at 70 degrees Fahrenheit; and they have their spheres, and may God prosper them. But we want in this great battle for God against the allied forces of perdition some John Knoxes, some Martin Luthers—men of nerve and faith and prowess, like the Huguenots and the Pilgrim Fathers and the Dutch at Leyden keeping back the enemy until the tides of the sea came in. Lord, God of the Rocks! help us in this awful struggle, in which heaven or hell is bound to beat. It is a mighty thing to have all heaven for reinforcement.

How much the rocks have had to do with the cause of God in all ages! In the wilderness God's Israel were fed with honey out of the rock. How the Rock of Horeb paid Moses back in gushing, rippling, sparkling water for the two stout strokes with which he struck it! And there stands the rock with name— I guess the longest word in the Bible—*sela-hammah-lekoth*—and it was worthy of a resounding, sesquipeda-lian nomenclature, for at that rock Saul was com-pelled to quit his pursuit of David and go home and look after the Philistines, who were making a flank movement. There were the rocks of Bozez and Seneh, between which Jonathan climbed up and sent flying in retreat the garrison of the uncircumcised. And yonder see David and his men hidden in the rocks of Adullam and En-gedi!

But while I go on with my study of the Geology of the Bible, or God among the Rocks, I get a more intelligent and helpful idea of Divine deliberation. These rocks, the growth of thousands of years—and Geology says, of millions of years—ought to show the prolongation of God's plans, and cure our impatience because things are not done in short order. Men, without seeing it, become critical of the Almighty and think "Why does he not do this and do that, and do it right away?" We feel sometimes as if we could not wait. Well, I guess we will have to wait. God is never in a hurry, except about two things. His plans, sweeping through eternity, are beyond our comprehension. They have such wide circle, such vastness of revolution, such infinitude, that we cannot compass them. Indeed, he would not be much of a God whom we could thoroughly understand. That would not be much of a father who had no thoughts or plans larger than his babe of one year could compass. If God takes millions of years to make one rock, do not let us become critical if he takes twenty years, or a century, or several centuries to do that which we would like to have done immediately. Do not repeat the folly of those who conclude there is no God, or that he is not in sympathy with the right and the good because he does not do certain things in the time we set apart for their performance. Do not let us hold up our little watch with its tiny hour hand and minute hand, and by it try to correct the clock of the universe, its pendulum taking five hundred years to swing this way, and five hundred years to swing that way. Do not let us set up our little spinning-wheel beside the loom in which God weaves sunrises and sunsets and auroras. We have the best of authority for saying that "one day with the Lord is as a thousand years, and a thousand years as one day." Do not expect that Uzzah's oxen, even if they do not shy off, but go straight ahead, can keep up with the fire-shod lightnings.

But that was not a slip of the tongue when I said that God is never in a hurry except in two things. Those two things are, when he goes to save a repentant sinner and comfort a praying mourner. The one divine hurry was set forth in the parable of the prodigal son, when it says, "the father ran." He was old, and I suppose he had as much as he could do to walk, but the sight of his bad boy coming home limbered the stiff knees and lengthened the shortened pace of the old man into an athletic stride. "The father ran!" Put it into your oratorios. Sound it with full orchestra. Repeat it through all heavens: "The father ran!" O, soul farthest off, come back! and God, your Father, will come out to meet you at full run! The other time when God is in a hurry is when a troubled soul calls for comfort. Then the Bible represents the divine gait and swing and velocity by the reindeer, saying: "Be thou like a roe or a young hart on the mountains of Bether." That parenthesis I put in, thinking that there may be some repentant sinner who wants to find pardon or some mourning soul who needs comfort, and therefore I mention the two things about which God is in a great hurry.

But concerning all the vast things of God's government of the universe, be patient with the carrying out of the plans beyond our measurement. Naturalists tell us that there are insects that are born and die within an hour, and that there are several generations of them in one day; and if one of those July insects of an hour should say: "How slow everything goes! I was told in the chrysalis state by a wondrous instinct that I would find in this world seasons of the year— spring, summer, autumn, and winter. But where are the autumnal forests upholstered in fire, and where are the glorious springtimes, with orchards waving their censers of perfume before the altars of the morning? I do not believe there are any autmns or springtimes;" if then a golden eagle, many years old, in a cage nearby, heard the hum of that complaining insect, it might well answer: "O, summer insect of an hour, though your life is so short that you cannot see the magnificent turn of the seasons, I can testify to their reality, for I have seen them roll. When I was young, and before I was imprisoned in this cage, I brushed their gorgeous leafage and their fragrant blossoms with my own wing. You live an hour: I have lived thirty years. But in one of my flights high up, the gate of heaven open for a soul to go in or a seraph to come out, I heard the choirs chanting, 'From everlasting to everlasting thou art God!' And it was an antiphonal in which all heaven responded, 'From everlasting to everlasting thou art God!'" O man! O woman! so far as your earthly existence is concerned, only the insect of an hour, be not impatient with the workings of the Omnipotent and the Eternal.

And now, for your solace and your safety, I ask you to come under the shelter, and into the deep clefts, and the almighty defense of a Rock that is higher than you, higher than any Gibraltar, higher than the Himalayas—the "Rock of Ages,"—that will shelter you from the storm, that will hide you from your enemies, that will stand when the earthquakes of the last day get their pry under the mountains and hurl them into seas boiling with the fires which are already burning their way out from red-hot centres toward the surfaces, which are already here and there spouting with fire amid the quaking of the mountains, under the look and touch of him, of whom it is said in the sublimest sentence ever written: "He looketh upon the mountains, and they tremble: He toucheth the hills and they smoke!"

Hie you one and all to the Rock of Ages! And now, as before this sermon on the Rocks I gave out the significant and appropriate hymn, "How firm a foundation ye saints of the Lord," I will give out after this sermon on the Rocks, the significant and appropriate hymn:

> Rock of Ages, cleft for me,
> Let me hide myself in thee!

THE SCULPTURE OF THE BIBLE; OR, GOD AMID THE CORAL-REEFS.

Job, 28: 18: " No mention shall be made of coral."

THE SCULPTURE OF THE BIBLE; OR, GOD AMID THE CORAL-REEFS.

Job, 28: 18: "No mention shall be made of coral."

Why do you say so, inspired dramatist? When you wanted to set forth the superior value of our religion, you tossed aside the onyx, which is used for making exquisite cameos, and the sapphire of deep blue and topaz of rhombic prism and the ruby of frozen blood, and here you say that the coral, which is a miracle of shape and a transport of color to those who have studied it, is not worthy of mention in comparison with our holy religion. "No mention shall be made of coral." At St. Johnsbury, Vt., in a museum built by the chief citizen, as I examined a specimen on the shelf, I first realized what a holy of holies God can build and has built in the temple of one piece of coral. I do not wonder that Ernst Hæckel, the great scientist, while in Ceylon was so entranced with the specimens which some Cingalese divers had brought up for his inspection that he himself plunged into the sea and went clear under the waves at the risk of his life, again and again and again, that he might know more of the coral, the beauty of which he indicates cannot even be guessed by those who have only seen it above water, and after the polyps, which are its sculptors and architects, have died and the chief glories of these submarine flowers have expired.

Job, in my text, did not mean to depreciate this divine sculpture in the coral reefs along the sea-coasts. No one can afford to depreciate these white palaces of the deep, built under God's direction. He never changes his plans for the building of the islands and shores; and for uncounted thousands of years the coral gardens, and the coral castles, and the coral battlements go on and up. I charge you that you will please God and please yourself if you will go into the minute examination of the corals—their foundations, their pinnacles, their aisles, their curves, their cleavages, their reticulation, their grouping—families of them, towns of them, cities of them, and continents of them. Indeed, you cannot appreciate the meaning of my text unless you know something of the coral. Labyrinthian, stellar, columnar, floral, dented like shields from battle, spotted like leopards, embroidered like lace, hung like upholstery—twilight and auroras and sunbursts of beauty! From deep crimson to milk-white are its colors. You may find this work of God amid the animalcules, whether eighty fathoms down, or amid the breakers, where the sea dashes the wildest and beats the mightiest and bellows the loudest. These sea-creatures are ever busy. Now they build islands in the centre of the Pacific Ocean. Now they lift barriers around the continent. Indian Ocean, Red Sea, and coast of Zanzibar have specimens of their infinitesimal but sublime masonry. At the recession of the tides you may in some places see the top of their Alpine elevations, while elsewhere nothing but the deep-sea soundings from the decks of *The Challenger*, *The Porcupine*, and *The Lightning* of the British expedition can detect them. The ancient Gauls employed the coral to adorn their helmets and the hilts of swords. In many lands it has been used as amulets. The Algerian reefs in one year (1873) had at work amid the coral 311 vessels, with 3,150 sailors, yielding in profit $565,000. But the secular and worldly value of the coral is nothing as compared with the moral and religious, as when, in my text, Job employs it in comparison. I do not know how any one can examine a coral the size of the thumb-nail without bethinking himself of God and worshiping him, and feeling the opposite of the great infidel surgeon, lecturing to the medical students in the dissecting-room upon a human eye which he held in his hand, showing its wonders of architecture and adaptation, when the idea of God flashed upon him so powerfully he cried out to the students: "Gentlemen, there is a God; but I hate him." Picking up a coral, I feel like crying out: "There is a God, and I adore him."

Nothing so impresses me with the fact that our God loves the beautiful. The most beautiful coral of the world never comes to human observation. Sunrises and sunsets he hangs up for nations to look at; he may green the grass, and round the dew into pearl, and set on fire autumnal foliage to please mortal sight, but those thousands of miles of coral achievement I think he has had built for his own delight. In those galleries he alone can walk. The music of those keys, played on by the fingers of the wave, he only can hear. The snow of that white and the bloom of that crimson he alone can see. Having garnitured this world to please the human race, and lifted a glorious heaven to please the angelic intelligences, I am glad that he has planted these gardens of the deep to please himself. But here and there God allows specimens of submarine glory to be brought up and set before us for sublime contemplation. While I speak, these great nations of zoophytes, meandrinas, and madrepores, with tentacles for trowel, are building just such coral as we find in our text. The diamond may be more rare, the crystal may be more sparkling, the chrysoprase may be more ablaze, but the coral is the long, deep, everlasting blush of the sea. Yet Job, who understood all kinds of precious stones, declares that the beauty and value of the coral are nothing compared with our holy religion, and he picks up this coralline formation and looks at it, and flings it aside with all the other beautiful things he has ever heard of, and cries out in ecstasy of admiration for the superior qualities of our religion: "No mention shall be made of coral."

Take my hand, and we will walk through this bower of the sea, while I show you that even exquisite coral is not worthy of being compared with the richer jewels of a Christian soul. The first thing that strikes me in looking at the coral is its long-continued accumulation. It is not turned up like Cotopaxi, but is an outputting and an outbranching of ages. In Polynesia there are reefs hundreds of feet deep and one thousand miles long. Who built these reefs, these islands? The zoophytes, the corallines. They who built the pyramids were not such workers as were these masons, these creatures of the sea. What small creations amounting to what vast aggregation! Who can estimate the ages between the time when the madrepores laid the foundations of the islands and the time when they put on the capstone of a completed work? It puzzles all the scientists to guess through how many years the corallines were building the Sandwich and Society Islands and the Marshall and Gilbert groups. But more slowly and wonderfully accumulative is grace in the heart. You sometimes get discouraged because the upbuilding by the soul does not go on more rapidly. Why, you have all eternity to build in! The little annoyances of life are zoophyte builders, and there will be small layer on top of small layer, and fossilized grief on the top of fossilized grief. Grace does not go up rapidly in your soul, but, blessed be God, it goes up. Ten thousand million ages will

not finish you. You will never be finished. On forever! Up forever! Out of the sea of earthly dis-
quietude will gradually rise the reefs, the islands, the
continents, the hemispheres of grandeur and glory.
Men talk as though only in this life we had time to
build; but what we build in this life, as compared with
what we shall build in the next life, is as a striped shell
to all Australia. You go into an architect's study and
there you see the sketch of a temple, the corner-stone
of which has not yet been laid. Oh, that I could have
an architectural sketch of what you will be after eternity has wrought upon you! What pillars of strength!
What altars of supernal worship! What pinnacles
thrusting their glittering spikes into the sun that never
sets! You do not scold the corallines because they
cannot build an island in a day. Why should you
scold yourself because you cannot complete a temple
of holiness for the heart in this short lifetime? You
tell me we do not amount to much now; but try us
after a thousand million ages of hallelujahs. Let us
hear the angels chant for a million centuries. Give
us an eternity with God, and then see if we do not
amount to something. More slowly and marvelously
accumulative is the grace in the soul than anything I
can think of. "No mention shall be made of coral."

Lord, help us to learn that which most of us are
deficient in—patience. If thou canst take, through
the sea-anemones, millions of years to build one bank
of coral, ought we not to be willing to do work
through ten years or fifty years without complaint,
without restlessness, without chafing of spirit? Patience with the erring; patience that we cannot have
the millennium in a few weeks; patience with assault
of antagonists; patience at what seems slow fulfillment
of Bible promises; patience with physical ailments;
patience under delays of Providence. Grand, glo-

rious, all-enduring, all-conquering patience! Without it life is an irritation, but with it life is a triumph. Patience like that which my now-ascended friend, Dr. Abel Stevens, describes when writing of one of Wesley's preachers, John Nelson, who, when a man had him put in prison on false charges, and being for a long time tormented by his enemy, said: "The Lord lifted up a standard when the anger was coming in like a flood, else I should have wrung his neck to the ground and set my foot upon it." Patience like that of Pericles, the Athenian statesman, who, when a man pursued him to his own door, hurling at him epithets, and arriving there when it had become dark, sent his servant with a torch to light his enemy back to his home. Patience like that eulogized by the Spanish proverb when it says: "I have lost the rings, but here are the fingers still." Patience! The sweetest sugar for the sourest cup; the balance-wheel for all mental and moral machinery; the foot that treads into placidity the stormiest lake; the bridle for otherwise rash tongues; the sublime silence that conquers the boisterous and blatant. Patience like that of the most illustrious example of all ages—Jesus Christ; patient under betrayal; patient under the treatment of Pilate's Oyer and Terminer; patient under the expectoration of his assailants; patient under flagellation; patient unto death. Under all exasperations employ it. Whatever comes, stand it; hold on, wait, bear up.

Take my hand again, and we will go a little further into this garden of the sea, and we shall find that in proportion as the climate is hot the coral is finest. Draw two isothermal lines at sixty degrees north and south of the equator, and you find the favorite home of the coral. Go to the hottest part of the Pacific seas and you find the finest specimens of coral. Coral is a child of fire. But more wonderfully do the heats and fires of trouble bring out the jewels of the Christian soul. Those are not the stalwart men who are asleep on the shaded lawn, but those who are pounding amid the furnaces. I do not know of any other way of getting a thorough Christian character. I will show you a picture. Here are a father and a mother thirty or thirty-five years of age, their family around them. It is Sabbath morning. They have prayers. They hear the children's catechism. They have prayers every day of the week. They are in humble circumstances. But, after awhile the wheel of fortune turns up, and the man gets his twenty thousand dollars. Now he has prayers on Sabbath and every day of the week, but he has dropped his catechism. The wheel of fortune turns up again, and he gets his eighty thousand dollars. Now he has prayers on Sabbath morning alone. The wheel of fortune keeps turning up, and he has two hundred thousand dollars, and now he has prayers on Sabbath morning when he feels like it and there is no company. The wheel of fortune keeps on turning up, and he has his three hundred thousand dollars and no prayers at all. Four-leaf clover in a pasture field is not so rare as family prayers in the houses of people who have more than three hundred thousand dollars. But now the wheel of fortune turns down, and the man loses two hundred thousand dollars out of the three hundred thousand. Now on Sabbath morning he is on a stepladder looking for a Bible under the old newspapers on the book-case. He is going to have prayers. His affairs are more and more complicated, and after a while crash goes his last dollar. Now he has prayers every morning, and he hears his grandchildren recite the catechism. Prosperity took him away from God; adversity drove him back to God. Hot climate to make the coral; hot and scalding trouble to make the jewels of grace in his soul. We all hate trouble, and yet it does a great deal for us. You have heard, perhaps, of that painter who wished to get an expression of great distress for his canvas, and who had his servant lash a man fast and put him to great torture, and then the artist caught the look on the victim's face and immediately transferred it to the canvas. Then he said to the servant, "More torture," and under more torture there was a more thorough expression of pain, and the artist said: "Stop there; wait till I catch that expression. There! Now I have it upon the canvas. Let loose the victim. I have a work that will last forever." "Oh," you say, "he was an inhuman painter." No doubt about it. Trouble is cruel and inhuman; but he is a great painter, and out of our tears and blood on his palette he makes colors that never die. Oh, that it might be a picture of Christian fortitude, of shining hope!

On the day I was licensed to preach the Gospel, an old Christian man took my hand and said: "My son, when you get in a tight corner on Saturday night, without any sermon, send for me, and I will preach for you." Well, it was a great encouragement to be backed up by such a good old minister, and it was not long before I got into a tight corner on Saturday night, without any sermon; and I sent for the old minister, and he came and preached; and it was the last sermon he ever preached. All the tears I cried at his funeral could not express my affection for that man, who was willing to help me out of a tight corner. Ah! that is what we all want—somebody to help us out of a tight corner. You are in one now. How do I know it? I am used to judging of human countenances, and I see beyond the smile and beyond the courageous look with which you hide your feelings from others. I know you are in a tight corner. What to do? Do as I did when I sent for old Doctor Scott.

Sculpture of the Bible

Do better than I did—send for the Lord God of Daniel, and of Joshua, and of every other man who got into a tight corner. "But," says some one, "why cannot God develop me through prosperity instead of through adversity?" I will answer your question by asking another. Why does not God dye our northern and temperate seas with coral? You say: "The water is not hot enough." There! In answering my question you have answered your own. Hot climate for richest specimens of coral; hot trouble for the jewels of the soul. The coral fishers going out from Torre del Grecco never brought ashore such fine specimens as are brought out from the scalding surges of misfortune. I look down into the tropical sea, and there is something that looks like blood, and I say: "Has there been a great battle down there?" Seeming blood scattered all up and down the reefs. It is the blood of the coral, and it makes me think of those who come out of great tribulation and have their robes washed in the Blood of the Lamb. But these gems of earth are nothing to the gems of heaven. "No mention shall be made of coral."

Again, I take your hand, and we walk on through this garden of the sea and look more particularly than we did at the beauty of the coral. The poets have all been fascinated with it. One of them wrote:

There, with a broad and easy motion,
  The fan coral sweeps through the clear deep sea,
And the yellow and scarlet tufts of the ocean
  Are bent like corn on the upland lea.

One specimen of coral is called the dendrophilia, because it is like a tree; another is called the astrara, because it is like a star; another is called the brain coral, because it is like the convolutions of the human brain; another is called fan coral, because it is like the instrument with which you cool yourself on a hot day;

another specimen is called the organ-pipe coral, because it resembles the king of musical instruments. All the flowers and all the shrubs in the gardens of the land have their correspondences in this garden of the sea. Corallum! It is a synonym for beauty. And yet there is no beauty in the coral compared with our religion. It gives physiognomic beauty. It does not change the features; it does not give features with which the person was not originally endowed, but it sets behind the features of the homeliest person a heaven that shines clear through. So that often, on first acquaintance, you said of a man: "He is the homeliest person I ever saw," when, after you came to understand him and his nobility of soul shining through his countenance, you said: "He is the loveliest person I ever saw." No one ever had a homely Christian mother. Whatever the world may have thought of her, there were two who thought well—your father, who had admired her for fifty years, and you, over whom she bent with so many tender ministrations. When you think of the angels of God, and your mother among them, she outshines them all. Oh, that our young people could understand that there is nothing that so much beautifies the human countenance as the religion of Jesus Christ! It makes everything beautiful. Trouble beautiful. Sickness beautiful. Disappointment beautiful.

Near my early home there was a place called the "Two Bridges." These bridges leaped the two streams. Well, my friends, the religion of Jesus Christ is two bridges. It bridges all the past. It arches and overspans all the future. It makes the dying pillow the landing-place of angels fresh from glory. It turns the sepulchre into a May-time orchard. It catches up the dying into full orchestra.

Sculpture of the Bible

Corallum! And yet that does not express the beauty: "No mention shall be made of coral."

I take your hand again and walk a little further on in this garden of the sea, and I notice the durability of the work of the coral. Montgomery speaks of it. He says: "Frail were their forms, ephemeral their lives, their masonry imperishable." Rhizopods are insects so small they are invisible, and yet they built the Apennines and they planted for their own monument the Cordilleras! It takes 187,000,000 of them to make one grain. Corals are changing the navigation of the sea, saying to the commerce of the world: "Take this channel," "Take that channel," "Avoid the other channel." Animalcules beating back the Atlantic and Pacific seas! If the insects of the ocean have built a reef a thousand miles long, who knows but that they may yet build a reef three thousand miles long, and thus, that by one stone bridge Europe shall be united with this continent on one side, and by another stone bridge Asia will be united with this continent on the other side; and the tourist of the world, without the turn of a steamer's wheel or the spread of a ship's sail, may go all around the world, and thus be fulfilled the prophecy, "There shall be no more sea."

But the durability of the coral's work is not at all to be compared with the durability of our work for God. The coral is going to crumble in the fires of the last day, but our work for God will endure forever. No more discouraged man ever lived than Beethoven, the great musical composer. Unmercifully criticised by brother artists and his music sometimes rejected. Deaf for twenty-five years, and forced, on his way to Vienna, to beg food and lodging at a very plain house by the roadside. In the evening the family opened a musical instrument and played and sang with great enthusiasm; and one of the numbers they rendered was so emotional that tears ran down their cheeks while they sang and played. Beethoven, sitting in the room, too deaf to hear the singing, was curious to know what was the music that so overpowered them, and when they got through he reached up and took the folio in his hand and found it was his own music—Beethoven's Symphony in A—and he cried out, "I wrote that!" The household sat and stood abashed to find that their poor-looking guest was the great composer. But he never left that house alive. A fever seized him that night, and no relief could be afforded, and in a few days he died. But just before expiring he took the hand of his nephew, who had been sent for and had arrived, saying: "After all, Hummel, I must have had some talent." Poor Beethoven! His work still lives, and in the twentieth century will be better appreciated than it was in the nineteenth; and as long as there is on earth an orchestra to play or an oratorio to sing, Beethoven's nine symphonies will be the enchantment of nations.

But you are not a composer, and you say that there is nothing remarkable about you—only a mother trying to rear your family for usefulness and heaven. Yet the song with which you sing your child to sleep will never cease its mission. You will grow old and die. That son will pass out into the world. The song with which you sang him to sleep last night will go with him while he lives, a conscious or unconscious restraint and inspiration here, and may help open to him the gate of a glorious and triumphant hereafter. The lullabies of this century will sing through all the centuries. The humblest good accomplished in time will last through eternity. I sometimes get discouraged, as I suppose you do, at the vastness of the work and at how little we are doing. And yet, do you suppose the rhizopod said: "There is no need of my working; I cannot build the Cordilleras?" Do you suppose the madrepore said: "There is no need of my working; I cannot build the Sandwich Islands?" Each one attended to his own business; and there are the Sandwich Islands, and there are the Cordilleras. Ah, my friends, the redemption of this world is a great enterprise. I did not see it start; I will not in this world see its close. I am only an insect as compared with the great work to be done, but yet I must do my part. Help build this eternal corallum I will. My parents toiled on this reef long before I was born. I pray God that my children may toil on this reef long after I am dead. Insects all of us, but honored by God to help heave up the reef of light across which shall break the ocean's immortal gladness. Better be insignificant and useful than great and idle. The mastodons and megatheriums of the earth, what did they do but stalk their great carcases across the land and leave their skeletons in the strata, while the corallines went on heaving up the islands all covered with fruitage and verdure. Better be a coralline than a mastodon. So now I am trying to make one little coralline. The polyp picks out of the wave that smites it carbonate of lime, and with that builds up its own insectile masonry. So out of the wave of your tears I take the salt; out of the bruise I take the blue, and out of your bleeding heart I take the red, and out of them altogether I make this coral, which I pray may not be disowned in the day when God makes up his jewels.

Little things decide great things. All that tremendous career of the last Napoleon hung on the hand of a brakeman who, on one of our American railways, caught him as he was falling between the cars of a flying train. The battle of Dunbar was decided against the Scotch because their matches had given out. Aggregations of little things that pull down or build up. When an army or a regiment come to a bridge they are always commanded to break ranks, for their simultaneous tread will destroy the strongest bridge. A bridge at Angiers, France, and a bridge at Broughton, England, went down because the regiments kept step while crossing. Aggregations of temptations, aggregations of sorrow, aggregations of assault, aggregations of Christian effort, aggregations of self-sacrifices! These make the irresistible power to demolish or to uplift, to destroy or to save. Little causes and great results. Christianity was introduced into Japan by the falling overboard of a pocket-Bible from a ship in the harbor of Tokio.

Written on the fly-leaf of one of my books, by one whom God took to himself out of our household, were the following words—I do not know who composed them; perhaps she composed them herself:

Not a sparrow falleth but its God doth know,
Just as when his mandate lays a monarch low;
Not a leaflet waveth but its God doth see;
Think not then, O trembler, God forgetteth thee.

For more precious surely than the birds that fly
Is a Father's image to a Father's eye;
E'en thine hairs are numbered; trust him full and free,
Cast thy care upon him, and he'll care for thee.

For the God that planted in thy breast a soul
On his sacred tables doth thy name enroll;
Cheer thine heart, thou trembler, never faithless be;
He that marks the sparrow will remember thee.

Oh, be encouraged! Do not any man say, "My work is so small." Do not any woman say, "My work is so insignificant; I cannot do anything for the upbuilding of God's kingdom." You can. Remember the corallines. A Christian mother sat sewing a garment, and her little girl wanted to help her, and so she sewed on another piece of the same garment and brought it to her mother, and the work was corrected. It was imperfect, and had to be all taken out again. But did the mother chide the child? Oh, no! She said, "She wanted to help me, and she did as well as she could." And so the mother blessed the child, and while she blessed the child, she thought of herself, and said: "Perhaps it may be so with my poor work at last. God will look at it. It may be very imperfect, and I know it is very crooked. He may have to take it all out; but he knows that I want to serve him, and he knows it is the best that I can do." So be comforted in your Christian work. Five thousand million corallines made one corallum. And then they passed away and other millions came, and the work is wonderful. But on the day when the world's redemption shall be consummated, and the names of all the millions of Christians who in all the ages have toiled on this structure shall be read, the work will appear so grand, and the achievement so glorious, and the durability so everlasting that "No mention shall be made of coral."

THE PRECIOUS STONES OF THE BIBLE; OR, GOD AMONG THE AMETHYSTS

Revelation, 21: 19: " The foundations of the wall of the city were garnished with all manner of precious stones."

THE PRECIOUS STONES OF THE BIBLE; OR, GOD AMONG THE AMETHYSTS

Revelation, 21: 19: " The foundations of the wall of the city
were garnished with all manner of precious stones."

Shall I be frank and tell you what are my de-
signs on you to-day? They are to make you homesick for heaven; to console you concerning your
departed Christian friends by giving you some idea of
the scenes in which they now commingle; to give all
who love the Lord a more elevated idea as to where
they are going to pass the most of the years of their
existence; and to set all the indifferent and neglectful
to quick and immediate preparation, that they may
have it likewise. It is to induce many of our young
people to study a volume of God that few ever open,
but without some acquaintance with which it is impossible to understand the Bible—I mean the precious
stones; their crystallization, their powers of refraction,
their cleavage, their fracture, their lustre, their phosphorescence, their transparency, their infinity of color
and shape, and what they had to do with the welfare
and doom of families and the destiny of nations; ay,
the positive revelation they make of God himself.

My text brings us into the presence of the most
stupendous splendor of the universe, and that is the
wall of heaven, and says of its foundations that they
are garnished with all manner of precious stones. All
the ancient cities had walls for safety, and heaven has
a wall for everlasting safety. You may say that a wall
made up of all manner of precious stones is figurative,

but you cannot understand the force and significance of the figure unless you know something about the real structure and color and value of the precious stones mentioned. Now, I propose, so far as the Lord may help me, to attempt to climb, not the wall of heaven, but the foundations of the wall, and I ask you to join me in the attempt to scale some of the heights. We shall only get part of the way up, but that is better than to stay down on the stupid level, where the most of us have all our lives been standing. We begin clear down at the bottom, where the wall begins.

The first layer of the foundation, reaching all around the city and for fifteen hundred miles is a layer of jasper. Indeed there is more of jasper in the wall of heaven than any other brilliant, because it not only composes a part of the foundation but makes up the chief part of the superstructure. The jasper is a congregation of many colors. It is brown; it is yellow: it is green; it is vermilion; it is red; it is purple; it is black; and is striped with colors so that much of it is called ribbon jasper. It is found in Siberia and Egypt, but it is rare in most lands and of great value, for it is so hard that ordinary processes cannot break it off from the places where it has been deposited. The workmen bore holes into the rock of jasper; then drive into these holes sticks of dry birch-wood, and then saturate the sticks and keep them saturated until they swell enough to split the rock, and the fragments are brought out and polished and transported and cut into cameos and put behind the glass doors of museums. The portraits of Roman emperors were cut into it. The finest intaglio ever seen is in the Vatican museum, the head of Minerva in jasper. By divine arrangement, jasper adorned the breastplate of the high priest in the ancient temple; but its most significant position is where it glows and burns and darkens and brightens and preaches from the lowest stratum of the wall of heaven. Glad am I that the very first row of stones in the wall of heaven is jasper of many colors, and if you like purple, it is purple, and if you like brown it is brown, and if you like green it is green, and if you like ochre-yellow it is ochre-yellow, and if you like vermilion it is vermilion, and if you like black it is black. It suggests to me that heaven is a place of all colors—colors of opinion, colors of creed, colors of skin, colors of taste.

But we must pass up in this inspection of the foundations of the great wall of heaven, and after leaving the jasper, the next precious stone reached is *2nd* sapphire, and it sweeps around the city fifteen hundred miles. All lapidaries agree in saying that the sapphire of the Bible is what we now call lapis lazuli. Job speaks with emotion of "The Place of Sapphires," and God thought so much of this precious stone that he put it in the breast-plate of the high priest, commanding: "The second row shall be an emerald, a sapphire, and a diamond." The sapphire is a blue, but varies from faintest hue to deepest ultramarine. It is found a pebble in the rivers of Ceylon. It is elsewhere in compact masses. Persia and Thibet and Burmah and New South Wales and North Carolina yield exquisite specimens. Its blue eye is seen in the valley of the Rhine. After a burial of thousands of years it has been brought to light in Egyptian monuments and Assyrian cylinders. At Moscow and St. Petersburg and Constantinople, I have seen great masses of the sapphire, commonly called lapis lazuli. The closer you study its veins, the more enchanting; and I do not wonder that the sapphire is called into the foundation of the wall of heaven. It makes a strong stone for the foundation, for it is the hardest of all minerals except the diamond. Sapphire based on jasper: a blue sky over a fiery sunset. St. John points to it in the Revelation, and says: "The second, sapphire;" and this suggests to me that though our earth and all its furniture of mountains and seas and atmospheres is to collapse and vanish, we will throughout all eternity have in some way kept the most beautiful of earthly appearances, whether you take this sapphire of the second layer as literal or figurative. The deep blue of our skies and the deep blue of our seas must not, will not, be forgotten. If, a thousand years after the world has gone to ashes, you or I want to recall how the earthly skies looked in a summer noon, or the mid-ocean in a calm, we will have only to look at the second row of the foundation of the wall of heaven. I am glad that St. John told us about it! "The second, sapphire!" While we are living in sight of that wall, spirits who have come from other worlds, and who never saw our earth, will visit us, and we will visit them, and some time we will be in converse about this earth when it was yet a-float and a-swing, and we shall want to tell them how it looked at certain times, and then it will be a great object lesson for all eternity, and we will say to our visitor from some other world, as we point toward the wall of heaven: "It looked like that stratum of foundation next to the lowest." The Revelation, 21st chapter and 19th verse: "The second, sapphire."

A step higher and you come to chalcedony, another layer in the foundation of the wall and running fifteen hundred miles around the heavenly city. Chalcedony! Translucent. A divine mixture of agates and opals and cornelians. Striped with white and gray. Dash of pallor blushing into red and darkening into purple. Iceland and Hebrides hold forth beautiful specimens of chalcedony.

But we must make a swift ascent to the top of the foundation wall, for we cannot minutely examine all the layers, and so, putting one foot on the chalcedony, of which we have been speaking, we spring to the emerald, and we are one-third of the way to the top of the foundation, for the fourth row is emerald. That, I would judge, is God's favorite among gems, because it holds what seems evident is his favorite color on earth, the green; since that is the color most widely diffused across all the earth's continents — the grass, the foliage, the every-day dress of nature. The emerald! Kings used it as a seal to stamp pronunciamentos. The rainbow around the Throne of God is by St. John compared to it. Conquerors have considered it the greatest prize to capture. What ruthlessness, when the soldiers of Pizarro pounded it with their hammers. Emeralds have had much to do with the destiny of Mexico. Five of them were presented by Cortez to his bride, one of them cut into the shape of a rose, another into the shape of a trumpet, another into the shape of a bell, with tongue of pearl, and this presentation aroused the jealousy of the throne and caused the consequent downfall of Cortez. But the depths of the sea were decorated with those emeralds, for in a shipwreck they went down off the coast of Barbary. Napoleon wore an emerald at Austerlitz. In the Kremlin Museum at Moscow, there are crowns and sceptres and outspread miracles of emerald. Ireland is called the Emerald Isle, not because of its verdure, but because it was presented to Henry the Second of England with an emerald ring. Nero had a magnifying glass of emerald through which he looked at the gladiatorial contests at Rome. But here are fifteen hundred miles of emerald, sweeping around the heavenly city in one layer.

Upward still, and you put your foot on a stratum of sardonyx, white and red, a seeming commingling of snow and fire; the snow cooling the fire, the fire melting the snow. Another climb, and you reach the sardius, named after the city of Sardis. Another climb, and you reach the chrysolite. A specimen of this, belonging to Epiphanus in the fourth century, was said to be so brilliant that it shone through whatever was put over to conceal it; and the Emperor of China has a specimen that is described as having such penetrating radiance that it makes the night as bright as the day. A higher climb, and you reach the beryl. Two thousand years ago the Greeks used this precious stone for engraving purposes. It was accounted among the royal treasures of Tyre. The hilt of Murat's sword was adorned with it. It glows in the imperial crown of Great Britain. Luther thought the beryl of the heavenly wall was turquoise. Kalisch thought it was chrysolite. Josephus thought it a golden-colored jewel. The wheels of Ezekiel's vision flamed with beryl, and were a revolving fire. The beryl appears in six-sided prisms, and is set in seals and intaglios, in necklaces and coronets. It was the joy of ancient jewelry. It ornamented the affluent with ear-drops. Charlemagne presented it to his favorites. Beautiful beryl! Exquisitely shaped beryl! Divinely colored beryl! It seems like congealed color. It looks like frozen fire.

But stop not here. Climb higher and you come to topaz, a bewilderment of beauty, and named after an island of the Red Sea. You must not be tempted to stop here amid the brilliance, but climb higher and you come to chrysoprasus, of greenish-golden hue and hard as flint. Climb higher, and you reach the jacinth, named after the flower hyacinth and of reddish-blue. Take one more step, and you reach the top, not of the wall, but the top of the foundations of the wall, and St. John cries out: "The twelfth, an amethyst!" This precious stone, when found in Australia or India or

Precious Stones of the Bible

Europe, stands in columns and pyramids. For color, it is a violet blooming in stone. For its play of light, for its deep mysteries of color, for its uses in Egyptian, in Etruscan, in Roman art, it has been honored. The Greeks thought this stone a preventive of drunkenness. The Hebrews thought it a source of pleasant dreams. For all lovers of gems, it is a subject of admiration and suggestiveness. Yes, the word amethyst means a prevention of drunkenness. Long before the New Testament made reference to the amethyst in the wall of heaven, the Persians thought that cups made out of amethyst would hinder any kind of liquor contained therein from becoming intoxicating. But of all the amethystine cups from which the ancients drank, not one had any such result of prevention. For thousands of years the world has been looking in vain for such a preventive amethystine cup. Staggering Noah could not find it. Convivial Ahasuerus, driving Vashti from the gates, could not find it. Nabal, breaking the heart of beautiful Abigail, could not find it. Belshazzar, the royal reveler, on the night that the Chaldeans took Babylon, could not find it. Not one of the millions of inebriates, whose skulls pave the continents and pave the depths of the sea, could find it. There is no such cup. Strong drink from hollowed amethyst imbrutes the same as strong drink from pewter mug. It is not the style of cup we drink out of, but that which the cup contains which decides the helpful or damning result of the beverage. All around the world last night and to-day, out of cups costlier than amethyst, men and women have been drinking their own doom and the doom of their children for this life and the next. Ah, it is the amethystine cups that do the wildest and worst slaughter. The smash of the filthy goblets of the rummeries would long ago have taken place by law, but the amethystine chalices prevent—the chalices out of which legislatures and congresses drink before and after they make the laws. Amethystine chalices have been the friends of intoxication instead of its foes. Over the fiery lips of the amethystine chalices is thrust the tongue of that which biteth like a serpent and stingeth like an adder. Drunkenness is a combination of apoplexy and dementia. The four hundred million victims of opium come out to meet the one hundred and fifty million victims of alcohol, and the two agents take the contract for tumbling the human race into perdition, but whether they will succeed in fulfilling the contract depends on the action of the amethystine cups, the amethystine demijohns, the amethystine ale pitchers, the amethystine flagons, the amethystine wine cellars. O, Persians! O, Assyrians! O, Greeks! O, Egyptians! You were wrong in thinking that a cup of amethyst would prevent inebriation.

But standing on the top of this amethystine layer of the foundation of the wall of heaven, I bethink myself of the mistake that many of the ancient Hebrews made when they thought that the amethyst was a producer of pleasant dreams. Just wear a piece of amethyst over your heart, or put it under your pillow, they said, and you would have your dreams filled with everything beautiful and entrancing. No, no! The style of pillow will not decide the character of the dream. The only recipe for pleasant dreams is to do right and think right when you are wide awake. Conditions of physical disease may give a good man a nightmare, but a man physically well, if he behave himself aright, will not be troubled with bad dreams. Nebuchadnezzar, with eagle's down under his head and Tyrian purple over it, struggled with a bad dream that made him shriek out for the soothsayers and astrologers to come and interpret it. Pharaoh, amid the marble palaces of Memphis, was confounded by a dream in which lean cows ate up the fat cows, and the small ears of corn devoured the seven large ears, and awful famine was prefigured. Pilate's wife, amid clouds of richest upholstery, had a startling dream, because of which she sent a message in hot haste to a court-room to keep her husband from enacting a judicial outrage. But Jacob, at Bethel, with a pillow of mountain rock, had a blissful dream of the ladder angel-blossoming. Bunyan, with his head on a hard plank of Bedford jail, saw the gates of the celestial city. St. John, on the barrenest island of the Ægean Sea, in his dream heard trumpets and saw cavalrymen on white horses and a new heaven and a new earth. No amount of rough pillow can disturb the night vision of a saint, and no amount of amethystine charm can delectate the dream of a miscreant.

But some one will say, "Why have you brought us to this amethyst, the top row of the foundation of the heavenly wall, if you are not able to accept the theory of the ancient Greeks, who said that the amethyst was a charm against intoxication, or if you are not willing to accept the theory of the ancient Hebrews that the amethyst was a producer of pleasant dreams?" My answer is, I have brought you to the top row, the twelfth layer of the foundation of the heavenly wall of fifteen hundred miles of circling amethyst, to put you in a position where you can get a new idea of heaven; to let you see that after you have climbed up twelve strata of glory, you are only at the base of the eternal grandeurs; to let you, with enchantment of soul, look far down and look far up; and to force upon you the thrilling question that if all our climbing has only shown us the foundation of the wall, what must the wall itself be; and if this is the outside of heaven, what must the inside be; and if all this is figurative, what must the reality be? Oh, this piled-up magnificence of the heavenly wall, this eternity of decoration, this opalescent, fluorescent, prismatic miracle of architecture! What enthronement of all colors! A mingling of the blue of the skies, and the surf of seas, and the green of meadows, and the upholstery of autumnal forests, and the fire of August sunsets. All the splendors of earth and heaven dashed into those twelve rows of foundation wall. All that, mark you, only typical of the spiritual glories that roll over heaven like the Atlantic and Pacific oceans swung in one billow.

Do you not see that it was impossible that you could understand a hundredth part of the suggestiveness of that twenty-first chapter of the Revelation without going into some of the particulars of the wall of heaven and dipping up some of its dripping colors, and running your eye along some of the wondrous crystallizations, and examining some of the frozen light in its turquoise, and feeling with your own finger the hardness of its sapphire, and shielding your eyes against the shimmering brilliance in its beryl, and studying the fifteen hundred miles of emerald without a flaw? Yet all this only the outside of heaven, and the poorest part of the outside; not the wall itself, but only the foot of the wall, for my text says: "The foundations of the wall of the city were garnished with all manner of precious stones." Oh, get down your harp, if you can play one. Get down a palm branch, if you can reach one. Why, it makes us all feel like crying out with James Montgomery:

> When shall these eyes thy heaven-built walls
> And pearly gates behold?

Oh, my soul! If my text shows us only the outside, what must the inside be? While riding one summer, a few years ago, through the emperor's park near St. Petersburg, Russia, I was captivated with the groves, transplanted from all zones, and the flower-beds, miles this way and miles that way, incarnadined with beauty, and the fountains bounding in such revels with the sunlight as nowhere else is seen. I said: "This is beautiful. I never saw anything like this before." But when I entered the palace and saw the pictured walls and the long line of statuary, and aquariums afloat with all bright scales, and aviaries a-chant with bird voices, and the inner doors of the palace were swung back by the chamberlain, and I saw the emperor and empress and princes and princesses, and they greeted me with a cordiality as of old acquaintanceship, I forgot all the groves and floral bewitchment I had seen outside before entrance. And now I ask, if the outside of heaven attracts our souls to-day, how much more will be the uplifting, when we get inside and see the King in his beauty and all the princes and princesses of the palaces of amethyst? Are you not glad that we did not stop in our ascent until we got to the top round of the foundation wall of heaven, the twelfth row, the amethyst?

Perhaps the ancient Hebrews were not, after all, so far out of the way when they thought that the touch of the amethyst gave pleasant dreams, for the touch of it this hour gives me a very pleasant dream. Standing on this amethyst, I dream a dream. I close my eyes and I see it all. We are there. This is heaven! Not the outside, but the inside of heaven. With what warmth of welcome our long-ago departed loved ones have kissed us. How they have changed in looks. They were so sick when they went away, and now they are so well. Look! Yonder is the palace of our Lord the King. Not kept a moment outside, we are ushered into the throne-room.

Stretching out his scarred hand, he says: "I have loved thee with an everlasting love," and we respond: "Whom have I in heaven but thee?" But, look! Yonder is the playground of the children. Children do not want a throne. A throne would not fit a child. There they are on the playgrounds of heaven—the children. Out of the sick cradle of earth, they came into this romping mirth of the eternal playgrounds. I clap my hands to cheer them in their glee. Yonder are the palaces of the martyrs, and before their doorway the flowers crimson as the bloody martyrdoms through which they waded up into glory. Yonder is Apostolic Row, and the highest turret is over the home of Paul. Here is Evangelist Place. Yonder are the concert halls in which the musicians of earth and heaven are taking part—Handel with organ and David with harp and Gabriel with trumpet and four and twenty elders with voices. And an angel of God says to me: "Where shall I take you? On what street of heaven would you like to live? What celestial habitation would you like to occupy?" And I answer: "Now that I have got inside the wall made up of all manner of precious stones, I do not care where you put me. Just show me where my departed loved ones are. I have seen the Lord, and next I want to see them. But here are those with whom I toiled in the Kingdom of God on earth. They are from my old parishes at Belleville and Syracuse and Philadelphia and Brooklyn and Washington and from many places on both sides the sea where I have been permitted to work with them and for them. Give them the best places you can find. I will help steady them as they mount the thrones. I will help you burnish their coronets. Take these, my old friends, to as good rooms as you can get for them in the House of Many Mansions, and with windows looking out upon the

Palace of the Great King. As for myself, anywhere in heaven is good enough for me. Hallelujah to the Lamb that was slain!" But I awake. In the ecstasy of the moment my foot slipped from the layer of amethyst—that so-called producer of dreams—and in the effort to catch myself, the vision vanished. And lo! it was but a dream!

THE CHRONOLOGY OF THE BIBLE; OR, GOD AMONG THE CENTURIES

Deut., 32: 7:   " Consider the years of many generations."

THE CHRONOLOGY OF THE BIBLE; OR, GOD AMONG THE CENTURIES

A New Year's sermon.

Deut., 32:7: "Consider the years of many generations."

At twelve o'clock last night, while so many good people were watching, an old friend passed out of our homes and a stranger entered. The old friend making valedictory was the departing year; the stranger arriving is the new. The old friend was garrulous with the occurrences of many days, but the stranger put his finger over his lip and said nothing and seemed charged with many secrets and mysteries. I did not see either the departure or the arrival, but was sound asleep, thinking that was for me the best way to be wide awake now. And I was confident that the transference from year to year would go on just as well as if I were watching. Good-bye, Old Year! Welcome, New Year!

As an army is divided into brigades and regiments and companies, and they observe this order in their march, and their tread is majestic, so the time of the world's existence is divided into an army, divinely commanded: the eras are the brigades, the centuries are the regiments, and the years are the companies. Forward! into the eternity past, out of the eternity to come. Forward! is the command, and nothing can halt them even though the world should die. While obeying my text, "Consider the years of many generations," I propose to speak of the "Chronology of the Bible, or God among the Centuries."

Sermons by T. DeWitt Talmage

We make a distinction between time and eternity, but time is only a piece of eternity, and chronology has been engaged in the sublime work of dividing up this portion of eternity that we call time into compartments, and putting events in their right compartment. It is as much an injustice against the past to wrongly arrange its events, as it would be an injustice if, through neglect of chronological accuracy, it should, in the far distant future, be said that America was discovered in 1776, and the Declaration of Independence was signed in 1492, and Washington born on the 22d of March, and the Civil War of the United States was fought in 1840. As God puts all the events of time in the right place, let us be careful that we do not put them in the wrong place. The chronology of the Bible takes six steps, but they are steps so long, it makes us hold our breath as we watch the movement. From Adam to Abraham. From Abraham to the exodus from Egypt. From the exodus to the foundation of Solomon's Temple. From the foundation of Solomon's Temple to the destruction of that Temple. From the destruction of the Temple to the return from Babylonish captivity. From Babylonish captivity to the birth of Christ. Chronology takes pen and pencil, and calling astronomy and history to help, says: "Let us fix one event, from which to calculate everything. Let it be a star, the Bethlehem star, the Christmas star." And from that we go back to see the world was created four thousand and four years before Christ, the deluge came two thousand three hundred and forty-eight years before Christ, the exodus from Egypt occurred one thousand four hundred and ninety-one years before Christ, and Solomon's temple was destroyed five hundred and eighty-six years before Christ. Chronology enters the first chapter of Genesis and says the day mentioned there is not a day of

Chronology of the Bible

twenty-four hours, but of ages; the word there translated as "day," in other places meaning ages, and so the Bible account of the creation and the geologists' account of the creation are completely harmonious. Chronology enters the book of Daniel, and says that words "time and a-half" mean a year and a-half. Chronology enters at another point and shows us that the seasons of the year were then only two—summer and winter. We find that the Bible year was three hundred and sixty days, instead of three hundred and sixty-five; that the day was calculated from six o'clock in the morning to six o'clock at night; that the night was divided into four watches, namely, the late watch, the midnight, the cock-crowing, the early watch. The clock and watch were invented so long after the world began that the day could not be very sharply divided in Bible times. Ahaz had a sun-dial, or a flight of stairs with a column at the top, and the shadow which that column threw on the steps beneath indicated the hour, the shadow lengthening or withdrawing from step to step.

But the events of life and the events of the world moved so slowly, for the most part in Bible times, that they had no need of such timepieces as we stand on our mantels or carry in our pockets in an age when a man may have a half dozen or a dozen engagements for one day and needs to know the exact minute for each one of them. The earth itself in Bible times was the chief timepiece, and it turned once on its axis and that was a day, and once around the sun and that was a year. It was not until the fourteenth century that the almanac was born, the almanac that we toss carelessly about, not realizing that it took the accumulated ingenuity of more than five thousand years to make one. Chronology had to bring into its service the monuments of Egypt, and the cylinders of Assyria, and the bricks of Babylon, and the pottery of Nineveh, and the medals struck at Antioch for the battle of Actium, and all the hieroglyphics that could be deciphered, and had to go into the extremely delicate business of asking the ages of Adam and Seth and Enoch and Methuselah who, after their three-hundredth year, wanted to be thought young. I think it must have been in recognition of the stupendous work of making an almanac that all the days of the week are named after the gods. Sunday, after the Sun, which was of old worshiped as a god; Monday, after the Moon, which was also worshiped as a god; Tuesday, after Tuesco, the god of War; Wednesday, after Woden, the chief god of the Scandinavians; Thursday, after Thor, the god of thunder; Friday, after Frea, the goddess of marriage, and Saturday, after Saturn. The old Bible year began with the 25th of March. Not until 1752 did the first of the month of January get the honor in legal documents in England of being called the first day of the year. Improvements all along have been made in chronology until the calendar and the almanac and the clock and the watch seem to have reached perfection, and all the nations of Christendom have similarity of time calculations and have adopted what is called the "New Style," except Russia, which keeps what is called the "Old Style," and is twelve days different, so that, writing from there, if you wish to be accurate, you date your letter January 1st and January 12th, or December 10th and December 22d.

It is something to thank God for that the modes are so complete for calculating the cycles, the centuries, the decades, the years, the months, the days, the hours, the seconds. Think of making appointments, as in the Bible days, for the time of the new moon. Think of making one of the watches of the night, in the Bible times, a rooster's crowing. The Bible says, "Before the cock crow thou shalt deny me thrice;" "If the Master cometh at cock-crowing;" and that was the way the midnight watch was indicated. The crowing of that barnyard bird has always been most uncertain. The crowing is at the lowest temperature of the night, and the amount of dew and the direction of the wind may bring the lowest temperature at eleven o'clock at night, or two o'clock in the morning, and at any one of six hours. Just before a rain, the crowing of chanticleer in the night is almost perpetual.

Compare these modes of marking time with our own modes, when twelve o'clock is twelve o'clock, and six o'clock is six o'clock, and ten o'clock is ten o'clock, independent of all weathers, and then thank God that you live now. But, notwithstanding all the imperfect modes of marking hours or years or centuries, Bible chronology never trips up, never falters, never contradicts itself, and here is one of the best arguments for the authenticity of the Scriptures. If you can prove an alibi in the courts, and you can prove beyond doubt that you were in some particular place at the time you were charged with doing or saying something in quite another place, you gain the victory, and Infidelity has tried to prove an alibi by contending that events and circumstances in the Bible ascribed to certain times must have taken place at some other time, if they took place at all. But this Book's chronology has never been caught at fault. It has been proved that when the Hebrews went into Egypt there were only seventy of them, and that when they came out there were two millions of them. "Now," says Infidelity, with a guffaw that it cannot suppress, "what an absurdity! They went down into Egypt seventy and came out two millions. That is a falsehood on the face of it. Nations do not increase in that ratio." But, my sceptical friend, hold a moment. The Bible says the Jews were 430 years in Egypt, and that explains the increase from seventy persons to two millions, for it is no more but rather less than the ordinary increase of nations. The Pilgrim Fathers came to America in the *Mayflower*, one small shipload of passengers, less than three hundred years ago, and now we have a nation of sixty millions. Where then is the so-called impossibility that the seventy Jews who went into Egypt in four hundred and thirty years became two millions? Infidelity wrong and Bible chronology right.

Now, stop and reflect, why is it that this sublime subject of Bible chronology has been so neglected, and that the most of you have never given ten minutes to the consideration of it and that this is the first sermon ever preached on this stupendous and overwhelming theme? We have stood by the half day or the whole day at grand reviews and seen armies pass. Again and again and again on the Champs Elysees, Frenchmen, by the hundreds of thousands, have stood and watched the bannered armies go by, and the huzza has been three miles long and until the populace were so hoarse they could huzza no longer. Again and again and again, the Germans, by hundreds of thousands, have stood on the palaced and statued Unter den Linden, Berlin, and strewn garlands under the feet of uniformed hosts led on by Von Moltke or Blucher or Frederick the Great. When Wellington and Ponsonby and the Scots Greys came back from Waterloo, or Wolseley from Egypt or Marlborough from Blenheim, what military processions through Regent street and along by the palaces of London and over the bridges of the Thames! What almost interminable lines of military on the streets of all our American capitals, while Mayors and Governors and Presidents, with uncovered heads, looked on. But put all those grand reviews together and they are tame compared with the reviews which on this New Year's Day you from the pew and I from the pulpit witness. Hear them pass in chronological order; all the years before the flood; all the years since the flood; decades abreast; centuries abreast; epochs abreast; millenniums abreast; Egyptian civilization, Babylonian populations, Assyrian dominions. Armies of Persian, Grecian, Peloponnesian and Roman wars: Byzantine empire, Saracenic hosts, Crusaders of the First, the Second, the Third and the last—avalanche of men: Dark Ages in sombre epaulettes and Brighter Ages with shields of silver and helmets of gold: Italy, Spain, France, Russia, Germany, England and America, past and present: dynasties, feudal domains, despotisms, monarchies, republics, ages on ages, ages on ages, passing to-day in a chronological review, until one has no more power to look upon the advancing columns, now brilliant, now squalid; now garlanded with peace, now crimson with slaughter; now horrid with ghastliness, now radiant with love and joy.

This chronological study affords, among many practical thoughts, especially two—the one encouraging to the last degree and the other startling. The encouraging thought is that the main drift of the centuries has been toward betterment, with only here and there a serious reversal. Grecian civilization was a vast improvement on Egyptian civilization, and Roman civilization a vast improvement on Grecian civilization, and Christian civilization is a vast improvement on Roman civilization. What was the boasted age of Pericles compared with the age of Longfellow and Tennyson? What was Queen Elizabeth as a specimen of moral womanhood compared with Queen

Victoria? What were the cruel warriors of olden times compared with the most distinguished warriors of the last half century, all of them as much distinguished for kindness and good morals as for prowess; the two military leaders of our Civil War on Northern and Southern side communicant members of Christian churches, and their home life as pure as their public life? Nothing impresses me in this chronological review more than the fact that the regiments of years are better and better regiments as the troops move on. I thank God that you and I were not born any sooner than we were born. How could we have endured the disaster of being born in the eighteenth or seventeenth or sixteenth century? Glad am I that we are in the regiment now passing the reviewing stand and that our children will pass the stand in a still better regiment. God did not build this world for a slaughter-house or a den of infamy. A good deal of cleaning house will be necessary before this world becomes as clean and sweet as it ought to be; but the brooms and the scrubbing brushes and the upholsterers and plumbers are already busy, and when the world gets fixed up as it will be, if Adam and Eve ever visit it—as I expect they will—they will say to each other: "Well, this beats Paradise when we lived there, and the pears and plums are better than we plucked from the first trees, and the wardrobes are more complete, and the climate is better." Since I settled in my own mind the fact that God was stronger than the devil, I have never lost faith in the emparadisation of this planet. With the exception of a retrogression in the Dark Ages, the movement of the world has been on and on, and up and up, and I have two jubilant hosannas—one for the closing year and the other for the new year.

But the other thought coming out of this subject

Chronology of the Bible

is that biblical chronology, and indeed all chronology, is urging the world to more punctuality and promptitude. What an unsatisfactory and indefinite thing it must have been for two business men in the time of Ahaz to make an appointment, saying: "We will settle that business matter to-morrow when the shadow on the dial of Ahaz reaches the tenth step from the top," or, "I will meet you in the street called Straight in Damascus in the time of the new moon," or, when asked in a court-room, what time an occurrence took place, should answer: "It was during the time of the latter rain," or, "It was at the time of the third crowing of the barnyard." You and I remember when ministers of the Gospel in the country, giving out a notice of an evening service, instead of saying at six or seven or eight o'clock would say, "The service will begin at early candle-light." Thank God for chronological achievements which have ushered in calendars and almanacs and clocks and watches, and at so cheap a rate all may possess them.

Chronology, beginning by appreciating the value of years and the value of days, has kept on until it cries out: "Man, immortal; woman, immortal; look out for that second!" The greatest fraud a man can commit is to rob another of his time. Hear it, ye laggards, and repent! All the fingers of chronology point to punctuality as one of the graces. The minister or the lecturer or business man who comes to his place ten minutes after the appointed time commits a crime, the enormity of which can only be estimated by multiplying the number of persons present by ten. If the engagement be made with five persons, he has stolen fifty minutes, for he is ten minutes late and he has robbed each of the five persons of ten minutes apiece, and ten times five are fifty. If there are five hundred persons present, and he be ten minutes late, he has committed a robbery of five thousand minutes, for ten times five hundred are five thousand, and five thousand minutes are eighty-three hours, which make more than three days. The thief of dry goods, the thief of bank bills is not half so bad as the thief of time.

Doctor Rush, the greatest and busiest physician of his day appreciated the value of time, and when asked how he had been able to gather so much information for his books and lectures, he replied: "I have been able to do it by economizing my time. I have not spent one hour in amusement in thirty years." And taking a blank book from his pocket, said, "I fill a book like this every week with thoughts that occur to me and facts collected in the rooms of my patients." Napoleon appreciated the value of time when the sun was sinking upon Waterloo, and he thought that a little more time would retrieve his fortunes, and he pointed to the sinking sun, and said: "What would I not give to be this day possessed of the power of Joshua and enabled to retard thy march for two hours?" Voltaire, the blatant French infidel, appreciated the value of time, when, in his dying moments, he said to his doctor: "I will give you half of what I am worth if you will give me six months of life," and when told that he could not live six weeks, he burst into tears and said: "Then, I shall go to hell." John Wesley appreciated the value of time when he stood on his steps waiting for a delayed carriage to take him to an appointment, saying: "I have lost ten minutes forever." Lord Nelson appreciated the value of time when he said: "I owe everything in the world to being always a quarter of an hour beforehand." A clockmaker in one of the old English towns appreciated the value of time when he put on the front of the town clock the words: "Now or when?" Mitchell, the astronomer, appreciated the value of time when he said: "I have been in the habit of calculating the value of a thousandth part of a second." They best appreciate the value of time whose Sabbaths have been wasted and whose opportunities of repentance and usefulness are all gone, and who have nothing left but memories, baleful and elegiac. They stand in the bleak September, with bare feet, on the sharp stubble of a reaped wheat field, crying: "The harvest is past," and the sough of an autumnal equinox moans forth in echo: "The harvest is past!"

But do not let us get an impression from chronology that because the years of time have been so long in procession they are to go on forever. Matter is not eternal! Oh, no! If you watch half a day, or a whole day, or two days, as I once did, to see a military procession, you remember the last brigade and the last regiment and the last company finally passed on, and as we rose to go we said to each other: "It is all over." So this mighty procession of earthly years will terminate. Just when, I have no power to prognosticate, but science confirms the Bible prophecy that the earth cannot always last. Indeed, there has been a fatality of worlds. The moon is merely the corpse of what it once was, and scientists have again and again gone up in their observatories to attend the death-bed of dying worlds, and have seen them cremated. So I am certain, both from the Word of God and science, that the world's chronology will sooner or later come to its last chapter. The final century will arrive and pass on, and then will come the final decade, and then the final year and the final month and the final day. The last spring will swing its censer of apple blossoms, and the last winter bank its snows. The last sunset will burn like Moscow, and the last morning radiate the hills.

Sermons by T. DeWitt Talmage

The clocks will strike their last hour, and the watches will tick their last second.

No incendiaries will be needed to run hither and yon with torches to set the world on fire. Chemistry teaches us that there is a very inflammable element in water. While oxygen makes up a part of the water, the other part of the water is hydrogen, and that is very combustible. The oxygen drawn out from the water may put instantly into conflagration the Hudsons and Savannahs and Mississippis and Rhines and Urals and Danubes, and the Atlantic and Pacific and Indian and Mediterranean Seas. And then the Angel of God, descending from the Throne, might put one foot in the surf of the sea and the other on the beach, and cry to the four winds of heaven: "Time was! But time shall be no longer!" Yet, found in Christ, pardoned and sanctified, we shall welcome the day with more gladness than we ever welcomed a Christmas or New Year's morn.

> When wrapt in fire, the realms of ether glow,
> And heaven's last thunder shakes the earth below;
> Thou, undismayed, shalt o'er the ruin smile,
> And light thy torch at nature's funeral pile.

THE LIGHTNING OF THE SEA

Job, 41: 32: " He maketh a path to shine after him."

THE LIGHTNING OF THE SEA

Job, 41: 32: " He maketh a path to shine after him."

If for the next thousand years ministers of religion should preach from this Bible there will yet be texts unexpounded and unexplained and unappreciated. What little has been said concerning this chapter in Job from which my text is taken, bears on the controversy as to what was really the leviathan described as disturbing the sea. What creature it was I know not. Some say it was a whale. Some say it was a crocodile. My own opinion is, it was a sea-monster now extinct. No creature now floating in Mediterranean or Atlantic waters corresponds to Job's description.

What most interests me is that as it moved on through the deep it left the waters flashing and resplendent. In the words of the text, "He maketh a path to shine after him." What was that illumined path? It was phosphorescence. You find it in the wake of a ship in the night, especially after rough weather. Phosphorescence is the lightning of the sea. That this figure of speech is correct in describing its appearance I am certified by an incident. After crossing the Atlantic the first time and writing from Basle, Switzerland, to an American magazine an account of my voyage, in which nothing more fascinated me than the phosphorescence in the ship's wake, I called it The Lightning of the Sea. Returning to my hotel, I found a book of John Ruskin, and the first sentence my eyes fell upon was his description of phosphorescence, in which he called it "The Lightning of the Sea." Down to the post-office I hastened to get the

manuscript, and with great labor and some expense
got possession of the magazine article and put quotation marks around that one sentence, although it was
as original with me as with John Ruskin.

I suppose that nine-tenths of you living so near the
sea-coast have watched this marine appearance called
phosphorescence, and I hope that the other tenth may
some day be so happy as to witness it. It is the
waves of the sea diamonded; it is the inflorescence
of the billows; the waves of the sea crimsoned, as was
the deep after the sea-fight of Lepanto; the waves of
the sea on fire. There are times when from horizon
to horizon the entire ocean seems in conflagration with
this strange splendor, as it changes every moment to
duller or more dazzling color on all sides of you. You
sit looking over the taffrail of the yacht or ocean
steamer watching and waiting to see what new thing
the God of beauty will do with the Atlantic. It is the
ocean in transfiguration; it is the marine world casting
its garments of glory in the pathway of the Almighty
as he walks the deep; it is an inverted firmament with
all the stars gone down with it. No picture can present it, for photographer's camera cannot be successfully trained to catch it, and before it the hand of the
painter drops its pencil, overawed and powerless. This
phosphorescence is the appearance of myriads of the
animal kingdom rising, falling, playing, flashing, living, dying. These luminous animalcules for nearly
one hundred and fifty years have been the study of
naturalists and the fascination and solemnization of
all who have brain enough to think. Now, God, who
puts in his Bible nothing trivial or useless, calls the
attention of Job, the greatest scientist of his day, to
this phosphorescence, and as the leviathan of the deep
sweeps past, points out the fact that "he maketh a
path to shine after him."

The Lightning of the Sea

Is that true of us now, and will it be true of us when we have gone? Will there be subsequent light or darkness? Will there be a trail of gloom or good cheer? Can any one between now and the next one hundred years say of us truthfully as the text says of the leviathan of the deep, "He maketh a path to shine after him?" For we are moving on. While we live in the same house, and transact business in the same store, and write on the same table, and chisel in the same studio, and thresh in the same barn, and worship in the same church, we are in motion, and are in many respects moving on, and we are not where we were ten years ago, nor where we will be ten years hence. Moving on! Look at the family record, or the almanac, or into the mirror, and see if any one of you is where you were. All in motion. Other feet may trip and stumble and halt, but the foot of not one moment for the last sixty centuries has tripped or stumbled or halted. Moving on! Society moving on! Heaven moving on! The universe moving on! Time moving on! Eternity moving on! Therefore, it is absurd to think that we ourselves can stop, as we must move with all the rest. Are we like the creature of the text, making our path to shine after us? It may be a peculiar question, but my text suggests it. What influence will we leave in this world after we have gone through it? "None," answer hundreds of voices; "we are not of the immortals. Fifty years after we are out of the world it will be as though we never inhabited it." You are wrong in saying that. I pass through an audience looking for some one whom I cannot find. I look for one who will have no influence in this world a hundred years from now. But I find the man who has the least influence, and I inquire into his history and I find that by a "yes" or a "no" he decided some one's eternity. In time of temptation he gave an affirmative or a negative to some temptation which another, hearing of, was induced to decide in the same way. Clear on the other side of the next million years may be the first you hear of the long-reaching influence of that "yes" or "no," but hear of it you will. Will that father make a path to shine after him? Will that mother make a path to shine after her? You will be walking along these streets, or along that country road two hundred years from now in the character of your descendants. They will be affected by your courage or your cowardice, your purity or your depravity, your holiness or your sin. You will make the path to shine after you or darken after you.

Why should they point out to us on some mountain two rivulets, one of which passes down into the rivers which pour out into the Pacific Ocean and the other rivulet flowing down into the rivers which pass out into the Atlantic Ocean? Every man, every woman, stands at a point where words uttered, or prayers offered, decide opposite destinies and opposite eternities. We see a man planting a tree, and treading the sod firmly on each side of it, and watering it in dry weather, and taking great care in its culture, and he never plucks any fruit from its bough; but his children will. We are all planting trees that will yield fruit hundreds of years after we are dead, orchards of golden fruit, or groves of deadly upas. I am so fascinated with the phosphorescence in the track of a ship that I have sometimes watched for a long while, and have seen nothing on the face of the deep but blackness, the mouth of watery chasms that looked like gaping jaws of hell. Not a spark as big as the firefly; not a white scroll of surf; not a taper to illuminate the mighty sepulchres of dead ships; darkness three thousand feet deep, and more thousands of feet long and wide. That is the kind of wake that a bad man leaves behind him as he plows through the ocean of this life toward the vaster ocean of the great future.

Now, suppose a man seated in a corner grocery, or business office among clerks, gives himself to hilarious scepticism. He laughs at the Bible, makes sport of the miracles, speaks of perdition in jokes, and laughs at revivals as a frolic, and at the passage of a funeral procession, which always solemnizes sensible people, says, "Boys, let's take a drink." There is in that group a young man who is making a great struggle against temptation, and prays night and morning, and reads his Bible, and is asking God for help day by day. But that guffaw against Christianity makes him lose his grip of sacred things and he gives up Sabbath and Church and morals, and goes from bad to worse, till he falls under dissipation, dies in a lazar house and is buried in the potter's field. Another young man who heard that merry scepticism made up his mind that "it makes no difference what we do or say, for we will all come out at last at the right place," and began, as a consequence, to purloin. Some money that came into his hands for others he applied to his own use, thinking perhaps he would make it straight some other time, and all would be well, even if he did not make it straight. He ends in the penitentiary. That scoffer who uttered the jokes against Christianity never realized what bad work he was doing, and he passed on through life, and out of it, and into a future that I am not now going to depict. I do not propose with a searchlight to show the breakers of the awful coast on which that ship is wrecked, for my business now is to watch the sea after the keel has plowed it. No phosphorescence in the wake of that ship, but behind it two souls struggling in the wave; two young men destroyed by reckless scepticism, an unillumined ocean beneath, and on all sides of them blackness of darkness. You know what a gloriously good man the Rev. John Newton was, the most of his life, but before his conversion he was a very wicked sailor, and on board the ship *Harwich* instilled in the mind of a young man infidelity and vice—principles which destroyed him. Afterward the two met and Newton tried to undo his bad work, but in vain. The young man became worse and worse, and died a profligate, horrifying with his profanities those who stood by him in his last moments. Better look out what bad influence you start, for you may not be able to stop it. It does not require very great force to ruin others. Why was it that many years ago a great flood nearly destroyed New Orleans? A crawfish had burrowed into the banks of the river until the ground was saturated, and the banks weakened until the flood burst.

But I find here a man who starts out in life with the determination that he will never see suffering without trying to alleviate it, and never see discouragement without trying to cheer it, and never meet with anybody without trying to do him good. Getting his strength from God, he starts from home with high purposes of doing all the good he can possibly do in one day. Whether standing behind the counter, or talking in the business office with a pen behind his ear, or making a bargain with a fellow-trader, or out in the fields discussing with his next neighbor the wisest rotation of crops, or in the shoemaker's shop pounding the sole-leather, there is something in his face and in his phraseology and in his manner that demonstrates the grace of God in his heart. He can talk on religion without awkwardly dragging it in by the ears. He loves God, and loves the souls of all whom he meets, and is interested in their present and eternal destiny. For fifty or sixty years he lives that kind of life, and then gets through with it and goes into heaven a ransomed soul. But I am not going to describe the port into which that ship has entered. I am not going to describe the Pilot who met him outside at the "lightship." I am not going to say anything about the crowds of friends who met him on the crystalline wharves up which he goes on steps of chrysoprasus. For God in his words to Job calls me to look at the path of foam in the wake of that ship, and it is all a-gleam with splendors of kindness done, and rolling with illumined tears that were wiped away, and a-dash with congratulations; and clear out to the horizon in all directions is the sparkling, flashing, billowing phosphorescence of a Christian life. "He maketh a path to shine after him."

And here I correct one of the mean notions which at some time takes possession of all of us, and that is as to the brevity of human life. When I bury some very useful man, clerical or lay, in his thirtieth or fortieth year, I say, "What a waste of energies! It was hardly worth while for him to get ready for Christian work, for he had so soon to quit it." But the fact is that I may insure any man or woman, who does any good on a large or small scale, for a life on earth as long as the world lasts. Sickness, trolley-car accidents, death itself, can no more destroy his life than they can tear down one of the rings of Saturn. You can start one good word, one kind act, one cheerful smile, on a mission that will last until the world becomes a bonfire, and out of that blaze it will pass into the heavens, never to halt as long as God lives.

There were in the seventeenth century men and women, whose names you never heard of, who are today influencing schools, colleges, churches, nations.

Sermons by T. DeWitt Talmage

You can no more measure the gracious results of their lifetime than you could measure the length and breadth and depth of the phosphorescence following the ship of a great ocean liner 1,500 miles out at sea. How the courage and consecration of others inspire us to follow, as a general in the American army, cool amid the flying bullets, inspired a trembling soldier, who said afterwards, "I was nearly scared to death, but I saw the old man's white moustache over his shoulder, and went on." Aye, we are all following somebody, either in right or wrong directions. One day I stood beside the garlanded casket of a Gospel minister, and in my remarks had occasion to recall a snowy night in a farmhouse when I was a boy, and an evangelist spending a night at my father's house, who said something so tender and beautiful and impressive that it led me into the kingdom of God, and decided my destiny for this world and the next. You will probably, before twenty-four hours go by, meet some man or woman with a big pack of care and trouble, and you may say something to him or her that will endure until this world shall have been so far lost in the past that nothing but the stretch of angelic memory will be able to realize that it ever existed at all. I am not talking of remarkable men and women, but of what ordinary folks can do. I am not speaking of the phosphorescence in the wake of a *Campania*, but of the phosphorescence in the track of a Newfoundland fishing-smack. God makes thunderbolts out of sparks, and out of the small words and deeds of a small life he can launch a power that will flash and burn and thunder through the eternities. How do you like this prolongation of your earthly life by deathless influence? Many a babe that died at six months of age, by the anxiety created in the parents' heart to meet that child in realms seraphic, is living

The Lightning of the Sea

yet in the transformed heart and life of those parents, and will live on forever in the history of that family.

If this be the opportunity of ordinary souls, what is the opportunity of those who have especial intellectual or social or monetary equipment? Have you any arithmetic capable of estimating the influence of our good and gracious friend now at rest—George W. Childs, of Philadelphia? From a newspaper that was printed for thirty years without one word of defamation or scurrility or scandal, and putting chief emphasis on virtue and charity and clean intelligence, he reaped a fortune for himself and then distributed a vast amount of it among the poor and struggling; putting his invalid and aged reporters on pensions, until his name stands everywhere for large-heartedness and sympathy and help and highest style of Christian gentleman. In an era which had in the chairs of its journalism a Horace Greeley and a Henry J. Raymond and a James Gordon Bennett and an Erastus Brooks and a George William Curtis and an Irenaeus Prime none of them will be longer remembered than George W. Childs. Staying away from the unveiling of the monument he had reared at large expense in Greenwood in memory of Professor Proctor, the astronomer, lest I should say something in praise of the man who had paid for the monument. By all acknowledged a representative of the highest American journalism. If you would calculate his influence for good you must count how many sheets of his newspaper have been published in the last quarter of a century, and how many people have read them, and the effect not only upon the readers, but upon all whom they shall influence for all time; while you add to all that the work of the churches he helped build, and of the institutions of mercy he helped found. Better give up before you start the measuring of the phosphorescence in the wake of that ship of the Celestial Line. Who can tell the post-mortem influence of a Savonarola, a Winklereid, a Guttenberg, a Marlborough, a Decatur, a Toussaint, a Bolivar, a Clarkson, a Robert Raikes, a Harlan Page, who had one hundred and twenty-five scholars, eighty-four of whom became Christians, and six of them ministers of the Gospel?

With gratitude and penitence and worship I mention the grandest Life that was ever lived. That ship of light was launched from the heavens nearly 1,900 years ago, angelic hosts chanting, and from the celestial wharves the ship sprang into the roughest sea that ever tossed. Its billows were made up of the wrath of men and devils, Herodic and Sanhedrimic persecutions stirring the deep with red wrath, and all the hurricanes of woe smote it, until on the rocks of Golgotha that life struck with a resound of agony that appalled the earth and the heavens. But in the wake of that life what a phosphorescence of smiles on the cheek of souls pardoned and lives reformed and nations redeemed. The millennium itself is only one roll of that irradiated wave of gladness and benediction. In the sublimest of all senses it may be said of him, "He maketh a path to shine after him."

But I cannot look upon that luminosity that follows ships without realizing how fond the Lord is of life. That fire of the deep is life, myriads of creatures all a-swim and a-play and a-romp in parks of marine beauty, laid out and parterred and roseated and blossomed by Omnipotence. What is the use of those creatures called by naturalists "crustaceans" and "copepods," not more than one out of hundreds of billions of which are ever seen by human eye? God created them for the same reason that he creates flowers in places where no human foot ever makes them tremble, and no human nostril ever inhales their redolence, and no human eye ever sees their charm. In the botanical world they prove that God loves flowers, as in the marine world the phosphori prove that he loves life, and he loves life in play, life in brilliancy of gladness, life in exuberance.

And so I am led to believe that he loves our life if we fulfil our mission as fully as the phosphori fulfil theirs. The Son of God came "that we might have life, and have it more abundantly." But I am glad to tell you that our God is not the God sometimes described as a harsh critic at the head of the universe, or an infinite scold; or a God that loves funerals better than weddings; or a God that prefers tears to laughter, an omnipotent Nero, a ferocious Nana Sahib; but the loveliest Being in the universe, loving flowers and life and play, whether of phosphori in the wake of the *Majestic*, or of the human race keeping a holiday.

But mark that the phosphorescence has a glow that the night monopolizes, and I ask you not only what kind of influence you are going to leave in the world as you pass through it, but what light are you going to throw across the world's night of sin and sorrow? People who are sailing on smooth sea and at noon do not need much sympathy, but what are you going to do for people in the night of misfortune? Will you drop on them shadow, or will you kindle for them phosphorescence? At this moment there are more people crying than laughing; more people on the round world this moment hungry than well-fed; more households bereft than homes unbroken. What are you going to do about it? "Well," says yonder soul, "I would like to do something toward illumining the great ocean of human wretchedness, but I cannot do much." Can you do as much as one of the phosphori in the middle of the Atlantic Ocean, creatures smaller than the point of a sharp pin? "Oh, yes," you say. Then do that. Shine! Stand before the looking-glass and experiment to see if you cannot get that scowl off your forehead, that peevish look out of your lips. Have at least one bright ribbon in your bonnet. Embroider at least one white cord somewhere in the midnight of your apparel. Do not any longer impersonate a funeral! Shine! Do say something cheerful about society, and about the world. Put a few drops of Heaven into your disposition. Once in awhile substitute a sweet orange for a sour lemon. Remember that pessimism is blasphemy, and that optimism is Christianity. Throw some light on the night ocean. If you cannot be a lantern swinging in the rigging, be one of the tiny phosphori back of the keel. Shine! "Let your light so shine before men that others seeing your good works may glorify your Father which is in Heaven." Make one person happy every day, and do that for twenty years and you will have made seven thousand, three hundred happy. You know a man who lost all his property by an unfortunate investment, or by putting his name on the back of a friend's note? Go and cheer up that man. You can, if God helps you, say something that will do him good after both of you have been dead a thousand years. Shine! You know of a family with a bad boy who has run away from home. Go before night and tell that father and mother the parable of the prodigal son, and that some of the illustrious and useful men now in Church and State had a silly passage in their lives and ran away from home. Shine! You know of a family that has lost a child, and the silence of the nursery glooms the whole house from cellar to garret. Go before night and tell them how much that child has happily escaped, since the most prosperous life on earth is a struggle. Shine! You know of some one who likes you, and you like him, and he ought to be a Christian. Go tell him what religion has done for you, and ask him if you can pray for him. Shine! Oh, for a disposition so charged with sweetness and light that we cannot help but shine! Remember, if you cannot be a leviathan, lashing the ocean into fury, you can be one of the phosphori, doing your part toward making a path of phosphorescence. Then I will tell you what impression you will leave as you pass through this life and after you are gone. I will tell you to your face and not leave it for the minister who officiates at your obsequies. The failure in all eulogium of the departed is that they cannot hear it. This, in substance, is what I or some one else will say of you on such an occasion: "We gather for offices of respect to this departed one. It is impossible to tell how many tears he wiped away; how many burdens he lifted; or how many souls he was, under God, instrumental in saving. His influence will never cease. We are all better for having known him. That pillow of flowers on the casket was presented by his Sabbath School class, all of whom he brought to Christ. That cross of flowers at the head was presented by the Orphan Asylum which he befriended. Those three single flowers—one was sent by a poor woman for whom he bought a ton of coal, and one was from a waif of the street whom he rescued through the midnight mission, and the other was from a prison cell which he had often visited to encourage repentance in a young man who had done wrong. Those three loose flowers mean quite as much as the costly garlands now breathing their aroma through this saddened home, crowded with sympathizers. 'Blessed are the dead who die in the Lord; they rest from their labors, and their works do follow them.'" Or if it should be the more solemn burial at sea, let it be after the sun has gone down, and the captain has read the appropriate liturgy, and the ship's bell has tolled, and you are let down from the stern of the vessel into the resplendent phosphorescence at the wake of the ship. Then let some one say, in the words of my text, "He maketh a path to shine after him."

THE FINGER OF GOD

Exodus, 8: 19: "The finger of God."

THE FINGER OF GOD

Exodus, 8: 19: "The finger of God."

Pharaoh was sulking in his marble throne room at Memphis. Plague after plague had come, and sometimes the Egyptian monarch was disposed to do better, but at the lifting of each plague, he was as bad as before. The necromancers of the palace, however, were compelled to recognize the divine movement, and after one of the most exasperating plagues of all the series, they cried out in the words of my text: "This is the finger of God," not the first nor the last time when bad people said a good thing. An old Philadelphia friend visiting me the other day, asked me if I had ever noticed the passage of Scripture from which I to-day speak. I told him no, and I said right away, "That is a good text for a sermon." In strange way sometimes God suggests to his servants useful discourse. It would be a great book that would give the history of sermons.

We all recognize the hand of God, and know it is a mighty hand. You have seen a man keep two or three rubber balls flying in the air, catching and pitching them so that none of them fell to the floor, and do this for several minutes, and you have admired his dexterity; but have you thought how the hand of God keeps thousands and thousands of round worlds vastly larger than our world flying for centuries without letting one fall? Wondrous power and skill of God's hand! But about that I am not to discourse. My text leads me to speak of less than a fifth of the divine hand. "This is the finger of God." Only in two other places does the Bible refer to this division of the Omnipotent hand. The rocks on Mount Sinai are basalt and very hard stone. Do you imagine it was a chisel that cut the ten commandments in that basalt? No, in Exodus we read that the tables of stone were "written with the finger of God." Christ says that he cast out devils with "the finger of God." The only instance that Christ wrote a word, he wrote not with a pen on parchment, but with his finger on the ground. Yet, though so seldom reference is made in the Bible to a part of God's hand, if you and I keep our eyes open and our heart right, we will be compelled often to cry out, "This is the finger of God."

To most of us gesticulation is natural. If a stranger accost you on the street and ask you the way to some place, it is as natural as to breathe for you to level your forefinger this way or that. Not one out of a thousand of you would stand with your hands by your side and make no motion with your finger. Whatever you may say with your lips is emphasized and reinforced and translated by your finger. Now, God, in the dear old Book, says to us innumerable things by the way of direction. He plainly tells us the way to go. But in every exigency of our life, if we will only look, we will find a providential gesture and a providential pointing, so that we may confidently say, "This is the finger of God." Two or three times in my life when perplexed on questions of duty after earnest prayer I have cast lots as to what I should do. In olden times the Lord's people cast lots. The land of Canaan was divided by lot; the cities were divided among the priests and Levites by lot; Matthias was chosen to the apostleship by lot. Now, casting lots is about the most solemn thing you can do. It should never be done except with solemnity, like that of the last judgment. It is a direct appeal to the Almighty. If, after earnest prayer, you do not seem to get the divine direction, I think you might, without sin, write upon one slip of paper "Yes" and upon another "No," or some other words appropriate to the case, and then obliterating from your mind the identity of the slips of paper, draw the decision and act upon it. In that case I think you have a right to take that indication as the finger of God. But do not do that except as the last resort, and with a devoutness that leaves absolutely all with God.

For much that concerns us we have no responsibility, and we need not make appeal to the Lord for direction. We are not responsible for most of our surroundings; we are not responsible for the country of our birth, nor for whether we are Americans or Norwegians or Scotchmen or Irishmen or Englishmen; we are not responsible for our temperament, be it nervous or phlegmatic, bilious or sanguine; we are not responsible for our features, be they homely or beautiful; we are not responsible for the height or smallness of our stature; we are not responsible for the fact that we are mentally dull or brilliant. For the most of our environments, we have no more responsibility than we have for the mollusks at the bottom of the Atlantic Ocean. I am very glad that there are many things that we are not responsible for. Do not blame one for being in his manner as cold as an iceberg or nervous as a cat amid a pack of Fourth of July crackers. If you are determined to blame somebody, blame our great-grandfathers, or our great-grandmothers, who died before the Revolutionary War, and who may have had habits depressing and ruinous. There are wrong things about all of us, which make me think that one hundred and fifty years ago there was some terrible crank in our ancestral

line. Realize that and it will be a relief, semi-infinite.
Let us take ourselves as we are this moment, and then
ask, "Which way?" Get all the direction you can
from careful and constant study of the Bible, and then
look up and look out and look around, and see if
you can find the finger of God.

It is a remarkable thing that sometimes no one can
see that finger but yourself. A year before Abraham
Lincoln signed the Proclamation of Emancipation,
the White House was thronged with committees and
associations, ministers and laymen, advising the President to make that Proclamation. But he waited and
waited, amid scoff and anathema, because he did not
himself see the finger of God. After awhile, and at
just the right time, he saw the divine pointing and
signed the Proclamation. The distinguished Confederates, Mason and Slidell, were taken off an English
vessel by the United States Government. "Don't
give them up," shouted all the Northern States.
"Let us have war with England rather than surrender
them," was the almost unanimous cry of the North.
But William H. Seward saw the finger of God leading in just the opposite direction, and the Confederates were given up, and we avoided a war with England, which at that time would have been the demolition of the United States Government. In other
words, the finger of God, as it directs you, may be invisible to everybody else. Follow the divine pointing, as you see it, although the world may call you a
fool. There has never been a man or woman who
amounted to anything that has not sometimes been
called a fool. Nearly all the mistakes that you and
I have made have come from our following the pointing of some other finger, instead of the finger of God.
But, now, suppose all forms of disaster close in upon
a man. Suppose his business collapses. Suppose he

The Finger of God

buys goods and cannot sell them. There are men of vast wealth who are as rich for heaven as they are for this world, but they are exceptions. If a man grows in grace, it is generally before he gets $100,000, or after he loses them. If a man has plenty of railroad securities and has applied to his banker for more; if the lots he bought have gone up fifty per cent. in value; if he had hard work to get the door of his fire-proof safe shut because of the new roll of securities he put in there just before locking up at night; if he be speculating in a falling market, or a rising market, and things take for him a right turn, he does not grow in grace very much that week. Suppose a cold spring or a late autumn or the coming of an epidemic corners a man, and his notes come due and he cannot meet them, and his rent must be paid and there is nothing with which to pay it, and the wages of the employees are due and there is nothing with which to meet that obligation, and the bank will not discount, and the business friends to whom he goes for accommodation are in the same predicament, and he bears up and struggles on, until, after a while, crash goes the whole concern. He stands wondering and saying: "I do not see the meaning of all this; I have done the best I could. God knows I would pay my debts if I could, but here I am hedged in and stopped." What should that man do in that case? Go to the Scriptures and read the promise about all things working together for good, and kindred passages? That is well. But he needs to do something beside reading the Scriptures. He needs to look for the finger of God that is pointing toward better treasures; that is pointing toward eternal release; that is urging him to higher realms. No human finger ever pointed to the East or West or North or South so certainly as the finger of God is pointing that troubled man to higher and better spiritual resources than he ever enjoyed. I am speaking of whole-souled men. Such men are so broken by calamity that they are humbled and fly to God for relief. Men who have no spirit and never expect anything are not much affected by financial changes. They are as apt to go into the kingdom under one set of circumstances as another. They are dead beats wherever they are. The only way to get rid of them is to lend them a dollar, and you will never see them again. I have tried that plan and it works well. But I am speaking of the effects of misfortune on high-spirited men. Nothing but trial will turn such men from earth to heaven.

Do you know what made the great revival of 1857, when more people were converted to God, probably, than in any year since Christ was born? It was the defalcations and bankruptcies which swept American prosperity so flat that it could fall no flatter. It is only through clouds and darkness and whirlwind of disaster such men can see the finger of God.

A most interesting, as well as a most useful, study is to watch the pointing of the finger of God. In the Seventeenth Century, South Carolina was yielding resin and turpentine and tar as her chief productions. But Thomas Smith noticed that the ground near his house in Charleston was very much like the places in Madagascar where he had raised rice, and some of the Madagascar rice was sown there and grew so rapidly that South Carolina was led to make rice her chief production. Can you not see the finger of God in that incident? Rev. John Fletcher, of England, many will know, was one of the most useful ministers of the Gospel who ever preached. Before conversion he joined the army and had bought his ticket on the ship for South America. The morning he was to sail someone spilled on him a kettle of hot water, and he was

The Finger of God

so scalded he could not go. He was very much disappointed, but the ship he was going to sail on went out and was never heard of again. Who can doubt that God was arranging the life of John Fletcher? Was it merely accident that Richard Rodda, a Cornish miner, who was on his knees praying, remained unhurt, though heavy stones fell before him and behind him and on each side of him, and another fell on top of these so as to make a roof over him? F. W. Robertson, the great preacher of Brighton, England, had his life-work decided by the barking of his dog. A neighbor, whose daughter was ill, was disturbed by the barking of that dog one night. This brought the neighbor into communication with Robertson. That acquaintanceship kept him from joining the dragoons, and going to India and spending his life in military service, and reserved him for a pulpit, the influence of which, for Gospelization, will resound for all time and all eternity. Why did not Columbus sink when, in early manhood, he was afloat six miles from the beach with nothing to sustain him till he could swim to land but a boat's oar? I wonder if his preservation had anything to do with America? Had the storm that diverted the *Mayflower* from the mouth of the Hudson, for which it was sailing, and sent it ashore at Cape Cod, no Divine supervisal? Does anarchy rule this world, or God?

St. Felix escaped martyrdom by crawling through a hole in the wall across which the spiders immediately afterward wove a web. His persecutors saw the hole in the wall, but the spiders' web put them off the track. A boy was lost by his drunken father, and could not for years find his way home. Nearly grown, he went into a Fulton street prayer-meeting and asked for prayers that he might find his parents. His mother was in the room, and rose, and recognized her long-

lost son. Do you say that these things "only happened so?" Tell that to those who do not believe in
a God and have no faith in the Bible. Do not tell
it to me. I said to an aged minister of much experience, "All the events of my life seem to have been
divinely connected. Do you suppose it is so in all
lives?" He answered, "Yes, but most people do not
notice the divine leadings." I stand here to say from
my own experience that the safest thing in all the
world to do is to trust the Lord. I never had a misfortune, or a persecution, or a trial, or a disappointment, however excruciating at the time, that God did
not make turn out for my good. My one wish is to
follow the divine leading. I want to watch the finger
of God.

Nations also would do well to watch for the finger
of God. What does the cholera scare in America
mean? Some say it means that the plague will sweep
our land next summer. I do not believe a word of it.
There will be no cholera here next summer. Four or
five summers ago there were those who said it would
surely be here the following summer because it was
on the way. But it did not come. The sanitary pre-
cautions established here will make next summer un-
usually healthful. Cholera never starts from the place
it stopped the season before, but always starts in the
filth of Asia, and if it starts next summer, it will start
there again; it will not start from New York quarantine. But it is evident to me that the finger of God is
in this cholera scare, and that he is pointing this nation to something higher and better. It has been
demonstrated, as never before, that we are in the
hands of God. He allowed the plague to come to our
very gates and then halted it. The quarantine was
right and necessary, but very easily the plague could
have leaped the barriers lifted against it. Thanks to

The Finger of God

the President of the United States, and thanks to the health officers, and thanks to the Thirteenth Regiment, and thanks to all who stood between this evil and our national health, but more than all, and higher than all, thanks to God! Out of that solemnity we ought to pass up to something better than anything that has ever yet characterized us as a nation. We ought to quit our national sins, our Sabbath breaking, and our drunkenness, and our impurities, and our corruptions of all sorts as a people. The tendency is in self-gratulation at our prosperity to forget the mercy of God that has kept us from being blotted out for our crimes, and that still multiplies our temporal prosperities. Forward, and upward! See you not the finger of God in this protecting mercy?

I rejoice that there are many encouraging signs for our nation, and one is that this presidential campaign has less malignity and abuse than any presidential campaign since we have been a nation. Turn over to the pictorials and the columns of the political sheets of the presidential excitements all the way back and see what contumely Washington and Jefferson and Madison and Monroe and Jackson went through. Now see the almost entire absence of all that. The political orators, I notice this year, are apt to begin by eulogizing the honesty and good intentions of the opposing candidate, and say that he is better than his party. Instead of vitriol, camomile flowers. That we seem to have escaped the degradation of the usual quadrennial billingsgate is an encouraging fact. Perhaps this betterment may have somewhat resulted from the sadness hovering over the home of one of the candidates, a sadness in which the whole nation sympathizes. Perhaps we have been so absorbed in paying honors to Christopher Columbus that we have forgotten to anathematize the prominent men of the present. No man in this country is fully honored until he is dead. Whatever be the reasons, this nation has escaped many of the horrors that ordinarily accompany the presidential contest. But let us not pause too long in hilarity about the present and forget the fact that there are not only temporal possibilities far greater than those attained, but higher moral and religious possibilities. The God of our fathers is the God of their children, and his finger points us to a higher national career than many have yet suspected. For our churches, our schools, our colleges, our institutions of mercy, the best days are yet to come.

But notice that this finger of God, almost always and in almost everything, points forward and not backward. All the way through the Bible, the lamb and pigeon on the altar, the pillar of fire poised above the wilderness, peace offering, sin offering, trespass offering, fingers of Joseph and Isaac and Joshua and David and Isaiah and Micah and Ezekiel, all together made the one finger of God pointing to the human, the divine, the gracious, the glorious, the omnipotent, the gentle, the pardoning and suffering and atoning Christ. And now the same finger of God is pointing the world upward to the same Redeémer and forward to the time of his universal domination. My hearers, get out of the habit of looking back and looking down and look up and look forward. It is useful once in awhile to look back, but you had better, for the most part of the time, stop reminiscence and begin anticipation. We have, most of us, hardly begun yet. If we love the Lord and trust him—and you may all love him and trust him from this moment on —we no more understand the good things ahead of us than a child at school studying his A B C can understand what that has to do with his reading John

The Finger of God

Ruskin's "Seven Lamps of Architecture," or Dante's "Divina Commedia." The satisfactions and joys we have as yet had are like the music a boy makes with his first lesson on the violin compared with what was evoked from his great orchestra by my dear and illustrious and transcendent, but now departed friend, Patrick Gilmore, when he lifted his baton and all the strings vibrated, and all the trumpets pealed forth, and all the flutes caroled, and all the drums rolled, and all the hoofs of the cavalry charge, which he imitated, were in full beat. Look ahead! The finger of God points forward.

"Oh, but," says some one, "I am getting old and I have a touch of rheumatism in that foot, and I believe something is the matter with my heart, and I cannot stand as much as I used to." Well, I congratulate you, for that shows you are getting nearer to the time when you are going to enter immortal youth and be strong enough to hurl off the battlements of heaven any bandit, who, by unheard-of burglary, might break into the Golden City. "But," says some one else, "I feel so lonely; the most of my friends are gone, and the bereavements of life have multiplied until this world, that was once so bright to me, has lost its charm." I congratulate you, for, when you go, there will be fewer here to hold you back and more there to pull you in. Look ahead! The finger of God is pointing forward.

We sit here in church, and by hymn and prayer and sermon and Christian association we try to get into a frame of mind that will be acceptable to God and pleasant to ourselves. But what a stupid thing it all is compared with what it will be when we have gone beyond psalm book and sermon and Bible, and we stand, our last imperfection gone, in the presence of that charm of the universe—the blessed Christ—

and have him look in our face and say: "I have been watching you and sympathizing with you and helping you all these years, and now you are here. Go where you please and never know a sorrow and never shed a tear. There is your mother now—she is coming to greet you—and there is your father, and there are your children. Sit down under this tree of life, and on the banks of this river talk it all over." I tell you there will be more joy in one minute of that than in fifty years of earthly exultation. Look ahead! Look at the finest house on earth and know that you will have a finer one in heaven. Look up the healthiest person you can find, and know you will yet be healthier. Look up the one who has the best eyesight of any one you have ever heard of, and know you will have better vision. Listen to the sweetest prima donna that ever trod the platform, and know that in heaven you will lift a more enrapturing song than ever enchanted earthly auditorium.

My friends, I do not know how we are going to stand it—I mean the full inrush of that splendor. Last summer I saw Moscow, in some respects the most splendid city under the sun. The Emperor afterward asked me if I had seen it, for Moscow is the pride of Russia. I told him yes, and that I had seen Moscow burn. I will tell you what I meant. After examining nine hundred brass cannons which were picked out of the snow after Napoleon retreated from Moscow, each cannon deep cut with the letter "N," I ascended a tower of some two hundred and fifty feet, just before sunset, and on each platform there were bells, large and small, and I climbed up among the bells, and then as I reached the top, all the bells underneath me began to ring, and they were joined by the bells of fourteen hundred towers and domes and turrets. Some of the bells sent out a faint tinkle of sound, a sweet tintinnabulation that seemed a bubbling of the air, and others thundered forth boom after boom, boom after boom, until it seemed to shake the earth and fill the heavens—sounds so weird, so sweet, so awful, so grand, so charming, so tremendous, so soft, so rippling, so reverberating—and they seemed to wreathe and whirl and rise and sink and burst and roll and mount and die. When Napoleon saw Moscow burn, it could not have been more brilliant than when I saw the fourteen hundred turrets aflame with the sunset; and there were roofs of gold, and walls of malachite, and pillars of porphyry, and balustrades of mosaic, and architecture of all colors mingling the brown of autumnal forests and the blue of summer heavens, and the conflagration of morning skies, and the emerald of rich grass, and the foam of tossing seas. The mingling of so many sounds was an entrancement almost too much for human nerves and human eyes and human ears. I expect to see nothing to equal it until you and I see heaven. But that will surpass it and make the memory of what I saw that July evening in Moscow almost tame and insipid. All heaven aglow and all heaven a-ring, not in the sunset, but in the sunrise. Voices of our own kindred mingling with the doxologies of empires. Organs of eternal worship responding to the trumpets that have wakened the dead. Nations in white. Centuries in coronation. Anthems like the voice of many waters. Circle of martyrs. Circle of apostles. Circle of prophets. Thrones of cherubim. Thrones of seraphim. Throne of archangel. Throne of Christ. Throne of God. Thrones! Thrones! Thrones! The finger of God points that way. Stop not until you reach that place. Through the atoning Christ, all I speak of and more may be yours and mine. Do you not now hear the chime of the bells of that metropolis of the universe? Do you not see the shimmering of the towers? Good morning.

RUBIES SURPASSED

Proverbs, 8: 11: "Wisdom is better than rubies."

RUBIES SURPASSED

Proverbs, 8: 11: " Wisdom is better than rubies."

You have all seen the precious stone commonly
called the ruby. It is of deep red color. The Bible
makes much of it. It glowed in the first row of the
high priest's breast plate. Under another name it
stood in the wall of heaven. Jeremiah compares the
ruddy cheek of the Nazarites to the ruby. Ezekiel
points it out in the robes of the king of Tyre. Four
times does Solomon use it as a symbol by which to
extol wisdom, or religion, always setting its value as
better than rubies.

The world does not agree as to how the precious
stones were formed. The ancients thought that amber was made of drops of perspiration of the goddess
Ge. The thunderstone was supposed to have dropped
from a storm-cloud. The emerald was said to have
been made of the fire-fly. The lapis lazuli was thought
to have been born of the cry of an Indian giant. And
modern mineralogists say that the precious stones
were made of gases and liquids. To me the ruby
seems like a spark from the anvil of the setting sun.

The home of the genuine ruby is Burmah, and
sixty miles from its capital, where lives and reigns the
ruler, called, "Lord of the Rubies." Under a careful
governmental guard are these valuable mines of ruby
kept. Rarely has any foreigner visited them. When
a ruby of large value was discovered it was brought
forth with elaborate ceremony, a procession was
formed, and with all bannered pomp, military guard

and princely attendants, the gem was brought to the king's palace.

Of great value is the ruby, much more so than diamond, as lapidaries and jewelers will tell you. An expert on this subject writes: "A ruby of perfect color weighing five carats is worth at the present day ten times as much as a diamond of equal weight." It was a disaster when Charles the Bold lost the ruby he was wearing at the Battle of Grandson. It was a great affluence when Rudolph the Second of Austria inherited a ruby from his sister, the Queen Dowager. It was thought to have had much to do with the victory of Henry the Fifth, as he wore it into the Battle of Agincourt. It is the pride of the Russian court to own the largest ruby of all the world, presented by Gustavus the Third to the Russian Empress. Wondrous ruby! It has electric characteristics, and there are lightnings compressed in its double six-sided prisms. What shall I call it? It is frozen fire! It is petrified blood! In all the world there is only one thing more valuable, and my text makes the comparison: "Wisdom is better than rubies."

But it is impossible to compare two things together unless there are some points of similarity as well as of difference. I am glad there is nothing lacking here. The ruby is more beautiful in the night and under the lamplight than by day. It is preferred for evening adornment. How the rubies glow, and burn, and flash as the lights lift the darkness! Catherine of Aragon had on her finger a ruby that fairly lanterned the night. Sir John Mandeville, the celebrated traveler of four hundred years ago, said that the Emperor of China had a ruby that made the night as bright as the day. The probability is that Solomon under some of the lamps that illumined his cedar palace by night, noticed the peculiar glow of the ruby as it appeared in

the hilt of a sword, or hung in some fold of the upholstery, or beautified the lip of some chalice, while
he was thinking at the same time of the excellency of
our holy religion as chiefly seen in the night of trouble,
and he cries out, "Wisdom is better than rubies."

Oh, yes, it is a good thing to have religion while
the sun of prosperity rides high and everything is
brilliant in fortune, in health, in worldly favor. Yet
you can at such time hardly tell how much of it is
natural exuberance and how much of it is the grace
of God. But let the sun set, and the shadows
avalanche the plain, and the thick darkness of sickness
or poverty or persecution or mental exhaustion fill
the soul and fill the house and fill the world; then you
sit down by the lamp of God's Word and under its
light the consolations of the Gospel come out; the
peace of God which passeth all understanding appears.
You never fully appreciated their power until in the
deep night of trouble the Divine Lamp revealed their
exquisiteness. Pearls and amethysts for the day, but
rubies for the night. Travelers tell us that in the
Arctic regions there are nights six months long, but
you and I have known people whose night lasted for
twelve months, and they needed especial comfort for
such prolongation.

All of the books of the Bible attempt in some way
the assuagement of misfortune. Of the one hundred
and fifty Biblical Psalms at least ninety allude to
trouble. There are sighings in every wind and tears
in every brook and pangs in every heart. It was
originally proposed to call the President's residence at
Washington "The Palace," or "The Executive Mansion," but after it was destroyed in the war of 1814
and rebuilt, it was painted white to cover up the marks
of the smoke and fire that had blackened the stone
walls. Hence it was called "The White House."

Sermons by T. DeWitt Talmage

Most of the things now white with attractiveness were once black with disaster. What the world most needs is the consolatory, and here it comes, our holy religion, with both hands full of anodynes and sedatives and balsams, as in Daniel's time to stop mouths leonine; as in Shadrach's time to cool blast furnaces; as in Ezekiel's time to console captivity; as in St. John's time to unroll an apocalypse over rocky desolations. Hear its soothing voice as it declares: "Weeping may endure for a night, but joy cometh in the morning;" "The mountains shall depart and the hills be removed, but my loving kindness shall not depart from you;" "Whom the Lord loveth he chasteneth;" "They shall hunger no more, neither thirst any more, neither shall the sun light on them, nor any heat; for the Lamb which is in the midst of the throne shall lead them to living fountains of water, and God shall wipe away all tears from their eyes."

The most wholesome thing on earth is trouble, if met in Christian spirit. To make Paul what he was it took shipwreck, and whipping on the bare back, and penitentiary, and pursuit of wild mobs, and the sword of decapitation. To make David what he was it took all that Ahithophel and Saul and Absalom and Goliath and all the Philistine hosts could do against him. It took Robert Chambers's malformation of feet to make him the literary conqueror. It was bereavement that brought William Haworth of Wesley's time from wickedness to an evangelism that won many thousands for heaven. The world would never have known what heroic stuff Ridley was made of had not the fires been kindled around his feet, and, not liking their slow work, he cried, "I cannot burn; let the fire come to me; I cannot burn." Thank God that there are gems that unfold their best glories under the lamplight! Thank God for the ruby!

Rubies Surpassed

Moreover, I am sure that Solomon was right in saying that religion, or wisdom, is better than rubies, from the fact that a thing is worth what it will fetch. Religion will fetch solid happiness, and the ruby will not. In all your observation did you ever find a person thoroughly felicitated by an encrustment of jewels. As you know more of yourself than any one else, are you happier now with worldly adornments and successes than before you won them? Does the picture that cost you hundreds or thousands of dollars on your wall bring you as much satisfaction as the engraving that at the expense of five dollars was hung upon the wall when you first began to keep house? Do all the cutlery and rare plate that glitter on your extension dining-table, surrounded by flattering guests, contain more of real bliss than the plain ware of your first table, at which sat only two? Does a wardrobe crowded with costly attire give you more satisfaction than your first clothes closet, with its four or five pegs? Did not the plain ring set on the third finger of your left hand on the day of your betrothal give more gladness than the ruby that is now enthroned on the third finger of your right hand? If in this journey of life we have learned anything, we have learned that this world neither with its emoluments nor gains can satisfy the soul.

Why, here come as many witnesses as I wish to call to the stand to testify that before high heaven and the world, in companionship with Jesus Christ and a good hope of heaven, they feel a joy that all the resources of their vocabulary fail to express. Sometimes it evidences itself in ejaculations of hosanna; sometimes in doxology; sometimes in tears. A converted native of India in a letter said: "How I long for my bed, not that I may sleep; I lie awake often and long but to hold sweet communion with my God."

Sermons by T. DeWitt Talmage

If so mighty is worldly joy that Julius the Second hearing his armies were triumphant, expired; and if Talva hearing that the Roman Senate had decreed him an honor, expired; and if Dionysius and Sophocles overcome of joy, expired; and if a shipwrecked purser, waiting on the coast of Guinea in want and starvation, at the sight of a vessel bringing relief, fell dead from shock of delight—is it any surprise to you that the joys of pardon and heaven rolling over the soul should sometimes be almost too much for the Christian to endure and live? An aged aunt said to me, "DeWitt, three times I have fainted dead away under too great Christian joy. It was in all three cases at the holy communion." An eminent Christian man while in prayer said, "Stop, Lord, I cannot bear any more of this gladness; it is too much for mortal. Withhold! Withhold!" We have heard of poor workmen or workwomen getting a letter suddenly telling them that a fortune had been left them, and how they were almost beside themselves with glee, taking the first ship to claim the estate. But, oh, what it is to wake up out of the stupor of a sinful life and through pardoning grace find that all our earthly existence will be divinely managed for our best welfare, and that then all heaven will roll in upon the soul. Compared with that a spring morning is stupid, and an August sunset is inane, and an aurora has no pillared splendor, and a diamond has no flash, and a pearl no light, and a beryl no aquamarine, and a ruby no ruddiness. My gracious Lord! My glorious God! My precious Christ! Roll over on us a few billows of that rapture. And now I ask you as fair-minded men and women, accustomed to make comparisons, is not such a joy as that worth more than anything one can have in a jeweled casket? Was not Solomon right when he said, "Wisdom is better than rubies?"

Rubies Surpassed

There is also something in the deep carmine of the ruby that suggests the sacrifice on which our whole system of religion depends. While the emerald suggests the meadows, and the sapphire the skies, and the opal the sea, the ruby suggests the blood of sacrifice. The most emphatic and startling of all colors hath the ruby. Solomon, the author of my text, knew all about the sacrifice of lamb and dove on the altars of the temple, and he knew the meaning of sacrificial blood, and what other precious stone could he so well use to symbolize it as the ruby? Red, intensely red, red as the blood of the greatest martyr of all time—Jesus of the centuries! Drive the story of the crucifixion out of the Bible and the doctrine of the atonement out of our religion, and there would be nothing of Christianity left for our worship or our admiration. Why should it be hard to adopt the Bible theory that our redemption was purchased by blood? What great bridge ever sprung its arches; what temple ever reared its towers; what nation ever achieved its independence; what mighty good was ever done without sacrifice of life? The great wonder of the world, the bridge that unites Brooklyn and New York, cost the life of the first architect. Ask the shipyards of Glasgow and New York how many carpenters went down under accidents before the steamer was launched; ask the three great transcontinental railroads how many in their construction were buried under crumbling embankments, or crushed under timbers, or destroyed by the powder-blast. Tabulate the statistics of how many mothers have been martyrs to the cradle of sick children. Tell us how many men sacrificed nerve and muscle and brain and life in the effort to support their households. Tell me how many men in England, in France, in Germany, in Italy, in the United States have died for their country. Vicarious suffering is as old as the world, but the most thrilling, the most startling, the most stupendous sacrifice of all time and eternity was on a bluff back of Jerusalem, when one Being took upon himself the sins, the agonies, the perdition of a great multitude that no man can number, between twelve o'clock of a darkened noon and three o'clock in the afternoon, purchasing the ransom of a ruined world. Dive in all the seas; explore all the mines; crowbar all the mountains, view all the crowned jewels of all the emperors, and find me any gem that can so overwhelmingly symbolize that martyrdom as the ruby.

Mark you, there are many gems that are somewhat like the ruby. So is the cornelian; so is the garnet; so is the spinel; so is the balas; so are the gems brought from among the gravels of Ceylon and New South Wales; but there is only one genuine ruby, and that comes from the mines of Burmah. And there is only one Christ, and he comes from heaven. One Redeemer, one Ransom, one Son of God; only "one Name given under heaven among men by which we can be saved." Ten thousand times ten thousand beautiful imitations of that ruby, but only one ruby. Christ had no descendant. Christ had no counterpart. In the lifted-up grandeur and glory and love and sympathy of his character he is the Incomparable, the Infinite One! "The Only Wise God, our Saviour." Let all hearts, all homes, all times, all eternities bow low before him! Let his banner be lifted in all our souls.

In olden times, Scotland was disturbed by freebooters and pirates. To rid the seas and ports of these desperadoes, the hero, William Wallace, fitted out a merchant vessel, but filled it with armed men, and put out to sea. The pirates with their flag inscribed of a death's-head, thinking they would get an easy prize,

Rubies Surpassed

bore down upon the Scottish merchantman, when the armed men of Wallace boarded the craft of the pirates and put them in chains, and then sailed for port under the Scotch flag flying. And so our souls assailed of sin and death and hell through Christ are rescued, and the black flag of sin is torn down and the striped flag of the Cross is hoisted. Blessed be God for any sign, for any signal, for any precious stone that brings to mind the price paid for such a rescue!

I like the coral, for it seems the solidified foam of breakers; and I like the jasper, for it gathers seventeen colors into its bosom; and I like the jet, for it compresses the shadows of many midnights; and I like the chrysolite, for its waves of color which seem on fire. But this morning nothing so impresses me as the ruby, for it depicts, it typifies, it suggests, "the blood of Jesus Christ that cleanseth from all sin;" "Without the shedding of blood there is no remission." Yea, Solomon was right when he said, "Wisdom is better than rubies."

To bring out a contrast that will illustrate my text, I put before you two last earthly scenes. The one is in a room with rubies, but no religion; and the other in a room with religion, but no rubies. You enter the first room, when an affluent and worldly man is about to quit this life. There is a ruby on the mantel, possibly among the vases. There is a ruby in the headdress of the queenly wife. On the finger of the dying man there is a ruby. The presence of these rubies implies opulence of all kinds. The pictures on the walls are heirlooms, or the trophies of European travel. The curtains are from foreign looms. The rugs are from Damascus or Cairo. The rocking-chairs roll backward and forward on lullabies. The pillows are exquisitely embroidered. All the appointments of the room are a peroration to a successful commercial or professional life. But the man has no religion; never has had, and never professed to have. There is not a Bible or one religious book in the room. The departing man feels that his earthly career is ended, and nothing opens beyond. Where he will land stepping off from this life is a mystery, or whether he will land at all, for it may be annihilation. He has no prayer to offer, and he does not know how to pray. No hope of meeting again in another state of existence. He is through with this life, and is sure of no other. The ruby on the mantel and the ruby on the wasted finger of the departing one say nothing of the ransoming blood which they so mightily typify. Midnight of utter hopelessness drops on all the scene.

Another room of mortal exit. Religion and no rubies. She never had money enough to buy one of these exquisites. Sometimes she stopped at a jeweler's show-window and saw a row of them incarnadining the velvet. She had keen taste enough to appreciate those gems, but she never owned one of them. She was not jealous or unhappy because others had rubies while she had none. But she had a richer treasure, and that was the grace of God that had comforted her along the way amid bereavements and temptations and persecutions and sicknesses and privations and trials of all sorts. Now she is going out of life. The room is bright, not with pictures or statues, not with upholstery, not with any of the gems of mountain or of sea, but there is a strange and vivid glow in the room; not the light of chandelier or star or noon-day sun, but something that outshines all of them. It must be the presence of supernaturals. From the appearance of her illumined face I think she must hear sweet voices. Yea, she does hear sweet voices—voices of departed kindred; voices apostolic and prophetic, and evangelic, but all of them over-

Rubies Surpassed

powered by the voice of Christ, saying, "Come, ye blessed of my Father, inherit the kingdom." From her illumined face, I think she does hear rapturous music, now soft as solos, now thunderous as orchestras; now a saintly voice alone, now the hundred and forty and four thousand in concert. From her illumined face, I think she must breathe redolence. Yea, she does inhale aroma from off the gardens whose flowers never wither, and from the blossoms of orchards, every tree of which bears twelve manner of fruits. From her illumined face, I think she must see a glorious sight. Yes, she sees the wall that has jasper at the base, and amethyst at the top, and blood-red rubies between. Good-bye, sweet soul! Why should you longer stay! Your work all done; your burdens all carried; your tears all wept! Forward into the light! Up into the joy! Out into the grandeur. And after you have saluted Christ and your kindred search out him of the palaces of Lebanon cedar, and tell him that you have found to be gloriously true what thousands of years ago he asserted in this morning's text: "Wisdom is better than rubies." In those burnished palaces of our God may we all meet. For I confess to you that my chief desire for heaven is not the radiance, or to take the suggestion of the text, not the rubescence of the scene. My one idea of heaven is the place to meet old friends, God our best Friend, and our earthly friends already transported. Ay! to meet the millions whom I have never seen, but to whom I have administered in the Gospel week by week through journalism on both sides of the sea, and throughout Christendom, and through many lands yet semi-barbaric. A gentleman tapped me on the shoulder summer before last on a street of Edinburgh, Scotland, and said, "I live in the Shetland Islands, North Scotland, and I read your sermons every Sabbath to an audience of neighbors, and my brother lives in Cape Town, South Africa, and he reads them every Sabbath to an audience of his neighbors." And I here and now say to the forty millions of the earth to whose eyes these words will come, that one of my dearest anticipations is to meet them in heaven. Ah! that will be better than rubies. Coming up from different continents, from different hemispheres, from opposite sides of the earth to greet each other in holy love in the presence of the glorious Christ who made it possible for us to get there. Our sins all pardoned, our sorrows all banished, never to weep, never to part, never to die! I tell you that will be better than rubies. Others may have the crowns and the thrones and the sceptres; give us our old friends back again, Christ, "the friend who sticketh closer than a brother," and all the kindred who have gone up from our bereft households, and all our friends whom we have never yet seen, and you may have all the rubies, for that will be "better than rubies." Instead of the dying kiss when they looked so pale and wan and sick, it will be the kiss of welcome on lips jubilant with song; while standing on floors paved with what exquisiteness, under ceilings hung with what glory, bounded by walls facing us with what splendor, amid gladness rolling over us with what Doxology. Far better, infinitely better, everlastingly better than rubies.

PARENTAGE OF THE SHOWER

Job, 38: 28: "Hath the rain a father?"

PARENTAGE OF THE SHOWER

Job, 38: 28: " Hath the rain a father?"

This book of Job has been the subject of un-
bounded theological wrangle. Men have made it the
ring in which to display their ecclesiastical pugilism.
Some say that this book of Job is a true history;
others, that it is an allegory; others, that it is an epic
poem; others, that it is a drama. Some say that Job
lived eighteen hundred years before Christ; others say
that he never lived at all. Some say that the author of
this book was Job; others, David; others, Solomon.
The discussion has landed some in blank infidelity.

Now, I have no trouble with the book of Job or the
Revelation—the two most mysterious books in the
Bible—because of a rule I adopted some years ago.
I wade down into a Scripture passage as long as I
can touch bottom, and when I cannot then I wade out.
I used to wade in until it was over my head, and then
I was drowned. I study a passage of Scripture so
long as it is a comfort and help to my soul; but when
it becomes a perplexity and a spiritual upturning, I
quit. In other words, we ought to wade in up to our
heart, but never wade in until it is over our head. No
man should ever expect to wade across this great
ocean of divine truth. I go down into that ocean as
I go down into the Atlantic Ocean at East Hampton,
Long Island, just far enough to bathe; then I come
out. I never had any idea that with my weak hand
and foot I could strike my way clear over to Liverpool. So while there is much in the book of Job I

cannot fathom, there is much that is beautiful and suggestive, and these passages we take for our instruction and comfort. One of these I have chosen for my text.

I suppose you understand your family genealogy. You know something about your parents, your grandparents, your great-grandparents. Perhaps you know where they were born, or where they died. Have you ever studied the parentage of the shower? "Hath the rain a father?" This question is not asked by a poetaster or a scientist, but by the Head of the Universe. To humble and to save Job, God asks him fourteen questions: about the world's architecture, about the refraction of the sun's rays, about the tides, about the snow-crystal, about the lightnings, and then he arraigns him with the interrogation of the text: "Hath the rain a father?" With the scientific wonders of the rain I have nothing to do. A minister gets through with that kind of sermons within the first three years, and if he has piety enough, he gets through with it in the first three months. A sermon has come to me to mean one word of four letters: "Help!"

You all know that the rain is not an orphan. You know it is not cast out of the gates of heaven a foundling. You would answer the question of my text in the affirmative. Safely housed during the storm, you hear the rain beating against the window-pane, and you find it searching all the crevices of the window sill. It first comes down in solitary drops, spattering the dust, and then it deluges the fields and angers the mountain torrents and makes the traveler implore shelter. You know that the rain is not an accident of the world's economy. You know it was born of the cloud. You know it was rocked in the cradle of the wind. You know it was sung to sleep by the storm.

Parentage of the Shower

You know that it is a flying evangel from heaven to earth. You know it is the gospel of the weather. You know that God is its father. A shower is not as might be supposed, the elements in a fit of angry passion.

If this be true, then, how wicked is our murmuring about climatic changes! The first eleven Sabbaths after I entered the ministry, it stormed. Through the week it was clear weather, but on the Sabbaths the old country meeting-house looked like Noah's ark before it landed. A few drenched people sat before a drenched pastor; but most of the farmers stayed at home and thanked God that what was bad for the church was good for the crops. I committed a good deal of sin in those days in denouncing the weather. Ministers of the Gospel sometimes fret about stormy Sabbaths or hot Sabbaths or inclement Sabbaths. They forget the fact that the same God who ordained the Sabbath and sent forth his ministers to announce salvation, also ordained the weather. Merchants, also, with their stores filled with new goods and their clerks hanging idly around the counters, commit the same transgression. There have been seasons when the whole spring and fall trade has been ruined by protracted wet weather. The merchants then examined the "weather probabilities" with more interest than they read their Bibles. They watched for a patch of blue sky. They went complaining to the store, and came complaining home again. In all that season of wet feet and dripping garments and impassable streets, they never once asked the question: "Hath the rain a father?"

So agriculturists commit this sin. There is nothing more annoying than to have planted corn rot in the ground because of too much moisture, or hay all ready for the mow dashed of a shower, or wheat almost ready for the sickle spoiled with the rust. How hard it is to bear the agricultural disappointments! God has infinite resources, but I do not think He has capacity to make weather to please all the. farmers. Sometimes it is too hot or it is too cold, it is too wet or it is too dry, it is too early or it is too late. They forget that the God who promised seedtime and harvest, summer and winter, cold and heat, also ordained all the climatic changes. There is one question that ought to be written on every barn, on every fence, on every farmhouse: "Hath the rain a father?"

If we only knew what a vast enterprise it is to provide appropriate weather for this world, we would not be so critical of the Lord. Isaac Watts, at ten years of age, complained that he did not like the hymns that were sung in the English chapel. "Well, Isaac," said his father, "instead of your complaining about the hymns, go and make hymns that are better." And he did go and make hymns that were better. Now I say to you, if you do not like the weather, do you think you could get up a weather company, and have a president and a secretary and a treasurer and a board of directors and ten million dollars of stock, and then provide weather that will suit all of us?

There is a man who has a weak head, and he cannot stand the glare of the sun. You must have a cloud always hovering over him. I like the sunshine; I cannot live without plenty of sunlight; so you must always have enough light for me. Two ships meet in mid-Atlantic. The one is going to Southampton, the other is going to New York. Provide weather that, while it is abaft for one ship is not a head wind for the other. There is a farm that is dried up for lack of rain, and here is a pleasure party going out for a field excursion. Provide weather that will suit the dry farm and the pleasure excursion. I will not take one dollar of stock in your weather company. There is only one Being in the universe who knows enough to provide the right kind of weather for this world. "Hath the rain a father?"

My text also suggests God's minute supervisal. You see the Divine Sonship in every drop of rain. The jewels of the shower are not flung away by a spendthrift who knows not how many he throws or where they fall. They are all shining princes of heaven. They all have eternal lineage. They are all the children of a King. "Hath the rain a father?" Well, then, I say if God takes notice of every minute raindrop, he will take notice of the most insignificant affair of my life.

It is the astronomical view of things that bothers me. We look up into the night heavens and we say: "Worlds! worlds!" and how insignificant we feel! We stand at the foot of Mount Washington or Mont Blanc, and we feel that we are only insects, and then we say to ourselves: "Though the world is so large, the sun is 1,400,000 times larger. If God wheels that great machinery through immensity, he will not take the trouble to look down at me." Infidel conclusion! Saturn, Mercury, and Jupiter are no more rounded and weighed and swung by the hand of God than are the globules on a lilac-bush the morning after a shower. God is no more in magnitudes than he is in minutiæ. If he has scales to weigh the mountains, he has balances delicate enough to weigh the infinitesimal. You can no more see him through the telescope than you can see him through the microscope—no more when you look up than when you look down. Are not the hairs of your head all numbered? And if Himalaya has a God, "Hath not the rain a father?"

I take this doctrine of a particular Providence, and I thrust it into the midst of your every-day life. If

Sermons by T. DeWitt Talmage

God fathers a raindrop, is there anything so insignificant in your affairs that God will not father that? When Druyse, the gunsmith, invented the needle-gun, which decided the battle of Sadowa, was it a mere accident? When a farmer's boy showed Blucher a short cut by which he could bring his army up soon enough to decide Waterloo for England, was it a mere accident? When Lord Byron took a piece of money and tossed it up to decide whether or not he should be affianced to Miss Millbank, was it a mere accident which side of the money was up and which was down? When the Protestants were besieged at Bezors, and a drunken drummer came in at midnight and rang the alarm bell, not knowing what he was doing, but waking up the host in time to fight their enemies that moment arriving, was it an accident? When, in the Irish rebellion, a starving mother, flying with her starving child, sank down and fainted on the rock in the night, and her hand fell on a warm bottle of milk, did that just happen so? God is either in the affairs of men, or our religion is worth nothing at all, and you had better take it away from us, and instead of this Bible, which teaches the doctrine, give us a secular book, and let us, as the famous Mr. Fox, the member of Parliament, in his last hour, cry out: "Read me the eighth book of Virgil." Let us rouse up to an appreciation of the fact that all the affairs of our life are under a king's command, and under a father's watch.

Alexander's war-horse Bucephalus would allow anybody to mount him when he was unharnessed; but as soon as they put on that war-horse, Bucephalus, the saddle and the trappings of the conqueror, he would allow no one but Alexander to touch him. And if a soulless horse could have so much pride in his owner, shall not we immortals exult in the fact that we are owned by a **King?**

Again, my subject teaches me that God's dealings with us are inexplicable. That was the original force of my text. The rain was a great mystery to the ancients. They could not understand how the water should get into the cloud, and getting there, how it should be suspended, or, falling, why it should come down in drops. Modern science comes along and says there are two portions of air of different temperature, and they are charged with moisture, and the one portion of air decreases in temperature, so that the water can no longer be held in vapor, and it falls. And they tell us that some of the clouds that look to be no larger than a man's hand, and to be almost quiet in the heavens, are great mountains of mist, 4,000 feet from base to top, and that they rush miles a minute. But after all the brilliant experiments of Dr. James Hutton and de Saussurre and other scientists, there is an infinite mystery about the rain. There is an ocean of the unfathomable in every raindrop, and God says to-day, as he said in the time of Job: "If you cannot understand one drop of rain, do not be surprised if my dealings with you are inexplicable."

Why does that aged man, decrepit, beggared, vicious, sick of the world, and the world sick of him, live on, while here is a man in mid-life, consecrated to God, hard-working, useful in every respect, who dies? Why does that old gossip, gadding along the street about everybody's business but her own, have such good health, while the Christian mother, with a flock of little ones about her, whom she is preparing for usefulness and for heaven—the mother who you think could not be spared an hour from that household— why does she lie down and die with a cancer? Why does that man, selfish to the core, who goes on adding fortune to fortune, consuming everything on himself, continue to prosper, while that man, who has been giving ten per cent. of all his income to God and the church, goes into bankruptcy?

Before we make stark fools of ourselves, let us stop pressing this everlasting "Why." Let us worship where we cannot understand. Let a man take that one question "Why," and pursue it far enough, and push it, and he will land in wretchedness and perdition. We want in our theology fewer interrogation marks and more exclamation points. Heaven is the place for explanation. Earth is the place for trust. If you cannot understand so minute a thing as a raindrop, how can you expect to understand God's dealings? "Hath the rain a father?"

My text makes me think that the rain of tears is of divine origin. Great clouds of trouble sometimes hover over us. They are black, and they are gorged, and they are thunderous. They are more portentous than Salvator or Claude ever painted—clouds of poverty or persecution or bereavement. They hover over us, and they get darker and blacker, and after a while a tear starts, and we think by a heavy pressure of the eyelid to stop that tear, but we cannot stop it. Others follow, and after a while there is a shower of tearful emotion. Yes, there is a rain of tears. "Hath that rain a father?"

"Oh," you say, "a tear is nothing but a drop of limpid fluid secreted by the lachrymal gland—it is only a sign of weak eyes." Great mistake! It is one of the Lord's richest benedictions to the world. There are people in Blackwell's Island Insane Asylum, and at Utica, and at all the asylums of this land, who are demented by the fact that they could not cry at the right time. Said a maniac in one of our public institutions, under a Gospel sermon that started the tears: "Do you see that tear? That is the first tear that I have wept for twelve years. I think it will help my brain." There are a great many in the grave who could not stand any longer under the glacier of trouble. If that glacier had only melted into weeping, they could have endured it.

There have been times in your life when you would have given the world, if you had possessed it, for one tear. You could shriek, you could blaspheme, but you could not cry. Have you never seen a man holding the hand of a dead wife who had been all the world to him? The temples livid with excitement, the eye dry and frantic, no moisture on the upper or lower lid. You saw there were bolts of anger in the cloud, but no rain. To your Christian comfort, he said: "Don't talk to me about God; there is no God; or if there is, I hate him. Don't talk to me about God. Would he have left me and these motherless children?" But a few days or hours after, coming across some pencil that she owned in life, or some letters which she wrote when he was away from home, with an outcry that appalls there bursts the fountain of tears; and as the sunlight of God's consolation strikes that fountain of tears, you find out that it is a tender-hearted, merciful, pitiful, and all-compassionate God who is the father of that rain.

"Oh," you say, "it is absurd to think that God is going to watch over tears." No, my friends; there are three or four kinds of them that God counts, bottles, and eternizes. First, there are all paternal tears, and there are more of these than of any other kind, because the most of the race die in infancy, and that keeps parents mourning all around the world. They never get over it. They may live to shout and sing afterward, but there is always a corridor in the soul that is silent, though it once resounded. My parents never mentioned the death of a child who died fifty years before without a tremor in the voice and a sigh, oh, how deep-fetched! It was better she should die. It was a mercy she should die. She would have been a lifelong invalid. But you cannot argue away a parent's grief. How often you hear the moan, "Oh, my child! my child!"

Then there are the filial tears. Little children soon get over the loss of parents. They are easily diverted with a new toy. But where is the man that has come to thirty or forty or fifty years of age who can think of the old people without having all the fountains of his soul stirred up? You may have had to take care of her a good many years, but you can never forget how she used to take care of you. Have you never heard of an old man, in the delirium of some sickness, call for his mother? The fact is, we get so used to calling for her the first ten years of our life, we never get over it, and when she goes away from us, it makes deep sorrow. Sometimes, perhaps, in the days of trouble and darkness, when the world would say, "You ought to be able to take care of yourself," you wake up from your dreams finding yourself saying, "Oh, mother! mother!"

Have these tears no divine origin? Why, take all the warm hearts that ever beat in all lands, and in all ages, and put them together, and their united throb would be weak compared with the throb of God's eternal sympathy. Yes, God also is the father of all those tears of repentance. Did you ever see a man repent? I see people going around, trying to repent. They cannot repent. Do you know, no man can repent until God helps him to repent? How do I know? By this passage: "Him hath God exalted to be a Prince and a Saviour to give repentance." Oh, it is a tremendous hour when one wakes up and says: "I am a bad man; I have not sinned against the laws of the land, but I have wasted my life; God asked me for my services, but I haven't given those services. Oh, my sins! God forgive me!" When that tear starts, it thrills all heaven. An angel cannot keep his eye off it, and the Church of God assembles around, and there is a commingling of tears—a rain of tears—and God is the father of that rain. The Lord, long-suffering, merciful, and gracious.

In a religious assemblage a man arose and said: "I have been a very wicked man; I broke my mother's heart; I became an infidel; but I have seen my evil ways, and I have surrendered my heart to God; yet it is a grief I can never get over, that my parents should never have heard of my salvation. I don't know whether they are living or dead." While yet he was standing in the audience, a voice from the gallery said: "Oh, my son! my son!" He looked up and recognized her. It was his old mother. She had been praying for him for a great many years, and when, at the foot of the cross, the prodigal son and the praying mother embraced each other, there was a rain, a tremendous rain of tears, and God was the father of those tears. Would that God would break us down with the sense of our sin, and then lift us with the appreciation of his mercy. Tears over our wasted life. Tears over a grieved Spirit. Tears over an injured Father. Repent! Repent!

The king of Carthage was dethroned. His people rebelled against him. He was driven into banishment. His wife and children were outrageously abused. Years went by, and the king of Carthage made many friends. He gathered up a great army. He marched again toward Carthage. Reaching the gates of Carthage, the best men of the place came out barefooted and bareheaded, and with ropes around their necks, crying for mercy. They said: "We abused you, and we abused your family, but we cry for mercy." The king of Carthage looked down upon the people from his chariot and said: "I came here to bless, I did not come to destroy. You drove me out, but this day I pronounce pardon for all the people. Open the gate and let the army come in." The king marched in and took the throne, and the people all shouted: "Long live the king!"

My friends, you have driven the Lord Jesus Christ, the King of the Church, away from your heart; you have been maltreating him all these years; but he comes back and he stands in front of the gates of your soul. If you will only pray for his pardon, he will meet you with his gracious spirit and he will say: "Thy sins and thine iniquities I will remember no more. Open wide the gate; I will take the throne. My peace I give unto you." And then, from the young and from the old, there will be a rain of tears, and God will be the father of that rain.

THE EAR

Psalm, 94: 9: " He that planted the ear, shall he not hear?"

THE EAR

Psalm, 94: 9: "He that planted the ear shall he not hear?"

Architecture is one of the most fascinating arts, and the study of Egyptian, Grecian, Etruscan, Roman, Byzantine, Moorish and Renaissance styles of building has been to many a man a sublime life-work. Lincoln and York cathedrals, St. Paul's and St. Peter's, and Arch of Titus, and Theban Temple, and Alhambra and Parthenon are the monuments to the genius of those who built them. But more wonderful than any arch they ever lifted, or any transept window they ever illumined or any Corinthian column they ever crowned, or any Gothic cloister they ever elaborated, is the human ear. No one but the infinite God could have fashioned it.

Among the most skilful and assiduous physiologists of our time have been those who have given their time to the examination of the ear and the studying of its arches, its walls, its floor, its canals, its aqueducts, its galleries, its intricacies, its convolutions, its divine machinery, and yet it will take another thousand years before the world comes to any adequate appreciation of what God did when he planned and executed the infinite and overmastering architecture of the human ear. The most of it is invisible, and the microscope breaks down in the attempt at exploration. The cartilage which we call the ear is only the storm-door of the great temple clear down out of sight, next door to the immortal soul. Such scientists as Helmholtz and Le Conte and de Blainville and Ranke and Buck have attempted to walk the Appian

Way of the human ear, but the mysterious pathway has never been fully trodden but by two feet—the foot of sound and the foot of God. Three ears on each side the head—the external ear, the middle ear, the internal ear—but all connected by most wonderful telegraphy.

The external ear in all ages adorned by precious stones or precious metals. The Temple of Jerusalem was partly built by the contribution of earrings; and Homer in the Iliad speaks of Hera wearing three bright drops, her glittering gems suspended from the ear; and many of the adornments of our day are only copies of ear jewels found to-day in Pompeiian museum and Etruscan vase. But while the outer ear may be adorned by human art, the middle and the internal ear are adorned and garnished only by the hand of the Lord God Almighty. The stroke of a key of this organ sets the air vibrating, and the ear catches the undulating sound, and passes it on through the bonelets of the middle ear to the internal ear, which is filled with liquid, and that liquid again vibrates until the three thousand fibres of the human brain take up the vibration and roll the sound on into the soul.

A part of the ear is called by physiologists "the hammer," for it is something to strike, and another part of the ear is called "the anvil," for it is something to be smitten, and another part is called "the stirrup," because it is like the stirrup of the saddle with which we mount the steed, and another part is called "the drum," for it is something to be beaten into sound. Coiled like a snail shell, by which one of the innermost passages of the ear is actually called; like a stairway, for the sound to ascend; like a bent tube of a heating apparatus, taking that which enters round and round; like a labyrinth with wonderful passages into which the thought enters only to be lost in bewilderment. The middle ear filled with air, the medium of the sound as it passes to the internal ear filled with liquid—a muscle contracting when the noise is too loud, just as the pupil of the eye contracts when the light is too glaring. The external ear is defended by wax, which, with its bitterness, discourages insectile invasion. The internal ear imbedded in what is by far the hardest bone of the human system, a very rock of strength and defiance.

The ear is so strange a contrivance that, by the estimate of one scientist, it can catch the sound of seventy-three thousand seven hundred vibrations in a second. The outer ear taking in all kinds of sound, whether the crash of an avalanche, or the hum of a bee. The sound passing to the inner door of the outside ear, halts until another mechanism, divine mechanism, passes it on by the bonelets of the middle ear, and coming to the inner door of that second ear, the sound has no power to come farther until another divine mechanism passes it on through into the inner ear, and then the sound swims the liquid until it comes to the rail-track of the brain branchlet, and rolls on and on until it comes to sensation, and there the curtain drops, and a hundred gates shut, and the voice of God seems to say to all human inspection: "Thus far and no farther."

In this vestibule of the palace of the soul, how many kings of thought, of medicine, of physiology, have done penance of lifelong study and got no farther than the vestibule. Mysterious home of reverberation and echo. Grand Central Depot of sound. Headquarters to which there come quick dispatches, part the way by cartilages, part the way by air, part the way by bone, part the way by water, part the way by nerve—the slowest dispatch plunging into the ear at the speed of one thousand and ninety feet a second.

Sermons by T. DeWitt Talmage

The ear is the small instrument of music on which is played all the music you ever hear, from the grandeurs of an August thunderstorm to the softest breathings of a flute. Small instrument of music, only a quarter of an inch of surface and the thinness of one two hundred and fiftieth part of an inch, and that thinness divided into three layers. In that ear musical staff, lines, spaces, bar and rest. A bridge leading from the outside natural world to the inside spiritual world; we seeing the abutment at this end the bridge, but the fog of an unlifted mystery hiding the abutment on the other end the bridge. Whispering gallery of the soul. The human voice is God's eulogy to the ear. That voice capable of producing seventeen trillion, five hundred and ninety-two billion, one hundred and eighty-six million, forty-four thousand, four hundred and fifteen sounds, and all that variety made, not for the regalement of beast or bird, but for the human ear.

You remember that Tuesday, in Venice, when there lay down in death one whom many consider the greatest musical composer of the century. Struggling on up from six years of age, when he was left fatherless, Wagner rose through the obloquy of the world, and oftentimes all nations seemingly against him, until he gained the favor of a king, and won the enthusiasm of the opera-houses of Europe and America. Struggling all the way on to seventy years of age, to conquer the world's ear.

In that same attempt to master the human ear and gain supremacy over this gate of the immortal soul, great battles were fought by Mozart, Gluck and Weber, and by Beethoven and Meyerbeer, by Rossini and by all the roll of German and Italian and French composers—some of them in the battle leaving their blood on the keynotes and the musical scores. Great

The Ear

battle fought for the ear, fought with baton, with organ-pipe, with trumpet, with cornet-a-piston, with all ivory and brazen and silver and golden weapons of the orchestra ; royal theatre and cathedral and academy of music the fortresses of the contest for the ear. England and Egypt fought for the supremacy of the Suez Canal, and the Spartans and Persians fought for the defile at Thermopylæ, but the musicians of all ages have fought for the mastery of the auditory canal and the defile of the immortal soul and the Thermopylæ of struggling cadences. For the conquest of the ear, Haydn struggled on up from the garret, where he had neither fire nor food, on and on until under the too great nervous strain of hearing his own oratorio of the "Creation" performed, he was carried out to die ; but leaving as his legacy to the world one hundred and eighteen symphonies, one hundred and sixty-three pieces for the barytone, fifteen masses, five oratorios, forty-two German and Italian songs, thirty-nine canzonets, three hundred and sixty-five English and Scotch songs with accompaniment, and one thousand five hundred and thirty-six pages of libretti. All that to capture the gate of the body that swings in from the tympanum to the snail shell lying on the beach of the ocean of the immortal soul.

To conquer the ear, Handel struggled on from the time when his father would not let him go to school, lest he learn the gamut and become a musician, and from the time when he was allowed in the organ loft just to play, after the audience had left, one voluntary, to the time when he left to all nations his unparalleled oratorios of "Esther," "Deborah," "Samson," "Jeph-thah," "Judas Maccabeus," "Israel in Egypt" and the "Messiah," the soul of the great German composer still weeping in the dead march of our great obsequies and triumphing in the raptures of every Easter morn.

To conquer the ear and take this gate of the immortal soul, Schubert composed his immortal "Serenade," writing the staves of the music on the bill of fare in a restaurant, and went on until he could leave as a legacy to the world over a thousand magnificent compositions in music. To conquer the ear and take this gate of the soul's castle, Mozart struggled on through poverty until he came to a pauper's grave; and one chilly, wet afternoon the body of him who gave to the world the "Requiem" and the "G-minor Symphony" was crunched in on the top of two other paupers into a grave which to this day is epitaphless.

For the ear everything mellifluous, from the birth hour when our earth was wrapped in swaddling clothes of light and serenaded by other worlds, from the time when Jubal thrummed the first harp and pressed a key of the first organ down to the music of this Sabbath morning. Yea, for the ear the coming overtures of heaven; for whatever other part of the body may be left in the dust, the ear, we know, is to come to celestial life; otherwise, why the "harpers harping with their harps?" For the ear, carol of lark and whistle of quail and chirp of cricket and dash of cascade and roar of tides oceanic and doxology of worshipful assembly and minstrelsy, cherubic, seraphic, and archangelic. For the ear, all Pandean pipes, all flutes, all clarionets, all hautboys, all bassoons, all bells, and all organs—Luzerne and Westminster Abbey and Freyburg and Berlin and all the organ pipes set across Christendom, and great Giant's Causeway for the monarchs of music to play on. For the ear, all chimes, all ticking of chronometers, all anthems, all dirges, all glees, all choruses, all lullabies, all orchestration.

The Ear

Oh, the ear!—the God-honored ear!—grooved with divine sculpture and poised with divine gracefulness and upholstered with curtains of divine embroidery, and corridored by divine carpentry, and pillared with divine architecture, and chiseled in bone of divine masonry, and conquered by processions of divine marshaling. The ear! A perpetual point of interrogation, asking how; a perpetual point of apostrophe, appealing to God. None but God could plan it; none but God could build it; none but God could work it; none but God could keep it; none but God could understand it; none but God could explain it. Oh, the wonders of the human ear!

How surpassingly sacred the human ear. You had better be careful how you let the sound of blasphemy or uncleanness step into that holy of holies. The Bible says that in the ancient temple the priest was set apart by the putting of the blood of a ram on the tip of the ear, the right ear of the priest. But, my friends, we need all of us to have the sacred touch of ordination on the hanging lobe of both ears, and on the arches of the ears, on the eustachian tube of the ear, on the mastoid cells of the ear, on the tympanic cavity of the ear, and on everything from the outside rim of the outside ear clear in to the point where sound steps off the auditory nerve and rolls on down into the unfathomable depths of the immortal soul. The Bible speaks of "dull ears," and of "uncircumcised ears," and of "itching ears," and of "rebellious ears," and of "open ears," and of those who have all the organs of hearing and yet who seem to be deaf, for it cries to them: "He that hath ears to hear, let him hear."

To show how much Christ thought of the human ear: He one day met a man who was deaf, came up to him and put a finger of the right hand into the orifice of the left ear of the patient, and put a finger of the left hand into the orifice of the right ear of the patient, and agitated the tympanum, and startled the bonelets, and with a voice that rang clear through into the man's soul, cried: "Ephphatha!" and the polyphoid growths gave way, and the inflamed auricle cooled off, and that man who had not heard a sound for many years, that night heard the wash of the waves of Galilee against the limestone shelving. To show how much Christ thought of the human ear, when the apostle Peter got mad and with one slash of his sword dropped the ear of Malchus into the dust, Christ created a new external ear for Malchus, corresponding with the middle ear and the internal ear, that no sword could clip away. And to show what God thinks of the ear, we are informed of the fact that in the millennial June which shall roseate all the earth, the ears of the deaf will be unstopped, all the vascular growths gone—all deformation of the listening organ cured, corrected, changed. Every being on earth will have a hearing apparatus as perfect as God knows how to make it, and all the ears will be ready for that great symphony in which all the musical instruments of the earth shall play the accompaniment, nations of earth and empires of heaven mingling their voices together, with the deep bass of the sea and the alto of the winds, and the barytone of the thunder: "Alleluia!" surging up meeting the "Alleluia!" descending.

Oh, yes! my friends, we have been looking for God too far away instead of looking for him close by and in our own organism. We go up into the observatory and look through the telescope and see God in Jupiter and God in Saturn and God in Mars; but we could see more of him through the microscope of an aurist. No king is satisfied with only one residence, and in France it has been St. Cloud and Versailles

The Ear

and the Tuileries, and in Great Britain it has been Windsor and Balmoral and Osborne. A ruler does not always prefer the larger. The King of earth and heaven may have larger castles and greater palaces, but I do not think there is any one more curiously wrought than the human ear. The heaven of heavens cannot contain him, and yet he says he finds room to dwell in a contrite heart, and, I think, in a Christian ear. We have been looking for God in the infinite; let us look for him in the infinitesimal. God walking the corridor of the ear, God sitting in the gallery of the human ear, God speaking along the auditory nerve of the ear, God dwelling in the ear to hear that which comes from the outside, and so near the brain and the soul he can hear all that occurs there. The Lord of hosts encamping under the curtains of membrane. Palace of the Almighty in the human ear. The rider on the white horse of the Apocalypse thrusting his hand into the loop of bone which the physiologist has been pleased to call the stirrup of the ear.

Are you ready now for the question of my text? Have you the endurance to bear its overwhelming suggestiveness? Will you take hold of some pillar and balance yourself under the semi-omnipotent stroke? "He that planted the ear, shall he not hear?" Shall the God who gives us the apparatus with which we hear the sounds of the world, himself not be able to catch up song and groan and blasphemy and worship? Does he give us a faculty which he has not himself? Doctors Wild and Gruber and Toynbee invented the acoumeter and other instruments by which to measure and examine the ear, and do these instruments know more than the doctors who made them? "He that planted the ear, shall he not hear?"

Jupiter of Crete was always represented in statuary and painting as without ears, suggesting the idea that he did not want to be bothered with the affairs of the world. But our God has ears. "His ears are open to their cry." The Bible intimates that two workmen on Saturday night do not get their wages. Their complaint instantly strikes the ear of God: "The cry of those that reaped hath entered the ears of the Lord of Sabaoth." Did God hear that poor girl last night as she threw herself on the prison bunk in the city dungeon and cried in the midnight: "God have mercy"? Do you really think God could hear her? Yes, just as easily as when fifteen years ago she was sick with scarlet fever, and her mother heard her when at midnight she asked for a drink of water. "He that planted the ear, shall he not hear?"

When a soul prays, God does not sit upright until the prayer travels immensity and climbs to his ear. The Bible says he bends clear over. In more than one place Isaiah said he bowed down his ear. In more than one place the Psalmist said he inclined his ear, by which I come to believe that God puts his ear so closely down to your lips that he can hear your faintest whisper. It is not God away off up yonder; it is God away down here, close up—so close up that when you pray to him it is not more a whisper than a kiss. Ah, yes! he hears the captive's sigh and the plash of the orphan's tear, and the dying syllables of the shipwrecked sailor driven on the Skerries, and the infant's "Now I lay me down to sleep," as distinctly as he hears the fortissimo of brazen bands in the Dusseldorf festival, as easily as he hears the salvo of artillery when the thirteen squares of English troops open all their batteries at once at Waterloo. He that planted the ear can hear.

Just as sometimes an entrancing strain of music will linger in your ears for days after you have heard it, and just as a sharp cry of pain I once heard while

The Ear

passing through Bellevue Hospital clung to my ear for weeks, and just as a horrid blasphemy in the street sometimes haunts one's ears for days, so God hears—not only hears, but holds—the songs, the prayers, the groans, the worship, the blasphemy. The phonograph is a newly-invented instrument which holds not only the words you utter, but the very tones of your voice, so that a hundred years from now, that instrument turned, the very words you now utter and the very tone of your voice will be reproduced. Wonderful phonograph. As of our beloved dead we keep a lock of hair, or picture of the features, so the time will come when we will be able to keep the tones of their voices and the words they uttered. So that if now dear friends should speak into the phonograph some words of affection, and then they should be taken away from us, years from now from that instrument we could unroll the words they uttered and the very tones of their voice. But more wonderful is God's power to hold, to retain. Ah! what delightful encouragement for our prayers. What an awful reproof for our hard speeches. What assurance of warm-hearted sympathy for all our griefs. "He that planteth the ear, shall he not hear?"

Better take that organ of your body away from all sin. Better put it under the best sound. Better take it away from all gossip, from all slander, from all innuendo, from all bad influence of evil association. Better put it to school, to church, to philharmonic. Better put that ear under the blessed touch of Christian hymnology. Better consecrate it for time and eternity to him who planted the ear. Rousseau, the infidel, fell asleep amid his sceptical manuscript lying all around the room, and in his dream he entered heaven and heard the song of the worshippers, and it was so sweet he asked an angel what it meant. The angel said: "This is the Paradise of God, and the song you hear is the anthem of the redeemed." Under another roll of the celestial music Rousseau wakened and got up in the midnight and as well as he could wrote down the strains of the music that he had heard in the wonderful tune called the "Songs of the Redeemed." God grant that it may not be to you and to me an infidel dream, but a glorious reality. When we come to the night of death and we lie down to our last sleep, may our ears really be wakened by the canticles of the heavenly temple, and the songs and the anthems and the carols and the doxologies that shall climb the musical ladder of that heavenly gamut.

THE EYE

Psalm, 94: 9: "He that formed the eye, shall he not see?"

THE EYE

Psalm, 94: 9: "He that formed the eye, shall he not see?"

The imperial organ of the human system is the eye. All up and down the Bible God honors it, extols it, illustrates it, or arraigns it. Five hundred and thirty-four times is it mentioned in the Bible. Omnipresence —"the eyes of the Lord are in every place." Divine care—"as the apple of the eye." The clouds—"the eyelids of the morning." Irreverence—"the eye that mocketh at its father." Pride—"oh, how lofty are their eyes." Inattention—"the fool's eye in the ends of the earth." Divine inspection—"wheels full of eyes." Suddenness—"in the twinkling of an eye at the last trump." Olivetic sermon—"the light of the body is the eye." This morning's text: "He that formed the eye, shall he not see?"

The surgeons, the doctors, the anatomists, and the physiologists understand much of the glories of the two great lights of the human face; but the vast multitudes go on from cradle to grave without any appreciation of the two great masterpieces of the Lord God Almighty. If God had lacked anything of infinite wisdom he would have failed in creating the human eye. We wander through the earth trying to see wonderful sights, but the most wonderful sight that we ever see is not so wonderful as the instruments through which we see it.

It has been a strange thing to me for thirty years that some scientist with enough eloquence and magnetism did not go through the country with illustrated lecture on canvas thirty feet square, to startle and thrill and overwhelm Christendom with the marvels of the human eye. Putting it on the worldly and the lowest ground, there is a fortune awaiting any such competent demonstrator. We want the eye taken from all its technicalities and some one who shall lay aside all talk about the pterygomaxillary fissures, the sclerotica, and the chiasma of the optic nerve, and in plain, common parlance which you and I and everybody can understand, present the subject. We have learned men who have been telling us what our origin is and what we were. Oh, if some one would come forth from the dissecting-table and from the classroom of the university and take the platform, and, asking the help of the Creator, demonstrate the wonders of what we are. If I refer to the physiological facts suggested by the former part of my text, it is only to bring out in plainer way the theological lessons of the latter part of my text. "He that formed the eye, shall he not see?"

I suppose my text referred to the human eye, since it excels all others in structure and in adaptation. The eyes of fish and reptiles and moles and bats are very simple things, because they have not much to do. There are insects with a score of eyes, but the twenty eyes have less faculty than the two human eyes. The black beetle swimming the summer pond has two eyes under the water and two eyes above the water, but the four insectile are not equal to the two human. Man placed at the head of all living creatures must have supreme equipment, while the blind fish in the Mammoth Cave of Kentucky have only an undeveloped organ of sight, an apology for the eye, which, if through some crevice of the mountain they should go into the sunlight, might be developed into positive eyesight.

In the first chapter of Genesis we find that God,

without any consultation, created the light, created the trees, created the fish, created the fowl, but when he was about to make man he called a convention of divinity, as though to imply that all the powers of Godhead were to be enlisted in the achievement. "Let us make man." Put a whole ton of emphasis on that word "us." "Let us make man." And if God called a convention of divinity to create man, I think the two great questions in that conference were how to create a soul and how to make an appropriate window for the emperor to look out of.

See how God honored the eye before he created it. He cried until chaos was irradiated with the utterance: "Let there be light!" In other words, before he introduced man into this temple of the world, he illumined it, prepared it for the eyesight. And so after the last human eye has been destroyed in the final demolition of the world, stars are to fall and the sun is to cease its shining, and the moon is to turn into blood. In other words, after the human eyes are no more to be profited by their shining, the chandeliers of heaven are to be turned out. God, to educate and to bless and to help the human eye, set on the mantel of heaven two lamps—a gold lamp and a silver lamp—the one for the day and the other for the night.

To show how God honors the eye, look at the two halls built for the residence of the eyes; seven bones making the wall for each eye, the seven bones curiously wrought together. Kingly palace of ivory is considered rich, but the halls for the residence of the human eyes are richer by so much as human bone is more sacred than elephantine tusk. See how God honored the eyes when he made a roof for them, so that the sweat of toil should not smart them, and the rain dashing against the forehead might not drip into them; the eyebrows not bending over the eye, but reaching to the right and to the left so that the rain and the sweat should be compelled to drop upon the cheek, instead of falling into this divinely protected human eyesight.

See how God honored the eye in the fact presented by anatomists and physiologists that there are eight hundred contrivances in every eye. For window-shutters, the eyelids opening and closing thirty thousand times a day. The eyelashes so constructed that they have their selection as to what shall be admitted, saying to the dust, "Stay out," and saying to the light, "Come in." For inside curtain the iris, or pupil of the eye, according as the light is greater or less, contracting or dilating. The eye of the owl is blind in the daytime, the eyes of some creatures are blind at night, but the human eye is so marvelously constructed it can see both by day and by night.

Many of the other creatures of God can move the eye only from side to side, but the human eye, so marvelously constructed, has one muscle to lift the eye and another muscle to lower the eye, and another muscle to roll it to the right, and another muscle to roll it to the left, and another muscle passing through a pulley to turn it round and round—an elaborate gearing of six muscles as perfect as God could make them.

There also is the retina, gathering the rays of light and passing the visual impression on to the sensorium and on into the soul. What a delicate lens, what an exquisite screen, what soft cushions, what wonderful chemistry of the human eye. The eye washed by a slow stream of moisture whether we sleep or wake, rolling imperceptibly over the pebble of the eye and emptying into a bone of the nostril; the eye a contrivance so wonderful that it can see the sun, ninety-five millions of miles away, and the point of a pin. Telescope and microscope in the same contrivance.

The Eye

The astronomer swings and moves this way and that, and adjusts and readjusts the telescope until he gets it to the right focus; the microscopist moves this way and that, and adjusts and readjusts the magnifying glass until it is prepared to do its work, but the human eye, without a touch, beholds the star and the smallest insect. The traveler among the Alps with one glance taking in Mont Blanc and the face of his watch to see whether he has time to climb it. Oh, this wonderful camera-obscura which you and I carry about with us, so to-day we can take in this audience, so from the top of Mount Washington we can take in New England, so at night we can sweep into our vision the constellations from horizon to horizon. So delicate, so semi-infinite, and yet the light coming ninety-five millions of miles at the rate of nearly two hundred thousand miles a second, is obliged to halt at the gate of the eye, waiting until the portcullis be lifted. Something hurled ninety-five millions of miles and striking an instrument which has not the agitation of even winking under the power of the stroke.

There, also, is the merciful arrangement of the tear-gland by which the eye is washed and through which rolls the tide which brings relief that comes in tears when some bereavement or great loss strikes us. The tear not an augmentation of sorrow, but the breaking up of the Arctic of frozen grief in the warm Gulf Stream of consolation. Incapacity to weep is madness or death. Thank God for the tear-glands and that the crystal gates are so easily opened.

Oh, the wonderful hydraulic apparatus of the human eye. Divinely constructed vision. Two light-houses at the harbor of the immortal soul, under the shining of which the world sails in and drops anchor. What an anthem of praise to God is the human eye! The tongue is speechless and a clumsy instrument of expression as compared with it. Have you not seen it flash with indignation, or kindle with enthusiasm, or expand with devotion, or melt with sympathy, or stare with fright, or leer with villainy, or droop with sadness, or pale with envy, or fire with revenge, or twinkle with mirth, or beam with love? It is tragedy and comedy and pastoral and lyric in turn. Have you not seen its uplifted brow of surprise, or its frown of wrath, or its contraction of pain? If the eye say one thing and the lips say another thing, you believe the eye rather than the lips. The eyes of Archibald Alexander and Charles S. Finney were the mightiest part of their sermon. George Whitefield enthralled great assemblages with his eyes, though they were crippled with strabismus. Many a military chieftain has with a look hurled a regiment to victory or to death. Martin Luther turned his great eye on an assassin who came to take his life, and the villain fled. Under the glance of the human eye the tiger, with five times a man's strength, snarls back into the African jungle.

But those best appreciate the value of the eye who have lost it. The Emperor Adrian by accident put out the eye of his servant, and he said to his servant, "What shall I pay you in money, or in lands? Anything you ask me; I am so sorry I put your eye out." But the servant refused to put any financial estimate on the value of the eye, and when the emperor urged and urged again the matter, he said: "O Emperor, I want nothing but my lost eye." Alas for those for whom a thick and impenetrable veil is drawn across the face of the heavens and the face of one's own kindred. That was a pathetic scene when a blind man lighted a torch at night and was found passing along the highway, and some one said, "Why do you carry that torch when you can't see?" "Ah!" said he, "I can't see, but I carry this torch that others may

The Eye

see me and pity my helplessness and not run me down." Samson, the giant, with his eyes put out of the Philistines is more helpless than the smallest dwarf with vision undamaged. All the sympathies of Christ were stirred when he saw Bartimeus with darkened retina, and the only salve he ever made that we read of was a mixture of dust and saliva, and a prayer with which he cured the eyes of a man blind from his nativity.

The value of the eye shown as much by its catastrophe as by its healthful action. Ask the man who for twenty years has not seen the sunrise. Ask the man who for half a century has not seen the face of a friend. Ask in the hospital the victim of ophthalmia. Ask the man whose eyesight perished in a powder blast. Ask the Bartimeus who never met a Christ, or the man born blind who is to die blind. Ask him.

The Earl of Bridgewater in his last will and testament bequeathed $40,000 for essays to be written on the power and wisdom and goodness of God as manifested in creation, and Sir Charles Bell, the British surgeon, fresh from Corunna and Waterloo, where he had been tending the wounded and studying the formation of the human body amid the amputating horrors of the battlefield, accepted the invitation to write one of those Bridgewater treatises, and he wrote his book on the human hand, a book that will live as long as the world lives. In my imperfect way, I have only hinted at the splendors, the glories, the wonders, the divine revelations, the apocalypses of the human eye, and I stagger back from the awful portals of the physiological miracle which must have taxed the ingenuity of a God, to cry out in your ears the words of my text: "He that formed the eye, shall he not see?" Shall Herschel not know as much as his telescope? Shall Fraunhofer not know as much as his spectroscope?

Shall Swammerdam not know as much as his microscope? Shall Dr. Hooke not know as much as his
micrometer? Shall the thing formed know more
than its maker? "He that formed the eye, shall he
not see?"

The recoil of this question is tremendous. We
stand at the centre of a vast circumference of observation. No privacy. On us, eyes of cherubim, eyes of
seraphim, eyes of archangel, eyes of God. We may
not be able to see the inhabitants of other worlds, but
perhaps they may be able to see us. We have not
optical instruments strong enough to descry them;
perhaps they have optical instruments strong enough
to descry us. The mole cannot see the eagle mid air,
but the eagle mid-sky can see the mole mid grass.
We are able to see mountains and caverns of another
world; but perhaps the inhabitants of other worlds
can see the towers of our cities, the flash of our seas,
the marching of our processions, the white robes of
our weddings, the black scarfs of our obsequies. It
passes out from the guess into the positive, when we
are told in the Bible that the inhabitants of other
worlds do come to this. Are they not all ministering
spirits sent forth to minister to those who shall be
heirs of salvation?

But human inspection and angelic inspection and
stellar inspection and lunar inspection and solar inspection are tame as compared with the thought of
divine inspection. "You converted me twenty years
ago," said a black man to my father. "How so?"
said my father. "Twenty years ago," said the other,
"in the old schoolhouse prayer-meeting at Bound
Brook, you said in your prayer, 'Thou God seest me,'
and I had no peace under the eye of God until I became a Christian." Hear it: "The eyes of the Lord
are in every place." "His eyelids try the children of

men." "His eyes were as a flame of fire." "I will guide thee with mine eye." Oh, the eye of God, so full of pity, so full of power, so full of love, so full of indignation, so full of compassion, so full of mercy. How it peers through the darkness; how it outshines the day; how it glares upon the offender; how it beams on the penitent soul. Talk about the human eye as being indescribably wonderful; how much more wonderful the great, searching, overwhelming eye of God! All eternity past and all eternity to come on that retina. The eyes with which we look into each other's face to-day suggest it. It stands written twice on your face and twice on mine, unless through casualty one or both have been obliterated. "He that formed the eye shall he not see?" Oh, the eye of God! It sees our sorrows to assuage them; sees our perplexities to disentangle them; sees our wants to sympathize with them. If we fight him back, the eye of an antagonist; if we ask his grace, the eye of an everlasting friend.

You often find in a book or manuscript a star calling your attention to a footnote or explanation. That star the printer calls an asterisk. But all the stars of the night-heavens are asterisks, calling your attention to God, an all observing God. Our every nerve a divine handwriting; our every muscle a pulley divinely swung; our every bone sculptured with divine suggestiveness; our every eye a reflection of the divine eye. God above us and God beneath us and God before us and God behind us and God within us. What a stupendous thing to live! What a stupendous thing to die! No such thing as hidden transgression.

A dramatic advocate in olden times at night in a court-room, persuaded of the innocence of his client, charged with murder, and of the guilt of the witness who was trying to swear the poor man's life away—

that advocate took up two bright lamps and thrust them close up to the face of the witness and cried: "May it please the court and gentlemen of the jury, behold the murderer!" and the man practically under that awful glare, confessed that he was the criminal instead of the man arraigned at the bar. Our most hidden sin is under a brighter light than that; it is under the burning eye of God.

He is not a blind giant stumbling through the heavens; he is not a blind monarch feeling for the step of his chariot. Are you wronged? He sees it. Are you poor? He sees it. Have you domestic perturbation of which the world knows nothing? He sees it. "Oh," you say, "my affairs are so insignificant I can't realize that God sees me and sees my affairs." Can you see the point of a pin? Can you see the eye of a needle? Can you see a mote in the sunbeam? And has God given you that power of minute observation and does he not possess it himself? "He that formed the eye, shall he not see?"

But you say, "God is in one world and I am in another world; he seems so far off from me I don't really think he sees what is going on in my life." Can you see the sun ninety-five million miles away? And do you not think God has as prolonged vision? But you say, "There are phases of my life and there are colors, shades of color in my annoyances and my vexations that I don't think God can understand." Does not God gather up all the colors and all the shades of color in the rainbow? And do you suppose there is any phase or any shade in your life that he has not gathered up in his own heart?

Beside that, I want to tell you it will soon all be over, this struggle. That eye of yours, so exquisitely fashioned and strung and hinged and roofed, will before long close in the last slumber. Loving hands will smooth down the silken fringes. So he giveth his beloved sleep. A legend of St. Frotobert is that his mother was blind, and he was so sorely pitiful for the misfortune that one day in sympathy he kissed her eyes, and by miracle she saw everything. But it is not a legend when I tell you that all the blind eyes of the Christian dead under the kiss of the resurrection morn shall gloriously open. Oh, what a day that will be for those who went groping through this world under perpetual obscuration, or were dependent on the hand of a friend, or with an uncertain staff felt their way; and for the aged of dim sight, about whom it might be said that "they which look out of the windows be darkened," when eternal daybreak comes in.

What a beautiful epitaph that was for a tombstone in a European cemetery: "Here reposes in God, Katrina, a saint, eighty-five years of age and blind. The light was restored to her May 10, 1840."

THE CIRCLE

Isaiah, 40: 22: "It is he that sitteth upon the circle of the earth."

THE CIRCLE

Isaiah, 40: 22: "It is he that sitteth upon the circle of the earth."

While yet people thought that the world was flat, and thousands of years before they found out that it was round, Isaiah, in my text, intimated the shape of it, God sitting upon the circle of the earth. The most beautiful figure in all geometry is the circle. God made the universe on the plan of a circle.

There are in the natural world straight lines, angles, parallelograms, diagonals, quadrangles; but these evidently are not God's favorites. Almost everywhere where you find him geometrizing, you find the circle dominant, and if not the circle, then the curve, which is a circle that died young! If it had lived long enough, it would have been a full orb, a periphery. An ellipse is a circle pressed only a little too hard at the sides.

Giant's Causeway in Ireland shows what God thinks of mathematics. There are over thirty-five thousand columns of rocks—octagonal, hexagonal, pentagonal. These rocks seem to have been made by rule and by compass. Every artist has his moulding room, where he may make fifty shapes; but he chooses one shape as preferable to all others. I will not say that the Giant's Causeway was the world's moulding room, but I do say, out of a great many figures, God seems to have selected the circle as the best. "It is he that sitteth on the circle of the earth." The stars in a circle, the moon in a circle, the sun in a circle, the universe in a circle, and the throne of God the centre of that circle. Full appreciation of this would correct the bungling architecture of churches, whose shape is a defiance of divine suggestion.

When men build churches, they ought to imitate the idea of the Great Architect, and put the audience in a circle, knowing that the tides of emotion roll more easily that way than in straight lines. Six thousand years ago God flung this world out of his right hand; but he did not throw it out in a straight line, but curvilinear, with a leash of love holding it so as to bring it back again. The world started from his hand pure and Edenic. It has been rolling on through regions of moral ice and distemper. How long it will roll God only knows, but it will in due time make complete circuit and come back to the place where it started—the hand of God—pure and Edenic.

The history of the world goes in a circle. Why is it that the shipping in our day is improving so rapidly? It is because men are imitating the old model of Noah's ark. A ship carpenter gives that as his opinion. Although so much derided by small wits, that ship of Noah's time beat the *Lucania* and the *Teutonic*, of which we boast so much. Where is the ship on the sea to-day that could outride a deluge in which the heaven and the earth were wrecked, landing all the passengers in safety?—two of each kind of living creatures, hundreds of thousands of species.

Pomology will go on with its achievements, until after many centuries the world will have plums and pears equal to the Paradisaical. The art of gardening will grow for centuries, and after the Downings and Mitchells of the world have done their best, in the far future the art of gardening will come up to the arborescence of the year one. If the makers of colored glass go on improving, they may in some centuries be able to make something equal to the east window of York Minster, which was built in the year 1290. We are six centuries behind those artists; but the world must keep on toiling until it shall make the complete circuit and come up to the skill of those very men.

If the world continue to improve in masonry, we shall have after a while, perhaps after the advance of centuries, mortar equal to that which I saw this summer in the wall of an exhumed English city, built in the time of the Romans, sixteen hundred years ago— that mortar to-day as good as the day in which it was made, having outlasted the brick and the stone. I say, after hundreds of years, masonry may advance to that point.

If the world stands long enough, we may have a city as large as they had in old times. Babylon, five times the size of London. You go into the potteries in England, and you find them making cups and vases after the style of the cups and vases exhumed from Pompeii. The world is not going back. Oh, no! but it is swinging in a circle, and will come around to the styles of pottery known so long ago as the days of Pompeii. The world must keep on progressing until it makes the complete circuit. The curve is in the right direction, the curve will keep on until it becomes the circle.

Well, now, my friends, what is true in the material universe is true in God's moral government and spiritual arrangement. That is the meaning of Ezekiel's wheel. All commentators agree in saying that the wheel means God's providence. But a wheel is of no use unless it turns, and if it turns it turns around, and if it turns around it moves in a circle.

What then? Are we parts of a great iron machine whirled around whether we will or not, the victims of inexorable fate? No! So far from that, I shall show you that we ourselves start the circle of good or bad actions, and that it will surely come around again to us unless by divine intervention it be hindered. Those bad or good actions may make the circuit of many years; but come back to us they will as certainly as that God sits on the circle of the earth.

Jezebel, the worst woman of the Bible—Shakespeare copying his "Lady Macbeth" from her picture —slew Naboth because she wanted his vineyard. While the dogs were eating the body of Naboth, Elijah the prophet put down his compass, and marked a circle from those dogs clear round to the dogs that should eat the body of Jezebel the murderess. "Impossible!" the people said; "that will never happen." Who is that being flung out of the palace window? Jezebel. A few hours after they came around, hoping to bury her. They find only the palms of the hands and the skull. The dogs that devoured Jezebel and the dogs that devoured Naboth. Oh, what a swift, what an awful circuit! But it is sometimes the case that this circle sweeps through a century, or through many centuries. The world started with a theocracy for government; that is, God was the president and emperor of the world. People got tired of a theocracy. They said, "We don't want God directly interfering with the affairs of the world; give us a monarchy." The world had a monarchy. From a monarchy it is going to have a limited monarchy. After a while, the limited monarchy will be given up, and the republican form of government will be everywhere dominant and recognized. Then the world will get tired of the republican form of government, and it will have an anarchy, which is no government at all. And then, all nations finding out that man is not capable of righteously governing man, will cry out again for theocracy, and say: "Let God come back and conduct the affairs of the world." Every step—monarchy, limited monarchy, republicanism, anarchy—only different steps between the first theocracy and the last theocracy, or segments of the great circle of the earth on which God sits.

But do not become impatient because you cannot see the curve of events, and therefore conclude that God's government is going to break down. History tells us that in the making of the Pyramids it took two thousand men two years to drag one great stone from the quarry and put it into the Pyramids. Well, now, if men short-lived can afford to work so slowly as that, cannot God in the building of the eternities afford to wait? What though God should take ten thousand years to draw a circle? Shall we take our little watch, which we have to wind up every night lest it run down, and hold it up beside the clock of eternal ages? If, according to the Bible, a thousand years are in God's sight as one day, then according to that calculation the six thousand years of the world's existence has been only to God as from Monday to Saturday.

But it is often the case that the rebound is quicker, the return is much quicker than that. The circle is sooner completed. You resolve that you will do what good you can. In one week you put a word of counsel in the heart of a Sabbath School child. During that same week you give a letter of introduction to a young man struggling in business. During the same week you make an exhortation in a prayer-meeting. It is all gone; you will never hear of it perhaps, you think. A few years after, a man comes up to you and says: "You don't know me, do you?" You say: "No,

Sermons by T. DeWitt Talmage.

I don't remember ever to have seen you." "Why," he says, "I was in the Sabbath School class over which you were the teacher; one Sunday you invited me to Christ; I accepted the offer. You see that church with two towers yonder?" "Yes," you say. He says: "That is where I preach," or, "Do you see that governor's house? That is where I live."

One day a man comes to you and says: "Good morning." You look at him and say: "Why, you have the advantage of me; I cannot place you." He says: "Don't you remember thirty years ago giving a letter of introduction to a young man—a letter of introduction to Moses H. Grinnell?" "Yes, yes, I do." He says: "I am the man; that was my first step toward a fortune; but I have retired from business now, and am giving my time to philanthropies and public interests. Come up to Yonkers and see me."

Or a man comes to you and says: "I want to introduce myself to you. I went into a prayer-meeting some years ago; I sat back by the door; you arose to make an exhortation; that talk changed the course of my life, and if I ever get to heaven, under God I will owe my salvation to you." In only ten, twenty, or thirty years, the circle swept out and swept back again to your own grateful heart.

But sometimes it is a wider circle, and does not return for a great while. I saw a bill of expenses for burning Latimer and Ridley. The bill of expenses says:

> One load of fire fagots............ 3s. 4d.
> Cartage for four loads of wood...... 2s.
> Item, a post...................... 1s. 4d.
> Item, two chains.................. 3s. 4d.
> Item, two staples................. 6d.
> Item, four laborers............... 2s. 8d.

making in all twenty-five shillings and eight pence. That was cheap fire, considering all the circumstances; but it kindled a light which shone all around the world and aroused the martyr spirit, and out from that burning of Latimer and Ridley rolled the circle wider and wider, starting other circles, convoluting, overrunning, circumscribing, overarching all heaven— a circle.

But what is true of the good is just as true of the bad. You utter a slander against your neighbor. It has gone forth from your teeth; it will never come back, you think. You have done the man all the mischief you can. You rejoice to see him wince. You say, "Didn't I give it to him!" That word has gone out, that slanderous word, on its poisonous and blasted way. You think it will never do you any harm. But I am watching that word, and I see it beginning to curve, and it curves around, and it is aiming at your heart. You had better dodge it. You cannot dodge it. It rolls into your bosom, and after it rolls in a word of an old book which says, "With what measure ye mete, it shall be measured to you again."

You maltreat an aged parent. You begrudge him the room in your house. You are impatient of his whimsicalities and garrulity. It makes you mad to hear him tell the same story twice. You give him food he cannot masticate. You wish he was away. You wonder if he is going to live forever. He will be gone very soon. His steps are shorter and shorter. He is going to stop. But God has an account to settle with you on that subject. After a while, your eye will be dim, and your gait will halt, and the sound of the grinding will be low, and you will tell the same story twice, and your children will wonder if you will never be taken away. They called you "father" once; now they call you the "old man." If you live a few years longer, they will call you the "old chap"! What are those rough words with which your children are accosting you? They are the echo of the very words you used in the ear of your old father forty years ago. What is that which you are trying to chew, but find it unmasticable, and your jaws ache and you surrender the attempt? Perhaps it may be the gristle which you gave to your father for his breakfast forty years ago.

A gentleman passing along the avenue saw a son dragging his father into the street by the hair of the head. The gentleman, outraged at this brutal conduct, was about to punish the offender, when the old man arose and said: "Don't hurt him; it's all right; forty years ago this morning I dragged out my father by the hair of his head!" It is a circle. My father lived into the eighties, and he had a very wide experience, and he said that maltreatment of parents was always punished in this world. Other sins may be adjourned to the next world, but maltreatment of parents is punished in this world.

The circle turns quickly, very quickly. Oh, what a stupendous thought that the good and the evil we start come back to us! Do you know that the judgment day will be only the points at which the circles join, the good and the bad we have done coming back to us—unless divine intervention hinder—coming back to us with welcome of delight or curse of condemnation?

Oh, I would like to see Paul, the invalid missionary, at the moment when his influence comes to full orb—his influence rolling out through Antioch, through Cyprus, through Lystra, through Corinth, through Athens, through Asia, through Europe, through America, through the first century, through five centuries, through twenty centuries, through earth,

The Circle

through heaven; and at last, the wave of influence, having made full circuit, strikes his soul. Oh, then I would like to see him! No one can tell the wide sweep of the circle of his influence, save the One who is seated on the circle of the earth.

I should not like to see the countenance of Voltaire when his influence comes to full orb. When the fatal hemorrhage seized him at eighty-three years of age, his influence did not cease. The most brilliant man of his century, he had used all his faculties for assaulting Christianity; his bad influence widening through France, widening out through Germany, widening through all Europe, widening through America, widening through the one hundred and nineteen years that have gone by since he died, widening through earth, widening through hell; until at last the accumulated influence of his bad life in fiery surge of omnipotent wrath will beat against his destroying spirit, and at that moment it will be enough to make the black hair of eternal darkness turn white with the horror. No one can tell how that bad man's influence girdled the earth, save the One who is seated on the circle of the earth—the Lord Almighty.

"Well, now," say the people in this audience, "this in some respects is a very glad theory, and in others a very sad one; we would like to have all the good we have ever done come back to us, but the thought that all the sins we have ever committed will come back to us fills us with affright." My brother, I have to tell you God can break that circle, and will do so at your call. I can bring twenty passages of Scripture to prove that when God for Christ's sake forgives a man, the sins of his past life never come back. The wheel may roll on and on, but you take your position behind the cross and the wheel strikes the cross and is shattered forever. The sins fly off from the circle into the perpendicular, falling at right angles with complete oblivion. Forgiven! Forgiven. The meanest thing a man can do is, after some difficulty has been settled, to bring it up again; and God will not be so mean as that. God's memory is mighty enough to hold all the events of the ages, but there is one thing that is sure to slip his memory, one thing he is sure to forget, and that is pardoned transgression. How do I know it? I will prove it. "Their sins and their iniquities will I remember no more." Come into that state this morning, my dear brother, my dear sister. "Blessed is he whose transgression is forgiven."

But do not make the mistake of thinking that this doctrine of the circle stops with this life; it rolls on through heaven. You might quote in opposition to me what St. John says about the city of heaven. He says it "lieth four square." That does seem to militate against this idea; but do you know there is many a square house that has a family circle facing each other, and in a circle moving, and I can prove that this is so in regard to heaven.

St. John says: "I heard the voice of many angels round about the throne, and the beasts and the elders." And again he says: "I saw round about the throne four and twenty seats." Again he says: "There was a rainbow round about the throne." The two former instances a circle; the last, either a circle or a semi-circle. The seats facing each other, the angels facing each other, the men facing each other. Heaven an amphitheatre of glory. Circumference of patriarch and prophet and apostle. Circumference of Scotch Covenanters and Theban legion and Albigenses. Circumference of the good of all ages. Periphery of splendor unimagined and indescribable. A circle! A circle!

But every circumference must have a centre, and

what is the centre of this heavenly circumference? Christ. His all the glory; his all the praise; his all the crowns. All heaven wreathed into a garland round about him.

Take off the imperial sandal from his foot, and behold the scar of the spike. Lift the coronet of dominion from his brow, and see where was the laceration of the briers. Come closer, all heaven. Narrow the circle around his great heart. O Christ, the Saviour! O Christ, the man! O Christ, the God! Keep thy throne forever, seated on the circle of the earth, seated on the circle of the heaven.

> On Christ, the solid rock, I stand;
> All other ground is shifting sand.

THE SNOW

Job, 38: 22:   " Hast thou entered into the treasures of the
snow?"

THE SNOW

Job, 38: 22: "Hast thou entered into the treasures of the snow?"

Grossly maligned is the season of winter. The spring and summer and autumn have had many admirers; but winter, hoary-headed and white-bearded winter, hath had more enemies than friends. Yet without winter the human race would be inane and effortless. You might speak of the winter as the mother of tempests; but I take it as the father of a whole family of physical, mental and spiritual energies. Most of the people that I know are strong in proportion to the number of snowbanks they had to climb over, or push through, in childhood, while their fathers drove the sled loaded with logs through the crunching drifts high as the fences. At the season of the year when we are so familiar with the snow—those frozen vapors, those falling blossoms of the sky, those white angels of the atmosphere, those poems of the storm, those Iliads and Odysseys of the wintry tempest—I turn over the leaves of my Bible and, though most of it was written in a clime where snow seldom or never fell—I find many references to these beautiful congelations. Though the writers may seldom or never have felt the cold touch of the snowflake on their cheek, they had in sight two mountains, the tops of which were suggestive. Other kings sometimes take off their crowns, but Lebanon and Mount Hermon all the year round and through the ages never lift the coronets of crystal from their foreheads. The first time we find a deep fall of snow in the Bible is where Samuel describes a fight between Benaiah and a lion in a pit; and though the snow may have crimsoned under the wounds of both man and brute, the shaggy monster rolled over dead and the giant was victor. But the snow is not fully recognized in the Bible until God interrogates Job, the scientist, concerning its wonders, saying: "Hast thou entered into the treasures of the snow?"

I rather think that Job may have examined the snowflake with a microscope; for, although it is supposed that the microscope was invented long after Job's time, there had been wonders of glass long before the microscope and telescope of later days were thought of. So long ago as when the Coliseum was in its full splendor, Nero sat in the emperor's box of that great theatre, which held a hundred thousand people, and looked at the combatants through a gem in his finger-ring which brought everything close up to his eye. Four hundred years before Christ, in the stores at Athens, were sold powerful glasses called "burning spheres," and Layard, the explorer, found a magnifying glass amid the ruins of Nineveh, and in the palace of Nimrod. Whether through magnifying instrument or with unaided eye, I cannot say, but I am sure that Job somehow went through the galleries of the snowflake and counted its pillars and found wonders, raptures, mysteries, theologies, majesties, infinities walking up and down its corridors, as a result of the question which the Lord had asked him, "Hast thou entered into the treasures of the snow?"

Oh, it is a wondrous meteor! Humboldt studied it in the Andes twelve thousand feet above the level of the sea. De Saussure reveled among these meteors in the Alps and Dr. Scoresby counted ninety-six varieties of snowflake amid the Arctics. They are in shape of stars, in shape of coronets, in shape of cyl-

The Snow

inders; are globular, are hexagonal, are pyramidal, are castellated. After a fresh fall of snow, in one walk you crush under your feet Tuileries, Windsor Castles, St. Pauls, St. Peters, St. Marks Cathedrals, Alhambras and Sydenham Palaces innumerable. I know it depends much on your own condition what impression these flying meteors of the snow make. I shall not forget two rough and unpretending wood-cuts which I saw in my boyhood, side by side—one picture of a prosperous farmhouse, with all signs of comfort, and a lad, warmly clothed, looking out of the door upon the first flurry of snow, and his mind no doubt filled with the sound of jingling sleigh-bells, and the frolic with playfellows in the deep banks, and he clapping his hands and shouting: "It snows! It snows!" The other sketch was of a boy, haggard and hollow-eyed with hunger, looking from the broken door of a wretched home, and seeing in the falling flakes prophecy of more cold and less bread and greater privation, wringing his hands and with tears rolling down his wan cheeks, crying: "Oh, my God! It snows! It snows!" Out of the abundance that characterizes most of our homes may there go speedy relief to all whom winter finds in want and exposure!

And now I propose for your spiritual and everlasting profit, if you will accept my guidance, to take you through some of these wonders of crystallization. And notice, first, God in the littles. You may take alpenstock and cross the *Mer de Glace*, the Sea of Ice, and ascend Mont Blanc, which rises into the clouds like a pillar of the Great White Throne, or with Arctic explorer ascend the mountains around the North Pole and see glaciers a thousand feet high grinding against glaciers three thousand feet high. But I will take you on a less pretentious journey and show you God in the snowflake. There is room enough between its pillars for the great Jehovah to stand. In that one frozen drop on the tip of your finger, you may find the throne-room of the Almighty. I take up the snow in my hand and see the coursers of celestial dominion pawing these crystal pavements. The telescope is grand, but I must confess that I am quite as much interested in the microscope. The one reveals the universe above us; the other, just as great a universe beneath us. But the telescope overwhelms me, while the microscope comforts me. What you want and I want especially is a God in littles. If we were seraphic or archangelic in our natures, we would want to study God in the great; but such small, weak, short-lived beings as you and I are, want to find God in the littles.

When I see the Maker of the universe giving himself to the architecture of a snowflake and making its shafts, its domes, its curves, its walls, its irradiations so perfect, I conclude he will look after our insignificant affairs. And if we are of more value than a sparrow, most certainly we are of infinitely greater value than an inanimate snowflake. So the Bible would chiefly impress us with God in the littles. It does not say, "Consider the clouds," but it says ,"Consider the lilies." It does not say, "Behold the tempests!" but "Behold the fowls!" and it applauds a cup of cold water, and the widow's two mites, and says the hairs of your head are all numbered. Do not fear, therefore, that you are going to be lost in the crowd. Do not think that because you estimate yourself as only one snowflake among a three-days' January snowstorm that you will be forgotten. The birth and death of a drop of chilled vapor is as certainly regarded by the Lord as the creation and demolition of a planet. Nothing is big to God and nothing is small. What makes the honey industries of South Carolina such a source of livelihood and wealth? It is because God teaches the ladybug to make an opening in the rind of the apricot for the bee, who cannot otherwise get at the juices of the fruit. So God sends the ladybug ahead to prepare the way for the honeybee. He teaches the ant to bite each grain of corn that she puts in the ground for winter food, in order that it may not take root and so ruin the little granary. He teaches the raven in dry weather to throw pebbles into a hollow tree, that the water far down and out of reach may come up within the reach of the bird's beak. What a comfort that he is a God in littles! The emperor of all the Russias in olden time was looking at a map spread before him of his vast dominions, and he could not find Great Britain on the map, and he called in his secretary and said: "Where is Great Britain that I hear so much about?" "It is under your thumb," said the secretary; and the emperor raised his hand from the map and saw the country he was looking for. And it is high time that we find this mighty realm of God close by and under our little finger. To drop you out of his memory would be to resign his omniscience. To refuse you his protection would be to abdicate his omnipotence. When you tell me that he is the God of Jupiter and the God of Mercury and the God of Saturn, you tell me something so vast that I cannot comprehend it. But if you tell me he is the God of the snowflake, you tell me something I can hold and measure and realize. Thus the smallest snowflake contains a jewel-case of comfort. Here is an opal, an amethyst, a diamond. Here is one of the treasures of the snow. Take it for your present and everlasting comfort.

Behold, also, in the snow the treasure of accumulated power. During a snowstorm let an apothecary accustomed to weigh most delicate quantities, hold his weighing scales out of the window and let one flake fall on the surface of the scales and it will not even make it tremble. When you want to express extreme triviality of weight you say, "Light as a feather;" but a snowflake is much lighter. It is just twenty-four times lighter than water. And yet the accumulation of these flakes once broke down, in sight of my house, six telegraph poles, made helpless police and fire departments, and halted rail-trains with two thundering locomotives. We have already learned so much of the power of electricity that we have become careful how we touch the electric wire, and in many cases a touch has been death. But the snow puts its hand on many of these wires and tears them down as though they were cobwebs. The snow says, "You seem afraid of the thunderbolt; I will catch it and hurl it to the ground. Your boasted electric lights adorning your cities with bubbles of fire, I will put out as easily as your ancestors snuffed out a tallow candle." The snow puts its finger on the lips of our cities that are talking with each other and they relapse into silence, uttering not a word. The snow mightier than the lightning!

In March, 1888, the snow stopped America. It said to Brooklyn, "Stay home!" to New York, "Stay home!" to Philadelphia, "Stay home!" to Washington, "Stay home!" to Richmond, "Stay home!" It put into a white sepulchre most of this nation. Commerce, whose wheels never stopped before, stopped then. What was the matter? Power of accumulated snowflakes. On the top of the Appenines one flake falls, and others fall, and they pile up, and they make a mountain of fleece on the top of a mountain of rock, until one day a gust of wind, or even the voice of a mountaineer, sets the frozen vapors into action and by awful descent they sweep everything in their course

The Snow

—trees, rocks, villages—as when, in 1827, the town of Briel in Valois was buried, and in 1624, in Switzerland, three hundred soldiers were entombed. These avalanches were made up of single snowflakes. What tragedies of the snow have been witnessed by the monks of St. Bernard, who, for ages have with the dogs been busy in extricating bewildered and overwhelmed travelers in Alpine storms, the dogs with blankets fastened to their backs and flasks of spirits fastened to their necks, to resuscitate the helpless travelers—one of these dogs decorated with a medal for having saved the lives of twenty-two persons, the brave beast himself slain of the snow on that day when accompanying a Piedmontese courier on the way to his anxious household down the mountain, the wife and children of the Piedmontese coming up the mountain in search of him, an avalanche covered all under pyramids higher than those under which the Egyptian monarchs sleep their sleep of the ages. Snowslides of our own Northwest, many perishing by them every spring; snowslides on Alaskan glaciers, forever entombing the unfortunate gold-seekers; the melting snows flooding our great rivers, till they overleap their banks and carry destruction and death through entire counties along the Mississippi, the Missouri, the Ohio and the Arkansas. What an illustration of the tragedies of the snow is found in that scene between Glencoe and Glencreran one February, in Scotland, where Ronald Cameron comes forth to bring to his father's house his cousin, Flora Macdonald, for the celebration of a birthday, and the calm day turns into a hurricane of white fury that leaves Ronald and Flora as dead, to be resuscitated by the shepherds. What an exciting struggle had Bayard Taylor among the wintry Appenines.

In the winter of 1812, by a similar force, the destiny of Europe was decided. The French army marched up toward Moscow, five hundred thousand men. What can resist them? Not bayonets, but the dumb elements overwhelm that host. Napoleon retreats from Moscow with about two hundred thousand men, a mighty nucleus for another campaign after he gets back to Paris. The morning of October 19th, when they start for home, is bright and beautiful. The air is tonic, and, although this Russian campaign has been a failure, Napoleon will try again in some other direction with his host of brave surviving Frenchmen. But a cloud comes on the sky, and the air gets chill, and one of the soldiers feels on his cheek a snowflake, and then there is a multiplication of these wintry messages, and soon the plumes of the officers are decked with another style of plume, and then all the skies let loose upon the warriors a hurricane of snow, and the march becomes difficult, and the horses find it hard to pull the supply train, and the men begin to fall under the fatigue, and many, not able to take another step, lie down in the drifts never to rise, and the cavalry horses stumble and fall, and one thousand of the army fall, and ten thousand perish, and twenty thousand go down, and fifty thousand, and a hundred thousand, and a hundred and twenty thousand, and a hundred and thirty-two thousand die, and the victor of Jena and bridge of Lodi and Eylau and Austerlitz, where three great armies commanded by three emperors surrendered to him, now himself surrenders to the snowflakes. Historians do not seem to recognize that the tide in that man's life turned from December the 16th, 1809, when he banished by hideous divorce his wife Josephine from the palace and so challenged the Almighty, and the Lord charged upon him from the fortresses of the sky with ammunition of crystal. Snowed under! Billions, trillions, quadrillions, quin-

The Snow

tillions of flakes did the work. And what a suggestion of accumulative power, and what a rebuke to all of
us who get discouraged because we cannot do much,
and therefore do nothing.

"Oh," says some one, "I would like to stop the
forces of sin and crime that are marching for the
conquest of the nations; but I am nobody, I have
neither wealth nor eloquence nor social power. What
can I do?" My brother, how much do you weigh?
as much as a snowflake? "Oh, yes." Then do your
share. It is an aggregation of small influences that
will yet put this lost world back into the bosom of a
pardoning God. Alas, that there are so many men
and women who will not use the one talent because
they have not ten, and will not give a penny because
they cannot give a dollar, and will not speak as well
as they can because they are not eloquent, and will not
be a snowflake because they cannot be an avalanche.
In earthly wars the generals get about all the credit,
but in the war for God and righteousness and heaven
all the private soldiers will get crowns of victory un-
failing. When we reach heaven—by the grace of
God may we all arrive there!—I do not think we will
be able to begin the new song right away, because of
the surprise we shall feel at the comparative rewards
given. As we are being conducted along the street
to our celestial residence, we will begin to ask where
live some of those who were mighty on earth. We
will ask, "Is so-and-so here?" And the answer will
be, "Yes, I think he is in the city, but we do not hear
much of him; he was good and he got in, but he took
most of his pay in earthly applause; he had enough
grace to get through the gate, but just where he lives
I know not. He squeezed through somehow, although I think the gates took the skirts of his gar-

ments. I think he lives in one of those back streets in one of the plainer residences."

Then we shall see a palace, the doorsteps of gold, and the windows of agate, and the tower like the sun for brilliance, and chariots before the door, and people who look like princes and princesses going up and down the steps, and we shall say, "Which of the hierarchs lives here? That must be the residence of a Paul or a Milton, or some one whose name resounds through all the planet from which we have just ascended." "No, no," says our celestial dragoman, "that is the residence of a soul whom you never heard of. When she gave a charity, her left hand knew not what her right hand did. She was mighty in secret prayer, and no one but God and her own soul knew it. She had more trouble than anybody in all the land where she lived, and without complaining she bore it, and though her talents were never great, what she had was all consecrated to God and helping others, and the Lord is making up for her earthly privation by especial raptures here, and the King of this country had that palace built especially for her. The walls began to go up when her troubles and privations and consecration began on earth, and it so happened— what a heavenly coincidence!—that the last stroke of the trowel of amethyst on those walls was given the hour she entered heaven. You know nothing of her. On earth her name was only once in the newspapers, and that among the column of the dead, but she is mighty up here. There she comes now, out of her palace grounds, in her chariot behind those two white horses, for a ride on the banks of the river that flows from under the throne of God. Let me see. Did you not have in your world below an old classic which says something about 'these are they who came out of great tribulation, and they shall reign forever and ever?'"

As we pass up the street I find a good many on foot, and I say to the dragoman, "Who are these?" And when their name is announced I recognize that some of them were on earth great poets and great orators and great merchants and great warriors, and when I express my surprise about their going afoot, the dragoman says, "In this country people are rewarded not according to the number of their earthly talents, but according to the use they made of what they had." And then I thought to myself: "Why, that theory would make a snowflake that falls cheerfully and in the right place, and does all the work assigned it, as honorable as a whole Mont Blanc of snowflakes." "Yes, yes," says the celestial dragoman, "Many of these pearls that you find on the foreheads of the righteous, and many of the gems in the jewel-case of prince and princess, are only the petrified snowflakes of earthly tempest, for God does not forget the promise made in regard to them: 'They shall be mine, saith the Lord of hosts, in that day when I make up my jewels.'" Accumulated power! All the prayers and charities and kindnesses and talents of all the good concentred and compacted will be the world's evangelization. This thought of the aggregation of the many smalls into that one mighty is another treasure of the snow.

Another treasure of the snow is the suggestion of the usefulness of sorrow. Absence of snow makes all nations sick. One snowless winter does not end its disasters, for many months. It puts tens of thousands into the grave and leaves others in homes and hospitals, gradually to go down. Called by a trivial name, the Russian "grip," it became an international plague. Plenty of snow means public health. There is no medicine that so soon cures the world's malarias as these white pellets that the clouds administer. Pellets small enough to be homoeopathic, but in such large doses as to be allopathic, and melting soon enough to be hydropathic. Like a sponge, every flake absorbs unhealthy gases. The tables of mortality immediately lessen when the snows of December begin to fall. The snow is one of the grandest and best of the world's doctors.

Yes; it is necessary for the land's productiveness. Great snows in winter are generally followed by great harvests the next summer. Scientific analysis has shown that snow contains a larger percentage of ammonia than the rain, and hence its greater power of enrichment. And besides that, it is a white blanket to keep the earth warm. An examination of snow in Siberia showed that it was a hundred degrees warmer under the snow than above the snow. Alpine plants perished in the mild winter of England for lack of enough snow to keep them warm. Snow strikes back the rich gases, which otherwise would escape in the air and be lost. Thank God for the snows, high and deep and wide and enriching; they bring the harvests which embroider with gold this entire American continent. But who with any analogical faculty can notice that out of such chill as the snow comes the wheat, without realizing that chilling sorrows produce harvests of grace! The strongest Christians, without exception, are those who, by bereavements or sickness or poverty or persecution, or all of them together, were snowed under, and again and again snowed under. These snowstorms of trouble! They kill the malarias of the soul. They drive us out of worldly dependence to God. Call the roll of all the eminently pious of all the ages and you will find them the sons and daughters of sorrow. The Maronites say that one

The Snow

characteristic of the cedar tree is that when the air is full of snow, and it begins to descend, the tree lifts its branches in a way better to receive the snow and bear up under it, and I know by much observation that the grandest cedars of Christian character lift higher their branches toward God, when the snows of trouble are coming. Lord Nelson's coffin was made out of the masts of the ship *L'Orient*, in which he had fought so bravely, and your throne in heaven, oh, suffering child of God, will be built out of conquered earthly disasters. What gave John Bunyan such a wondrous dream of the celestial city? The Bedford penitentiary. What gave Richard Baxter such power to tell of the Saints' Everlasting Rest, and give his immortal Call to the Unconverted? Physical disease which racked every nerve of his body. What made George Whitefield so mighty in saving souls, bringing ten thousand to God when others brought a hundred? Persecution that caricatured and assailed him all up and down England, and dead vermin thrown in his face when he was preaching. What mellowed and glorified Wilberforce's Christian character? A financial misfortune that led him to write: "I know not why my life is spared so long, except it be to show that a man can be as happy without a fortune as with one." What gave John Milton such deep spiritual eyesight that he could see the battle of angels? Extinguishment of physical eyesight. What is the highest observatory for studying the stars of hope and faith and spiritual promise? The believer's sick-bed. What proclaims the richest and most golden harvests that wave on all the hills of heavenly rapture? The snows, the deep snows, the awful snows of earthly calamity. And that thought is one of the treasures of the snow.

Another treasure of the snow is the suggestion

that this mantle covering the earth is like the soul after it is forgiven. "Wash me," said the Psalmist, "and I shall be whiter than snow." My dear friend, Gasherie De Witt, went over to Geneva, Switzerland, for the recovery of his health, but the Lord had something better for him than earthly recovery. Little did I think when I bade him good-by one lovely afternoon on the other side the sea, to return to America, that we would not meet again till we meet in heaven. As he lay one Sabbath morning on his dying pillow in Switzerland, the window open, he was looking out upon Mont Blanc. The air was clear. That great mountain stood in its robe of snow, glittering in the morning light, and my friend said to his wife: "Jennie, do you know what that snow on Mont Blanc makes me think of? It makes me think that the righteousness of Christ and the pardon of God cover all the sins and imperfections of my life, as that snow covers up that mountain; for the promise is that though our sins be as scarlet, they shall be as white as snow." Was not that glorious? I do not care who you are, or where you are, you need as much as I do that cleansing which made Gasherie De Witt good while he lived and glorious when he died. Do not take it as the tenet of an obsolete theology that our nature is corrupt. We must be changed. We must be made over again.

The ancients thought that snow-water had especial power to wash out deep stains. All other water might fail, but melted snow would make them clean. Well, Job had great admiration for snow, but he declares in substance that if he should wash his soul in melted snow, he would still be covered with mud like a man down in a ditch. Job, 9:30: "If I wash myself with snow-water, and make my hands never so clean, yet shalt thou plunge me in the ditch and mine own clothes shall abhor me." We must be washed in the fountain of God's mercy, before we can be whiter than snow. "Without holiness, no man shall see the Lord." Oh, for the cleansing power!

If there be among us one man or woman whose thoughts have always been right, whose words always right, and whose actions always right, let such a one declare it. Not one! All we, like sheep, have gone astray. Unclean! unclean! And yet we may be made whiter than snow, whiter than that which, on a cold winter's morning, after a night of storm, clothes the tree from bottom of trunk to top of highest branch; whiter than that which makes the Adirondacks and the Sierra Nevada and Mount Washington heights of pomp and splendor fit to enthrone an archangel.

In the time of Grahame, the essayist, in one mountain district of Scotland, an average of ten shepherds perished every winter in the snow-drifts, and so he proposed that, at the distance of every mile, a pole fifteen feet high and with two cross-pieces be erected, showing the points of the compass, and that a bell be hung at the top, so that every breeze would ring it, and the lost one on the mountains would hear the sound and take the direction given by this pole with the cross-pieces and get safely home. Whether that proposed plan was adopted or not, I do not know; but I declare to all who are in the heavy and blinding drifts of sin and sorrow that there is a cross near-by that can direct you to home and peace and God. Hear you not the ringing of the Gospel bell hanging on that cross, saying: "This is the way, walk ye in it?" No wonder that the sacred poet put the Psalmist's thought into rhythm, with that ringing chorus we have so often sung:

Dear Jesus, I long to be perfectly whole;
I want thee forever to live in my soul.

Break down very idol, cast down every foe!
Now wash me, and I shall be whiter than snow!
Whiter than snow! yes, whiter than snow!
Now wash me, and I shall be whiter than snow!

Get that prayer answered, and we will be fit not only for earth, but for the heaven where everything is so white because everything is so pure. You know that the redeemed in that land wear robes that are white, and the conquerors in that land ride horses that are white, and John in vision says of Christ, "his head and his hairs were white," and the throne on which he sits is a Great White Throne. By the pardoning and sanctifying grace of God, may we all at last stand amid that radiance!

Ten thousand times ten thousand,
In glittering armor bright,
The armies of the living God,
Throng up the steeps of light.
'Tis finished, all is finished,
Their fight with death and sin:
Throw open wide the golden gates,
And let the conquerors in.

EQUIPAGE OF CLOUD

Ps., 104: 3: "Who maketh the clouds his chariot."

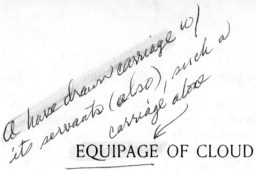

a have drawn carriage w/
its servants (also), such a
carriage also

EQUIPAGE OF CLOUD

Ps., 104: 3: "Who maketh the clouds his chariot."

Brutes are constructed so as to look down. Those earthly creatures that have wings, when they rise from the earth, still look down; and the eagle searches for mice in the grass, and the raven for carcases in the field. Man alone is made to look up. To induce him to look up, God makes the sky a picture-gallery, a Dusseldorf, a Louvre, a Luxembourg, a Vatican, that eclipses all that German or French or Italian art ever accomplished. But God has failed so far to attract the attention of most of us by the scenery of the sky. We go into raptures over flowers in the soil, but have little or no appreciation of the "morning-glories" that bloom on the wall of the sky at sunrise, or the dahlias in the clouds at sunset. We are in ecstasies over a gobelin tapestry or a bridal veil of rare fabric or a snowbank of exquisite curve; but we see not at all, or see without emotion, the bridal veils of mist that cover the face of the Catskills or the swaying upholstery around the couch of the dying day or the snowbanks of vapor piled up in the heavens.

My text bids us lift our chin three or four inches and open the two telescopes which, under the forehead, are put on swivel easily turned upward, and see that the clouds are not merely uninteresting signs of wet or dry weather, but that they are embroidered canopies of shade; that they are the conservatories of the sky; that they are thrones of pomp; that they are crystalline bars; that they are paintings in water-color; that they are the angels of the mist; that they are great cathedrals of light with broad aisles for angelic beings to walk through and bow at altars of amber and alabaster; that they are the mothers of the dew; that they are ladders for ascending and descending glories, Cotopaxis of belching flame, Niagaras of color; that they are the masterpieces of the Lord God Almighty.

The clouds are a favorite Bible simile, and the sacred writers have made much use of them. After the Deluge, God hung on a cloud in concentric bands the colors of the spectrum, saying: "I do set my bow in the cloud." As a mountain is sometimes entirely hidden by the vapors, so, says God, "I have blotted out as a thick cloud thy transgressions." David measured the divine goodness, and found it so high he apostrophized: "Thy faithfulness reacheth unto the clouds." As sometimes there are thousands of fleeces of vapor scurrying across the heavens, so, says Isaiah, will be the converts in the millennium "as clouds and as doves." As in the wet season, no sooner does the sky clear than there comes another obscuration; so, says Solomon, one ache or ailment of old folks has no more than gone than another pain comes "as clouds return after the rain."

A column of illumined cloud led the Israelites across the wilderness. In the Book of Job, Elihu, watching the clouds, could not understand why they did not fall, or why they did not all roll together, the laws of evaporation and condensation then not being understood, and he cries out: "Dost thou know the balancing of the clouds?" When I read my text, it suggests to me that the clouds are the Creator's equipage, and their whirling masses are the wheels, and the tongue of the cloud is the pole of the celestial vehicle, and the winds are the harnessed steeds, and God is the Royal occupant and driver, "who maketh the clouds his chariot."

Equipage of Cloud

To understand the Psalmist's meaning in the text, you must know that the chariot of old was sometimes a sculptured brilliancy, made out of ivory, sometimes of solid silver, and rolled on two wheels, which were fastened to the axle by stout pins; and the awful defeat of Œnomaus by Pelops was caused by the fact that a traitorous charioteer had inserted a linch-pin of wax instead of a linch-pin of iron. All of the six hundred chariots of Pharaoh lost their linch-pins in the Red Sea, for the Bible says: "The Lord took off their wheels." Look at the long flash of Solomon's fourteen hundred chariots, and the thirty thousand chariots of the Philistines.

If you have ever visited the buildings where a king or queen keeps the coaches of state, you know that kings and queens have a great variety of turnouts. The keeper tells you: "This is the state carriage, and used only on great occasions." "This is the coronation carriage, and in it the king rode on the day he took the throne." "In this the queen went to open Parliament." "This is the coach in which the Czar and the Sultan rode on the occasion of their visit." All costly and tessellated and enriched and emblazoned are they, and when the driver takes the reins of the ten white horses in his hands, and amid mounted troops and bands in full force sounding the national air, the splendor starts, and rolls on under arches entwined with banners, and amid the huzza of hundreds of thousands of spectators, the scene is memorable. But my text puts all such occasions into insignificance, as it represents the King of the Universe coming to the door of his palace, and the gilded vapors of the heavens rolling up to his feet, and he, stepping in and taking the reins of the galloping winds in his hand, starts in triumphal ride under the arches of sapphire, and over the atmospheric highways of opal and chrysolite, the clouds his chariot.

Do not think that God belittles himself when he takes such conveyance. Do you know that the clouds are among the most wondrous and majestic things in the whole universe? Do you know that they are flying lakes and rivers and oceans? God waved his hand over them and said: "Come up higher!" and they obeyed the mandate. That cloud, instead of being, as it seems, a small gathering of vapor a few yards wide and high, is really seven or eight miles across, and is a mountain, from its base to its top, fifteen thousand feet, eighteen thousand feet, twenty thousand feet, and cut through with ravines five thousand feet deep. No, David did not make a fragile or unworthy representation of God in the text, when he spoke of the clouds as his chariot. But, as I suggested in the case of an earthly king, he has his morning-cloud chariot and his evening-cloud chariot—the cloud chariot in which he rode down to Sinai to open the law, and the cloud chariot in which he rode down to Tabor to honor the Gospel, and the cloud chariot in which he will come to judgment. When he rides out in his morning chariot he puts golden coronets on the dome of cities, and silvers the rivers, and out of the dew makes a diamond ring for the fingers of every grass blade, and bids good cheer to invalids who in the night said: "Would God it were morning." From this morning cloud chariot he distributes light —light for the earth and light for the heavens, light for the land and light for the sea; great bars of it, great wreaths of it, great columns of it, a world full of it. Hail him in worship as every morning he drives out in his chariot of morning cloud, and cry with David: "My voice shalt thou hear in the morning, in the morning will I direct my prayer unto thee and look up." I rejoice in these Scripture ejaculations: "Joy cometh in the morning." "My soul waiteth for thee more than they that watch for the morning." "If I take the wing of the morning." "The eyelids of the morning." "The morning cometh." "Who is she that looketh forth as the morning." "His going forth is prepared as the morning." "As the morning spread on the mountains." "That thou shouldest visit him every morning." What a mighty thing the king throws from his chariot when he throws us the morning!

He has his evening cloud chariot. It is made out of the saffron and the gold and the purple and the orange and the vermilion and upshot flame of the sunset. That is the place where the splendors that have marched through the day, having ended the procession, throw down their torches and set the heavens on fire. That is the only hour of the day when the atmosphere is clear enough to let us see the wall of the heavenly city with its twelve manner of precious stones, from foundation of jasper to middle strata of sardius and on up to the coping of amethyst. At that hour, without any of Elisha's supernatural vision, we see horses of fire and chariots of fire and banners of fire and ships of fire and cities of fire and seas of fire, and it seems as if the last conflagration had begun and there is a world on fire. When God makes these clouds his chariot let us all kneel. Another day past, what have we done with it? Another day dead, and this is its gorgeous catafalque. Now is the time for what David called the "evening sacrifice," or Daniel called the "evening oblation."

Oh! what a chariot made out of evening cloud! Have you hung over the taffrail on the ocean and seen this cloudy vehicle roll over the pavements of a calm summer sea, the wheels dripping with the magnificence? Have you, from the top of Ben Lomond or the Cordilleras or the Berkshire hills, seen the day pillowed for the night, and yet had no aspiration of praise and homage? What a rich God we have, who can put on one evening sky pictures that excel Michael Angelo's "Last Judgment," and Ghirlandjo's "Adoration of the Magi," and whole galleries of Madonnas, and for only an hour, and then throw them away, and the next evening put on the same sky something that excels all that the Raphaels and the Titians and the Rembrandts and the Corregios and the Leonardo da Vincis ever executed, and then draw a curtain of mist over them, never again to be exhibited! How rich God must be to have a new chariot of clouds every evening!

But the Bible tells us that our King also has his black chariot. "Clouds and darkness," we are told, "are round about him." That chariot is cloven out of night, and that night is trouble. When he rides forth in that black chariot, pestilence and earthquake and famine and hurricane and woe attend him. Then let the earth tremble. Then let nations pray. Again and again he has ridden forth, in that chariot of black clouds, across England and France and Italy and Russia and America, and over all nations. That which men took for the sound of cannonading at Sebastopol, at Sedan, at Gettysburg, at Tel-el-Kebir, at Bunker Hill, was only the rumblings of the black chariot of storm-cloud armed with thunderbolts, and neither man nor angel nor devil nor earth nor hell nor heaven can resist him. On those boulevards of blue, this chariot never turns aside for anything. No one else drives there. Under one wheel of that chariot, Babylon was crushed, and Baalbec fell dead, and the Roman Empire was prostrated, and Atlantis—a whole continent that once connected Europe with America—

sank clear out of sight, so that the longest anchor of ocean steamer cannot touch the top of its highest mountains. The throne of the Cæsars was less than a pebble under the right wheel of this chariot, and the Austrian despotism less than a snowflake under the left wheel. And over destroyed worlds on worlds, that chariot has rolled without a jar or jolt. This black chariot of war-cloud rolled up to the northwest of Europe in 1812, and four hundred thousand men marched to take Moscow; but that chariot of clouds rolled back, and only twenty-five thousand out of the four hundred thousand troops lived to return. No great snowstorm like that ever before or since visited Russia.

The chariot of the Lord is irresistible. There is only one thing that can halt or turn any of his chariots, and that is prayer. Again and again it has stopped it, wheeled it around, and the chariot of black clouds, under that sanctified human breath, has blossomed into such brightness and color that men and angels had to veil their faces from its brightness. Mark you, the ancient chariot which David uses as a symbol in my text, had only two wheels, and that was that they might turn quickly, two wheels taking less than half the time to turn that four wheels would have taken. And our Lord's chariot has only two wheels, and that means instant reversal and instant help and instant deliverance. While the combined forces of the universe in battle array could not stop his black chariot a second, or diverge it an inch, the driver of that chariot says: "Call upon me in the day of trouble, and I will deliver thee." "While they are yet speaking, I will hear." Two-wheeled chariot, one wheel justice and the other wheel mercy. Ay, they are swift wheels. A cloud—whether it belongs to the cirrus, the clouds that float the highest; or belongs to the stratus, the central ranges; or to the cumulus, the lowest ranges— seems to move slowly along the sky if it moves at all. But many of the clouds go at such a speed that a vestibule, limited, lightning express-train would seem lethargic, so swift is the chariot of our God; yea, swifter than the storm, swifter than the light. Yet a child ten years old has been known to reach up, and with the hand of prayer take the courser of that chariot by the bit and slow it up or stop it or turn it aside or turn it back. The boy Samuel stopped it. Elijah stopped it; Hezekiah stopped it; Daniel stopped it; Joshua stopped it; Esther stopped it; Ruth stopped it; Hannah stopped it; Mary stopped it; my father stopped it; my mother stopped it; my sister stopped it; and we have have in our Sabbath Schools children who again and again and again have stopped it.

Notice that these old-time chariots, which my text uses for symbol, had what we would call a high dash- board at the front, but were open behind. And the king would stand at the dash-board and drive with his own hands. And I am glad that he, whose chariot the clouds are, drives himself. He does not let fate drive, for fate is merciless. But our Father King drives himself, and he puts his loving hand on the reins of the flying coursers, and he has a loving ear open to the cry of all who want to catch his attention. Oh! I am so glad that my Father drives, and never drives too fast, and never drives too slow, and never drives off the precipice; and that he controls, by a bit that never breaks, the wildest and most raging cir- cumstances. I heard of a ship-captain who put out with his vessel with a large number of passengers from Buffalo, on Lake Erie, very early in the season and while there was much ice. When they were well out, the captain saw, to his horror, that the ice was closing in on him upon all sides, and he saw no way out from destruction and death. He called into the cabin the passengers, and all the crew that could be spared from their posts, and told them that the ship must be lost unless God interposed, and although he was not a Christian man, he said: "Let us pray," and they all knelt, asking God to come for their deliverance. They went back to the deck, and the man at the wheel shouted: "All right, Cap'n, it's blowing nor' by nor'west now." While the prayer was going on in the cabin the wind changed and blew the ice out of the way. The mate asked: "Shall I put on more sail, Cap'n?" "No!" responded the captain. "Don't touch her. Some one else is managing this ship." Oh, men and women, shut in on all sides by icy troubles and misfortunes, in earnest prayer put all your affairs in the hands of God. You will come out all right. Some one else is managing the ship!

It did not merely happen so that when Leyden was besieged, and the Duke of Alva felt sure of his triumph, that suddenly the wind turned, and the swollen waters compelled him to stop the siege, and the city was saved. God that night drove along the coast of the Netherlands in a black chariot of storm-cloud. It did not merely happen so that Luther rose from the place where he was sitting just in time to escape from being crushed by a stone that the instant after fell on the very spot. Had he not escaped where would have been the Reformation? It did not merely happen so that, when George Washington was in Brooklyn, N. Y., a great fog settled down over all the place where my church once stood, and over all that end of Long Island, and that under that fog he and his army escaped from the clutches of Generals Howe and Clinton. In a chariot of mist and cloud the God of American Independence rode along that place. What solace in a theme like this. It is a sedative, a tonic, a stimulus.

On that pillow of consolation I put down my head to sleep at night. On that solid foundation I build when I see this nation in political paroxysm every four years, not because they care two cents about whether it is a high tariff or low tariff or no tariff at all, but only whether the Democrats or the Republicans shall have the salaried offices. When European nations are holding their breath, wondering whether Russia or Germany will launch a war that will incarnadine a continent, I fall back on the faith that my Father drives. Yea, I cast this as an anchor, and plant this as a column of strength, and lift this as a telescope, and build this as a fortress, and propose without any perturbation to launch upon an unknown future, triumphant in the fact that my Father drives. Yes, he drives very near. I know that many of the clouds you see in summer are far off, the bases of some of them five miles above the earth. High on the highest peaks of the Andes, travelers have seen clouds far higher than where they were standing. Gay Lussac, after he had risen in a balloon twenty-three thousand feet, saw clouds above him. But there are clouds that touch the earth and discharge their rain; and, though the clouds out of which God's chariot is made may sometimes be far away, often they are close by, and they touch our shoulders, and they touch our homes, and they touch us all over. I have read of two rides that the Lord took in two different chariots of clouds, and of another that he will take. One day, in a chariot of clouds that were a mingling of fog and smoke and fire, God drove down to the top of a terrible crag fifteen hundred feet high, now called Jebel-Musa, then called Mount Sinai, and he stepped out of his chariot among the split shelvings of rock. The mountain shook as with an ague, and there were ten volleys of thunder, each of the ten emphasizing a tremendous "Thou shalt," or "Thou shalt not." Then the Lord resumed his chariot of cloud and drove up the hills of heaven. They were dark and portentous clouds that made that chariot at the giving of the law. But one day he took another ride, and this time down to Mount Tabor; the clouds out of which his chariot was made, bright clouds, roseate clouds, illumined clouds; and music rained from all of them, and the music was a mingling of carol and chant and triumphal march: "This is my beloved Son, in whom I am well pleased." Transfiguration chariot!

"Oh," say hundreds of you, "I wish I could have seen those chariots—the black one that brought the Lord to Jebel-Musa, at the giving of the law, and the white one that brought him down to Tabor!" Never mind, you will see something grander than that, and it will be a mightier mingling of the sombre and the radiant, and the pomp of it will be such that the chariots in which Trajan and Diocletian and Zenobia and Cæsar and Alexander and all the conquerors of all ages rode, will be unworthy of mention; and what stirs me the most is, that when he comes in that chariot of cloud and goes back, he will ask you and me to ride with him both ways. How do I know that the judgment chariot will be made out of clouds? Revelation 1: 7: "Behold he cometh with clouds." Oh, he will not then ride through the heavens alone as he does now. He is going to bring along with him escort of ten full regiments. Inspiration says: "Behold the Lord cometh with ten thousand of his saints." But these figures simply mean that there will be a great throng. And as we shall probably, through the atonement of Christ, be in heaven before that, I hope that we can come down in that escort of chariot. Christ in the centre chariot, but chariots before him to clear the way and chariots behind him and chariots on either side of him. Perhaps the prophets and patriarchs of the old dispensation may ride ahead, each one charioted—Abraham and Moses and Ezekiel and David and Joshua, who foretold his first coming. On either side of the central chariot, apostles and martyrs, who, in the same or approximate centuries, suffered for him—Paul, Stephen and Ignatius and Polycarp and Justin Martyr, and multitudes who went up in chariot of fire, now coming in chariot of cloud, while in the rear of the central chariot shall be the multitudes of later days and of our own time, who have tried to serve the Lord—ourselves, I hope, among them. "Behold the Lord cometh, with ten thousand of his saints."

Yes; although all unworthy of such companionship, we want to come with him on that day to see the last of this old world which was once our residence. Coming through the skies, myriads of chariots rolling on and rolling down. By that time how changed this world will be! Its deserts all flowers, its rocks all mossed and lichened, its poorhouses all palaces, its sorrows all joys, its sins all virtues; and in the same pasture-field, lion and calf; and on the same perch, hawk and dove. Now the chariots of cloud strike the earth, filling all the valleys and covering all the mountain-sides, and halting in all the cemeteries and graveyards, and over the waters deep, where the dead sleep in coral sarcophagus. A loud blast of the Resurrection trumpet is given and the bodies of the dead rise and join the spirits from which they have long been separated. Then Christ our king, rising in the centre chariot of cloud, with his scarred hands waves the signal, and the chariots wheel and come into line for glorious ascent. Drive on! Drive up! Chariots of

Equipage of Cloud

cloud ahead of the king, chariots of cloud on either side of the king, chariots of cloud following the king. Upward and a-past starry hosts, and through immensities, and across infinitudes, higher, higher, higher! unto the gates, the shining gates. Lift up your heads, ye Everlasting Gates! For him who maketh the clouds his chariot, and who, through condescending, and uplifting grace, invites us to mount and ride with him!

PAGEANTRY OF THE WOODS

Isaiah, 64: 6: "We all do fade as a leaf."

PAGEANTRY OF THE WOODS

Isaiah, 64: 6: "We all do fade as a leaf."

It is so hard for us to understand religious truth that God constantly reiterates. As the schoolmaster takes a blackboard, and puts upon it figures and diagrams, so that the scholar may not only get his lesson through the ear, but also through the eye, so God takes all the truths of his Bible, and draws them out in diagram on the natural world. Champollion, the famous Frenchman, went down into Egypt to study hieroglyphics on monuments and temples. After much labor he deciphered them, and announced to the learned world the result of his investigations. The wisdom, goodness, and power of God are written in hieroglyphics all over the earth and all over the heaven. God grant that we may have understanding enough to decipher them! There are Scriptural passages, like my text, which need to be studied in the very presence of the natural world. Habakkuk says, "Thou makest my feet like hinds' feet," a passage which means nothing save to the man that knows that the feet of the red deer, or hind, are peculiarly constructed, so that they can walk among slippery rocks without falling. Knowing that fact, we understand that, when Habakkuk says, "Thou makest my feet like hinds' feet," he sets forth that the Christian can walk amid the most dangerous and slippery places without falling.

Those know but little of the meaning of the natural world, who have looked at it through the eyes of others, and from book or canvas taken their impression. There are some faces so mobile that photographers cannot take them; and the face of Nature has such a flush and sparkle and life that no human description can gather them. No one knows the pathos of a bird's voice unless he sometime sat at summer evening-tide at the edge of a wood, and listened to the cry of the whip-poor-will. This accounts for the fact that nearly all the real poets of the world were born in the country.

There is to-day more glory in one branch of sumach than a painter could put on a whole forest of maples. God hath struck into the autumnal leaf a glance that none see but those who come face to face —the mountain looking upon the man, and the man looking upon the mountain.

For several autumns I have made a tour to the Far West, and one autumn I saw that which I shall never forget. I have seen the autumnal sketches of Cropsey and other skilful painters, but that week I saw a pageant two thousand miles long. Let artists stand back when God stretches his canvas! A grander spectacle was never kindled before mortal eyes. Along by the rivers, and up and down the sides of the great hills, and by the banks of the lakes, there was an indescribable mingling of gold and orange and crimson and saffron, now sobering into drab and maroon, now flaming into solferino and scarlet. Here and there the trees looked as if just their tips had blossomed into fire. In the morning light the forests seemed as if they had been transfigured, and in the evening hour they looked as if the sunset had burst and dropped upon the leaves. In more sequestered spots, where the frosts had been hindered in their work, we saw the first kindling of the flames of color in a lowly sprig; then they rushed up from branch to branch, until the glory of the Lord submerged the forest. Here you would find a tree just making up its mind to change, and there one looked as if, wounded at every pore, it stood bathed in carnage. Along the banks of Lake Huron, there were hills over which there seemed pouring cataracts of fire, tossed up and down, and every whither by the rocks. Through some of the ravines we saw occasionally a foaming stream, as though it were rushing to put out the conflagration. If at one end of the woods, a commanding tree would set up its crimson banner, the whole forest prepared to follow. If God's urn of colors were not infinite, one swamp that I saw along the Maumee would have exhausted it forever. It seemed as if the sea of divine glory had dashed its surf to the tiptop of the Alleghanies, and then it had come dripping down to lowest leaf and deepest cavern.

Most persons preaching from this text find only in it a vein of sadness. I find that I have two strings to this Gospel harp, a string of sadness and a string of joy infinite. "We all do fade as a leaf."

First, like the foliage, we fade gradually. The leaves which have already felt the frost, day by day, change in tint, yet for many days cling to the bough, waiting for the fist of the wind to strike them. Suppose you that the pictured leaf which you hold in your hand took on color in an hour or in a day or in a week? No. Deeper and deeper the flush, till all the veins of its life now seem opened and bleeding away. After a while, leaf after leaf, they fall. Now those on the outer branches, then those most hidden, until the last spark of the gleaming forge shall have been quenched.

So gradually we pass away. From day to day we hardly see the change. But the frosts have touched us. The work of decay is going on. Now a slight cold; now a season of over-fatigue; now a fever; now a stitch in the side; now a neuralgic thrust; now a rheumatic twinge; now a fall. Little by little; pain by pain; less steady of limb; sight not so clear; ear not so alert. After a while we take staff; then, after much resistance, we come to spectacles. Instead of bounding into the vehicle, we are willing to be helped in. At last the octogenarian falls. Forty years of decaying. No sudden change; no fierce cannonading of the batteries of life; but a fading away—slowly—gradually. As the leaf! As the leaf!

Again, like the leaf we fade, to make room for others. Next year's forests will be as grandly foliaged as this. There are other generations of oak leaves to take the place of those which this autumn perish. Next May, the cradle of the wind will rock the young buds. The woods will be all a-hum with the chorus of leafy voices. If the tree in front of your house, like Elijah, takes a chariot of fire, its mantle will fall upon Elisha. If, in the blast of the autumnal batteries, so many ranks fall, there are reserve forces to take their place to defend the fortress of the hills. The beaters of gold leaf will have more gold leaf to beat. The crown that drops to-day from the head of the oak will be picked up and handed down for other kings to wear. Let the blasts come. They only make room for other life.

So, when we go, others take our spheres. We do not grudge the future generations their places. We will have had our good time. Let them come on and have their good time. There is no sighing among these leaves to-day, because other leaves are to follow them. After a lifetime of preaching, doctoring, selling, sewing, or digging, let us cheerfully give way for those who come on to do the preaching, doctoring, selling, sewing, and digging. God grant that their life may be brighter than ours has been! As we get older, do not let us be affronted if young men and women crowd us a little. We will have had our day and we must let them have theirs. When our voices get cracked, let us not snarl at those who can warble. When our knees are stiffened, let us have patience with those who go fleet as the deer. Because our leaf is fading, do not let us despise the unfrosted. Autumn must not envy the spring; old men must be patient with the boys. Dr. Guthrie stood up in Scotland and said, "You need not think I am old because my hair is white; I never was so young as I am now." I look back to my childhood days, and remember when, in winter nights, in the sitting-room, the children played, the blithest and the gayest of all the company were father and mother. Although reaching fourscore years of age, they never got old.

Do not be disturbed as you see good and great men die. People worry when some important personage passes off the stage, and say, "His place will never be filled." But neither the Church nor the State will suffer for it. There will be others to take their places. When God takes one man away, he has another right back of him. God is so rich in resources that he could spare five thousand Summerfields and Saurins, if there were so many. There will be other leaves as green, as exquisitely veined, as gracefully etched, as well-pointed. However prominent the place we fill, our death will not jar the world. One falling leaf does not shake the Adirondacks. A ship is not well manned unless there be an extra supply of hands—some working on deck; some sound asleep in their hammocks. God has manned this world very well. There will be other seamen on deck when you and I are down in the cabin, sound asleep in the hammocks.

Sermons by T. DeWitt Talmage

Again, as with the leaves, we fade and fall amid myriads of others. One cannot count the number of plumes which the frosts pluck from the hills. They strew all the streams; they drift into caverns; they soften the wild beast's lair, and fill the eagle's eyrie. All the aisles of the forest will be covered with their carpet, and the steps of the hills glow with a wealth of color and shape that will defy the looms of Axminster. What urn could hold the ashes of all these dead leaves? Who could count the hosts that burn on this funeral pyre of the mountains?

So we die in concert. The clock that strikes the hour of our going will sound the going of many thousands. Keeping step with the feet of those who carry us out, will be the tramp of hundreds doing the same errand. Between fifty and seventy people every day lie down in Greenwood cemetery. That place has over two hundred thousand of the dead. I said to the man at the gate, "Then if there are so many here, you must have the largest cemetery." He said there were two Catholic cemeteries in Brooklyn, each of which had more than this. We are all dying. London and Pekin are not the great cities of the world. The grave is the great city. It hath mightier population, longer streets, brighter lights, thicker darknesses. Cæsar is there, and all his subjects; Nero is there, and all his victims. City of kings and paupers! It has swallowed up in its immigration Thebes and Tyre and Babylon, and will yet swallow all our cities. Great City of Silence. No voice; no hoof; no wheel; no clash; no smiting of hammer; no clack of flying loom; no jar; no whisper. Great City of Silence! Of all its million million hands, not one of them is lifted; of all its million million eyes, not one of them sparkles; of all its million million hearts, not one pulsates. The living are in the small minority.

Pageantry of the Woods

If, in the movement of time, some great question between the living and the dead should be put, and God called up all the dead and the living to decide it, as we lifted our hands, and from all the resting-places of the dead they lifted their hands, the dead would outvote us. Why, the multitude of the dying and the dead are as the autumnal leaves drifting under our feet. We march on toward eternity, not by companies of a hundred, or regiments of a thousand, or brigades of ten thousand, but sixteen hundred millions abreast! Marching on! Marching on!

Again, as with variety of appearance the leaves depart, so do we. You have noticed that some trees, at the first touch of the frost, lose all their beauty; they stand withered and uncomely and ragged, waiting for the northeast storm to drive their leaves into the mire. The sun shining at noonday gilds them with no beauty. Ragged leaves! Dead leaves! No one stands to study them. They are gathered in no vase; they are hung on no wall. So death smites many. There is no beauty in their departure. One sharp frost of sickness, or one blast off the cold waters, and they are gone. No tinge of hope; no prophecy of heaven. Their spring was all abloom with bright prospects; their summer thick foliaged with opportunities; but October came, and their glory went. Frosted! In early autumn the frosts come; but do not seem to damage vegetation. They are light frosts. But some morning you look out of the window and say, "There was a black frost last night," and you know that from that day everything will wither. So men seem to get along without religion, amid the annoyances and vexations of life that nip them slightly here and nip them there. But after a while death comes. It is a black frost, and all is ended. Oh, what withering and scattering death makes among those not prepared to meet it! They leave everything pleasant behind them, their house, their families, their friends, their books, their pictures, and step out of the sunshine into the shadow. They quit the presence of bird and bloom and wave, to go unbeckoned and unwelcomed. The bower in which they stood and sang and wove chaplets, and made themselves merry, has gone down under an awful equinoctial. No bell can toll one-half the dolefulness of their condition. Frosted!

But thank God that is not the way people always die. Tell me, on what day of all the year the leaves of the woodbine are as bright as they are to-day? So Christian character is never so attractive as in the dying hour. Such go into the grave, not as a dog, by frown and harsh voice, driven into a kennel; but they pass away calmly, brightly, sweetly, grandly! As the leaf! As the leaf!

Why go to the deathbed of distinguished men, when there is hardly a house on this street from which a Christian has not departed? When your baby died, there were enough angels in the room to have chanted a coronation. When your father died, you sat watching, and after awhile felt of his wrist, and then put your hand under his arm to see if there were any warmth left, and placed the mirror to the mouth to see if there were any sign of breathing; and when all was over, you thought how grandly he slept—a giant resting after a battle. Oh! there are many Christian deathbeds. The chariots of God, come to take his children home, are speeding every-whither. This one halts at the gate of the almshouse; that one at the gate of princes. The shout of captives breaking their chains comes on the mountain air. The heavens ring again and again with the coronation. The twelve gates of heaven are crowded with the ascending righteous. I see the accumulated glories of a thousand Christian death-beds—an autumnal forest illumined by an autumnal sunset! They died not in shame, but in triumph! As the leaf! As the leaf!

Lastly, as the leaves fade and fall only to rise, so do we. All this golden shower of the woods is making the ground richer, and in the juice and sap and life of the tree the leaves will come up again. Next May the south wind will blow the resurrection trumpet, and they will rise. So we fall in the dust only to rise again. "The hour is coming when all who are in their graves shall hear his voice and come forth." It would be a horrible consideration to think that our bodies were always to lie in the ground. However beautiful the flowers you plant there, we do not want to make our everlasting residence in such a place.

I have with these eyes seen so many of the glories of the natural world, that I do not want to think that when I close them in death I shall never open them again. It is sad enough to have a hand or foot amputated. In a hospital, after a soldier had had his hand taken off, he said, "Good-by, dear old hand, you have done me a great deal of good service," and burst into tears. It is a more awful thing to think of having the whole body amputated from the soul forever. I must have my body again, to see with, to hear with, to walk with. With this hand I must clasp the hand of my loved ones when I have passed clean over Jordan, and with it wave the triumphs of my King. Aha! we shall rise again—we shall rise again. As the leaf! As the leaf!

Crossing the Atlantic, the ship may founder, and our bodies be eaten by the sharks; but God tameth leviathan, and we shall come again. In awful explosion of factory boiler our bodies may be shattered into a hundred fragments in the air; but God watches the disaster, and we shall come again. He will drag the deep, and ransack the tomb, and upturn the wilderness, and torture the mountain, but he will find us, and fetch us out and up to judgment and to victory. We shall come up with perfect eye, with perfect hand, with perfect foot, and with perfect body. All our weaknesses left behind.

We fall, but we rise; we die, but we live again! We moulder away, but we come to higher unfolding! As the leaf! As the leaf!

THE GARDENS OF THE SEA

Jonah, 2: 5: "The weeds were wrapped about my head."

THE GARDENS OF THE SEA

Jonah, 2: 5: " The weeds were wrapped about my head."

In all our theological seminaries, where we make ministers, there ought to be professors to give lessons in Natural History. Physical Science ought to be taught side by side with Revelation. It is the same God who inspires the page of the natural world as the page of the Scriptural world. What a freshening up it would be to our sermons to press into them even a fragment of Mediterranean seaweed. We should have fewer sermons awfully dry if we imitated our blessed Lord; and in our discourses, like him, we would let a lily bloom, or a crow fly, or a hen brood her chickens, or a crystal of salt flash out the preservative qualities of religion. The trouble is that in many of our theological seminaries men who are so dry themselves they never could get people to come and hear them preach, are now trying to teach young men how to preach, and the student is put between two great presses of dogmatic theology and squeezed until there is no life left in him. Give the poor victim at least one lesson on the Botany of the Bible.

That was an awful plunge that the recreant prophet Jonah made when, dropped over the gunwale of the Mediterranean ship, he sank many fathoms down into a tempestuous sea. Both before and after the monster of the deep swallowed him, he was entangled in seaweed. The jungles of the deep threw their cordage of vegetation around him. Some of this seaweed was anchored to the bottom of the watery abysm, and some of it was afloat and swallowed by the great sea-monster, so that, while the prophet was at the bottom of the deep after he was horribly imprisoned, he could exclaim, and did exclaim in the words of my text: "The weeds were wrapped about my head." Jonah was the first to record that there are growths upon the bottom of the sea, as well as upon land. The first picture I ever owned was a handful of seaweed pressed on a page, and I called them "The Shorn Locks of Neptune." These products of the deep, whether brown or green or yellow or purple or red or inter-shot of many colors, are most fascinating. They are distributed all over the depths, and from Arctic to Antarctic. That God thinks well of them, I conclude from the fact that he has made six thousand species of them. Sometimes these water-plants are four hundred or seven hundred feet long, and they cable the sea. One specimen has a growth of fifteen hundred feet. On the northwest shore of our country is a seaweed with leaves thirty or forty feet long, amid which the sea-otter makes his home, resting himself on the buoyancy of the leaf and stem. The thickest jungles of the tropics are not more full of vegetation than the depths of the sea. There are forests down there and vast prairies all abloom, and God walks there as he walked in the Garden of Eden "in the cool of the day." What entrancement, this sub-aqueous world! Oh, the God-given wonders of the seaweed! Its birthplace is a palace of crystal. The cradle that rocks it is the storm. Its grave is a sarcophagus of beryl and sapphire. There is no night down there. There are creatures of God on the bottom of the sea so constructed that, strewn all along, they make a firmament besprent with stars, constellations and galaxies of imposing lustre. The sea-feather is a lamplighter; the gymnotus is an electrician, and he is surcharged with electricity, and makes the deep bright with the lightning of the sea; the gorgona flashes like jewels. There are sea anemones ablaze with light; there is the star-fish and the moon-fish, so called because they so powerfully suggest stellar and lunar illumination. Oh! these midnight lanterns of the ocean caverns; these processions of flame over the white floor of the deep; these illuminations three miles down under the sea; these gorgeously upholstered castles of the Almighty in the under-world! The author of the text felt the pull of the hidden vegetation of the Mediterranean, whether or not he appreciated its beauty, as he cries out: "The weeds were wrapped about my head."

Let my subject cheer all those who had friends who have been buried at sea or in our great American lakes. Which of us brought up on the Atlantic coast has not had kindred or friend thus sepulchred? We had the useless horror of thinking that they were denied proper resting-place. We said: "Oh, if they had lived to come ashore, and had then expired! What an alleviation of our trouble it would have been to put them in some beautiful family plot, where we could have planted flowers and trees over them." Why, God did better for them than we could have done for them. They were let down into beautiful gardens. Before they had reached the bottom they had garlands about their brow. In more elaborate and adorned place than we could have afforded them, they were put away for the last slumber. Hear it, mothers and fathers of sailor boys, whose ship went down in hurricane! There are no Greenwoods or Laurel Hills or Mount Auburns so beautiful on the land as there are banked and terraced and scooped and hung in the depths of the sea. The bodies of our foundered and sunken friends are girdled and canopied and housed with such glories as attend no other necropolis. They were swamped in life-boats, or they struck on Goodwin Sands or Deal Beach or the Skerries, and were never heard of, or disappeared with the *City of Boston* or the *Ville de Havre* or the *Cymbria*, or were run down in a fishing-smack that put out from Newfoundland. But dismiss your previous gloom about the horrors of ocean entombment.

When Sebastopol was besieged in the Crimean war, Prince Mentschikoff, commanding the Russian navy, saw that the only way to keep the English out of the harbor was to sink all of the Russian ships of war in the roadstead, and so one hundred vessels sank. When, after the war was over, our American engineer, Gowan, descended to the depths in a diving-bell, it was an impressive spectacle. One hundred buried ships! But it is that way nearly all across the Atlantic Ocean. Ships sunk not by command of admirals, but by the command of cyclones. But they all had sublime burial, and the surroundings amid which they sleep the last sleep are more imposing than the Taj Mahal, the mausoleum with walls encrusted with precious stones, and built by the Great Mogul of India over his Empress. Your departed ones were buried in the Gardens of the Sea, fenced off by hedges of coralline.

The greatest obsequies ever known on the land were those of Moses, where no one but God was present. The sublime report of that entombment is in the Book of Deuteronomy, which says that the Lord buried him, and of those who have gone down to slumber in the deep the same may be said—"The Lord buried them." As Christ was buried in a garden, so your shipwrecked friends, and those who could not survive till they reached port, were put down amid iridescence—"In the midst of the garden

The Gardens of the Sea

there was a sepulchre." It has always been a mystery what was the particular mode by which George G. Cookman, the pulpit orator of the Methodist Church and the Chaplain of the American Congress, left this life after embarking for England on the steamship *President*, March 11, 1841. That ship never arrived in port. No one ever signaled her, and on both sides of the ocean it has for fifty years been questioned what became of her. But this I know about Cookman, that whether it was an iceberg, or conflagration mid-sea, or collision, he had more garlands on his ocean tomb than if, expiring on land, each of his million friends had put a bouquet on his casket. In the midst of the garden was his sepulchre.

But that brings me to notice the misnomer in this Jonahitic expression of the text. The prophet not only made a mistake by trying to go to Tarshish when God told him to go to Nineveh, but he made a mistake when he styled as weeds these growths that enwrapped him on the day he sank. A weed is something that is useless. It is something you throw out from the garden. It is something that chokes the wheat. It is something to be grubbed out from among the cotton. It is something unsightly to the eye. It is an invader of the vegetable or floral world. But this growth that sprang up from the depth of the Mediterranean, or floated on its surface, was among the most beautiful things that God ever makes. It was a water-plant known as the red-colored Alga, and no weed at all. It comes from the loom of infinite beauty. It is planted by heavenly love. It is the star of a sunken firmament. It is a lamp which the Lord kindled. It is a cord by which to bind whole sheaves of practical suggestion. It is a poem all of whose cantos are sung by divine goodness. Yet we all make the mistake that Jonah made in regard to it, and call it a weed. "The weeds were wrapped about my head." Ah! that is the trouble on the land as on the sea. We call those weeds that are flowers.

Pitched up on the beach of society are children without home, without opportunity for anything but sin, seemingly without God. They are washed up helpless. They are called ragamuffins. They are spoken of as the rakings of the world. They are waifs. They are street Arabs. They are flotsam and jetsam of the social sea. They are something to be left alone, or something to be trod on, or something to give up to decay. Nothing but weeds. They are up the rickety stairs of that garret. They are down in the cellar of that tenement house. They swelter in summers when they see not a blade of green grass, and shiver in winters that allow them not one warm coat or shawl or shoe. Such, a city missionary found in one of our New York city rookeries, and when the poor woman was asked if she sent her children to school, she replied: "No, sir, I never did send 'em to school. I know it, they ought to learn, but I couldn't. I try to shame him sometimes (it is my husband, sir), but he drinks and then beats me—look at that bruise on my face—and I tell him to see what is comin' to his children. There's Peggy, goes sellin' fruit every night in those cellars in Water Street, and they're hells, sir. She's learning all sorts of bad words there, and don't get back till twelve o'clock at night. If it wasn't for her earnin' a shillin' or two in them places, I should starve. Oh, I wish they was out of the city. Yes, it is the truth; I would rather have all my children dead than in the street, but I can't help it." Another one of those poor women, found by a reformatory association, recited her story of want and woe, and looked up and said: "I felt so hard to lose the children when they died, but now I'm glad they're gone."

The Gardens of the Sea

Ask any one of a thousand such children on the streets: "Where do you live?" and they will answer: "I don't live nowhere." They will sleep to-night in ash-barrels, or under outdoor stairs, or on the wharf, kicked and bruised and hungry. Who cares for them? Once in a while a city missionary or a tract distributor or a teacher of ragged schools will rescue one of them, but for most people they are only weeds. Yet, Jonah did not more completely misrepresent the red algæ about his head in the Mediterranean than most people misjudge these poor and forlorn and dying children of the street. They are not weeds. They are immortal flowers. Down in the deep sea of woe, but flowers. When society and the Church of God come to appreciate their eternal value, there will be more C. L. Braces and more Van Meters and more Angels of Mercy spending their fortunes and their lives in the rescue. Hear it, oh, ye philanthropic and Christian and merciful souls; not weeds, but flowers. I adjure you as the friends of all newsboys' lodging houses, of all industrial schools, of all homes for friendless girls, and for the many reformatories and humane associations now on foot. How much they have already accomplished. Out of what wretchedness, into what good homes. Of twenty thousand of these picked up out of the streets and sent into country homes, only twelve children turned out badly. In the last thirty years an army of the vagrants that no man can number have been lifted into respectability and usefulness and a Christian life. Many of them have homes of their own. Though ragged boys once and street girls, now at the head of prosperous families, honored on earth and to be glorious in heaven. Some of them have been governors of States. Some of them are ministers of the Gospel. In all departments of life those who were thought to be weeds have turned out to be flowers. One of those rescued lads from the streets of our cities wrote to another, saying: "I have heard you are studying for the ministry; so am I."

I implead you for the newsboys of the streets, many of them the brightest children of the city, but no chance. Do not step on their bare feet. Do not, when they steal a ride, cut behind. When the paper is two cents, once in a while give them a five-cent piece, and tell them to keep the change. I like the ring of the letter the newsboy sent back from Indiana, where he had been sent to a good home, to a New York newsboys' lodging house: "Boys, we should show ourselves that we are no fools, that we can become as respectable as any of the countrymen, for Franklin and Webster and Clay were poor boys once, and even George Law and Vanderbilt and Astor. And now, boys, stand up, and let them see you have got the real stuff in you. Come out here and make respectable and honorable men, so they can say: 'There, that boy was once a newsboy.'" My hearers, join the Christian philanthropists who are changing organ-grinders and bootblacks and newsboys and street Arabs and cigar girls into those who shall be kings and queens unto God forever. It is high time that Jonah finds out that that which is about him is not weeds, but flowers.

As I examine this red alga which was about the recreant prophet down in the Mediterranean depths, when, in the words of my text, he cried out: "The weeds were wrapped about my head," and I am led thereby to further examine this submarine world, I am compelled to exclaim, what a wonderful God we have! I am glad that, by diving-bell and "Brooks' Deep-Sea Sounding Apparatus" and ever improving machinery, we are permitted to walk the floor of the

The Gardens of the Sea

ocean and report the wonders wrought by the great God. Study these gardens of the sea. Easier and easier shall the profounds of the ocean become to us, and more and more its opulence of color and plant unroll especially as "Villeroy's Submarine Boat" has been constructed making it possible to navigate under the sea almost as well as on the surface of the sea, and unless God in his mercy banishes war from the earth, whole fleets of armed ships will yet far down under the water move on to blow up the argosies that float the surface. May such submarine ships be used for laying open the wonders of God's workings in the great deep and never for human devastation! Oh, the marvels of the water-world! These so-called seaweeds are the pasture fields and the forage of the innumerable animals of the deep. Not one species of them can be spared from the economy of nature.

Valleys and mountains and plants miles underneath the waves are all covered with flora and fauna. Sunken Alps and Apennines and Himalayas of Atlantic and Pacific oceans. A continent that once connected Europe and America, so that in the ages past men came on foot across from where England is to where we now stand, all sunken, and now covered with the growths of the land. England and Ireland once all one piece of land, but now much of it so far sunken as to make a channel, and Ireland has become an island. The islands, for the most part, are only the foreheads of sunken continents. The sea conquering the land all along the coasts, and crumbling the hemispheres, wider and wider become the subaqueous dominions. Thank God that skilled hydrographers have made us maps and charts of the rivers and lakes and seas, and shown us something of the work of the Eternal God in the water-worlds. Thank God that the great Virginian, Lieutenant Maury, lived to give

Sermons by T. DeWitt Talmage.

us "The Physical Geography of the Sea," and that men of genius have gone forth to study the so-called weeds that wrapped about Jonah's head and have found them to be coronals of beauty, and when the tide receded, these scientists have waded down and picked up divinely pictured leaves of the ocean, the naturalists, Pike and Hooper and Walters, gathering them from the beach of Long Island Sound, and Dr. Blodgett preserving them from the shores of Key West, and Professors Emerson and Gray finding them along Boston Harbor, and Professor Gibbs gathering them from Charleston Harbor, and for all the other triumphs **of algology, or** the science of seaweed. Why confine ourselves to the old and hackneyed illustrations of the wonder-workings of God, when there are at least five great seas full of illustrations as yet not marshaled, every root and frond and cell and color and movement and habit of oceanic vegetation crying out: "God! God! He made us. He clothed us. He adorned us. He was the God of our ancestors clear back to the first sea-growth, when God divided the waters which were above the firmament from the waters which were under the firmament, and shall be the God of our descendants clear down to the day when the sea shall give up its dead. We have heard his command and we have obeyed: 'Praise the Lord, dragons and all deeps.'"

There is a great comfort that rolls over upon us from this study of the so-called seaweed, and that is the demonstrated doctrine of a particular Providence. When I find that the Lord provides in the so-called seaweed the pasturage for the thronged marine world, so that not a fin or scale in all that oceanic aquarium suffers need, I conclude he will feed us, and if he suits the algæ to the animal life of the deep, he will provide the food for our physical and spiritual needs. And if

The Gardens of the Sea

he clothes the flowers of the deep with richness of robe that looks bright as fallen rainbows by day, and at night makes the underworld look as though the sea were on fire, surely he will clothe you: " O, ye of little faith!" And what fills me with unspeakable delight is that this God of depths and heights, of ocean and of continent, may, through Jesus Christ, the divinely appointed means, be yours and mine, to help, to cheer, to pardon, to save, to emparadise. What matters who in earth or hell is against us, if he is for us? Omnipotence to defend us, Omnipresence to companion us, and Infinite love to enfold and uplift and enrapture us. And when God does small things so well, seemingly taking as much care with the coil of a seaweed as the out-branching of a Lebanon cedar, and with the color of a vegetable growth which is hidden fathoms out of sight as he does with the solferino and purple of a summer sunset, we will be determined to do well all we are called to do, though no one see or appreciate us. Mighty God! Roll in upon our admiration and holy appreciation more of the wonders of this submarine world.

My joy is that after we are quit of all earthly hindrances we may come back to this world and explore what we cannot now fully investigate. If we shall have power to soar into the atmospheric without fatigue I think we shall have power to dive into the aqueous without peril, and that the pictured and tessellated sea-floor will be as accessible as now is to the traveler the floor of the Alhambra; and all the gardens of the deep will then swing open to us their gates as now to the tourist Chatsworth opens on public days its cascades and statuary and conservatories for our entrance. "It doth not yet appear what we shall be." You cannot make me believe that God hath spread out all that garniture of the deep merely for the polyps and crustacea to look at.

And if the unintelligent creatures of the Mediterranean and the Atlantic Ocean, he surrounds with such beautiful grasses of the deep, what a heaven we may expect for our uplifted and ransomed souls when we are unchained of the flesh and rise to realms beatific. Of the flora of that "Sea of glass mingled with fire," I have no power to speak, but I shall always be glad that, when the prophet of the text, flung over the gunwale of the Mediterranean ship, descended into the boiling sea, that which he supposed to be weeds wrapped about his head were not weeds but flowers. And am I not right in this glance at the Botany of the Bible in adding to Luke's mint, anise and cummin, and Matthew's tares, and John's vine, and Solomon's cluster of camphire, and Jeremiah's balm, and Job's bulrush, and Isaiah's terebinth, and Hosea's thistle, and Ezekiel's cedar, and "the hyssop that springeth out of the wall," and the "Rose of Sharon and the Lily of the Valley," and the frankincense and myrrh and cassia which the astrologers brought to the manger, at least one stalk of the Algæ of the Mediterranean? And now I make the marine doxology of David my peroration, for it was written about forty or fifty miles from the place where the scene of the text was enacted. "The sea is his and he made it! and his hands formed the dry land. Oh, come, let us worship and bow down; let us kneel before the Lord our Maker. For he is our God, and we are the people of his pasture." Amen.

SONG OF BIRDS

Psalm, 104: 12: " By them shall the fowls of the heaven have their habitation, which sing among the branches."

SONG OF BIRDS

Psalm, 104: 12: " By them shall the fowls of the heaven have their habitation, which sing among the branches."

There is an important and improving subject to which most people have given no thought, and concerning which pulpits rarely make allusion, namely, the Song of Birds. If all that has been written concerning music by human voice or about music sounded on instrument by finger or breath were put together, volume by the side of volume, it would fill a hundred alcoves of the national libraries. But about the song of birds there is as much silence as though, a thousand years ago, the last lark had, with his wing, swept the door-latch of heaven, and as though never a whip-poor-will had sung its lullaby to a slumbering forest at nightfall. We give a passing smile to the call of a bobolink or the chirp of a canary, but about the origin, about the fibre, about the meaning, about the mirth, about the pathos, about the inspiration, about the religion in the song of birds, the most of us are either ignorant or indifferent. A caveat I this morning file in the High Court of Heaven against that almost universal irreligion. We ought to realize that the first Bible that God ever wrote, and long before the Old Testament and the New Testament, was the Book of Nature.

First, I remark that which will surprise many, that the song of birds is a regulated and systematic song, capable of being written out in note and staff and bar and clef, as much as anything that Wagner or Schumann or Handel ever put on paper. As we pass the grove where the flocks are holding matin or vesper service, we are apt to think that the sounds are extemporized, the rising or falling tone is a mere accident, it is flung up and down by haphazard, the bird did not know what it was doing, it did not care whether it was a long metre psalm or a madrigal. What a mistake! The musician never put on the music rack before him Mendelssohn's "Elijah" or Beethoven's "Concerto in G" or Spohr's "B flat Symphony" with more definite idea as to what he was doing than every bird that can sing at all confines himself to accurate and predetermined rendering. The oratorios, the chants, the carols, the overtures, the interludes, the ballads, the canticles, that this morning were heard or will this evening be heard in the forest, have rolled down through the ages without a variation. Even the chipmunk's song was ordained clear back in the eternities. At the gates of Paradise it sang in sounds like the syllables "Kuk! Kuk! Kuk!" just as this morning in a Long Island orchard it sang "Kuk! Kuk! Kuk!" The thrush at the creation uttered sounds like the words "Teacher! Teacher! Teacher!" as now it utters sounds like "Teacher! Teacher! Teacher!" In the summer of the year one, the yellow-hammer trilled that which sounded like the words "If! If! If!" as in this summer it trills "If! If! If!" The Maryland yellow-throat inherits and bequeaths the tune sounding like the words "Pity me! Pity me! Pity me!" The white sparrow's "Tseep, tseep" woke our great-grandfathers as it will awaken our great-grandchildren. The "Tee-ka-tee-ka-tee-ka" of the birds in the first century was the same as the "Tee-ka-tee-ka-tee-ka" of the nineteenth century.

The goldfiinch has for six thousand years been singing "De-ree-dee-ee-ree." But these sounds, which we put in harsh words, they put in cadences rhythmic, soulful and enrapturing. Now, if there is this order and systematization and rhythm all through God's creation, does it not imply that we should have the same characteristics in the music we make or try to make? Is it not a wickedness that so many parents give no opportunity for the culture of their children in the art of sweet sound? If God stoops to educate every bluebird, oriole and grosbeak in song, how can parents be so indifferent about the musical development of the immortals in their household? While God will accept our attempts to sing, though it be only a hum or a drone, if we can do no better, what a shame that, in this last decade of the nineteenth century, when so many orchestral batons are waving and so many academies of music are in full concert and so many skilled men and women are waiting to offer instruction, there are so many people who cannot sing with any confidence in the house of God, because they have had no culture in this sacred art, or, while they are able to sing a fantasia at a piano amid the fluttering fans of social admirers, nevertheless feel utterly helpless when, in church, the surges of an Ariel or an Antioch roll over them. The old-fashioned country singing school, now much derided and caricatured (and indeed sometimes it was diverted from the real design into the culture of the soft emotions rather than the voice), nevertheless did admirable work, and in our churches we need singing schools to prepare our Sabbath audiences for prompt and spontaneous and multipotent psalmody. This world needs to be stormed with hallelujahs. We want a hemispheric campaign of hosannahs. From hearing a blind beggar sing, Martin Luther went home at forty years of age to write his first hymn. If the church of God universal is going to take this world for righteousness, there must be added a hundredfold more harmony, as well as a hundredfold more volume to sacred music.

Further, I notice in the song of birds that it is a divinely-taught song. The rarest prima donna of all the earth could not teach the robin one musical note. A kingfisher, flying over the roof of a temple a-quake with harmonies, would not catch up one melody. From the time that the first bird's throat was fashioned on the banks of the Gihon and Hiddekel until to-day on the Hudson or Rhine, the winged creature has learned nothing from the human race in the way of carol or anthem. The feathered songsters learned all their music direct from God. He gave them the art in a nest of straw or moss or sticks, and taught them how to lift that song into the higher heavens and sprinkle the earth with its dulcet enchantments. God-fashioned, God-tuned, God-launched, God-lifted music! And there is a kind of music that the Lord only can impart to you, my hearer. There have been depraved, reprobate and blasphemous souls which could sing till great auditoriums were in raptures. There have been soloists and bassos and barytones and sopranos whose brilliancy in concert halls has not been more famous than their debaucheries. But there is a kind of song which, like the song of birds, is divinely fashioned. Songs of pardon; songs of divine comfort; songs of worship; "songs in the night," like those which David and Job mentioned; songs full of faith and tenderness and prayer, like those which the Christian mother sings over the sick cradle; songs of a broken heart being healed; songs of the dying flashed upon by opening portals of amethyst; songs like that which Paul commended to the Colossians when he said, "Admonish one another in psalms and hymns and spiritual songs, singing, with grace in your

Song of Birds

hearts, to the Lord"; songs like Moses sang after the tragedy of the Red Sea; songs like Deborah and Barak sang at the overthrow of Sisera; songs like Isaiah heard the redeemed sing as they came to Zion. O God, teach us that kind of song which thou only canst teach, and help us to sing it on earth and sing it in heaven. It was the highest result of sweet sound when under the playing of Paganini one auditor exclaimed reverently, "O God!" and another sobbed out, "O Christ!"

Further, I remark in regard to the song of birds, that it is trustful, and without any fear of what may yet come. Will you tell me how it is possible for that wren, that sparrow, that chickadee to sing so sweetly, when they may any time be pounced on by a hawk and torn wing from wing? There are cruel beaks in thicket and in sky ready to slay the song birds. Herods on the wing. Modocs of the sky. Assassins armed with iron claw. Murderers of song floating up and down the heavens. How can the birds sing amid such perils? Beside that, how is the bird sure to get its food? Millions of birds have been starved. Yet it sings in the dawn without any certainty of breakfast or dinner or supper. Would it not be better to gather its food for the day before vocalizing? Beside that, the hunters are abroad. Bang! goes a gun in one direction. Bang! goes a gun in another direction. The song will attract the shot and add to the peril. Beside that, yonder is a thundercloud, and there may be hurricane and hail to be let loose, and what then will become of you, the poor warbler? Beside that, winter will come, and it may be smitten down before it gets to the tropics. Have you never seen the snow strewn with the birds belated in their migration? The titmouse mingles its voice with the snowstorms as Emerson describes the little thing he found in tempestuous January:

> Here was this atom in full breath
> Hurling defiance at vast death;
> This scrap of valor just for play
> Fronts the north wind in waistcoat gray.

For every bird, a thousand perils and disasters hovering and sweeping round and round. Yet, there it sings, and it is a trustful song. The bird that has it the hardest, sings the sweetest. The lark, from the shape of her claws, may not perch on a tree. In the grass her nest is exposed to every hoof that passes. One of the poorest shelters of all the earth is the lark's nest. If she sing at all, you will expect her to render the saddest of threnodies. No, no! She sings exultingly an hour without a pause and mounting three thousand feet without losing a note. Would God we all might learn the lesson. Whatever perils, whatever bereavements, whatever trials are yet to come; sing, sing with all your heart and sing with all your lungs. If you wait until all the hawks of trouble have folded their wings and all the hunters of hate have unloaded their guns and all the hurricanes of disaster have spent their fury, you will never sing at all. David, the pursued of Absalom, and the betrayed of Ahithophel, and the depleted of "sores that ran in the night," presents us the best songs of the Bible. John Milton, not able to see his hand before his face, sings for us the most famous poem of all literature, and some of the most cheerful people I have ever met have been Christian people under physical, or domestic, or public torment. The songs of Charles Wesley, which we now calmly sing in church, were composed by him between mobs.

Further, in the sky-galleries there are songs adapted to all moods. The meadow-lark is mournful and the goldfinch joyous and the grosbeak prolonged of note. But the libretto of nature is voluminous. Are you sad? you can hear from the bowers the echo of your grief. Are you glad? you can hear an echo of your happiness. Are you thoughtful? you can hear that which will plunge you into deeper profound. Are you weary? you may catch a restful air. So the songs of birds are administrative in all circumstances. And we do well to have a hymnology for all changes of condition. You may sing your woes into peace and rouse your joys into greater altitudes. Upon every condition of body and soul, let us try the power of song. The multitudinous utterances of grove and orchard and garden and forest suggest most delightful possibilities.

Further, I notice that the song of birds is a family song. Even those of the feathered throngs which have no song at all make what utterances they do in sounds of their own family of birds. The hoot of the owl, the clatter of the magpie, the crow of the chanticleer, the drumming of the grouse, the laugh of the loon in the Adirondacks, the cackle of the hen, the scream of the eagle, the croak of the raven, are sounds belonging to each particular family; but when you come to those which have real songs, how suggestive that it is always a family song. All the skylarks, all the nightingales, all the goldfinches, all the blackbirds, all the cuckoos, prefer the song of their own family and never sing anything else. So the most deeply impressive songs we ever sing are family songs. They have come down from generation to generation. You were sung to sleep in your infancy and childhood by songs that will sing in your soul forever. Where was it, my brother or sister, that you heard the family song—on the banks of the Ohio or the

Alabama or the Androscoggin or the Connecticut or the Tweed or the Thames or the Danube? That song at eventide, when you were tired out—indeed, too tired to sleep, and you cried with leg-ache, and you were rocked and sung to sleep—you hear it now, the soft voice from sweet lips, she as tired, perhaps, more tired than you, but she rocked and you slumbered. Oh, those family songs! The songs that father sang, that mother sang. They roll on us to-day with a reminiscence that fills the throat, as well as the heart, with emotion. In our house, in my childhood, it was always a religious song; I do not think that the old folks knew anything but religious songs; at any rate, I never heard them sing anything else. It was "Jesus, Lover of My Soul," or "Rock of Ages," or "There is a Fountain Filled with Blood," or "Mary to the Saviour's Tomb." Mothers, be careful what you sing your children to sleep with. Let it be nothing frivolous or silly. Better have in it something of Christ and Heaven; better have in it something that will help that boy thirty years from now to bear up under the bombardment of temptation; better have in it something that will help that daughter thirty years from now when upon her come the cares of motherhood and the agonies of bereavement and the brutal treatment of one who swore before high heaven that he would cherish and protect. Do not waste the best hour for making an impression upon your little one, the hour of dusk, the beach between the day and the night.

Sing not a doleful song, but a suggestive song, a Christian song, a song you will not be ashamed to meet when it comes to you in the eternal destiny of your son and daughter. The oriole has a loud song and the chewink a long song and the bluebird a short song, but it is always a family song; and let your

Song of Birds

gloaming song to your children, whether loud or long or short, be a Christian song. These family songs are about all we keep of the old homestead. The house where you were born will go into the hands of strangers. The garments that were carefully kept as relics will become moth-eaten. The family Bible can go into the possession of only one of the family. The lock of gray hair may be lost from the locket, and in a few years all signs and mementoes of the old homestead will be gone forever. But the family songs, those that we heard at two years of age, at five years of age, at ten years of age, will be indestructible, and at forty or fifty or sixty or seventy years of age will give us a mighty boost over some rough place in the path of our pilgrimage. Many years ago a group of white children were captured and carried off by the Indians. Years after a mother, who had lost two children in that capture, went among the Indians, and there were many white children in line, but so long a time had passed, the mother could not tell which were hers, until she began to sing the old nursery songs, and her two children immediately rushed up, shouting "Mamma!" "Mamma!" Yes, there is an immortality in a nursery song. Hear it, all you mothers, an immortality of power to rescue and save. What an occasion that must have been in this city, December 17, 1850, when Jenny Lind sang "Home, Sweet Home," the author of those words, John Howard Payne, seated before her. She had rendered her other favorite songs, "Casta Diva," and her "Flute Song," with fine effect, but when she struck "Home, Sweet Home," John Howard Payne rose under the power, and President Fillmore and Henry Clay and Daniel Webster, and the whole audience rose with him. Anything connected with home ransacks our entire nature with a holy power, and songs that get well started in the nursery, or by the family hearth, roll on after the lips that sung them are forever silent and the ears that first heard them forever cease to hear.

I preach this sermon just before many of you will go out to pass days or weeks in the country. Be careful how you treat the birds. Remember they are God's favorites, and if you offend them, you offend him. He is so fond of their voices that there are forests where for a hundred miles no human foot has ever trod and no human ear has ever listened. Those interminable forests are concert halls with only one auditor—the Lord God Almighty. He builded those auditoriums of leaves and sky, and supports all that infinite minstrelsy for himself alone. Be careful how you treat his favorite choir. In Deuteronomy, he warns the people: "If a bird's nest chance to be before thee in the way in any tree, or on the ground, whether they be young ones or eggs, thou shalt not take the dam with the young, that it may be well with thee, and that thou mayest prolong thy days." So you see your own longevity is related to your treatment of birds. Then go forth and attend the minstrelsy. Put off startling colors, which frighten the winged songsters into silence or flight, and move noiselessly into the woods, further and further from the main road, and have no conversation, for many a concert in and out of doors has been ruined by persistent talkers, and then sit down on a mossy bank:

> Where a wild stream with headlong shock
> Comes brawling down a bed of rock."

And after perhaps a half an hour of intense solitude there will be a tap of a beak on a tree branch far up, sounding like the tap of a musical baton, and then first there will be a solo, followed by a duet or quartet, and afterward by doxologies in all the tree tops and amid all the branches, and if you have a Bible along with you, and you can, without rustling the leaves, turn to the 148th Psalm of David, and read: "Praise the Lord, beasts, and all cattle, creeping things and flying fowl," and then turn over quietly to my text, and read: "By them shall the fowls of the heaven have their habitation, which sing among the branches;" or, if under the power of the bird voices you are transported, as when Dr. Worgan played so powerfully on the organ at St. John's that Richard Cecil said he was in such blessed bewilderment he could not find in his Bible the first chapter of Isaiah, though he turned the leaves of the book over and over, and you shall be so overcome with forest harmony that you cannot find the Psalms of David, never mind, for God will speak to you so mightily it will make no difference whether you hear his voice from the printed page or the vibrating throat of one of his plumed creatures.

While this summer more than usual out of doors, let us have what my text suggests, an out-of-doors religion. What business had David, with all the advantages of costly religious service, and smoking incense on the altar, to be listening to the chantresses among the tree branches? Ah! he wanted to make himself and all who should come after him more alert and more worshipful amid the sweet sounds and beautiful sights of the natural world. There is an old church that needs to be re-dedicated. It is older than St. Paul's or St. Peter's or St. Mark's or St. Sophia's or St. Isaac's. It is the cathedral of Nature. That is the church in which the services of the millennium will be held. The buildings fashioned out of stone and brick and mortar will not hold the people. Again the Mount of Olives will be the pulpit; again the Jordan will be the baptistry; again the mountains will be the galleries; again the skies will be the blue ceiling; again the sunrise will be the front door and the sunset the back door of that temple; again the clouds will be the upholstery and the morning mist the incense; again the trees will be the organ-loft where "the fowls of heaven have their habitation which sing among the branches."

St. Francis d' Assisi preached a sermon to birds and pronounced a benediction upon them, but all birds preach to us, and their benediction is almost supernal. While, this summer, amid the works of God, let us learn responsiveness. Surely, if we cannot sing, we can hum a tune; and if we cannot hum a tune, we can whistle. If we cannot be an oriole, we can be a quail. In some way let us demonstrate our gratitude to God. Let us not be beaten by the chimney swallow and the humming bird and the brown thresher. Let us try to set everything in our life to music, and if we cannot give the carol of the song sparrow, take the plaint of the hermit thrush. Let our life be an anthem of worship to the God who created us and the Christ who ransomed us and the Holy Ghost who sanctifies us. And our last song! May it be our best song! The swan was thought by the ancients never to sing except when dying. In the time of Edward IV no one was allowed to own a swan except he were a king's son, or had considerable estate. Through one or two hundred years of life that bird was said never to utter anything like music, until its last moment came, and, then, lifting its crested beauty, it would pour forth a song of almost matchless thrill, resounding through the groves. And so, although the struggle of life may be too much for us, and we may find it hard to sing at all, when the last hour comes to you and me, may there be a radiance from above and a glory settling round that shall enable us to utter a song on the

Song of Birds

wings of which we will shall mount to where the music never ceases and the raptures never die.

What is that mother? The swan, my love;
He is floating down from his native grove.
No loved one, no nestling nigh;
He is floating down by himself to die.
Death darkens his eye and unplumes his wings,
Yet the sweetest song is the last he sings.
Live so, my child, that when death shall come,
Swan-like and sweet, it may waft thee home!

CHANT AT THE CORNER-STONE

Job, 38: 6, 7: " Who laid the corner-stone thereof, when the
morning stars sang together? "

CHANT AT THE CORNER-STONE

Job, 38: 6, 7: " Who laid the corner-stone thereof, when the morning stars sang together? "

We have all seen the ceremony at the laying of the corner-stone of church, asylum or Masonic temple. Into the hollow of the stone were placed scrolls of history and important documents, to be suggestive if, one or two hundred years after, the building should be destroyed by fire or torn down. We remember the silver trowel or iron hammer that smote the square piece of granite into sanctity. We remember some venerable man who presided, wielding the trowel or hammer. We remember also the music as the choir stood on the scattered stones and timber of the building about to be constructed. The leaves of the note-books fluttered in the wind, and were turned over with a great rustling, and we remember how the bass, bary-tone, tenor, contralto and soprano voices commingled. They had for many days been rehearsing the special programme that it might be worthy of the corner-stone laying. The music at the laying of corner-stones is always impressive.

In my text God, addressing the poet of Uz. calls us to a grander ceremony—the laying of the founda-tion of this great temple of a world. The corner-stone was a block of light and the trowel was of celestial crystal. All about and on the embankments of cloud stood the angelic choristers unrolling the r librettos of overture, and other worlds clapped shining cymbals while the ceremony went on, and God, the architect, by stroke of light after stroke of light, dedicated this great cathedral of a world, with mountains for pillars, and sky for frescoed ceiling, and flowering fields for floor, and sunrise and midnight aurora for upholstery. "Who laid the corner-stone thereof, when the morning stars sang together?"

The fact is that the whole universe was a complete cadence, an unbroken dithyramb, a musical portfolio. The great sheet of immensity had been spread out, and written on it were the stars, the smaller of them minims, the larger of them sustained notes. The meteors marked the staccato passages, the whole heavens a gamut with all sounds, intonations and modulations; the space between the worlds a musical interval, trembling of stellar light a quaver, the thunder a base clef, the wind among trees a treble clef. That is the way God made all things a perfect harmony.

But one day a harp-string snapped in the great orchestra. One day a voice sounded out of tune. One day a discord, harsh and terrific, grated upon the glorious antiphone. It was sin that made the dissonance, and that harsh discord has been sounding through the centuries. All the work of Christians and philanthropists and reformers of all ages is to stop that discord and get all things back into the perfect harmony which was heard at the laying of the corner-stone when the morning stars sang together. Before I get through, if I am divinely helped, I will make it plain that sin is discord and righteousness is harmony. That things in general are out f tune is as plain as to a musician's ear is the unhappy clash of clarionet and bassoon in an orchestral rendering. The world's health out of tune: weak lung and the atmosphere in collision, disordered eye and noonday light in quarrel, rheumatic limb and damp weather in struggle, neuralgias and pneumonias and consumptions and epilepsies in flocks swoop upon neighborhoods and cities. Where you find one person with sound throat and keen eyesight and alert ear and easy respiration and regular pulsation and supple limb and prime digestion and steady nerves, you find a hundred who have to be very careful because this or that or the other physical function is disordered. The human intellect out of tune: the judgment wrongly swerved or the memory leaky or the will weak or the temper inflammable and the well-balanced mind exceptional. Domestic life out of tune: only here and there a conjugal outbreak of incompatibility of temper through the divorce courts, or a filial outbreak about a father's will through the surrogate's court, or a case of wife-beating or husband-poisoning through the criminal courts, but thousands of families with June outside and January within. Society out of tune: labor and capital, their hands on each other's throat. Spirit of caste keeping those down in the social scale in a struggle to get up, and putting those who are up in anxiety lest they have to come down. No wonder the old pianoforte of society is all out of tune, when hypocrisy and lying and subterfuge and double dealing and sycophancy and charlatanism and revenge have all through the ages been banging away at the keys and stamping the pedals.

On all sides there is a perpetual shipwreck of harmonies. Nations in discord without realizing it, so antipathetic is the feeling of nation for nation, that symbols chosen are fierce and destructive. In this country, where our skies are full of robins and doves and morning larks, we have for our national symbol, the fierce and filthy eagle, as immoral a bird as can be found in all the ornithological catalogues. In Great Britain, where they have lambs and fallow deer, their symbol is the merciless lion. In Russia, where from between her frozen North and blooming South all kindly beasts dwell, they chose the growling bear; and in the world's heraldry a favorite figure is the dragon, which is a winged serpent, ferocious and dreadful. And so fond is the world of contention, that we climb out through the heavens and baptize one of the other planets with the spirit of battle and call it Mars, after the god of war, and we give to the eighth sign of the zodiac the name of the scorpion, a creature which is chiefly celebrated for its deadly sting. But, after all, these symbols are expressive of the way nation feels toward nation. Discord wide as the continent and bridging the seas.

I suppose you have noticed how warmly in love dry-goods stores are with other dry-goods stores, and how highly grocerymen think of the sugars of the grocerymen on the same block. And in what a eulogistic way allopathic and homeopathic doctors speak of each other, and how ministers will sometimes put ministers on that beautiful cooking instrument which the English call a spit, an iron roller with spikes on it, and turned by a crank before a hot fire, and then if the minister who is being roasted cries out against it, the men who are turning him say: "Hush, brother, we are turning this spit for the glory of God and the good of your soul, and you must be quiet, while we close the service with:

> Blest be the tie that binds
> Our hearts in Christian love.

The earth is diametered and circumferenced with discord, and the music that was rendered at the laying of the world's corner-stone, when the morning stars sang together, is not heard now; and though here and there, from this and that part of society, and from this and that part of the earth, there comes up a thrilling solo of love, or a warble of worship, or a sweet duet of patience, they are drowned out by a discord that shakes the earth.

Paul says: "The whole creation groaneth," and while the nightingale and the woodlark and the canary and the plover sometimes sing so sweetly that their notes have been written out in musical notation, and it is found that the cuckoo sings in the key of D, and that the cormorant is a basso in the winged choir, yet sportsmen's gun and the autumnal blast often leave them ruffled and bleeding or dead in meadow or forest. Paul was right, for the groan in nature drowns out the prima-donnas of the sky.

Tartini, the great musical composer, dreamed one night that he made a contract with Satan, the latter to be ever in the composer's service. He thought in his dream that he handed to Satan a violin, on which Diabolus played such sweet music that the composer was awakened by the emotion and tried to reproduce the sounds, and therefrom was written Tartini's most famous piece, "The Devil's Sonata;" a dream ingenious but faulty, for all melody descends from heaven, and only discords ascend from hell. All hatreds, feuds, controversies, backbitings and revenges are the devil's sonata, are diabolic fugue, are demoniac phantasy, are grand march of doom, are allegro of perdition.

But if in this world things in general are out of tune to our frail ear, how much more so to ears angelic and deific. It takes a skilled artist fully to appreciate disagreement of sound. Many have no capacity to detect a defect of musical execution, and, though there were in one bar as many offenses against harmony as could crowd in between the low F of the bass and the high G of the soprano, it would give them no discomfort; while on the forehead of the educated artist beads of perspiration would stand out as a result of the harrowing dissonance. While an amateur was performing on a piano and had just struck the wrong chord, John Sebastian Bach, the immortal composer, entered the room, and the amateur rose in embarrassment, and Bach rushed past the host who stepped forward to greet him, and before the strings had stopped vibrating, put his adroit hands upon the keys and changed the painful inharmony into glorious cadence. Then Bach turned and gave salutation to the host who had invited him.

But worst of all is moral discord. If society and the world are painfully discordant to imperfect man, what must they be to a perfect God. People try to define what sin is. It seems to me that sin is getting out of harmony with God, a disagreement with his holiness, with his purity, with his love, with his commands; our will clashing with his will, the finite dashing against the infinite, the frail against the puissant, the created against the Creator. If a thousand musicians, with flute and cornet-a-piston and trumpet and violincello and hautboy and trombone and all the wind and stringed instruments that ever gathered in a Dusseldorf jubilee should resolve that they would play out of tune, and put concord on the rack, and make the place wild with shrieking and grating and rasping sounds, they could not make such a pandemonium as that which a sinful soul produces in the ears of God when he listens to the play of its thoughts, passions and emotions—discord, lifelong discord, maddening discord!

The world pays more for discord than it does for consonance. High prices have been paid for music. One man gave two hundred and twenty-five dollars to hear the Swedish songstress in New York, and another six hundred and twenty-five dollars to hear her in Boston, and another six hundred and fifty dollars to hear her in Providence. Fabulous prices have been paid for sweet sounds, but far more has been paid for discord. The Crimean war cost one billion, seven hundred million dollars, and our American civil war over nine and a half billion dollars, and our war with Spain cost us about three hundred million dollars, and the war debts of professed Christian nations are about fifteen billion dollars. The world pays for this red ticket, which admits it to the saturnalia of broken bones, and death agonies and destroyed cities and ploughed graves and crushed hearts, any amount of money Satan asks. Discord! Discord!

But I have to tell you that the song that the morning stars sang together at the laying of the world's corner-stone is to be resumed. Mozart's greatest overture was composed one night when he was several times overpowered with sleep, and artists say they can tell the places in the music where he was falling asleep, and the places where he awakened. So the overture of the morning stars, spoken of in my text, has been asleep, but it will awaken and be more grandly rendered by the evening stars of the world's existence than by the morning stars, and the vespers will be sweeter than the matins. The work of all good men and women and of all good churches and all reform associations is to bring the race back to the original harmony. The rebellious heart to be attuned, social life to be attuned, commercial ethics to be attuned, internationality to be attuned, hemispheres to be attuned.

In olden time the choristers had a tuning fork with two prongs, and they would strike it on the back of pew or music rack, and put it to the ear, and then start the tune, and all the other voices would join. In modern orchestra the leader has a perfect instrument, rightly attuned and he sounds that, and all the other performers tune the keys of their instruments to make them correspond, and sound the bow over the string and listen, and sound it out over again, until all the keys are screwed to concert pitch, and the discord melts into one great symphony, and the curtain hoists, and the baton taps, and audiences are raptured with Schumann's "Paradise and the Peri," or Rossini's "Stabat Mater," or Bach's "Magnificat" in D or Gounod's 'Redemption."

Now our world can never be attuned by an imperfect instrument. Even a Cremona would not do. Heaven has ordained the only instrument, and it is made out of the wood of the cross, and the voices that accompany it are imported voices, cantatrices of the first Christmas night, when heaven serenaded the earth with: "Glory to God in the highest and on earth peace, goodwill to men." Lest we start too far off, and get lost in generalities, we had better begin with ourselves, get our own hearts and lives in harmony with the eternal Christ. Oh, for his almighty Spirit to attune us, to chord our will and his will, to modulate our life with his life, and bring us into unison with all that is pure and self-sacrificing and heavenly. The strings of our nature are all broken and twisted, and the bow is so slack it cannot evoke anything mellifluous. The instrument made for heaven to play on has been roughly twanged and struck by influences worldly and demoniac. Oh, master hand of Christ, restore this split and fractured and despoiled and unstrung nature until first it shall wail out for our sin and then trill with divine pardon.

The whole world must also be attuned by the same power. A few days ago I was in the Fairbanks Weighing Scale Manufactory, of Vermont. Six hundred hands, and they have never made a strike. Complete harmony between labor and capital, the operatives of scores of years in their beautiful homes near-by the mansions of the manufacturers, whose invention and Christian behavior made the great enterprise. So, all the world over, labor and capital will be brought into euphony. You may have heard what is called the Anvil Chorus, composed by Verdi, a tune played by hammers, great and small, now with mighty stroke, and now with heavy stroke, beating a great iron anvil. That is what the world must come to—anvil chorus, yard-stick chorus, shuttle chorus, trowel chorus, crowbar chorus, pick-axe chorus, gold-mine chorus, railtrack chorus, locomotive chorus. It can be done, and it will be done. So all social life will be attuned by the Gospel harp. There will be as many classes in society as now, but the classes will not be regulated by birth or wealth or accident, but by the scale of virtue and benevolence, and people will be assigned to their places as good or very good or most excellent. So, also, commercial life will be attuned, and there will be twelve in every dozen, and sixteen ounces in every pound, and apples at the bottom of the barrel will be as sound as those on the top, and silk goods will not be cotton, and sellers will not have to charge honest people more than the right price because others will not pay, and goods will come to you corresponding with the sample by which you purchased them, and coffee will not be chickoried, and sugar will not be sanded, and milk will not be chalked, and adulteration of food will be a State-prison offense. Ay, all things shall be attuned. Elections in England and the United States will no more be a grand carnival of defamation and scurrility, but the elevation of righteous men in a righteous way.

In the sixteenth century the singers called the Fischer Brothers reached the lowest bass ever recorded, and the highest note ever trilled was by La Bastardella, and Catalini's voice had a compass of three and a half octaves; but Christianity is more wonderful; for it runs all up and down the greatest heights and the deepest depths of the world's necessity, and it will compass everything and bring it in accord with the song which the morning stars sang at the laying of the world's corner-stone. All the sacred music in homes, concert halls and churches tends towards this consummation. Make it more and more hearty. Sing in your families. Sing in your places of business. If we with proper spirit use these faculties, we are rehearsing for the skies.

Heaven is to have a new song, an entirely new song, but I should not wonder if as sometimes on earth a tune is fashioned out of many tunes, or it is one tune with the variations, so some of the songs of the glorified of heaven may have playing through them the songs of earth; and how thrilling, as coming through the great anthem of the saved, accompanied by the harpers with their harps and trumpeters with their trumpets, if we should hear some of the strains of Antioch and Mount Pisgah and Coronation and Lenox and St. Martin's and Fountain and Ariel and Old Hundred. How they would bring to mind the praying circles and communion days and the Christmas festivals and the church worship in which on earth we mingled! I have no idea that when we bid farewell to earth, we are to bid farewell to all these grand old Gospel hymns, which melted and raptured our souls for so many years.

Now, my friends, if sin is discord, and righteousness is harmony, let us get out of the one and enter the other. At the Washington Peace Jubilee, to commemorate the close of our war with Spain, tens of thousands of spectators viewed the festivities and listened to the splendid musical festival that followed. Twenty States participated in that great celebration. After our dreadful Civil War was over, and in the sum-

Chant at the Corner-Stone

mer of 1869, a great National Peace Jubilee was held
in Boston, and as an elder of this church had been honored by the selection of some of his music, to be rendered on that occasion, I accompanied him to the jubilee. Forty thousand people sat and stood in the great
Coliseum erected for that purpose. Thousands of wind
and stringed instruments. Twelve thousand trained
voices. The masterpieces of all ages rendered, hour
after hour, and day after day—Handel's "Judas Mac-
cabæus," Sphor's "Last Judgment," Beethoven's
"Mount of Olives," Haydn's "Creation," Mendelssohn's "Elijah," Meyerbeer's "Coronation March,"
rolling on and up in surges that billowed against the
heavens. The mighty cadences within were accompanied on the outside by the ringing of the bells of the
city and cannon on the commons, discharged by electricity, in exact time with the music, thundering their
awful bars of a harmony that astounded all nations.
Sometimes I bowed my head and wept. At other
times I stood up in the enchantment, and there were
moments when the effect was so overpowering I felt I
could not endure it. When all the voices were in full
chorus, and all the batons in full wave, and all the orchestra in full triumph, and a hundred anvils under
mighty hammers were in full clang, and all the towers
of the city rolling in their majestic sweetness, and the
whole building quaked with the boom of thirty cannon,
Parepa Rosa, with a voice that will never again be
equaled on earth until the archangelic voice proclaims
that time shall be no longer, rose above all other
sounds in her rendering of our national air, the Star
Spangled Banner. It was too much for a mortal, and
quite enough for an immortal, to hear, and while some
fainted, one womanly spirit, released under its power,
sped away to be with God.

O Lord, our God, quickly usher in the whole

world's peace jubilee, and all islands of the sea join the five continents, and all the voices and musical instruments of all nations combine, and all the organs that ever sounded requiem of sorrow sound only a grand march of joy, and all the bells that tolled for burial ring for resurrection, and all the cannon that ever hurled death across the nations sound to eternal victory, and over all the acclaim of earth and minstrelsy of heaven there will be heard one voice sweeter and mightier than any human or angelic voice, a voice once full of tears, but then full of triumph, the voice of Christ saying: "I am Alpha and Omega, the beginning and the end, the first and the last." Then, at the laying of the top-stone of the world's history, the same voices shall be heard as when at the laying of the world's corner-stone "the morning stars sang together."

VOICES OF NATURE

Isa., 60: 13: " The glory of Lebanon shall come unto thee, the fir-tree, the pine-tree, and the box together, to beautify the place of my sanctuary."

VOICES OF NATURE

Isa., 60: 13: " The glory of Lebanon shall come unto thee, the fir-tree, the pine-tree, and the box together, to beautify the place of my sanctuary."

ON our way from Damascus we saw the mountains of Lebanon white with snow, and the places from which the cedars were hewn, and then drawn by ox-teams down to the Mediterranean Sea, and then floated in great rafts to Joppa, and then again drawn by ox-teams up to Jerusalem to build Solomon's temple. Those mighty trees in my text are called the " glory of Lebanon." Inanimate nature felt the effects of the first transgression. When Eve touched the forbidden tree, it seems as if the sinful contact had smitten not only that tree, but as if the air caught the pollution from the leaves, and as if the sap had carried the virus down into the very soil until the entire earth reeked with the leprosy. Under that sinful touch nature withered. The inanimate creation, as if aware of the damage done it, sent up the thorn and briar and nettle to wound, and fiercely oppose, the human race. Now, as the physical earth felt the effects of the first transgression, so it shall also feel the effects of the Saviour's mission. As from that one tree in Paradise a blight went forth through the entire earth, so from one tree on Calvary another force shall speed out to interpenetrate and check, subdue and override, the evil. In the end it shall be found that the tree of Calvary has more potency than the tree of Paradise. As the nations are evangelized, I think a corresponding change will be effected in the natural world. I verily believe that the trees, and the birds, and the rivers, and the skies will have their millennium. If man's sin affected the ground, and the vegetation, and the atmosphere, shall Christ's work be less powerful or less extensive?

Doubtless God will take the irregularity and fierceness from the elements so as to make them congenial to the race, which will then be symmetrical and evangelized. The ground shall not be so lavish of weeds and so grudgeful of grain. Soils which now have peculiar proclivities toward certain forms of evil production will be delivered from these besetting sins. Steep mountains, ploughed down into more gradual ascents, shall be girdled with flocks of sheep and shocks of corn. The wet marsh shall become the deep-grassed meadow. Cattle shall eat unharmed by caverns once haunted of wild beasts. Children will build play houses in what was once a cave of serpents; and, as the Scripture saith, "The weaned child shall put his hand on the cockatrice's den."

Oh, what harvests shall be reaped when neither drouth, nor excessive rain, nor mildew, nor infesting insects shall arrest the growth, and the utmost capacity of the fields for production shall be tested by an intelligent and athletic yeomanry. Thrift and competency characterizing the world's inhabitants, their dwelling-places shall be graceful and healthy and adorned. Tree and arbor and grove around about will look as if Adam and Eve had got back to Paradise. Great cities, now neglected and unwashed, shall be orderly, adorned with architectural symmetry and connected with far distant seaports by present modes of transportation carried to their greatest perfection, or by new inventions yet to spring up out of the water or drop from the air at the beck of a Morse or of a Robert Fulton belonging to future generations. Isaiah

in my text seems to look forward to the future condition of the physical earth as a condition of great
beauty and excellence, and then prophesies that as the
strongest and most ornamental timber in Lebanon
was brought down to Jerusalem and constructed into
the ancient temple, so all that is beautiful and excellent
in the physical earth shall yet contribute to the Church
now being built in the world. "The glory of Lebanon
shall come unto thee; the fir-tree, the pine-tree, and
the box together, to beautify the place of my sanctuary."

Much of this prophecy has already been fulfilled, and
I proceed to some practical remarks upon the contributions which the natural world is making to the
kingdom of God, and then draw some inferences. The
first contribution that nature gives to the Church is
her testimony in behalf of the truth of Christianity.
This is an age of profound research. Nature cannot
evade men's inquiries as once. In chemist's laboratory
she is put to torture and compelled to give up her
mysteries. Hidden laws have come out of their hiding
place. The earth and the heavens, since they have
been ransacked by geologist and botanist and
astronomer, appear so different from what they once
were that they may be called "the new heavens and
the new earth." This research and discovery will have
powerful effect upon the religious world. They must
either advance or arrest Christianity, make men better
or make them worse, be the Church's honor or the
Church's overthrow. Christians, aware of this in the
early ages of discovery, were nervous and fearful as
to the progress of science. They feared that some
natural law, before unknown, would suddenly spring
into harsh collision with Christianity. Gunpowder
and the gleam of swords would not so much have
been feared by religionists as electric batteries, voltaic

piles, and astronomical apparatus. It was feared that Moses and the prophets would be run over by sceptical chemists and philosophers. Some of the followers of Aristotle, after the invention of the telescope, refused to look through that instrument, lest what they saw would overthrow the teachings of that great philosopher. But the Christian religion has no such apprehension now. Bring on your telescopes and microscopes, and spectroscopes — and the more the better. The God of nature is the God of the Bible, and in all the universe, and in all the eternities, He has never once contradicted Himself. Christian merchants endow universities, and in them Christian professors instruct the children of Christian communities. The warmest and most enthusiastic friends of Christ are bravest and most enthusiastic friends of science. The Church rejoices as much over every discovery as the world rejoices. Good men have found that there is no war between science and religion. That which at first has seemed to be the weapon of the infidel has turned out to be the weapon of the Christian.

Scientific discussions may be divided into those which are concluded, and those which are still in progress, depending for decision upon future investigation. Those which are concluded have invariably rendered their verdict for Christianity, and we have faith to believe that those which are still in prosecution will come to as favorable a conclusion. The great systems of error are falling before these discoveries. They have crushed everything but the Bible and they have reinforced Christianity. Mohammedanism and paganism in their ten thousand forms have been proved false, and by great natural laws shown to be impositions. Buried cities have been exhumed, and the truth of God found written on their coffin-lids. Bartlett, Robinson, and Layard, Piazzi

Smyth and Flinders Petric, have been not more the apostles of science than the apostles of religion. The dumb lips of the pyramids have opened to preach the gospel. Expeditions have been fitted out for Palestine, and explorers have come back to say that they have found among mountains, and among ruins, and on the shore of waters, living and undying evidences of our glorious Christianity.

Men who have gone to Palestine infidels have come back Christians. They who were blind and deaf to the truth at home have seemed to see Christ again preaching upon Olivet, and have beheld in vivid imagination the Son of God again walking the hills about Jerusalem. Caviglia once rejected the truth, but afterward said, " I came to Egypt, and the Scriptures and the pyramids converted me." When I was in Beyrout, Syria, last December, our beloved American missionary, Rev. Dr. Jessup, told me of his friend who met a sceptic at Joppa, the seaport of Jerusalem, and the unbeliever said to his friend: " I am going into the Holy Land to show up the folly of the Christian religion. I am going to visit all the so-called ' sacred places,' and write them up, and show the world that the New Testament is an imposition upon the world's credulity." Months after, Dr. Jessup's friend met the sceptic at Beyrout, after he had completed his journey through the Holy Land. " Well, how is it? " asked the aforesaid gentleman of the sceptic. The answer was: " I have seen it all, and I tell you the Bible is true! Yes, it is all true! " The man who went to destroy came back to defend. After what I myself saw during my recent absence, I conclude that anyone who can go through the Holy Land and remain an unbeliever, is either a bad man or an imbecile. God employed men to write the Bible, but He took many of the same truths which they recorded, and with His own almighty hand He gouged them into the rocks, and drove them down into dismal depths, and, as documents are put in the corner-stone of a temple, so in the very foundation of the earth He folded up and placed the records of heavenly truth. The earth's corner-stone was laid, like that of other sacred edifices, in the name of the Father, and of the Son, and of the Holy Ghost. The Author of revelation, standing among the great strata, looked upon Moses, and said, "Let us record for future ages the world's history; you write it there on papyrus; I will write it here on the boulders."

Again, nature offers an invaluable contribution to Christianity by the illustration she makes of divine truth. The inspired writers seized upon the advantages offered by the natural world. Trees and rivers and clouds and rocks broke forth into holy and enthusiastic utterances. Would Christ set forth the strength of faith, He points to the sycamore, whose roots spread out, and strike down, and clinch themselves amid great depths of earth, and He said that faith was strong enough to tear that up by the roots. At Hawarden, England, Mr. Gladstone, while showing me his trees during a prolonged walk through his magnificent park, pointed out a sycamore, and with a wave of the hand said, "In your visit to the Holy Land did you see any sycamore more impressive than that?" I confessed that I had not. Its branches were not more remarkable than its roots. It was to such a tree as that Jesus pointed when He would illustrate the power of faith. "Ye might say unto this sycamore tree, Be thou plucked up by the roots and be thou cast into the sea, and it would obey you." One reason why Christ has fascinated the world as no other teacher, is because instead of using severe argument He was always telling how something in the spiritual world was like unto something in the natural world. Oh, these wonderful "likes" of our Lord! Like a grain of mustard seed. Like a treasure hid in a field. Like a merchant seeking goodly pearls. Like unto a net that was cast into the sea. Like unto a householder. Would Christ teach the precision with which He looks after you, He says He counts the hairs of your head. Well, that is a long and tedious count if the head have the average endowment. It has been found that if the hairs of the head be black there are about one hundred and twenty thousand, or if they be flaxen there are about one hundred and forty thousand. But God knows the exact number: "The hairs of your head are all numbered." Would Christ impress us with the divine watchfulness and care, he speaks of the sparrows that were a nuisance in those times. They were caught by the thousands in the net. They were thin and scrawny, and had comparatively no meat on their bones. They seemed almost valueless, whether living or dead. Now, argues Christ, if my Father takes care of them will he not take care of you? Christ would have the Christian despondent over his slowness of religious development go to his corn-field for a lesson. He watches first the green shoot pressing up through the clods, gradually strengthening into a stalk, and last of all the husk swelling out with the pressure of the corn: "First the blade, then the ear, after that the full corn in the ear." Would David set forth the freshness and beauty of genuine Christian character — he sees an eagle starting from its nest just after the moulting season, its old feathers shed, and its wings and breast decked with new down and plumes, its body as finely feathered as that of her young ones just beginning to try the speed of their wings. Thus rejuvenated and replumed is the Christian's faith and hope, by every season of communion with God. "Thy youth is renewed like the eagle's." Would Solomon represent the annoyance of a contentious woman's tongue, he points to a leakage in the top of his house or tent, where, throughout the stormy day the water comes through, falling upon the floor — drip! drip! drip! And he says, " A continual dropping in a very rainy day and a contentious woman are alike." Would Christ set forth the character of those who make great profession of piety, but have no fruit, he compares them to barren fig-trees, which have very large and showy leaves, and nothing but leaves. Would Job illustrate deceitful friendships, he speaks of brooks in those climes, that wind about in different directions, and dry up when you want to drink out of them: " My brethren have dealt deceitfully as a brook, and as the stream of brooks they pass away." David, when he would impress us with the despondency into which he had sunk, compares it to a quagmire of those regions, through which he had doubtless sometimes tried to walk, but sunk in up to his neck, and he cried, " I sink in deep mire where there is no standing." Would Habakkuk set forth the capacity which God gives the good man to walk safely amid the wildest perils, he points to the wild animal called the hind walking over slippery rocks, and leaping from wild crag to wild crag, by the peculiar make of its hoofs able calmly to sustain itself in the most dangerous places: " The Lord God is my strength, and he will make my feet like hind's feet."

Job makes all natural objects pay tribute to the royalty of his book. As you go through some chapters of Job you feel as if it were a bright spring morning, and, as you see the glittering drops on the grass under your feet, you say with that patriarch, " Who hath begotten the drops of the dew?" And now, as you read on, you seem in the silent midnight to behold the waving of a great light upon your path, and you look up to find it the aurora borealis, which Job described so long ago as "the bright light in the clouds and the splendor that cometh out of the north." As you read on, there is darkness hurtling in the heavens, and the showers break loose till the birds fly for hiding-place and the mountain torrents in red fury foam over the rocky shelving; and with the same poet you exclaim, "Who can number the clouds in wisdom, or who can stay the bottles of heaven?" As you read on, you feel yourself coming in frosty climes, and, in fancy, wading through the snow, you say, with that same inspired writer, "Hast thou entered into the treasures of the snow?" And while the sharp sleet drives in your face, and the hail stings your cheek, you quote him again: "Hast thou seen the treasures of the hail?" In the Psalmist's writings I hear the voices of the sea: "Deep calleth unto deep;" and the roar of forests: "The Lord shaketh the wilderness of Kadesh;" and the loud peal of the black tempest: "The God of glory thundereth;" and the rustle of the long silk on the well-filled husks: "The valleys are covered with corn;" and the cry of wild beasts: "The young lions roar after their prey;" the hum of palm-trees and cedars: "The righteous shall flourish like a palm-tree, he shall grow like a cedar in Lebanon;" the sough of wings and the swirl of fins: "Dominion over the fowl of the air and the fish of the sea."

The truths of the gospel might have been presented in technical terms, and by the means of dry definitions, but under these the world would not have listened or felt. How could the safety of trusting upon Christ have been presented, were it not for the figure of a rock? How could the gladdening effect of the gospel have been set forth, had not Zacharias thought of the dawn of the morning, exclaiming, "The day-spring from on high hath visited us to give light to them that sit in darkness." How could the soul's intense longing for Christ have been presented so well as by the emblem of natural hunger and natural thirst? As the lake gathers into its bosom the shadow of hills around, and the gleam of stars above, so, in these great deeps of divine truth, all objects in nature are grandly reflected. We walk forth in the spring-time, and everything breathes of the resurrection. Bright blossom and springing grass speak to us of the coming up of those whom we have loved, when in the white robes of their joy and coronation they shall appear. And when in the autumn of the year nature preaches thousands of funeral sermons from the text, "We all do fade as a leaf," and scatters her elegies in our path, we cannot help but think of sickness and the tomb. Even winter, "being dead, yet speaketh." The world will not be argued into the right. It will be tenderly illustrated into the right. Tell them what religion is like. When the mother tried to tell her dying child what heaven was, she compared it to light. "But that hurts my eyes," said the dying girl. Then the mother compared heaven to music. "But any sound hurts me; I am so weak," said the dying child. Then she was told that heaven was like mother's arms. "Oh, take me there!" she said. "If it is like mother's arms, take me there!" The appropriate simile had been found at last.

Another contribution which the natural world is making to the kingdom of Christ, is the defense and aid which the elements are compelled to give to the Christian personally. There is no law in nature but is sworn for the Christian's defense. In Job this thought is presented as a bargain made between the inanimate creation and the righteous man: "Thou shalt be in league with the stones of the field." What a grand thought that the lightnings, and the tempests, and the hail, and the frosts, which are the enemies of unrighteousness, are all marshaled as the Christian's body-guard. They fight for him. They strike with an arm of fire, or clutch with their fingers of ice. Everlasting peace is declared between the fiercest elements of nature and the good man. They may in their fury seem to be indiscriminate, smiting down the righteous with the wicked, yet they cannot damage the Christian's soul, although they may shrivel his body. The wintry blast that howls about your dwelling, you may call your brother, and the south wind coming up on a June day by way of a flower-garden, you may call your sister. Though so mighty in circumference and diameter, the sun and the moon have a special charge concerning you. "The sun shall not smite thee by day, nor the moon by night." Elements and forces hidden in the earth are now harnessed and at work in producing for you food and clothing. Some grain-field that you never saw presented you this day with your morning meal. The great earth and the heavens are the busy loom at work for you; and shooting light, and silvery stream, and sharp lightning are only woven threads in the great loom, with God's foot on the shuttle. The same Spirit that converted your soul has also converted the elements from enmity toward you into inviolable friendship, and furthest star and deepest cavern, regions of everlasting cold as well as climes of eternal summer, all have a mission of good, direct or indirect, for your spirit.

Now I infer from this that the study of natural objects will increase our religious knowledge. If David and Job and John and Paul could not afford to let go without observation one passing cloud, or rift of snow, or spring blossom, you cannot afford to let them go without study. Men and women of God most eminent in all ages for faith and zeal, indulged in such observations — Rutherford and Thomas à Kempis and Cecil and Hannah More. That man is not worthy the name of Christian who saunters listlessly among these wonderful disclosures of divine power around, beneath, and above us, stupid and uninstructed. Such persons are not worthy to live in a desert, for that has its fountains and palm-trees; nor in regions of everlasting ice, for even there the stars kindle their lights, and auroras flash, and huge icebergs shimmer in the morning light, and God's power sits upon them as upon a great white throne. Yet there are Christians in the Church who look upon all such tendencies of mind and heart as soft sentimentalities, and because they believe this printed Revelation of God are content to be infidels in regard to all that has been written in this great Book of the universe, written in letters of stars, in paragraphs of constellations, and illustrated with sunset and thunder-cloud and spring morning.

I infer, also, the transcendent importance of Christ's religion. Nothing is so far down, and nothing is so high up, and nothing so far out, but God makes it pay tax to the Christian religion. If snow and tempest and dragon are expected to praise God, suppose you he expects no homage from your soul? When God has written his truth upon everything around you, suppose you he did not mean you to open your eyes and read it?

Finally, I learn from this subject what an honorable position the Christian occupies when nothing is so great and glorious in nature but it is made to edify, defend, and instruct him. Hold up your heads, sons and daughters of the Lord Almighty, that I may see how you bear your honors. Though now you may think yourself unbefriended, this spring's soft wind, and next summer's harvest of barley, and next autumn's glowing fruits, and next winter's storms, all seasons, all elements, zephyr and euroclydon, rose's breath and thunder-cloud, gleaming light and thick darkness, are sworn to defend you, and cohorts of angels would fly to deliver you from peril, and the great God would unsheathe his sword and arm the universe in your cause rather than that harm should touch you with one of its lightest fingers. "As the mountains around about Jerusalem, so the Lord is around about his people from this time forth for evermore."

We need more sympathy with the natural world, and then we should always have a Bible open before us, and we could take a lesson from the most fleeting circumstances, as when a storm came down upon England, Charles Wesley sat in a room watching it through an open window, and frightened by the lightning and the thunder a little bird flew in, and nestled in the bosom of the sacred poet, and as he gently stroked it and felt the wild beating of its heart, he turned to his desk and wrote that hymn which will be sung while the world lasts:

> Jesus, lover of my soul,
>   Let me to Thy bosom fly,
> While the nearer waters roll
>   While the tempest still is high:
> Hide me, O my Saviour, hide,
>   Till the storm of life be past,
> Safe into the haven guide,
>   O receive my soul at last.

THE MISSION OF THE FROST

Job, 37: 10: " By the breath of God frost is given."

THE MISSION OF THE PROS?

THE MISSION OF THE FROST

Job, 37: 10: " By the breath of God frost is given."

Nothing is more embarrassing to an organist or a pianist than to put his finger on a key of the instrument and have it make no response. Though all the other keys are in full play, that one silence spoils the music. So in the great cathedral of nature if one part fail to praise the Lord the harmony is halted and lost. While fire and hail, snow and vapor, respond to the touch of inspiration, if the frost made no utterance, the orchestral rendering would be hopelessly damaged and the harmony forever incomplete. I am more glad than I can tell that the white key of the frost sounds forth as mightily as any of the other keys, and when David touches it in the Psalm, it sounds forth the words: "He scattereth the hoar frost like ashes," and when Job touches it in my text, it resounds with the words: "By the breath of God frost is given."

As no one seems disposed to discuss the mission of frost, depending on divine help, I undertake it. This is the first Sabbath of winter. The leaves are down. The warmth has gone out of the air. The birds have made their winged march southward. The landscape has been scarred by the autumnal equinox. The huskers have rifled the corn-shocks. The night sky has shown the usual meteoric restlessness of November. Three seasons of the year are past, and the fourth and last has entered. Another element now comes in to bless and adorn and instruct the world. It is the frost. The palaces of this king are far up in the Arctic. Their walls are glittering congelation.

Sermons by T. DeWitt Talmage

Windsor Castles and Tuileries and Winter Palaces and Kenilworths and Alhambras of ice. Temples with pendant chandeliers of ice. Thrones of iceberg, on which eternal silence reigns. Theatres on whose stage eternal cold dramatizes eternal winter. Pillars of ice. Arches of ice. Crowns of ice. Chariots of ice. Sepulchres of ice. Mountains of ice. Dominions of ice. Eternal frigidity! From those hard, white, burnished portals King Frost descends, and waves his silvery sceptre over our temperate zone. You will soon hear his heel on the skating pond. You already feel his breath in the night wind. By most considered an enemy, coming here to benumb and hinder and slay, I shall show you that the frost is a friend, with benediction divinely pronounced, and charged and surcharged with lessons potent, beneficent and tremendous. The Bible seven times alludes to the frost, and we must not ignore it. "By the breath of God frost is given."

First, I think of Frost as a painter. He begins his work on the leaves and continues it on the window-panes. With palette covered with all manner of colors in his left hand, and pencil of crystal in his right hand, he sits down before humblest bush in the latter part of September, and begins the sketching of the leaves. Now he puts upon the foliage a faint pallor, and then a touch of brown, and then a hue of orange, and last a flame of fire. The beech and ash and oak are turned first into sunrises and then into sunsets of vividness and splendor. All the leaves are penciled one by one, but sometimes a whole forest in the course of a few days shows great velocity of work. Weenix, the Dutch painter, could make in a summer day three portraits of life-size, but the frost in ten days can paint ten mountains in life-size. He makes the last days of an autumnal wood the days

The Mission of the Frost

of his chiefest glory. Luxembourgs in the Adirondacks; Louvres in the Sierra Nevadas; Vaticans in the White Mountains. The work of other painters you must see in the right light to fully appreciate; but the paintings of the frost in all lights are enchanting, and from the time when the curtain of the morning lifts to the time when the curtain of the night drops. Michael Angelo put upon one ceiling his representation of the Last Judgment, but the frost represents universal conflagration upon three thousand miles of stretched-out grandeur. Leonardo da Vinci put upon a few feet of canvas our Lord's "Last Supper" for all ages to admire, but the frost puts the gleaming chalices of the imperial glories of the Last Supper of the dying year on the heights and lengths and breadths of the Alleghanies. When Titian first gazed upon a sketch of Correggio he was wrought up into such ecstasy that he cried out: "If I were not Titian I would be Corregio;" and so great and overpowering are the autumnal scenes of our American forests that one force of nature might well exclaim to another: "If I were not the sunlight I would be the frost." Rugendas, the German painter, suffering from weakness in his right hand, laboriously learned to paint with his left hand; but the frost paints with both hands, and has in them more skill than all the Rembrandts and Rubens and Wests and Poussins and Albert Durers and Paul Veroneses and Claudes gathered in one long art gallery.

But the door of that great museum of autumnal coloring is now closed for a twelvemonth, and another spectacle just as wonderful is about to open. I put you on the alert and ask you to put your children on the alert. Tired of working on the leaves, the frost will soon turn to the window-panes. You will soon waken on a cold morning and find that the windows of your home have during the night been adorned with curves, with coronets, with exquisiteness, with pomp, with almost supernatural spectacle. Then you will appreciate what my text says, as it declares, "By the breath of God frost is given." You will see on the window-pane, traced there by the frost, whole gardens of beauty: ferns, orchids, daffodils, heliotropes, china-asters, fountains, statues, hounds on the chase, roebucks plunging into the stream, battle-scenes with dying and dead, catafalques of kings, triumphal processions; and as the morning sun breaks through you will see cities on fire, and bombardment with bursting shell, and illuminations as for some great victory, coronations, and angels on the wing. All night long, while you were sleeping, the frost was working, and you ought not to let the warmth obliterate the scene until you have admired it, studied it, absorbed it, set it up in your memory for perpetual refreshment, and realized the force and magnitude and intensity of my text: " By the breath of God frost is given."

Oh, what a God we have! What resources are implied by the fact that he is able to do that by the finger of the frost fifty times in one winter and on a hundred thousand window-panes for thousands of winters! The great art galleries of Venice and Naples and Dresden are carefully guarded, and governments protect them, for, once lost, they can never be reproduced; but God sets up the Royal Galleries of the Frost, pictures such as no human art could ever produce, hundreds of thousands of them, only for four or five hours, and then rubs them out, making the place clear for a display just as magnificent the next morning. No one but a God could afford to do that. It would bankrupt everything but infinity and omnipotence.

Standing here between the closed doors of the pictured woods and the opening doors of the transfigured

The Mission of the Frost

window-glass, I want to cure my folly and your folly of longing for glorious things in the distance, while we neglect appreciation of glorious things close by. "Oh, if I could only go and see the factories of lace at Brussels," says some one. Why, within twenty feet of where you awaken some December morning, you will see richer lace interwoven for your window-panes by Divine fingers. "Oh, if I could see the factories of silk at Lyons," says some one. Why, without leaving your home, on the north side of your own house on Christmas morning you may see where the Lord has spun silken threads about your windows this way and that. Embroideries such as no one but God can work. Alas! for this glorification of the distant and this belittling of the close-by! This crossing of oceans and paying a high admission in expenses to look at that which is not half as well done as something we can see by crossing our own room, and free of charge. This praising of Raphaels hundreds of years gone, when the greater Raphael, the Frost, will soon be busy at the entrances to your own home.

Next I speak of the frost as a physician. Standing at the gates of New York harbor, autumn before last, the frost drove back the cholera, saying, "Thus far shalt thou come and no farther." From Memphis and New Orleans and Jacksonville, he smote the fever plague till it reeled back and departed. The frost is a physician that doctors cities, nations and continents. He medicines the world. Quinine for malaria, antifebrile for typhoids, sulphonal for sleeplessness, antispasmodic for disturbed nerves; but in all therapeutics there is no remedy like the small pellets prepared by the cold, and no physician so skilful or so mighty as the frost. Scotland has had great physicians, but her greatest doctors have been the Abernethies and Abercrombies that have come down over the Highlands horsed on the north wind. England has had her great physicians, but her greatest doctors have been the Andrew Clarkes and the Mackenzies who appeared the first night the fields of England were rimed with white. America has had its great physicians, but her greatest doctors have been the Willard Parkers and Valentine Motts who landed from bleak skies while our fingers were benumbed and our ears tingled with the cold. Oh, it is high time that you add another line to your liturgy. It is high time that you make an addendum to your prayers. It is high time that you enlarge the catalogue of your blessings. Thank God for frost! It is the best of all germicides. It is a factor in bacteriology. It is the medicament of continents. It is the salvation of our temperate zone. It is the best tonic that God ever gave the human race. It is the only strong stimulant which has no reaction. The best commentary on it I had while walking out one cool morning with my brother John, who spent the most of his life as a missionary in China, and in that part of it where there are no frosts. He said there was a tingling gladness in his nerves indescribable, and an almost intoxication of delight from the fact that it was the first time for years he had felt the sensation of frost. We complain of it, we scold it, we frown upon it, when we ought to be stirred by it to gratitude, and hoist it on a doxology.

But I must go further and speak of the frost as a jeweler. As the snow is frozen rain, so the frost is frozen dew. God transforms it from a liquid into a crystal. It is the dew glorified. In the thirty-eighth chapter of that inspired drama, the book of Job, God says to the inspired dramatist, with ecstatic interrogation: "The hoary frost of heaven, who hath gendered it?" God there asks Job if he knows the parentage of the frost. He inquires about its pedigree. He

The Mission of the Frost

suggests that Job study up the frost's genealogical line. A minute before God had asked about the parentage of a rain-drop in words that have already given me a suggestive text for a sermon: "Hath the rain a father?" But now the Lord Almighty is catechising Job about the frost. He practically says: "Do you know its father? Do you know its mother? In what cradle of the leaves did the wind rock it? 'The hoary frost of heaven, who hath gendered it?'" He is a stupid Christian who thinks so much of the printed and bound Bible that he neglects the Old Testament of the fields and does not read the wisdom and kindness and beauty of God written in blossoms on the orchard, in sparkles on the lake, in stars in the sky, in frost on the meadows. The greatest jeweler of all the earth is the frost. There is nothing more wonderful in all crystallography. Some morning in December a whole continent is found besprent with diamonds, the result of one night's work by this jeweler. Do you make the depreciatory remark that the frost is impermanent and will last only two or three hours? What of that? We go into London Tower and look at the crown jewels of England, but we are in a procession that the guards keep moving on, and five minutes or less are your only opportunity of looking at those crown jewels; but at the crown jewels bestarred of the frost in parks and fields, you may stand to look deliberately and for hours, and no one to tell you to move on.

Oh, these regalias and diadems of beauty flung out of heaven! Kings and queens on celebrative days have come riding through the streets, throwing handfuls of silver and gold among the people; but the Queen of the Winter Morning is the only queen rich enough to throw pearls, and the King of Frost the only king rich enough to throw opals and sapphires and diamonds. Homer describes a necklace of amber given to Penelope; but the frost necklaces a continent. The carcanet of precious stones given to Harmonia had pinions of orange jasper and white moonstone and Indian agate, but it brought misfortune to any one who owned or inherited it, and its history, generation after generation, was a history of disaster; but the regalia of frost is the good fortune of every morning that owns it. The imperial household of Louis XVI could not afford the diamond necklace which had been ordered for Queen Marie Antoinette, and it was stolen and taken apart and lost; but the necklace that the frost puts on the wintry morning, though made of as many brilliants as the withered grass blades, is easily afforded by divine opulence, and is never lost, but after its use in the coronation of the fields is taken back to heaven. O men and women, accustomed to go into ecstasy when in foreign travel you come upon the historical gems of nations, whether the jewel be called "The Mountain of Glory" or the "Sea of Light" or "The Crown of the Moon" or "The Eye of Allah" or "The Star of Sarawak" or "The Koh-i-noor," I implead you study the jewels strewn all 'round your wintry home, and realize that "By the breath of God frost is given."

But I go a step further and speak of the frost as an evangelist, and a text of Scripture is not of much use to me unless I can find the Gospel in it. The Israelites in the wilderness breakfasted on something that looked like frozen dew. The manna fell on the dew, and the dew evaporated and left a pulverized material, white, and looking like frost, but it was manna, and of that they ate. So now this morning, mixed with the frozen dew of my text, there is manna on which we may breakfast our souls. You say the frost kills. Yes, it kills some things, but we have already seen that it gives health and life to others. This Gos-

The Mission of the Frost

pel is the savor of life unto life or of death unto death. As the frost is mighty, the Gospel is mighty. As the frost descends from heaven, the Gospel descends from heaven. By the breath of God frost is given. As the frost prepares for food many things that otherwise would be inedible, so the frost of trial ripens and prepares food for the soul. In the tight grip of the frost the hard shells of walnut and chestnut and hickorynut open, and the luxuries of the woods come into our laps or upon our tables; so the frost of trial takes many a hard and prickly shell and crushes it until that which stung the soul now feeds it.

There are passages of Scripture that once were enigmas, puzzles, riddles, and impossible for you to understand; but the frosts of trouble after awhile exposed the full meaning to your soul. You said, "I do not see why David keeps rolling over in his Psalms the story of how he was pursued and persecuted." He describes himself as surrounded by bees. He says: "They compassed me about like bees; yea, they compassed me about like bees." You think what an exaggerating thing for him to exclaim, "Out of the depths of hell have I cried unto thee, O Lord." And there is so much of that style of lamentation in his writings you think he overdoes it; but after awhile the frost comes upon you in the shape of persecution, and you are pierced with this censure and wounded with that defamation and stung with some falsehood, and lies in swarms are buzzing, buzzing about your ears, and at last you understand what David meant when he said: "They compassed me about like bees; yea, they compassed me about like bees," and you go down under nervous prostration, and feel that you are as far down as David when he cried: "Out of the depths of hell." What opened all those chapters that hitherto had no appropriateness?

Frosts! For a long while the Bible seemed lop-sided and a disproportionate amount of it given up to the consolatory. Why page after page and chapter after chapter and book after book in the Bible taken up with alleviations, with pacifications, with condolences? The Book seems like an apothecary store with one-half of the shelves occupied with balsams. Why such a superfluity of balsams? But after awhile the membranous croup carries off your child, or your health gives way under the grip, or your property is swept off by a bad investment, or perhaps all three troubles come at once—bankruptcy, sickness and bereavement. Now the consolatory parts of the Bible do not seem to be disproportionate. You want something off almost all the shelves of that sacred Dispensary. What has uncovered and exposed to you the usefulness of so much of the Bible that was before hidden? The frosts have been fulfilling their mission.

Put down all the promises of the Bible on a table for study, and put on one side the table a man who has never had any trouble, or very little of it, but pile upon the table beside him all encyclopædias and all dictionaries and all archæologies and all commentaries; and on the other side of the table put a man who has had trial upon trial, disaster upon disaster, and let him begin the study of the promises without lexicon, without commentary, without any book to explain or help, and this latter man will understand far more of the height and depth and length and breadth of these promises than the learned exegete opposite almost submerged in sacred literature. The one has the advantage over the other because he has felt the Mission of the Frosts. Oh, take the consolation of this theme, ye to whom life is a struggle and a disappointment and a gauntlet and a pang. That is a beauti-

The Mission of the Frost

ful proverb among the Hebrews which says: "When the tale of bricks is doubled, then Moses comes."

Mild doses of medicine will do for mild sickness, but violent pains need strong doses, and so I stand over you and count out some drops that will alleviate your worst troubles if you will only take the medicine, and here it is: "In the world ye shall have tribulation, but be of good cheer; I have overcome the world." "Weeping may endure for a night, but joy cometh in the morning." Thank God for frosts. What helped make Milton the greatest of poets? The frost of blindness. What helped make Washington the greatest of generals? The frosts of Valley Forge. What made it appropriate for one passing John Bunyan's grave to exclaim, "Sleep on, thou prince of dreamers"? The frosts of imprisonment. The greatest college from which we can graduate is the College of Frosts. Especial trial fits for especial work. Just now watch, and you will see that trouble is preparative and educational. That is the grindstone on which battle-axes are sharpened. I have always noticed in my own case that when the Lord had some especial work for me to do, it was preceded by especial attack upon me. This is so proverbial in my own house that if for something I say or do I get poured upon me a volley of censure and anathema, my wife always asks, "I wonder what new opportunity of usefulness is about to open? Something good and grand is surely coming!"

What is true in my case is true on a larger or smaller scale in the history of every man and woman who wants to serve the Lord. Without complaint take the hard knocks. You will see after awhile though you may not appreciate it now, that by the breath of a good and loving God frost is given.

Sermons by T. DeWitt Talmage

Let the corners of your mouth so long drawn down in complaint be drawn up in smiles of content.

For many years poets and essayists have celebrated the grace and swiftness of the Arabian horse. The most wonderful exhibition of horsemanship that I ever witnessed was just outside the city of Jerusalem—an Arab steed mounted by an Arab. Do you know where these Arab horses got their fleetness and poetry of motion? Long centuries ago, Mohammed, with thirty thousand cavalry on the march, could find for them not a drop of water for three days. Coming to the top of a hill a river was in sight. With wild dash the thirty thousand horses started for the stream. A minute after an armed host was seen advancing, and at Mohammed's command one hundred bugles blew for the horses to fall in line, but all the thirty thousand continued the wild gallop to the river, except five, and they, almost dead with thirst, wheeled into line of battle. Nothing in human bravery and self-sacrifice excels that bravery and self-sacrifice of those five Arabian war-horses. Those five splendid steeds Mohammed chose for his own use, and from those five came that race of Arabian horses for ages the glory of the equestrian world. And let me say that, in this great war of truth against error, of holiness against sin, and heaven against hell, the best war horses are descended from those who, under pang and self-denial and trouble, answered the Gospel trumpet and wheeled into line. Out of great tribulation, out of great fires, out of great frosts, they came. And let me say it will not take long for God to make up to you in the next world for all you have suffered in this. As you enter heaven he may say: "Give this man one of those towered and colonnaded palaces on that ridge of gold overlooking the Sea of Glass. Give this woman a home among those amaranthine blooms and between those fountains tossing in the everlasting sunlight. Give her a couch canopied with rainbows to pay her for all the fatigues of wifehood and motherhood and housekeeping, from which she had no rest for forty years. Cup-bearers of heaven, give these newly-arrived souls from earth the costliest beverages and roll to their door the grandest chariots, and hang on their walls the sweetest harps that ever responded to fingers seraphic. Give to them rapture on rapture, celebration on celebration, jubilee on jubilee, heaven on heaven. They had a hard time on earth earning a livelihood, or nursing sick children, or waiting on querulous old age, or battling falsehoods that were told about them, or were compelled to work after they got short-breathed and rheumatic and dim-sighted. Chamberlains of heaven! Keepers of the King's robes! Banqueters of eternal royalty! Make up to them a hundredfold, a thousandfold, a millionfold for all they suffered from swaddling clothes to shroud, and let all those who, whether on the hills or in the temples or on the thrones or on jasper wall, were helped and sanctified and prepared for this heavenly realm by the Mission of the Frosts stand up and wave their sceptres!" And I looked, and behold! nine-tenths of the ransomed rose to their feet, and nine-tenths of the sceptres swayed to and fro in the light of the sun that never sets, and then I understood, far better than I ever did before, that trouble comes for beneficent purpose, and that on the coldest nights the aurora is brightest in the northern heavens, and that "By the breath of God frost is given."

ILLUMINED CLOUDS

Job, 37: 21: " And now men see not the bright light which
is in the clouds."

ILLUMINED CLOUDS

Job, 37: 21: "And now men see not the bright light which is in the clouds."

Wind east. Barometer falling. Storm-signals out. Ship reefing maintopsail. Awnings taken in. Prophecies of foul weather everywhere. The clouds congregate around the sun, proposing to abolish him. But after a while he assails the flanks of the clouds with flying artillery of light, and here and there is a sign of clearing weather. Many do not observe it. Many do not realize it. "And now men see not the bright light which is in the clouds." In other words, there are a hundred men looking for storm where there is one man looking for sunshine. My object is to get you and myself into the delightful habit of making the best of everything.

You may have wondered at the statistics showing that in India, in one year, there were over nineteen thousand people slain by wild beasts, and in another year there were in India over twenty thousand people destroyed by wild animals. But there is a monster in our own land which is year by year destroying more than that. It is the old bear of melancholy, and with Gospel weapons I propose to chase it back to its midnight caverns. I mean to do two sums — a sum in subtraction and a sum in addition — a subtraction from your days of depression and an addition to your days of joy. If God will help me I will compel you to see the bright light that there is in the clouds, and compel you to make the best of everything.

In the first place, you ought to make the very best

of all your financial misfortunes. During the panic a few years ago you all lost money. Some of you lost it in most unaccountable ways. For the question, " How many thousands of dollars shall I put aside this year? " you substituted the question, " How shall I pay my butcher, and baker, and clothier, and landlord? " You had the sensation of rowing hard with two oars, and yet all the time going down stream. You did not say much about it, because it was not politic to speak much of financial embarrassment; but your wife knew. Less variety of wardrobe, more economy at the table, self-denial in art and tapestry. Compression; retrenchment. Who did not feel the necessity of it? My friend, did you make the best of this? Are you aware of how narrow an escape you made? Suppose you had reached the fortune toward which you were rapidly going? What then? You would have been as proud as Lucifer.

How few men have succeeded largely in a financial sense and yet maintained their simplicity and religious consecration! Not one man out of a hundred. There are glorious exceptions, but the general rule is that in proportion as a man gets well off for this world he gets poorly off for the next. He loses his sense of dependence on God. He gets a distaste for prayer-meetings. With plenty of bank stocks and plenty of government securities, what does that man know of the prayer, " Give me this day my daily bread? " How few men largely successful in this world are bringing souls to Christ, or showing self-denial for others, or are eminent for piety? You can count them all upon your eight fingers and two thumbs. One of the old covetous officials, when he was sick unto death, used to have a basin filled with gold brought in, and his sole amusement and the only relief he got for his inflamed hands was running them down through the gold and turning it up in the basin. Oh, what infatuation and what destroying power money has for many a man! You were sailing at thirty knots the hour towards these vortices of worldliness — what a mercy it was, that honest business collapse! The same divine hand that crushed your storehouse, your bank, your office, your insurance company, lifted you out of destruction. The day you honestly suspended in business made your fortune for eternity.

You say, "I could get along very well myself, but I am so disappointed that I cannot leave a competence for my children." The same financial misfortune that is going to save your soul will save your children. With the anticipation of large fortune how much industry would your children have? — without which habit of industry there is no safety. The young man would say, "Well, there is no need of my working; my father will soon step out, and then I'll have just what I want." You cannot hide from him how much you are worth. You think you are hiding it; he knows all about it. He can tell you almost to a dollar. Perhaps he has been to the county office and searched the records of deeds and mortgages, and he has added it all up, and he has made an estimate of how long you will probably stay in this world, and is not as much worried about your rheumatism and shortness of breath as you are. The only fortune worth anything that you can give your child is the fortune you put in his head and heart. Of all the young men who started life with forty thousand dollars capital, how many turned out well? I do not know half a dozen. The best inheritance a young man can have is the feeling that he has to fight his own battle, and that life is a struggle in which he must throw body, mind, and soul, or be disgracefully worsted.

Where are the burial-places of the men who started life with a fortune? Some of them in the potter's field; some in the suicide's grave. But few of these men reached thirty-five years of age. They drank, they smoked, they gambled. In them the beast destroyed the man. Some of them lived long enough to get their fortunes, and went through them. The vast majority of them did not live to get their inheritance. From the gin-shop or house of infamy they were brought home to their father's house, and in delirium began to pick off loathsome reptiles from the embroidered pillow, and to fight back imaginary devils. And then they were laid out in highly upholstered parlor, the casket covered with flowers by indulgent parents — flowers suggestive of a resurrection with no hope.

As you sat this morning at your breakfast-table, and looked into the faces of your children, perhaps you said within yourself, " Poor things! How I wish I could start them in life with a competence! How I have been disappointed in all my expectations of what I would do for them!" Upon that scene of pathos I break with a pæan of congratulation, that by your financial losses your own prospect for heaven, and the prospect for heaven of your children, is mightily improved. You may have lost a toy, but you have won a palace. " How hardly shall they that have riches enter into the kingdom of God!" " It is easier for a camel to go through a needle's eye than for a rich man to enter the kingdom of heaven." What does that mean? It means that the grandest blessing God ever bestowed upon you was to take your money away from you.

Do not put much stress on the treasures of this

world. You cannot take them along with you. **At**
any rate, you cannot take them more than two **or**
three miles; you will have to leave them at the cemetery. Attila had three coffins. So fond was he of this
life, that he decreed that first he should be buried in a
coffin of gold, and that then that should be enclosed
in.a coffin of silver, and that should be enclosed in a
coffin of iron, and then a large amount of treasure
should be thrown in over his body. And so he was
buried, and the men who buried him were slain, so
that no one might know where he was buried, and no
one might there interfere with his treasures. Oh, men
of the world, who want to take your money with you,
better have three coffins!

Again, I remark, you ought to make the very best
of your bereavements. The whole tendency is to
brood over these separations, and to give much time
to the handling of mementoes of the departed, and to
make long visitations to the cemetery, and to say,
" Oh, I can never look up again; my hope is gone;
my courage is gone; my religion is gone; my faith in
God is gone! Oh, the wear and tear and exhaustion
of this loneliness!" The most frequent bereavement
is the loss of children. If your departed child had
lived as long as you have lived, do you not suppose
that he would have had about the same amount of
trouble and trial you have had? If you could make a
choice for your child between forty years of annoyance, loss, vexation, exasperation, and bereavement,
and forty years in heaven, would you take the responsibility of choosing the former? Would you snatch
away the cup of eternal bliss and put into that child's
hand the cup of many bereavements? Instead of the
complete safety into which that child has been lifted,
would you like to hold it down to the risks of this
mortal state? Would you like to keep it out on a sea

in which there have been more shipwrecks than safe voyages? Is it not a comfort to you to know that that child, instead of being besoiled and flung into the mire of sin, is swung clear into the skies? Are not those children to be congratulated that the point of celestial bliss which you expect to reach by a pilgrimage of fifty or sixty or seventy years, they reached at a flash? If the last ten thousand children who have entered heaven had gone through the average length of human life on earth, are you sure all those ten thousand children would have finally reached the blissful terminus? Besides, you are to look at this matter as a self-denial on your part for their benefit. If your children want to go off in a May-day party, if they want to go on a flowery and musical excursion, you consent. You might prefer to have them with you, but their jubilant absence satisfies you. Well, your departed children have only gone out in a May-day party, amid flowery and musical entertainment, amid joys and hilarities forever. That ought to quell some of your grief, the thought of their glee.

So it ought to be that you could make the best of all bereavements. The fact that you have so many friends in heaven will make your own departure very cheerful. When you are going on a voyage, everything depends upon where your friends are — if they are on the wharf that you leave, or on the wharf toward which you are going to sail. In other words, the more friends you have in heaven the easier it will be to get away from this world. The more friends here, the more bitter goodbyes; the more friends there, the more glorious welcomes. Some of you have so many brothers, sisters, children, friends in heaven, that I hardly know how you are going to crowd through. When a vessel came from foreign lands, and brought a prince to our harbor, the ships were covered with bunting, and you remember how the men-of-war thundered broadsides; but there was no joy there compared with the joy which shall be demonstrated when you sail up the broad bay of heavenly salutation. The more friends you have there, the easier your own transit. What is death to a mother whose children are in heaven? Why, there is no more grief in it than there is in her going into a nursery amid the romp and laughter of her household. Though all around may be dark, see you not the bright light in the clouds — that light the irradiated faces of your glorified kindred?

So also, I would have you make the best of your sickness. When you see one move off with elastic step and in full physical vigor, sometimes you become impatient with your lame foot. When a man describes an object a mile off, and you cannot see it at all, you become impatient of your dim eye. When you hear of a well man making a great achievement you become impatient with your depressed nervous system or your dilapidated health. I will tell you how you can make the worst of it. Brood over it; brood over all all these illnesses, and your nerves will become more twitchy, your dyspepsia more aggravated, and your weakness more appalling. But that is the devil's work, to tell you how to make the worst of it; it is my work to show you a bright light in the clouds.

Which of the Bible men most attract your attention? You say, Moses, Job, David, Jeremiah, Paul. Why, what a strange thing it is that you have chosen those who were physically disordered! Moses — I know he was nervous from the clip he gave the Egyptian. Job — his blood was vitiated and diseased, and his skin distressfully eruptive. David — he had a running sore which he speaks of when he says, " My sore ran in the night and ceased not." Jeremiah had enlargement of the spleen. Who can doubt it who reads Lamentations. Paul — he had a lifetime sickness which the commentators have been guessing about for years, not knowing exactly what the apostle meant by " a thorn in the flesh." I do not know either; but it was something sharp; something that pierced him.

I gather from all this that physical disorder may be the means of grace to the soul. You say you have so many temptations from bodily ailments, and if you were only well you think you could be a good Christian. While your temptations may be different, they are no more than those of the man who has an appetite three times a day, and sleeps eight hours every night. From my observation, I judge that invalids have a more rapturous view of the next world than well people, and will have higher renown in heaven. The best view of the delectable mountains is through the lattice of the sickroom. There are trains running every hour between pillow and throne, between hospital and mansion, between bandages and robes, between crutch and palm branch. Oh, I wish some of you people who are compelled to cry, " My head, my head! my foot, my foot! my back, my back!" would try some of the Lord's medicine! You are going to be well anyhow before long. Heaven is an old city, but has never yet reported one case of sickness or one bill of mortality. No ophthalmia for the eye. No pneumonia for the lungs. No pleurisy for the side. No neuralgia for the nerves. No rheumatism for the muscles. "The inhabitant shall never say, I am sick." "There shall be no more pain."

Again, you ought to make the best of life's finality. Now, you think I have a very tough subject. You do not see how I am to strike a spark of light out of the flint of the tombstone. There are many people who have an idea that death is the submergence of

Illumined Clouds

everything pleasant by everything doleful. If my subject could close in the upsetting of all such preconceived notions, it would close well. Who can judge best of the features of a man — those who are close by him, or those who are afar off? "Oh," you say, "those can judge best of the features of a man who are close by him!" Now, who shall judge of the features of death — whether they are lovely or whether they are repulsive? You? You are too far off. If I want to get a judgment as to what really the features of death are, I will not ask you; I will ask those who have been within a month of death, or a week of death, or an hour of death, or a minute of death. They stand so near the features, they can tell. They give unanimous testimony, if they are Christian people, that death, instead of being demoniac, is cherubic. Of all the thousands of Christians who have been carried through the gates of Greenwood, gather up their dying experiences, and you will find that they nearly all bordered on a jubilate. How often you have seen a dying man join in the psalm being sung around his bedside, the middle of the verse opening to let his ransomed spirit free!— long after the lips could not speak, he looking and pointing upward.

Some of you talk as though God had exhausted Himself in building this world, and that all the rich curtains He ever made He hung around this planet, and all the flowers He ever grew He has woven into the carpet of our daisied meadows. No. This world is not the best thing God can do; this world is not the best thing that God has done. One week of the year is called blossom week — called so all throughout the land because there are more blossoms in that week than in any other week of the whole year. Blossom week! And that is what the future world is to which the Christian is invited — blossom week forever. It is as far ahead of this world as Paradise is ahead of Dry Tortugas; and yet here we stand shivering and fearing to go out, and we want to stay on the dry sand, and amid the stormy petrels, when we are invited to arbors of jessamine and birds of paradise.

One season I had two springtimes. I went to New Orleans in April, and I marked the difference between going toward New Orleans and then coming back. As I went on down toward New Orleans the verdure, the foliage, became thicker and more beautiful. When I came back, the further I came toward home the less the foliage, and less and less it became until there was hardly any. Now, it all depends upon the direction in which you travel. If a spirit from heaven should come toward our world, he is travelling from June toward December, from radiance toward darkness, from hanging gardens toward icebergs. And one would not be very much surprised if a spirit of God sent forth from heaven toward our world should be slow to come. But how strange it is that we dread going out toward that world when going is from December toward June — from the snow of earthly storm to the snow of Edenic blossom — from the Arctics of trouble toward the tropics of eternal joy!

Oh, what an ado about dying! We get so attached to the malarial marsh in which we live that we are afraid to go up and live on the hilltop. We are alarmed because vacation is coming. Eternal sunlight, and best programme of celestial minstrels and hallelujah, no inducement. Let us stay here and keep cold and ignorant and weak. Do not introduce us to Elijah, and John Milton, and Bourdaloue. Keep our feet on the sharp cobble-stones of earth instead of planting them on the bank of amaranth in heaven. Give us this small island of a leprous world instead of the immensities of splendor and delight. Keep our hands full of nettles, and our shoulder under the burden, and our neck in the yoke, and hopples on our ankles, and handcuffs on our wrists. " Dear Lord," we seem to say, " keep us down here, where we have to suffer, instead of letting us up where we might live and reign and rejoice." I am amazed at myself and at yourself for this infatuation under which we all rest. Men you would suppose would get frightened at having to stay in this world, instead of getting frightened at having to go toward heaven. I congratulate anybody who has a right to die. By that I mean through sickness you cannot avert, or through accident you cannot avoid — your work consummated. "Where did they bury Lily?" said one little child to another. " Oh," she replied, " they buried her in the ground." " What! in the cold ground?" " Oh, no, no; not in the cold ground, but in the warm ground, where ugly seeds become beautiful flowers." " But," says some one, " it pains me so much to think that I must lose the body with which my soul has so long companioned." You do not lose it. You no more lose your body by death than you lose your watch when you send it to have it repaired, or your jewel when you send it to have it reset, or the faded picture when you send it to have it touched up, or the photograph of a friend when you have it put in a new locket. You do not lose your body. Paul will go to Rome to get his, Payson will go to Portland to get his, President Edwards will go to Princeton to get his, George Cookman will go to the bottom of the Atlantic to get his, and we will go to the village churchyards and the city cemeteries to get ours; and when we have our perfect spirit rejoined to our perfect body, then we will be the kind of men and women that the resurrection morning will make possible.

So you see you have not made out any doleful

story yet. What have you proved about death? What is the case you have made out? You have made out just this — that death allows us to have a perfect body, free of all aches, united forever with a perfect soul free from all sin. Correct your theology. What does it all mean? Why, it means that moving-day is coming, and that you are going to quit cramped apartments and be mansioned forever. The horse that stands at the gate will not be the one lathered and bespattered, carrying bad news, but it will be the horse that St. John saw in apocalyptic vision — the white horse on which the King comes to the banquet. The ground around the palace will quake with the tires and hoofs of celestial equipage, and those Christians who in this world lost their friends, and lost their property, and lost their health, and lost their life, will find out that God was always kind, and that all things worked together for their good, and that those were the wisest people on earth who made the best of everything. See you not now the bright light in the clouds?

CONTENTS.

PAGE.

AMERICA FOR GOD. - - - - - - 9

TEXT: *And I beheld another beast coming up out of the earth; and he had two horns like a lamb and he spake as a dragon.*— Revelation 13: 11.

America in the Bible — Bible most popular book of the day — America can be taken for God — The American eagle a tired bird — Area of our country — Early morning of nation's life — Some of the enemy's strongholds — Our leader in the onslaught — Birth and life — The armies that have followed him — Many ramparts already taken — Large fortunes no obstacle — Foreign immigration an ally — Conglomerate population a blessing — The weapons of our warfare — The Bible — Gospel batteries — The grand march — Finale.

FROM OCEAN TO OCEAN. - - - - - 21

TEXT: *He shall have dominion also from sea to sea.*— Psalm 72: 8.

America for God — Immensity of the possession — Let in the Territories — Reclamation predicted — Progress and value of irrigation — Wonders of construction — Monarchs of foliage — Older than the Christian centuries — Scenery of the Yosemite — A throne of Jehovah — Chorus of the mountains — The geologists' paradise — Boiling geysers — Pictorial splendors — Jehovah surpassing himself — Sunrise and sunset married — Testament of the rocks — A hall for the Last Judgment — The sweep of the American continent — Bridge of Bering straits — Satan no right to America — Diabolic nomenclature — To Christianize America.

THE AMERICAN SHEAF. - - - - - 37

TEXT: *We were binding sheaves in the field, and lo, my sheaf arose, and also stood upright; and, behold, your sheaves stood round about, and made obeisance to my sheaf.*— Genesis 37: 7.

America the Joseph of the nations — Sheaves of old world not equal to our sheaf — Atmospheric blessings — Drawbacks of tropical regions — The paradise of industry — Better political condition — Fabulous cost of royalty — Less monopolistic oppression — Foreign monopoly of the soil — 5000 millionaires in the U. S.— Illimitable resources — American peace — Abundance of room — No foes to fight — Silent fortresses, idle warships — Less burdensome national debt — Our sheaf larger than ever.

THE DECORATION OF GRAVES. - - - - 53

TEXT: *The tower of David builded for an armory, whereon there hang a thousand bucklers, all shields of mighty men.*— Song of Solomon 4: 4.

The church compared to an armory — Night with stellar illumination — A brave private — "Don't shoot" — Gray and Blue blended — A gen-

Contents

eration since the war — Missing, missing — Might have been avoided
— War the champion curse — Courage honored — Graves of the
"Unknown" — Liberty — Decoration implies defense — No room save
for Canada — A good neighbor — Foreign invasion and sectional strife —
Beautify all tombs — David's cry better than Jacob's — Greenwood's
quaint epitaph.

HALF A PLANET. - - - - - - - - 67

TEXT : *Lift up thine eyes westward.*— Deuteronomy 3 : 27.

Columbus's mother-in-law — God's will to the discoverer — Drift from
another hemisphere — The can't-be-dones — A Friday expedition — A
Friday morning look-out — Calumny and chains — Columbus celebration — America a religious discovery — The doxology on the beach —
Interstellar communication — Startling possibilities — Spoiled for fishermen — Meeting a prophet — Mrs. Murray's wit — The
soldier of Resaca — A benediction on the skippers.

RESERVATION OF AMERICA. - - - - - 83

TEXT : *And hath made of one blood all nations.*—Acts 17 : 26.

One blood, one origin — America an exposition of the text — Madcap
cries — A nation of immigrants — Heaven for the Heavenians — Not to
be a convict colony — No parlor exclusiveness — Give the millions the
wish-bone — Overcrowding impossible — Commingling of the races —
America's salvation — Bury race prejudice — What foreigners should
do — Our debt to Europe — Dedication.

ALLEVIATIONS OF WAR. - - - - - 99

TEXT : *Though war shall rise against me, in this will I be confident.*—
Psalm 27 : 3.

War in the Old Testament — Alleviations of war — Consolidation
achieved — Most unselfish war of the ages — Twentieth century's
demand — A war for advancement of liberty — A great victory — Thanks
due to God — Might on the side of right — The Maine atrocity — A God
to whom to commend the imperiled — Communication with the distant
via the throne of God — Shipwrecked sailor's thirst — Turn Spain out
— The Spanish Armada destroyed — History to be repeated — Christ the
world's great want.

POLITICS AND RELIGION. - - - - - 113

TEXT : *Then the king commanded and they brought Daniel and cast him
into the den of lions.*— Daniel 6 : 16.

Daniel's high office — Secretary of state — Jealousy excited — Ruse to
get rid of Daniel — A King's insomnia — Daniel's deliverance — Fate of
his foes — The crime of success — Value of decision of character —
Indecision illustrated — Religion in worldly business — Too busy to be
religious ! — The more business, the more opportunities — Religion in
politics — Daniel's unpopular platform — Lions cannot hurt a good man
— Lions of misfortune — Fears and pearls — Knighthood's tests.

THE BRIDE OF NATIONS. - - - - - 125

TEXT : *Thy land shall be married.*— Isaiah 62 : 4.

Final destiny of this nation — A funeral or a wedding — Suitors for
America — How a railroad company secured donation of public lands
— Monopoly, its grasping character — Nihilism's destructive tendencies
— An enemy of the working man — Infidelity's perilous propositions —
Source of all right impulse — Christ a suitor for America — This nation
Christ's from its birth — Its immeasurable prosperities — High class of
immigration — The Rocky Mountains as a marriage altar.

Contents

PAGE.

BEFORE THEY ADJOURN. - - - - - - 139

TEXT: *And teach his senators wisdom.*— Psalm 105 : 22.

A suggestion from Joseph's state policy — Teaching senators wisdom
— Wholesale defamation of public men — Washington's high type of
citizenship — Good men in Congress — God's name in Constitution —
Recognition of Divine intervention — Past and future need of it — Sectarian appropriations out of place — God in national political platforms —
Our country belongs to God — Taken possession of in his name — North
and South praying in their own way — God answering in his own way —
A copy of our national documents for every immigrant — Christian
patriotism to be cultivated.

THE NATION'S WOE. - - - - - - 155

TEXT: *Comfort ye, comfort ye, my people, saith your God.*— Isaiah 40 : 1.

Garfield shot — Comfort in calamity — Prepared for death — Bible
reading at college — Most pronounced Christian President since Washington — Family will be provided for — National prosperity not affected
— Successor will carry out leading principles of present administration
— Prayers for will be answered — Escaping years of abuse — Pacification
of North and South accomplished — Office-hunting a disreputable business — Need of human sacrifice — Potent warning.

THE NATION KNEELING. - - - - - 169

TEXT: *And Isaiah said, Take a lump of figs. And they took and laid it
on the boil, and he recovered.*— II. Kings 20 : 7.

Hezekiah, given up to die, but spared — Garfield must die — Pains,
poultices, prayers — Spared — A nation in prayer — God's intervention
— Prince of Wales saved by prayer — Prayer and the crops — When to
cease praying — Answers to prayer — Revelation of woman's courage —
Not exceptional — A wife's prompt measures for husband's life — Too
many pistols — Danger of carrying — The ordination of suffering — Its
beneficent fruitage — A lesson of contentment — An ungrateful public
— Daniel Webster's stinging arraignment.

MIGHTIER DEAD THAN ALIVE, - - - - 185

TEXT: *So the dead which he slew at his death were more than they
which he slew in his life* — Judges 16 : 30.

Garfield's influence in death exceeding that of life — His death effective for good — Christian religion emphatically eulogized — His heroic
endurance — Good will between North and South strengthened — Wonders of human frame never before so emphasized — Popular interest in
— Death cannot be turned aside — Possible effect of Garfield's death on
national purification — Sympathy for the bereaved.

WERE THE PRAYERS FOR PRESIDENT GARFIELD
A FAILURE? - - - - - - - - 197

TEXT: *I besought the Lord thrice that it might depart from me. And
he said unto me, my grace is sufficient for thee.*— II. Corinthians
12 : 8, 9.

Paul and his affliction — Presumably disease of the eyes — No right
prayer unanswered — Prayers for President Garfield not a failure —
Would have been permanently disabled if spared — Insurmountable
difficulties of office under the circumstances — Difficulty of paying off
favors shown — Prayer answered in Garfield's bettered condition — Sanctifying influences upon whole nation — Possible sanitary influence on
Mormonism — Good effects of exemplary home life in White House —
Future national blessings from prayers of the people assured — Prayers
not lost — God gives better than we ask — National guardian angels.

Contents

PAGE.

EPIDEMIC OF STRIKES. - - - - - - 213

TEXT: *The eye cannot say to the hand I have no need of thee.*— I. Corinthians 12 : 21.

Society an interdependent mechanism — Injury retroactive — Labor and capital — Identical interests — Laborers who become capitalists — Advantages of co-operative associations — Thomas Brassey on co-operation — Lord Derby and John Stuart Mill on labor question — How workingmen could have a surplus — Trades-unions good and bad — No stimulants needed — Money that burns — Eyesight for a sealskin sacque — The Centennial and the mortgaged farms — Abraham Van Nest — Talmage's present for books — Savings banks and insurance — Confidence called for — How Talmage's friend avoided strikes — A democratic Gospel — Investments for eternity — Sweat drops turned to pearls — Working people in heaven.

LAST DECADE OF THE CENTURY. - - - 229

TEXT: *Amen! Alleluia.*— Revelation 19 : 4.

Almanac a solemn book — Division of time wise — Great events in closing years of centuries — World to be taken for God — When God changes his mind — God a father — Fighting at too long range — The millennium can be hastened — God is ready — Enough workers can be had — The professor's figures — God cares for mathematics — Work for all denominations — All requisite machinery possessed — Abundance of money — The victorious procession — Universal glee of a redeemed planet — Fitting climax to century — Clouds of helpers.

A FAVORED NATION. - - - - - - 247

TEXT: *Thou hast increased the nation, O Lord, thou hast increased the nation.*— Isaiah 26 : 15.

A shadow in the sky — Official harvest records — Statistics of wheat, corn, cotton, etc.— Nation's lap filled with blessing — Full organ on Thanksgiving day — Municipal frauds — Exposition — Betterment — War before the war — A new state of feeling — America not yet fully discovered — Coal fields, iron mines — Two black world-shaking giants — Source of our safety — Manners and customs improving — Old-time drinking and dissipations — No such wars as of old — The favored land.

NATIONAL RUIN. - - - - - - - 263

TEXT: *Alas, alas, that great city Babylon, that mighty city! for in one hour is thy judgment come.* — Revelation 18 : 10-13.

Buried Babylon, that great city — Walls, gardens, streets, river, wealth, sin — Its capture — Death of nations — Calling the roll — A warning to this nation — Perils that beset — Election bribery — Buying up a State — Sectional antagonisms ridiculous and perilous — Low ebb of public morals — Politics have touched bottom — Society folks not good enough to sweep Sodom — San Francisco's curse — Licentiousness of cities — The ship crushing cephaloptera — When the dumb son spoke — Hope still in God — Contending for a continent.

THE TIMES WE LIVE IN. - - - - - 277

TEXT: *Who knoweth whether thou art come to the kingdom for such a time as this?* — Esther 4 : 14.

Esther's mission — Our mission — Dry technicalities not wanted — Our magnificent destiny — Piety needs fresh air — A hint from a Carolina cactus — Flower-pot Christians — The parsimonious century plant — Sin rampant — The haystack society — Adapting the work — Excursioning on rhetorical stilts — The world converting the Church — Hedley Vicars, the undaunted — Havelock and his candles — Peter Croy's praying — The final triumph.

Contents

PAGE.

WASHINGTON FOR GOD. - - - - - - 289

TEXT: *Beginning at Jerusalem.*— Luke 24 : 47.

First sight of Jerusalem — Most interesting city ever built — Beginning at Washington — America for God or for Apollyon — Downward or upward — Curfew's message — Washington central — The place of representative men — Congress improved — Potent influences of Gospel — One soul worth more than another — 1857 ; its wonderful revival — A Washington daily prayer-meeting — Great work at the capital — All hands to the beam — Wonderful news.

MORAL CHARACTER OF CANDIDATES. - - 303

TEXT: *The Ten Commandments.*— Exodus 20 : 1-17.

The first law library — Letting loose the Ten Commandments — Testing the candidates — Contradictory newspapers — One standard for all — Caution against mean charges — No tampering with the scales — Sins in droves — Measuring God's thunderbolts — The commandments in small type — Village of Ardericca — Keeping the decalogue in sight — Slain by the Ten Commandments — Lot and Sodom's candidates — The kite and the doves — A diet of pigeons — The ten drops of Moses — Calvary answers Sinai — Etna's open way for rescuers of parents — The Ramsgate lifeboat.

THE MISSION OF THE WHEEL. - - - - 319

TEXT: *As for the wheels, it was cried unto them in my hearing, O wheel !* — Ezekiel 10 : 13.

Victories of peace — The wheel in the Bible — Triumphs of machinery — Idleness and ruin — The sewing machine — Bondage of the needle — The wheel in agriculture — Whitney, Chichester and the cotton gin — In the traveling world — John Fitch's dilemma — Sir H. Davy on gas project — The Clermont on the Hudson — Sanderson's stage — George Stephenson's first locomotive — The bicycle — The printing-press — A platform of plenty — Convention of kings

HEROES OF THE NAVY. - - - - - 337

TEXT: *Behold also the ships.*— James 3 : 4.

American ships of to-day — Old-time naval battles — Navy of 1861 — Latest naval heroes — Hail to the heroes — Christ the great admiral — Veterans in hospitals — Reviewing the four navies — Foote's Christian work and dying words — Farragut and his father's rebuke — The Tecumseh's loss — Captain Philip at Santiago — Importance of battle of Manila bay — A country lad — Nelson and Dewey — Strip for the last battle.

MUST THE CHINESE GO ? - - - - - 353

TEXT: *Who is my neighbor ?* — Luke 10 : 29.

Christ and the lawyer — All the world one neighborhood — Talmage visits San Francisco's Chinatown — How to extirpate the Chinese evils — Unequaled laundrymen — Do they injure American labor ? — Chinese financial contributions — Bones sent home — Queues not exclusively Chinese — Chinese dress a religious question — Talmage's sermon in a Chinese church — Arts and literature among the Chinese in past ages — Richest country in all the earth — Must the Americans go ? — Nations confounded at Babel ; to be made one at the cross — Unreasonable planks — Ambassador Burlingame's success — China to be evangelized — A temple of liberty.

Contents

PAGE.

TWO DECADES: 1864 AND 1884 - - - - - 371

TEXT: *And the Lord commanded the angel; and he put up his sword again into the sheath thereof.*—I. Chronicles 21 : 27.

The destroying angel—The sword scabbarded—1864 and 1884 compared and contrasted—President Samuel K. Talmage's prayer in the Confederate Congress—Lions of war silenced—Changes in domestic life—Leaving home in 1864—A Crimean soldier's cruel letter—Figures in crystal—Rosy-cheeked numerals—Contrast in national condition—Garlands for the dead—Reveille of the Last Judgment.

SETTLED IN HEAVEN. - - - - - - 385

TEXT: *Forever, O Lord, thy word is settled in heaven.*— Psalm 119 : 89.

A changing world—Five things settled—The cemetery of dead nations—National destiny settled in heaven—Happiness a matter of spiritual condition—Jealousy at others' success—A dying President's declaration—Not alarmed by the fire-bell—Two kinds of graduates—The world to be made over—God's reserved forces—The tidal wave of 1868—The tidal wave of Calvary—The fallen king and crowned earl—Irrelevant questions—Christ the great essential—Pompey's triumph—Belisarius's procession—Aurelian's triumph and gold-fettered Zenobia.

The following indexes will be found at the end of volume twenty:

        INDEX OF TEXTS,

        INDEX OF TITLES AND TEXTS,

        INDEX OF ANECDOTAL AND HISTORICAL ILLUSTRATIONS,

        INDEX OF SUBJECTS.

AMERICA FOR GOD

Rev., 13: 11: "And I beheld another beast coming up out of the earth; and he had two horns like a lamb and he spake as a dragon."

Is America mentioned in the Bible? Learned and consecrated men, who have studied the inspired books of Daniel and Revelation more than I have, and understand them better, agree in saying that the leopard mentioned in the Bible meant Grecia, and the bear meant Medo-Persia, and the lion meant Babylon, and the beast of the text coming up out of the earth with two horns like a lamb, and the voice of a dragon means our country; because, among other reasons, it seemed to come up out of the earth when Columbus discovered it, and it has been for the most part at peace, like a lamb, unless assaulted by foreign foe, in which case it has had two horns strong and sharp, and the voice of a dragon loud enough to make all nations hear the roar of its indignation. Is it reasonable to suppose that God would leave out from the prophecies of his Book this whole Western Hemisphere? No, no! "I beheld another beast coming up out of the earth and he had two horns like a lamb, and he spake as a dragon." Germany for scholarship. England for manufactories. France for manners. Egypt for antiquities. Italy for pictures. But America for God!

I start with the cheering thought that the most popular book on earth to-day is the Bible, the most popular institution on earth to-day is the church, and the most popular name on earth to-day is Jesus. From this audience hundreds of men and women would, if need be, march out and die for him. Am I too confident in saying "America for God?" If the Lord will help me I will show the strength and extent of the long line of fortresses to be taken, and give you my reasons for saying it can be done and will be done. Let us decide, in this battle for God, whether we are at Bull Run or at Gettysburg. There is a Fourth of Julyish way of bragging about this country, and the most tired and plucked bird that ever flew through the heavens is the American eagle; so much so that Mr. Gladstone said to me facetiously, at Hawarden: "I hear that the fish in your American lakes are so large that, when one of them is taken out, the entire lake is perceptibly lowered;" and at a dinner given in Paris an American offered for a sentiment: "Here is to the United States—bounded on the north by the aurora borealis, on the south by the procession of the equinoxes, on the east by primeval chaos, and on the west by the Day of Judgment." The effect of such grandiloquence is to discredit the real facts which are so tremendous they need no garnishing. The worst thing to do in any campaign, military or religious, is to underestimate an enemy, and I will have no part in such attempt at belittlement. Indeed, the obstacles in the way are so multitudinous and vast that were it not for promised supernatural aid we would now surrender.

This land to be taken for God, according to Hassel, the statistician, has fourteen million two hundred and nineteen thousand nine hundred and sixty-seven square miles, a width and a length that none but the Omniscient can appreciate. Four Europes put together and capable of holding and feeding, as it will hold and feed, according to Atkinson, the statistician, if the world continues in existence and does not run

America for God

afoul of some other world or get consumed by the fires already burning in the cellars of the planet—capable, I say, of holding and feeding more than one billion of inhabitants. For you must remember it must be held for God as well as taken for God, and the last five hundred million inhabitants must not be allowed to swamp the religion of the first five hundred million. Not much use in taking the fortress if we cannot hold it. It must be held until the Archangel's trumpet bids living and dead arise from this foundering planet.

You must remember it is only about seven o'clock in the morning of our nation's life. Great cities are to flash and roar among what are called the "Bad Lands" of the Dakotas and the great "Columbia Plains" of Washington State, and that on which we put our schoolboy fingers on the map and spelled out as the "Great American Desert," is, through systematic and consummating irrigation, to bloom like Chatsworth Park and be made more productive than those regions dependent upon uncertain and spasmodic rainfall. All those regions, as well as these regions already cultivated, to be inhabited! That was a sublime thing said by Henry Clay, while crossing the Alleghany Mountains, and he was waiting for the stage horses to be rested, as he stood on a rock, arms folded, looking off into the valley, and some one said to him: "Mr. Clay, what are you thinking about?" He replied, "I am listening to the on-coming tramp of the future generations of America." Have you laid your home missionary scheme on such an infinitude of scale? If the work of bringing one soul to God is so great, can a thousand million be captured? In this country, already planted and to be overcome, Paganism has built its altar to Brahma, and the Chinese are already burning incense in their temples, and Mohammedanism, drunk with the red wine of human blood in Armenia, is trying to get a foothold here, and from the minarets of her mosques will yet mumble her blasphemies, saying, "Allah is great, and Mohammed is his prophet." Then there are the vaster multitudes with no religion at all. They worship no God, they live with no consolation, and they die with no hope. No star of peace points down to the manger in which they are born, and no prayer is uttered over the grave into which they sink. Then there is Alcoholism, its piled-up demijohns and beer barrels, and hogsheads of fiery death, a barricade high and long as the Alleghanies and Rockies and Sierra Nevadas, pouring forth day and night their ammunition of wretchedness and woe. When a German wants to take a drink he takes beer. When an Englishman wants to take a drink he takes ale. When a Scotchman wants to take a drink he takes whisky. But when an American wants to take a drink he takes anything he can lay his hands on.

Plenty of statistics to tell how much money is spent in this country for rum, and how many drunkards die, but who will give us the statistics of how many hearts are crushed under the heel of this worst demon of the centuries? How many hopes blasted? How many children turned out on the world, accursed with the stigma of a debauched ancestry? Until the worm of the distillery becomes the worm that never dies, and the smoke of the heated wine vats becomes the smoke of the torment that ascendeth up forever and ever, Alcoholism, swearing—not with hand uplifted toward heaven, for from that direction it can get no help, but with right hand stretched down toward perdition from which it came up—swearing that it will not cease as long as there are any homesteads to despoil, any magnificent men and women to destroy, any immortal souls to damn, any more nations to balk, any more civilizations to extinguish.

Then there is what in America we call Anarchism, in France Communism, and in Russia Nihilism—the three names for one and the same thing—and having but two doctrines in its creed: first, there is no God; second, there shall be no rights of property. One of their chief journals printed this sentiment: "Dynamite can be made out of the dead bodies of capitalists, as well as out of hogs." One of the leaders of Communism left inscribed on his prison wall, where he had been justly incarcerated, these words: "When once you are dead, there is an end of everything; therefore, ye scoundrels, grab whatever you can— only don't let yourselves be grabbed. Amen!" There are in this country hundreds of thousands of these lazy scoundrels. Honest men deplore it when they cannot get work, but those of whom I speak will not do work when they can get it. I tried to employ one who asked me for money. I said, "Down in my cellar I have some wood to saw, and I will pay you for it." For a little while I heard the saw going, and then I heard it no more. I went downstairs and found the wood, but the workman had disappeared, taking for company both buck and saw. Anarchism, Communism and Nihilism mean, "Too wicked to acknowledge God, and too lazy to earn a living," and among the mightiest obstacles to be overcome are those organized elements of domestic, social, and political ruin.

There also are the fastnesses of infidelity and atheism and fraud and political corruption and multiform, hydra-headed, million-armed abominations all over the land. While the mightiest agencies for righteousness on earth are good and healthful newspapers and good and healthful books, and our chief dependence for intelligence and Christian achievement is upon them, what word among the more than one hundred thousand words in our vocabulary can describe the work of that archangel of mischief, a corrupt literature? What man, attempting anything for God and humanity, has escaped a stroke of its filthy wing? What good cause has escaped its hinderment? What other obstacle in all the land so appalling? But I cannot name more than one-half the battlements, the bastions, the intrenchments, the redoubts, the fortifications to be stormed and overcome if this country is ever taken for God. The statistics are so awful that if we had nothing but the multiplication table and the arithmetic, the attempt to evangelize America would be an absurdity higher than the Tower of Babel before it dropped on the plain of Shinar.

Where are the drilled troops to march against those fortifications as long as the continent? Where are the batteries that can be unlimbered against these walls? Where are the guns of large enough calibre to storm these gates? Well, let us look around and see, first of all, who is our Leader and will be our Leader until the work is done. Garibaldi, with a thousand Italians, could do more than another commander with ten thousand Italians. General Sherman, on one side, and Stonewall Jackson on the other, each with ten thousand troops, could do more than some other generals with twenty thousand troops apiece. The rough boat in which Washington crossed the icy Delaware with a few half-frozen troops was mightier than the ship of war that, during the American Revolution came through the Narrows, a gun at each porthole, and sunk in Hell Gate.

Our Leader, like most great leaders, was born in an obscure place, and it was a humble home, about five miles from Jerusalem. Those who were out of doors that night said that there was stellar commotion, and music that came out of the clouds, as though the front door of heaven had been set open, and that the camels heard his first infantile cry. Then he came to the fairest boyhood that mother was ever proud of, and from twelve to thirty years of age was off in India (if traditions there are accurate) and then returned to his native land, and for three years had his pathway surrounded by blind eyes that he illumined, and epileptic patients to whom he gave rubicund health, and tongues that he loosed from silence into song, and those whose funerals he stopped that he might give back to bereaved mothers their only boys, and those whose fevered pulses he had restored into rhythmic throb, and whose paralytic limbs he had warmed into healthful circulation—pastor at Capernaum, but flaming evangelist everywhere, hushing crying tempests and turning rolling seas into solid sapphire, and, for the rescue of a race, submitted to court-room filled with howling miscreants, and to a martydom at the sight of which the sun fainted and fell back in the heavens, and then treading the clouds homeward, like snowy mountain-peaks, till heaven took him back again, more a favorite than he had ever been. But, coming again, he is on earth now, and the nations are gathering to his standard. Following him were the Scotch covenanters, the Theban legion, the victims of the London Haymarket, the Piedmontese sufferers, the Pilgrim Fathers, the Huguenots, and uncounted multitudes of the past, joined by about four hundred millions of the present, and with the certainty that all nations shall huzzah at his chariot-wheel, he goes forth, the moon under his feet and the stars of heaven for his tiara—the Mighty Leader, he of Drumclog and Bothwell Bridge and Bannockburn, and the One who whelmed Spanish Armada, "Coming up from Edom, with dyed garments from Bozrah, traveling in the greatness of his strength, mighty to save," and behind whom we fall into line to-day and march in the campaign that is to take America for God. Hosanna! Hosanna! Wave all the palm branches! At his feet put down your silver and your gold, as in heaven you will cast before him your coronets.

With such a Leader do you not think we can do it? Say, do you think we can? Why, many ramparts have already been taken. Where is American slavery? Gone, and the South, as heartily as the North, prays "Peace to its ashes." Where is bestial polygamy? Gone, by the fiat of the United States Government, urged on by Christian sentiment; and Mormonism, having retreated in 1830 from Fayette, New York, to Kirkland, Ohio, and in 1838 retreated to Missouri, and in 1846 retreated to Salt Lake City, now divorced from its superfluity of wives, will soon retreat into the Pacific, and no basin smaller than an ocean could wash out its pollutions. Its recent attempt to invade Congress aroused the resentment of that body and the indignation of the whole country. Illiteracy going down under the work of Slater and Peabody funds, and the Sabbath-schools of all the churches of all denominations! Corruption at the ballot-box, by law of registration and other safeguards, made almost impossible! Churches twice as large as the old ones, the enlarged supply to meet the greatly enlarged demand! Great cities, so often mentioned as great obstacles—the center of crime and the reservoirs of all iniquities—are to lead in the work of Gospelization. Who give most to home missions, to asylums, to religious education, to all styles of humanitarian and Christian institutions? The cities. From what places did the most relief go at the time of Johnstown flood and Michigan fires and Charleston earthquake and Ohio freshets? From the cities. What place will do more than any other place, by its contribution of Christian men and women and means, in this work of taking America for God? New York city. The way Paris goes, goes France. The way Berlin goes, goes Germany. The way London goes, goes England. The way New York and a couple of other cities go, goes America. May the Eternal God wake us up to the stupendous issue!

Another thing quoted pessimistically is the vast and overtopping fortunes in this country, and they say it means concentrated wealth and luxuriousness and display and moral ruin. It is my observation that it is people who have but limited resources who make the most splurge; and I ask you, who are endowing colleges and theological seminaries? Did you ever hear of Peter Cooper and James Lenox and sainted William E. Dodge and the Lawrences, Amos and Abbott, while I refrain from mentioning living benefactors who, quite as generous and Christian, are at this moment planning what they can do in these days, and in their last will and testament in this campaign that proposes taking America for God? The time is coming—hasten it, Lord!—and I think you and I will see it, when, as Joseph, the wealthy Arimathean, gave for the dead Christ a costly mausoleum, the affluent men and women of this country will rise in their strength and build for our King, one Jesus, the throne of this American continent.

Another thing quoted for discouragement, but which I quote for encouragement, is foreign immigration. Now that from the New York Barge Office we turn back by the first steamship the foreign vagabondism, we are getting people, the vast majority of whom come to make an honest living; among them some of the bravest and the best. If you should turn back from this land to Europe the foreign ministers of the Gospel and the foreign attorneys and the foreign merchants and the foreign philanthropists, what a robbery of our pulpits, our court-rooms, our store-houses, and our beneficent institutions, and what a putting back of every monetary, merciful, moral, and religious interest of the land! This commingling here of all nationalities under the blessing of God will produce in seventy-five or one hundred years the most magnificent style of man and woman the world ever saw. They will have the wit of one race, the eloquence of another race, the kindness of another, the generosity of another, the æsthetic taste of another, the high moral character of another; and when that man and woman step forth, their brain and nerve and muscle an intertwining of the fibres of all nationalities, nothing but a new electric photographic apparatus, that can see clear through body, mind and soul, can take of them an adequate picture. But the foreign population of America is less than fifteen per cent. of all our population, and why all this fuss about foreign immigration?

Now what are the weapons by which, under our Omnipotent Leader, the real obstacles in the way of our country's evangelization, the ten thousand mile Sebastopols, are to be leveled? The first columbiad, with range enough to sweep from eternity to eternity, is the Bible, millions of its copies going out, millions on millions. Then there are all the Gospel batteries, manned by seventy thousand pastors and home missionaries, over the head of each one of whom is the shield of divine protection, and in the right hand of each one the gleaming, two-edged sword of the Infinite Spirit! Hundreds of thousands of private soldiers for Christ, marching under the one-starred, blood-striped flag of Emmanuel! On our side, the great and mighty theologians of the land, the heavy artillery;

and the hundreds of thousands of Christian children, the infantry. They are marching on! Episcopacy, with the sublime roll of its liturgies; Methodism, with its battle-cry of "The sword of the Lord and John Wesley;" the Baptist Church, with its glorious navy sailing up our Oregons and Sacramentos and Mississippis; and Presbyterianism, moving on with the battle-cry of "The sword of the Lord and John Knox." And then, after awhile will come the great tides of revival, sweeping over the land, the five hundred thousand conversions in 1857 eclipsed by the salvation of millions in a day, and the four American armies of the Lord's host marching toward each other, the Eastern army marching West, the Western army marching East, the Northern army marching South, the Southern army marching North; shoulder to shoulder! Tramp! tramp! tramp! until they meet mid-continent, having taken America for God!

The thunder of the bombardment is already in the air, and when the last bridge of opposition is taken, and the last portcullis of Satan is lifted, and the last gun spiked, and the last tower dismantled, and the last charger of iniquity shall have been hurled back upon its haunches, what a time of rejoicing! We will see it, not with these eyes, which before that will be closed in blessed sleep, but with strong and better vision, when the Lord once in awhile gives us a vacation among the doxologies to come down and see the dear old land, which I pray may always be the lamb of the text, mild and peaceful, inoffensive; but in case foreign nations assail it, having two horns of army and navy strong enough to hook them back and hook them down, and a voice louder than a dragon, yea, louder than ten thousand thunders, saying to the billows of Asiatic superstition and European arrogance, "Thus far shalt thou go, and no farther, and here shall thy proud waves be stayed!"

FROM OCEAN TO OCEAN

Ps., 72: 8: " He shall have dominion also from sea to sea."

FROM OCEAN TO OCEAN

Ps., 72: 8: " He shall have dominion also from sea to sea."

What two seas are referred to? Some might say
that the text meant that Christ was to reign over all
the land between the Arabian Sea and Caspian Sea, or
between the Red Sea and the Mediterranean Sea, or
between the Black Sea and the North Sea. No; in
such case my text would have named them. It meant
from any large body of water on the earth clear across
to any other large body of water. And so I have a
right to read it: "He shall have dominion from Atlantic to Pacific."

First, consider the immensity of this possession.
I unroll before you the map of the regions to be traversed and conquered. If it were only a small tract
of land capable of nothing better than sage-brush, and
with ability only to support prairie-dogs, I should not
have much enthusiasm in wanting Christ to have it
added to his dominion. But its immensity and affluence no one can imagine, unless, in immigrant wagon
or stage-coach, or in rail-train of the Union Pacific or
the Northern Pacific or the Canadian Pacific or the
Southern Pacific, he has traversed it. Having been
privileged six times to cross this continent, and twice
this summer, I have come to some appreciation of its
magnitude. California, which I supposed in my boyhood, from its size on the map, was a few yards across;
a ridge of land on which one must walk cautiously lest
he hit his head against the Sierra Nevada on one side,
or slip off into the Pacific waters on the other—California, the thin slice of land, as I supposed it to be in

boyhood, I have found to be larger than all the States of New England and all New York State and all Pennsylvania added together; for if you add them together their square miles fall far short of California. North and South Dakota, Montana, Idaho, Wyoming and Washington Territory, since launched into Statehood, were giants at their birth. Let the Congress of the United States strain a point and soon admit New Mexico. What is the use keeping them out in the cold any longer? Let us have the whole continent divided into States, with Senatorial and Congressional representatives, and we will all be happy together. If some of them have not quite the requisite number of people, fix up the Constitution to suit these cases. Even Utah, by dropping polygamy, has been permitted to enter. Monogamy has triumphed in parts of Utah. Turn all the Territories into States, and if some of the sisters are smaller than the elder sisters, give them time and they will soon be as large as any of them. Because some of the daughters of a family may be five feet in stature and the others only four feet, do not let the daughters five feet high shut the door in the faces of those who are only four feet high. Among the dying utterances of our good friend, the wise statesman and great author, the brilliant orator and magnificent soul, S. S. Cox, was the expressed determination to move in Congress for the transference of more of our Territories into States.

"But," says some one, "in calculating the immensity of our continental acreage you must remember that vast reaches of our public domain are uncultivated heaps of dry sand, and the 'Bad Lands' of Montana and the Great American Desert." I am glad you mentioned that. Within twenty-five years there will not be between the Atlantic and Pacific coasts a hundred miles of land not reclaimed either by farmers'

plow or miners' crowbar. By irrigation, the waters
of the rivers and the showers of heaven, in what are
called the rainy season, will be gathered into great
reservoirs, and through aqueducts let down where and
when the people want them. Utah is an object lesson. Some parts of that territory which were so barren that a spear of grass could not have been raised
there in a hundred years, are now rich as Lancaster
County farms of Pennsylvania, or Westchester farms
of New York, or Somerset County farms of New Jersey. Experiments have proved that ten acres of
ground irrigated from waters gathered in great hydro-
logical basins will produce as much as fifty acres from
the downpour of rain as seen in our regions. We have
our freshets and our droughts; but in those lands
which are to be scientifically irrigated there will be
neither freshets nor droughts. As you take a pitcher
and get it full of water, and then set it on a table and
take a drink out of it when you are thirsty, and never think of drinking a pitcherful all at once, so Montana and Wyoming and Idaho will catch the rains
of their rainy season and take up all the waters of their
rivers in great pitchers of reservoirs, and drink out of
them whenever they will and refresh their land whenever they will. The work has already been grandly
begun by the United States Government. Over four
hundred lakes have already been officially taken
possession of by the nation for the great enterprise of
irrigation. Rivers that have been rolling idly through
these regions, doing nothing on their way to the sea,
will be lassoed and corralled and penned up until such
time as the farmers need them. Under the same processes the Ohio, the Mississippi, and all the other
rivers will be taught to behave themselves better; and
great basins will be made to catch the surplus of waters in times of freshet, and keep them for times of

drought. The irrigating process by which all the arid lands between the Atlantic and Pacific oceans are to be fertilized is no new experiment. It has been going on successfully hundreds of years in Spain, in China, in India, in Russia, in Egypt. About eight hundred million of people of the earth to-day are kept alive by food raised on irrigated land. And here we have allowed to lie waste, given up to rattlesnake and bat and prairie-dog, lands enough to support whole nations of industrious population. The work begun will be consummated. Here and there exceptional lands may be stubborn and refuse to yield any wheat or corn from their hard fists; but if the hoe fail to make an impression, the miner's pickax will discover the reason for it, and bring up from beneath those unproductive surfaces coal and iron and lead and copper and silver and gold. God speed the geologists and the surveyors, the engineers and the senatorial commissions, and the capitalists and the new settlers and the husbandmen, who put their brain and hand and heart to this transfiguration of the American continent!

But while I speak of the immensity of the continent, I must remark it is not an immensity of monotone or tameness. The larger some countries are, the worse for the world. This continent is not more remarkable for its magnitude than for its wonders of construction. What a pity the United States Government did not take possession of Yosemite, California, as it has of Yellowstone, Wyoming, and of Niagara Falls, New York! Yosemite and the adjoining California regions! Who that has seen them can think of them without having his blood tingle? Trees now standing there that were old when Christ lived! These monarchs of foliage reigned before Cæsar or Alexander, and the next thousand years will not shatter their scepter! They are the masts of the continent, their canvas spread on the winds; while the old ship bears on its way through the ages! Their size, of which travelers often speak, does not affect me so much as their longevity. Though so old now, the branches of some of them will crackle in the last conflagration of the planet. That valley of the Yosemite is eight miles long and a half-mile wide and three thousand feet deep. It seems as if it had been the meaning of Omnipotence to crowd into as small a place as possible some of the most stupendous scenery of the world. Some of the cliffs you do not stop to measure by feet, for they are literally a mile high. Steep, so that neither foot of man or beast ever scaled them, they stand in everlasting defiance. If Jehovah has a throne on earth, these are its white pillars. Standing down in this great chasm of the valley you look up, and yonder is Cathedral Rock; vast, gloomy minster built for the silent worship of the mountains. Yonder is Sentinel Rock, three thousand two hundred and seventy feet high, bold, solitary; standing guard among the ages, its top seldom touched, until a bride, one Fourth of July, mounted it and planted the national standard, and the people down in the valley looked up and saw the head of the mountain turbaned with the Stars and Stripes. Yonder are the Three Brothers, four thousand feet high; Cloud's Rest, North and South Dome, and the heights never captured save by the fiery bayonets of the thunder-storm.

No pause for the eye, no stopping-place for the mind. Mountains hurled on mountains. Mountains in the wake of mountains. Mountains flanked by mountains. Mountains split. Mountains ground. Mountains fallen. Mountains triumphant. As though Mount Blanc and the Adirondacks and Mount Washington were here uttering themselves in one magnificent chorus of rock and precipice and waterfall. Sifting and dashing through the rocks, the water comes down. The Bridal Veil Falls so thin you can see the face of the mountain behind it. Yonder is Yosemite Falls, dropping two thousand six hundred and thirty-four feet—sixteen times greater descent than that of Niagara. These waters dashed to death on the rocks, so that the white spirit of the slain waters ascending in robe of mist seeks the heavens. Yonder is Nevada Falls, plunging seven hundred feet, the water in arrows, the water in rockets, the water in pearls, the water in amethysts, the water in diamonds. That cascade flings down the rocks enough jewels to array all the earth in beauty, and rushes on until it drops into a very hell of waters, the smoke of their torment ascending forever and ever.

But the most wonderful part of this American continent is the Yellowstone Park. My visit there last month made upon me an impression that will last forever. After all poetry has exhausted itself, and all the Morans and Bierstadts and the other enchanting artists have completed their canvas, there will be other revelations to make, and other stories of its beauty and wrath, splendor and agony, to be recited. The Yellowstone Park is the geologists' paradise. By cheapening of travel may it become the nation's playground! In some portions of it there seems to be the anarchy of the elements. Fire and water, and the vapor born of that marriage terrific. Geyser cones or hills of crystal that have been over five thousand years growing! In places the earth, throbbing, sobbing, groaning, quaking with aqueous paroxysm. At the expiration of every sixty-five minutes one of the geysers tossing its boiling water one hundred and eighty-five feet in the air and then descending into swinging rainbows. Caverns of pictured walls large enough for the sepulchre of the human race. Formations of stone in shape and color of calla lily, of heliotrope, of rose, of cowslip, of sunflower, and of gladiolus. Sulphur and arsenic and oxide of iron, with their delicate pencils, turning the hills into a Luxemburg, or a Vatican picture-gallery. The so-called Thanatopsis Geyser, exquisite as the Bryant poem it was named after, and Evangeline Geyser, lovely as the Longfellow heroine it commemorates. The so-called Pulpit Terrace, from its white elevation, preaching mightier sermons of God than human lips ever uttered. The so-called Bethesda Geyser, by the warmth of which invalids have already been cured, the angel of health continually stirring the waters. Enraged craters, with heat at five hundred degrees, only a little below the surface. Wide reaches of stone of intermingled colors, blue as the sky, green as the foliage, crimson as the dahlia, white as the snow, spotted as the leopard, tawny as the lion, grizzly as the bear; in circles, in angles, in stars, in coronets, in stalactites, in stalagmites. Here and there are petrified growths, or the dead trees and vegetation of other ages, kept through a process of natural embalmment. In some places waters as innocent and smiling as a child making a first attempt to walk from its mother's lap, and not far off as foaming and frenzied and ungovernable as a maniac in struggle with his keepers.

But after you have wandered along the geyserite enchantment for days, and begin to feel that there can be nothing more of interest to see, you suddenly come upon the peroration of all majesty and grandeur, the Grand Canyon. It is here, that it seems to me—and I speak it with reverence—Jehovah seems to have surpassed himself. It seems a great gulch let down into eternities. Here, hung up and let down and spread abroad, are all the colors of land and sea and sky. Upholstering of the Lord God Almighty. Best work of the Architect of worlds. Sculpturing by the Infinite. Masonry by an omnipotent trowel. Yellow! You never saw yellow unless you saw it there. Red! You never saw red unless you saw it there. Violet! You never saw violet unless you saw it there. Triumphant banners of color. In a cathedral of basalt, Sunrise and Sunset married by the setting of rainbow ring.

Gothic arches, Corinthian capitals and Egyptian basilicas built before human architecture was born. Huge fortifications of granite constructed before war forged its first cannon. Gibraltars and Sebastopols that never can be taken. Alhambras, where kings of strength and queens of beauty reigned long before the first earthly crown was empearled. Thrones on which no one but the King of heaven and earth ever sat. Fount of waters at which the hills are baptized, while the giant cliffs stand 'round as sponsors. For thousands of years before that scene was unveiled to human sight, the elements were busy, and the geysers were hewing away with their hot chisel, and glaciers were pounding with their cold hammers, and hurricanes were cleaving with their lightning strokes, and hailstones giving the finishing touches, and after all these forces of nature had done their best, in our century the curtain dropped, and the world had a new and divinely inspired revelation, the Old Testament written on papyrus, the New Testament written on parchment, and now this last Testament written on the rocks.

Hanging over one of the cliffs I looked off until I could not get my breath, then retreating to a less exposed place I looked down again. Down there is a pillar of rock that in certain conditions of the atmosphere looks like a pillar of blood. Yonder are fifty feet of emerald on a base of five hundred feet of opal. Wall of chalk resting on pedestals of beryl; turrets of light tumbling on floors of darkness; the brown lightening into golden; snow of crystal melting into fire of carbuncle; flaming red cooling into russet; cold blue warming into saffron; dull gray kindling into solferino; morning twilight flushing midnight shadows; auroras crouching among rocks.

Yonder is an eagle's nest on a shaft of basalt. Through an eyeglass we see in it the young eagles, but the stoutest arm of our group cannot hurl a stone near enough to disturb the feathered domesticity. Yonder are heights that would be chilled with horror but for the warm robe of forest foliage with which they are enwrapped; altars of worship at which nations might kneel; domes of chalcedony on temples of porphyry. See all this carnage of color up and down the cliffs; it must have been the battlefield of the war of the elements. Here are all the colors of the wall of heaven, neither the sapphire, nor the chrysolite, nor the topaz, nor the jacinth, nor the amethyst, nor the jasper, nor the twelve gates of twelve pearls, wanting. If spirits bound from earth to heaven could pass up by way of this canyon, the dash of heavenly beauty would not be so overpowering. It would only be from glory to glory. Ascent through such earthly scenery, in which the crystal is so bright, and the red so flaming, would be fit preparation for the "sea of glass mingled with fire."

Standing there in the Grand Canyon of the Yellowstone Park, one August morning, for the most part we held our peace, but after a while it flashed upon me with such power I could not help but say to my comrades: "What a hall this would be for the last Judgment!" See that mighty cascade with the rainbows at the foot of it! Those waters congealed and transfixed with the agitation of that day, what a place they would make for the shining feet of a Judge of quick and dead! And those rainbows look now like the crowns to be cast at his feet. At the bottom of this great canyon is a floor on which the nations of the earth might stand, and all up and down these galleries of rock the nations of heaven might sit. And what reverberation of archangels' trumpet there would be through all these gorges, and from all these caverns, and over all these heights. Why should not the greatest of all the days the world shall ever see close amid the grandest scenery Omnipotence ever built?

Oh, the sweep of the American continent! Sailing up Puget Sound, its shores so bold that for fifteen hundred miles a ship's prow would touch the shore before its keel touched the bottom, I said: "This is the Mediterranean of America." Visiting Portland, and Tacoma and Seattle and Victoria and Fort Townsend and Vancouver and other cities of the Northwest region, I thought to myself: these are the Bostons, New Yorks, Charlestons, and Savannahs of the Pacific coast. But after all this summer's journeying, and my other journeys westward in other summers, I found that I had seen only a part of the American continent, for Alaska is as far west of San Francisco as the coast of Maine is east of it, so that the central city of the American continent is San Francisco.

I have said these things about the magnitude of the continent, and given you a few specimens of some of its wonders, to let you know the comprehensiveness of the text when it says that Christ is going to have dominion from sea to sea; that is, from the Atlantic to the Pacific. Besides that, the salvation of this continent means the salvation of Asia, for we are only thirty-six miles from Asia at the northwest. Only

From Ocean to Ocean

Bering Straits separate us from Asia, and these will be spanned by a great bridge before another century closes, and probably long before that. The thirty-six miles of water between these two continents are not all deep sea, but have three islands, and there are also shoals which will allow piers for bridges, and for the most of the way the water is only about twenty fathoms deep. The Americo-Asiatic bridge which will yet span those straits will make America, Asia, Europe and Africa one continent. The trans Siberian railroad, which the Czar is now building, and which will be finished in 1904, will meet this trans-oceanic bridge. So, you see, America evangelized, Asia will be evangelized; Europe taking Asia from one side and America taking it from the other side. Our great grandchildren will cross that bridge. America and Asia and Europe, all one, what subtraction from the pangs of seasickness! And the prophecies in Revelation will be fulfilled: "There shall be no more sea." But do I mean literally that this American continent is going to be all Gospelized? I do. Christopher Columbus, when he went ashore from the *Santa Maria*, and his second brother Alonzo, when he went ashore from the *Pinta*, and his third brother Vincent, when he went ashore from the *Nina*, took possession of this country in the name of the Father and the Son and the Holy Ghost. Satan has no more right to this country than I have to your pocketbook. To hear him talk on the roof of the Temple, where he proposed to give Christ the kingdoms of this world and the glory of them, you might suppose that Satan was a great capitalist, or that he was loaded up with real estate, when the old miscreant never owned an acre or an inch of ground on this planet. For that reason I protest against something I heard and saw while traveling in Montana and Oregon and Wyoming and Idaho and Colorado and California. They have given diabolic names to many places in the West and Northwest. As soon as you get in Yellowstone Park or California you have pointed out to you places cursed with such names as "The Devil's Slide," "The Devil's Kitchen," "The Devil's Thumb," "The Devil's Pulpit," "The Devil's Mush Pot," "The Devil's Teakettle," "The Devil's Sawmill," "The Devil's Machine-shop," "The Devil's Gate," and so on. Now it is very much needed that geological surveyor, or Congressional committee, or group of distinguished tourists go through Montana and Wyoming and California and Colorado, and give other names to these places. All these regions belong to the Lord and to a Christian nation, and away with such Plutonic nomenclature!

But how is this continent to be Gospelized? The pulpit and a Christian printing-press harnessed together will be the mightiest team for the first plow. Not by the power of cold, formalistic theology; not by ecclesiastical technicalities. I am sick of them, and the world is sick of them. But it will be done by the warm-hearted, sympathetic presentation of the fact that Christ is ready to pardon all our sins, and heal all our wounds, and save us both for this world and the next. Let your religion of glaciers crack off and fall into the Gulf Stream and get melted. Take all your creeds of all denominations and drop out of them all human phraseology and put in only Scriptural phraseology, and you will see how quick the people will jump after them. On the Columbia River we saw the salmon jump clear out of the water in different places; I suppose for the purpose of getting the insects. And if when we want to fish for men we could only have the right kind of bait, they will spring out above the flood of their sins and sorrows to reach it. The Young Men's Christian Associations of America will also do part of the work. All over the continent I saw their new buildings rising. In Vancouver I asked: "What are you going to put on that sightly place?" The answer was: "A Young Men's Christian Association building." At Lincoln, Neb., I said: "What are they making those excavations for?" Answer: "For our Young Men's Christian Association building." At Des Moines, Ia., I saw a noble structure rising, and I asked for what purpose it was being built, and they told me for the Young Men's Christian Association. These institutions are going to take the young men of this nation for God; these institutions seem in better favor with God and man than ever before. Business men and capitalists are awaking to the fact that they can do nothing better in the way of living beneficence, or in last will and testament, than to do what Mr. Marquand did for Brooklyn when he made the Young Men's Christian palace possible. These institutions will get our young men all over the land into a stampede for heaven. Thus we will all in some way help on the work, you with your ten talents, I with five, somebody else with three. It is estimated that to irrigate the arid and desert lands of America, as they ought to be irrigated, it will cost about one hundred million dollars to gather the waters into reservoirs. As much contribution and effort as that would irrigate with Gospel influences all the waste places of this continent. Let us by prayer and contribution and right living all help to fill the reservoirs. You will carry a bucket, and you a cup, and even a thimbleful would help. And after a while God will send the floods of mercy so gathered, pouring down over all the land, and some of us on earth and some of us in heaven will sing with Isaiah, "In the wilderness waters have broken out, and streams in the deserts," and with David, "There is a river the streams whereof shall make glad the City of God." Oh, fill up the reservoirs!

THE AMERICAN SHEAF

A Thanksgiving Sermon.

Genesis, 37: 7: "We were binding sheaves in the field, and lo, my sheaf arose, and also stood upright; and, behold, your sheaves stood round about, and made obeisance to my sheaf."

THE AMERICAN SHEAF

A Thanksgiving Sermon.

Genesis, 37: 7: " We were binding sheaves in the field, and lo, my sheaf arose, and also stood upright; and, behold, your sheaves stood round about, and made obeisance to my sheaf."

A Josephic dream! At seventeen years of age, and when life is most roseate, Joseph, in vision, saw a great harvest field, himself and his brethren at work in it, and after a while the sheaf that he was binding rose up with an imperial air, and the sheaves of the other harvesters fell flat on their faces as the over-awed subjects of an empire might fall down on their faces before a king. The dream was fulfilled when there was famine in Egypt and Joseph had the care of all the corn-cribs, and his brethren came and implored food from him. Sure enough, all their sheaves bowed to his sheaf. A Thanksgiving Day vision! I am away out in the center of a field where the harvests of all nations are reaping. Here is the great American sheaf. Sheaf of wheat, sheaf of rice, sheaf of corn, sheaf floral; agricultural, homological, mineralogical, literary and moral prosperities—all bound together in one great sheaf. It is kingly, and on its brow is the golden coronal of all the year's sunshine, and in its presence all the sheaves of European and Asiatic harvests bend and fall down, feeling their littleness. Oh, the sheaf, the golden sheaf, the overtopping sheaf of American prosperity! Other nations far surpass ours in antiquities, in cathedrals, in titled pomp, in art galleries; but in most things their sheaves must bow to our sheaf. I have an idea that the most favored constellation of immensity is the one of which the earth is a star, and of the hemispheres the western is the most favored, and that of the zones the temperate is the more desirable, and the United States are the best part of the American continent. The best place on earth to live is here. Had it not been so, there would have been three hundred thousand Americans last year moving into Europe, instead of three hundred thousand Europeans moving into America.

Human nature has a strong tendency to fault-finding. The pessimists outnumber the optimists. Where there is one man who sings and whistles and laughs, there are ten men who sigh and groan and complain. We are more apt to compare our condition with those who are better off than with those who are worse off.

I propose this Thanksgiving morning, for the purpose of stirring your gratitude, to show you how much preferable is the condition of this nation to all other nations, and how the Italian sheaf and the British sheaf and the Spanish sheaf and the French sheaf and all the other sheaves, must bow down to our American sheaf.

Have you realized your superior blessings atmospheric? Have you thought of the fact that most of the millions of the human race are in climates frigid or torrid or horrid? Take up the map, and thank God that you are are so far off from Arctic icebergs on the one side and seven-feet-long cobras on the other. For what multitudes of the human race, life is an Arctic expedition! Underground huts. Immeasurable barrenness. Life a prolonged shiver. Our front door-steps on a January night are genial compared with their climate. Ask some of the Arctic explorers about the luxuries of life around the North

Pole. Instead of killing so many brave men in Polar expeditions, we had better send messengers to persuade those pale inhabitants of polar climates to say good-by to the eternal snows and abandon those realms of earth to the walrus and white bear, and shut up those gates of crystal and come down into a realm where the thermometer seldom drops below zero. Oh, the beauties of Baffin's Bay, only six weeks in the year open! What a delightful thing when, in those Arctic regions, they milk their cows and milk only ice-cream! Let all those who, like yourselves, live between thirty and fifty degrees of north latitude, thank God and have sympathy for the vast population of both hemispheres who freeze between sixty and eighty degrees of latitude. Then compare our atmosphere with the heated air, infested with reptilian and insectile life, in which most of the human race suffer. Think of India and China and Ethiopia. Travelers tell you of the delicious orange groves, but ask them about the centipedes. They tell of the odor of the forests, but ask them about the black flies. They tell you about the rich plumage of the birds, but ask them about the malarias. They tell you about the fine riders, but ask them about the Bedouins and bandits. They tell you about the broad piazzas, but ask them about the midnights with the thermometer at an insufferable 110. Vast cities of the torrid clime without sewerage, without cleansing, packed and piled-up wretchedness, and all discomfort. What beautiful hyenas! What fascinating scorpions! What sociable tarantulas! What captivating lizards! What wealth of bugs! What an opportunity to study comparative anatomy and herpetology! What a chance to look into the open countenance of the pleasing crocodile. Hundreds of millions of people in such surroundings! I would rather live in one of these

American cities in a house with two rooms than to live in the torrid lands and own all Brazil, all Hindustan, all Arabia, all China.

There is not a land where wages and salaries are so large for the great masses of the people as here. In Ireland, in some parts, eight cents a day for wages; in England, a dollar a day good wages, vast populations not getting as much as that; in other lands, fifty cents a day and twenty-five cents a day, clear on down to starvation and squalor. An editor in England told me that his salary was seven hundred and fifty dollars a year, and he seemed satisfied! Look at the great populations coming out of the factories of other lands, and accompany them to their homes, and see what privation the hard-working classes on the other side the sea suffer.

The laboring classes here are ten per cent. better off than in any other country under the sun—twenty per cent., forty per cent., fifty per cent., seventy-five per cent. The toilers with hand and foot have better homes and better furnished. I do not talk an abstraction. I know what I have seen. The stonemasons, and carpenters, and plumbers, and mechanics, and artisans of all styles in America have finer residences than the majority of the professional men in Great Britain. You enter the laborer's house on this side the sea and you will find upholstery and pictures and instruments of music. His children are educated at the best schools; his life is insured so that in case of his sudden demise the family shall not be homeless. Let all American workmen know that while their wages may not be as high as they would like to have them, America is the paradise of industry.

Again, there is no land on the earth where the political condition is so satisfactory as here. Every two years in the State and every four years in the nation we clean house. After a vehement expression of the people at the ballot-box in the autumnal election, they all seem satisfied; and if they are not satisfied, at any rate they smile.

An Englishman asked me in an English rail train this question: "How do you people stand it in America with a revolution every four years? Wouldn't it be better for you, like us, to have a Queen for a lifetime and everything settled?" England changes government just as frequently as we do. At some adverse vote in Parliament out goes the Conservative and in comes the Liberal; and after a while there will be another admonitory vote in Parliament, and out will go the Liberal, and in will come the Conservative. Administrations change there, but not as advantageously as here, for there they may change almost any day, while here a party in power continues in power four years.

It is said that in this country we have more political dishonesty than in any other land. The difference is that in this country almost every official has a chance to steal, while in other lands a few people absorb so much that the others have no chance at appropriation! The reason they do not steal is they cannot get their hands on it! The governments of Europe are so expensive that after the salaries of the royal families are paid there is not much left to misappropriate.

The Emperor of Russia has a nice little salary of eight million two hundred and ten thousand dollars; the Emperor of Austria has a yearly salary of four million dollars; Victoria, the Queen, has a salary of two million two hundred thousand dollars; the royal plate at St. James' palace is worth ten million dollars; the Queen's hairdresser gets ten thousand dollars a year for combing the royal locks, while the most of us have to comb our hair at less than half that expense, if we have any to comb!

Over there, there is a host of attendants, all on salaries, some of them five thousand and six thousand dollars a year; Master of Buck Hounds, seven thousand five hundred dollars a year. (I translate pounds into dollars.) Gentlemen of the Wine and Beer Cellars, Controller of the Household, Groom of the Robes, Mistress of the Robes, Captain of Gold Stick, Lieutenant of Gold Stick, Lieutenant of Silver Stick, Clerk of the Powder Closet, Pages of the Back Stairs, Maids of Honor, Master of Horse, Chief Equerry, Equerries in Ordinary, Crown Equerry, Hereditary Grand Falconer, Vice Chamberlain, Clerk of Kitchen, Master of Forks, Grooms in Waiting, Lords in Waiting, Grooms of the Great Chamber, Sergeant-at-Arms, Barge Master and Waterman, Eight Bedchamber Women, Eight Ladies of the Bedchamber, Ten Grooms of the Great Chain, and so on, and so on, *ad infinitum, ad nauseam*.

All this is only a type of the fabulous expense of foreign governments. All this paid out of the sweat and the blood of the people. Are the people satisfied? However much the Germans like William, and the Spaniards like their young King, and England likes her glorious Queen, these stupendous governmental expenses are built on a groan of dissatisfaction as wide as Europe. If it were left to the people of England, of Germany, of Austria, of Spain, of Russia, whether these expensive establishments should be kept up, do you doubt what the vote would be?

Now, is it not better that we be overtaxed and the surplus be distributed all over the land among the lobby men, and that it go into the hands of hundreds and thousands of people—is there not a better chance of its finally getting down into the hands of honest people, than if it were all built up, piled up inside gardens and palaces?

Again, the monopolistic oppression is less here than anywhere else. The air here is full of protest because great houses, great companies, great individuals, are building such over-towering fortunes. Stephen Girard and John Jacob Astor stared at in their time for their august fortunes, would not now be pointed at in the streets of Philadelphia or New York as anything remarkable. These vast fortunes for some imply pinchedness of want for others. A great protuberance on a man's head implies the illness of the whole body. These estates of disproportioned size weaken all the body politic. But the evil is nothing here compared with the monopolistic oppression abroad. Just look at their ecclesiastical establishments. Look at those great cathedrals built at fabulous expense and supported by ecclesiastical machinery at vast expense, and sometimes in an audience room that would hold a thousand people, twenty or thirty people gather for worship. The pope's income is eight million dollars. Cathedrals of statuary and braided arch and walls covered with masterpieces of Rubens and Raphael and Michael Angelo, against all the walls dashing seas of poverty, and crime, and filth, and abomination.

Ireland to-day one vast monopolistic devastation. About thirty-five millions of people in Great Britain, and yet all the soil owned by about thirty-two thousand. Statistics enough to shake the earth, Duke of Devonshire owning ninety-six thousand acres in Derbyshire, Duke of Richmond owning three hundred thousand acres at Gordon Castle, Marquis of Breadalbane going on a journey of one hundred miles in a straight line, all on his own property; Duke of Sutherland has an estate as wide as Scotland, which dips into the sea on both sides. Bad as we have it here, it is a thousand times worse there.

Beside that, if here a few fortunes overshadow all others, we must remember there is a vast throng of

Sermons by T. DeWitt Talmage

other people being enriched, and this fact shows the
thriftiness of the country. It is estimated that there
are over five thousand millionaires in the United
States. In addition to this, you must remember that
there are successes on less extended scale. Tens of
thousands of people worth five hundred thousand dollars; scores of thousands of people worth
one hundred thousand dollars each. Yea, the majority of the people of the United States are on their
way to fortunes. They will either be rich themselves
or their children will be rich. If I should leave to
some men the question: "Will you have a fortune
and your children struggle on through their lives in
the struggle you have had to make—will you have
the fortune, or would you rather that they should have
the fortune?" Scores of men would say: "I am willing to fight this battle all the way through and give my
children a chance; I don't care so much about myself;
it's only for ten or twenty years, anyhow; give my
children a chance." If anything stirs my admiration
it is to see a man without any education himself sending his sons to college, and without any opportunity
for luxury himself, resolved that though he may have
it hard all the days of his life, his children shall have
a good start. And I tell you, although some of you
may have sore commercial struggle, there is going to
be a great opening for your sons and your daughters
as they come on to take their places in society.

Besides that, the domains of Europe and Asia are
already full. Every place occupied unless it be desert
or volcano or condemned barrens, while here we have
plenty of room, and the resources are only just opening. In other lands, if fortunes fatten they must fatten on others; but here they can fatten out of illimitable prairies and out of inexhaustible mines.

We have only just begun to set the Thanksgiving
table in this country. We have just put on one silver

fork, and one salt cellar, and one loaf of bread, and one smoking platter. Wait until the fruits come in from all the orchards, and the meats from all the markets, and the vegetables from all the gardens, and the silver from all the mines, and the dinner bell rings, saying: "Thanksgiving table spread. Come all the people from between the two oceans. Come from between the Thousand Isles and the Gulf of Mexico. Come and dine!" The prospects are so magnificent that for centuries to come all the other sheaves will have to bow to our sheaf.

Again, the nation is more fully at peace than any other. At least fifteen million men belonging to the standing armies of Europe to-day. Since we had our conflict, on the other side the sea they have had Zulu war, Afghan war, Egyptian war, Russo-Turkish war, German-French war. No certainty about the future. All the governments of Europe watching each other lest one of them get too much advantage. Diplomacy all the time nervously at work. Four nations watching the Suez Canal as carefully as four cats could watch one rat.

In order to keep peace, intermarriage of royal families; some bright princess compelled to marry some disagreeable foreign dignitary in order to keep the balance of political power in Europe, the ill-matched pair fighting out on a small scale that which would have been international contests, sometimes the husband holding the balance of power, sometimes the wife holding the balance of power. One unwise stroke of Gladstone's pen after Garnet Wolseley had captured Tel-el-Kebir and all Europe would have been one battlefield. Crowded cities, crowded governments, crowded learned institutions, crowded great cities, close by each other. You get in the cars here and you ride one hundred or one hundred and fifty miles; then you come to a great city, as from here to Philadelphia, as from here to Albany, as from here to Boston.

I got on the cars at Manchester and closed my eyes for a long sleep before I got to Liverpool. In forty minutes I was aroused out of sleep by some one saying: "We are here; this is Liverpool." The cities crowded; the populations crowded, packed in between the Pyrenees and the Alps, packed in between the English Channel and the Adriatic so closely they cannot move without treading either on each other's heels or toes. Sceptres clashing, chariot wheels colliding. The nations of Asia and Europe this moment wondering what next.

But on this continent we have plenty of room and nobody to fight. Eight million square miles in North America, and all but one-seventh capable of rich cultivation, implying what fertility and what commerce! Four great basins pouring their waters into the Atlantic, Pacific, Arctic, and Gulf of Mexico. Shore line of twenty-nine thousand nine hundred and sixty-nine miles. The one State of Texas with more square miles than all France, than all Germany.

That our continent might have plenty of elbow room, and not be jostled by the effete governments of Europe, God sank to the depths of the sea a whole continent that once ran from off the coast of Europe to the coast of America—the continent of Atlantis— which allowed the human race to pass from Europe to America on foot, with little or no shipping; that continent dimly described in history, but the existence of which has been proved by archæological evidences innumerable; that whole continent sunken so that a fleet of German, British, and American vessels had to take deep sea soundings to touch the top of it; that highway from Europe to America entirely removed so that for the most part only the earnest, and the persevering, and the brave, could reach America, and that through long sea voyage.

Did I say the whole continent of ours, this North American continent? Governments on the southern end of this continent are gradually coming to the time when they will beg annexation. On the other hand, beautiful and hospitable Canada. The vast majority of the people there are more republican than monarchical in their feelings, and the chief difference between them and us is that they live on one side the St. Lawrence and we on the other. The United States Government will offer hand and heart in marriage to beautiful and hospitable Canada, and Canada will blush and look down, and thinking of her allegiance across the sea, will say: "Ask mother." Peace all over the continent, and nothing to fight about. What a pity that slavery is gone! While that lasted we had something over which the orators could develop their muscles of vituperation and calumny.

We are so hardly put to it for military demonstration that guns and swords and cannon were called out when we celebrated the bicentennial of William Penn, the peaceful Quaker for whom a gun would never have been of any use except to hang his broad brim hat on. Oh, what shall we do for a fight? Will not somebody strike us? We cannot draw swords on the subject of civil service reform, or free trade, or "corners" in wheat. Our ships of war are cruising around the ocean, hoping for something interesting to turn up. Sumter and Moultrie and Pulaski and Fort Lafayette and Fortress Monroe and all the other shaggy lions of war sound asleep on their iron paws. Gunpowder out of fashion, and not even allowed the juvenile population on Fourth of July. Fire-crackers a sin.

Sermons by T. DeWitt Talmage

The land is struck through and through with peace. There is hardly a Northern city where there are not Confederate generals in its law offices, or commercial establishments, or insurance companies. There you sit or stand to-day, side by side—you who wore the blue and you who wore the gray; you who kindled fires on the opposite side of the Potomac in the winter of 1862; you who followed Stonewall Jackson toward the North; and you who followed General Sherman toward the South. Why are you not breaking each other's heads?

Ah! you have irreparably mixed up your politics. The Northern man married a Southern wife, and the Southern man married a Northern wife, and your children are half Mississippian and half New Englander; and to make another division between the North and the South possible you would have to do with your child as Solomon proposed with the child brought before him in judgment—divide it with the sword, giving half to the North and half to the South. No, sir; there is nothing so hard to split as a cradle. Intermarriage will go on and consanguinal ties will be multiplied, and the question for generations to come will be, how we people in this generation got into such an awful wrangle and went to digging such an awful grave trench.

But there is now—look! no blood on the cotton, no mark of cavalry hoof on the wheat. Twenty years ago could the wheat sheaf and the palmetto have stood on the same platform? No. Every grain of this wheat would have been a bullet, and every leaf of the palmetto a sword. "Peace on earth, good will to men." Apple and orange; how the colors blend. In the great harvest field of the world's tranquility all sheaves bowing to our sheaf.

Again, we are better off than other nations in

matters of national debt, our debt less than one-half of that of England, and not more than a third that of France. We have for many years, every day, paid one hundred and forty-two thousand dollars toward the liquidation of the national debt. It is going all to melt away like a snowbank under an April sun.

Again, we have a better climate than in any other nation. We do not suffer from anything like the Scotch mist, or the English fogs, or from anything like the Russian ice blast, or from the awful typhus of Southern Europe, or the Asiatic cholera. Epidemics here are exceptional, very exceptional. Plenty of wood and coal to make a roaring fire in winter time; easy access to sea beach or mountain top when the ardors of summer come down; Michigan wheat for the bread; Long Island corn for the meal; New Jersey pumpkins for the pies; Carolina rice for the queen of puddings; prairie fowl from Illinois; fish from the Hudson and the James; hickory, and hazel, and walnuts from all our woods; Louisiana sugar to sweeten our beverages; Georgia cotton to keep us warm; oats for the horses; carrots for the cattle; and oleomargarine butter for the hogs! In our land all products and all climates that you may desire. Are your nerves weak and in need of bracing up? Go North. Is your throat delicate and in need of balmy airs? Go South. Do you feel crowded and want more room? Go West. Are you tempted to become office-seekers? Go to jail! Almost anything you want you can have. Plenty to eat, plenty to wear, plenty to read.

"It has been well the past year," says the loom. "It has been well," says the type. "It has been well," say pen and chisel and hammer and plough and fishing-net. "It has been well," answer the groves and orchards and studios and factories and workshops and harvest fields of America.

Sermons by T. DeWitt Talmage

Our national sheaf is larger this year, and more regal, and riper, and more richly grained, than at any time since the Pilgrim Fathers settled New England, or the Hollanders founded New York, or the Huguenots took possession of the Carolinas. Sheaf of sheaves. While all others bow before it, let it bow in turn before the good Lord of the unparalleled American harvest. Before him come down all the corn shocks; before him come down the sheaf of governmental sceptres, the sheaf of battle-spears, the sheaf of barbaric arrows, the sheaf of commercial yardsticks, the sheaf of joy, the sheaf of family reunion, the sheaf of thanksgiving. All the sheaves of the harvest field bowing down low at the feet of the great Husbandman.

You have in hackneyed phrase heard over and over again that America is the asylum of the oppressed. This glorious Thanksgiving morning I declare it to be the wardrobe of the earth, the wheat-bin of the hemispheres, the corn-crib of all nations.

THE DECORATION OF GRAVES

Solomon's Song, 4: 4: "The tower of David builded for an armory, whereon there hang a thousand bucklers, all shields of mighty men."

THE DECORATION OF GRAVES

(Preached on the Sunday before Decoration Day.)

Solomon's Song, 4: 4: "The tower of David builded for an armory, whereon there hang a thousand bucklers, all shields of mighty men."

The Church is here compared to an armory, the walls hung with trophies of dead heroes. Walk all about this tower of David and see the dented shields and the twisted swords and the rusted helmets of terrible battle. So we turn our Church to-day into an armory adorned with memories of our departed braves. Blossom and bloom, oh, walls, with stories of self-sacrifice; the shadows gathered into this drapery typical of our grief for the dead, and the light clustered into these constellations symbolical of our national deliverance. You see it is not the blackness of darkness, but night with stellar illumination.

By unanimous decree of the people of the United States of America, the graves of all the Northern and Southern dead are every year decorated. The nation comes forth with garlands for the graves of the departed and consolation for the bereft who are living. All acerbity and bitterness have gone out of the national solemnity, and as the men and women of the South one month ago floralized the cemeteries and graveyards, so to-morrow we the men and women of the North shall put upon the tombs of our dead the kiss of patriotic affection. Bravery always appreciates bravery, though it fight on the other side; and if a soldier of the Federal army had been a month ago at Savannah he would not have been ashamed to march in the floral processions to the cemetery. And if to-morrow there be a Confederate soldier walking in Greenwood, he will be glad to put a sprig of heart's-ease on the silent heart of our dead.

In a battle during our last war, the Confederates were driving back the Federals, who were in swift retreat, when a Federal officer dropped wounded. One of his men stopped at the risk of his life, and put his arms around the officer to carry him from the field. Fifty Confederate muskets were aimed at the young man who was picking up the officer. But the Confederate captain shouted, "Hold! Don't fire! That fellow is too brave to shoot." And as the Federal officer, held up by his private soldier, went limping slowly off the field, the Confederates gave three cheers for the brave private; and just before the two disappeared behind a barn, both the wounded officer and the brave private lifted their caps in gratitude to the Confederate captain. Shall the Gospel be less generous than the world? We stack arms, the bayonet of our Northern gun facing this way, the bayonet of the Southern gun facing the other way, and as the gray of the morning melts into the blue of noon, so the typical gray and blue of old war-times have blended at last, and they quote in the language of King James's translation without any revision: "Glory to God in the highest, and on earth peace, good will to men." That you may act intelligently in this matter, I shall make this an ordination service to the beautiful ceremonies of to-morrow.

What do we mean by this great observance? First, we mean instruction to one whole generation. Subtract 1865, when the war ended, from our 1881 and you will realize what a vast number of people were born since the war, or were so young as to have no vivid appreciation. No one under twenty-six years

The Decoration of Graves

of age has any adequate memory of that prolonged horror. Young man, do you remember it? "Well," you say, "I only remember that mother swooned away while she was reading the newspaper, and that they brought my father home wrapped in the flag, and that a good many people came in the house to pray, and that mother faded away after that until again there were many people in the house, and they told me she was dead."

There are others who cannot remember the roll of a drum or the tramp of a regiment, or a sigh or a tear of that tornado of woe that swept the nation again and again until there was one dead in each house. Now it is the religious duty of those who do remember it to tell those who do not. My young friends, there were such partings at rail-car windows and steamboat wharves, and at front doors of comfortable homes as I pray God you may never witness. Oh, what a time it was, when fathers and mothers gave up their sons, never expecting to see them again, and never did see them again until they came back mutilated and crushed and dead! Four years of blood. Four years of hostile experiences. Four years of ghastliness. Four years of grave-digging. Four years of funerals, coffins, shrouds, hearses, dirges. Mourning! mourning! mourning! It was hell let loose. What a time of waiting for news! Morning paper and evening paper scrutinized for intelligence from the boys at the front. First, announcement that the battle must occur the next day. Then the news of the battle's going on. On the following day still going on. Then news of thirty thousand slain, and of the names of the great generals who had fallen, but no news about the private soldiers. Waiting for news! After many days a load of wounded going through the town or city, but no news from our boy. Then a long list of wounded and a long list of the dead, and a long list of the missing. And among the last list, our boy. When missing? How missing? Who saw him last? Missing! Missing! Was he in the woods or by the stream? How was he hurt? Missing! missing! What burning prayers that he may yet be heard from. In that awful waiting for news many a life perished. The strain of anxiety was too great. That wife's brain gave way that first week after the battle, and ever and anon she walks the floor of the asylum or looks out of the window as though she expected some one to come along the path and up the steps, as she soliloquizes, "Missing! missing!"

What made matters worse, all this might have been avoided. There was no more need of that war than that this moment I should plunge a dagger through your heart. There were a few Christian philanthropists in those days, scoffed at both by North and South, who had the right of it. If they had been heard on both sides we should have had no war and no slavery. It was advised by those Christian philanthropists, "Let the North pay in money for the slaves as property, and set them free." The North said, "We cannot afford to pay." The South said, "We will not sell the slaves anyhow." But the North did pay in war expenses enough to purchase the slaves, and the South was compelled to give up slavery anyhow. Might not the North better have paid the money and saved the lives of five hundred thousand brave men, and might not the South better have sold out slavery and saved her five hundred thousand brave men? While there are wars that are necessary, and when such wars are forced on us, we must fight in self-defense, I here declare that out of one hundred wars ninety-nine of them are unnecessary, and I swear you by the graves of your fathers and brothers,

The Decoration of Graves

and sons to a new hatred for the champion curse of the universe—war! O Lord God, with the hottest bolt of thine omnipotent indignation, strike that monster down forever and ever. Imprison it in the deepest dungeon of the eternal penitentiary. Bolt it in with all the iron ever forged in cannon or moulded into howitzers. Cleave it with all the sabres that ever glittered in battle, and wring its soul with all the pangs which it ever caused. Let it feel all the conflagration of the homesteads it ever destroyed. Deeper down let it fall, and in fiercer flame let it burn, till it has gathered into its heart all the suffering of eternity as well as time. In the name of the millions of graves of its victims, I curse it! The nations need more the spirit of treaty and less of the spirit of war, less of the Disraelian and more of the Gladstonian.

Again, by this national ceremony we mean to honor courage. Many of these departed soldiers were volunteers, not conscripts, and many of those who were drafted might have provided a substitute or got off on furlough or have deserted. The fact that they lie in their graves is proof of their bravery. Brave at the front, brave at cannon's mouth, brave on lonely picket duty, brave in cavalry charge, brave before the surgeon, brave in the dying message to the home circle. We to-morrow put a garland on the brow of courage. The world wants more of it. The Church of God is in woeful need of men who can stand under fire. The lion of worldly derision roars and the sheep tremble. In great reformatory movements at the first shot how many fall back! The great obstacle to the Church's advancement is the inanity, the vacuity, the soft prettiness, the namby-pambyism of professed Christians. Great on a parade, cowards in battle. Afraid of getting their plumes ruffled, they carry a parasol over their helmet. They go into battle not with warriors' gauntlet, but with kid gloves; not clutching the sword-hilt too tightly, lest the glove split at the back. Deliver us from a womanish man, his hair done up with curling tongs and his feet going with girlish steps. In all our reformatory and Christian work the great want is more backbone, more mettle, more daring, more prowess. We would in all our churches like to trade off a hundred do-nothings for one do-everything. "Quit yourselves like men; be strong."

> Thy saints in all this glorious war
>   Shall conquer, though they die;
> They see the triumph from afar,
>   And seize it with their eye.

Again, we mean by this national observance to honor self-sacrifice for others. To all these departed men home and kindred were as dear as our home and kindred are to us. Do you know how they felt? Just as you and I would feel starting out to-morrow morning with nine chances out of ten against our returning alive; for the intelligent soldier sees not only battle ahead, but malarial sickness and exhaustion. Had these men chosen, they could have spent last night in their homes, and to-day have beeen seated where you are. They chose the camp, not because they liked it better than their own house; and followed the drum and fife, not because they were better music than the voices of the domestic circle. South Mountain and Murfreesboro, and the swamps of Chickahominy were not playgrounds.

These heroes risked and lost all for others. There is no higher sublimity than that. To keep three-quarters for ourselves and give one-quarter to others is honorable. To divide even with others is generous. To keep nothing for ourselves and give all for others is magnanimity Christ-like. Put a girdle around your body and then measure the girdle and see if you are fifty or sixty inches round. And is that the circle of your sympathies—the size of yourself? Or, to measure you around the heart, would it take a girdle large enough to encircle the land and encircle the world? You want to know what we dry theologians mean when we talk of vicarious suffering. Look at the soldiers' graves to-morrow and find out. Vicarious! pangs for others, wounds for others, homesickness for others, blood for others, sepulchre for others.

Those who visit the national cemeteries to-morrow at Arlington Heights and at Richmond and Gettysburg will see one inscription on soldiers' tombs oftener repeated than any other—"Unknown." When, six or seven years ago, I was called to deliver the oration at Arlington Heights, Washington, I was not as much impressed with the minute guns that shook the earth, or with the attendance of President and Cabinet and foreign ministers and generals of the army and commodores of the navy as with the pathetic and overwhelming suggestiveness of that epitaph on so many graves at my feet. "Unknown!" "Unknown!" Oh, is it not almost time to take off that epitaph? It seems to me that the time must come when the Government of the United States shall take off that epitaph. They are no more unknown! We have found them out at last. They are the beloved sons of the Republic.

Would it not be well to take the statue of the heathen goddess off the top of the Capitol at Washington (for I have no faith in the morals of a heathen goddess) and put one great statue in all our national cemeteries—a statue of liberty in the form of a Christian woman with her hand on an open Bible and her foot on the Rock of Ages, with the other hand pointing down to the graves of the unknown, saying, "These are my sons who died that I might live." Take off the misnomer. Everybody knows them. It is of comparatively little importance what was the name given them in baptism of water. In the holier and mightier baptism of blood we know them, and to-morrow the nation puts both arms around them and hugs them to her heart, crying, "Mine forever!"

Again, by this national ceremony we mean the future defense of this nation. By every wreath of flowers on the soldiers' graves we say, "Those who die for the country shall not be forgotten," and that will give enthusiasm to our young men in case our nation should in the future need to defend itself in battle. We shall never have another war between North and South. The old decayed bone of contention, American slavery, has been cast out; although here and there a depraved politician takes it up to see if he can't gnaw something off it. We are floating off farther and farther from the possibility of sectional strife. Rutherford B. Hayes wrought four years toward pacification, and President Garfield has no better man in his Cabinet than Secretary Hunt, of New Orleans, Louisiana. The great sectional contest which raged from Canada to the Gulf of Mexico and from the Atlantic to the Pacific, for many years, has dwindled down and dwindled down till there is so little of it that a bear-garden at Albany to-day attracts the attention of all the nation.

No possibility of civil war. But about foreign invasion I am not so certain. When I spoke against war I said nothing against self-defense. An inventor told me the other day at Washington that he had invented a style of weapon which could be used in self-defense, but not in aggressive warfare. I said, "When you get the nations to adopt that weapon you have introduced the millennium." I have no right to go on

The Decoration of Graves

my neighbor's premises and assault him, but if some ruffian break into my house for the assassination of my family, and I can borrow a gun and load it in time and aim it straight enough, I will shoot him.

There is no room on this continent for any other nation—except Canada, and a better neighbor no one ever had. If you do not think so, go to Montreal and Toronto, and see how well they will treat you. Other than that there is absolutely no room for any other nation. I have been across the continent again and again, and know that we have not a half inch of ground for the gouty foot of foreign despotism to stand on. But I am not so sure that some of the arrogant nations of Europe may not some day challenge us. I do not know that those forts around New York Bay are to sleep all through the next century. I do not know that Barnegat lighthouse will not yet look off upon a hostile navy. I do not know but that a half dozen nations, envious of our prosperity, may want to give us a wrestle. During our Civil War there were two or three nations that could hardly keep their hands off us. It is very easy to pick national quarrels, and if our nation escapes much longer it will be the exception. If foreign foe should come, we want men like those of 1812 and like those of 1861 to meet them. We want them all up and down the coast, Pulaski and Fort Sumter in the same chorus of thunder as Fort Lafayette and Fort Hamilton. Men who will not only know how to fight, but how to die. When such a time comes, if it ever does come, the generations on the stage of action will say, "My country will care for my family as they did in the soldiers' asylums for the orphans in the Civil War, and my country will honor my dust as it honored those who preceded me in patriotic sacrifice, and once a year at any rate, on Decoration Day, I shall be resurrected into the remembrance of those for whom I died. Here I go for God and my country!"

I have sometimes thought it might need a foreign invasion to make us forget all our sectional strife—I mean, to entirely and forever forget it. If such an invasion should ever come, you would see the North, the South, the East, the West, side by side, as though they had never had any quarrel. I see them in imagination going to the conflict: Fifteenth New York volunteers, Tenth Alabama cavalry, Fourteenth Pennsylvania riflemen, Tenth Massachusettts artillery, Seventh South Carolina sharpshooters. And such a strong conjunction of officers: Blaine and Conkling and Garfield and Grant and Mahone and Cornell and Sherman, and all the stalwarts and half-breeds and full-bloods. I do not know but it may require the attack of some foreign foe to make us forget our absurd sectional wrangling. I have no faith in the cry, "No North, no South, no East, no West." Let all four sections keep their peculiarities and their preferences, each doing its own work and not interfering with each other, each of the four carrying its part in the great harmony—the bass, the alto, the tenor, the soprano— in the grand march of Union.

Once more, this great national ceremony means the beautification of the tombs, whether of those who fell in battle or accident, or who have expired in their beds or in our arms or on our laps. I suppose you have noticed that many of the families take this season as the time for the adornment of their family plots. This national observance has secured the arboriculture and floriculture of the cemeteries, the straightening up of many a slab planted thirty or forty years ago; and has swung the scythe through the long grass and has brought the stonecutter to call out the half-obliterated epitaph. This day is the benediction of the resting

place of father, mother, son, daughter, brother, sister
It is all that we can do for them now. Make their
resting places attractive, not absurd with costly outlay,
but in quiet remembrance. You know how. If you
can afford only one flower, that will do. It shows
what you would do if you could. One blossom from
you may mean more than the Duke of Wellington's
catafalque. Oh, we cannot afford to forget them.
They were so lovely to us. We miss them so much.
We will never get over it. Blessed Lord Jesus, comfort our broken hearts. From every bank of flowers
breathes promise of resurrection.

In olden times the Hebrews, returning from their
burial-place, used to pluck the grass from the field
three or four times, then throw it over their heads, suggestive of the resurrection. We pick not the grass,
but the flowers; and instead of throwing them over our
heads, we place them before our eyes, right down over
the silent heart that once beat with warmest love toward us, or over the still feet that ran to service, or
over the lips from which we took the kiss at the
anguish of the last parting. O my glorified father! O
my sainted mother! O my beloved brothers and sisters!
O my son! My son! My son! If you pass to-morrow near the new entrance of Greenwood, you who
knew him will find his new-made grave. If you go
that way, drop a flower on that mound. Your grief is
mine, and my grief is yours. But stop! We are not
infidels. Our bodies will soon join the bodies of our
departed in the tomb, and our spirits shall join their
spirits in the land of the rising sun. We cannot long
be separated. Instead of crying with Jacob for
Joseph, "I will go down into the grave unto my son,
mourning," let us cry with David, "I shall go to him."
On one of the gates of Greenwood is the quaint inscription, "A night's lodging on the way to the city

of the New Jerusalem." Comfort one another with these words. May the hand of him who shall wipe away all tears from all eyes wipe your cheek with softest tenderness. The Christ of Mary and Martha and Lazarus will enfold you in his arms. The white-robed angels who sat at the tomb of Jesus will yet roll the stone from the door of your dead in radiant resurrection. The Lord himself shall descend from heaven with a shout and the voice of the archangel. So the Dead March in Saul shall become the Hallelujah Chorus.

HALF A PLANET

Deut., 3: 27: " Lift up thine eyes westward."

HALF A PLANET

Deut., 3: 27: "Lift up thine eyes westward."

So God said to Moses in Bible times, and so he said to Christoforo Colombo, the son of a wool-comber of Genoa, more than four hundred years ago. As if to condemn the slur that different ages put upon mothers-in-law, the mother-in-law of Columbus gave him the sea-charts and maps and other navigators' materials out of which he ciphered America. The nations had been looking chiefly toward the East. The sculpture of the world, the architecture of the world, the laws of the world, the philosophy of the world, the civilization of the world, the religion of the world came from the East. But, while Columbus, as his name was called after it was Latinized, stood studying maps and examining globes and reading cosmography, God said to him: "Lift up thine eyes toward the West." The fact was it must have seemed to Columbus a very lop-sided world. Like a cart with one wheel, like a scissors with one blade, like a sack on one side of a camel, needing a sack on the other side to balance it. Here was a bride of a world with no bridegroom. When God makes a half of anything he does not stop there. He makes the other half. We are all obliged sometimes to leave things only half done. But God never stops half-way, because he has the time and the power to go all the way. I do not wonder that Columbus was not satisfied with half a world, and so went to work to find the other half. The pieces of carved wood that were floated to the shores of Europe by a westerly gale, and two dead human faces, unlike anything he had seen before, likewise floated from the West, were to him the voice of God, saying: "Lift up thine eyes toward the West."

But the world then as now had plenty of Can't-be-Done's. That is what keeps individuals back and enterprises back and the church back, and nations back —ignominious and disgusting and disheartening Can't-be-Done's. Old navigators said to young Columbus, "It can't be done." The republic of Genoa said, "It can't be done." Alphonso V. said, "It can't be done." A committee on maritime affairs, to whom the subject was submitted, declared, "It can't be done." Venetians said, "It can't be done." After a while the story of this poor but ambitious Columbus reaches the ear of Queen Isabella, and she pays eighty dollars to buy him a decent suit of clothes, so that he may be fit to appear before royalty. The interview in the palace was successful. Money enough was borrowed to fit out the expedition.

There they are, the three ships, in the Gulf of Cadiz, Spain. If you ask me which have been the most famous boats of the world I would say, first, Noah's ship, that wharfed on Mount Ararat; second, the boat of bulrushes, in which Moses floated the Nile; third, the Mayflower, that put out from Plymouth with the Pilgrim Fathers; and now these three vessels that on this, the Friday morning, August 3, 1492, are rocking on the ripples. I am so glad it is Friday, so that the prows of those three ships shall first run down the superstition that things begun or voyages started on Friday must necessarily be disastrous. Show me any Monday or Tuesday or Wednesday or Thursday or Saturday that ever accomplished as much as this expedition that started on Friday. With the idea that there will be perils connected with the expedition, the Sacrament of the Lord's Supper is administered.

Half a Planet.

Do not forget that this voyage was begun under religious auspices. There is the *Santa Maria,* only ninety feet long, with four masts and eight anchors. The captain walking the deck is fifty-seven years old, his hair white, for at thirty-five he was gray, and his face is round, his nose aquiline and his stature a little taller than the average. I know from his decided step and the set of his jaw that he is a determined man. That is Captain Christopher Columbus. Near-by, but far enough off not to run into each other, are the smaller ships, the *Pinta* and the *Nina,* about large enough and safe enough to cross the Hudson River or the Thames in good weather. There are two doctors in this fleet of ships, and a few landsmen, adventurers who are ready to risk their necks in a wild expedition. There are enough provisions for a year. "Captain Columbus, where are you sailing for?" "I do not know." "How long before you will get there?" I cannot say." "All ashore that are not going," is heard, and those who wish to remain behind go to the land. Now the anchors of the three ships are being weighed and the ratlines begin to rattle and the sails to unfurl. The wind is dead east, and it does not take long to get out to sea. In a few hours the adventurers wish they had not started. The ships begin to roll and pitch. Oh, what a delightful sensation to landsmen! They begin to bother Christopher Columbus with questions. They want to know what he thinks of the weather. They want to know when he thinks they will probably get there. Every time when he stands taking observations of the sun with an astrolabe they wonder what he sees and ask more questions. The crew are rather grouty. Some of them came on under four months' advance pay and others were impressed into the service. For sixteen days the wind is dead east, and that pleases the captain, because it blows them further and further away from the European coast, and further on toward the shore of another country, if there is any. After a while there comes a calm day and the attempt is made to fathom the ocean, and they cannot touch bottom though the line and lead run down 200 fathoms. More delightful sensations for those who are not good sailors! A fathom is six feet and two hundred fathoms are one thousand and two hundred feet, and below that it may be many hundred fathoms deeper. To add interest to the voyage, on the twentieth day out, a violent storm sweeps the sea, and the Atlantic Ocean tries what it can do with the ships *Santa Maria*, the *Pinta* and the *Nina*. Some of you know something of what a sea can do with the *Umbria*, the *Majestic*, the *Teutonic* and the *Paris*, and you must imagine what the ocean could do with those three small ships of olden times. You may judge what the ocean was then by what it is now; it has never changed its habits. It can smile like the morning, but often it is the archangel of wrath, and its most rollicking fun is a shipwreck. The mutinous crew would have killed Columbus had it not been for the general opinion on shipboard that he was the only one that could take them back home in safety. The promise of a silk waistcoat and forty dollars in money to the man who should first discover land, appeased them somewhat, but the indignation and blasphemy and threats of assassination must have been awful. Yet God sustained the great sailor commanding the *Santa Maria*. Every evening on shipboard they had prayers and sung a vesper hymn. But, after all the patience of those on board the ships had been exhausted, and the great captain or admiral had been cursed by every anathema that human lips could frame, one night a sailor saw a light moving along the shore, and then moving up and down, and then disappearing. On Friday morning, October 12, 1492, a gun from the *Pinta* signaled "Land ahead." At two o'clock, just long enough after Thursday to make it sure it was Friday, and to give another blow at the world's ideas of unlucky days. Then the ships lay to, and the boats were lowered, and Captain Christopher Columbus first stepped upon the shore, amid the song of birds and the air a surge of redolence, and took possession in the name of the Father and the Son and the Holy Ghost. So the voyage that began with the sacrament ended with Gloria in Excelsis Deo.

From that day onward, you say there can be nothing for Columbus but honors, rewards, rhapsodies, palaces and world-wide applause. No, no! On his way back to Spain the ship was so wrenched by the tempest and so threatened with destruction that he wrote a brief account of his discovery and put it in a cask and threw it overboard, that the world might not lose the advantage of his adventures. Honors awaited him on the beach; but he undertook a second voyage and with it came all maligning and persecution and denunciation and poverty. He was called a land-grabber, a liar, a cheat, a fraud, a deceiver of nations. Speculators robbed him of his good name, courtiers depreciated his discoveries, and there came to him ruined health and imprisonment and chains, of which he said while he rattled them on his wrists: "I will wear them as a memento of the gratitude of princes." Amid keen appreciation of the world's abuse and cruelty, and with body writhing in the tortures of gout, he groaned out his last words: "In manus tuas Domine commendo spiritum meum:" "Into thy hands, Oh, Lord, I commend my spirit."

Of course he had regal obsequies. That is the way the world tries to atone for its mean treatment of great benefactors. Many a man has had a fine ride to his grave who during this life had to walk all the way. A big funeral, and instead of bread they give him a stone—that is, a tombstone. But death that brings quiet to the body of others did not bring quiet to his. First buried in the church of Santa Maria. Seven years afterward removed to Seville. Twenty-three years afterward removed to San Domingo. Finally removed to Cuba. Four post-mortem journeys from sepulchre to sepulchre. I wish his bones had been transported to our own shores, where they belong, and that in the fifth century after his decease the American continent might have built a mausoleum worthy of him who picked this jewel of a hemisphere out of the sea and set it in the crown of the world's geography.

Four Re-Burials

But the bright noonday sun of that old sailor's prosperity went down in thickest night, and though here and there a monument has been lifted in his memory, and here and there a city called after him, the continent that he was the means of founding was named after another name and no fitting commemoration of his work has been proposed until nearly four hundred years after his body turned to dust. May the imposing demonstration now being made in his honor on the Atlantic coast, and to be made next year in his honor mid-continent, be brilliant enough and far-resounding enough and Christian enough and magnificent enough to atone for the neglect of centuries. May the good Lord allow that most illustrious sailor of all time to look over the amethystine battlements long enough to see some of the garlands wreathed around his name and hear something of the hemispheric shout that shall greet his memory.

What most impresses me in all that wondrous life, which, for the next twelve months, we will be commemorating by sermon and song and military parade and World's Fair and Congress of Nations, is something I have never heard stated, and that is, that the discovery of America was a religious discovery and in the name of God. Columbus, by the study of prophecies and by what Zechariah and Micah and David and Isaiah had said about the "ends of the earth," was persuaded to go out and find the "ends of the earth," and he felt himself called by God to carry Christianity to the "ends of the earth." Then, the administration of the Last Supper before they left the Gulf of Cadiz, and the evening prayers during the voyage, and the devout ascription as soon as they saw the new world, and the doxologies with which they landed, confirm me in saying that the discovery of America was a religious discovery. Atheism has no right here; infidelity has no right here; vagabondism has no right here. And as God is not apt to fail in any of his undertakings (at any rate, I have never heard of his having anything to do with a failure), America is going to be gospelized, and from the Golden Gate of California to the Narrows of New York Harbor, and from the top of North America to the foot of South America, from Behring Straits to Cape Horn, this is going to be Immanuel's Land. All the forms of irreligion and abomination that have cursed other parts of the world will land here—yea, they have already landed—and they will wrangle for the possession of this hemisphere, and they will make great headway and feel themselves almost established. But at what time they feel themselves secure of domination they will be made to bite the dust. God will not forget the prophecies which encouraged Columbus about the "ends of the earth seeing the salvation of God," nor the Christian anthem which Columbus led on the morning of the 12th of October, 1492, on the coast of San Salvador. Like that flock of land birds which met the *Santa Maria*, and the *Pinta*, and the *Nina* far out at sea, indicating to the commanders of that fleet that they were approaching some country, so a whole flock of promises and hopes, golden-winged and songful, this morning alight around us, assuring us that we are approaching the glorious period of American evangelization. A Divine influence will yet sweep the continent that will make iniquity drop like slacked lime, and will make the most blatant infidelity declare it was only joking when it said the Bible was not true, and the worst atheism announce that it always did believe in the God of Nations. Let others call for Requiem and Dead March; I call for George Frederick Handel's Hallelujah Chorus.

There has been much talk of late about communication with other worlds. Mars has come so near we can see its canals, and it has been hoped that by signals after a while we may communicate with other stars. Ah, that will not be possible until our world has been reformed and evangelized. It would not do for our world in its lost and ruined state to have communication with other worlds. It would spoil their morals. But wait until this world is fully redeemed, as it will be, and then perhaps interstellar correspondence may be opened. Till then, this smitten and sickened world of ours must be quarantined from coming too near the unfallen worlds. But, thank God! the prophecies which cheered Columbus in his undertaking cheer us. America for God! Yea, the round world for God! There can be no doubt about it.

That great Italian navigator also impresses me with the idea that when one does a good thing, he cannot appreciate its ramifications. To the moment of his death, Columbus never knew that he had discovered America, but thought that Cuba was a part of Asia. He thought the Island of Hispaniola was the

Half a Planet

Ophir of Solomon. He thought he had only opened a new way to old Asia. Had he known what North and South America were and are, and that he had found a country three thousand miles wide, ten thousand miles long, of near sixteen million square miles, and four times as large as Europe, the happiness would have been too much for mortal man to endure. He had no idea that the time would come when a nation of sixty million people on this side of the sea would be joined by all the intelligent nations on the other side the sea, for the most part of the year reciting his wonderful deeds. It took centuries to reveal the result of that one transatlantic voyage. So it has always been. Could Paul, on that June day, when he was decapitated, have had any idea of what effect his letters and the account of his life would have on Christendom? Could Martin Luther have had any idea of the echoes that would ring through the ages from the bang of his hammer nailing the Latin theses against a church door at Wittenberg? Could Eli Whitney have realized the continents of wealth that would be added to the South by the invention of his cotton gin? Could John Guttenberg, toiling year after year, making type, and laboriously setting them side by side, and with presses changed now this way and that, and sued by John Faust for money loaned, and many of the people trying to cheat Guttenberg out of his invention, he toiling on until he produced the Mazarin Bible, have any idea that, as a result of his invention, there would be librairies that, placed side by side, would again and again engirdle the earth, or the showers of newspapers that snow the world under? When Manhattan Island was sold to the Dutch for twenty-four dollars, neither they who sold, nor they who bought, could have forseen New York, the commercial metropolis of America, that now stands on it.

Sermons by T. DeWitt Talmage

Can a man who preaches a sermon, or a woman who distributes tracts; or a teacher who instructs a class, or a passer-by who utters encouraging words, realize the infinitudes of useful result? The teacher at Harrow School, who toiled with William Jones, the most stupid boy in school, and at the foot of his class, did not know that he was fitting for his work the greatest Oriental scholar of modern times; his statue now in St. Paul's Cathedral, London. Every move you make for God, however insignificant in your own eyes, or in the eyes of others, touches worlds larger than the one Columbus discovered. Why talk about unimportant things? There are no unimportant things. Infinity is made up of infinitesimals. On a clear night the smallest dew-drop holds a star. Each one of you is at the centre of a universe, and all you say and do somehow vibrates to the extreme of that universe in all directions.

I promise everlasting renown to those who will go forth with Christian and sympathetic words. After the battle of Copenhagen, Nelson, the admiral, went into a hospital and halted at the bed of a wounded sailor who had lost his arm, and said: "Well, Jack, what is the matter with you?" and the sailor replied: "Lost my right arm, your honor;" and Nelson looked down at his own empty sleeve and said: "Well, Jack, then you and I are both spoiled for fishermen. Cheer up, my brave fellow!" and that sympathetic word cheered the entire hospital. Before you die, you can, out of your own misfortunes, cheer a hundred souls, and start unending echoes. You can no more appreciate the far-reaching results of your life than Columbus could see this continent from Arctic to Antarctic. I say this not to make you proud and arrogant, but to make you tremble with your responsibilities, and put you on your guard as to what you do and what you say.

While studying the life of this Italian navigator, I am also reminded of the fact that while we are diligently looking for one thing, we find another. Columbus started to find India, but found America. Go on and do your duty diligently and prayerfully, and if you do not find what you looked for, you will find something better. Saul was hunting for the strayed animals of his father's barnyard, but met Samuel, the prophet, who gave him a crown of dominion. Nearly all the great inventions and discoveries were made by men who, at the time, were looking for something else. Professor Morse gone to Europe to perfect himself in chemistry, on returning happens to take the packet-ship *Sully* from Havre, and while in conversation with a passenger learns of some experiments in France, which suggests to him the magnetic telegraphy. He went to Europe to learn the wisdom of others and discovered the telegraph. Hargreaves by the upsetting of a machine, and the motion of its wheels while upset, discovered the spinning-jenny. So, my friend, go on faithfully and promptly with your work, and if you do not get the success you seek, and your plans upset, you will get something just as good and perhaps better. Sail ahead on the voyage of life, keep a correct log-book, brave the tempest, make the best use of the east wind, keep a sharp lookout, and I warrant you in the name of the God of Columbus that if you do not find just what you want of an earthly nature, you will find heaven, and that will be better. What was wornout India, crouching under a tropical sun, compared with salubrious and radiant and almost illimitable America; and what is all that this little world in which we live can afford you compared with that supernal realm, whose foliage, and whose fruits, and whose riches, and whose population, and whose grandeurs, and whose worship, and whose Christ, make up an affluence that the most rapturous vocabulary fails to utter?

Another look at the career of that Admiral of the *Santa Maria* persuades me that it is not to be expected that this world will do its hard workers full justice. If any man ought to have been treated well from first to last, it was Columbus. He had his faults. Let others depict them. But a greater soul the centuries have not produced. This continent ought to have been called Columbia, after the hero who discovered it, or Isabelliana, after the queen who furnished the means for the expedition. No. The world did not do him justice, while he was alive, and why should it be expected to do him justice after he was dead. Columbus in a dungeon! What a thought. Columbus in irons! What a spectacle. The wife of Robert Murray, after whom Murray Hill, New York, was named, never has received proper credit for detaining at a very rich luncheon the officers of the opposing army until Washington and his army could escape. Mrs. Murray saved American independence. How the wrong men and the wrong women get credit that does not belong to them, while God's heroes and God's heroines go ungarlanded. You have heard of the brave words of dying chieftains, but you probably never heard of what a private soldier said, fallen at Resaca, and bleeding under a shell wound in his mouth, and who though suffering dreadfully from thirst, when a cup of water was offered him declined to drink, saying, "My mouth is all bloody, sir, and it might make the tin-cup bad for others!"

The world knows little or nothing of the bravest words and the bravest deeds. In one of the last letters which Columbus sent to his son, he wrote this lamentation: "I receive nothing of the revenue due me. I live by borrowing. Little have I profited by twenty years of service with such toils and perils, since at present I do not own a roof in Spain. If I desire to eat or sleep, I have no recourse but the inn, and, for the most times, have not wherewithal to pay my bill." Be not surprised, my hearer, if you suffer injustice. You are in the best of company; the men and women who wrought mightily for God and the world's improvement, and got for it chiefly misrepresentation and abuse while they lived, although afterward they have had a long row of carriages at the obsequies, and a gilt-edged set of resolutions unanimously adopted for the consolation of the bereft household. Do your full duty, expecting no appreciation in this world, but full reward in the world to come.

And, now, while I am thinking of this illustrious ship captain of Genoa, let me bespeak higher appreciation for the ship captains now in service, many of them this moment on the sea, the lives of tens of thousands of passengers in their keeping. What an awful responsibility is theirs! They go out through the Narrows, or start from Queenstown or Southampton or Glasgow, not knowing what cyclones, or collisions, or midnight perils are waiting for them. It requires bravery to face an army of men, but far more bravery to face an army of Atlantic surges led on by hurricanes. A more stupendous scene is not to be witnessed than that of a ship captain walking the bridge of a steamer in the midst of a cyclone. Remember those heroes in your prayers; and when worn out in the service, and they have to command inferior craft, or return to the land and go out of service, do them full honor for what they once were. Let the ship companies award them pensions worthy of what they endured until they start on their last voyage from this world to the next. Ay, that voyage we must all take, landsmen as well as seafarers. Let us be sure that we have the right pilot, and the right chart, and the right captain, and that we start in the right direction. It will be to each of us who love the Lord a voyage more wonderful for discovery than that which Columbus took, for, after all we have heard about that other world, we know not where it is, or how it looks; and it will be as new as San Salvador was to the glorious captain of the *Santa Maria*. "Eye hath not seen, nor ear heard, neither have entered into the heart of man." May the light from that Golden Beach flash on the darkness, and we be able to step ashore amid groves and orchards and aromas, such as the world's atmosphere never ripened or breathed. Ay, fellow-mariners, over the rough sea of life, through the fogs and mists of earth, see you not already the outline of the better country? Land ahead! Land ahead! Nearer and nearer we come to heavenly wharfage. Throw out the planks and step ashore into the arms of your kindred, who have been waiting and watching for the hour of your disembarkation. Through the rich grace of Christ, our Lord, may we all have such blissful arrival!

RESERVATION OF AMERICA

Acts, 17: 26: "And hath made of one blood all nations."

RESERVATION OF AMERICA

Acts, 17: 26: "And hath made of one blood all nations."

That is, if for some reason general phlebotomy were ordered, and standing in a row were an American, an Englishman, a Scotchman, and an Irishman, a Frenchman, a German, a Norwegian, an Icelander, a Spaniard, an Italian, a Russian, and representatives of all other nationalities bared their right arm, and a lancet were struck into it, the blood let out would have the same characteristics, for it would be red, complex, fibrin, globulin, chlorin, and containing sulphuric acid, potassium, phosphate of magnesia, and so on; and Harvey, and Sir Astley Cooper, and Richardson, and Zimmerman, and Brown-Sequard, and all the scientific doctors, allopathic, homeopathic, hydropathic, and eclectic, would agree with Paul, as, standing on Mars Hill, his pulpit a ridge of limestone rock fifty feet high, and among the proudest, and most exclusive, and undemocratic people of the earth, he crashed into all their prejudices by declaring, in the words of my text, that God had made "of one blood all nations." The countenance of the five races of the human family may be different as a result of climate, or education, or habits, and the Malay will have the projecting upper jaw, and the Caucasian the oval face and small mouth, and the Ethiopian the retreating forehead and large lip, and the Mongolian the flat face of olive hue, and the American Indian the copper-colored complexion, but the blood is the same, and indicates that they all had one origin, and that Adam and Eve were their ancestor and ancestress.

Sermons by T. DeWitt Talmage

I think God built this American continent and organized this United States republic to demonstrate the stupendous idea of the text. A man in Persia will always remain a Persian; a man in Switzerland will always remain a Swiss; a man in Austria will always remain an Austrian, but all foreign nationalities coming to America were intended to be Americans. This land is the chemical laboratory where foreign bloods are to be inextricably mixed up and race prejudices and race antipathies are to perish; and this sermon is an ax by which I hope to help kill them. It is not hard for me to preach such a sermon, because, although my ancestors came to this country about two hundred and fifty years ago; some of them came from Wales, and some from Scotland, and some from Holland, and some from other lands, and I am a mixture of so many nationalities, that I feel at home with people from under every sky, and have a right to call them blood relations. There are madcaps and patriotic lunatics in this country who are ever and anon crying out, "America for Americans!" Down with the Germans! down with the Irish! down with the Jews! down with the Chinese! are in some directions the popular cries, all of which vociferations I would drown out by the full organ of my text, while I pull out the stops and put my foot on the pedal that will open the loudest pipes, and run my fingers over all the four banks of ivory keys, playing the chant, "God hath made of one blood all nations." For national selfishness God has nothing but hot indignations.

There are not five men in this audience, nor five men in any audience to-day in America, except it be on an Indian reservation, who were not descended from foreigners, if you go far enough back. The only native Americans are the Modocs, the Shawnees, the Chippewas, the Cherokees, the Chickasaws, the Seminoles, and such like. If the principle, America only for Americans, be carried out, then you and I have no right to be here, and we had better charter all the steamers and clippers and men-of-war and yachts and sloops and get out of this country as quick as possible. The Pilgrim Fathers were all immigrants, the Huguenots all immigrants. The cradle of most every one of our families was rocked on the bank of the Clyde or the Rhine or the Shannon or the Seine or the Tiber. Had the watchword, "America for Americans!" been an early and successful cry, where now stand our cities would have stood Indian wigwams; and canoes instead of steamers would have tracked the Hudson and the Connecticut; and, instead of the Mississippi being the main artery of the continent, it would have been only a trough for deer, and antelope, and wild pigeons to drink out of. What makes the cry of "America for Americans!" the more absurd, and the more inhuman, is that some in this country, who themselves arrived here in their boyhood, or arrived here only one or two generations back, are joining in the cry. Escaped from foreign despotisms themselves, they say, "Shut the door of escape for others." Getting themselves on our shores in a lifeboat from the shipwreck, saying, "Haul the boat on the beach, and let the rest of the passengers go to the bottom!" Men who have yet on them a Scotch or German or English or Irish brogue, crying out, "America for Americans!" What if the native inhabitants of Heaven—I mean the angels, the cherubim, the seraphim, born there—should stand in the gate, and when they see us coming up at last should say, "Go back! Heaven for the Heavenians!"

Of course we do well not to allow foreign nations to make this country a convict colony. We would have a wall built as high as heaven and as deep as hell against foreign thieves, pickpockets, and anarchists. We would not let them wipe their feet on the mat of the outside door of Ellis Island. If England, or Russia, or Germany, or France, send here their desperadoes to get clear of them, we would have these desperadoes sent back in chains to the places where they came from. We will not have America become the dumping-place for foreign vagabondism. But you build up a wall at the Narrows before New York Harbor, or at the Golden Gate before San Francisco, and forbid the coming of the industrious and hard working and honest populations of other lands who want to breathe the air of our free institutions, and get opportunity for better livelihood; and it is only a question of time when God will tumble that wall flat on our own heads with red-hot thunderbolts of his omnipotent indignation.

You are a father, and you have five children. The parlor is the best room in your house. Your son Philip says to the other four children, "Now, John, you live in the small room in the end of the hall, and stay there; George, you live in the garret, and stay there; Mary, you live in the cellar, and stay there; Fanny, you live in the kitchen, and stay there. I, Philip, will take the parlor; it suits me exactly. I like the pictures on the wall; I like the lambrequins at the windows; I like the Axminster on the floor. Now, I, Philip, propose to occupy this parlor and I command you to stay out. The parlor only for Philippians." You, the father, hear of this arrangement, and what will you do? You will get red in the face, and say, "John, come out of that small room at the end of the hall; George, come down out of the garret; Mary, come up from the cellar; Fanny, come out of the kitchen, and go into the parlor, or anywhere you choose; and, Philip, for your greediness and unbrotherly behavior, I put you for two hours in the dark closet under the stairs." God is the Father of the human race. He has at least five sons—a North American, a South American, a European, an Asiatic, and an African. The North American sniffs the breeze, and he says to his four brothers and sisters: "Let the South American stay in South America; let the European stay in Europe; let the Asiatic stay in Asia; let the African stay in Africa; but America is for me. I think it is the parlor of the whole earth. I like its carpets of grass, and its upholstery of the front window, namely, the American sunrise; and the upholstery of the back window, namely, the American sunset. Now, I want you all to stay out, and keep to your places." I am sure the Father of the whole human race would hear of it, and chastisement would come; and whether by earthquake, or flood, or drought, or heaven-darkening swarms of locust and grasshopper, or destroying angel of pestilence, God would rebuke our selfishness as a nation, and say to the four winds of heaven: "This world is my house, and the North American is no more my child than is the South American, and the European, and the Asiatic, and the African. And I built this world for all the children, and the parlor is theirs, and all is theirs." For, let me say, whether we will or not, the population of other lands will come here. There are harbors all the way from Baffin's Bay to Galveston, and if you shut fifty gates, there will be other gates unguarded; and if you forbid foreigners from coming on the steamers, they will take sailing vessels; and if you forbid them coming on sailing vessels, they will come in boats; and if you will not let them come in boats, they will come on rafts; and if you will not allow wharfage to the raft, they will leave it outside Sandy Hook and swim for free America. Stop them?

You might as well pass a law forbidding a swarm of summer bees from lighting on the clover-tops, or pass a law forbidding the tides of the Atlantic to rise when the moon puts under it silver grappling-hooks, or a law that the noonday sun should not irradiate the atmosphere. They have come; they are coming now; they will come. And if I had a voice loud enough to be heard across the seas, I would put it to the utmost tension, and cry: "Let them come!" You stingy, selfish, shriveled up, heartless souls, who sit before your silver dinner-plate piled up with breast of roast turkey incarnadined with cranberry, your fork full and your mouth full, and cramming down the superabundance till your digestive organs are terrorized, let the millions of your fellow-men have at least the wishing-bone!

But some of this cry, "America for Americans!" may arise from an honest fear lest this land be over-crowded. Such persons had better take the Northern Pacific, or Union Pacific, or Southern Pacific, or Atlantic and Charlotte air line, or Texas and Sante Fe, and go a long journey and find out that no more than a tenth part of this continent is fully cultivated. If a man with a hundred acres of farm land should put all his cultivation on one acre, he would be cultivating a larger ratio of his farm than our nation is now cultivating. Pour the whole human race, Europe, Asia, Africa, and all the islands of the sea, into America, and there would be room to spare. All the Rocky Mountain barrennesses and all the other American deserts are to be fertilized; and as Salt Lake City and much of Utah once yielded not a blade of grass, now by artificial irrigation have become gardens, so a large part of this continent that now is too poor to grow even a mullein stalk or a Canada thistle, will through artificial irrigation, like an Illinois prairie, wave with wheat, or like a Wisconsin farm rustle with corn tassels. Besides that, after perhaps a century or two more, when this continent is quite well occupied, the tides of immigration will turn the other way. Politics and governmental affairs being corrected on the other side of the waters; Ireland, under different regulation, turned into a garden, will invite back another generation of Irishmen; and the wide wastes of Russia cultivated, will, with her own green fields, invite back another generation of Russians. And there will be hundreds of thousands of Americans every year settling on the other continents. And after a number of centuries, all the earth full and crowded, what then? Well, at that time, some night, a panther meteor wandering through the heavens will put its paw on our world and stop it; and putting its panther tooth into the neck of its mountain range, will shake it lifeless, as the rat-terrier a rat. So I have no more fear of America being overcrowded than that the porpoises in the Atlantic Ocean will become so numerous as to stop shipping.

It is through mighty addition of foreign population to our native population that I think God is going to fill this land with a race of people ninety-five per cent. superior to anything the world has ever seen. Intermarriage of families and intermarriage in nations is depressing and crippling. Marriage outside of one's own nationality and with another style of nationality is a mighty gain. What makes the Scotch-Irish second to no pedigree for brain and stamina of character, so that such blood goes right up to Supreme Court bench, and to the front rank in jurisprudence and merchandise and art? Because nothing under heaven can be more unlike than a Scotchman and an Irishman, and the descendants of these two conjoined nationalities, unless rum flings them, go right to the tip-top in everything. All nationalities coming to this land, the opposites will all the while be affianced, and French and German will unite, and that will stop all the quarrel between them, and one child they will call Alsace, and the other Lorraine. And hot-blooded Spaniard will unite with cool-blooded Polander, and romantic Italian with matter-of-fact Norwegian, and a hundred and fifty years from now the race occupying this land will be, in stature, in purity of complexion, in liquidity of eye, in gracefulness of poise, in dome-like brow, in taste, in intelligence, and in morals, so far ahead of anything now known on either side the seas that this last quarter of the nineteenth century will seem to them like the Dark Ages. Oh, then how they will legislate and bargain and pray and preach and govern! This is the land where, by the mingling of races, the race prejudice is to get its death blow. How Heaven feels about it, we may conclude from the fact that Christ, the Jew, and descended from a Jewess, nevertheless provided a religion for all races; and that Paul, though a Jew, became the chief apostle of the Gentiles; and that recently God has allowed to burst in splendor upon the attention of the world Hirsch, the Jew, who, after giving ten million dollars to Christian churches and hospitals, has called a committee of nations, and furnished them with forty million dollars for schools to elevate his race in France and Germany and Russia to higher intelligence, and abolish, as he says, the prejudices against their race; these fifty million dollars not given in a last will and testament, and at a time when a man must leave his money anyhow, but by donation at fifty-five years of age, and in good health; utterly eclipsing all benevolence since the world was created.

I must confess there was a time when I entertained race prejudice, but, thanks to God, that prejudice has

gone; and if I sat in church, and on one side of me
there was a black man, and on the other side of me
was an Indian, and before me was a Chinaman, and
behind me a Turk, I would be as happy as I am now
standing in the presence of this brilliant audience; and
I am as happy now as I can be and live. The sooner
we get this corpse of race prejudice buried, the healthier will be our American atmosphere. Let each one
fetch a spade, and let us dig its grave clear on down
deeper and deeper till we get as far down as the centre
of the earth and half-way to China, but no farther lest
it poison those living on the other side the earth.
Then into this grave let down the accursed carcase of
race prejudice, and throw on it all the mean things
that have ever been said and written between Jew and
Gentile, between Turk and Russian, between English
and French, between Mongolian and anti-Mongolian,
between black and white, and put over that grave for
tombstone some scorched and jagged chunk of scoriæ
spit out by some volcanic eruption, and chisel on it
for epitaph: "Here lies the carcase of one who cursed
the world. Aged near six thousand years. Departed
this life for the perdition from whence it came. No
peace to its ashes!"

Now, in view of this subject, I have two point-
blank words to utter, one suggesting what foreigners
ought to do for us, and the other what we ought to
do for foreigners. First, to foreigners: Lay aside
all apologetic air, and realize you have as much right
as any man who was not only himself born here, but
his father and his grandfather and great-grandfather
before him. Are you an Englishman? Though during the Revolutionary War your fathers treated our
fathers roughly, England has more than atoned for
that by giving to this country at least two denominations of Christians, the Church of England and the

Methodist Church. Witness the magnificent liturgy of the one, and hear the Wesleyan hallelujahs of the other. And who shall ever pay England for what Shakespeare and John Milton and Wordsworth and a thousand other authors, have done for America? Are you a Scotchman? Thanks for John Knox's Presbyterianism; the balance-wheel of other denominations. And how shall Americans ever pay your native land for what Thomas Chalmers, and Macintosh, and Robert Burns, and Christopher North, and Robert McCheyne, and Candlish, and Guthrie, have done for Americans? Are you a Frenchman? We cannot forget your Lafayette, who, in the most desperate time of our American revolution, New York surrendered, and our armies flying in retreat, espoused our cause, and at Brandywine and Monmouth and Yorktown, put all America under eternal obligation. And we cannot forget the coming to the rescue of our fathers of Rochambeau and his French fleet with six thousand armed men. Are you a German? We have not forgotten the eleven wounds through which Baron De Kalb poured out his life-blood at the head of the Maryland and Delaware troops in the disastrous battle at Camden, and after we have named our streets, and our cities, and counties, after him, we have not paid a tithe of what we owe Germany for his valor and self-sacrifice. And what about Martin Luther, the giant German, who made way for religious liberty for all lands and ages? Are you a Polander? How can we forget your brilliant Count Pulaski, whose bones were laid in Savannah River after a mortal wound, gotten while in the stirrups of one of the fiercest cavalry charges of the American Revolution? But with no time to particularize, I say, "All hail to the men and women of other lands who come here with honest purpose!" Renounce all obligation to foreign despots; take the oath of American allegiance; get out your naturalization papers. Don't talk against our institutions, for the fact that you came here, and stay, shows that you like ours better than any other. If you do not like them, there are steamers going out of our ports almost every day, and the fare is cheap, and, lest you should be detained for parting civilities, I bid you good-by now; but if you like it here, then I charge you, at the ballot-box, in legislative hall, in churches, and everywhere, be out-and-out Americans. Do not try to establish here the loose foreign Sabbaths, or transcendentalism spun into a religion of mush and moonshine, or foreign libertinism, or that condensation of all thievery, scoundrelism, lust, murder, and perdition, which, in Russia, is called Nihilism, and in France called Communism, and in America called Anarchism. Unite with us in making, by the grace of God, the fifteen million square miles of America, on both sides the Isthmus of Panama, the paradise of virtue and religion.

My other word suggests what Americans ought to do for foreigners. By all possible means explain to them our institutions. Coming here, the vast majority of them know about as much concerning republican or democratic form of government as you in the United States know about the politics of Denmark, or France, or Italy, or Switzerland, namely, nothing. Explain to them that liberty in this country means liberty to do right, but not liberty to do wrong. Never in their presence say anything against their native land, for, no matter how much they may have been oppressed there, in that native land there are sacred places, cabins or mansions, around whose doors they played, and perhaps somewhere there is a grave into which they would like, when life's toils are over, to be let down, for it is mother's grave; and it would be like going again into the loving arms that first held them, and against the bosom that first pillowed them. My! my! how low down a man must have descended to have no regard for the place where his cradle was rocked. Do not mock their brogue, or their stumbling attempts at the hardest of all languages to learn, namely, the English language. I warrant you they speak English as well as you could speak Scandinavian. Treat them in America as you would like to be treated, if, for the sake of your honest principles or a better livelihood for yourself or your family, you had moved under the shadow of Jungfrau, or the Rigi, or the Giant's Causeway, or the Bohemian Forest, or the Franconian Jura. If they get homesick, as some of them are, suggest to them that God is as near to help them here as he was near them before they crossed the Atlantic, and that the soul's final flight is less than a second, whether from the beach of the Caspian Sea, or the banks of Lake Erie. Evangelize their adults through the churches, and their children though the schools, and let home missions, and tract societies, and the Bible, translated in all the languages of these foreign people, have full swing.

Rejoice as Christian patriots that, instead of being an element of weakness, the foreign people, thoroughly evangelized, will be our mightiest defence against all the world. The Congress of the United States built new forts all up and down our American coasts, and a new navy was projected. But let me say that three hundred million dollars expended in coast defence will not be so mighty as a vast foreign population living in America. With hundreds of thousands of Germans living in New York, Germany would as soon think of bomb-shelling Berlin as attacking us; with hundreds of thousands of Frenchmen in New York, France would as soon think of firing on

Paris; with hundreds of thousands of Englishmen in New York, England would as soon think of destroying London. The mightiest defence against European nations is a wall of Europeans reaching all up and down the American continent—a wall of heads and hearts consecrated to free government. A bulwark of foreign humanity heaved up all along our shores, reinforced by the Atlantic Ocean, armed as it is with tempests, and Caribbean whirlwinds and giant billows ready to fling mountains from their catapult, we need as a nation fear no one in the universe but God; and, if found in his service, we need not fear him. As six hundred million people will yet sit down at our national table, let God preside. To him be dedicated the metal of our mines, the sheaves of our harvest-fields, the fruits of our orchards, the fabrics of our manufactories, the telescopes of our observatories, the volumes of our libraries, the songs of our churches, the affections of our hearts, and all our lakes become baptismal fonts, and all our mountains altars of praise, and all our valleys amphitheatres of worship; and our country having become fifty nations consolidated in one, may its every heart-throb be a pulsation of gratitude to him who made "of one blood all nations," and ransomed that blood by the payment of the last drop of his own.

ALLEVIATIONS OF WAR

Ps., 27: 3: "Though war should rise against me, in this will
I be confident."

ALLEVIATIONS OF WAR

Ps., 27: 3: "Though war should rise against me, in this will
I be confident."

The ring of battle-axes, and the clash of shields,
and the tramp of armies, are heard all up and down
the Old Testament; and you find godly soldiers like
Moses, and Joshua, and Caleb, and Gideon, and
scoundrelly soldiers like Sennacherib, and Shalma-
neser, and Nebuchadnezzar. The High Priest would
stand at the head of the army, and say: "Hear, O
Israel, ye approach this day unto battle against your
enemies, let not your hearts faint, fear not, and do not
tremble, neither be ye terrified because of them!" and
then the officers would give command to the troops,
saying: "What man is there that hath built a new
house, and hath not dedicated it? Let him go and
return to his house, lest he die in the battle and another
man dedicate it? And what man is he that hath planteth a vineyard and hath not eaten of it? Let him also
go and return unto his house, lest he die in the battle
and another man eat of it. And what man is there that
hath betrothed a wife and hath not taken her? Let
him go and return unto his house, lest he die in the
battle and another man take her." Great armies
marched and fought. In time of Moses and Joshua all
the men were soldiers. When Israel came out of
Egypt they were six hundred thousand fighting men.
Abijah commanded four hundred thousand, Jeroboam
commanded eight hundred thousand men, of whom
five hundred thousand were slain in one battle. Some
of these wars God approved, for they were for the res-

cue of oppressed nations, and some of them he denounced, but in all cases it was a judgment upon both victors and vanquished. David knew just what war was when he wrote in the text: "Though war should rise against me, in this will I be confident."

David is encouraging himself in stormy times, and before approaching battles administers to himself this consolation. So to-day my theme is the "Alleviations of War." War is organized atrocity. It is the science of assassination. It is the convocation of all horrors. It is butchery wholesale. It is murder glorified. It is Death on a throne of human skeletons. It is the coffin in ascendancy. It is diabolism at a game of skulls. But war is here, and it is time now to preach on its alleviations, and make up our mind what ought to be the style of our behavior while passing through this national ordeal.

First, I find an alleviation in the fact that it has consolidated the North and the South after long-continued strained relations. It is thirty-four years since our Civil War closed, and the violences are all gone and the severities have been hushed. But ever and anon, in oration, in sermon, in newspaper editorial, in magazine article, on political stump, and in congressional hall, the old sectional difference has lifted its head; and for the first time within my memory, or the memory of any one who hears or reads these words, the North and the South are one. By a marvelous providence, the family that led in opposition to our government thirty years ago is represented at the front in this present war. Nothing else could have done the work of unification so suddenly or so completely as this conflict between the United States and Spain. At Tampa, at Chattanooga, at Richmond, and in many other places, the regiments are forming, and it will be side by side, Massachusetts and Alabama,

Alleviations of War

New York and Georgia, Illinois and Louisiana, Maine and South Carolina. Northern and Southern men will together unlimber the guns and rush upon the fortification and charge upon the enemy and shout the triumph. The voices of military officers who were under Sidney Johnson and Joseph Hooker will give the command on the same side. The old sectional grudges forever dead. The name of Grant on the Northern side and of Lee on the Southern side exchanged for the names of Grant and Lee on the same side. The veterans in Northern and Southern homes and asylums are stretching their rheumatic limbs to see whether they can again keep step in a march, and are testing their eyesight to find whether they can again look along the gun-barrel to successfully take aim and fire. The old war cry of "On to Richmond!" and "On to Washington!" has become the war-cry of "On to Havana!" "On to Porto Rico!" "On to the Philippine Islands!" The two old rusty swords that in other days clashed at Murfreesboro and South Mountain and Atlanta, are now lifted to strike down Hispanic abominations.

Another alleviation of the war is the fact that it is the most unselfish war of the ages. While the commercial rights of our wronged citizens will be vindicated, that is not the chief idea of this war. It is the rescue of hundreds of thousands of people from starvation and multiform maltreatment. At least two hundred thousand graves are calling to us to come on and remember by what process their occupants died. It is the twentieth century crying out to the nineteenth: "Do you mean to pass down to me the curse with which you have been blasted? Or will you let me begin under new auspices and turn the island of desolation into an island Edenic?" It is a war inspired by mercy, which is an attribute in man imitative of the same attribute of God. In no other age of the world could such a war have been waged. The Gospel of kindness needed to be recognized throughout Christendom in order to make such a war possible. The chief reason why most of the European nations are not now banded together against us is because they dare not take the part of that behemoth of cruelty, the Spanish government, against the crusade of mercy which our nation has started. Had it been on our part a war of conquest, a war of annexation, a war of aggrandizement, there would have been by this time enough flying squadrons coming to this country across the Atlantic to throw into panic every city on our American seaboard. Most of the wars of the world have been wars of ambition or conquest; but in this Hispanic-American war every drummer-boy or picket or gunner or standard-bearer or skirmisher or sharpshooter or cavalryman or artilleryman or engineer who falls, falls in the cause of mercy, and becomes a martyr for God and his country.

Another alleviation of this war is that it is for the advancement of the sublime principle of liberty, which will yet engirdle the earth. Not only will this war free Cuba, but finally will free Spain. By what right does a dynasty like that stand, and a corrupt court dominate a people for centuries, taxing them to death, riding in gilded chariot over the necks of a beggared population? There are ten thousand boys in Spain growing up with more capacity to govern that nation than the weak boy now in the Madrid palace will ever possess. Before this conflict is over, the Spanish nation will be well on toward the time when a constitutional convention will assemble to establish a free government, instead of the worn-out dynasty that now afflicts the people. The liberty of all nations, trans-Atlantic as well as cis-Atlantic, if not already established, is on the way, and it cannot be stopped. Napoleon III thought he had successfully driven the principle out of France, when, on the second day of December, 1851, he rode down the Champs Elysees of Paris, constitutional government seemingly crushed under the hoofs of his steed. But did it stay crushed? Let the batteries on the heights above Sedan answer, and the shout of two hundred and fifty thousand triumphant troops and the letter of surrender to Emperor William tell the story. "Sire, my Brother: Not having been able to die in the midst of my troops, it only remains for me to place my sword in your Majesty's hands. I am, your Majesty, your good brother, Napoleon. Sedan, 1 September, 1870." That monarchy having fallen, then the French Republic resumed its march.

Another alleviation is that the war opens with a great victory for the United States. It took our government four years to get over the fiasco at Bull Run. A defeat at the start of this present war would have been disheartening to the last degree, and would have invited foreign intervention to stop the war before anything practical for God and humanity had been accomplished, and would have prolonged the strife, for which we are hoping a quick termination. In the most jubilant manner let this victory of our navy be celebrated. With the story of the exploding battleship fresh in the minds of the world, it required no ordinary courage to sail into the harbor of Manila and attack the Spanish ships. That harbor, crowded with sunken weaponry of death; to enter it was running a risk enough to make all nations shiver. But Manila is ours, and the blow has shaken to the foundation the palaces of Madrid, and for policy's sake the doubtful nations are on our side. For Commodore Dewey and all who followed him let the whole nation utter its most resounding huzza; and more than that, let us thank the Lord of hosts for his guiding and protecting power. "Praise ye the Lord! Let everything that hath breath praise the Lord!"

Another alleviation is the fact that in this war the might is on the side of the right. Again and again have liberty and justice and suffering humanity had the odds against them. It was so when Benhadad's Syrian hosts, who were in the wrong, at Aphek, came upon the small regiments of Israel, who were in the right, the Bible putting it in one of those graphic sentences for which the book is remarkable: "The children of Israel pitched before them like two little flocks of kids, but the Syrians filled the whole country." It was so in the awful defeat of the Lord's people at Gilboa and Megiddo. It was so recently when gallant and glorious Greece was in conflict with gigantic Mohammedanism, and the navies of Europe hovering about the Bosphorus were in practical protection of the Turkish government, fresh from the slaughter of one hundred thousand Armenians. It was so when, in 1776, the thirteen colonies, with no war shipping and a few undrilled and poorly-clad soldiers were brought into a contest with the mightiest navy of all the earth, and an army that commanded the admiration of nations. It was so when Poland was crushed. It was so when Hungary went under. It has been so during all the struggles heretofore for Cuban independence. But now it is our powerful navy against a feeble group of incompetent ships, crawling across the Atlantic to meet our flotillas, which have enough guns to send them as completely under as when the Red Sea submerged Pharaoh's army. It is so in these times, when only a few thousand Spaniards at most can reach our hemisphere, and we go out to meet them with one hundred and twenty-five thousand armed men, to be backed up speedily with five hundred thousand more if needed. We do not have to ask for any miracle, but only a fair shot at the ships headed this way, and time enough to demolish them. This is one of the cases in the world's history where might and right are shoulder to shoulder.

Another alleviation is the fact that such an atrocity as the destruction of two hundred and sixty-six lives in Havana harbor in time of peace cannot with impunity be perpetrated in this age of the world's civilization. The question as to who did that infernalism is too well settled to need any further discussion. But what a small crime it was, compared with the systematic putting into their graves of hundreds of thousands of Cubans, or leaving them unburied for the buzzards to take care of! If Spain could destroy two hundred thousand men, women and children, the slaughter of two hundred and sixty-six people was not a very great undertaking. But this one last deed will result in the liberation of Cuba, and the driving of Spain from this hemisphere.

There was danger that the long-continued oppression of our neighbors in Cuba might be continued from generation to generation without sufficient protest on our part and the pronounced execration of people on both sides of the Atlantic, but that bursting volcano of destruction in the harbor of Havana fired the nation and shocked the whole civilized world. All nations will learn that such an act cannot be repeated without the anathema of all Christendom. As individual criminals must be punished for the public good, and we have for them courts of oyer and terminer, and penitentiaries, and electric chairs, and hangman's gallows, so governments committing high crimes against God and humanity must be scourged and hung up for the world's indignation. When in Spanish waters our battleship, looking after our commercial interests and intending nothing but quietude, was hurled into demolition, and the men on board, without time to utter one word of prayer, were dashed into the eternal world, the final doom of the reigning house of Spain was pronounced in tones louder than the thunder of explosion which that night rolled out over the sea.

Another alleviation is the fact that we have a God to go to in behalf of all those of our countrymen who may be in especial exposure at the front, for we must admit the perils. It is no trifling thing for one hundred thousand young men to be put outside of home restraints and sometimes into evil companionship. Many of the brave of the earth are not the good of the earth. To be in the same tent with those who have no regard for God or home; to hear their holy religion sometimes slurred at; to be placed under influences calculated to make one reckless; to have no Sabbath, or such a Sabbath as in most encampments amounts to no Sabbath at all; to go out from homes where all sanitary laws are observed into surroundings where questions of health are never discussed; to invade climes where pestilence holds possession; to make long marches under blistering skies; to stand on deck and in the fields under fire, at the mercy of shot and shell—we must admit that those thus exposed need especial care, and to the Omnipresent God we have a right to commend them and will commend them. Postal communication may be interrupted, and letters started from camps or homes may not arrive at the right destination, but however far away our loved ones may be from us, and however wide and deep the seas that separate us, we may hold communication with them *via* the throne of God.

A shipwrecked sailor was found floating on a raft

near the coast of California. While in hospital he told his experience, and said that he had a companion on the same raft for some time. While that companion was dying of thirst he said to him: "George, where are you going?" and the dying sailor said: "I hope I am going to God." "If you do," said the rescued sailor, "will you ask him to send some water?" After the death of his companion, the survivor said, the rain came in torrents, and slaked his thirst and kept him alive until he was taken to safety. The survivor always thought it was in answer to the message he had sent to heaven asking for water. Thank God we may have direct and instantaneous communication with the Lord Almighty through Jesus Christ, his only begotten Son, and in that faith we may secure the rescue of our imperiled kindred. Is not that a mighty alleviation?

Until this conflict is ended let us be much in prayer for our beloved country. Do not let us depend upon the friendship of foreign nations. Our hope is in God. Out of every misfortune, he has brought this nation to a better moral and financial condition, and so let us pray that he will lift us out of this valley of trouble into a higher mountain of blessing.

It is a mystery that, just as this country was recovering from a long season of hard times, so many of our industries should now be halted; that business men who thought they could see their way to pay their debts and build up more prosperous enterprises and endow their homes with more advantages should have to halt and wait until the perfidious oppressor of Cuba shall be turned back. But individual and national life is always clothed with mysteries, and we make ourselves miserable by stabbing ourselves with sharp interrogation points, and plying the everlasting questions of "Why?" and "How?" and "What?" and

"When?" While we must, of course, try to be intelligent on all public affairs, it is a glorious thing to do our duty, and then fully and confidently trust all in the hands of God, who has proved himself the friend of our country from the time when the Spanish government fitted out an expedition to discover it, to this time, when Spaniards would like to destroy it.

Morning, noon and night, let us commend this beloved land to the care of a gracious God. That he answers prayer is so certain that your religion is an hallucination if he does not answer it. Pray that in reply to such supplications, the farmers' boys may get home again in time to reap the harvest of next July; that our business men may return in time to prepare for a fall trade such as has never yet filled the stores and factories with customers, and that all the homes in this country, now saddened by the departure of father or brother or son, may months before the Thanksgiving and Christmas holidays be full of joy at the arrival of those who will for the rest of their lives have stories to tell of double-quick march, and narrow escape, and charges up the parapets, and nights set on fire with bombardment, and our flag hauled up to places from which other flags were hauled down.

Now that we have started on the work, let us make that Spanish government get out of this hemisphere. We do not want her any more, with her injustices and barbarism, and stilettos of cruelty, hanging around the shores of this free land. She must not breathe her foul breath on our winds; she must not again redden our seas with her butcheries. There bids fair to be a scene on the deep as disastrous to the Spanish as that which whelmed their Armada in 1588. Philip the Second, King of Spain, resolved on the conquest of Europe, and already in the compass of his dominions, besides Spain, were Naples and Sicily, and the Netherlands, and the East Indies, and the Canary and Molucca and Sunda and Philippine Islands, and Mexico and Cuba and some of the most splendid parts of America. All the nations of the earth, except England, were to her underlings, and the Spanish king resolved that even England must bow the knee. Although the destructive strength of modern battleships was then unknown, the Spanish Armada started for the subjection of England with about one hundred and forty great ships, with two thousand six hundred guns, four thousand cavalry horses, and thirty-two thousand men. The battleships were provisioned with one hundred and forty-seven thousand casks of wine, and six months of provisions. The commanders and officers of these war vessels were dukes and marquises and noblemen.

A storm such as had never swept the coast of England or aroused the ocean swooped down upon that Spanish Armada. Most of the ships soon went down under the sea, while others were driven helplessly along, to be splintered on the coasts of England, Ireland, Scotland and Norway. Another Spanish Armada is crossing the Atlantic, and we are ready to meet them. The same God who destroyed the Armada in 1588 reigns in 1898. May he, in his might, either through human arm or dumb element, defeat their squadron, and give victory to the old flag of Admiral Farragut and David Porter!

Yet what the world most wants is Christ, who is coming to take possession of all hearts, all homes, all nations; but the world blocks the wheels of his chariot. I would like to see this century, which is now almost wound up, find its peroration in some mighty overthrow of tyrannies and a universal building up of liberty and justice. Almost all the centuries have ended with some stupendous event that transformed nations and changed the map of the world. It was so at the close of the fourteenth century; it was so at the close of the fifteenth century; at the close of the sixteenth, at the close of the seventeenth, at the close of the eighteenth century. May it be more gloriously so at the close of the nineteenth century! "Blessed be the Lord God of Israel from everlasting to everlasting, and let the whole earth be filled with his glory." Amen.

POLITICS AND RELIGION

Daniel, 6: 16: " Then the king commanded, and they brought
Daniel, and cast him into the den of lions."

POLITICS AND RELIGION

Daniel, 6: 16: " Then the king commanded, and they brought
Daniel, and cast him into the den of lions."

Darius was king of Babylon, and the young man
Daniel was so much a favorite with him that he made
him Prime Minister, or Secretary of State. But no
man could gain such a high position without exciting
the envy and jealousy of the people. There were
demagogues in Babylon who were so appreciative of
their own abilities that they were affronted at the elevation of this young man. Old Babylon was afraid
of young Babylon. The taller the cedar the more apt
it is to be riven of the lightning. These demagogues
asked the king to make a decree that anybody that
made a petition to any one except the king during a
period of thirty days should be put to death. King
Darius, not suspecting any foul play, makes that
decree. The demagogues have accomplished all they
want, because they know that no one can keep Daniel
from sending petitions before God for thirty days.

So far from being afraid, Daniel goes on with his
supplications three times a day, and is found on his
housetop making prayer. He is caught in the act.
He is condemned to be devoured by the lions. Rough
executioners of the law seize him and hasten him to
the cavern. I hear the growl of the wild beasts, and
I see them pawing the dust, and as they put their
mouths to the ground the solid earth quakes with their
bellowing. I see their eyes roll, and I almost hear the
fiery eyeballs snap in the darkness. These monsters
approach Daniel. They have an appetite keen with

hunger. With one stroke of their paw or one snatch of their teeth, they may leave him dead at the bottom of the cavern. But what a strange welcome Daniel receives from these hungry monsters. They fawn around him, they lick his hand, they bury his feet in their long mane. That night he has calm sleep with his head pillowed on the warm necks of the tamed lions.

But not so well does Darius, the king, sleep. He has an attack of terrific insomnia. He loves Daniel, and hates this stratagem by which he has been condemned. All night long the king walks the floor. He cannot sleep. At the least sound he starts, and his flesh creeps with horror. He is impatient for the dawning of the morning. At the first streak of the daylight Darius hastens forth to see the fate of Daniel. The heavy palace doors open and clang shut long before the people of the city waken. Darius goes to the den of the lions; he looks in. All is silent. His heart stops. He feels that the very worst has happened; but gathering all his strength, he shouts through the rifts of the rock, "O Daniel! is thy God whom thou servest continually able to deliver thee?" There comes rolling up from the deep darkness a voice which says: "O king! live forever. My God has sent his angel to shut the lions' mouths that they have not hurt me." Then Daniel is brought out from the den. The demagogues are hurled into it, and no sooner have they struck the bottom of the den than their flesh was rent, and their bones cracked, and their blood spurted through the rifts of the rock, and as the lions make the rocks tremble with their roar, they announce to all ages that while God will defend his people, the way of the ungodly shall perish.

Learn first from this subject that the greatest crime that you can commit in the eyes of many is the crime

of success. What had Daniel done that he should be
flung to the lions? He got to be Prime Minister.
They could not forgive him for that, and behold in
that a touch of unsanctified human nature as seen in
all ages of the world. So long as you are pinched in
poverty, so long as you are running the gauntlet between landlord and tax-gatherer, so long as you find
it hard work to educate your children, there are people who will say: "Poor man, I am sorry for him;
he ought to succeed, poor man." But after a while
the tide turns in your favor. That was a profitable
investment you made. You bought just at the right
time. Fortune becomes good humored and smiles
upon you. Now you are in some department successful, and your success chills some one. Those men who
used to sympathize with you stand along the street,
and they scowl at you from under the rim of their
hats. You have more money or more influence than
they have, and you ought to be scowled at from under
the rim of their hats. You catch a word or two as you
pass by them. "Stuck up," says one; "Got it dis-
honestly," says another; "Will burst soon," says a
third. Every stone in your new house is laid on their
hearts. Your horses' hoofs went over their nerves.
Every item of your success has been to them an item
of discomfiture and despair. Just as soon as in any
respect you rise above your fellows, if you are more
virtuous, if you are more wise, if you are more influen-
tial, you cast a shadow on the prospect of others. The
road to honor and success is within reach of the enemy's guns. Jealousy says: "Stay down, or I'll knock
you down." "I do not like you," says the snowflake
to the snowbird. "Why don't you like me?" said the
snowbird. "Oh," said the snowflake, "you are going
up and I am coming down." Young merchants,
young lawyers, young doctors, young mechanics,

young artists, young farmers, at certain times there are those to sympathize with you, but now that you are becoming a master of your particular occupation or profession, how is it now, young lawyers, young doctors, young artists, young farmers—how is it now? The greatest crime that you can commit is the crime of success.

Again, my subject impresses me with the value of decision of character in any department. Daniel knew that if he continued his adherence to the religion of the Lord he would be hurled to the lions, but having set his compass well, he sailed right on. For the lack of that element of decision of character, so eminent in Daniel, many men are ruined for this world, and ruined for the world to come. A great many at forty years of age are not settled in any respect, because they have not been able to make up their minds. Perhaps they will go West; perhaps they will go East; perhaps they will not; perhaps they will go North; perhaps they may go South; perhaps they will not; perhaps they may make that investment in real estate or in railroads; perhaps they will not. They are like a steamer that should go out of New York harbor, starting for Glasgow, and the next day should change for Havre de Grace, and the next for Charleston, and the next for Boston, and the next for Liverpool. These men on the sea of life everlastingly tacking ship and making no headway. Or they are like a man who starts to build a house in the Corinthian style and changes it to Doric, and then completes it in the Ionic, the curse of all styles of architecture. Young man, start right and keep on. Have decision of character. Character is like the goldfinch of Tonquin; it is magnificent while standing firm, but loses all its beauty in flight. How much decision of character in order that these young men may be Christians! Their old associates make sarcastic flings at them. They go on excursions, and they do not invite them. They prophesy that he will give out. They wonder if he is not getting wings. As he passes, they grimace, and wink, and chuckle, and say, "There goes a saint." O, young man! have decision of character. You can afford in this matter of religion to be laughed at. What do you care for the scoffs of these men, who are affronted because you will not go to hell with them? When the grave cracks open under their feet, and grim messengers push them into it, and eternity comes down hard upon their spirit, and conscience stings, and hopeless ruin lifts them up to hurl them down, will they laugh then?

I learn also from my subject that men may take religion into their worldly business. This is a most appropriate thought at this season of the year, when business is brightening, and so many men are starting out in new enterprises. Daniel had enough work to do to occupy six men. All the affairs of state were in his hands: questions of finance, questions of war, of peace; all international questions were for his settlement or adjustment. He must have had a correspondence vast beyond all computation. There was not a man in all the earth who had more to do than Daniel, the Secretary of State, and yet we find him three times a day bowing before God in prayer. There are men in our day who have not a hundredth part of Daniel's engagements, who say they are too busy to be religious. They have an idea somehow that religion will spoil their worldly occupation, that it will trip the accountant's pen, or dull the carpenter's saw, or confuse the lawyer's brief, or disarrange the merchant's store shelf. They think religion is impertinent. They would like to have it very well seated beside them in church on the Sabbath, to find the place in the Psalm book, or to nudge them awake when they get sleepy under the didactic discourse; or they would like to leave it in the pew on Sabbath evening, as they go out, closing the door, saying, "Good-night, religion; I'll be back next Sunday!" But to have religion go right along by them all through life, to have religion looking over their shoulder when they are making a bargain, to have religion take up a bag of dishonest gold and shake it, and say, "Where did you get that?" They think that is an impertinent religion. They would like to have a religion to help them when they are sick, and when the shadow of death comes over them, they would like to have religion as a sort of night-key with which to open the door of heaven; but religion under other circumstances they take to be impertinence.

Now, my friends, religion never robbed a man of a dollar. Other things being equal, a mason will build a better wall, a cabinet-maker will make a better chair, a plumber will make a better pipe, a lawyer will make a better plea, a merchant will sell a better bill of goods. I say, other things being equal. Of course when religion gives a man a new heart, it does not propose to give him a new head, or to intellectualize him, or to change a man's condition when his ordinary state is an overthrow of the philosophical theory that a total vacuum is impossible; but the more letters you have to write, the more burdens you have to carry, the more miles you have to travel, the more burdens you have to lift, the more engagements you have to meet, the more disputes you have to settle, the more opportunity you have of being a Christian. If you have a thousand irons in the fire, you have a thousand more opportunities of serving God than if you only had one iron in the fire. Who so busy as Christ? And yet who a millionth part as holy? The busiest men the best men.

Politics and Religion

All the persons converted in Scripture busy at the time of their being converted. Matthew attending to his custom-house duties; the Prodigal Son feeding swine; Lydia selling purple; Simon Peter hauling in the net from the sea; Saul spurring his horse toward Damascus, going down on his law business. Busy! busy! Daniel with all the affairs of state weighing down upon his soul, and yet three times a day worshiping the God of heaven.

Again, I learn from this subject that a man may take religion into his politics. Daniel had all the affairs of state on hand, yet a servant of God. He could not have kept his elevated position unless he had been a thorough politician; and yet all the thrusts of officials and all the danger of disgrace did not make him yield one iota of his high-toned religious principle. He stood before that age, he stands before all ages, a specimen of a godly politician. So there have been in our day and in the days of our fathers men as eminent in the service of God as they have been eminent in the service of the state. Such was Benjamin F. Butler, Attorney-General of New York in the time of your fathers. Such was John McLean, of the Supreme Court of the United States. Such was George Briggs, of Massachusetts. Such was Theodore Frelinghuysen, of New Jersey—men faithful to the state at the same time faithful to God. It is absurd to expect that men who have been immersed in political wickedness for thirty or forty years shall come to reformation; and our hope is in the young men who are coming up, that they have patriotic principle and Christian principle side by side when they come to the ballot-box and cast their first vote, and that they swear allegiance to the government of heaven as well as the government of the United States. We would have Bunker Hill mean less to them than Calvary, and Lexington mean less to them than Bethlehem. But because there are bad men around the ballot-box is no reason why Christian men should retreat from the arena. The last time you ought to give up your child or forsake your child is when it is surrounded by a company of Choctaws; and the last time to surrender the ballot-box is when it is surrounded by impurity and dishonesty and all sorts of wickedness.

Daniel stood on a most unpopular platform. He stood firmly, though the demagogues of the day hissed at him and tried to overthrow him. We must carry our religion into our politics. But there are a great many men who are in favor of taking religion into national politics who do not see the importance of taking it into city politics; as though a man were intelligent about the welfare of his neighborhood, and had no concern about his own home.

My subject also impresses me with the fact that lions cannot hurt a good man. No man ever got into worse company than Daniel got into when he was thrown into the den. What a rare morsel that fair young man would have been for the hungry monsters! If they had plunged at him, he could not have climbed into a niche beyond the reach of their paw or the snatch of their tooth. They came pleased all around about him, as hunters' hounds at the well-known whistle come bounding to his feet. You need not go to Numidia to get many lions. You all have had them after you—the lion of financial distress, the lion of sickness, the lion of persecution. You saw that lion of financial panic putting his mouth down to the earth, and he roared until all the banks and all the insurance companies quaked. With his nostril he scattered the ashes on the domestic hearth. You have had trial after trial, misfortune after misfortune, lion after lion; and yet they have never hurt you if you put your trust in God, and they never will hurt you. They did not hurt Daniel, and they cannot hurt you. The Persians used to think that spring rain falling into sea-shells would turn into pearls; and I have to tell you that the tears of sorrow turn into precious gems when they drop into God's bottle. You need be afraid of nothing, putting your trust in God. Even death, that monster lion whose den is the world's sepulchre, and who puts his paw down amid thousands of millions of the dead, cannot affright you. When in olden times a man was to get the honors of knighthood, he was compelled to go fully armed the night before, among the tombs of the dead, carrying a sort of spear, and then when the day broke he would come forth, and, amid the sound of cornet and great parade, he would get the honors of knighthood. And so it will be with the Christian in the night before heaven, as fully armed with spear and helmet of salvation, he will wait and watch through the darkness until the morning dawns, and then he will take the honors of heaven amid that great throng with snowy robes, streaming over seas of sapphire.

THE BRIDE OF NATIONS

Isa., 62: 4: "Thy land shall be married."

THE BRIDE OF NATIONS

Isa.. 62:4: " Thy land shall be married."

As the greater includes the less, so does the circle of future joy around our entire world include the epicycle of our own republic. Bold, exhilarant, unique, divine imagery of the text. At the close of a week in which for three days our National Capitol was a pageant, and all that grand review, and bannered procession, and National Anthems could do, celebrated peace, it may not be inapt to anticipate the time when the Prince of Peace and the Heir of Universal Dominion shall take possession of this nation, and "thy land shall be married."

In discussing the final destiny of this nation, it makes all the difference in the world whether we are on the way to a funeral or a wedding. The Bible leaves no doubt on this subject. In pulpits, and on platforms, and in places of public concourse, I hear so many of the muffled drums of evil prophecy sounded, as though we were on the way to national interment, and beside Thebes and Babylon and Tyre in the cemetery of dead nations our republic was to be entombed, that I wish you to understand it is not to be obsequies, but nuptials; not mausoleum, but carpeted altar; not cypress, but orange-blossoms; not requiem, but wedding march; for "thy land shall be married." I propose to name some of the suitors who are claiming the hand of this republic. This land is so fair, so beautiful, so affluent, that it has many suitors, and it will depend much upon your advice whether this or that shall be accepted or rejected. Even if your advice in regard to national betrothal is not regarded, you will have discharged your responsibility.

In the first place, I remark: there is a greedy, all-grasping monster who comes in as suitor seeking the hand of this republic, and that monster is known by the name of Monopoly. His sceptre is made out of the iron of the rail track and the wire of telegraphy. He does everything for his own advantage and for the robbery of the people. Things went on from bad to worse until in the three legislatures of New York, New Jersey and Pennsylvania, for a long time Monopoly decided everything. If Monopoly favor a law, it passes; if Monopoly oppose a law, it is rejected. Monopoly stands in the railroad depot, putting into his pockets in one year two hundred million of dollars in excess of all reasonable charges for services; Monopoly holds in his one hand the steam power of locomotion, and in the other the electricity of swift communication; Monopoly has the Republican party in one pocket and the Democratic party in the other pocket; Monopoly decides nominations and elections —city elections, State elections, national elections. With bribes he secures the votes of legislators, giving them free passes, giving appointments to needy relatives to lucrative positions, employing them as attorneys if they are lawyers, carrying their goods fifteen per cent. less if they are merchants; and if he find a case very stubborn, as well as very important, puts down before him the hard cash of bribery.

But Monopoly is not so easily caught now as when, during the term of Mr. Buchanan, the legislative committee in one of our States explored and exposed the manner in which a certain railway company had obtained a donation of public land. It was found out that thirteen of the senators of that State received one hundred and seventy-five thousand dollars among them, sixty members of the lower

The Bride of Nations

house of that State received between five thousand dollars and ten thousand dollars each, the Governor of that State received fifty thousand dollars, his clerk received five thousand dollars, the Lieutenant-Governor received ten thousand dollars, all the clerks of the Legislature received five thousand dollars each, while fifty thousand dollars were divided among the lobby agents. That thing on a larger or smaller scale is all the time going on in some of the States of the Union; but it is not so blundering as it used to be, and therefore not so easily exposed or arrested. I tell you that the overshadowing curse of the United States to-day is Monopoly. He puts his hand upon every bushel of wheat, upon every sack of salt, upon every ton of coal, and every man, woman and child in the United States feels the touch of that moneyed despotism. I rejoice that in twenty-four States of the Union already anti-monopoly leagues have been established. God speed them in the work of liberation.

I have nothing to say against capitalists; a man has a right to all the money he can make honestly; I have nothing to say against corporations as such; without them no great enterprise would be possible; but what I do say is that the same principles are to be applied to capitalists and to corporations that are applied to the poorest man and the plainest laborer. What is wrong for me is wrong for great corporations. If I take from you your property without any adequate compensation, I am a thief; and if a railway damages the property of the people without making any adequate compensation, that is a gigantic theft. What is wrong on a small scale is wrong on a large scale. Monopoly in England has ground hundreds of thousands of her best people into semi-starvation, and in Ireland has driven multitudinous tenants almost to madness, and in the United States proposes to take the wealth of sixty or seventy millions of people and put it in a few silken wallets.

Sermons by T. DeWitt Talmage

Monopoly, brazen-faced, iron-fingered, vulture-hearted Monopoly, offers his hand to this republic. He stretches it out over the lakes, and up the great railroads, and over the telegraph poles of the continent, and says: "Here is my heart and hand; be mine forever." Let the millions of the people North, South, East and West forbid the banns of that marriage, forbid them at the ballot-box, forbid them on the platform, forbid them by great organizations, forbid them by the overwhelming sentiment of an outraged nation, forbid them by the protest of the Church of God, forbid them by prayer to high heaven. That Herod shall not have this Abigail. It shall not be to all-devouring Monopoly that this land is to be married.

Another suitor claiming the hand of this republic is Nihilism.

He owns nothing but a knife for universal cutthroatery, and a nitro-glycerine bomb for universal explosion. He believes in no God, no government, no heaven, and no hell, except what he can make on earth! He slew the Czar of Russia, keeps many a king practically imprisoned, killed Abraham Lincoln, would put to death every king and president on earth; and if he had the power, would climb up until he could drive the God of heaven from his throne and take it himself, the universal butcher. In France it is called Communism; in the United States it is called Anarchism; in Russia it is called Nihilism, but that last is the most graphic and descriptive term. It means complete and eternal smash-up. It would make the holding of property a crime, and it would drive a dagger through your heart, and put a torch to your dwelling and turn over this whole land into the possession of theft, and lust, and rapine, and murder.

Where does this monster live? In all the towns

and cities of this land. It offers its hand to this fair republic; it proposes to tear to pieces the ballot-box, the legislative hall, the Congressional assembly; it would take this land and divide it up, or, rather, divide it down; it would give as much to the idler as to the worker, to the bad as to the good. Nihilism! This panther having prowled across other lands, has set its paw on our soil, and it is only waiting for the time in which to spring upon its prey. It was Nihilism that burned the railroad property at Pittsburg during the great riots; it was Nihilism that slew black people in our Northern cities during the war; it was Nihilism that mauled to death the Chinese immigrants years ago; it is Nihilism that glares out of the windows of the drunkeries upon sober people as they go by. Ah! its power has never yet been tested. I pray God its power may never be fully tested. It would, if it had the power, leave every church, chapel, cathedral, schoolhouse and college in ashes.

Let me say it is the worse enemy of the laboring classes in any country. The honest cry for reform lifted by oppressed laboring men is drowned out by the vociferation for anarchy. The criminals and vagabonds who range though our cities talking about their rights, when their first right is the penitentiary; if they could be hushed up, and the downtrodden laboring men of this country could be heard, there would be more bread for hungry children. In this land, riot and bloodshed never gained any wages for the people or gathered up any prosperity. In this land the best weapon is not the club, not the shillalah, not firearms, but the ballot. Let not our oppressed laboring men be beguiled to coming under the bloody banner of Nihilism. It will make your taxes heavier, your wages smaller, your table scantier, your children hungrier, your suffering greater. Yet this Nihilism, with feet red of slaughter, comes forth and offers its hand for this republic. Shall the banns be proclaimed? If so, where shall the marriage altar be? and who will be the officiating priest? and what will be the music? That altar will have to be white with bleached skulls, the officiating priest must be a dripping assassin, the music must be the smothered groan of multitudinous victims, the garlands must be twisted of nightshade, the fruits must be apples of Sodom, the wine must be the blood of St. Bartholomew's massacre. No! It is not to Nihilism, the sanguinary monster, that this land is to be married.

Another suitor for the hand of this nation is Infidelity. When the midnight ruffians despoiled the grave of A. T. Stewart in St. Mark's churchyard, everybody was shocked; but Infidelity proposes something worse than that, the robbing of all the graves of Christendom of the hope of a resurrection. It proposes to chisel out from the tombstones of your Christian dead the words, "Asleep in Jesus," and substitute the words, "Obliteration—annihilation." Infidelity proposes to take the letter from the world's Father, inviting the nations to virtue and happiness, and tear it up into fragments so small that you cannot read a word of it. It proposes to take the consolation from the broken-hearted, and the soothing pillow from the dying. Infidelity proposes to swear in the President of the United States, and the Supreme Court, and the Governors of States, and the witnesses in the court room with their right hand on Paine's "Age of Reason," or Voltaire's "Philosophy of History." It proposes to take away from this country the Book that makes the difference between the United States and the Kingdom of Dahomey, between American civilization and Bornesian cannibalism. If infidelity could destroy the Scriptures, it would in two hundred years turn the civilized nations back to semi-barbarism, and then from semi-barbarism into midnight savagery, until the morals of a menagerie of tigers, rattlesnakes and chimpanzees would be better than the morals of the shipwrecked human race.

The only impulse in the right direction that this world has ever had has come from the Bible. It was the mother of Roman law and of healthful jurisprudence. That book has been the mother of all reforms and all charities—mother of English Magna Charta and American Declaration of Independence. Benjamin Franklin, holding that holy Book in his hand, stood before an infidel club in Paris and read to them out of the prophecies of Habakkuk, and the infidels, not knowing what book it was, declared it was the best poetry they had ever heard. That book brought George Washington down on his knees in the snow at Valley Forge, and led the dying Prince Albert to ask some one to sing "Rock of Ages."

I tell you that the worst attempted crime of the century is the attempt to destroy this book; yet Infidelity, loathsome, stenchful, leprous, pestiferous, rotten monster, stretches out its hand, ichorous with the second death, to take the hand of this republic. It stretches it out through seductive magazines, and through lyceum lectures, and through caricatures of religion. It asks for all that part of the continent already fully settled, and the two-thirds not yet occupied. It says: "Give me all east of the Mississippi, with the keys of the church and with the Christian printing presses; then give me Wyoming, give me Alaska, give me Montana, give me Colorado, give me all the States west of the Mississippi, and I will take those places and keep them by right of possession long before the Gospel can be fully entrenched.

And this suitor presses his case persistently. Shall

the banns of that marriage be proclaimed? "No!" say the home missionaries of the West, a martyr band of whom the world is not worthy, toiling amid fatigues and malaria and starvation. "No! not if we can help it. By what we and our children have suffered, we forbid the banns of that marriage!" "No!" say all patriotic voices, "our institutions were bought at too dear a price and were defended at too great a sacrifice to be so cheaply surrendered." "No!" says the God of Bunker Hill and Independence Hall and Gettysburg, "I did not start this nation for such a farce." "No!" cry ten thousand voices, "to Infidelity this land shall not be married."

But there is another suitor that presents his claim for the hand of this republic. He is mentioned in the verse following my text where it says: "As the bridegroom rejoiceth over the bride, so shall thy God rejoice over thee." It is not my figure; it is the figure of the Bible. Christ is so desirous to have this world love him that he stops at no humiliation of simile. He compares his grace to spittle on the eyes of the blind man. He compares himself to a hen gathering the chickens, and in my text he compares himself to a suitor begging a hand in marriage. Does this Christ, the King, deserve this land? Behold Pilate's hall and the insulting expectoration on the face of Christ. Behold the Calvarean massacre and the awful hemorrhage of five wounds. Jacob served fourteen years for Rachel, but Christ, my Lord, the King, suffered in torture thirty-three years to win the love of this world. As often princesses at their very birth are pledged in treaty of marriage to princes of kings of earth, so this nation at its birth was pledged to Christ for divine marriage.

Before Columbus and his one hundred and twenty men embarked on the *Santa Maria*, the *Pinta*, and the

Nina, for their wonderful voyage, what was the last thing they did? They sat down and took the holy sacrament of the Lord Jesus Christ. After they caught the first glimpse of this country and the gun of one ship had announced it to the other vessels that land had been discovered, what was the song that went up from all the three decks? *Gloria in excelsis.* After Columbus and his one hundred and twenty men had stepped from the ship's deck to the solid ground, what did they do? They all knelt and consecrated the new world to God. What did the Huguenots do after they landed in the Carolinas? What did the Holland refugees do after they had landed in New York? What did the Pilgrim fathers do after they landed in New England? With bended knee, and uplifted face, and heaven besieging prayer, they took possession of this continent for God. How was the first American Congress opened? By prayer, in the name of Jesus Christ. From its birth this nation was pledged for holy marriage with Christ.

And then see how good God has been to us! Just open the map of the continent, and see how it is shaped for immeasurable prosperities. Navigable rivers, more in number and greater than of any other land, rolling down on all sides into the sea, prophesying large manufactures and easy commerce. Look at the great ranges of mountains timbered with wealth on the top and sides, metaled with wealth underneath. One hundred and eighty thousand square miles of coal; one hundred and eighty thousand square miles of iron. The land so contoured that extreme weather hardly ever lasts more than three days—extreme heat or extreme cold. Climate for the most part bracing and favorable for brawn and brain. All fruits, all minerals, all harvests. Scenery displaying an autumnal pageantry that no land on earth pretends to rival. No

South American earthquakes; no Scotch mists; no London fogs; no Egyptian plagues; no Germanic divisions. The people of the United States are happier than any people on earth. It is the testimony of every man that has traveled abroad. For the poor, more sympathy; for the industrious, more opportunity. Oh, how good God was to our fathers, and how good he has been to us and our children. To him! Blessed be his mighty name! To him of Cross and triumph, to him who still remembers the prayers of the Huguenots, and Holland refugees, and the Pilgrim Fathers—to him shall this land be married. Oh! you Christian patriots, by your contributions and your prayers, hasten on the fulfilment of the text.

We have been turning an important leaf in the mighty tome of our national history. One year at the gates of this continent over five hundred thousand immigrants arrived; I was told by the Commissioner of Immigration that the probability was that in that one year six hundred thousand immigrants would arrive at the different gates of commerce. Who were they, the paupers of Europe? No. At Kansas City I was told by a gentleman, who had opportunity for large investigation, that a great multitude had gone through there, averaging in worldly estate eight hundred dollars. I was told by an officer of the Government, who had opportunity for authentic investigation, that thousands and thousands had gone, averaging one thousand dollars in possession each. I was told by the Commissioner of Immigration that twenty families that had recently arrived brought eighty-five thousand dollars with them. Mark you, families, not tramps. Additions to the national wealth, not subtractions therefrom. I saw some of them reading their Bibles and their hymn books, thanking God for his kindness in helping them cross the sea. Some of them had Christ in the steerage all across the waves, and they will have Christ in the rail trains which at five o'clock every afternoon start for the great West. They are being taken by the Commissioner of Immigration in New York, taken from the vessels, protected from the Shylocks and the sharpers, and in the name of God and humanity passed on to their destination; and there they will turn your wildernesses into gardens, if you will build for them churches and establish for them schools, and send to them Christian missionaries.

Are you afraid this continent is going to be overcrowded with this population? Ah, that shows you have not been to California; that shows you have not been to Oregon; that shows you have not been to Texas. A fishing smack to-day on Lake Ontario might as well be afraid of being crowded by other shipping before night as for any one of the next ten generations of Americans to be afraid of being overcrowded by foreign populations in this country. The one State of Texas is far larger than all the Austrian Empire, yet the Austrian Empire supports thirty-five million people. The one State of Texas is larger than all France, and France supports thirty-six million people. The one State of Texas far surpasses in size the Germanic Empire, yet the Germanic Empire supports forty-one million people. I tell you the great want of the Western States is more population.

While some people may stand at the gates of the city saying, "Stay back!" to foreign populations, I press out as far beyond those gates as I can press out beyond them and beckon to foreign nations, saying: "Come, come! all ye people who are honest and industrious and God-loving!" But say you: "I am so afraid that they will bring their prejudices for foreign governments and plant them here." Absurd. They are sick of the governments that have oppressed them, and they want free America! Give them the great gospel of welcome. Throw around them all Christian hospitalities. They will add their industry and hard-earned wages to this country, and then we will dedicate all to Christ, and "thy land shall be married." But where shall the marriage altar be? Let it be the Rocky Mountains, when, through artificial and mighty irrigation, all their tops shall be covered, as they will be, with vineyards, and orchards, and grain fields. Then let the Bostons, and the New Yorks, and the Charlestons of the Pacific coast come to the marriage altar on the one side, and then let the Bostons and the New Yorks and the Charlestons of the Atlantic coast come to the marriage altar on the other side, and there between them let this bride of nations kneel; and then if the organ of the loudest thunders that ever shook the Sierra Nevadas on the one side, or moved the foundations of the Alleghanies on the other side, should open full diapason march, that organ of thunders could not drown the voice of him who would take the hand of this bride of nations, saying, "as a bridegroom rejoiceth over a bride, so thy God rejoiceth over thee." At that marriage banquet the platters shall be of Nevada silver, and the chalices of California gold, and the fruits of Northern orchards, and the spices of Southern groves, and the tapestry of American manufacture, and the congratulations from all the free nations of earth and from all the triumphant armies of heaven. "And so thy land shall be married."

BEFORE THEY ADJOURN

Psalm, 105: 22: "And teach his senators wisdom."

BEFORE THEY ADJOURN*

Psalm, 105: 22: "And teach his senators wisdom."

Senators in this text stand for law-makers. Joseph was the Lord Treasurer of the Egyptian government, and among other great things which he did, according to my text, was to teach his senators wisdom; and if any men on earth ought to be endowed with wisdom, it is senators, whether they stand in congresses or parliaments or reichstags or assemblies or legislatures. By their decisions nations go up or down. Law-makers are sometimes so tempted by prejudices, by sectional preferences, by opportunity of personal advancement, and sometimes what is best to do is so doubtful that they ought to be prayed for and encouraged in every possible way, instead of severely criticised and blamed and excoriated, as is much of the time the case. Our public men are so often the target to be shot at, merely because they obtain eminence which other men wanted but could not reach, that more injustices are hurled at our national Legislature than the people of the United States can possibly imagine. The wholesale belying of our public men is simply damnable. By residence in Washington I have come to find out that many of our public men are persistently misrepresented, and some of the best of them, the purest in their lives and most faithful in the discharge of their duties, are the worst defamed. Some day I want to preach a sermon from the text in II. Peter: "They are not afraid to speak evil of

---

* Preached in Washington on the eve of the adjournment of the Fifty-fifth Congress.

dignities. Whereas angels, which are greater in power and might, bring not railing accusation against them before the Lord. But these, as natural brute beasts, made to be taken and destroyed, speak evil of the things that they understand not." So constant and malignant is this work of depreciation and scandalization in regard to our public men that all over the land there are those who suppose that the city of Washington is the centre of all corruption; while, what with its parks, and its equestrian statuary, and its wide streets, and its architectural symmetries, and its lovely homes, it is not only the most beautiful city under the sun, but has the highest style of citizenship. I saw but one intoxicated man in the first six months of my residence, and I do not think any man can give similar testimony of any other city on the American continent. The depressing things written and spoken concerning this Capitol are inspired by reasons not at all complimentary to those who utter them.

The gavels of our two houses of national legislature will soon fall, and adjournment of two bodies of men as talented, as upright, and as patriotic as ever graced the Capitol, will take place. The two or three unfortunate outbreaks which you have noticed only make more conspicuous the dignity, the fraternity, the eloquence, the fidelity which have characterized those two bodies during all the long months of important and anxious deliberation. We put a halo around great men of the past because they were so rare in their time. Our Senate and House of Representatives have five such men where they once had one. But it will not be until after they are dead that they will get appreciated. The world finds it safer to praise the dead than the living, because the departed, having a heavy pile of marble above them, may not rise to become rivals. But, before the gavels of adjournment drop and the doors of Capitol Hill shut, there are one or two things that ought to be done, and let us pray God that they may be accomplished. More forcibly than ever before, Congress has been implored to acknowledge God in our Constitution. The Methodist Church—a church that is always doing glorious things—has in its recent Wilmington conference requested our Congress to amend the immortal document which has been the foundation and wall and dome of our United States government, by inserting the words, "Trusting in Almighty God." If that amendment is made, it will not only please all the good people of the country, but will please the heavens. It was only an oversight or a mental accident that the fathers who made the Constitution did not insert a divinely worshipful sentence. They all, so far as they amounted to anything, believed in "God, the Father Almighty, the Maker of heaven and earth, and in Jesus Christ, his only begotten Son." The Constitution would have been a failure had it not been for the Divine interference. The members of the convention could agree on nothing until, in response to Benjamin Franklin's request that the meetings be opened by prayer, the Lord God was called on to interfere and help, and then the way was cleared, and all the States signed the document—an historical fact that all the rat-terriers of modern infidelity cannot bark out of existence.

I know that there was an exception to the fact that the prominent men of those times were good men. Tom Paine, a libertine and a sot, did not believe in anything good until he was dying, and he shrieked out for God's mercy. And Ethan Allen, from one of whose descendants I have received within a few days a confirmation of the incident I mentioned in a recent sermon, as saying to his dying daughter that she had better take her mother's Christian religion than his own infidelity. The article sent me says: "The story has been denied by some of the Allen family, but the Bronson family, some of whom were with the dying girl, affirm that it is substantially true. In such a matter one confirmation is worth more than many denials." So says the article sent me. But all the decent men of the Revolution believed in God, and our American Congress, now assembled, will only echo the sentiments of the fathers when they enthrone the name of God in the Constitution. We have now more reason for inserting that acknowledgment of Divinity than our fathers had. Since then the continent has been peopled and great cities from the Atlantic to the Pacific built, and all in peace, showing that there must have been supernal supervisal. Since then the War of 1812, and ours the victory! Since then great financial prostrations, out of which we came to greater prosperity than anything that preceded. Since then sanguinary 1861, 1862, 1863, 1864 and 1865, and, notwithstanding the fact that all the foreign despotisms were planning for our demolition, we are a united people, and to-morrow you will find in both houses of Congress the men who fought for the North and the South, now sitting side by side, armed with no weapon except the pen, with which they write home to their constituents who want to be appointed postmasters. The man who cannot see God in our American history is as blind of soul as he would be blind of body if he could not at twelve o'clock of unclouded noon see the sun in the heavens. As a matter of gratitude to Almighty God, gentlemen of the American Congress, be pleased to insert the four words suggested by the Methodist Conference!

Not only because of the kindness of God to this nation in the past should such a reverential insertion be made, but because of the fact that we are going to want Divine interposition still further in our national history. This gold and silver question will never be settled until God settles it. This question of tariff and free trade will never be settled until God settles it. This question between the East and the West which is getting hotter and hotter, and looks towards a republic of the Pacific will not be settled until God settles it. We needed God in the one hundred and twenty years of our past life, and we will need him still more in the next one hundred and twenty years. Lift up your heads, ye everlasting gates of our glorious Constitution, and let the King of Glory come in! Make one line of that immortal document radiant with Omnipotence! Spell at least one word with Thrones! At the beginning, or at the close, or in the centre, recognize him from whom as a nation we have received all the blessings of the past and upon whom we are dependent for the future. Print that word "God," or "Lord," or "Eternal Father," or "Ruler of Nations," somewhere between the first word and the last. The Great Expounder of the Constitution sleeps at Marshfield, Massachusetts, the Atlantic Ocean still humming near his pillow of dust its prolonged lullaby; but is there not some one now living, who, in the white marble palace of the nation on yonder hill, not ten minutes away, will become the Irradiator of the Constitution by causing to be added the most tremendous word of our English vocabulary, the name of that Being before whom all nations must bow or go into defeat and annihilation— "God"?

Again, before the approaching adjournment of our American Congress, it ought to be decidedly and forever settled that no appropriations be made to sectarian schools, and that the courtship between Church and State in this country be forever broken up. That question already seems temporarily settled. I wish it might be completely and forever settled. All schools and all institutions, as well as all denominations, should stand on the same level before American law. Emperor Alexander of Russia, at his Peterhof Palace, asked me how many denominations of religion there were in America, and I recited their names as well as I could. Then he asked me the difference between them, and there I broke down. But when I told him that no religious denomination in America had any privileges above the others, he could hardly understand it. The Greek Church first in Russia. The Lutheran Church first in Germany. The Episcopal Church first in England. The Catholic Church first in Rome. Mohammedanism first in Constantinople. The Emperor wondered how it was possible that all the denominations in America could stand on the same platform. But so it is, and so let it ever be. Let there be no preference, no partiality, no attempt to help one sect an inch higher than another. Washington and Jefferson and all the early Presidents, and all the great statesmen of the past, have lifted their voice against any such tendency. If a school or an institution cannot stand without the prop of national appropriation, then let that school or that institution go down. On the other side of the sea the world has had plenty of illustration of Church and State united. Let us have none of the hypocrisy and demoralization born of that relation on this side of the Atlantic. Let that denomination come out ahead which does the most for the cause of God and humanity; men, institutions, and religions getting what they achieve by their own right arm of usefulness, and not by the favoritism of government. As you desire the welfare and perpetuity of our institutions, keep politics out of religion.

But now that I am speaking of national affairs from a religious standpoint, I bethink myself of the fact that two other gavels will soon lift and fall, the one at St. Louis and the other at Chicago, and before those national conventions adjourn, I ask that they acknowledge God in the platforms. The men who construct those platforms are here this morning or will read these words. Let no political party think it can do its duty unless it acknowledges that God, who built this continent, and revealed it at the right time to the discoverer, and who has reared here a prosperity which has been given to no other people. "Oh," says some one, "there are people in this country who do not believe in a God, and it would be an insult to them." Well, there are people in this country who do not believe in common decency or common honesty or any kind of government, preferring anarchy. Your very platform is an insult to them. You ought not to regard a man who does not believe in God, any more than you should regard a man who refuses to believe in common decency. Your pocket-book is not safe a moment in the presence of an atheist. God is the only source of good government. Why not, then, say so, and let the chairman of the Committee on Resolutions in your national conventions take a pen full of ink and with bold hand head the document with one significant "Whereas" acknowledging the goodness of God in the past, and invoking his kindness and protection for the future?

This country belongs to God, and we ought in every possible way to acknowledge it. From the moment that, on an October morning in 1492, Columbus looked over the side of the ship and saw the carved staff which made him think he was near an inhabited country, and saw also a thorn and a cluster of berries (type of our history ever since, the piercing sorrows and cluster of national joys), until this hour our country has been bounded on the north, south, east and west by the goodness of God. The Huguenots took possession of the Carolinas, in the name of God. William Penn settled Philadelphia, in the name of God. The Hollanders took possession of New York, in the name of God. The Pilgrim Fathers settled New England, in the name of God. Preceding the first gun of Bunker Hill, at the voice of prayer all heads uncovered. In the War of 1812, an officer came to Gen. Andrew Jackson and said: "There is an unusual noise in the camp; it ought to be stopped." General Jackson said, "What is the noise?" The officer said, "It is the voice of prayer and praise." Then the General said, "God forbid that prayer and praise should be an unusual noise in the encampment. You had better go and join them." Prayer at Valley Forge. Prayer at Monmouth. Prayer at Atlanta. Prayer at South Mountain. Prayer at Gettysburg. "Oh!" says some infidel, "the Northern people prayed on one side and the Southern people prayed on the other side, and so it did not amount to anything." And I have heard good Christian people confounded with the infidel statement, when it is as plain to me as my right hand. Yes; the Northern people prayed in one way, and the Southern people prayed in another way, and God answered in his own way, giving to the North the reestablishment of the government, and giving to the South larger opportunities, larger than she had ever anticipated, the harnessing of her rivers in great manufacturing interests, until the Mobile and the Tallapoosa and the Chattahoochee are Southern Merrimacs, and the unrolling of great Southern mines of coal and iron, of which the world knew nothing, and opening before her opportunities of wealth which will give ninety-nine per cent. more of affluence than she ever possessed; and instead of the black hands of American slaves, there are the more industrious black hands of the coal and iron mines of the South, which are achieving for her fabulous and unimagined wealth.

And there are domes of white blossoms where spread the white tent,
And there are ploughs in the track where the war wagons went,
And there are songs where they lifted up Rachel's Lament.

Oh, you are a stupid man if you do not understand how God answered Abraham Lincoln's prayer in the White House, and Stonewall Jackson's prayer in the saddle, and answered all the prayers of all the cathedrals on both sides of Mason and Dixon's Line. God's country all the way past; God's country now. Put his name in your pronunciamentos. Put his name on your ensigns. Put his name on your city and State and national enterprises. Put his name in your hearts. We cannot sleep well the last sleep, until we are assured that the God of our American institutions in the past will be the God of our American institutions in the days that are to come. Oh, when all the rivers that empty into Atlantic and Pacific seas shall pull on factory bands; when all the great mines of gold and silver and iron and coal shall be laid bare for the nation; when the last swamp shall be reclaimed, and the last jungle cleared, and the last American desert Edenized, and from sea to sea the continent shall be occupied by more than twelve hundred million souls, may it be found that moral and religious influences were multiplied in more rapid ratio than the population. And then there shall be four doxologies coming from North and South and East and West, four doxologies rolling toward each other, and meeting mid-continent, with such dash of holy joy that they shall mount to the Throne—

Sermons by T. DeWitt Talmage

And Heaven's high arch resound again
With peace on earth, good will to men.

I take a step further, and say that before the gavels of our Senate and House of Representatives and our political conventions pound adjournment, there ought to be passed a law or adopted a plank of intelligent helpfulness for the great foreign populations which are coming among us. It is too late now to discuss whether we had better let them come. They are here. They are coming this moment through the Narrows. They are this moment taking the first full inhalation of the free air of America. And they will continue to come as long as this country is the best place to live in. You might as well pass a law prohibiting summer bees from alighting on a field of blossoming buckwheat; you might as well prohibit the stags of the mountain from coming down to the deerlick, as to prohibit the hunger-bitten nations of Europe from coming to this land of bread—as to prohibit the people of England, Ireland, Scotland, Italy, Norway, Sweden and Germany, working themselves to death on small wages on the other side the sea, from coming to this land where there are the largest compensations under the sun. Why did God spread out the prairies of the Dakotas and roll the precious ore into Colorado? It was that all the earth might come and plough, and come and dig. Just as long as the centrifugal force of foreign despotisms throw them off, just so long will the centripetal force of American institutions draw them here. And that is what is going to make this the mightiest nation on the earth. Intermarriage of nationalities! Not circle intermarrying circle, and nation intermarrying nation. But it is going to be Italian and Norwegian, Russian and Celt, Scotch and French, English and American. The

Before they Adjourn

American of a hundred years from now is to be different from the American of to-day. German brain, Irish wit, French civility, Scotch firmness, English loyalty, Italian æsthetics packed into one man, and he an American! It is this intermarriage of nationalities that is going to make the American nation the greatest nation of the ages. But what are we doing for the moral and intellectual culture of the five hundred thousand foreigners who came in one year, and the six hundred thousand who came in another year, and the eight hundred thousand who came in another year, and the one million who are coming into our various American ports? What are we doing for them? Many of them have no acquaintance with our laws. Now, I say, let the Government of the United States, so commanded by one political party or both political parties, give to every immigrant who lands here a volume, in good type and well bound for long usage—a volume containing the Declaration of Independence, the Constitution of the United States, and a chapter on the spirit of our Government. Let there be such a book on the shelf of every free library in America. While the American Bible Society puts into the right hand of every immigrant a copy of the Holy Scriptures, let the Government of the United States, commanded by some political party, put into the left hand of every immigrant a volume instructing him in the duties of good citizenship. There are thousands of foreigners in this land who need to learn that the ballot-box is not a foot-stool, but a throne—not something to put your foot on, but something to bow before.

There are three great reasons why you and I should do our best for this country—three great reasons: Our fathers' graves, our cradle, our children's birthright. When I say your father's graves, your pulses run quickly. Whether they sleep in city cemetery or country graveyard, their dust is very precious to you. I think they lived well and that they died right. Never submit to have any government over their tombs other than that government under which they lived and died. And then this country is our cradle. It may have rocked us very roughly, but it was a good cradle to be rocked in. Oh, how much we owe to it! Our boyhood and girlhood, it was spent in this blessed country. I never have any patience with a man who talks against this country. Glorious place to be born in, and a glorious place to live in. It has been our cradle. Ay! it is to be our children's birthright. You and I will soon be through. We will perhaps see a few more spring blossoms, and we will perhaps see a few more summer harvests, and we will perhaps gather a few more autumnal fruits; but we are to hand this government to our children as it was handed to us—a free land, a happy land, a Christian land. They are not to be trampled by despotism. They are not to be frightened by anarchies. We must hand this government to them over the ballot-box, over the school-desk, over the church altar, as we have received it, and charge them solemnly to put their life between it and any keen stroke that would destroy it.

And thou, Lord God Almighty! We put, with a thousand-armed prayer, into thy protection this nation. Remember our fathers' bleeding feet at Valley Forge. Remember Marion and Kosciusko. Remember the cold, and the hunger, and the long march, and the fever hospital. Remember the fearful charge at Bunker Hill. Remember Lexington, and Yorktown, and King's Mountain, and Gettysburg. Remember Perry's battle on the lake, and Hampton Roads, where the Cumberland went down. Remember Washington's prayer by the camp-fire. Remember Plymouth Rock, and the landing amid the savages. Remember Independence Hall, and how much it cost our fathers to sign their names. Remember all the blood and tears of three wars—1776, 1812, 1862. And more than all, remember the groan that was mightier than all other groans, and the thirst that stung worse than all other thirsts, and the death that was ghastlier than all other deaths, the Mount on which Jesus died to make all men happy and free. For the sake of all this human and divine sacrifice, O God, protect this nation! And whosoever would blot it out, and whosoever would strike it down, and whosoever would turn his back, let him be accursed!

Go home to-day in high hopes of the future. The Eternal God is on the side of this nation. Our brightest days are yet to come.

He hath sounded forth the trumpet that will never call retreat,
He is sifting out the hearts of men before the Judgment-seat.
Be swift my soul to answer him, be jubilant my feet.
    Our God is marching on.

THE NATION'S WOE

Isa., 40: 1: " Comfort ye, comfort ye, my people, saith your
God."

THE NATION'S WOE*

Isa., 40: 1: "Comfort ye, comfort ye my people, saith your God."

This reiterated command to the ministers of religion centuries ago is just as appropriate this terrible morning, while we are awaiting tidings from the suffering couch of our chief magistrate.

"The President shot!" was sounded through the rail-train as we halted a few moments on the morning of July 2d, at Williamstown, Mass., the place at which the President was expected in three days. "Absurd and impossible," I said. I asked then, as I ask you now, Why should any one want to kill him? He had nothing but that which he had earned with his own brain and hand. He had fought his own way up from country home to college hall, and from college hall to the House of Representatives, and from House of Representatives to the Senate Chamber, and from the Senate Chamber to the Presidential chair. Why should any one want to kill him? He was not a despot who had been treading on the rights of the people. There was nothing of the Nero or the Robespierre in him. He had wronged no man. He was free and happy himself and wanted all the world free and happy. Why should any one want to kill him? He had a family to shepherd and educate, a noble wife and a group of little children leaning on his arm, and holding his hand, and who needed him for many years to come. If any one must shoot him, why shoot

---

* Preached August 18, 1881, during the anxious time when the nation waited the result of the shooting of President Garfield.

him then, just as after with indescribable perplexity and fatigue, he had launched his administration and was off for a few days of recreation which he had so dearly earned? How any man could take steady aim at such a good, kind, sympathetic heart, and draw the trigger and see him fall is inexplicable.

But the deed is done. There is a black shadow on every hearthstone in America. It seems as if there were one dead in each house. Again and again we have prayed as we prayed this morning, "Father, if it be possible, let this cup pass from us." God will hear our prayer, if not in one way, then in another. God's way is sometimes different from man's way, but it is always the best way.

I am thankful to my friends who have sent me a great multitude of telegrams this morning, showing their interest in this subject—telegrams from gentlemen who are my friends, and from others who are strangers, official telegrams from the public office of telegraphy—and they give a ray of hope. Who knows but our President may come forth again and ride through these very streets in triumph? God grant it! But the indications are not in that direction. I have hastened before my time of expected return, because I wanted in your presence to obey the text, "Comfort ye, comfort ye my people, saith your God." While I comfort you I must comfort my own soul, for no public event has ever so overwhelmed me. My personal acquaintance with him, though not intimate, filled me with faith in his capacity to guide and bless this nation.

I could dwell on the aggravations of this event, and say, what a pity that he could not have carried out the excellent policy proposed; what a pity that he could not longer have enjoyed the high honor bestowed by the suffrages of the people; what a pity that he should go out of life by the hand of violence; what an awful thing for his family and the nation and the world if he should die. But instead of dwelling upon the aggravations I shall obey my text, "Comfort ye, comfort ye my people," and present only the alleviations of this stupendous horror.

Alleviation the first: James A. Garfield is prepared to exchange worlds if God sees fit to call him. Long ago he settled that matter. He was not dependent for happiness upon the course of a bullet or the whim of an assassin. On his knees and in days of health and with deliberation he had made all right for eternity. There has been nothing of cant or whining or lugubriousness in his religion, but a manly out and out profession of faith in God. Yea! he has preached this very Gospel. A minister said to me the other day, "I heard him preach; he preached for me in my own pulpit." I said, "What style of sermon was it?" He responded, "Excellent, excellent." But in all places he had preached—in Wall Street to the excited throng the day after Lincoln was shot; at Chickamauga among the wounded soldiers; in the Congress of the United States in many a noble speech.

Religion was with him no new thing. When a college boy, and encamped among the mountains for summer recreation, at eventide he takes out his Bible and says: "Boys, at this time of evening I am apt to read a passage of the Scripture; if you would like to hear it, I will read a chapter now." And then one of the comrades was called upon for prayer, and they all knelt in their summer tent. The last thing he did before leaving Mentor for Washington, was to take the holy sacrament of our Lord Jesus Christ, the tears of emotion rolling down the cheek of the communicant. The first opportunity he had after he was shot, he declared that he trusted all in the Lord's hand—was ready to die or to live. Surely he was ready then.

After these eight weeks of purifying distress, he is ready now.

I want all the world to mark that this illustrious bed, if it be a death-bed—illustrious for patience, illustrious for courage, illustrious for gentleness—is no infidel's death-bed, no scoffer's death-bed, a Christian death-bed. Though canopied and surrounded with the elegance of a ruler's mansion, it is the same kind of pillow that your old Christian father and mother died on, and the same pillow which shall be offered in our last sickness, however humble our lot may be. It puts me more than ever in love with the old Gospel— the Gospel of the One who died at the hand of cruel assassins. O! thou assassinated Christ, by thy own wounds in the side and the hands and the feet and the brow, pity the head, the feet, the side, the physical anguish of our beloved President!

There have been other Christian men in the Presidential chair of this country, but the most pronounced Christian since the days of Washington, in the Presidential chair, is James A. Garfield. If he go—God forbid that he should go now—but if he go, he goes straight to the bosom of a merciful God. Death will be promotion. He will lose nothing, but gain everything. On the steps of the Capitol, that stormy day in March, he took the oath of high office. If he go now, at the gate of heaven he will take the crown of triumph. Whether he live or die, I shout for him, "Victory, through our Lord Jesus Christ!"

Alleviation the second: his family will be magnificently provided for. It is an awful thing when the bread-winner of a family falls, if there be no estate left, and the wife must go forth, with her helpless children at her back, to fight for a livelihood. The mother, weak and sick with long watching, goes out to look for a place, and the children are taken by friends who, perhaps, get tired of the burden they assumed under sudden impulse of sympathy. But the more than one hundred and fifty thousand dollars already subscribed to the Garfield fund are a hint that there is not one of us amid the fifty millions of America who will allow that afflicted family to suffer need. If this stroke come, the widow, the children, the aged mother will be the sacred charge of this nation. I see so many bereft women in the awful struggle for bread dying by inches, and finding no rest until they get inside the grave, that I am sure I am right when I present among the alleviations of this great sorrow the complete financial deliverance of our President's family.

Alleviation the third: if our President die, this nation, without a moment's halting, will march right on in its career of prosperity. The death of rulers in other lands often means bloody revolution. This nation endured the death of Presidents Harrison and Taylor and Lincoln, when it was not half as strong as it is now, and it will not be discomfited by this calamity. It will take more than one murderous wretch to stop this nation, when God commands it to march on. If on that awful second of July the President had been instantly slain, I know not what would have occurred. There would have been other pistol shots and panic, and perhaps national delirium. How good God was to spare our President these two months, until the nation could gather its equipoise; for I tell you that while the heart of this nation is very sore, its head is level.

There will be but one life taken, and that by the hand of the law. I have no admiration for the organizations that I hear are forming to tear down the Washington jail, and maul the desperado. No, no! Let the judge of the court take his place and the jury be impaneled, and the witnesses testify, and the verdict be rendered, and the judge, amid a silence like the grave, give the sentence, and the scaffold be raised, and, with a stout rope, this accursed Guiteau be hung by the neck until he be dead. All that excitement will soon be in the rear, and the nation chastened by this affliction, will move on and up.

"But," you say, "what if the President die, what of his successor?" I answer, I have no acquaintance with the one who would be the incoming President, but I beg of you, the American people, to give him a fair chance; do as you would like to be done by if you were put in the same crisis. The nation would make nothing by throwing any impediments in his way. Others make a prophecy in regard to this incoming President in case of the death of our present ruler—I make a prophecy. They make prophecy from a political standpoint—I make mine from a religious standpoint. If our President die, judging from what seems God's design of kindness to this nation, I think he will give especial blessing for especial emergency, and the chief ideas of President Garfield's administration will be carried out by President Arthur's administration.

There are men now in the Cabinet who have inaugurated such a great work that they will certainly be retained. Postmaster General James has sent such consternation among the scoundrels of the Star Routes, saving our country millions of dollars, and making his department more illustrious than have any of his predecessors, that I know his hand will be kept in that reformation. Secretary Windom has wrought what merchants and bankers all over the land have called a miracle of financiering, and I am sure he will not be dethroned while he is saving the land more millions than I dare to state. Robert Lincoln, Secretary of War, admired by all parties, first for his own sake and next for his martyred father's sake, will, I am sure, continue in the councils of the nation.

And others of the Cabinet, whose brilliant and world-renowned services cannot afford to be stopped, will stay in their places; and with all the Episcopal churches of America, by the command of their liturgy, praying Sabbath by Sabbath for the President of the United States, and all the non-liturgical churches of America uniting in the same supplication, I am sure upon the new Chief Magistrate would come, straight from God, the spirit of good government. You say that his position, if called to it, will be one of great delicacy. I know it. But it will be one of unlimited and unparalleled opportunity. Mark that. Fellow citizens, fellow patriots, fellow Christians, fellow mourners, now is the time to trust God.

Alleviation the fourth: if our President die, he dies at what must be the best time. It does not seem to suit me, it does not seem to suit you; but God's time is always the best. Do you say this is the teaching of fatalism? It is the teaching of your Bible and my Bible that God sets the limit of our life. Had it been best, the President by this time would have been amid the cooling sea-breezes of Long Branch. Men with more bullets in them and in worse directions, are walking your streets to-day.

If he die—God avert the sorrow!—if he die, he will go at the time when he has the love of all the people. If he live he could not be an exception to the universal rule, that a brisk and decisive and reformatory administration rouses rancor and invective. Look up the files of the newspapers and see what surges of obloquy rolled over Lincoln and Madison and Monroe and Jefferson and Washington. Do you suppose Mr. Garfield could have carried out his intention of extirpating Mormonism, and that there would have been no wincing under the national surgery? He had other plans revolutionary for good.

It seems to me he suffered enough abuse in the political campaign of last autumn to suffice for one lifetime. If in addition to that there should be the insults of three or four years of contumely, it would be more than his share of bombardment. If James A. Garfield now dies, he dies in time to escape more insult than was ever heaped upon any of his predecessors, for by so much as he proposed greater reforms, he must have had to endure worse outrage. I was with him a few days before the bloody assault. I never saw a more anxious or perturbed countenance, and it seemed a relief to him to talk to my child, turning his back on the perplexities of State. What he has escaped, or seems about to escape, God only knows. The storm is lulled. If he goes, ours will be the grief —his the congratulation.

Six months seems to be a very short administration, but in those six months he has accomplished what forty years of his predecessors failed to do—the complete and eternal pacification of the North and South. There are more public meetings of sympathy in the South than in the North, on this subject. His sick bed, in eight weeks, has done more for the sisterhood of States than if he had lived out eight years, namely, two terms of the Presidency. The North, the South, the East, the West, stand on the four sides of his bed looking into each other's eyes with a kindliness that never before characterized them. If he expire, do not think his administration, because of its brevity, is a failure. There has gone out from the sick room an influence that will be felt as long as the American Government continues. Oh! measure not a man's life by days, or months, or years; measure it by the sweep of its influence. Out of six months of time a good man may build an eternity.

Alleviation the fifth: this calamity makes the business of office seeking disgustingly disreputable. Guiteau was no more crazy than thousands of other place-hunters. He had been refused an office, and he was full of unmingled and burning revenge. There was nothing else the matter with him. It was just this: "You haven't given me what I want; now I'll kill you." For months after each presidential inauguration the hotels of Washington are roosts for these buzzards. They are the crawling vermin of this nation. Guiteau was no rarity. There were hundreds of Guiteaus in Washington after the inauguration, except that they had not the courage to shoot. I saw them some two months after, or six weeks after. They were mad enough to do it. I saw it in their eyes.

They killed two other Presidents, William Henry Harrison and Zachary Taylor. I know the physicians called the disease congestion of the lungs or liver, but the plain truth was that they were worried to death; they were trampled out of life by place-hunters. Now, in God's name, let this thing stop. Three Presidents sacrificed to this one demon are enough. Let the Congress of the United States at the next session start a work of presidential emancipation. Four Presidents have recommended civil service reform, and it has amounted to little or nothing. But this assassination will compel speedy and decisive action, and so some good will come of it.

But is it not sadly strange that the world makes no advance except through the sacrifice of human life? The Church is to be reformed, but Wycliffe and John Oldcastle must perish; and the scenes of Piedmont and Brussels market-place must be enacted. The French depotism must be destroyed; but the streets of Paris must be incarnadined with human gore. The United States are to be separated from foreign rulers; but the frosts of Valley Forge must devour, and the bayonets of Yorktown must stab. National contests about slavery must be settled; but a million brave Northern and Southern men must die. Official patronage is to be regulated; but James A. Garfield must be assassinated. Alas! alas! without the shedding of blood there seems to be no reformation for the suffering state, and no atonement for the sin-cursed world. It seems for every reformation there must be a Messiah born in a manger and dying on a cross.

Alleviation the sixth: this calamity has resulted in an outburst of sympathy glorious and sublime. There never was anything like it since the world stood. You tell me this is a selfish world, and it is every man for himself, and there is no kindness or generosity left. You make a mistake. Throne and cottage, Victoria and the village schoolgirls, parlor and kitchen, trans-Atlantic and cis-Atlantic, trans-Pacific and cis-Pacific, Protestantism and Roman Catholicism, Eastern hemisphere and Western hemisphere, have by voice, by pen, by telephone, by telegram, by day, by night, poured forth sympathy for our President and his family and the nation. That man expressed the feeling of many in this country when last week he offered to spare part or all the blood from his veins, if it was necessary, to invigorate the President. We go back to ancient history to find a scene like that, and we speak of it in poetry and in song. We need not go so far back now. There are men here to-day who, wrought upon by the same power in this great sorrow, would bare their arm for the lancet, crying, like that old hero of centuries ago: "Pour my blood into his veins that he die not." I think we must be brothers and sisters all; I think that nations must belong to one family, and that they must have the same great mother—God. A little fore-taste this of the good time when all misunderstanding shall cease and everybody shall say pleasant things about everybody else, and the embroidered eagle and lion and bear will be taken off the banners, and there shall be substituted the lamb and the dove. How strange that one sick-bed should have given us such a glimpse of a millennium!

The President's son was said to be keeping a scrap-book with all the expressions of sympathy and kind-ness, that he might show them to his father after he got well. Unsuccessful attempt! No book that ever went forth from earthly bindery would be large enough to contain the story. It will require the in-finite book of God's remembrance to keep the record of the earthly and celestial sympathy that has hovered these long, dreadful weeks over the emaciated form of our suffering President.

Alleviation the last: the fact that this nation has impressed upon it as never before the uncertainty of human life starting out on a holiday tour—coming back in an ambulance. Strong health no warrant against fatality. The President had a model physique. Out of a hundred men you would have selected him as the most healthy. Fine intellect no warrant. He was decidedly the most brilliant mind that ever occu-pied the White House. Able to select what food he would, what residence he would, what defence he would, yet we have been told more than once during the last two or three days that he is dying. Out of all this come lessons of perpetual readiness. It was a wonderful eulogy day before yesterday pronounced by the surgeons when they said: "There is no need of telling him he has to die, for he said at the start he had no preparations to make." Be ye also ready, so that whether by flying bullet or falling scaffold, or colliding rail-trains, or in gradual decrease of ordinary sickness ye be called away you may not die unprepared.

I have this morning tried, at the behest of my text, to comfort you by the rehearsal of the alleviations of the national calamity; but, after all, there will remain in all our hearts a grief for many a day. I know just what you all feel. Oh, that he only could get well! How we would ring the bells and thunder the cannon, and set the night afire with pyrotechnic display. Oh! if he only could get well! But it does not seem to me at this crisis—although I have been hopeful until now—that he will recover.

I fear the message very soon will come shuddering along the lines: "President Garfield is dead!" If so, then with the pomp of great processions, and the tolling of bells, and the booming of minute guns, his silent form will move through these great cities toward his western home. He started from it with the congratulations of his country neighbors only a few months ago. They will at the same depot take up his palled casket, and with blinding tears carry it to the quiet graveyard and lay it down among his old friends.

We have no Westminster Abbey in which to bury kings, but we have a great national heart in which we enshrine those who have suffered for our land. Into that great shrine of the national heart we will carry our beloved President, and lay him down beside Adams and Lincoln and Washington and the other mighty men who loved God and toiled for the betterment of the race. Then we will sound forth, partly in requiem and partly in grand march of triumph, the words which Garfield employed after another famous assassination: "The Lord reigneth. Though clouds and darkness are around about him, righteousness and judgment are the habitation of his throne." God save the President! God save the nation!

THE NATION KNEELING

II Kings, 20: 7: "And Isaiah said, Take a lump of figs. And they took and laid it on the boil, and he recovered."

THE NATION KNEELING*

II Kings, 20: 7: "And Isaiah said, Take a lump of figs. And they took and laid it on the boil, and he recovered."

Good Hezekiah had been given up to die by the surgeons and by the clergy. Recovery was pronounced an impossibility. Then God came to the rescue and prescribed for the illness, and a great change took place. A lump of figs was the cool and strong poultice applied to the carbuncle, and Hezekiah rises from his sick bed for fifteen more years of earthly existence.

Our afflicted United States President in his sufferings has been the anxiety of all Christendom for the last eight weeks. More recently attention was diverted from the wound by the assassin to the virulent swelling which resisted the poultice, and the danger which the doctors said was imminent and the worst. Convalescence after convalescence, relapse after relapse, and last Saturday a week he was given up to die. All the six or seven surgeons decided that he must die; all the medical men throughout the United States, so far as heard from, declared that death was just at hand; all the newspapers said that soon the President would pass out of life. Those who had been most hopeful became despairing. Just in that darkest hour, in answer to the prayers that have been going up day and night from church and store-house, from rail-train and ship's deck, from all the civilized nations of the earth, a change took place, and the symptoms of the patient are more promising now than at any time since

* Preached during the illness of President Garfield.

the murderous revolver attempted its work. I rejoice with trembling, but I rejoice and hope, that President Garfield will get well. But never within your memory or mine has there been such a conspicuous and indisputable evidence of the fact that God honors prayer. Men who for forty years had not offered a supplication bent the knee during the last eight weeks. People who had no suspicion that they were praying, at the first calamity cried out, "God help us!" And last Sabbath afternoon, when the cheerful bulletin came in, exclaimed, "Thank God!" You may call that what you will; I call it prayer. Sublimest of all spectacles! We have seen nations in controversy, and nations in war, but here was a nation in prayer.

In that corps of six or seven surgeons there is some of the most eminent talent of this land, and of all lands —some of them of more ability, and others of less ability, but all admit they have done their very best. When I have thought of those surgeons under the nervous strain of the last eight weeks, all nations seeming to hold them responsible for the life of their illustrious patient, toiling on day and night amid the most depressing circumstances, all my sympathies have been aroused in their behalf, and my daily prayer has been, "God help and inspire and sustain and reward the doctors!" But, my friends, it was after all that combined medical and surgical skill had been defeated God stepped in; and he shall have all the glory, whether of present improvement, or in case of final restoration.

An unbeliever comes and says: "Oh! it was the result of natural causes; it was from subsidence of the parotid gland." My wise friend, who made the parotid gland go down? If the Divine Physician, at the call of prayer, had not come to the bedside, the obsequies of your President would have already been concluded.

The Nation Kneeling

This is the way God deals with nations. The Prince of Wales was down with typhoid fever. Worse and worse the case, until the official bulletin announced that he could not survive three hours. Meanwhile, his queenly mother was at prayer, and all England was at prayer, cathedral and coal shaft, House of Lords and the factory operatives, the mighty and the mean at prayer, and the tides of life which had been going out so rapidly suddenly began to rise, and the Prince of Wales got well. Had it not been for the prayers of the Christian people of this country, I believe that leaden bullet would seven weeks ago have completed its work. As surely as there is a God in Heaven, he heard prayer on the first Sabbath after the calamity, and the second Sabbath and the third Sabbath and the fourth Sabbath and the fifth and the sixth and the seventh and the eighth. I demand that you hereafter acknowledge prayer as an important factor in national prosperity. Have you not noticed in this case that every Saturday it seemed to dip to the lowest point, as if God on Sabbath morning would call upon the nation for prayer, saying, "You have called upon me in the day of trouble, and I will answer!" And then almost invariably Monday morning has presented a cheerful bulletin.

We have had in this country four great consecutive harvests, and everybody supposed that the same natural causes would produce the same results, and this year we would have larger crops than ever before, because more corn had been planted, and more wheat had been sown, and more fruit had been grafted; but in all the year I have not heard one audible prayer for a great harvest. What is the consequence? The corn crop, the wheat crop, the fruit crop, almost a failure in Michigan, almost a failure in Iowa, almost a failure in Pennsylvania; and the Associated Press reports giving to us the information from Cincinnati and from Toronto and from Pittsburg and from Chicago and from the great centres of trade, "no rain here in three weeks," "no rain here in four weeks," "no rain here in six weeks," "no rain here all summer." What does it mean? Why, it means that we want some Elijah to go up on the mountain top, and with strong hands of prayer squeeze out the sponge of the cloud on the dry and thirsty land. "Oh!" you say, "we haven't any such man as Elijah now." We have. The Bible distinctly says he was a poor, sinful man like ourselves. How does it read? "Elias was a man subject to like passions as we are; and he prayed earnestly that it might not rain; and it rained not on the earth by the space of three years and six months. And he prayed again, and the heavens gave rain, and the earth gave forth her fruit." I remember in my boyhood days that the Governor of New Jersey proclaimed a day of fasting and prayer on account of a great drought. We gathered in the country meeting-house, and I remember well that before the close of the service the sky began to darken with clouds, and that night the earth was saturated. "Oh!" you say, "it just happened so." Well, if you want to worship the blind god Fate, the helpless god Fate, who is the crippled idiot of the universe, you can worship him. I am glad to know that the vast multitudes of the American people during the past few weeks have preferred to worship the God of Elijah, the God of Hezekiah, the God of earth and Heaven, the God sympathetic, as well as omnipotent; Father, as well as King.

"But," says some one, "suppose now there should be a bad turn in the President's case, and, what is possible, that he should die, then your prayer would be a failure." Ah, no! What do we mean when we pray for the President? We mean his welfare and the welfare of this nation; and if God takes him it will be because it is best for his welfare, and, in some inscrutable way, best for this nation. You and I cannot understand it, but there is where Christian faith comes in. Two things you can always depend on. One is that God is always good. The other is that God is always right. Agassiz says that America was first created. So it seems that this continent is the senior of Europe, Asia and Africa—the Yosemite older than the Alps, Lake Cayuga older than Lake Como. Now, if Agassiz be right in this great geological fact that America was the continent first created, then I say let it be the first in loyalty to God, first in worship, first in consecration to all that is good and holy and Christian.

The first great use of this national calamity is that it has driven the nation to prayer. If you ask me what to do next, I say, Go on as now, pray and pray and pray. Queen Elizabeth said to Walter Raleigh: "Walter, when will you cease begging?" Raleigh replied: "When your Majesty ceases giving." The time for us to stop imploring the divine mercy in our behalf, and in behalf of the nation, is the time when God's ear becomes deaf, and his heart becomes hard, and his hand, now open in supply, is clenched in eternal denial. Have you not noticed that just as the sceptics of this country and the infidels thought that they had fully persuaded the great masses of the people in America that prayer is an absurdity, the wounding of the President makes millions of people cry to God for help? What a scene it was when the Roman army was surrounded and water was inaccessible, and the twelfth legion, all made up of Christians, knelt before God and prayed for rain. It is not a Christian record, but it is a profane record that very soon the clouds gathered and the rains descended in torrents, and these soldiers caught the rain in their helmets, holding the helmet with the left hand and then drinking, while with their right hand they continued to fight. So let this nation ever be looking up for the rain of divine help, while at the same time it goes right on in the struggle of righteousness and order and good will to men.

Another great use of this national calamity is a revelation of woman's courage, woman's faith in God, and woman's endurance. It is the domestic side of this calamity that has most deeply stirred the people. There never was a more difficult position opened before any woman than on the fourth of March last at the White House was opened before Mrs. Garfield. The position had been occupied four years by a very queen of womanly character and attractiveness, a model of simplicity, her presence in this nation a constant rebuke to the hollowness of fashion and the womanly extravagance which more than once directly or indirectly has plunged this nation into bankruptcy. It was no easy thing to be the successor of Mrs. President Hayes. But this national calamity has made a dark background to a beautiful picture of womanly courage and womanly sacrifice and womanly faith in God. Those two queens of modern society will go down side by side through history.

But what I want to impress upon you this morning is that all this is only a revelation of what is in woman's nature, and that in ten thousand inconspicuous spheres of which you have never heard, there is just as much faith in God, womanly faith in God, womanly self-sacrifice, womanly courage. The story has never been told, and it will never be told on earth; it will be told in Heaven. Of course, there are among women fools, as there are fools among men; but you have known many a wife who would sit four months, six months, by the bedside of a sick husband, giving the medicine at just the right time, no professional nurse to help, no encouraging bulletins placarded, no help from outside; with her own needle at the same time earning a livelihood for the household, buying medicines and bread, coughing her own life away in slow consumption until she dropped a martyr into the grave.

Now, while you admire, as you ought to admire, the womanly courage and faith in God, as seen in the White House, do not think it is exceptional. Greenwood is full of them; Mount Auburn is full of them; Laurel Hill is full of them; the graveyards and cemeteries of the earth are full of them. Women who lived, toiled, sacrificed, suffered, died for others. Are you surprised that one good woman should expect her husband's recovery after all the world said he must die? I have seen that a score of times in my parishes. After all the physicians said there was no hope, she had hope; and when death had set the signal on the brow and the life was gone, still violently resisting anything that implied that he was dead, saying: "He is not dead; he is no more dead than you are; he will come to." Rev. Dr. Burchard, the useful minister of Christ, admired by all who know him, and many of you were baptized by him, and received into the church of Christ, and the pronunciation of his name makes you reverential — Dr. Burchard, after severe surgery, was pronounced dead by a group of surgeons who stood in the room. One of the surgeons was deputed to go to another room and tell his wife of the death of her husband. He went with that information, and she came into the room where her husband lay. She said: "He is not dead; he will preach the Gospel yet for many a long year." She took command of the scene and of the occasion. She told one surgeon to inflate the lungs; she told another surgeon to apply friction to the hands and to the limbs, appointing to each one his work; and they, to gratify the wish, and what would seem to be the insane wish, of a bereft wife, went to work, and after three-quarters of an hour had passed, he breathed. I suppose this very Sabbath morning he is preaching the Gospel, as he has been for twenty years since that supposed death-scene.

That is woman in awful crisis of suffering. The heroine, God's heroine. Why, there are five hundred women in this house this morning who have within them the elements of the heroine—Ida Lewises and Grace Darlings, not with oar of lifeboat on raging sea, but on the awful surge of domestic calamity, if God called them to it. I say this not in any compliment or flattery. I say it because I want every honest man to know what a grand and glorious blessing God has given him if he have a good wife. She may be a little fretful and nervous under household cares, but you get down flat on your back with pneumonia, or fever, or under the wounds of an assassin, and you know better than I can tell you who would be the best watcher, and who would speak the brightest encouragement, and who for you would drop dead in her tracks. I thank God for this revelation from the White House of woman's courage and woman's faith in God and woman's endurance, not a revelation of something new, but a revelation of something very old.

Another practical use of this great national calamity is that it has disgusted more than ever people with this free use of firearms. There is too much shooting going on in this country. If a man insults you, shoot him; if a man doubts your veracity, shoot him; if a man stand in the way of your advancement, shoot him. It is bang, bang, bang! And there are Guiteaus in all the towns and villages and cities of this country.

The Nation Kneeling

There are too many pistols, and human life is too cheap. I wish that this Washington ruffian going about with a navy revolver in his pocket, practising at a mark so as not to fail hitting the heart of the President, might disgust all our young men with the habit of carrying deadly weapons.

On the frontier, or if it is your business as an officer of the law to make arrest of desperados, you had better be armed. Armed police, armed sheriffs, armed explorers, armed jail-keepers, are well enough; but it is high time that all respectable citizens snap in two their sword canes and unload their deadly weapons. If you move in reputable society in Brooklyn or New York or Washington or London you have no need of any more weapons than the two weapons which God gave you, two honest fists. If you feel the need of having a pistol in your pocket, you are a miserable coward. If you are afraid to go down the street unarmed, you had better get your grandmother with her knitting needles to go with you! I am glad that the Common Council of Brooklyn last week passed an ordinance forbidding the carrying of deadly weapons, or gave new emphasis to a law previously enacted. A pistol is the meanest and most infernal weapon ever invented. It is compact and portable murder. There is some dignity about a sword. If you are going to take a man's life with a sword you have to expose your own life, and so some courage is demanded; but a pistol is the weapon of a sneak. I would as soon carry a toad in my vest pocket! And what is more, the people who carry deadly weapons in this country are people of ungovernable temper. Now, if a man be cold and phlegmatic and calculating in his nature, there is not much danger in his carrying deadly weapons; but if a man be quick and sharp and irritable and violent and gunpowdery and explosive in his nature, he ought not to carry anything more dangerous than a dull jack-knife. You do not know what, under temptation, you might do. Away with this pistol business. Let Charles Guiteau and John Wilkes Booth have all the honors of assassination.

Another practical use of this great national calamity is the ordination of suffering. If President Garfield get well—and he has conquered so many occasions of relapse and collapse that I shall expect him to get well until I know he is buried—if the President get well, he will go forth to his work with an ordination such as no President ever had. Ordination, not by the laying on of human hands, but ordination by the laying on of hands of pain, hands of fever, hands of midnight anguish, hands of national solicitude, hands of mercy, both hands of God. During these whole eight weeks our President has looked over into the next world and he will feel his responsibility; if he comes back to us, he will come as from the very presence of God; and though all this year should be absorbed in convalescence, from fourth of March to fourth of March, he would have left three full, round years in which to scourge the seven devils of American politics and bury the putrescent carcass of Mormonism where it can no longer poison the nation.

If he get well, I say, he will have an ordination that no other man ever had. Our other Presidents, for the most part, so far as reform has been concerned, have been divided into two classes—those who had the moral disposition but not the courage, and those who had the courage but not the moral disposition. President Garfield, during the past eight weeks, has shown he has the courage, for if a man is not afraid of death, he is not afraid of anything, and he has shown also that he has the moral disposition. If he shall come forth from the sick bed under this ordination of suffering, look out, political corruption; look out, polygamy, look out. There will be hundreds of people who, now praying that he may live, will pray that he may die. If fully recovered, he goes forth from this ordination of suffering, he will be a thunderbolt in the right hand of God launched against the gigantic evils that are afflicting this country. But, my friends, we have all felt this ordination of suffering, and are we not ready to do better work as patriots, as reformers, as philanthropists, and as Christians? National suffering, political suffering, financial suffering, domestic suffering, ought to be ordination. It is not health, it is not gladness, it is not prosperity, which qualify for especial work, but suffering, sharp suffering, intense suffering, long-continued suffering. Fire of pain, fire of persecution, fire of bereavement, are ordination. It was not until Beethoven had become so deaf he could not hear the fortissimo of a full orchestra that he composed his chief oratorio. It was not until John Milton had become stone-blind that he could dictate the sublimest poem of the ages. It was not until Walter Scott was kicked off the horse and confined to the house for many days that he could write the "Lay of the Last Minstrel." The painter who mixes his colors with blood from his own broken heart makes the best pictures. The mightiest men of all the ages have been mightiest in their agonies. Oh, my friend, do not think that God sent trouble on you to break you down; it is for inspiration and for lifting up. God grant that this national trouble may be national ordination!

I remark once more, this great calamity ought to teach us to be contented with our humble lot. What a time our new President has had! Not one moment of rest, or quiet, or peace since he stepped into the White House. Weary, worn out, shot. There is not one person in this house this morning, who, so far as comfort and quiet are concerned, but is better off than he. Public men are targets to be shot at, belied, pursued, misinterpreted, assassinated. But it is no new story; it has always been so. I was surprised to read what Macaulay wrote in one of his intense sentences, after all his bright career in the English Parliament, and after being renowned the world over by all who could admire fine writing and great thought—Macaulay says: "Every friendship which a man may have becomes precarious as soon as he engages in politics." Daniel Webster, after his wonderful career and in the close of his life, writes: "If I were to live my life over again, with my present experiences, I would under no considerations allow myself to enter public life. The public are ungrateful. The man who serves the public most faithfully receives no adequate reward. In my own history those acts which have been before God most disinterested, and the least stained by selfish considerations, have been precisely those for which I have been most freely abused. No, no, have nothing to do with politics. Sell your iron, eat the bread of independence, support your family with the rewards of honest toil, do your duty as a private citizen to your country, but let politics alone. It is a hard life, a thankless life. I have had in the course of my political life, which is not a short one, my full share of ingratitude; but the unkindest cut of all, the shaft that has sunk the deepest in my heart, has been the refusal of this administration to grant my request for an office of small pecuniary consideration for my only son."

That is the testimony of a man who ought to know. My friends, better stay down than be shot down. He who has a good occupation, a good home, a good character, a good field of usefulness, and a good hope in Jesus Christ has all that is worth having. More

The Nation Kneeling

than that is exposure, is chagrin, is worriment, is exhaustion, is death. By the turmoil, and the consternation, and the horror of the White House, for the last eight weeks, I solemnly charge you, "Be content with such things as you have; you brought nothing into the world, and it is very certain you can carry nothing out. Having food and raiment, be therewith content."

MIGHTIER DEAD THAN ALIVE.

Judges, 16: 30: "So the dead which he slew at his death were more than they which he slew in his life."

MIGHTIER DEAD THAN ALIVE*

Judges, 16: 30: " So the dead which he slew at his death were more than they which he slew in his life."

Samson in the text was deified and became the Hercules of Greece. He was a giant warrior, born to be a leader, and Paul applauds him as a man who "through faith subdued kingdoms." He was a friend of God and an enemy of unrighteousness. But the most memorable scene in his life was the death-scene. The Philistines, his enemies, gathered round him in a great building to mock him. With supernatural strength he laid hold of the pillars and flung everything into ruin, destroying the lives of the three thousand scoffers, among them the lords of Philistia. He had slain many of the enemies of God during his life; but my text says his last achievement was the mightiest. "So the dead which he slew at his death were more than they which he slew in his life." It is sometimes the case that after a most industrious, useful, and eminent life, the last hours are more potent than the long years that preceded.

In the overshadowing event of this day we find illustrations of my text. President Garfield, as many orators will say, was all his life the enemy of sin, the enemy of sectionalism, the enemy of everything small-hearted, impure and debasing, and he made many a crushing blow against those moral and political Philistines, but in his death he made mightier conquest. The eleven weeks of dying have made more illustrious record than the fifty years of living. "So the dead

* Preached after the death of President Garfield.

which he slew at his death were more than they which he slew in his life."

As a matter of inspiration and comfort, I propose to show you that President Garfield's expiration is a mightier good than a prolonged lifetime possibly could be. Mind you, there was no time at which his death-bed could have been so emphatic. If he had died a few years before, his departure would not have been so conspicuous. If he had died one month before, his administration would not have been fairly launched. If he had died six months later, his advanced policy of reform would have cut the friendship of a great multitude, and if he had died years after, he would have been out of office and in the decline of life. But he died at the time when all parties had turned to him with unparalleled expectation. There has not been a time in all the fifty years of his past when his death-bed could have been so effective; and in the next fifty years there could not have been a time when his death-bed would have been so overwhelmingly impressive. "So the dead which he slew at his death were more than they which he slew in his life."

First, our President's death, more than his life, eulogizes the Christian religion. We all talk about the hope of the Christian and the courage of the Christian and the patience of the Christian. Put all the sermons on these subjects for the last twenty years together, and they would not make such an impression as the magnificent demeanor of this dying Chief Magistrate.

He was no more afraid to die than you are to go home this morning. Without one word of complaint he endures an anguish that his autopsy alone could reveal to the astonished world. For eighty days in inquisition of pain, yet often smiling, often facetious, always calm, giving military salute to a soldier who happened to look in at the window, talking with Cabinet officers about the affairs of state, reading the public bulletins in regard to his condition, watching his own pulse; and so undisturbed of soul that I warrant you if it had not been for his dependent family and the nation, whom he wanted to serve, he would have been glad to depart any time right up to the God who made him, and the Christ who redeemed him, and the Holy Ghost who comforted him.

Oh, sirs! all he ever did in confirmation of religion in days of health was nothing compared with what he did for it in this last crisis. James A. Garfield learned his religion from his mother in the days when she was trying in widowhood and poverty to bring up her boys aright; from that same old mother that sat with her Bible in her lap in her bedroom last Tuesday morning, when the dreadful news came that her son was dead. James A. Garfield had no new religion to experiment with in his last hours. It was the same Gospel into the faith of which he was baptized, when in early manhood he was immersed in the river in the name of the Father, and of the Son, and of the Holy Ghost. That religion had stood the test through all the buffetings and persecutions, through the hard work of life, and did not forsake him in the solemn close. There have been thousands of death-beds as calm and beautiful as this, but they were not so conspicuous. This electrifies Christendom. This encourages all the pain-struck in hospitals, and scattered all up and down the world, to suffer patiently. The consumptive, the cancered, and the palsied, and the fevered, and the dying of all nations lift their heads from their hot pillows, and bless this heroic, this triumphant, this illustrious sufferer. The religion that upheld him under surgeon's knife, and amid the appalling days and nights at Long Branch and at Washington, is a good religion to have. Show us in all the ages among the enemies of Christianity a death-bed that will compare with this radiant sunset!

Again, our President's death will do more for the consummation of right feeling between North and South than all his administration of four years could have accomplished. This is not "shaking hands across the bloody chasm," according to the rhetoric of campaign documents. This is shaking hands across the palpitating heart that was large enough to take in both sections. This expiring man took the hand of the North and the hand of the South and joined them together, and practically said, with a dying pathos that can never be forgotten: "Be brothers!" Where now are the flags at half mast? At New Orleans and Boston, Chicago and Charleston. There is absolutely today no Republican party and no Democratic party. A new party has swallowed up all—a party of national sympathy. The bulletins on the south side of Mason and Dixon's line have been as carefully watched as on the north side. We have been trying to arbitrate old difficulties and settle old grudges, yet the old quarrel has ever and anon broken out in a new place. But this requiem which shakes the land forever drowns out all sectional discords. After all that has been done and said during the last eleven weeks the people of the South will be welcome in all our homes as we shall be welcome in theirs. He who tries hereafter to kindle the old fires of hatred will find little fuel and no sulphurous match. Alabama and Massachusetts, stand up and be married! South Carolina and New York, join hands in betrothal! Georgia and Ohio, I pronounce you one! Whom God hath joined together let no man put asunder. The seal is set by the cold, emaciated hand of our dead President. No living man could have accomplished it. More of the sectional prejudices, and the misinterpretations, and the bitternesses of old war times have perished in the last eleven weeks than in all the seventeen years since the war ended; and so the dead which Garfield slew at his death were more than they which he slew in his whole life.

Again, President Garfield's sickness and death have educated the world, as all his life and the life of a thousand men beside could not have educated it in the wonders of the human body. For the last two months all Christendom has been studying anatomy and physiology. Never since the world stood has there been so much known about respiration, about pulsation, about temperature, about gunshot wounds, about febrile rise, about digestion, about convalescence. The vast majority of the race have hitherto wandered about stupidly ignorant of this masterpiece of God, the human mechanism. The last eleven weeks have educated ten thousand nurses for the sick. The invalids of all lands for this experience will have better attendance, more kindness, more opportunity for restoration. Never has there been such examination of dictionaries to find the meaning of a medical phrase. One new word of the morning bulletins has set the leaves of all the lexicons in America a-flutter. Garfield, during his life, had often talked on these themes in college class-rooms and on lecture platforms, and he was a scientist in these things, but he did more for the slaying of popular ignorance on this subject in his death than he did in all his life.

Since the time when David the Psalmist, probably returned from an Oriental dissecting-room, wrote the autopsy, "We are fearfully and wonderfully made," and Solomon, who was wise in physiology as well as in everything else, called the spinal marrow the silver cord (or "ever the silver cord be loosed"), and called the head the "golden bowl," because the skull is round like a bowl, and the membrane which contains the brain is yellow like gold (or "the golden bowl be broken"); and called the veins of the human body a pitcher, because they carry the crimson liquid from the heart, the fountain, all through all the organs of the body (or "the pitcher be broken at the fountain"); and called the lungs a wheel, because they draw to themselves and let go away like a well-bucket, and called the stomach the cistern (the "wheel broken at the cistern") and showed that he knew what Harvey thought he was discovering thousands of years after concerning the circulation of the blood—I say since those obscure times down to these days, when all physicians are busy instructing the people, and all medical colleges, and all high schools, are scattering physiological and anatomical information, there has never been so much wisdom on these subjects as to-day; and the most potent of all the teachers has been the sick and dying bed of our President, mightier in his death than in his life.

Again, these last scenes must impress the world, as no preachment ever did, that when our time comes to go, the most energetic and skilful physicians cannot hinder the event. Was there ever so much done to save a man's life as the life of President Garfield? Is the season too hot, there is manufactured for his sick room in August an October day. Is he to be transported to the seaside? all the wheels and all the steam whistles and all the voices along the line of progress are hushed for two hundred miles, and a new section of railroad is built to let him pass over. Added to the medical skill of the Capital are the skill of Philadelphia and New York. All the medical ingenuity of the last three hundred years flashes its electric light upon the wound. Paris and London and Edinburgh applaud the treatment. He had all the courage that comes from the hand of a wife who was sure he would get well. He had physicians who did not stand with cold, scientific calculation, studying the case; but splendid men whose hearts grew strong or faint as the patient's pulse was strong or faint, and they were as great nurses as they were great surgeons. But the doctors could not keep him. His wife could not keep him. All the arms of five children hung around his neck could not keep him. His great spirit pushes them all back from the gates of life, and soars away into the infinities. My Lord and My God! solemnize us with this consideration.

My hearer, if you and I were sick I am sure we would have good medical attendance and good nursing, plenty of watchers and plenty of attendants. The world is naturally very kind to the sick. We who have good homes would have sympathetic though trembling hands to hold ours in the last exigency. We all have those who love us as we love them, but when the time fixed by the merciful God arrives we must be off. There is no need of our getting nervous about it or fretting about it. All we have to do is to keep our hearts right with God and do our best, and then be as unfluttered as was our dying President. After the mightiest surgery of America and the world had to surrender on that Monday night at the stroke of the Death Angel, surely we cannot resist it!

In the emphasizing of all these great truths, James A. Garfield is mightier lying on his catafalque at Cleveland than in the White House receiving the honors of foreign embassage. Who knows but that his death will save millions of people for this world and the next? Fifty millions of people—nay, North and South America, and Europe, and parts of Asia—called to thoughts of mortality and the great future! Who knows but it may awaken whole nations from the death of sin to the life of the Gospel? When last week I saw one line of mourning from Detroit, Michigan, to Brooklyn, I wondered if God would not use this great grief for the purification of the nation. O Lord, revive thy work in the midst of the nation! Enough the Sabbath breakings, and the impurities, and the blasphemy, and the official corruption in this country! By the result of this terrific event let these dogs of hell be driven back to their fiery kennels. Against all these evils the Presidential giant is mightier dead than when alive.

But while the nation has this comfort there are three words that will leap to our lips, and they have been reiterated oftener than any other words for the past few days. Poor Mrs. Garfield! More pathetic words I never read than these in the Friday newspapers which said that with two of her children she had gone over to the White House to get the property of her family and have it sent to her home in Ohio. Can you imagine anything more full of torture than to walk through the room filled with associations of her husband's kindness, of her husband's anxieties, and of her husband's long-continued physical anguish?

She had with her womanly arms fought by his side all the way up the steep of life. She had helped him in their economies when they were very poor; with her own needle clothing their family, with her own hands making him bread. When the world frowned upon him in the days of scandalous assault she never forsook his side. They had together won the battle, and had seated themselves at the very top to enjoy the victory. Then the blow came. What a reversal of fortune! From what midnoon to what midnight! It is said that this will kill her. I do not believe it. The God who has helped her thus far will help her all the way through. When the broken circle gathers in the future days at the old home at Mentor, the mighty God who protected James A. Garfield at Chickamauga and in the fiery hell of many battles will protect his wife, his children, and his old mother.

Upon all the seven broken hearts let the comfort descend! What consolations they have! It was a great thing to have had such a son! It was a great thing to have been the wife of such a man! It was a great thing to have been the children of such a father! While theirs and ours is the grief, I am glad on his account that he has gone. He had suffered enough. Enough the cut of the lancets, and the thrusts of the catheter, and the pangs of head and side and feet and back! Ascend, oh, disenthralled spirit, and take thy place with those who came out of great tribulation, and had their robes made white in the blood of the Lamb!

This Samson of intellectual strength, this giant of moral power, had—like the one in the text—in other days slain the lion of wrathful opposition, and had carried off the gates of wrong from the rusted hinges. But the peroration of his life is stronger than any passage which went before. The dead which this giant slew in his death were more than those whom he slew in his life.

May we all learn the practical lessons with which our subject is filled! Behold the contrast between Friday, the fourth of March, 1881, and Friday, the twenty-third of September, 1881! On the former day Washington was ablaze with banners. Each State of the Union had its triumphal arch. Great men of this country and vast populations filled the streets! Procession such as had never moved from the White House and the Capitol! Military display that would have confounded hostile nations. The city shaken with cannonading by day, and the night on fire with pyrotechnics! Thousands of all political parties who congratulated the President pronounced that fourth of March the brightest day that had ever shone on American institutions. That night, or soon after, in some room of the Presidential mansion, I warrant you, there assembled husband and wife and five children, and the aged mother, taking a long breath after the excitement of the inauguration. The highest point of honor that mortal man can reach had been won.

But behold Friday, September 23d, the dead President in the Rotunda, his bereaved wife at a friend's house; a dangerously sick child four hundred miles away at Williamstown, Mass.; military on guard around the casket; hundreds of thousands of people gazing on the face so emaciated that none would know it; the poor black woman falling on her knees beside the coffin, expressing the anguish of speechless multitudes when she said: "Oh, dear! how he must have suffered!" Friday, fourth of March, 1881! Friday, September 23, 1881!

To the words of comfort I have uttered to-day I add this lesson, which seems to sound out from the tramp of pall-bearers and from the rolling of the draped rail-train moving westward, and from the open grave now waiting to receive our dead President: "Put not your trust in princes nor in the son of man, in whom there is no help. His breath goeth forth, he returneth to his earth; in that very day his thoughts perish." Fare thee well, departed chieftain!

WERE THE PRAYERS FOR PRESIDENT GARFIELD A FAILURE

II Corinthians, 12: 8, 9: " I besought the Lord thrice that it might depart from me. And he said unto me, My grace is sufficient for thee."

WERE THE PRAYERS FOR PRESIDENT GARFIELD A FAILURE

II Corinthians, 12: 8, 9: "I besought the Lord thrice that it might depart from me. And he said unto me, My grace is sufficient for thee."

There was something the matter with Paul in the text. He spoke of something that irritated him, or annoyed him or hurt him or mortified him, under the figure of a "thorn in the flesh." Some think it was a crooked back. Others think it was a stuttering tongue. More persons think, and among them the learned Kitto and Dr. John Brown, the Scotch essayist, that it was diseased eyes, amounting almost to total blindness. They think this because he almost always wrote by the hand of an amanuensis, once mentioning it as a rare occurrence that he had written a large letter with his own hand; and they think this also because he was always accompanied wherever he went, although he was much of the time a poor man and could not have paid attendants; and also because he seems to refer to his trouble with his eyes when, in describing the enthusiastic love of the Galatians he says: "ye would have plucked out your own eyes and have given them to me." In other words, "you love me so much you would have been willing to trade off your good eyes for my poor eyes." Those lands always have been afflicted with ophthalmia, and damaged eyesight was as common there and then as good eyesight here and now. But whatever may have been the trouble, Paul prayed to have it cured. I suppose he prayed hundreds of times on this matter, but he made three agonizing prayers. Did God answer those prayers? He did, by giving something better than Paul asked for. Not by straightening the back, or by unloosing the tongue, or by curing the disordered eyesight, but by giving him grace to turn into glorious advantage that which had been an irritating detriment. Instead of curing the physical misfortune, he sanctified that trouble until Paul became the greatest apostle of the Gentiles, the greatest and the grandest Christian of all the centuries. "I besought the Lord thrice that it might depart from me. And he said unto me, My grace is sufficient for thee." So it was then—so it is now. In the six thousand years of the world's existence there have not been one hundred right-hearted prayers unanswered. Nor fifty, nor ten, nor five, nor has there been one. If there had in six thousand years been just one right-hearted prayer unanswered, it would have impeached the character of God. If there be any truth well set forth in the Bible it is that God answers prayers. God gives you what you ask for always, or something better; and there is no exception.

During the eleven painful weeks of our President's suffering, all good people prayed for his recovery. The Sabbaths were full of supplication. Days were set forth for special fasting and prayer. There never was so much prayer offered on any one subject in any eleven weeks since the world by the wings of the Almighty was brooded out of chaos. And yet the body of President Garfield lies in the Lakeview Cemetery at Cleveland. "Your prayers were a dead failure," says the sceptic. "Your prayers were a dead failure," think a thousand men who do not just like to say so. "You wasted your breath. The laws of nature had their way. Don't hereafter mix theology and medicine." But I will undertake to show you this morning that all the right-hearted prayers made in behalf of the President may be divided into two classes—those which have been answered, and those which will be answered. Every right-hearted prayer in that direction had two ideas—the President's welfare and the best interests of this nation. Has the first half of your prolonged prayer of eleven weeks in behalf of the President's welfare been answered?

The autopsy declares if he had been continued in life he would have been a paralytic—that he never again could have walked—that he would have been incompetent for the work of his high office. But suppose a miracle had been performed and he had come forth in entire health? Could he have met the expectations aroused in regard to him? Not if he had been an angel from heaven, with the power of a hundred Garfields. Could he in a prolonged administration, in which thousands of questions would arise, have pleased everybody? Oh, no, no! Suppose that, during that prolonged administration, a question had arisen as between the Democratic party and the Republican party, both of which parties were equally sympathetic and equally eulogistic and equally helpful in all those eleven weeks of sickness, he certainly would have had to decide against one of the parties. Then that party, in remembrance of its sympathy during the weeks of sickness, would have pronounced him an ingrate, and there would have been a vehemence against him that has never been witnessed within our memory. They would say, "Here, this is the pay we get for all our sympathy for you, and all our kindness for you, and all our prayers for you;" and he would have been in an awful plight as between the two great parties. Suppose a question during the three coming years had arisen as between monopoly and anti-monopoly, as it will arise, how could he have met those questions? On the one side, leading anti-monopolists of the country, during all those eleven weeks of sickness, especially kind, especially sympathetic, especially helpful, especially eulogistic; while on the other hand, among the monopolists, was the Pennsylvania Railroad Company, that had given him the free rail-train to Long Branch, and extended the railroad when it was not long enough; and among those monopolists many in New York and throughout the country who had subscribed their five hundred dollars and their one thousand dollars and their five thousand dollars to Mrs. Garfield, and if you think that she did not tell him all about it in his better moments it is because you have never been married. Suppose he had been restored to health, how could he have met the expectations of monopolists and anti-monopolists? Suppose a question of international right had arisen, as between England and the United States. In the memory of the fact that from the first day of his wounding, the Queen and the Court and the mighty men and women of England had been bending over his suffering couch in sympathy— how could he have adjusted questions as between England and the United States? How could he have been impartial? How could he have acted at all?

Besides that, during his illness, he was put under obligation to a great multitude of people—some in one way and some in another way, and the hotels in Washington, and a new line of hotels encircling the city of Washington would not have held the people who would come to get reward for their favors. "I gave you an invalid chair; give me a consulship." "I manufactured the cooling apparatus; give me a post-office." "I subscribed five thousand dollars to Mrs. Garfield; recognize my services." "I wrote the mightiest editorials of sympathy during your sickness;

send me to Belgium." "I got the Washington malaria waiting on your case as a newspaper correspondent; send me to some place within reach of the air that blows off the Alps." The kindnesses and sympathies of those eleven weeks would have surrounded his administration with embarrassments mountain high; and in his inability to reward his benefactors, and in his adoption of an independent policy, he would have aroused feelings different from those which now exist; and instead of being the centre of the nation's admiration and the object almost of its idolatry, he would, during the three coming years, have been more denounced and more caricatured and more hated than any man that ever occupied the Presidential chair. He will have escaped during the next three years enough calumny to have covered up these continents with vituperative newspapers from Baffin's Bay to Terra del Fuego. If Washington and Adams and Monroe and Jefferson and Lincoln could not escape, much less could Garfield have escaped; for there were larger and more unreasonable expectations excited in regard to him than in regard to any of his predecessors. If, therefore, the first half of your prolonged prayers of eleven weeks meant the President's welfare, your prayers have been answered, completely answered, grandly answered, gloriously answered, triumphantly answered, forever answered, and could have been answered in no other way. His body never rested so well as now in the cemetery of Ohio. His soul never rested so well as now in the bosom of his God. Your prayers have been answered. *Quod erat demonstrandum.*

But has the last half of your prolonged prayer of eleven weeks been answered—the part of the prayer that pertained to the welfare of the nation? I remark, in the first place: the nation has never been so sanctified under trial and trouble as it is this very moment. When Booth shot Lincoln, the nation had been for four years drunk on war and massacre and blood, and that assassination seemed only another paragraph in a book of horrors. Before that time I never could endure to look upon a scene of suffering, and since that time I have never for a long while been able to continue looking upon a scene of suffering; and yet I went down to Sharpsburg during the conflict and preached to fifty Federals shattered and dying, and in a barn to a hundred Confederates shattered and dying, and somehow I got through the discourse. You say it was especial grace. Ah! yes, but I think the whole nation, constantly standing in the presence of blood and bruises and wounds and death, got hardened. But this last assassination comes at a time of peace, and the nation falls prostrate and sick under the calamity. The nation was never so chastened, never so gentle, never so sympathetic, never so worshipful as now. Blasphemers have gone down on their knees before God, and men who had not prayed since they knelt at the trundle-bed in childhood have formulated appropriate petition. While the nation's heart is far from what it ought to be, it is a better nation to-day than it has ever been. So that section of your prayer has been answered.

Another consideration: after what you know of our late Chief Magistrate, you must know that the paragraph in his inaugural which spoke against Mormonism was the most earnest paragraph in it. That institution is an insult to every home in America. James A. Garfield felt ordained of God, not only as President of the United States, but as a husband and a father, to annihilate that abomination. Within one year the lightning would have struck it. By an enactment of Congress the President would have proclaimed that that institution of Mormonism is at war with our best interests as a government, and while the polyga-mist, considering the present complications, might have remained in the possession of his numerous wives, it would have been understood by law that after that any one who attempted to select more marital companionship than is allowed in other States would go to prison and be denied his vote. Just back of Salt Lake City is the United States military encamp-ment, with guns that could rake that Sodom into ashes, in one forenoon; and that regiment, aided by other regiments, could have enforced the law. You say President Buchanan failed to do the work. I know he did. Great and good man, but he was a bachelor, and it needed a father and a husband like Garfield, understanding the value of a Christian home, to annihilate that abomination of Mormonism. But perhaps the time had not quite come. Perhaps it was necessary that the indignation of this nation should be aroused to a greater pitch against Mormonism before the work should be thoroughly attempted, and the death of Garfield under these circumstances ought to arouse the nation. Do you know that while all good people throughout the world were praying for our President's recovery, the Mormons were praying for his death? In Utah, in Wyoming, in Arizona, in New Mexico, praying for his death!—some of their papers utterly ignoring the whole subject, or else slily congratulatory at the prospect of our President's early decease. Why? Mormonism decreed long ago that its potent enemies should perish, if not in one way, then in another; and the whole work should be done in the name of the Lord! Brigham Young declared in his church, in a sermon which I could show you, that he who destroys the life of an anti-Mormon does God a service. Mountain Meadow massacre, wherein hundreds of men, women, children, and the little babes had their throats cut, and then were left unburied for the ravens and the wolves—that was all done in the name of the Lord! Dr. Robinson and Almand Babbitt and the Parishes all butchered by the Mormons, they said, in the name of the Lord! The assassins Hickman and Brigham Young, and that group of men called "Destroying Angels," because their only work is assassination—they did all their work in the name of the Lord. Now I will not say that Guiteau was a Mormon, nor will I dare to say that he was not a paid emissary. He says he shot Garfield in the name of the Lord. Everything he has said and written on the subject implies that it was done by divine commission, and in the name of the Lord. I will not say that he was a Mormon, but he has all the Mormon theories. He was a member of the Oneida Community, the chief doctrine of which is that it is right to have a profusion of wives. He had the ugliness of a Mormon, the licentiousness of a Mormon, the cruelty of a Mormon, the murderous spirit of a Mormon, the infernalism of a Mormon. Why, he says he sat in the park opposite the President's house, in the name of the Lord, and he went to the Baltimore depot on the second of July, and aimed at the heart of our beloved Chief Magistrate, and fired in the name of the Lord! I say there is an ugly sound in that cry when a man goes out to do the work of darkness in the name of the Lord.

I suppose that his crime originally started from his revenge at not getting a consulship; but I should not wonder if, in the great day when all secret things are revealed, it should be found that he was a paid agent of that old hag of hell which sits, making mouths at high heaven, between the Rocky Mountains and the Sierra Nevada. If the death of Garfield shall arouse the nation to more hatred of that institution of Mormonism, which was Garfield's especial disgust, he will not have died in vain, and another section of your prayer is answered.

Again I remark: your prayers have been answered in the sanctification of the home circle. Husband, wife, son, daughter, brother, sister were beautiful names before; but they never meant so much in this country as they do now. What an example we have had in the White House of a model Christian home! There have been Christian homes in the White House before this, but this by circumstances was more conspicuous as a Christian home. Well, you see as a nation we need toning up on that subject. For the last twenty-five years the country has been filled with trash about free-lovism and elective affinity, and divorce made easy. There has nothing happened in your day or mine that has done so much for the homes of America as that beautiful and overwhelming example we have recently had in the White House.

Where are things going? I suppose New England is as good a part of the country as any other—perhaps better. In 1878, in the State of Maine, there were four hundred and seventy-eight divorces; in the State of Connecticut, four hundred and one divorces; in New Hampshire, two hundred and forty-one divorces; in Rhode Island, one hundred and ninety-six divorces; in Massachusetts, six hundred divorces, making an aggregate of two thousand one hundred and thirteen divorces, in 1878 in New England. In Cook County, Illinois, last year, eight hundred and thirty divorce cases began. We need toning up on the subject of the family relation. You know that in some circles it gives a little piquancy to a man's character if he is said to be a little loose in his morals. Right in this time, when the nation needs so much instruction in the right direction on this important theme, we have this revelation of a Christian home circle. God grant that that influence may be potent for all years that are to come. The influence already felt in every home of this congregation, in every home of America, proves that your prayers have been answered.

Again, I want you to understand, my friends, that, in addition to the prayers which have already attained a blessing, from your prayers and from the prayers of the nation during the last few months, there will be born blessings for a thousand years to come, if American institutions stand so long. The astronomer tells us that worlds ages ago created have just reached us with their light, and so there are blessings which are a thousand years in flight. God gathers up all these prayers. He gathers them from the north and from the south; he gathers them from this side of the sea and the other side of the sea, from this side of the Atlantic and from the other side of the Atlantic; he gathers them all up in a reservoir at the foot of the throne—a great suspended blessing, a flood made up of the tears of many generations, and then at his own good time, from that reservoir of divine remembrance the streams of blessings will pour down upon the nations, and their harvests will be richer, and their schools will be better, and their institutions will be more prospered, and the Christian religion will be more triumphant. I should not wonder if it took God many centuries fully to answer the three hundred million hearted prayers of two hemispheres. The sins of the nation cry to heaven for vengeance; but the prayers of the nation cry to heaven for mercy; and the latter are going to overbalance the former. Does not the Psalmist intimate that God takes the tears of one of his children and puts them in a bottle, and then am I far out of the way when I suppose that God gathers up the tears of nations in a reservoir?

I am very glad that God does not answer all the prayers in our time. I am not so anxious about our present condition as a nation as I am anxiously concerned about the future. You and I can get along very well during the few years of our allotted time on earth, even if we do not like American politics. But how about the generations following? There are forces of darkness struggling to get possession of this continent, and I want some great storehouse of prayer filled for that exigency. Only the first wheel, as it were, has begun to turn in our manufacturing capacity. We have gathered only the first sheaf of agricultural resources, we have picked up only the first lump of coal or iron or copper or silver or gold of our American mining. What will be the condition of this country when the last arable acre is doing its very best, and when all our rivers are pulling their utmost at the factory bands, and when Nevada and Colorado and California and Arizona shall have disgorged all their treasures, and from ocean to ocean the continent shall be fully peopled? During the next twenty-five years there will be one hundred million people on this continent. During the next century, at the close of a century from now, there will be at least three hundred million people in the United States. What is to be the character of that population? You cannot shirk the responsibility, nor can I shirk it. Your prayers this morning and your prayers during those eleven weeks, and the prayers of all your past time, and your patriotic prayers for the future, and the prayers of the good of all ages, will help decide that question. Columbus, two hours before midnight, said to Pedro Gutierrez, of the king's wardrobe, "Look, look! see the light on the shore; that must be a continent!" But gladder will be the man who two hours before the daybreak of national purification shall hail the morning of regenerated America. I tell you the signs are most encouraging. The prayers of God's people are going to hand over this continent. I am just as certain of it as that I stand here and you sit there. Have you noticed the rapidly increasing momentum? During the first fifty years of this century, in our country there were three million converts added to the evangelical churches. There have been as many added to the evangelical churches in America during the last ten years. In other words, the last ten years have been equal to the first fifty years of this century. Clear the track for the Lord's chariot. The white horses that draw the chariot started on a slow walk. For the last few years they have been upon a gallop. They will soon be down to full run.

"Oh!" say you, "I can't see how my poor prayers are going to have any effect upon that grand result." Well, rivers might as well, when the mist rises and is drawn up and floats away into the heavens, say: "That moisture will never be heard of again." God would say: "Be patient;" and when the earth wanted rain then this despised mist would take the form of an angel of the shower and would float down through the air, and from the silver chalice of a cloud would dip the water and baptize all the valleys, while the mountains stood up as sponsor. So the Sun of righteousness exhales our prayers, and so they come back again in gracious distillation. Your prayers have been answered, your prayers will be answered.

It is something like this: I say God answers prayer, if not giving just what you want, giving something greater. It is as though a son should say: "Father, give me five thousand dollars," and the father should say: "I hear your request; I will do better than that; I will put that five thousand dollars into an education, and then it will be worth to you ten times five thousand dollars." It is as though a wayward son had come home and found his mother dying, and he should kneel by the bedside and pray for her recovery, and God should say to that wayward young man, "I hear your prayer, but I will do better than what you ask for. I will, by your mother's death, give you reformation, and give you an eternal home with her in heaven." So I meet this question differently from the way it is usually met. I declare now, and it is beyond all controversy, God always gives what you ask for in a right spirit, or gives something better. In all theologies it is believed that every individual has a guardian angel sent forth to protect, to defend and to foster. The Jewish rabbins say that Adam's guardian angel was named Razaiel, and that Abraham's guardian angel was Zakiel, and that Isaac's guardian angel was Raphael, and that Jacob's guardian angel was Peniel. If every individual has a guardian angel, shall not a Christian nation have guardian angels? Who shall they be? Those who never knew us? Those who never fought in behalf of our institutions? Those who never suffered for our land? No, no! Descend, ye spirits of the martyr Presidents, and ye mighty men of the councils of the past, ye who defended our country on land and sea. Descend, ye who preached and prayed as well as ye who fought! Mighty spirits of departed patriots, descend—come down out of the ineffable light into the shadows of earth, and lead the way. Washington and Everett, and Sumner and Garfield, and Lincoln and Burnside, and Lyon and Witherspoon, and Mason and Channing—descend, descend! Speak with lips once quieted. Strike with arms once palsied. Ride down into this fight in which earth and hell and heaven are in battle array. Thou mighty God of our fathers and brothers who fell at

Lexington and Yorktown, and South Mountain, and Gettysburg, descend and strike back national evil, and bring national good, and prove thyself the same God who answered the prayers of Hezekiah, and of Elijah, and of Deborah, and of Joshua. Thine, O Lord, is the Kingdom!

EPIDEMIC OF STRIKES

I Cor., 12: 21: "The eye cannot say to the hand I have no need of thee."

EPIDEMIC OF STRIKES

I Cor., 12: 21: " The eye cannot say to the hand I have no need of thee."

Fifty thousand workmen in Chicago ceasing work in one day; Brooklyn stunned by the attempt to halt its railroad cars; Cleveland in the throes of a labor agitation; and restlessness among toilers all over the land have caused an epidemic of strikes; and somewhat to better things I apply the Pauline thought of my text.

You have seen an elaborate piece of machinery with a thousand wheels and a thousand bands and a thousand pulleys all controlled by one great waterwheel, the machinery so adjusted that when you jar one part of it you jar all parts of it. Well, human society is a great piece of mechanism controlled by one great and ever-revolving force—the wheel of God's providence. You harm one part of the machinery of society, and you harm all parts. All professions interdependent. All trades interdependent. All classes of people interdependent. Capital and labor interdependent. No such thing as independence. Dives cannot kick Lazarus without hurting his own foot. They who threw Shadrach into the furnace got their own bodies scorched. Or, to come back to the figure of the text, what a strange thing it would be if the eye should say, "I oversee the entire physical mechanism. I despise the other members of the body. If there is anything I am disgusted with it is with those miserable. low-lived hands." Or, what if the hand should say, "I am the boss workman of the whole physical economy; I have no respect for the other members of the body. If there is anything I despise it is the eye seated under the dome of the forehead doing nothing but look." I come in and wave the flag of truce between these two contestants, and I say: "The eye cannot say to the hand, 'I have no need of thee.'"

That brings me to the first suggestion, and that is that Labor and Capital are to be brought to a better understanding by a complete canvass of the whole subject. They will be brought to peace when they find that they are identical in their interests. When one goes down, they both go down. When one rises, they both rise. There will be an equilibrium after a while. There never has been an exception to the rule. That which is good for one class of society eventually will be good for all classes of society, and that which is bad for one class of society will eventually prove to be bad for all. Every speech that Labor makes against Capital postpones the day of permanent adjustment. Every speech that Capital makes against Labor postpones the day of permanent adjustment. When Capital maligns Labor, it is the eye cursing the hand. When Labor maligns Capital, it is the hand cursing the eye. As far as I have observed, the vast majority of capitalists are successful laborers. If the capitalists would draw their glove, you would see the broken finger-nail, the scar of an old blister, the stiffened finger-joint. The great publishers of the country for the most part were bookbinders or typesetters on small pay. The great carriage manufacturers for the most part sandpapered wagon-bodies in wheelwright shops. While, on the other hand, in all our large manufacturing establishments you will find men on wages who once employed a hundred or five hundred hands. The distance between Capital and Labor is not a great gulf over which is swung a Niagara suspension bridge; it is only a step; and the capitalists are crossing over to become laborers, and the laborers are crossing over to become capitalists. Would God they might shake hands while they cross. On the other hand, laborers are the highest kind of capitalists. Where are their investments—in banks? No. In the railroads? No. Their nerve, their muscle, their bone, their mechanical skill, their physical health are magnificent capital. He who has two eyes, two ears, two feet, two hands, ten fingers, has machinery that puts into nothingness carpet and screw and cotton factory, and all the other implements of the planet. The capitalists are laborers, the laborers are capitalists. The sooner we understand that the better.

Again, there is to come relief to the laboring classes of this country through co-operative associations. I am not at this moment speaking of trades unions, but of that plan by which laborers put their savings together and become their own capitalists. Instead of being dependent upon the beck of this capitalist or that capitalist, they manage their own affairs. In England and Wales there are eight hundred and thirteen co-operative associations. They have three hundred and forty thousand members, they have a capital equivalent to eighteen million dollars, and they do a business annually having a gross return of sixty-three million dollars. Thomas Brassey, one of the foremost men in the British Parliament, on the subject says: "Co-operation is the one and the only relief for the laboring populations. This is the path, I believe, by which they are to come up from the hand-to-mouth style of living to reap the rewards and the honors of our advanced civilization." Lord Derby and John Stuart Mill, who gave half their lives to the study of the labor question, believed in co-operative institutions. The co-operative institution formed in Troy,

Sermons by T. DeWitt Talmage

New York, stood long enough to illustrate the fact that great good might come of such an institution if it were rightly carried on and mightily developed.

"But," says some one, "haven't these institutions sometimes been a failure?" Yes. Every great movement has been a failure at some time. Application of the steam power a failure, electro-telegraphy a failure, railroading a failure, but now the chief successes of the world.

"But," says some one, "why talk of savings being put by laborers into co-operative associations when the vast multitude of toilers of this country are struggling for their daily bread, and they have no surplus?" I reply: put into my hand the money spent by the laboring classes of America for rum and tobacco, and I will establish co-operative associations in all parts of this land, some of them mightier than any financial institutions of the country. We spend in this country over one hundred million dollars every year for tobacco. We spend over one billion five hundred million dollars directly or indirectly for rum. The laboring classes spend their share of this money. Now, suppose the laboring man who has been expending his money in those directions should just add up how much he has expended during these past few years; and then suppose that that money be put into a co-operative association; and then suppose he should have all his friends in toil, who had made the same kind of expenditure, do the same thing, and that should be added up and put into a co-operative association. And then take all that money expended for overdress and overstyle and overliving on the part of toiling people in order that they may appear as well as persons who have more income—gather that all up, and you could have co-operative associations all over this land.

I am not saying anything now about trade-unions.

Epidemic of Strikes

You want to know what I think of trade-unions. I think they are most beneficial in some directions, and they have a specific object; and in this day, when there are vast monopolies—a thousand monopolies concentring the wealth of the people into the possession of a few men — unless the laboring men of this country band together they will go under. There is a lawful use of a trade-union, but then there is an unlawful use of a trade-union. If it means sympathy in time of sickness, if it means finding work for people when they are out of work, if it means the improvement of the financial, the moral or the religious condition of the laboring classes, that is all right. Do not artists band together in an art-union? Do not singers band together in Handel and Haydn societies? Do not newspaper men band together in press clubs? Do not ministers of religion band together in conferences and associations? There is not in all the land a city where clergymen do not come together — many of them once a week — to talk over affairs. For these reasons you should not blame labor guilds. When they are doing their legitimate work they are most admirable; but when they come around with drum and fife and flag and drive people off from their toil, from their scaffoldings, from their factories, then they are nihilistic, then they are communistic, then they are barbaric, then they are a curse. If a man wants to stop work, let him stop work; but he cannot stop me from work.

But now suppose all the laboring classes banded together for beneficent purposes in co-operative association, under whatever name they put their means together. Suppose they take the money that they waste in rum and tobacco and use it for the elevation of their families, for the education of their children, for their moral, intellectual and religious improvement? What a different state of things we would have in this country, and they would have in Great Britain!

Do you not realize the fact that men work better without stimulant? You say, "Will you deny the laboring men this help which they get from strong drink, borne down as they are with many anxieties and exhausting work?" I would deny them nothing that is good for them. I would deny them strong drink, if I had the power, because it is damaging to them. My father said: "I became a temperance man in early life because I found that in the harvest-field, while I was naturally weaker than the other men, I could hold out longer than any of them. They took stimulant and I took none."

Everybody knows they cannot endure great fatigue —men who indulge in stimulants. All our young men understand that. When they are preparing for the regatta or the ball club or the athletic wrestling they abstain from strong drink. Now, suppose all this money that is wasted were gathered together and put into co-operative institutions—oh, we would have a very different state of things from what we have now!

I remark again, the laboring classes of this country are to find great relief when they learn — all of them learn — forecast and providence. Vast numbers of them put down their income and they put down their expenses, and if the income meets the expenses that is all that is necessary. I know laboring men who are in a perfect fidget until they have spent their last dollar. They fly around everywhere until they get it spent. A case came under my observation where a young man was receiving seven hundred dollars a year, and earned it by very hard work. The marriage day came. The bride had received five hundred dollars as an inheritance from her grandfather. She put the five hundred dollars in wedding equipment. Then the twain hired two rooms on the third story. Then this man, who had most arduous employment—just as much as he could possibly endure — got evening employment so he could earn a few dollars more; and by this extra evening employment almost extinguished his eyesight. Why did he take this extra evening employment? Was it to lay by something for a rainy day? No. Was it to get a life-insurance so that if he should die his wife would not be a pauper? No. It was for the one purpose of getting his wife a one-hundred-and-fifty-dollar sealskin sacque! I am just giving you a fact I know. The sister of this woman, although she was a very poor girl, was not to be eclipsed; and so she went to work day and night, and toiled and toiled and toiled almost into the grave, until she got a one-hundred-and-fifty-dollar sealskin sacque! Well, the news went abroad all through the street. Most of the people on that street were laboring, hardworking people, and they were not to be outshone in this way, and they all went to work in the same direction, and practically said, though not literally: "Though the heavens fall, we must have a sealskin sacque!"

A clergyman in Iowa told me that his church and the entire neighborhood had been ruined by the fact that the people mortgaged their farms in order to go down to the Philadelphia Centennial, in 1876. First, one family would go, then another family; and finally it was not respectable not to go to the Centennial at Philadelphia, and they mortgaged their farms. The church and the neighborhood ruined in that way. Now, between such fools and pauperism there is only a very short step. In time of peace, prepare for war. In time of prosperity, prepare for adversity. Yet how many there are who drive on the verge of the precipice, and at the least touch of accident or sickness over they go. Ah! my friends, it is not right, it is not honest. He that provideth not for his own, and especially those of his own household, is worse than an infidel. A man has no right to live in luxury and have all comforts and all brightness around him—taking his family with him at that rate—everything bright and beautiful and luxuriant, until he stumbles against a tomb and falls in, and the family go to the poorhouse. That is not common honesty. I am no advocate of skinflint saving; I abhor it. But I plead for Christian providence. There are some people who are disgusted if they see anything like economy, such as a man might show in turning down the gas in the parlor when he goes out. There are families actually embarrassed if you ring their door-bell before they have the hall lighted. There are people who apologize if you surprise them at the table. Now, it is mean or it is magnificent to save, just according to what you save for. If it is for the miserly hoarding of it, then it is despicable; but if it means better education for your children, if it means more house-help for your wife when she is not strong enough to do much work, if it means that the day of your death shall not be a horror beyond all endurance because it is to throw your family into disruption and annihilation and the poorhouse—then it is magnificent, if it is to avoid all that.

Some of the older persons remember very well Abraham Van Nest, of New York, one of its Christian merchants. He was often called mean, because he calculated so closely. Why did he calculate closely? That he might have the more to give. There was not a Bible society, or a tract society or a reformatory institution in the city of New York but he had his hand in supporting it. He denied himself many luxuries that he might give to others the necessities. He has been many years reaping his reward in heaven;

but I shall never forget the day when I, a green country lad, came to his house and spent the evening; and at the close of the evening, as I was departing, he accompanied me to the door, accompanied me to the steps, came down off the steps and said: "Here, De Witt, is forty dollars for books; don't say anything about it." It is mean or it is magnificent to save, according as you save for a good or for a bad object.

I know there are many people who have much to say against savings-banks and life-insurances. I have to tell you that the vast majority of the homesteads of this country have been the result of such institutions; and I have to tell you also that the vast majority of the homesteads of the future for the laboring classes will be the result of such institutions. It will be a great day for the working classes of England and the United States when the workingman can buy a barrel of flour, instead of flour by the small sack; when he can buy a barrel of sugar, instead of sugar by the pound; when he can pay cash for coats and hats and shoes, rather than pay an additional amount for the reason that he has to get it all charged.

Again I remark, great relief is to come for the laboring classes of this country by perception on the part of employers that they had better take their employees into their confidence. I can see very easily, looking from my standpoint, what is the matter. Employees seeing the employer in seeming prosperity do not know all the straits, all the hardships, all the losses, all the annoyances. They look at him and they think, "Why, he has it easy and we have it hard." They do not know that at that very moment the employer is at the last point of desperation to meet his engagements.

I know a gentleman very well who has over a thousand hands in his employ. I said to him some years ago, when there was great trouble in the labor market: "How are you getting on with your men?" "Oh," he said, "I have no trouble." "Why," I said, "have not you had any strikes?" "Oh, no," he said. "I never had any trouble." "What plan do you pursue?" He said: "I will tell you. All my men know every year just how matters stand. Every litttle while I call them together and say, 'Now, boys, last year I made so much; this year I made less; so you see I cannot pay you as much as I did last year. Now, I want to know what you think I ought to have as a percentage out of this establishment, and what wages I ought to give you. You know I put all my energy in this business, put all my fortune in it and risked everything. What do you really think I ought to have and you ought to have?' By the time we come out of that consultation we are unanimous; there never has been an exception. When we prosper we all prosper together; when we suffer, we all suffer together, and my men would die for me." Now, let all employers be frank with their employees. Take them into your confidence. Let them know just how matters stand. There is an immense amount of common sense in the world. It is always safe to appeal to it.

I remark again: great relief will come to the laboring classes of this country through the religious ratification of it. Labor is honored and rewarded in proportion as a community is Christianized. Why is it that our smallest coin in this country is a penny, while in China it takes a half-dozen pieces of coin, or a dozen, to make one of our pennies in value, so the Chinese carry the cash, as they call it, like a string of beads around the neck? We never want to pay less than a penny for anything in this country. They must pay that which is worth only the sixth part or the twelfth part of a penny. Heathenism and iniquity and infidelity depress everything. The Gospel of Jesus Christ elevates everything. How do I account for this? I account for it with the plainest philosophy. The religion of Jesus Christ is a democratic religion. It tells the employer that he is a brother to all the operatives in his establishment—made by the same God, to lie down in the same dust, and to be saved by the same supreme mercy. It does not make the slightest difference how much money you have, you cannot buy your way into the kingdom of heaven. If you have the grace of God in your heart, you will enter heaven. So you see it is a democratic religion. Saturate our populations with this Gospel, and labor will be respectful, labor will be rewarded, labor will be honored, capital will be Christian in all its behavior, and there will be higher tides of thrift setting in. Let me say a word to all capitalists: be your own executors. Make investments for eternity. Do not be like some of those capitalists I know who walk around among their employees with a supercilious air, or drive up to the factory in a manner which seems to indicate they are the autocrat of the universe with the sun and the moon in their vest pockets, chiefly anxious when they go among laboring men not to be touched by the greasy or smirched hand and have their broadcloth injured. Be a Christian employer. Remember those who are under your charge are bone of your bone and flesh of your flesh; that Jesus Christ died for them and that they are immortal. Divide up your estates, or portions of them, for the relief of the world before you leave it. Do not go out of the world like that man died in New York, leaving in his will forty million dollars, yet giving how much to the Church of God? how much for the alleviation of human suffering? He gave some money a little while before he died; that was well. But in all this will of forty million dollars how much? One million? No. Five hundred thousand? No. One hundred dollars? No. Two cents? No. One cent? No. These great cities groaning in anguish, nations crying out for the bread of everlasting life. A man in a will giving forty million dollars, and not one cent to God! It is a disgrace to our civilization. Or, as illustrated in a letter which I have concerning a man who departed this life leaving between five and eight million of dollars. Not one dollar was left, this writer says, to comfort the aged workmen and workwomen, not one dollar to elevate and instruct the hundreds of pale children who stifled their childish growth in the heat and clamor of his factory. Is it strange that the curse of the children of toil follow such ingratitude? How well could one of his many millions have been disbursed for the present and the future benefit of those whose hands had woven literally the fabric of the dead man's princely fortune! Oh, capitalists of the United States, be your own executors. Be a George Peabody, if need be, on a small scale. God has made you a steward; discharge your responsibility.

My word is to all laboring men in this country: I congratulate you at your brightening prospects. I congratulate you on the fact that you are getting your representatives at Albany, at Harrisburg and at Washington. I have only to mention such a man of the past as Henry Wilson, the shoemaker; as Andrew Johnson, the tailor; as Abraham Lincoln, the railsplitter. The living illustrations easily occur to you. This will go on until you will have representatives at all the headquarters, and you will have full justice. Mark that. I congratulate you also on the opportunities for your children. I congratulate you that you have to work, and that when you are dead your children will have to work.

Epidemic of Strikes

I also congratulate you because your work is only prefatory and introductory. You want the grace of Jesus Christ, the carpenter of Nazareth. He toiled himself, and he knows how to sympathize with all who toil. Get his grace in your heart and you can sing on the scaffolding amid the storm, in the shop shoving the plane, in the mine plunging the crowbar, on shipboard climbing the ratlines. He will make the drops of sweat on your brow glittering pearls for the eternal coronet. Are you tired, he will rest you. Are you sick, he will give you help. Are you cold, he will wrap you in the mantle of his love. Who are they before the Throne. "Ah!" you say, "their hands were never calloused with toil." Yes, they were. You say, "Their feet were never blistered with the long journey." Yes, they were; but Christ raised them to that high eminence. Who are these? "These are they that came out of great tribulation and had their robes washed and made white in the blood of the Lamb." That for every Christian working man and for every Christian working woman will be the beginning of eternal holiday.

LAST DECADE OF THE CENTURY

Rev., 19: 4: " Amen! Alleluia! "

LAST DECADE OF THE CENTURY*

Rev., 19: 4: " Amen! Alleluia! "

The nineteenth century is departing. After it has
taken a few more steps, if each year be a step, it will be
gone into the eternities. In a short time we shall be in
the last decade of this century, which fact makes the
solemnest book outside the Bible the almanac, and the
most sugges ve and the most tremendous piece of
machinery in all the earth, the clock. The last decade
of this century, upon which we shall soon enter, will be
the grandest, mightiest, and most decisive decade in
all the chronologies. I am glad it is not to come immediately, for we need by a new baptism of the Holy
Ghost to prepare for it. Does any one say that this
division of time is arbitrary? Oh, no; in other ages
the divisions of time may have been, but our years date
from Christ. Does any one say that the grouping of
ten together is an arrangement arbitrary? Oh, no;
next to the figure seven, ten is with God a favorite
number. Abraham dwelt ten years in Canaan. Ten
righteous men would have saved Sodom. In the ancient tabernacle were ten curtains, their pillars ten and
their sockets ten. In the ancient temple were ten la-
vers and ten candlesticks and ten tables and a molten
sea of ten cubits. And the Commandments written on
the granite of Mount Sinai were ten, and the kingdom
of God was likened to ten virgins, and ten men should
lay hold of him that was a Jew, and the reward of the
greatly faithful is that they shall reign over ten cities,
and in the effort to take the census of the New Jerusa-

---

* Preached in the Brooklyn Tabernacle, in 1890.

lem the number ten swings around the thousands, crying "ten thousand times ten thousand." So I come to look toward the closing ten years of the nineteenth century with an intensity of interest I can hardly describe. I have also noticed that the favorite time for great events in many of the centuries was the closing fragment of the century. There is apt to be at such a time a concentration of downfalls or enthronements, of splendors or horrors. Is America to be discovered— it must be in the last decade of the fifteenth century, namely, 1492. Was free constitutional government to be well established in America—the last years of the eighteenth century must achieve it. Were three cities to be submerged by one pitch of scoriæ—Herculaneum and Stabiæ and Pompeii in the latter part of the first century must go under. The fourth century closed with the most agitating ecclesiastical war of history— Urban the Sixth against Clement the Seventh. Alfred the Great closes the ninth century, and Edmund Ironsides the eleventh century, with their resounding deeds. The sixteenth century closed with the establishment of religious independence in the United Netherlands. The French Revolution with its Reign of Terror, the bloodiest upheaval of all time, at the close of the eighteenth century. Ay, almost every century has had its peroration of overtowering achievements.

As the closing years of the centuries seem a favorite time for great scenes of emancipation or disaster, and as the number ten seems a favorite number in the Scriptures, written by divine direction, and as we are soon to enter upon the last ten years of the nineteenth century, what does the world propose? What does the Church of Christ propose? What do reformers propose? I know not; but now in the presence of this consecrated assembly I propose that we make ready, get all our batteries planted, and all our plans well laid, in what remains of this decade, and then in the last decade of the nineteenth century march up and take this round world for God.

When I say we, I mean the five hundred million Christians now alive. But, as many of them will not have enough heart for the work, let us copy Gideon, and as he had thirty-two thousand men in his army to fight the Midianites, but many of them were not made of the right stuff, and he promulgated a military order, saying: "Whosoever is fearful and afraid let him return and depart early from Gilead," and twenty-two thousand were afraid of getting hurt, and went home, and only ten thousand were left, and God told him that even this reduced number was too large a number, for they might think they had triumphed independent of divine help, and so the number must be still further reduced, and only those should be kept in the ranks who in passing the river should be so in haste for victory over their enemies that, though very thirsty, they would, without stopping a second, just scoop up the water in the palm of their right hand, and scoop up the water in the palm of their left hand, and only three hundred men with the battle-shout, "The sword of the Lord and of Gideon," scattered the Midianites like leaves in an equinox—so out of the five hundred million nominal Christians of to-day let all unbelievers and cowards go home and get out of the way. And suppose we have only four hundred million left, suppose only two hundred million left, suppose only one hundred million left, yea, suppose we only have fifty million left, we will undertake the divine crusade, and each one just scooping up a palm full of the river of God's mercy in one hand, and a palm full of the river of God's strength in the other, let us with the cry, "The sword of the Lord and of Gideon," the sword of the Lord and of John Knox, the sword of the Lord and of Matthew Simpson, the sword of the Lord and of Bishop McIlvaine, the sword of the Lord and of Adoniram Judson, the sword of the Lord and of Martin Luther, go into the last decade of the nineteenth century.

Is it audacious for me to propose it? Oh, no; a captive servant in the kitchen of Naaman told the commander-in-chief where he could get rid of the blotches of his awful leprosy, and his complexion became as fair as a babe's. And did not Christ, in order to take the ophthalmia out of the eyes of the blind man, use a mixture of spittle and dust? And who showed Blucher a short-cut for his army, so that instead of taking the regular road, by which he would have come up too late, he came up in time to save Waterloo and Europe? Was it not an unknown lad, who perhaps could not write his own name? And so I, "who am less than the least of all saints," propose a short-cut to victory, and am willing to be the expectoration on some blind eye, and tell some of the brigadier-generals of the Lord of hosts how this leprosied world may in the final decade of the nineteenth century have its flesh come again as the flesh of a little child.

Is there anything in prophecy to hinder this speedy consummation? No. Some one begins to quote from Daniel about, "time, times and a half time," and takes from Revelation the seven trumpets, blowing them all at once in my ear. But, with utmost reverence, I take up all the prophecies and hold them toward heaven and say, God never has and never will stop consecrated effort and holy determination and magnificent resolve, and that if the Church of God will rise up to its full work, it can make Daniel's time twenty years and his half time ten years. Neither Isaiah, nor Ezekiel, nor Micah, nor Malachi, nor Jeremiah, nor any of the major or minor prophets will hinder us a second.

Last Decade of the Century

Suppose the Bible had announced the millennium to begin the year 3889, that would be no hindrance. In one sense God never changes his mind, being the same yesterday, to-day and forever. But in another sense he does change his mind, and times without number, every day, and that is when his people pray. Did he not change his mind about Nineveh? By God's command Jonah, at the top of his voice, while standing on the steps of the merchants' exchange, and the palatial residences of that city, cried out, "Yet forty days and Nineveh shall be overthrown." Was it overthrown in forty days? No. The people gave up their sins and cried for mercy, and though Jonah got mad because his whole course of sermons had been spoiled and went into a disgraceful pouting, we have the record so sublime, I cannot read it without feeling a nervous chill running through me. "God saw their works that they turned from their evil way, and God repented of the evil that he had said he would do unto them, and he did it not." God is a father, and some of us know what that means; and some time when we have promised chastisement and our child deserved it, the little darling has put her arms around our necks and expressed such sorrow and made such promises of doing better, that her tears landed on the lips of our kiss; and we have held her a half-hour after on our knees, and would as soon think of slapping an angel in the face as of even striking her with the weight of our little finger. God is a father, and while he has promised this world scourgings, though they were to be for a thousand or five thousand years, he would, if the world repented, substitute benediction and divine caress. God changed his mind about Sodom six times. He had determined on its destruction. Abraham asked him if he would not spare it, if fifty righteous people were found there; and, narrowing down the number, if forty-five people were found there; if forty people; if thirty people; if twenty people; if ten people were found there. And each of the six times the Lord answered "Yes." Oh, why did not Abraham go on just two steps further and say if five be found there and if one be found there? Then, for the sake of Lot, its one good citizen, I think Sodom would have been spared. Eight times does the Bible say that God repented when he had promised punishments, and that he withheld the stroke. Was it a slip of Paul's pen when he spoke of God's cutting short the work in righteousness? No; Paul's pen never slipped. There is nothing in the way of prophecy to hinder the crusade I have proposed for the last decade of the nineteenth century.

The whole trouble is that we put off the completion of the world's redemption to such long and indefinite distances. The old proverb, that "what is everybody's business is nobody's business," might be changed a little, and be made truthfully to say what is the Gospel business of all the ages is the Gospel business of no age. We are so constituted that we cannot get up much enthusiam about something five hundred years from now, or a thousand years from now. We are fighting at too long a range. That gun called the "Swamp Angel" was a nuisance. It shot six miles, but it hardly ever hit anything. It did its chief destructive work when it burst and killed those who were setting it off. Short range is the effective kind of work, whether it be for worldly or religious purposes. Some man with is eyes half shut drones out to me the Bible quotation, "A thousand years are as one day;" that is, ten centuries are not long for the Lord. But why do you not quote the previous sentence, which says that one day is with the Lord as a thousand years? That is, he could do the work of ten centuries in twenty-four hours. The mightiest obstacle to Christian work is the impression that the world's evangelization is away off. And we take the telescope and look on and on through centuries until we see two objects near each other, and we strain our vision and guess what they are; and we call great conventions to guess what they are, and we get down our heaviest theological book and balance our telescope on the lid, and look, and finally conclude that they are two wild beasts that we see, and the one has hairs and the other has wool, and we guess it must be the lion and the lamb lying together. In that great cradle of postponement and somnolence, we rock the church as though it were an impatient child and say, "Hush, my dear, do not be impatient; do not get excited by rivals; do not cry. Your father is coming; do not cry; your father is coming. Do not get uneasy. He will be here in two or three or ten or twenty thousand years." And we act as though we thought that when Macaulay's famous New Zealander in the far distance is seated on a broken arch of London bridge sketching the ruins of St. Paul's, his grandchild might break in and jolt his pencil by asking him if he thought the millennium ever would appear. Men and women of the eternal God! sons and daughters of the Lord Almighty? we may have it start in the decade that is soon to commence, and it will be done if we can persuade the people to get ready for the work.

What makes me think it can be done? First, because God is ready. He needs no long persuasion to do his work, for if he is not willing that any should perish, he is not willing that any of the people of the next decade shall perish; and the whole Bible is a chime of bells ringing out "Come! come! come!" And you need not go round the earth to find out how much he wants the world to come, but just walk around one stripped and bare and leafless tree, with two branches, not arched but horizontal. But he is waiting, as he said he would, for the co-operation of the Church. When we are ready, God is ready. And he certainly has all the weaponry ready to capture this world for the truth, all the weapons of kindness or devastation. On the one hand the Gospel and sunshine, and power to orchardize and gardenize the earth, and fountains swinging in rainbow and Chatsworthian verdure, and aromas poured out of the vials of heaven; while on the other hand, he has the weaponry of devastation, thunderbolt and conflagration, and forces planetary, solar, lunar, stellar, or meteoric, that with loose rein thrown on the neck for a second would leave constellations and galaxies so many split and shivered wheels on the boulevards of heaven. And that God is on our side, all on our side. Blessed be his glorious name!

If you continue to ask me why I think that the world can be saved in the final decade of the nineteenth century, I reply, because it is not a great undertaking, considering the number of workers that will go at it if once persuaded it can be done. We have sifted the five hundred million of workers down to four hundred million, and three hundred million, and two hundred million, and one hundred million, and to fifty million. I went to work to cipher out how many souls that number could bring to God in ten years if each one brought a soul every year, and if each soul so brought should bring another each succeeding year. I found out, aided by a professor in mathematics, that we did not need anything like such a number of workers enlisted. You see it is simply a question of mathematics and in geometrical progression. Then I gave to the learned professor this problem: how many persons would it require to start with if each one brought a soul into the kingdom each year for ten years, and each one brought another, each succeeding year, in order to have fourteen hundred million people saved, or the population of the earth at present? His answer was, two million seven hundred and fifty-four thousand three hundred and seventy-five workers. So you see that when I sifted the five hundred million nominal Christians of the earth down to fifty million and stopped there, I retained for this work forty-seven million people too many. There it is in glorious mathematics. *Quod erat demonstrandum.*

Do you tell me that God does not care for mathematics? Then you have never seen the Giant's Causeway, where God shows his regard for the hexagonal in whole ranges of rocky columns with six sides and six angles. Then you have not studied the geometry of a bee's honeycomb with six sides and six angles. Then you have not noticed what regard God has for the square, the altar of the ancient tabernacle four square, the breastplate four square, the court of the temple in Ezekiel's vision four square, the New Jerusalem laid out four square. Or you have not noticed his regard for the circle by making it his throne, "sitting on the circle of the earth," and fashioning sun and moon and stars in a circle, and sending our planetary system around other systems in a circle, and the whole universe sweeping around the throne of God in a circle. And as to his regard for mathematical numbers, he makes the fourth book in his Bible the book of numbers, and numbers the hosts of Israel and numbers the troops of Sennacherib and numbers the hewers in the forest, and numbers the spearmen, and numbers the footmen, and numbers the converted at Pentecost, and numbers the chariots of God rolling down the steeps of heaven. So I have a right to enlist mathematics for the demonstration of the easy possibility of bringing the whole world to God in the coming decade by simple process of solicitation, each one only having to bring one a year; although I want to take in forty thousand, and I know men now alive who, I think, by pen or voice, or both, directly or indirectly, will take hundreds of thousands each. So you see that that will discharge some of the two million seven hundred and fifty-four thousand three hundred and seventy-five from the necessity of taking any.

Another reason why I know it can be done is that we may divide the work up among the denominations. God does not ask any one denomination to do the work or any dozen denominations. The work can be divided, and is being divided up, not geographically, but according to the temperaments of the human family. We cannot say to one denomination, "You take Persia," and another, "You take China," and another, "You take India," because there are all styles of temperaments in all nations. And some denominations are especially adapted to work with people of sanguine temperament or phlegmatic temperament or choleric temperament or bilious temperament or nervous temperament or lymphatic temperament. The Episcopal Church will do its most effective work with those who by taste prefer the stately and ritualistic. The Methodist Church will do its best work among the emotional and demonstrative. The Presbyterian Church will do its best work among those who like strong doctrine, and the stately service softened by the emotional. So each denomination will have certain kinds of people whom it will especially affect. So let the work be divided up. There are the nine hundred and fifty thousand Christians of the Presbyterian Church North, and other hundreds of thousands in the Presbyterian Church South, and all foreign Presbyterians, more especially Scotch, English and Irish, making, I guess, about two million Presbyterians; the

Methodist Church is still larger; the Church of England on both sides of the sea still larger; and many other denominations as much, if not more, consecrated than any I have mentioned. Divide up the world's evangelization among these denominations after they are persuaded it can be done before the nineteenth century is dead, and the last Hottentot, the last Turk, the last Japanese, the last American, the last European, the last Asiatic, the last African, will see the salvation of God before he sees the opening gate of the twentieth century.

Again, the whole world can be saved in the time specified, because we have all manner of machinery requisite. It is not as though we had to build the printing presses; they are all built, and running day and night, those printing religious papers (nine hundred and twenty-five of those religious papers in this country), those printing religious tracts and those printing religious books. And thousands of printing presses now in the service of the devil could be bought and set to work in the service of God. Why was the printing press invented? To turn out bill-heads, and circulars of patent medicines, and tell the news which in three weeks will be of no importance? From the old-time Franklin printing press, on up to the Lord Stanhope press, and the Washington press, and the Victory press, to Hoe's perfecting printing press, that machine has been improving for its best work, and its final work, namely, the publication of the glad tidings of great joy which shall be to all people. We have the presses, or can have them before the first of January, when the new decade is to begin, to put a Bible in the hand of every son and daughter of Adam and Eve now living.

But this brings me to the adjoining thought, namely, we have the money to do the work. I mean the fifty million of Christians have it. Ay, the two million seven hundred and fifty-four thousand Christians have it; and the dam which is beginning to leak will soon break and there will be rushing floods of hundreds and millions and billions of dollars in holy contribution when you persuade the wealthy men of the kingdom of God that the speedy conversion of the world is a possibility. I have no sympathy with this bombardment of rich men. We would each one be worth five million dollars if we could, and by hard persuasion, perhaps might be induced to take fifteen million. Almost every paper I take up tells of some wealthy man who has endowed a college, or built a church or a hospital or a free library, and that thing is going to multiply until the treasury of all our denominations and reformatory organizations will be overwhelmed with munificence, if we can persuade our men of wealth that the world's evangelization is possible, and that they may live to see it with their own eyes.

I have always cherished the idea that when the world is converted we would be allowed to come out on the battlements of heaven and see the bannered procession and the bonfires of victory. But I would like to see the procession closer by and just be permitted myself to throw on a fagot for a bigger bonfire. And if you persuade our men of wealth that there is a possibility for them to join on earth in the universal glee of a redeemed planet, instead of laborious beseeching for funds, and arguing and flattering, in order to get a contribution for Christian objects, our men of wealth will stand in line as at a post-office window or a railroad ticket-office, but in this case waiting for their turn to make charitable deposit. The Gentiles are not long going to allow themselves to be eclipsed by Baron Hirsch, the Jew, who gave forty million dollars for schools in France, Germany, and Russia, besides endowing schools and training institutions in America. I rejoice that so much of the wealth of the world is coming into the possession of Christian men and women. And although the original Church was very poor, and its members were fish-dealers on the banks of Galilee, and had only such stock on hand as they could take in their own net, to-day in the hands of Christian men and women there is enough money to print Bibles and build churches and support missionaries under God in ten years to save the world.

Again, I think that the world's evangelization can be achieved in the time specified, because we have already the theological institutions necessary for this work. We do not have to build them; they are built, and they are filled with thousands of young men, and there will be three sets of students who will graduate into the ministry before the close of this century; and once have them understand that instead of preaching thirty or forty years, and taking into the kingdom of God a few hundred souls, right before them is the Sedan, is the Armageddon, and these young men, instead of entering the ministry timid, and with apologetic air, will feel like David, who came up just as the armies were set in array, and he left his carriage and shouted for the battle, and cried: "Who is this uncircumcised Philistine, that he should defy the armies of the living God?" and with five gravel stones skilfully flung, sent sprawling the bragging ten-footer, his mouth into the dust, and his heels into the air.

What but such a consummation could be a fit climax to this century? You notice a tendency in history and all about us to a climax. The creation week rising from herbs to fish, and from fish to bird, and from bird to quadruped, and from quadruped to immortal man. The New Testament rising from quiet genealogical table in Matthew to apocalyptic doxology in Revelation. Now, what can be an appropriate climax to this century, which has heard the puff of the first steamer, and the throb of the first stethoscope, and the click of the first telegraph, and the clatter of the first sewing-machine, and saw the flash of the first electric light, and the revolution of the first steam plough, and the law of storms was written, and the American Bible Society and the American Tract Society were born; and instead of an audience laughing down Dr. Carey for advocating foreign missions, as was done at Northampton in England in the last century, now all denominations vying with each other as to who shall go the furthest and the soonest into the darkest of the New Hebrides; and three hundred thousand souls have been born to God in the South Sea Islands; and Micronesia and Melanesia and Malayan Polynesia have been set in the crown of Christ, and David Livingstone has unveiled Africa, and the last bolted gate of barbaric nations has swung wide open to let the Gospel in. What, I ask, with a thousand interrogation points uplifted, can be a fit, an appropriate and sufficient climax except it be a world redeemed?

Yea, I believe it can be done if we get prepared for it, because the whole air and the whole heaven is full of willing help. "Are they not all ministering spirits sent forth?" We make an awful mistake if we calculate only on the forces we can see. The mightiest army is in the air. So much of selfishness and pride and rivalry and bad motives of all kinds get into our work here that we are hindered. But the mighty souls that have gone up to the flying armies of the sky have left all imperfection behind; and these souls are with us, and, without a fault and with perfect natures, are on our side. You cannot make me believe that, after toiling here for long years for the redemption of the world, until from exhaustion some of them fell into their graves, they have ceased their interest in the stupendous conflict now raging, or that they will decline their help.

Irenæus Prime! honored on earth, but now glorified in heaven, have you forgotten the work toward which you gave for more than half a century your gracious life, your loving voice, and your matchless pen? No! Then come down and help. Alexander Duff, have you forgotten the millions of India for whose salvation you suffered in Hindoo jungle and thundered on missionary platform? No! Then come down and help. David Brainerd, have you forgotten the aborigines to whom you preached and for whom you prayed until you could preach and pray no more, lying down delirious amid the miasmas of the swamp? No! Then come down and help. Moncrieff and Freeman and Campbell, have you forgotten Lucknow and Cawnpore? No! Then come down and help. I rub out of my eyes the stupidity and unbelief, and I, the servant of these great Elishas in the Gospel, see the mountains all round about full of horses of fire and chariots of fire; and they head this way. Hovered over are we by clouds of witnesses and helpers! Clouds of apostles in the air led on by Paul! Clouds of martyrs in the air led on by Stephen! Clouds of prophets in the aid led on by Isaiah! Clouds of patriarchs in the air led on by Abraham! Clouds of ancient warriors in the air led on by Joshua; and that Bible warrior at whose prayer astronomy once halted over Ajalon and Gibeon seems now to lift one hand toward the descending sun of this century, and the other hand toward the moon of the last decade, saying: "Stand thou still till the Church of God gets the final victory!"

Then let us take what remains of this decade to get ready for the final decade of the nineteenth century. You and I may or may not live to see that decade. We may or may not live to see its close, but that shall not hinder me from declaring the magnificent possibility. I confess that the mistake of my life has been, not that I did not work hard — for I could not have worked harder and lived, as God knows and my family know—but that I have not worked under the realization that the salvation of this world was a near-by possibility. But whether we see the beginning or the closing of that decade is of no importance, if only that decade can get the coronation; and then all decades shall kneel before this enthroned decade, and even the gray-grown centuries will cast their crowns before it, and it will be the most honored decade between the time when the morning stars sang together as the libretto of worlds was opened, and the time when the mighty angel, robed in cloud and garlanded in rainbow, shall, with one foot on the sea and the other foot on the land, swear by him that liveth forever and ever that time shall be no longer. Alleluia! Amen!

A FAVORED NATION

Isa., 26: 15: "Thou hast increased the nation, O Lord, thou hast increased the nation."

A FAVORED NATION*

Isa., 26: 15: "Thou hast increased the nation, O Lord, thou hast increased the nation."

As sometimes in the summer noon when all the harvest-fields are flooded with light the air is suddenly darkened and you look up to find that it is the wing of hawk or eagle flying over the plain, so these sheaves of Northern wheat and Southern rice gathered in this Thanksgiving service are suddenly shadowed with the black wing of Death. Our beloved Vice-President, Thomas A. Hendricks, has departed. But it would be unwise to make this occasion sombre and funereal, and so I adjourn until my lecture to-morrow night the tribute to my warm personal friend, Thomas A. Hendricks. For surely if the departed Governor, who had by his own proclamation again and again called the people to thanksgiving, were allowed to speak, he would charge the officiating clergy to-day to stir the gladness and joy and gratitude of the people by recital of our national blessings, and in no wise be hindered by personal griefs.

The optimists and pessimists and grain merchants and fruit dealers and dry-goods men and farmers have told us such diverse stories about the real condition of this country, that I was in a great fog on the subject; so that last week I appealed to the headquarters at Washington for accurate information, and I have now not the surmises or the guesses to present, but the facts received yesterday by letter from the United

---

* A Thanksgiving sermon delivered in 1885. The church was decorated with specimens of harvests and fruits from all parts of the country.

States Department of Agriculture, and I hereby publicly acknowledge my indebtedness to those obliging and skilful officials, especially Mr. Nesbit and Mr. Dodge. On this day, celebrative of temporal blessings, we will take larger liberty of thought and illustration than we allow ourselves in the Sabbath pulpit.

As a firm foundation on which to build your thanksgivings to-day observe:

Fact the first: That the wheat crop of the country yields this year three hundred and fifty million bushels. And add to that the surplus which we had over from last year, and you will find that America owns more wheat to-day than ever before since the world stood. All grain this year will make an aggregate of three million bushels more than ever.

Fact the second: The corn crop exceeds all its predecessors in absolute quantity. Though not as much per acre, yet more acres have yielded, and so the corn-bin of the nation is better filled to-day than ever before.

Fact the third: Unmanufactured cotton exported this year is valued at two hundred and one million nine hundred and sixty-two thousand five hundred and eighty-eight dollars, being five million dollars more sent to other countries this year than last, the exports of cotton this year twenty-nine million pounds more than last.

Fact the fourth: The tobacco crop is so luxuriant that we exported twenty-seven million pounds more this year than last year. A well-known and popular weed that is good for many things, tobacco is—to kill moths in wardrobes, and tick in sheep, and to strangulate all kinds of vermin, and to fumigate pestiferous places, and is death to all other malodors by its own superior power of stench, an article so useful to others that I wish we could export the entire crop.

Fact the fifth: The sugar crop is so large that we have sent abroad this year one hundred and seventy-

A Favored Nation

six million five hundred thousand pounds more than last. In 1884 we exported seventy-six million pounds, receiving for it five million four hundred thousand dollars, while this year we sent abroad two hundred and fifty-two million five hundred thousand pounds, getting for them sixteen million dollars. I put the sixteen million dollars of this year against the five million dollars of last year and the two hundred and fifty-two million five hundred thousand pounds of this year against the seventy-six million pounds of last year.

The so-called bears in the grain market and all the other markets are such persistent, chronic, and hemispheric croakers, that the great masses of the people have no idea, until now I tell them, of what God is doing for this country. We had a bad winter, it was said. Yes. We had a bad spring, it was said. Yes. We had a bad summer. Yes. But we had a good God, and, notwithstanding all the deluges, and all the droughts, and all the frosts, and all the insects, and all the political excitements—Republican, Democratic, and Mugwumpian—the lap of the nation is filled with blessing. Shall we, then, render to-day a jeremiad or a grand march? It will all depend upon the way you look at things. There are two ways of putting things:

Raindrop the first: "Always chill and wet, tossed by the wind, devoured by the sea."

Raindrop the second: "Aha! the sun kissed me, the flowers caught me, the fields blessed me."

Brook the first: "Alas, me! struck of the rock, dashed of the mill-wheel."

Brook the second: "I sang the miller to sleep, I ground the grist; oh, this gay somersault over the wheel?"

Horse the first: "Pull, pull, pull. This tugging in traces and holding back in the breeching, and standing at a post with a sharp wind hanging icicles from my nostrils."

Sermons by T. DeWitt Talmage

Horse the second gives a horse laugh: "Useful life I have been permitted to live. See that corn! I helped break the sod and run out the furrows, and on a starlight night I filled the ravines and mountains with the voices of jingling bell and the laugh of the sleigh-riding party. Then to have the children throw in an extra quart at my winnowing, and to have Jane pat me on the nose, and say: 'Poor Charlie!' To bound along with arched neck and flaming eye and clattering hoof; what an exhilaration."

Bird the first: "Weary of emigration; no one to pay me for song. Only here to be shot at."

Bird the second: "I have banquet of a thousand wheat-fields; cup of lily to drink out of, aisle of forest to walk in, Mount Washington under foot and a continent at a glance."

Different ways of putting things.

Give us full organ to-day. Pull out all the glad stops, and while we pray and while we sing let us make a joyful noise unto the Rock of our salvation. Gather your families together. Let your children be arrayed in their brightest robes. In the morning let the temples of God ring with hosannas, and in the night let your homes be filled with congratulation, laughter and song. Turn on all the lights; bracket, chandelier, and candelabra. Throw another armful of firewood on the hearth and let the fire blaze out cheerily. When you and I are gone and our children go out and look at the place where we sleep, may they be enabled to say: "There rest the father and mother who knew how to make their children happy on Thanksgiving Day."

On such a time as this shall we not render thanksgiving to God? What a wonderful change? It was not a great while ago when governments forbade religious assemblages; now they evoke them. The father, the husband, and the brother sit now at the end

A Favored Nation

of the pew through custom—a custom established in the dark ages of persecution, when it was necessary for the male members of the family to sit at the head of the church pew, armed for defence of those who could not defend themselves. Now, on Thanksgiving Day we meet in churches at the call of secular authority.

I find great cause of congratulation in our municipal propects. Our present Mayor retires from office with the kind wishes of our citizens, and our new Mayor will enter with the moral support of all good people of all parties. Municipal reform is a perpetual work, and every few years there need to be official brooms to sweep the city halls. For lack of it you know how in former years New York suffered. Never since God corrected the politics of Sodom by burying the city in brimstone were there greater outrages enacted on earth than in these clusters of cities under the disguise of municipal government. Frauds about parks, about pavements, about station-houses, about pipes, about city halls, about aqueducts, about courts, about election-frauds about everything. Fraudulent men applied for contracts of fraudulent officials, who wrote the contracts upon paper they had stolen, and then went home over pavements every stone of which had been put down in dishonesty, and in carriages every spoke and rivet of which were the evidences of their crime. Fraudulent election inspectors sat around fraudulent ballot-boxes and took fraudulent votes and made fraudulent returns, and sent to our State Legislatures men fit only for the idiot asylum or the penitentiary. Things went on until the decent people in all our cities were for ten years under saddest depression. The newspapers did not dare speak out for fear they would lose the public printing. The pulpits did not dare to speak out because there were prominent men in the churches who had one hand on the spoils and the other on the throat of the clergy, telling them they had better be prudent and keep quiet. Matters were beyond all human redemption, and no statesmanship, no human skill could ever have met the crises. But the Lord Almighty rose up and he put it into the hearts of the best men of both parties to band together and lay their hands to the work. The monstrosities were exposed, the vagabonds of fraud were arrested, and the work extended from New York until Brooklyn and Philadelphia and Boston and Chicago and all the cities felt the moral earthquake.

But every few years the work needs to be done over again in all our cities. Our Brooklyn city government costs too much and our taxes are infamous. Do you say that the city has enlarged and therefore it costs more to govern it? Yes, it has mightily enlarged, but the taxable property has also mightily increased, and it ought not to cost as much to govern a city with six hundred thousand inhabitants as when it held three hundred thousand, because there are more now to bear the burden. There is something wrong in the neighborhood of the City Hall. May the incoming administration discover and extirpate it. For the brightening prospects in all our cities we may this day appropriately lift the Jubilate.

I have much also to congratulate you upon in the condition and prospects of the nation. We have the most thorough feeling of amity in this country that we ever had. The hatred between North and South is not only healed, but the scars are gone. The oldest man among us never saw such brotherhood as to-day. Is it not a pity that the North and South have nothing to quarrel about? What a dismal failure the campaign orators made in the last Presidential election in their attempt to stir up the old feuds. We were for a great many years before the war and some years after the

A Favored Nation

war under the delusion that we were at peace in this country, but there never has been any peace until within the past ten years.

Even at the time that Brooks was cudgeling Sumner and chains were stretched around Boston Court House to keep fugitives from escaping from the hands of the Marshal, and all our Northern cities were in riot and bloodshed about the relation of black men to their owners, we were under the delusion that we were at peace. Monstrous absurdity. It was war perpetual. Pennsylvania Hall burned on account of this political agitation in the city of Philadelphia—was that peace? The printing press of the Alton *Observer* was thrown into the river—was that peace? In 1820, when the air was hot with sectional imprecation about the admission of Missouri as a slave State—was that peace? The burning of a college in New Hampshire in 1835 because colored youth were admitted—was that peace? South Carolina nullification—was that peace? Presbyterian and Methodist churches North and South split with a fracture that shook all Christendom on account of political agitation—was that peace? No; all billingsgate and scorn and vituperation and hatred and revenge and blasphemy on both sides were exhausted. It was war of tongue, war of pen, war of trade, war of Church, war bitter, furious, consuming, relentless.

Thank God, that time has gone by! We have come to a new state of feeling and brotherhood such as we have never enjoyed, and our Congress, instead of spending nine-tenths of its time wasting the public treasury, discussing sectional difficulties as it used, will give nine-tenths of its time to the discussion of the agricultural, the mining, the manufacturing, the commercial, the literary, and the moral interests of this nation. Are we not to be thankful to God for this state of feeling? He has not dealt so with any other nation. Praise him all ye people!

I find further cause of congratulation in the development of our national resources. Our wisest men in all departments of merchandise say that business is looking up and that our greatest prosperities are yet to come. It is the inevitable law of nature, which is also the law of God, that the material resources of this country must in the future produce material wealth. You will hear the anvil ring with a sturdier blow. You will see the furnaces glow with a fiercer fire. You will see the wheel strike with a swifter dash. America has not yet been fully discovered. Various Americas have been found, but there are better ones perhaps to come. Columbus found only the shell of this country. Agassiz came along and discovered fossiliferous America. Silliman came and discovered geological America. Longfellow came and discovered poetic America. But there are other Americas yet to be found. Our resources have not all been tested. We have a land capable of supporting three thousand six hundred million of people.

We have just begun to open the outside door of this great underground vault in which nature holds its treasures, the copper, the zinc, the coal, the iron, the gold, the silver. If you have ever crossed the mountains to California you have some idea of it. The rail trains have only just begun to bring the harvests of the West down to our seaboard. The American fishermen have only just begun to cast their net on the right side of the ship. The dry-docks have just begun to set the keels and clamp the spars of our trading vessels.

What populations, what enterprises, what wealth, what civilization, what an advance from the time when under King Edward a man was put to death for burning coal and from the time when the House of Commons forbade the use of what was called the noxious fuels, and these days, when the long trains rush down from the mines and fill our coal-bins and gorge the furnaces of our ocean steamers. One hundred and sixty thousand square miles of coal-fields. Two fields of coal, one reaching from Illinois, down through Missouri, into Iowa, and the other from Pennsylvania down into Alabama, while side by side with these great coal-fields are the mines of iron; these two great giants, these two Titans of the earth, iron and coal, insuring perpetual wealth to the nation, standing side by side to help each other; the iron to excavate and pry up the coal, and the coal to smelt and forge and mould the iron—eight hundred thousand tons of iron sent forth from the mines in one year in this country; thirty-two million tons of coal sent out from the mines of this country in a year. And all this only a prophecy of a larger yield when we shall come on with larger trains and more miners and stronger machinery to develop and to gather up, to transfer and to employ all this treasure. Make this calculation for yourselves, if you can make it: If England's coal-field, thirty-two miles long by eight miles wide, can keep, as it does, seventeen million six hundred thousand spindles at work in that small island, what may we not expect of our national industries when these one hundred and sixty thousand square miles of coal shall unite with one hundred and sixty thousand square miles of iron, both stretching themselves up to full height and strength—two black, world-shaking giants.

Lift up thine eyes, oh, nation of God's right hand, at the glorious prospects. Build larger your barns for the harvests. Dig deeper the vats for the spoil of the vineyards, enlarge the warehouses for the merchandise. Multiply galleries of art for the pictures and statues. Advance, oh, nation of God's right hand. But remember that national wealth, if unsanctified, is sumptuous waste, is ruin, is debauchery, is magnificent woe, is splendid rottenness, is gilded death. Woe to us for the wine-vats if drunkenness wallows in them. Woe to us for the harvests if greed gathers them. Woe to us for the merchandise if avarice swallows it. Woe to us for the cities if misrule walks there. Woe to the land if God-defying crime debauches it. Our only safety is in more Bibles, more churches, more free schools, more consecrated men, more pure printing-presses, more of the glorious Gospel of the Son of God, that corrects all wrongs and is the source of all blessedness.

I congratulate you also on the fact that the manners and customs of society are improving. This is going to be a better world to live in. Take it all in all, it has vastly improved. I know that there are people who long for the good old times. They say, "Just think of the pride of people at this day! Just look at the ladies' hats, how big they are!" Why, there is nothing in the ladies' hats of to-day to equal the coal-scuttle hats a hundred years ago. They say, "Just look at the way the people dress their hair!" Why, the extremest style of to-day will never equal the top-knots which our great-grandmothers rolled up with high combs that we would have thought would have made our great-grandfathers die with laughter. The hair was lifted into a pyramid a foot high. On the top of that tower lay a rosebud. Shoes of bespangled white kid and heels two or three inches high. Grandfather went out to meet her on the floor with coat of sky-blue silk and vest of white satin embroidered with gold lace, lace ruffles around his wrists and his hair falling in a queue. Oh, you modern hair-dressers, stand aghast at the locks of our ancestry!

A Favored Nation

They say our ministers are all askew, but just think of our clergymen entering the pulpit with their hair fixed up in the shape of one of the ancient bishops. The great George Washington had his horse's hoofs blackened when about to appear on parade, and wrote to Europe ordering sent for the use of himself and family one silver-laced hat, one pair of silver shoe-buckles, a coat made of fashionable silk, one pair of gold sleeve-buttons, six pairs of kid gloves, one dozen most fashionable cambric handkerchiefs, besides ruffles and tucker.

I once said to my father, an aged man: "Are people so much worse now than they used to be?" He made no answer for a minute, for the old people do not like to confess much to the boys. But after awhile his eye twinkled and he said: "Well, DeWitt, the fact is that people were never any better than they ought to be."

Talk about dissipations, ye who ever have seen the old-fashioned sideboard. Did not I have an old relative who always, when visitors came, used to go upstairs and take a drink, through economical habits, not offering anything to the visitors. Many of the fancy drinks of to-day were unknown to them; but their hard cider, mint julep, metheglin, hot toddy and lemonade, in which the lemon was not at all prominent, sometimes made lively work for the broad-brimmed hats and silver knee-buckles. Talk of dissipating parties of to-day and keeping of late hours. Why, did they not have their bees and sausage-stuffings and tea-parties and dances that for heartiness and uproar truly eclipsed all the waltzes, lances, and redowas and breakdowns of the nineteenth century, And they never went home till morning. And as to old-time courtships, Washington Irving describes them.

Talk about the dishonesties of to-day! Fifty years ago, the Governor of New York State had to disband the Legislature because of its utter corruption. Think of Aaron Burr, Vice-President of the United States and coming within one vote of being President. Think of the ministry having in it such men as Dean Swift and Sterne, their genius only equaled by their nastiness. Why, society was so much worse than it now is that I do not see how our fathers and mothers could have been induced to stay in it, although on our account I am glad they consented.

"But," say the deprecators of our time, "just think of the awful wars we have in these days, one half of the nation rising up to kill the other half." Yet, there has been no war in modern times so ghastly as in the olden. Think of Austerlitz, where thirty thousand fell; of Fontenoy, where one hundred thousand fell; of Chalons, where three hundred thousand fell; of Marius's fight, in which two hundred and ninety thousand fell, and the tragedy at Herat, where Genghis Khan massacred one million six hundred thousand; of Neishar, where he slew one million seven hundred and forty-seven thousand, and the eighteen millions this monster slew in fourteen years as he went forth declaring his purpose of exterminating the entire Chinese nation and making the empire a pasture for cattle. Think of the death-throes of the five million men sacrificed in one campaign of Xerxes. Think of the one hundred and thirty thousand that perished in the siege of Ostend, of the three hundred thousand dead at Acre, of one million one hundred thousand dead at Jerusalem, of one million eight hundred and sixteen thousand dead at Troy. What may come of the threatened conflict on the other side the sea I know not, but up until the present time there has been no war compared with the wars of the ancients.

This Thanksgiving morning finds this land above all others in a position to be grateful. What are we

A Favored Nation

coming to in abundance when I tell you that only a part of this continent yields anything? Now that the Northern Pacific Railroad is through, all our resources are to be multiplied illimitably. Mr Dalrymple, in the Dakota Territory, has a farm of forty thousand acres; in harvest time he has one hundred and twenty reapers and binders going at the same time. The different divisions of his farm are connected by telephone; thirty steam threshing-machines, men in corps like an army, his farm one year yielding four hundred and thirty-two thousand bushels of wheat—nine hundred car-loads; the Grandon farm, twenty-five thousand acres; the Case farm, fifteen thousand acres; the Cheney, fifteen thousand acres; the Williams farm, fifteen thousand acres—the product of all these regions only limited by the means of transportation to market. Our land enriched by a vast multitude of foreigners who came here, not the tramps or the tatterdemalions of other lands, but tens of thousands of them their best citizens. Let us this morning thank God for the prospects opening before this nation.

Oh, wheel into the ranks, all ye people! North, South, East, West; all decades, all centuries, all millenniums. Forward, the whole line! Huzza! Huzza!

NATIONAL RUIN

Rev., 18: 10: "Alas, alas, that **great** **city** Babylon, that
mighty city! for in one hour is thy judgment come."

NATIONAL RUIN

Rev., 18: 10: "Alas, alas, that **great** city Babylon, that mighty city! for in one hour is thy judgment come."

On cis-Atlantic shores a company of American scientists are now landing, on their way to find the tomb of a dead empire holding in its arms a dead city, mother and child of the same name—Babylon. The ancient mounds will invite the spades and shovels and crowbars, while the unwashed natives look on in surprise. Our scientific friends will find yellow bricks still impressed with the name of Nebuchadnezzar, and they will go down into the sarcophagus of a monarchy buried more than two thousand years ago. May the explorations of Rawlinson and Layard and Chevalier and Opperto and Loftus and Chesney be eclipsed by the present archæological uncovering.

But is it possible that this is all that remains of Babylon? A city once five times larger than London, and twelve times larger than New York, Walls three hundred and seventy-three feet high, and ninety-three feet thick. Twenty-five burnished gates on each side, with streets running clear through to corresponding gates on the other side. Six hundred and twenty-five squares. More pomp and wealth and splendor and sin than could be found in any five modern cities combined. A city of palaces and temples. A city having within it a garden on an artificial hill four hundred feet high, the sides of the mountain terraced. All this built to keep the king's wife, Amyitis, from becoming homesick for the mountainous region in which she had spent her girlhood. The waters of the Euphrates spouted up to irrigate this great altitude into fruits and flowers and arborescence unimaginable. A great river running from north to south clear through the city, bridges over it, tunnels under it, boats on it. A city of bazaars and of market-places, unrivaled for aromatics and unguents and high-mettled horses, with grooms by their side, and thyme wood, and African evergreen, and Egyptian linen, and all styles of costly textile fabric, and rarest purples extracted from shell-fish on the Mediterranean coast, and rarest scarlets taken from brilliant insects in Spain, and ivories brought from successful elephantine hunts in India, and diamonds whose flash was a repartee to the sun. Fortress within fortress, embattlement rising above embattlement. Great capital of the ages. But one night, while honest citizens were asleep, but all the saloons of saturnalia were in full blast, and at the king's castle they had filled the tankards for the tenth time, and reeling, and guffawing, and hiccoughing, around the state table were the rulers of the land, General Cyrus ordered his besieging army to take shovels and spades, and they diverted the river from its usual channel into another direction, so that the forsaken bed of the river became the path on which the besieging army entered. When the morning dawned the conquerors were inside the outside trenches. Babylon had fallen, and hence the sublime threnody of the text: "Alas, alas, that great city Babylon, that mighty city, for in one hour is thy judgment come."

But do nations die? Oh, yes, there is great mortality among monarchies and republics. They are like individuals in the fact that they are born, they have a middle life, they have a decease; they have a cradle and a grave. Some of them are assassinated, some destroyed by their own hand. Have we a right to conclude that because our republic is alive to-day it will be alive forever? Let me call the roll of some of the dead civilizations and some of the dead cities and let some one answer for them. Egyptian civilization, stand up. "Dead!" answer the ruins of Karnak and Luxor, and from seventy pyramids on the east side of the Nile there comes a chorus crying: "Dead, dead!" Assyrian Empire, stand up, and answer. "Dead!" cry the charred ruins of Nineveh. After six hundred years of magnificent opportunity, dead. Israelitish kingdom, stand up. After two hundred and fifty years of divine interposition, and of miraculous vicissitude and of heroic behavior, and of appalling depravity, dead. Phœnicia, stand up and answer. After inventing the alphabet and giving it to the world, and sending out her merchant caravans in one direction to Central Asia, and sending out navigators to the Atlantic Ocean in another direction, dead. Pillars of Hercules, and rocks on which the Tyrian fishermen dried their nets, all answer, "Dead Phœnicia." Athens, after Phidias, after Demosthenes, after Miltiades, dead. Sparta, after Leonidas, after Eurybiades, after Salamis, after Thermopylæ, dead. Roman Empire, stand up and answer. Empire once bounded by the British Channel on the north, by the Euphrates on the east, by the great Sahara Desert in Africa on the south, by the Atlantic Ocean on the west. Home of three great civilizations, owning all the then discovered world that was worth owning—Roman Empire, answer. Gibbon, in his "Rise and Fall of the Roman Empire," says: "Dead!" and the forsaken seats of the ruined Coliseum, and the skeleton of the aqueducts, and the miasma of the Campagna, and the fragments of the marble baths, and the useless piers of the Bridge Triumphalis, and the Mamartine prison, holding no more apostolic prisoners, and the silent Forum, and Basilica of Constantine, and the Arch of Titus and the Pantheon come in with great chorus, crying:

Sermons by T. DeWitt Talmage

"Dead, dead!" After Horace, after Virgil, after Tacitus, after Cicero, dead. After Horatius on the bridge, and Cincinnatus, the farmer oligarch, after Pompey, after Scipio, after Cassius, after Constantine, after Cæsar, dead. The war eagle of Rome flew so high it was blinded by the sun, and came whirling down through the heavens, and the owl of desolation and darkness built its nest in the forsaken eyrie. Mexican Empire, dead. French Empire, dead.

You see, my friends, it is no unusual thing for a government to perish, and in the same necrology of dead nations, and in the same graveyard of expired governments will go the United States of America unless there be some potent voice to call a halt and unless God in his mercy interfere, and through a purified ballot-box and a widespread Christian sentiment the catastrophe be averted. This nation is about to go to the ballot-box to exercise the right of suffrage, and I propose this morning, and in following Sabbath mornings, to set before you the evils that threaten to destroy the American government, and to annihilate American institutions, and if God will help me I will show you before I get through with these discourses the mode in which each and every one may do something to arrest that appalling calamity. And I shall plough up the whole field.

The first evil that threatens the annihilation of our American institutions is the fact that political bribery, which once was considered a crime, has by many come to be considered a tolerable peccadillo. Whole States swept by the scourge of political bribery. The pedlers carrying gold from Wall Street, gold from Third Street, gold from State Street, and gold from the Brewers' Association, are at all the political headquarters of the doubtful States, dealing out the infamous inducement. Then it is not only the money spent for votes, but the success of the election will be used as a bribe for the whole nation, inducing the multitude of men who sit on the fence to jump off and run with the triumphant party for the one hundred thousand offices at disposal. Such an election will not let you know whom the State wants for President of the United States. It will only indicate which party has the largest exchequer.

After one Presidential election a banquet was spread in New York to celebrate the victory, and in the presence of many of the mightiest men of the nation it was announced that one of the States had been bought up—had been carried in the election by bribery. Another word was used than the word bribery, but everybody understood. There was no surprise. Everybody knew which State had been bought. There used to be bribery, but it held its head in shame. It was under the utmost secrecy that many years ago a railroad company bought up the Wisconsin Legislature and many other public officials in that State. The Governor of the State at that time received fifty thousand dollars for his signature. His private secretary received five thousand dollars. Thirteen members of the Senate received one hundred and seventy-five thousand dollars in bonds. Sixty members of the other house received from five to ten thousand dollars each. The Lieutenant-Governor received ten thousand dollars. The clerks of the house received from five to ten thousand dollars each. The Bank Comptroller received ten thousand dollars. Two hundred and fifty thousand dollars were divided among the legislators and officials by the lobbyists. You see, the railroad company was very generous. But all that was hidden, and only through the severest scrutiny on the part of a legislative committee was this iniquity displayed. Now, political bribery defies you, dares you, is arrogant, and will probably decide the election on the first Tuesday of next November. Unless this diabolism ceases in this country, Bartholdi's statue, on Bedloe's Island, with uplifted torch to light other nations into the harbor, had better be changed, and the torch dropped as a symbol of universal incendiarism. Unless this purchase and sale of suffrage shall cease, the American Government will expire, and you might as well be getting ready the monument for another dead nation, and let my text inscribe upon it these words: "Alas! alas! for Babylon, that great city, that mighty city, for in one hour is thy judgment come." If you have not noticed that political bribery is one of the ghastly crimes of this day, you have not kept your eyes open.

Another evil which in former years threatened the destruction of American institutions, but which has now fortunately disappeared, was the solidifying of the sections against each other. A solid North, a solid South. If this had gone on, we should after a while have had a solid East against a solid West, solid Middle States against solid Northern States, a solid New York against a solid Pennsylvania, and a solid Ohio against a solid Kentucky. It is many years since the war closed, and yet at every Presidential election the old antagonism has been aroused.

When Garfield died, and all the States gathered around his casket in sympathy and in tears, and as hearty telegrams of condolence came from New Orleans and from Charleston as from Boston and Chicago, I said to myself: "I think sectionalism is dead." But alas! no. The difficulty will never be ended until each State of the nation is split up into two or three great political parties. This country cannot exist unless it exists as one body, the national capital the heart, sending out through all the arteries of communication warmth and life to the very extremities. This nation cannot exist unless it exists as one family, and

National Ruin

you might as well array solid brothers against solid sisters, and a solid bread-tray against a solid cradle, and a solid nursery against a solid dining-room; and you might as well have solid ears against solid eyes, and solid head against solid foot. What is the interest of Georgia is the interest of Massachusetts; what is the interest of New York is the interest of South Carolina. Does the Ohio River change its politics when it gets below Louisville? It is not possible for these sectional antagonisms to continue for a great many years without permanent compound fracture.

Another evil threatening the destruction of our American institutions is the low state of public morals. What killed Babylon of my text? What killed Phœnica? What killed Rome? Their own depravity; and the fraud and the drunkenness and the lechery which have destroyed other nations will destroy ours, unless a merciful God prevent. To show you the low state of public morals, I have to call your attention to the fact that many men nominated for offices in the State and nation at different times are entirely unfit for the positions for which they have been nominated. We have now ten persons nominated for the offices of President and Vice-President. Two of them are women. They are good. But three out of the eight men nominated for the offices of President and Vice-President have no more qualification for them than a wolf has qualification to be professor of pastoral theology in a flock of sheep, or a blind mole has qualification to lecture a class of eagles on optics, or than a vulture has qualification to chaperon a dove. The mere pronunciation of some of their names makes a demand for carbolic acid and fumigation! Yet Christian men will follow right on under the political standards.

Sermons by T. DeWitt Talmage

I have to tell you what you know already, that American politics have sunken to such a low depth that there is nothing beneath. What we see in some directions we see in nearly all directions. The peculation and the knavery hurled to the surface by the explosion of banks and business firms are only specimens of great Cotopaxis and Strombolis of wickedness that boil and roar and surge beneath, but have not yet regurgitated to the surface. When the heaven-descended Democratic party enacted the Tweed rascality it seemed to eclipse everything; but after a while the heaven-descended Republican party outwitted pandemonium with the Star Route infamy.

We have in this country people who say the marriage institution amounts to nothing. They scoff at it. We have people walking in polite parlors in our day who are not good enough to be scavengers in Sodom! I went over to San Francisco four or five years ago—that beautiful city, that queen of the Pacific. May the blessing of God come down upon her great churches and her noble men and women! When I got into the city of San Francisco, the mayor of the city and the president of the Board of Health called on me and insisted that I go and see the Chinese quarters; no doubt so that on my return to the Atlantic coast I might tell what dreadful people the Chinese are. But on the last night of my stay in San Francisco, before thousands of people in their great opera house, I said: "Would you like me to tell you just what I think, plainly and honestly?" They said: "Yes, yes, yes!" I said: "Do you think you can stand it all?" They said: "Yes, yes, yes!" "Then," I said, "my opinion is that the curse of San Francisco is not your Chinese quarters, but your millionaire libertines!" And two of them sat right before me—Felix and Drusilla. And so it is in all the cities. I never swear, but when I see a man go unwhipt of justice, laughing over his shame and calling his damnable deeds gallantry and peccadillo, I am tempted to hurl red-hot anathema and to conclude that if, according to some people's theology, there is no hell, there ought to be!

There is enough out-and-out licentiousness in American cities to-day to bring down upon them the wrath of that God who, on the 24th of August, 79, buried Herculaneum and Pompeii so deep in ashes that the eighteen hundred subsequent years have not been able to complete the exhumation. There are in American cities to-day whole blocks of houses which the police know to be infamous, and yet by purchase they are silenced, by hush money; so that such places are as much under the defence of the government as public libraries and asylums of mercy. These ulcers on the body politic bleed and gangrene away the life of the nation, and public authority in many of the cities looks the other way. You cannot cure such wounds as these with a silken bandage. You will have to cure them by putting deep in the lancet of moral surgery and burning them out with the caustic of holy wrath and with most decisive amputation cutting off the scabrous and putrefying abominations. As the Romans were after the Celts, and as the Normans were after the Britons, so there are evils after this nation which will attend the obsequies unless we first attend theirs.

Superstition tells of a marine reptile, the cephaloptera, which enfolded and crushed a ship of war; but it is no superstition when I tell you that the history of many of the dead nations proclaims to us the fact that our ship of state is in danger of being crushed by the cephaloptera of national depravity. Where is the Hercules to slay this hydra? Is it not time to speak by pen, by tongue, by ballot-box, by the rolling of the prison door, by hangman's halter, by earnest prayer, by Sinaitic detonation? A son of King Crœsus is said to have been dumb and to have never uttered a word until he saw his father being put to death. Then he broke the shackles of silence, and cried out: "Kill not my father, Crœsus!" When I see the cheatery and the wantonness and the manifold crime of this country attempting to commit patricide—yea, matricide—upon our institutions, it seems to me that lips that heretofore have been dumb ought to break the silence with thunderous tones of fiery protest.

I want to put all of the matter before you, so that every honest man and woman will know just how matters stand, and what they ought to do if they vote, and what they ought to do if they pray. This nation is not going to perish. Alexander, when he heard of the wealth of the Indies, divided Macedonia among his soldiers. Some one asked him what he had kept for himself, and he replied: "I am keeping hope." And that jewel I keep bright and shining in my soul, whatever else I shall surrender. "Hope, thou, in God." He will set back these oceanic tides of moral devastation.

Do you know what is the prize for which contention is made to-day? It is the prize of this continent. Never since the hour when, according to Milton, Satan was

> Hurled headlong flaming from the ethereal sky,
> With hideous ruin and combustion down,

have the powers of darkness been so determined to win this continent as they are now. What a jewel it is—a jewel carved in relief, the cameo of this planet! On one side of us the Atlantic Ocean, dividing us from the worn-out governments of Europe. On the other side the Pacific Ocean, dividing us from the superstitions of Asia. On the north of us the Arctic Sea, which is the gymnasium in which the explorers and navigators develop their courage. A continent ten thousand five hundred miles long, seventeen million square miles, and all of it but about one-seventh capable of rich cultivation. One hundred millions of population on this continent of North and South America—one hundred millions, and room for many hundred millions more. All flora and all fauna, all metals, and all precious woods, and all grains and all fruits. The Appalachian range the backbone and the rivers the ganglia carrying life all through and out to the extremities. Isthmus of Darien the narrow waist of a giant continent, all to be under one government, and all free and all Christian, and the scene of Christ's personal reign on earth if, according to the expectation of many good people, he shall at last set up his throne in this world. Who shall have this hemisphere—Christ or Satan? Who shall have the shore of her inland seas, the silver of her Nevadas, the gold of her Colorados, the telescopes of her observatories, the brain of her universities, the wheat of her prairies, the rice of her savannas, the two great ocean beaches—the one reaching from Baffin's Bay to Terra del Fuego, and the other from Behring Straits to Cape Horn—and all the moral, and temporal, and spiritual, and everlasting interests of a population vast beyond all computation save by him with whom a thousand years are as one day? Who shall have the hemisphere? You and I will decide that, or help to decide it, by conscientious vote, by earnest prayer, by maintenance of Christian institutions, by support of great philanthropies, by putting body, mind and soul on the right side of all moral, religious, and national movements.

Ah! it will not be long before it will not make any difference to you or to me what becomes of this continent, so far as earthly comfort is concerned. All we will want of it will be seven feet by three, and that will take in the largest, and there will be room and to spare. That is all of this country we will need very soon, the youngest of us. But we have an anxiety about the welfare and the happiness of the generations that are coming on, and it will be a grand thing if, when the archangel's trumpet sounds, we find that our sepulchre, like the one Joseph of Arimathea provided for Christ, is in the midst of a garden. By that time this country will be all Paradise, or all Dry Tortugas. Eternal God, to thee we commit the destiny of this people!

THE TIMES WE LIVE IN

Esther, 4: 14: " Who knoweth whether thou art come to
the kingdom for such a time at this? "

THE TIMES WE LIVE IN

Esther, 4: 14: " Who knoweth whether thou art come to the kingdom for such a time at this? "

Esther the beautiful was the wife of Ahasuerus the abominable. The time had come for her to present a petition to her infamous husband in behalf of the Jewish nation, to which she had once belonged. She was afraid to undertake the work, lest she should lose her own life; but her cousin Mordecai, who had brought her up, encouraged her with the suggestion that probably she had been raised up of God for that peculiar mission. "Who knoweth whether thou art come to the kingdom for such a time as this." Esther had her God-appointed work; you and I have ours. It is my business to tell you what style of men and women you ought to be in order that you may meet the demand of the age in which God has cast your lot. If you have come expecting to hear abstractions discussed, or dry technicalities of religion glorified, you have come to the wrong church, but if you really would like to know what this age has a right to expect of you as Christian men and women, then I am ready, in the Lord's name, to look you in the face.

When two armies have rushed into battle, the officers of each army do not want a philosophical discussion about the chemical properties of human blood or the nature of gunpowder; they want some one to man the batteries and swab out the guns. And now, when all the forces of light and darkness, of heaven and hell, have plunged into the fight, it is no time to give ourselves to the definitions and formulas and technicalities and conventionalities of religion. What we want is practical, earnest, concentrated, enthusiastic and triumphant help.

In the first place, in order to meet the special demand of this age, you need to be unmistakably aggressive Christians. Of half-and-half Christians we do not want any more. The Church of Jesus Christ would be better without ten thousand of them. They are the chief obstacles to the Church's advancement. I am speaking of another kind of Christian. All the appliances for your becoming an earnest Christian are at your hand, and there is a straight path for you into the broad daylight of God's forgiveness. You may have come into the Church the bondmen of the world, and yet before you go out you may become princes of the Lord God Almighty.

You remember what excitement there was in this country when the Prince of Wales came here—how the people rushed out by hundreds of thousands to see him. Why? Because they expected that some day he would sit upon the throne of England. But what was all that honor compared with the honor to which God calls you—to be sons and daughters of the Lord Almighty—yea, to be queens and kings unto God? "They shall reign with him forever and forever." But you need to be aggressive Christians, and not like persons who spend their lives in hugging their Christian graces and wondering why they do not make any progress. How much robustness of health would a man have if he hid himself in a dark closet? A great deal of the piety of the day is too exclusive. It hides itself. It needs more of fresh air, more out-door exercise. There are many Christians who are giving their entire life to self-examination. They are feeling their pulses to see what is the condition of their spiritual health. How long would a man have robust physical health if he kept all the days and weeks and months and years of his life feeling his pulse, instead of going out into earnest, active, every-day work? I have been among the wonderful and bewitching cactus growths of North Carolina, where I never was more bewildered with the beauty of flowers. Yet, when I would take up one of these cactuses and pull the leaves apart, the beauty was all gone. You could hardly tell that it had been a flower. And there are a great many Christian people in this day just pulling apart their own Christian experiences to see what there is in them, and there is nothing left of them. This style of self-examination is a damage instead of an advantage to their Christian character. I remember, when I was a boy, I used to have a small piece in the garden that I called my own, and I planted corn there, and every few days I would pull it up to see how fast it was growing. Now, there are a great many Christian people in this day whose self-examination merely amounts to the pulling up of that which they only yesterday or the day before planted. If you want to have a stalwart Christian character, plant it right out of doors in the great field of Christian usefulness, and though storms may come upon it, and though the hot sun of trial may try to consume it, it will thrive until it becomes a great tree, in which the fowls of heaven may have a habitation. I have no patience with these flower-pot Christians. They keep themselves under shelter, and all their Christian experience in a small and exclusive circle, when they ought to plant it in the great garden of the Lord, so that the whole atmosphere would be aromatic with their Christian piety. The century plant is wonderfully suggestive and wonderfully beautiful; but I never look at it without thinking of its parsimony. It lets whole generations go by before it puts forth one blossom; so I have really more heartfelt admiration when I see the dewy tears in the

Average Life Span
32 yrs?

blue eyes of the violets, for they come every spring. Time is going by so rapidly that we cannot afford to be idle. A recent statistician says that human life now has an average of thirty-two years. From these thirty-two years you must subtract all the time you take for sleep and the taking of food and recreation; that will leave you about sixteen years. From these sixteen years you must subtract all the time that you are necessarily engaged in the earning of a livelihood; that will leave you about eight years. From these eight years you must take all the days and weeks and months—all the length of time that is passed in sickness—leaving you about seven years in which to work for God. O my soul, wake up! How darest thou sleep in harvest-time, and with so few hours in which to reap? So I state it as a simple fact that all the time that the vast majority of you will have for the exclusive service of God will be less than seven years.

"But," says some man, "I liberally support the Gospel, and the Gospel is preached; all the spiritual advantages are spread before men, and if they want to be saved let them come to be saved; I have discharged all my responsibility." Is that the Master's spirit? Is there not an old Book somewhere that commands us to "go out into the highways and hedges and compel the people to come in?" What would have become of you and me if Christ had not come down off the hills of heaven, and if he had not come through the door of the Bethlehem caravansary, and if he had not with the crushed hand of the crucifixion knocked at the iron gate of the sepulchre of our spiritual death, crying, "Lazarus, come forth!"

Oh, friends, this is no time for inertia, when all the forces of darkness seem to be in full blast, when steam printing presses are publishing infidel tracts, when express railroad trains are carrying messengers of sin, when fast clippers are laden with opium and rum, when the night air of our cities is polluted with the laughter that breaks up from the ten thousand saloons of dissipation and abandonment. The fires of the second death already are kindled in the cheeks of some who only a little while ago were incorrupt. Oh, never since the curse fell upon the earth has there been a time when it was such an unwise, such a cruel, such an awful thing for the Church to sleep! The great audiences are not gathered in the Christian temples; they are gathered in temples of sin—tears of unutterable woe, their baptism; the blood of crushed hearts, the awful wine of their sacrament; blasphemies, their litany; and the groans of the lost world, the organ-dirge of their worship.

Again, if you want to be qualified to meet the duties which this age demands of you, you must on the one hand avoid reckless iconoclasm, and on the other hand, not stick too much to things because they are old. The air is full of new plans, new projects, new theories of government, new theologies; and I am amazed to see how many Christians want only novelty in order to recommend a thing to their confidence, and so they vacillate, and swing to and fro, and are useless, and they are unhappy. New plans—secular, ethical, philosophical, religious, cis-Atlantic, trans-Atlantic, long enough to make a line reaching from the German universities to the great Salt Lake City! Ah, do not take hold of a thing merely because it is new. Try it by the realities of a judgment day. But, on the other hand, do not adhere to anything merely because it is old. There is not a single enterprise of the Church or the world but has sometimes been scoffed at. There was a time when men derided even Bible societies; and when a few young men met near a haystack in Massachusetts and organized the first missionary society ever organized in this country, there went laughter and ridicule all around the Christian Church. They said the undertaking was preposterous. And so also the ministry of Jesus Christ was assailed. People cried out: "Who ever heard of such theories of ethics and government? Who ever listened to such a style of preaching as Jesus has?" Ezekiel had talked of mysterious wings and wheels. Here came a man from Nazareth and Capernaum and Genessaret and he drew his illustrations from the lakes, from the sand, from the raven, from the lilies, from the cornstacks. How the Pharisees scoffed! How Herod derided! And this Jesus they plucked by the beard, and they spat in his face, and they called him "this fellow." All the great enterprises in and out of the Church have at times been scoffed at, and there have been a great multitude who have thought that the chariot of God's truth would fall to pieces if it once got out of the old rut.

And so there are those who have no patience with anything like improvement in church architecture, or with anything like good, hearty, earnest church singing, and they deride every form of religious discussion which goes down walking with every-day men rather than that which makes an excursion on rhetorical stilts. Oh, that the Church of God would wake up to an adaptability of work! We must admit the simple fact that the churches of Jesus Christ in this day do not reach the great masses of mankind. There are fifty thousand people in Edinburgh who never hear the Gospel. There are two hundred thousand people in Glasgow who never hear the Gospel. There are one million people in London who never hear the Gospel. There are at least three hundred thousand souls in the city of Brooklyn who come not under the immediate ministration of Christ's truth; and the

Church of God to this day, instead of being a place full of "living epistles read and known of all men," is more like a "dead-letter" post-office.

"But," say the people, "the world is going to be converted; you must be patient; the kingdoms of this world are to become the kingdoms of Christ." Never, unless the Church of Jesus Christ puts on more speed and energy. Instead of the Church converting the world, the world is converting the Church! Here is a great fortress. How shall it be taken? An army comes and sits around about it, cuts off the supplies and says, "Now we will just wait until, from exhaustion and starvation, they will have to give up." Weeks and months, and perhaps a year, pass along, and finally the fortress surrenders through that starvation and exhaustion. But the fortresses of sin are never to be taken in that way. If they are taken for God, it will be by storm. You will have to bring up the great siege guns of the Gospel to the very wall and wheel the flying artillery into line, and when the armed infantry of heaven shall confront the battlements, you will have to give the quick command, "Forward, charge!"

There is work for you and for me right before us. Here is my pulpit and my preaching. Your pulpit is the bank. Your pulpit is the store. Your pulpit is the editorial chair. Your pulpit is the anvil. Your pulpit is the house scaffolding. Your pulpit is the mechanic's shop. I may stand in the pulpit, and through cowardice or through self-seeking may keep back the word I ought to utter, while you, with sleeve rolled up and brow besweated with toil, may utter the word that will bring on the shout of a great victory.

Oh, that you all might feel that the Lord Almighty was putting upon you the hands of ordination! Go forth and preach this Gospel. You have as much right to preach as I have, or as any man has. Only find out the pulpit where God would have you preach, and there preach. Hedley Vicars was a wicked man in the English army. The grace of God came to him. He became an earnest and eminent Christian. They scoffed at him and said, "You are a hypocrite; you are as bad as ever you were." Still he kept his faith in Christ, and after a while, finding that they could not turn him aside by calling him a hypocrite, they said to him, "Oh, you are nothing but a Methodist." That did not disturb him. He went on performing his Christian duty until he had formed all his troop into a Bible class, and the whole encampment was shaken with the presence of God. So Havelock went into the heathen temple in India, while the English army was there, and put a candle into the hands of each of the heathen gods that stood around in the heathen temple, and by the light of those candles held up by the idols, General Havelock preached righteousness, temperance and judgment to come. And who will say, on earth or in heaven, that Havelock had not the right to preach?

In the minister's house where I prepared for college there worked a man by the name of Peter Croy. He could neither read nor write, but he was a man of God. Often theologians would stop in the house— grave theologians—and at family prayer Peter Croy would be called upon to lead; and all those wise men sat around, wonder-struck at his religious efficiency. When he prayed he reached up and seemed to take hold of the very throne of the Almighty, and he talked with God until the very heavens were bowed down into the sitting-room. If I were dying I would rather have plain Peter Croy kneel by my bedside and commend my immortal spirit to God than the greatest arch-

bishop arrayed in costly canonicals! Go preach this
Gospel. You say you are not licensed. In the name
of the Lord Almighty, I license you. Go preach this
Gospel—preach it in the Sabbath schools, in the prayer
meetings, in the highways, in the hedges. Woe be
unto you if you preach it not!

I remark again that in order to be qualified to
meet your duty in this particular age, you want un-
bounded faith in the triumph of the truth and in the
overthrow of wickedness. How dare the Christian
Church ever get discouraged? Have we not the Lord
on our side? How long did it take God to slay the
hosts of Sennacherib, or burn Sodom, or shake down
Jericho? How long will it take God, when he once
arises in his strength, to overthrow all the forces of
iniquity? Between this time and that there may be
long seasons of darkness, the chariot wheels of God's
Gospel may seem to drag heavily; but there is the
promise, and yonder is the throne, and when Omniscience has lost its eyesight, and Omnipotence falls
back impotent, and Jehovah is driven from his throne,
then the Church of Jesus Christ can afford to be despondent, but never until then.

Despots may plan and armies may march and the
congresses of the nations may seem to think they are
adjusting all the affairs of the world, but the kings
of the earth are only the dust of the chariot wheels of
God's providence. And I hope that before the sun of
this century shall have set the last tyranny will fall,
and with a splendor of demonstration that shall be the
astonishment of the universe, God will set forth the
brightness and pomp and glory and perpetuity of
his eternal government. Out of the starry flags and
the emblazoned insignia of this world God will
make a path for his own triumph, and returning from

universal conquest, he will sit down, the grandest, strongest, highest throne of earth his footstool.

> Then shall all nations' song ascend
> To thee, our Father, Ruler, Friend,
> Till heaven's high arch resound again
> With peace on earth, good will to men.

I preach this sermon because I want to encourage all Christian workers in every possible department. Hosts of the living God, march on! march on! His spirit will bless you. His shield will defend you. His sword will strike for you. March on! march on! The despotisms will fall, and paganism will burn its idols, and Mohammedanism will give up its false prophet, and Judaism will confess the true Messiah, and the great walls of superstition will come down in thunder and in wreck at the long, loud blast of the Gospel trumpet. March on! march on! The besiegement will soon be ended. Only a few more steps on the long way; only a few more sturdy blows; only a few more battle-cries; and then God will put the laurel upon your brow, and from the living fountains of heaven will bathe off the sweat and the heat and the dust of the conflict. March on! march on! For you the time for work will soon be passed, and amid the outflashings of the judgment throne, and the trumpeting of the resurrection angels, and the upheaving of a world of graves, and the hosanna and the groaning of the saved and the lost, we shall be rewarded for our faithfulness or punished for our stupidity. Blessed be the Lord God of Israel, from everlasting to everlasting, and let the whole world be filled with his glory!

WASHINGTON FOR GOD

Luke, 24: 47: " Beginning at Jerusalem,"

WASHINGTON FOR GOD*

Luke, 24: 47: "Beginning at Jerusalem."

"There it is," said the driver, and we all instantly and excitedly rose in the carriage to catch the first glimpse of Jerusalem, so long the joy of the whole earth. That city, coroneted with temple and palace and radiant, whether looked up at from the valley of Jehoshaphat or gazed at from adjoining hills, was the capital of a great nation. Clouds of incense had hovered over it. Chariots of kings had rolled throt ;h it. Battering-rams of enemies had thundered against it. There Isaiah prophesied, and Jeremiah lamented, and David reigned, and Paul preached, and Christ was martyred. Most interesting city ever built since masonry rung its first trowel, or plumb-line tested its first wall, or royalty swung its first sceptre. What Jerusalem was to the Jewish kingdom, Washington is to our own country—the capital, the place to which all the tribes come up, the great national heart whose throb sends life or death through the body politic, clear out to the geographical extremities.

What the resurrected Christ said in my text to his disciples, when he ordered them to start on the work of Gospelization, "beginning at Jerusalem," it seems to me God says now, in his Providence, to tens of thousands of Christians in this city. Start for the evangelization of America, "beginning at Washington." America is going to be taken for God. As surely as God lives, and he is able to do as he says he

* This sermon was preached by Dr. Talmage in the First Presbyterian Church of Washington, of which he was then pastor.

will, this country will be evangelized from the mouth of the Potomac to the mouth of the Oregon, from the Highlands of Navesink to the Golden Horn, from Baffin's Bay to the Gulf of Mexico; and Christ will walk every lake, whether bestormed or placid, and be transfigured on every mountain, and the night skies, whether they hover over groves of magnolia or over Alaskan glacier, shall be filled with angelic overture of "Glory to God and good-will to men." Warned by the doom of nations which declined the mission on which they were sent and perished, I pray that this nation may accept its high work of emancipating the hemispheres.

Again and again does the old Book promise that all the earth shall see the salvation of God, and as the greater includes the lesser, that takes America gloriously in. Can you not see that if America is not taken for God by his consecrated people, it will be taken for Apollyon! The forces engaged on both sides are so tremendous that it cannot be a drawn battle. It is coming, the Armageddon! Either the American Sabbath will perish and this nation be handed over to Herods and Hildebrands and Diocletians and Neros of baleful power; and Alcoholism will reign, seated upon piled-up throne of beer barrels, his mouth foaming with domestic and national curse; and crime will lift its unhindered knife of assassination, and rattle keys of worst burglary, and wave torch of wildest conflagration, and our cities be turned into Sodoms, waiting for Almighty tempests of fire and brimstone, and one tidal wave of abominations will surge across the continent—or our Sabbaths will take on more sanctity, and the newspapers will become apocalyptic wings of benediction, and penitentiaries will be abandoned for lack of occupants, and holiness and happiness, twin son and daughter of heaven, shall

292

walk through the land, and Christ reign over this nation either in person or by agency so glorious that the whole country will be one clear, resounding echo of heaven. It will be one or the other. By the throne of him who liveth forever and ever, I declare it will be the latter. If the Lord will help me, as he always does—blessed be his glorious name!—I will show you how a mighty work of grace begun at Washington would have a tendency to bring the whole continent to God, and before this century closes.

William the Conqueror ordered the curfew, the custom of ringing the bell at midnight, at which all the fires on the hearths were to be banked, and all the lights extinguished, and all the people retire to their pillows. I pray God that the curfew of this century may not be sounded and the fires be banked and the lights extinguished, as the clock strikes the midnight hour that divides the nineteenth century from the twentieth century, until this beloved land, which was to most of us a cradle and which will be to most of us a grave, shall come into the full possession of him who is so glorious that William the Conqueror could not be compared to him, even the One who rideth forth, "conquering and to conquer."

Why would it be especially advantageous if a mighty work of grace started here, "beginning at Washington?" First, because this city is on the border between the North and the South. It is neither Northern nor Southern. It commingles the two climates. It brings together the two elements of population. It is not only right, but beautiful, that people should have especial love for the latitude where they were born and brought up. With what loving accentuation the Alabamian speaks of his orange groves! And the man from Massachusetts is sure to let you know that he comes from the land of the Adamses—Samuel and John and John Quincy. Did you ever know a Virginian or Ohioan whose face did not brighten when he announced himself from the Southern or Northern State of Presidents? If a man does not like his native clime, it is because while he lived there, he did not behave well. Our capital stands where, by its locality and political influence, it stretches forth one hand toward the North and the other toward the South, and if it had another it would be held out to the great West, so that a mighty work of grace starting here would probably be a national awakening. Georgia would clasp the hand of New Hampshire, and Maine the hand of Louisiana, and California the hand of New York, and say: "Come, let us go up and worship the God of Nations, the Christ of Golgotha, the Holy Ghost of the pentecostal three thousands." It had often been said that the only way the North and the South could be brought into complete accord, would be to have a war with some foreign nation, in which both sections, marching side by side, should forget everything but the foe to be overcome. Well, so it has proved. The war with Spain has made the sections forget past controversies; but what is needed is a war against unrighteousness, such as a universal religious awakening would declare. What we want is a battle for souls, in which about forty million Northerners and Southerners shall be on the same side, and shoulder to shoulder. In no other city on the continent can such a war be declared so appropriately, for all the other great cities are either Northern or Southern or Western. This is neither, or, rather, it is all.

Again, it would be especially advantageous if a mighty work of grace started here, because more representative men are in Washington than in any other city between the oceans. Of course there are accidents in politics, and occasionally there are men who get into the Senate and House of Representatives and other important places who are fitted for the positions in neither head nor heart; but this is exceptional and more exceptional now than in other days. There is not a drunkard in the National Legislature, although there were times when Kentucky, Virginia, Delaware, Illinois, New York, and Massachusetts had men in Senate or House of Representatives who went maudlin and staggering drunk across those high places. Never nobler group of men sat in Senate or House of Representatives than sat there yesterday and will sit there to-morrow, while the highest judiciary, without exception, has now upon its bench men beyond criticism for good morals and mental endowment. So in all departments of official position, with here and there an exception, are to-day the brainiest men and most honorable men of America. Now, suppose the Holy Ghost power should fall upon our capital city, and these men from all parts of America should suddenly become pronounced for Christ! Do you say the effect would be electrical? More than that, it would be omnipotent! Do you say that such learned and potent men are not wrought upon by religious influence? That shows that you have not observed what has been going on in past years. Commodore Foote, representing the navy; General Grant and Robert E. Lee, representing the Northern and Southern armies; Chief Justice Chase, representing the Supreme Court; the Frelinghuysens, Theodore and Frederick, representing the United States Senate; William Pennington and scores of others, representing the House of Representatives, have surrendered to that Gospel, which will, in this capital of the American nation, if we are faithful in our prayers and exertions, turn into the kingdom of God men of national and international power, their tongues of eloquence becoming the tongues of fire in another Pentecost. There are on yonder hill those who by the grace of God will become John Knoxes, and Chrysostoms, and Fenelons, and Bourdeloues, when once regenerated. There is a delusion I have heard in prayer-meetings, and heard in pulpits, that a soul is a soul—one soul worth as much as another. I deny it. The soul of a man who can bring a thousand or ten thousand souls into the kingdom of God, is worth a thousand times or ten thousand times more than the soul of a man who can bring no one into the kingdom. A great outpouring of the Holy Spirit in this capital, reaching the chief men of America, would be of more value to earth and heaven than in any other part of the nation, because it would reach all the States, cities, towns, and neighborhoods of the continent. Oh, for the outstretched right arm of God Almighty in the salvation of this capital!

Some of us remember 1857, when, at the close of the worst monetary distress this country has ever felt, compared with which the hard times of the last three years were a boom of prosperity, right on the heels of that complete prostration came an awakening in which five hundred thousand people were converted in different States of the Union. Do you know where one of its chief powers was demonstrated? In Washington. Do you know on what street? This street. Do you know in what church? This church. I picked up an old book a few days ago, and was startled, and thrilled, and enchanted to read these words, written at that time by the Washington correspondent of a New York paper. He wrote: "The First Presbyterian Church can scarce contain the people. Requests are daily preferred for an interest in the prayers offered, and the reading of these forms is one of the ten-

derest and most effective features of the meetings.
Particular pains are taken to disclaim and exclude
everything like sectarian feeling. General astonishment is felt at the unexpected rapidity with which the
work has thus far proceeded, and we are beginning to
anticipate the necessity of opening another church."
Why, not have that again, and more that that? There
are many thousands more of inhabitants now than
then. Beside that, since then, the telephone, with its
quasi-omnipresence, and the swift cable-car, for assem-
bling the people. I believe that the mightiest revival
of religion that this city has ever seen is yet to come,
and the earth will tremble from Capitoline Hill to the
boundaries on all sides with the footsteps of God as
he comes to awaken, and pardon, and save, these great
populations. People of Washington, meet us next
Thursday night, at half-past seven o'clock, to pray for
this coming of the Holy Ghost—not for a pentecostal
three thousand, that I have referred to, but thirty
thousand. Such a fire as that would kindle a light
that would be seen from the sledges crunching
through the snows of Labrador to the Caribbean Sea,
where the whirlwinds are born. Let our cry be that
of Habakkuk, the blank verse poet of the Bible: "O
Lord, revive thy work in the midst of the years, in the
midst of the years make known; in wrath remember
mercy." Let the battle-cry be, Washington for God!
the United States for God! America for God! the
world for God! We are all tired of skirmishing. Let
us bring on a general engagement. We are tired of
fishing with hook and line. With one sweep of the
Gospel net let us take in many thousands. This vast
work must begin somewhere. Why not here? Some
one must give the rallying cry, why may not I, one of
the Lord's servants? By providential arrangement,
I am every week in sermonic communication with

every city, town, and neighborhood of this country, and I now give the watchword to North and South, and East and West. Hear and see it, all people—this call to a forward movement, this call to repentance and faith, this call to a continental awakening!

This generation will soon be out of sight. Where are the mighty men of the past who trod your Pennsylvania avenue and spake in yonder National Legislature, and decided the stupendous questions of the supreme judicatory? Ask the sleepers in the Congressional Cemetery. Ask the mausoleums all over the land. Their tongues are speechless, their eyes closed, their arms folded, their opportunities gone, their destiny fixed. How soon time prorogues parliaments and adjourns senates and disbands cabinets and empties pulpits and dismisses generations! What we would do, we must do quickly or not at all. I call upon people who cannot come forth from their sick-beds to implore the heavens in our behalf from their midnight pillows, and I call upon the aged who cannot, even by the help of their staff, enter the churches, to spend their last days on earth in supplicating the salvation of this nation, and I call upon all men and women who have been in furnaces of trouble, as was Shadrach, and among lions, as was Daniel, and in dungeons of trouble, as was Jeremiah, to join in the prayer, and let the Church of God everywhere lay hold of the Almighty Arm that moves nations. Then Senators of the United States will announce to the State legislatures that sent them here, and Members of the House of Representatives will report to the Congressional districts that elected them, and the many thousands of men and women now and here engaged in the many departments of national service will write home, telling all sections of the country that the Lord is here, and that he is on the march for the redemption of America. Hallelujah! the Lord is coming! I hear the rumbling of his chariot wheels. I feel on my cheeks the breath of the white horses that draw the Victor! I see the flash of His lanterns through the long night of the world's sin and sorrow!

We want in this country, only on a larger scale, that which other centuries have seen of God's workings: as in the Reformation of the sixteenth century, when Martin Luther and Philip Melancthon led on; as in the awakening of the seventeenth century, when Bunyan and Flavel, and Baxter led on; as in the awakening of the eighteenth century, when Tennant, and Edwards, and the Wesleys led on; as in the awakening of 1857, led on by Matthew Simpson, the seraphic Methodist, and Bishop MacIlvaine, the Apostolic Episcopalian, and Albert Barnes, the consecrated Presbyterian, and others, just as good, in all demoninations. Oh, will not some of those glorious souls of the past come down and help us? Come down off your thrones, Nettleton and Finney and Daniel Baker and Edward Payson and Truman Osborne and Earle and Knapp and Inskip and Archibald Alexander—that Alexander the Great of the Christian Churches. Come down! How can you rest up there when the world is dying for lack of the Gospel? Come down and agonize with us in prayer. Come down and help us to preach in our pulpits. Come down and inspire our courage and faith. Heaven can get along without you better than we can. But more than all (and overwhelmed with reverent emotion we ask it), come, thou of the deeply-dyed garments of Bozrah, traveling in the greatness of thy strength, mighty to save! Lord God of Joshua! Let the sun of this century stand still above Gibeon, and the moon above the valley of Ajalon until we can whip out the five kings of hell, tumbling them down the precipices

as the other five kings went over the rocks of Beth-
horon. Ha! Ha! It will so surely be done that I
cannot restrain the laugh of triumph.

From where the seaweed is tossed on the beach by
the stormy Atlantic, to the sands laved by the quiet Pacific, this country will be Emmanuel's land, the work
beginning at Washington, if we have the faith and
holy push, and the consecration requisite. First of
all, we ministers must get right. That was a startling
utterance of Mr. Swinnock, when he said: "It is a
doleful thing to fall into hell from under the pulpit,
but, oh! how dreadful a thing to drop thither out of
the pulpit." That was an all-suggestive thing that
Paul wrote to the Corinthians: "lest by any means,
when I have preached to others, I myself should be a
castaway." That was an inspiring motto with which
Whitefield sealed all his letters: "We seek the stars."
Lord God! Wake up all our pulpits, and then it will
be as when Venn preached and it was said that men
fell before the Word like slacked lime. Let us all, lay-
man and clergyman, to the work. What Washington
wants most of all is an old-fashioned revival of religion, but on a vaster scale, so that the world will be
compelled to say, as of old, "We never saw it on
this fashion!"

But there is a human side as well as a divine side
to a revival. Those of us brought up in the country
know what is called "a raising," the neighbors gathered together to lift the heavy frame for a new house,
after the timbers are ready to be put into their places.
It is dangerous work, and there are many accidents.
The neighbors had gathered for such a raising, and
the beams had all been fitted to their places except
one, which was very heavy. That one, on the long
pikes of the men, had almost reached its place, when
something went wrong, and the men could hoist it no

higher. But if it did not go in its place it would fall back upon the men who were lifting it. It had already begun to settle back. The boss-carpenter shouted: "Lift men or die! All together! Yo—heave!" With mightier push they tried to send the beam to its place, but failed. Still they held on, all the time their strength lessening. The wives, and mothers, and daughters stood in horror looking on. Then the boss-carpenter shouted to the women, "Come and help!" They came, and womanly arms became the arms of giants, for they were lifting to save the lives of husbands, and fathers, and sons, as well as their own. Then the boss-carpenter mounted one of the beams and shouted: "Now! Altogether! Lift or die! Yo—heave!" And with a united effort that almost burst the blood-vessels, the great beam went to its place, and wild cheering was heard. That is the way it sometimes seems in the churches. Temples of righteousness are to be reared, but there is a halt, a stop, a catch somewhere. A few are lifting all they can, but we want more hands at this raising, and more hearts. More Christian men to help, ay, more Christian women to reinforce. If the work fail, it means the death of many souls. All together! Men and women of God! Lift or die! The top-stone must come to its place "with shoutings of grace, grace unto it." God is ready to do his part; are we ready to do our part? There is work not only for the knee of prayer, but for the shoulder of upheaval.

I would like to see, this hour, that which I have never seen, but hope to see—a whole audience saved under one flash of the Eternal Spirit. Before you go out of any of these doors, enter the door of Mercy. Father and mother, come in and bring your children with you. Newly-married folks, consecrate your life-time to God, and be married for eternity as well as time. Young man, you will want God before you get through this world, and you want him now. Young woman, without God this is a hard world for women. One and all, I lift my voice so that you can hear it, out in the corridors, and on the street, and say, in the words of the Mediterranean ship captain, "Call upon thy God, if so be that God will think upon us, that we perish not." Oh, what news to tell, what news to relate to your old father and mother, what news to telegraph to your friends on the other side of the mountains, what news with which to thrill your loved ones in heaven! It was of such news that a man read in a noonday meeting in Philadelphia. He arose, and unrolling a manuscript, read:

> Where'er we meet, you always say
>   What's the news? what's the news?
> Pray what's the order of the day?
>   What's the news? what's the news?
> Oh! I have got good news to tell;
> My Saviour hath done all things well,
> And triumphed over death and hell,
>   That's the news! that's the news!
>
> The Lamb was slain on Calvary,
>   That's the news! that's the news!
> To set a world of sinners free,
>   That's the news! that's the news!
>
> And now, if any one should say,
>   What's the news? what's the news?
> Oh, tell him you've begun to pray —
>   That's the news! that's the news!
> That you have joined the conquering band,
> And now with joy at God's command,
> You're marching to the better land,
>   That's the news! that's the news!

MORAL CHARACTER OF CANDIDATES

Exodus, 20: 1–17: " The Ten Commandments."

MORAL CHARACTER OF CANDIDATES

Exodus, 20: 1–17: "The Ten Commandments."

The lightnings and earthquakes united their forces to wreck a mountain of Arabia Petræa in olden time, and travelers to-day find heaps of porphyry and greenstone rocks, boulder against boulder, the remains of the first law library, written, not on parchment or papyrus, but on shattered slab of granite. The corner-stones of all morality, of all wise law, of all righteous jurisprudence, of all good government, are the two tablets of stone on which were written the Ten Commandments. All Roman law, all French law, all English law, all American law that is worth anything, all common law, civil law, criminal law, martial law, law of nations, were rocked in the cradle of the twentieth chapter of Exodus. And it would be well in these times of great political agitation if the newspapers would print the Decalogue some day in place of the able editorial. But let the Ten Commandments loose upon the great political parties of our day and there would be wild panic.

The fact is that some people suppose that the law has passed out of existence, and some are not aware of some of the passages of that law, and others say this or that is of the more importance, when no one has any right to make such an assertion. These laws are the pillars of society, and if you remove one pillar you damage the whole structure. I have noticed that men are particularly vehement against sins to which they are not particularly tempted, and find no especial wrath against sins in which they themselves indulge.

They take out one gun from this battery of ten guns, and load that and unlimber that and fire that. They say: This is an Armstrong gun, and this is a Krupp gun, and this is a Nordenfelt five-barreled gun, and this is a Gatling ten-barreled gun, and this is a Martini thirty-seven barreled gun." But I have to tell them that they are all of the same calibre, and that they shoot from eternity to eternity.

Many questions are before the people in the coming elections all over the land, but I shall try to show you that the most important thing to be settled about all these candidates is their personal moral character. To-day, in this brief course of sermons I am preaching on national affairs, and within a few days of the Presidential election, I propose to test the character of persons nominated for office in city, State and nation, and to test them by the Decalogue. Many of the clergymen have gone on the political platform in these times —and I have no criticism to offer in regard to them— some going on one political platform and some on the opposite political platform. I hope they are all better than I am, yet I have not felt called of God to copy their example, but rather in a few Sabbath morning sermons, omitting all personalities, to lay down certain principles which will stand the test of the Judgment Day. The Decalogue forbids idolatry, image making, profanity, maltreatment of parents, Sabbath desecration, murder, theft, incontinence, lying, and covetousness. That is the Decalogue by which you and I will have to be tried, and by that same Decalogue you and I must try candidates for office.

Of course we shall not find anything like perfection. If we do not vote until we find an immaculate nominee we will never vote at all. We have so many faults of our own we ought not to be censorious or maledictory or hypercritical in regard to the faults of others. The Christly rule is as appropriate for November as any other month in the year, and for the fourth year as for the three preceding years: "Judge not that ye be not judged, for with what measure ye mete it shall be measured to you again.

Most certainly are we not to take the statement of red-hot partisanship as the real character of any man. From nearly all the great cities of this land I receive daily or weekly newspapers, sent to me regularly and in compliment, so I see both sides—I see all sides—and it is most entertaining, and my regular amusement, to read the opposite statements. The one statement says the man is an angel, and the other says he is a devil; and I split the difference, and I find him half-way between. There has never been an honest or respectable man running for the United States Presidency since the foundations of the American Government, if we may believe the old files of newspapers in the museums. What a mercy it is that they were not all hung before inauguration day! If a man believe one-half of what he sees in the newspapers in these times, his career will be very short outside of Bloomingdale Insane Asylum. I was absent during this last week, and I was dependent entirely upon what I read in regard to what had occurred in these cities, and I read there was a procession in New York of five thousand patriots, and a minute after I read in another sheet that there were seventeen thousand; and then I read in regard to another procession that there were ten thousand, and then I read in another paper that there were sixty thousand. A campaign orator in the Rink or the Academy of Music received a very cold reception—a very chilling reception—said one statement. The other statement said the audience rose at him; so great was the enthusiam that for a long while the orator could not be heard, and it was only after lifting his hand that the vociferation began to subside! One statement will twist a letter one way, and another statement will twist it another way. You must admit it is a very difficult thing in times like these to get a very accurate estimate of a man's character, and I charge you, as your religious teacher, I charge you to caution, and to mercifulness, and to prayer.

I warn you also against the mistake which many are making, and always do make, of applying a different standard of character for those in high place and of large means from the standard they apply for ordinary persons. However much a man may have, and however high the position he gets, he has no especial liberty given him in the interpretation of the Ten Commandments. A great sinner is no more to be excused than a small sinner. Do not charge illustrious defection to eccentricity, or chop off the Ten Commandments to suit especial cases. The right is everlastingly right and the wrong is everlastingly wrong. If any man nominated for any office in this city, State, or nation differs from the Decalogue, do not fix up the Decalogue, but fix him up. This law must stand whatever else may fall.

I call your attention also to the fact that you are all aware of, that the breaking of one commandment makes it the more easy to break all of them, and the philosophy is plain. Any kind of sin weakens the conscience, and if the conscience is weakened, that opens the door for all kinds of transgression. If, for instance, a man go into this political campaign wielding scurrility as his chief weapon, and he believes everything bad about a man, and believes nothing good, how long before that man himself will get over the moral depression? Neither in time nor eternity. If I utter a falsehood in regard to a man I may damage him, but I get for myself tenfold more damage. That is a gun that kicks. If, for instance, a man be profane, under provocation he will commit any crime. I say under provocation. For if a man will maltreat the Lord Almighty, would he not maltreat his fellow-man? If a man be guilty of malfeasance in office he will, under provocation, commit any sin. He who will steal will lie, and he who will lie will steal. If, for instance, a man be unchaste, it opens the door for all other iniquity, for in that one iniquity he commits theft of the worst kind, and covetousness of the worst kind, and falsehood—pretending to be decent when he is not—and maltreats his parents by disgracing their name, if they were good. Be careful, therefore, how you charge that sin against any man either in high place or low place, either in office or out of office, because when you make that charge against a man you charge him with all villainies, with all disgusting propensities, with all rottenness. A libertine is a beast lower than the vermin that crawl over a summer carcass—lower than the swine, for the swine has no intelligence to sin against. Be careful, then, how you charge that against any man. You must be so certain that a mathematical demonstration is doubtful as compared with it.

And, then, when you investigate a man on such subjects, you must go the whole length of investigation, and find out whether or not he has repented. He may have been down on his knees before God and implored the divine forgiveness, and he may have implored the forgiveness of society and the forgiveness of the world; although if a man commit that sin at thirty or thirty-five years of age there is not one case out of a thousand where he ever repents. You must in your investigation see if it is possible that the one case investigated may not have been the glorious exception. But do not chop off the seventh commandment to suit the case. Do not change Fairbanks's scale to suit what you are weighing with it. Do not cut off a yardstick to suit the dry goods you are measuring. Let the law stand, and never tamper with it.

Above all, I charge you do not join in the cry that I have heard—for .fifteen, twenty years I have heard it—that there is no such thing as purity. If you make that charge you are a foul-mouthed scandaler of the human race. You are a leper. Make room for that leper! When a man, by pen or type or tongue, utters such a slander on the human race that there is no such thing as purity, I know right away that that man himself is a walking lazaretto, a reeking ulcer, and is fit for no society better than that of devils damned. We may enlarge our charities in such a case, but in no such case let us shave off the Ten Commandments. Let them stand as the everlasting defense of society and of the Church of God.

The committing of one sin opens the door for the commission of other sins. You see it every day. Those Wall Street embezzlers, those bank cashiers absconding as soon as they are brought to justice, develop the fact that they were in all kinds of sin. No exception to the rule. They all kept bad company, they nearly all gambled, they all went to places where they ought not. Why? The commisson of the one sin opened the gate for all the other sins. Sins go in flocks, in droves, and in herds. You open the door for one sin, that invites in all the miserable segregation. The campaign orators this autumn, some of them, bombarding the suffering candidates all the week, will think no wrong in Sabbath-breaking. All the week hurling the eighth commandment at one candidate, the seventh commandment at another candidate, and the ninth commandment at still another. They think no wrong in riding all Sunday, and they are at this moment, many of them, in the political headquarters calculating the chances. All the week hurling one commandment at Mr. Blaine, another commandment at Mr. Cleveland, and another commandment at Mr. St. John—what are they doing with the fourth commandment, "Remember the Sabbath day to keep it holy"? Breaking it. Is not the fourth commandment as important as the eighth, as the seventh, as the ninth? Some of these political campaign orators, as I have seen them reported, and as I have heard in regard to them, bombarding the suffering candidates all the week, yet tossing the name of God from their lips recklessly, guilty of profanity. What are they doing with the third commandment? Is not the third commandment, which says, "Thou shalt not take the name of the Lord thy God in vain, for the Lord will not hold him guiltless that taketh his name in vain"—is not the third commandment as important as the other nine? Oh, yes, we find in all departments men are hurling their indigation against sins perhaps to which they are not especially tempted —hurling it against iniquity toward which they are not particularly drawn.

I have this book for my authority when I say that the man who swears or the man who breaks the Sabbath is as culpable before God as either of those candidates is culpable if the things charged on him are true. What right have you and I to select which commandment we will keep and which we will break? Better not try to measure the thunderbolts of the Almighty, saying this has less blaze, this has less momentum. Better not play with the guns, better not experiment much with the divine ammunition. Cicero said he saw the Iliad written on a nut-shell, and you and I have seen the Lord's prayer written on a five-cent piece; but the whole tendency of these times is to write the Ten Commandments so small nobody can see them. I protest this day against the attempt to revise the Decalogue which was given on Mount Sinai amid the blast of trumpets and the cracking of the rocks and the paroxysm of the mountain of Arabia Petræa.

I bring up the candidates for city, State and national power, I bring them up, and I try them by this Decalogue. Of course, they are imperfect. We are all imperfect. We say things we ought not to say, we do things we ought not to do. We have all been wrong, we have all done wrong. But I shall find out one of the candidates who comes, in my estimation, nearest to obedience of the Ten Commandments, and I will vote for him, and you will vote for him unless you love God less than your party; then you will not.

Herodotus said that Nitocris, the daughter of Nebuchadnezzar, was so fascinated with her beautiful village of Ardericca, that she had the river above Babylon changed so it wound this way and wound that, and curved this way and curved that, and though you sailed on it for three days every day you would be in sight of that exquisite village. Now, I do not care which way you sail in morals, or which way you sail in life, if you only sail within sight of this beautiful group of divine commandments. Although they may sometimes seem to be a little angular, I do not care which way you sail, if you sail in sight of them you will never run aground and you will never be shipwrecked.

I never felt more impressed from God than I do this moment of the importance of what I am saying to this audience. Society needs toning up on all these subjects. I tell you there is nothing worse to fight than the ten regiments, with bayonets and sabres of fire, marching down the side of Mount Sinai. They always gain the victory, and those who fight against them go under. There are thousands and tens of thousands of men being slain by the Decalogue. What is the matter with that young man of whom I read, dying in his dissipations? In his dying delirium he said: "Now, fetch on the dice. It is mine! No, no! It is gone, all is gone! Bring on more wine! Bring on more wine! Oh, how they rattle their chains! Fiends, fiends, fiends! I say you cheat! The cards are marked! Oh, death! oh, death! oh, death! Fiends, fiends, fiends!" And he gasped and was gone. The Ten Commandments slew him.

Let not ladies and gentlemen in this nineteenth century revise the Ten Commandments, but let them in society and at the polls put to the front those who come the nearest to this God-lifted standard. On Tuesday morning next read the twentieth chapter of Exodus at family prayers. The moral or the immoral character of the next President of the United States will add seventy-five per cent. unto or subtract seventy-five per cent. from the national morals. You and I cannot afford to have a bad President; the young men of this country cannot afford to have a bad President; the commercial, the moral, the artistic, the agricultural, the manufacturing, the religious interests of this country, cannot afford to have a bad President; and if you, on looking over the whole field, cannot find a man who, in your estimation, comes within reasonable distance of obedience of the Decalogue, stay at home, do not vote at all.

I suppose when in the city of Sodom there were four candidates put up for office, and Lot did not believe in any of them, he did not register. I suppose if there came a crisis in the politics of Babylon, where Daniel did not believe in any of the candidates, he stayed at home on election day, praying with his face toward Jerusalem. But we have no such crisis, we have no such exigency, thank God. Yet I have to say to you to-day that the moral character of a ruler always affects the ruled; and I appeal to history. Wicked King Manasseh depressed the moral tone of all the nation of Judah, and threw them into idolatry. Good King Josiah lifted up the whole nation by his excellent example. Why is it that to-day England is higher up in morals than at any point in her national history? It is because she has the best ruler in all Europe, all the attempts to scandalize her name a failure. The political power of Talleyrand brooded all the political tricksters of the last ninety years. The dishonest Vice-Presidency of Aaron Burr blasted this nation until important letters were written in cipher, because the people could not trust the United States mail. And let the court circles of Louis XV and Henry VIII march out, followed by the debauched nations.

The higher up you put a bad man the worse is his power for evil. The great fabulist says that the pigeons were in fright at a kite flying in the air, and so these pigeons hovered near the dovecote; but one day the kite said, "Why are you so afraid? why do you pass your life in terror? make me king, and I'll destroy all your enemies." So the pigeons made the kite king, and as soon as he got the throne his regular diet was a pigeon a day. And while one of the victims was waiting for its turn to come, it said: "Served us right!" The malaria of swamps rises from the plain to the height, but moral malaria descends from the mountain to the plain. Be careful, therefore, how you elevate into authority men who are in any wise antagonistic to the Ten Commandments.

As near as I can tell, the most important thing now

to be done is to have about forty million copies of the Sinaitic Decalogue printed and scattered throughout the land. It was a terrible waste when the Alexandrian library was destroyed, and the books were taken to heat four thousand baths for the citizens of Alexandria. It was very expensive heat. But without any harm to the Decalogue, you could with it heat a hundred thousand baths of moral purification for the American people. I say we want a tonic—a mighty tonic—a corrective—an all-powerful corrective—and Moses in the text, with steady hand, notwithstanding the jarring mountains and the full orchestra of the tempest and the blazing of the air, pours out the ten drops—no more, no less—which this nation needs to take for its moral convalescence.

But I shall not leave you under the discouragement of the Ten Commandments, because we have all offended. There is another mountain in sight, and while one mountain thunders the other answers in thunder; and while Mount Sinai, with lightning, writes doom, the other mountain, with lightning, writes mercy. The only way you will ever spike the guns of the Decalogue is by the spikes of the cross. The only rock that will ever stop the Sinaitic upheaval is the Rock of Ages. Mount Calvary is higher than Mount Sinai. The English Survey Expedition, I know, say that one Sinaitic peak is seven thousand feet high and another eight thousand and another nine thousand feet high, and travelers tell us that Mount Calvary is only a slightly raised knoll outside of the wall of Jerusalem; but Calvary in moral significance overtops and over-shadows all the mountains of the hemispheres, and Mount Washington and Mount Blanc and the Himalayas are hillocks compared with it. You know that sometimes one fortress will silence another fortress. Moultrie silenced Sumter; and against the mountain of the law I put the mountain of the cross. "The soul that sinneth, it shall die," booms one, until the earth jars under the cannonade. "Save them from going down to the pit, I have found a ransom," pleads the other, until earth and heaven and hell quake under the reverberation. And Moses, who commands the one, surrenders to Christ, who commands the other.

> Once by the law our hopes were slain,
> But now in Christ we live again.

Aristotle says that Mount Etna erupted one day and poured torrents of scoria upon the villages at the base, but that the mountain divided its flame and made a lane of safety for all those who came to rescue their aged parents. And this volcanic Sinai divides its fury for all those whom Christ has come to rescue from the red ruin on both sides. Standing as I do to-day, half-way between the two mountains—the mountain of the 20th of Exodus and the mountain of the 19th of John—all my terror comes into supernatural calm, for the uproar of the one mountain subsides into quiet, and comes down into so deep a silence that I can hear the other mountain speak—ay, I can hear it whisper: "The blood, the blood, the blood that cleanseth from all sin."

The Survey Expedition says that the Sinaitic mountains have wadys, or water courses—Alleyat and Ajelah—emptying into Feiran. But those streams are not navigable. No boat put into those rocky streams could sail. But I have to tell you this day that the boat of Gospel rescue comes right up amid the water courses of Sinaitic gloom and threat, ready to take us off from under the shadows into the calm sunlight of God's pardon and into the land of peace. Oh, if you could see that boat of Gospel rescue coming this day, you would feel as John Gilmore, in his book, "The Storm Warriors," says that a ship's crew felt on the Kentish Knock Sands, off the coast of England, when they were being beaten to pieces and they all felt they must die! They had given up all hope, and every moment washed another plank from the wreck, and they said, "We must die, we must die!" But after a while they saw a Ramsgate lifeboat coming through the breakers for them, and the man standing highest up on the wreck said: "Can it be? Can it be? It is, it is, it is, it is! Thank God! It is the Ramsgate lifeboat! It is, it is, it is, it is!" And the old Jack tar, describing that lifeboat to his comrades after he got ashore, said: "Oh, my lads, what a beauty it did seem, what a beauty it did seem coming through the breakers that awful day!" May God, through the mercy in Jesus Christ, take us all off the miserable wreck of our sin into the beautiful lifeboat of the Gospel!

THE MISSION OF THE WHEEL

Ezekiel, 10: 13: "As for the wheels, it was cried unto them in my hearing, O wheel!"

THE MISSION OF THE WHEEL

A Thanksgiving Sermon.

Ezekiel, 10: 13: "As for the wheels, it was cried unto them in my hearing, O wheel!"

Next Thursday will, by proclamation of President and Governors, be observed in Thanksgiving for temporal mercies. With what spirit shall we enter upon it? For nearly a year and a half this nation has been celebrating the triumph of sword and gun and battery. We have sung martial airs and cheered returning heroes and sounded the requiem for the slain in battle. Methinks it will be a healthful change if this Thanksgiving week, in church and homestead, we celebrate the victories of peace: for nothing was done at Santiago or Manila that was of more importance than that which in the last year has been done in farmer's field, and mechanic's shop, and author's study, by those who never wore an epaulette or shot a Spaniard or went a hundred miles from their own door-sill. And now I call your attention to the wheel of the text.

Man, a small speck in the universe, was set down in a big world, high mountains rising before him, deep seas arresting his pathway, and wild beasts capable of his destruction; yet he was to conquer. It could not be by physical force, for, compare his arm with the ox's horn and the elephant's tusk, and how weak he is! It could not be by physical speed, for compare him to the antelope's foot and ptarmigan's wing, and how slow he is! It could not be by physical capacity to soar or plunge, for the condor beats him in one direction, and the porpoise in the other. Yet he was to conquer the world. Two eyes, two hands, and two feet were insufficient. He must be reinforced, so God sent the wheel.

Twenty-two times is the wheel mentioned in the Bible. Sometimes, as in Ezekiel, illustrating providential movement; sometimes, as in the Psalms, crushing the bad; sometimes, as in Judges, representing God's charioted progress. The wheel that started in Exodus, rolls on through Proverbs, through Isaiah, through Jeremiah, through Daniel, through Nahum, through the centuries — all the time gathering momentum and splendor, until, seeing what it has done for the world's progress and happiness, we clap our hands in thanksgiving, and employ the apostrophe of the text, crying, " O Wheel! "

I call on you in this Thanksgiving week to praise God for the triumphs of machinery, which have revolutionized the world and multiplied its attractions. Even Paradise, though very picturesque, must have been comparatively dull. Hardly anything going on. No agriculture needed, for the harvest was spontaneous. No architecture required, for they slept under the trees. No manufacturer's loom necessary for the weaving of apparel, for the fashions were exceedingly simple. To dress the garden could not have required ten minutes a day.

Having nothing to do, they got into mischief, and ruined themselves and the race. It was a sad thing to be turned out of Paradise, but, once turned out, a beneficent thing to be compelled to work. To help man up and on, God sent the wheel. If turned ahead, the race advances; if turned back, the race retreats. To arouse your gratitude and exalt your praise, I would show you what the wheel has done for the domestic world, for the agricultural world, for the traveling world, for the literary world. "As for the wheels, it was cried unto them in my hearing, O wheel!"

In domestic life the wheel has wrought revolution. Behold the sewing machine! It has shattered the housewife's bondage and prolonged woman's life, and added immeasurable advantages. The needle for ages had punctured the eyes and pierced the side, and made terrible massacre. To prepare the garments of a whole household in the spring for summer and in the autumn for winter was an exhausting process. "Stitch! stitch! stitch!" Thomas Hood set it to poetry, but millions of persons have found it agonizing prose.

Slain by the sword, we buried the hero with "Dead March in Saul," and flags half-mast. Slain by the needle, no one knew it but the household that watched her health giving way. The winter after that the children were ragged and cold and hungry, or in the almshouse. The hand that wielded the needle had forgotten its cunning. Soul and body had parted at the seam. The thimble had dropped from the palsied finger. The thread of life had snapped and let a suffering human life drop into the grave. The spool was all unwound. Her sepulchre was digged, not with sexton's spade, but with a sharper and shorter implement — a needle. Federal and Confederate dead have ornamented graves at Arlington Heights and Richmond and Gettysburg, thousands by thousands; but it will take the archangel's trumpet to find the million graves of the vaster army of women needle-slain.

Besides all the sewing done for the household at home, there are hundreds of thousands of sewing women. The tragedy of the needle is the tragedy of hunger and cold and insult and homesickness and suicide — five acts.

But I hear the rush of a wheel. Woman puts on the band and adjusts the instrument, puts her foot on the treadle and begins. Before the whirr and rattle, pleurisies, consumptions, headaches, backaches, heartaches are routed. The needle, once an oppressive tyrant, becomes a cheerful slave. Roll and rumble and roar until the family wardrobe is gathered, and winter is defied, and summer is welcomed, and the ardors and severities of the seasons are overcome. Winding the bobbin, threading the shuttle, tucking, quilting, ruffling, cording, embroidering, underbraiding set to music. Lock-stitch, twisted loop-stitch, crochet stitch, a fascinating ingenuity. All honor to the memory of Alsop and Duncan and Greenough and Singer and Wilson and Grover and Wilcox for their efforts to emancipate woman from the slavery of toil! But more than that, let there be monumental commemoration of Elias Howe, the inventor of the first complete sewing machine. What it has saved of sweat and tears God only can estimate. In the making of men's and boys' clothing in New York city in one year it saved seven million five hundred thousand dollars; and in Massachusetts, in the making of boots and shoes, in one year it saved seven million dollars.

No wonder that at some of the learned institutions, like the New Jersey State Normal School, and Rutgers' Female Institute, and Elmira Female College, acquaintance with the sewing-machine is a requisition, a young lady not being considered educated until she understands it. Winter is coming on, and the household must be warmly clad. The "Last Rose of Summer" will sound better played on a sewing-machine than on a piano. Roll on, O wheel of the sewing-machine! until the last shackled woman of toil shall be emancipated. Roll on!

Secondly, I look into the agricultural world to see

what the wheel has accomplished. Look at the stalks of wheat and oats, the one bread for man, the other bread for horses. Coat off, and with a cradle made out of five or six fingers of wood and one of sharp steel, the harvester went across the field, stroke after stroke, perspiration rolling down forehead and cheek and chest, head blistered by the consuming sun, and lip parched by the merciless August air. At noon, the workmen lying half dead under the trees. The grain brought to the barn, the sheaves were unbound and spread on a threshing-floor, and two men with flails stood opposite each other hour after hour, and day after day, pounding the wheat out of the stalk. Two strokes, and then a cessation of sound. Thump! thump! thump! thump! thump! thump! Pounded once and then turned over to be pounded again. Slow, very slow. The hens cackled and clucked by the door, and picked up the loose grains, and the horses, half asleep and dozing over the mangers where the hay had been.

But, hark! to the buzz of wheels in the distance! The farmer has taken his throne on a reaper. He once walked, now he rides. Once worked with arm of flesh, now with arm of iron. He starts at the end of the wheat field, heads his horses to the opposite end of the field, rides on. At the stroke of his iron chariot the gold of the grain is surrendered; the machine rolling this way and rolling that, this way and that, until the work which would have been accomplished in many days is accomplished in a few hours. The grain field prostrate before the harvesters.

What quick, clean work the wheel of the reaper does make! Soon after, the horses are fastened to the threshing-machine back of the barn. The iron-toothed cylinders are ready for their prey. The horses start, the unbound wheat is plunged into the vortex, and the broken straw is in one place, and the pure St. Louis wheat is in another place. The driving-wheel strapped, the cylinder humming with terrible velocity, the inexperienced warned off for fear of accident, the ground aquake with the mighty revolution, I stand in awe and thanksgiving at the agricultural conquest, and cry out with the text, " O, wheel! "

Can you imagine anything more beautiful than the Sea Island cotton? I take up the unmelted snow in my hand. How beautiful it is! But do you know by what painstaking and tedious toil it passed into anything like practicality? If you examined that cotton you would find it full of seeds. It was a severe process by which the seed was to be extracted from the fibre. Vast populations were leaving the South because they could not make any living out of this product. One pound of green seed-cotton was all that a man could prepare in one day; but Eli Whitney, a Massachusetts Yankee, woke up, got a handful of cotton, and went to constructing a wheel for the parting of the fibre and the seed. Teeth on cylinders, brushes on cylinders, wheels on wheels. South Carolina gave him fifty thousand dollars for his invention, and instead of one man taking a whole day to prepare a pound of cotton for the market, now he may prepare three hundred weight, and the South is enriched, and the commerce of the world is revolutionized, and over eight million bales of cotton were prepared this year, enough to keep at work in this country fourteen million three hundred thousand spindles, employing two hundred and seventy thousand hands, and enlisting two hundred and eighty-one million four hundred thousand dollars of capital.

Thank you, Eli Whitney, and L. S. Chichester, of New York, his successor. Above all, thank God for their inventive genius, that has done so much for the

The Mission of the Wheel

prosperity of the world. When I see coming forth from this cotton production and cotton manufacture enough cloth to cover the tables of a nation, and enough spool thread to sew every rent garment, and enough hosiery to warm the nation's feet, and enough cordage to fly the sails of all the shipping, and enough wadding to supply the guns of all the American sportsmen, and enough twine to fly all the kites outside of Wall street, and enough tape to tie up all the briefs of all the attorneys, and enough flannels to blanket a slumbering world, I thank God.

For the fifty thousand dollars received for his cotton-gin, Whitney gave a wealth that makes the word "millions" imbecile. Strange that one machine should work such marvels. Have you noticed the construction of the cotton-gin? On one side of it I count three wheels, and on another side I count three wheels, while on the third side there is a wheel on top of a wheel, and the salutation of the text bursts from my lips, while I cry in ecstasy, and admiration of gratitude, "O wheel!"

Thirdly, I look to see what the wheel has done for the traveling world. No one can tell how many noble and self-sacrificing inventors have been crushed between the coach-wheel and the modern locomotive, between the paddle and the ocean steamer.

I will not enter into the controversy as to whether John Fitch, or Robert Fulton, or Thomas Somerset was the inventor of the steam engine. They all suffered and were martyrs of the wheel, and they shall all be honored. John Fitch wrote:

"The 21st of January, 1743, was the fatal time of bringing me into existence. I know of nothing so perplexing and vexatious to a man of feeling as a turbulent wife and steamboat building. I experienced the former and quit in season, and had I been in my right senses I should undoubtedly have treated the latter in the same manner; but for one man to be teased with both, he must be looked upon as the most unfortunate man in the world."

Surely John Fitch was in a bad predicament. If the steamboat boiler did not blow him up, his wife would! In all ages there are those to prophesy the failure of any useful invention. You do not know what the inventors of the day suffer. When it was proposed to light London with gas, Sir Humphrey Davy, the great philosopher, said that he should as soon think of cutting a slice from the moon and setting it upon a pole to light the city. Through all abuse and caricature Fitch and Fulton went until yonder the wheel is in motion, and the *Clermont*, the first steamboat, is going up the North river, running the distance — hold your breath while I tell you — from New York to Albany in thirty-two hours. But the steamboat wheel multiplied its velocities until the *Lucania* of the Cunard, and the *Majestic* of the White Star line, and the *New York* of the American line, and the *Kaiser Wilhelm* of the North German Lloyd line cross the Atlantic ocean in six days or less. Communication between the two countries is so rapid and so constant, that whereas once those who had been to Europe took on airs for the rest of their mortal lives — and to me for many years the most disagreeable man I could meet was the man who had been to Europe, despising all American pictures and American music and American society, because he had seen European pictures and heard European music and mingled in European society — now a transatlantic voyage is so common that a sensible man would no more boast of it than if he had been to New York or Boston.

All the rivers and lakes and seas have turned white with rage under the smiting of the steamboat wheel.

The Mission of the Wheel

In the phosphorescent wake of it sail the world's commercial prosperities. Through the axle of that wheel nations join hands, and America says to Venice: "Give me your pictures"; and to France, "Give me your graceful apparel"; and to England, "Give me your Sheffield knives and Nottingham laces and Manchester goods, and I will give you breadstuffs, corn and rye and rice. I will give you cotton for your mills; I will give you cattle for your slaughter-houses. Give me all you have to spare and I will give you all I have to spare," and trans-Atlantic and cis-Atlantic nations grasp each other's hands in brotherhood.

What a difference between John Fitch's steamboat, sixty feet long, and the *Oceanic*, seven hundred and four feet long! The ocean wheel turns swifter and swifter, filling up the distance between the hemispheres, and hastening the time spoken of in the Book of Revelation, when there shall be no more sea.

While this has been doing on the water, James Watts' wheel has done as much on the land. How well I remember Sanderson's stage-coach, running from New Brunswick to Easton, as he drove through Somerville, New Jersey, turning up to the post-office and dropping the mail-bags with ten letters and two or three newspapers; on the box, Sanderson, himself, six feet two inches, and well proportioned, long lash-whip in his hand, the reins of six horses in the other, the "leaders" lathered along the lines of the traces, foam dripping from the bits. It was the event of the day when the stage came. It was our highest ambition to become a stage-driver. Some of the boys climbed on the great leathern boot of the stage, and those of us who could not get on shouted "Cut behind!" I saw the old stage-driver not long ago, and I expressed to him my surprise that one around whose head I had seen a halo of glory in my boyhood time was only a man like the rest of us. Between Sanderson's stage-coach and a Chicago express train, what a difference! All the great cities of the nation strung on an iron thread of railways!

At Doncaster, England, I saw George Stephenson's first locomotive. If in good repair it could run yet, but because of its make and size it would be the burlesque of all railroaders. Between that rude machine, crawling down the iron track, followed by a clumsy and bouncing train, and one of our Rocky Mountain locomotives, with a village of palace-cars, becoming drawing-rooms by day and princely dormitories by night, what bewitching progress!

See the train move out from one of our great depots for a thousand miles' journey! All aboard. Tickets clipped and baggage checked, and porters attentive to every want. Under tunnels dripping with dampness that never saw the light. Along ledges where an inch off the track would be the difference between a hundred men living and a hundred dead. Full head of steam, and two men in the locomotive charged with all the responsibility of whistle and Westinghouse brake. Clank, clank! go the wheels. Clank, clank! echo the rocks. Small villages only hear the thunder and see the whirlwind as the train shoots past. A city on the wing! Thrilling, startling, sublime, magnificent spectacle — a rail train in lightning procession.

When, years ago, the railroad men " struck " for wages our country was threatened with annihilation, and we realized what the railroad wheel had done for this country. Over one hundred and eighty thousand miles of railroad in the United States. In one year over a billion dollars received from passengers and freight. White Mountains, Alleghany Mountains, Rocky Mountains, Sierra Nevadas bowing to the iron

The Mission of the Wheel

yoke. All the rolling stock of New York Central, Erie, Pennsylvania, Michigan Central, Georgia, Great Southern, Union Pacific, and all the other wheels of the tens of thousands of freight cars, wrecking cars, cabooses, drawing-room cars, sleeping cars, passenger cars, of all the accommodation, express and special trains, started by the wheel of the grotesque locomotive that I saw at Doncaster. For what it has done for all Christendom, I ejaculate in the language of the text, " O wheel! "

While the world has been rolling on the eight wheels of the rail car, or the four wheels of the carriage, or the two wheels of the gig, it was not until 1876, at the Centennial Exposition, at Philadelphia, that the miracle of the nineteenth century rolled in — the bicycle. The world could not believe its own eyes, and not until quite far on in the eighties were the continents enchanted with the whirling, flashing, dominating spectacle of a machine that was to do so much for the pleasure, the business, the health, and the profit of nations. The world had needed it for six thousand years. Man's slowness of locomotion was a mystery. Was it of more importance that the reindeer or the eagle rapidly exchanged jungles or crags than that man should get swiftly from place to place? Was the business of the bird or the roebuck more urgent than that of the incarnated immortal? No! At last we have the obliteration of distances by pneumatic tire. At last we have wings. And what has this invention done for woman? The cynics and constitutional growlers would deny her this emancipation, and say: " What better exercise can she have than a broom, or a duster, or a churn, or rocking a cradle, or running up and down stairs, or a walk to church with a prayer book under her arm? " And they rather rejoice to find her disabled with broken pedal or punctured tire half way out to Chevy Chase or Coney Island. But all sensible people who know the tonic of fresh air, and the health in deep respiration, and the awakening of disused muscles, and the exhilaration of velocity, will rejoice that wife, and mother, and daughter, may have this new recreation. Indeed, life to so many is a hard grind that I am glad at the arrival of any new mode of healthful recreation. We need have no anxiety about this invasion of the world's stupidity by the vivacious, and laughing, and jubilant wheel, except that we always want it to roll in the right direction — toward place of business, toward good recreation, toward philanthropy, toward usefulness, toward places of divine worship, and never toward immorality or Sabbath desecration. My friend, Will Carleton, the poet, said what I like when he wrote of this new velocity:

> We claim a great utility that daily must increase;
> We claim from inactivity a sensible release;
> A constant mental, physical, and moral help, we feel,
> That bids us turn enthusiast, and cry, God bless the wheel!

Never yet having mounted one of those rolling wonders, I stand by the wayside, far enough off to avoid being run over, and in amazement and congratulation cry out, in Ezekiel's phraseology of the text, " O wheel!"

Fourthly, I look into the literary world and see what the wheel has accomplished. I am more astounded with this than anything that has preceded. Behold the almost miraculous printing-press. Do you not feel the ground shake with the machinery of the New York, Brooklyn, Boston, Philadelphia, Washington, and Western dailies? Some of us remember when the hand ink-roller was run over the cylinder, and by great haste eight hundred copies of

The Mission of the Wheel

the village newspaper were issued in one day and no lives lost; but invention has crowded invention, and wheel jostled wheel, stereotyping, electrotyping, taking their places, Benjamin Franklin's press giving way to the Lord Stanhope press; and the Washington press, and the Victory press, and the Hoe perfecting press have been set up. Together with the newspaper come the publication of innumerable books of history, of poetry, of romance, of art, of travel, of biography, of religion, dictionaries, encylopedias, and bibles. Some of these presses send forth the most accursed stuff, but the good predominates. Turn on with wider sweep and greater velocity, O wheel! Wheel of light, wheel of civilization, wheel of Christianity, wheel of divine momentum.

On those four wheels — that of the sewing-machine, that of the reaper, that of travel, that of the printing-press — the world has moved up to its present prosperity. I call on you to thank God for the triumphs of machinery as seen in our home comforts and added national grandeur.

And now I gather on an imaginary platform, as I literally did gather them on Thanksgiving days when I preached in Brooklyn, specimens of our American products. Here is corn from the West, a foretaste of the great harvest that is to come down to our seaboard; enough for ourselves and for foreign shipment. Here is rice from the South, never a more beautiful product grown on the planet, mingling the gold and green. Here are two sheaves, a sheaf of Northern wheat and a sheaf of Southern rice bound together. May the band never break! Here is cotton, the wealthiest product of America. Here is sugar-cane, enough to sweeten the beverages of an empire. Who would think that out of such a homely stalk there would come such a luscious product. Here are palmetto trees that have in their pulses the warmth of Southern climes. Here is the cactus of the South, so beautiful and so tempting it must go armed. Here are the products of American mines. This is iron, this is coal — the iron representing a vast yield, our country sending forth one year eight hundred thousand tons of it; the coal representing a hundred and sixty thousand square miles of it — the iron prying out the coal, the coal smelting the iron. This is silver, silver from Colorado and Nevada — those places able yet to yield silver napkin-rings, and silver knives, and silver castors, and silver platters for all our people. Here is mica from the quarries of New Hampshire. How beautiful it looks in the sunlight! Here is copper from Lake Superior, so heavy I dare not lift it. Here is gold from Virginia and Georgia. Here are apples, making you think of the long winter nights of your boyhood, when the neighbors came in, and you had apples and hickory nuts and cider. Here is corn from New Jersey. State of Theodore Frelinghuysen and William L. Dayton and Samuel L. Southard — the State of New Jersey, sometimes caricatured by people who are mad because they were not fortunate enough to have been born there! Here are lemons and oranges. Here are bananas from Florida. What a magnificent growth this is! What a leaf! implying shadow, comfort and refuge.

I look around me on this imaginary platform, and it seems as if the waves of agricultural, mineralogical, pomological wealth dash to the platform, and there are four beautiful beings that walk in, and they are all garlanded. And one is garlanded with wheat and blossoms of snow, and I find she is the North. And another comes in, and her brow is garlanded with rice and blossoms of magnolia, and I find she is the South. And another comes in, and I find she is gar-

The Mission of the Wheel

landed with seaweed and blossoms of spray, and I find she is the East. And another comes in, and I find she is garlanded with silk of corn and radiant with California gold, and I find she is the West. And coming face to face, they take off their garlands, and they twist them together into something that looks like a wreath, but it is a wheel, the wheel of national prosperity, and I say in an outburst of Thanksgiving joy for what God has done for the North and the South and the East and the West, " O wheel! "

At different times in Europe they have tried to get a Congress of kings at Berlin, or at Paris, or at St. Petersburg; but it has always been a failure. Only a few kings have come. But on this imaginary platform that I have built we have a convention of all the kings — King Corn, King Cotton, King Rice, King Wheat, King Oats, King Iron, King Coal, King Silver, King Gold, and they all bow before the King of Kings, to whom be all the glory of this year's wonderful production.

HEROES OF THE NAVY

James, 3: 4: " Behold also the ships."

HEROES OF THE NAVY*

James, 3: 4: " Behold also the ships."

IF this exclamation was appropriate about eighteen hundred and seventy-two years ago, when it was written concerning the crude fishing smacks that sailed Lake Galilee, how much more appropriate in an age which has launched from the dry docks for purposes of peace the *Oceanic* of the White Star Line, the *Lucania* of the Cunard Line, the *St. Louis* of the American Line, the *Kaiser Wilhelm der Grosse* of the North-German Lloyd Line, the *Augusta Victoria* of the Hamburg-American Line; and in an age, which, for purposes of war, has launched the screw-sloops like the *Idaho*, the *Shenandoah*, the *Ossipee*, and our ironclads like the *Kalamazoo*, the *Roanoke*, and the *Dunderberg*, and those which have already been buried in the deep like the *Monitor*, the *Housatonic*, and the *Weehawken*, the tempests ever since sounding a volley over their watery sepulchres, and the *Oregon* and the *Brooklyn*, and the *Texas*, and the *Olympia*, the *Iowa*, the *Massachusetts*, the *Indiana*, the *New York*, the *Marietta*, of the last war, and the scarred veterans of war shipping, like the *Constitution*, or the *Alliance*, or the *Constellation* that have swung into the naval yards to spend their last days, their decks now all silent of the feet that trod them, their rigging all silent of the hands that clung to them, their port-holes silent of the brazen throats

---

* Sermon for the Sabbath after Admiral Dewey and his men arrived in New York harbor, and the whole nation was stirred with patriotic emotion.

that once thundered out of them. If in the first century, when war vessels were dependent on the oars that paddled at the side of them for propulsion, my text was suggestive, with how much more emphasis and meaning and overwhelming reminiscence we can cry out, as we see the *Kearsarge* lay across the bows of the *Alabama* and sink it, teaching foreign nations they had better keep their hands off our American fight, or as we see the ram *Albemarle* of the Confederates running out and in the Roanoke, and up and down the coast, throwing everything into confusion as no other craft ever did, pursued by the *Miami*, the *Ceres*, the *Southfield*, the *Sassacus*, the *Mattabesett*, the *Whitehead*, the *Commodore Hull*, the *Louisiana*, the *Minnesota*, and other armed vessels, all trying in vain to catch her, until Captain Cushing, twenty-one years of age, and his men blew her up, himself and only one other escaping, and as I see the flag-ship *Hartford*, and the *Richmond*, and the *Monongahela*, with other gun-boats, sweep past the batteries of Port Hudson, and the Mississippi flows forever free to all Northern and Southern craft, and under the fire of Dewey and his men the Spanish ships at Manila burn or sink, and the fleet rushing out of Santiago harbor are demolished by our guns, and the brave Cervera surrenders, I cry out with a patriotic emotion that I cannot suppress if I would, and would not if I could, " Behold also the ships."

Full justice has been done to the men who at different times fought on the land, but not enough has been said of those who on ship's deck dared and suffered all things. Lord God of the rivers and the sea, help me in this sermon! So, ye admirals, commanders, captains, pilots, gunners, boatswains, sailmakers, surgeons, stokers, messmates and seamen of all names, to use your own parlance, we might as well get under way and stand out to sea. Let all land lubbers go ashore. Full speed now! Four bells!

Never since the sea fight of Lepanto, where three hundred royal galleys, manned by fifty thousand warriors, at sunrise, September 6th, 1571, met two hundred and fifty royal galleys, manned by one hundred and twenty thousand men, and in the four hours of battle eight thousand fell on one side, and twenty-five thousand on the other; yea, never since the day when at Actium, thirty-one years before Christ, Augustus with two hundred and sixty ships scattered the two hundred and twenty ships of Mark Antony and gained universal dominion as the prize; yea, since the day when at Salamis the twelve hundred galleys of the Persians, manned by five hundred thousand men, were crushed by Greeks with less than a third of that force; yea, never since the time of Noah, the first ship captain, has the world seen such a miraculous creation as that of the American navy in 1861.

There were about two hundred available seamen in all the naval stations and receiving ships, and here and there an old vessel. Yet orders were given to blockade thirty-five hundred miles of sea coast, greater than the whole coast of Europe, and beside that the Ohio, Tennessee, Cumberland, Mississippi, and other great rivers, covering an extent of two thousand more miles, were to be patrolled. No wonder the whole civilized world burst into guffaws of laughter at the seeming impossibility. But the work was done, done almost immediately, done thoroughly, and done with a speed and consummate skill that eclipsed all the history of naval architecture. What brilliant achievements are suggested by the mere mention of the names of the rear admirals! If all they did should be written, every one, I suppose that even the world itself could not contain the books that should be written. But these names have received the honors due. The most of them went to their graves under the cannonade of all the forts, navy yards, and men-of-war, the flags of all the shipping and capitals at half-mast.

I recite to-day the deeds of our naval heroes, many of whom have not yet received appropriate recognition. "Behold also the ships." As we will never know what our national prosperity is worth until we realize what it cost, I recall the unrecited fact that the men of the navy in all our wars ran especial risks. They had not only the human weaponry to contend with, but the tides, the fog, the storm. Not like other ships could they run into harbor at the approach of an equinox, or a cyclone, or a hurricane, because the harbors were hostile. A miscalculation of a tide might leave them on a bar, and a fog might overthrow all the plans of wisest commodore and admiral, and accident might leave them not on the land ready for an ambulance, but at the bottom of the sea, as when in our civil war the torpedo blew up the *Tecumseh* in Mobile Bay, and nearly all on board perished. They were at the mercy of the Atlantic and Pacific oceans, which have no mercy. Such tempests as wrecked the Spanish Armada might any day swoop upon the squadron. No hiding behind the earthworks. No digging in of cavalry spurs at the sound of retreat. Mightier than all the fortresses on all the coasts is the ocean when it bombards a flotilla.

In the cemeteries for Federal and Confederate dead are the bodies of most of those who fell on the land. But where those are who went down in the war vessels will not be known until the sea gives up its dead. The Jack tars knew that while loving arms might carry the men who fell on the land, and bury them with solemn liturgy, and the honors of war, for the bodies of those who dropped from the ratlines into the sea, or went down with all on board under the stroke of a gun-boat, there remained the shark and the whale and the endless tossing of the sea which cannot rest. Once a year, in the decoration of the graves, those who fell in the land were remembered; but how about the graves of those who went down at sea; Nothing but the archangel's trumpet shall reach their lowly bed. A few of them are gathered into naval cemeteries of the land, and we every year garland the sod that covers them; but who will put flowers on the fallen crew of the exploded *Westfield* and *Shawsheen*, and the sunken *Southfield*, and the *Winfield Scott?* Bullets threatening in front, bombs threatening from above, torpedoes threatening from beneath, and the ocean, with its reputation of six thousand years for shipwreck, lying all around, am I not right in saying it required a special courage for the navy in 1863 as it required especial courage in 1898?

It looks picturesque and beautiful to see a war vessel going out through the Narrows, sailors in new rig singing,

> A life on the ocean wave,
> A home on the rolling deep!

the colors gracefully dipping to passing ships, the decks immaculately clean, and the guns at Quarantine firing parting salute. But the poetry is all gone out of that ship as it comes out of that engagement, its decks red with human blood, wheel-house gone, the cabins a pile of shattered mirrors and destroyed furniture, steering-wheel broken, smoke-stack crushed, a hundred-pound Whitworth rifle shot having left its mark from port to starboard, the shrouds rent away, ladders splintered and decks ploughed up, and smoke-blackened and scalded corpses lying among those who

Sermons by T. DeWitt Talmage

are gasping their last gasp far away from home and kindred, whom they love as much as we love wife and parents and children.

Oh, men of the American navy returned from Manila, and Santiago, and Havana, as well as those who are survivors of the naval conflicts of 1863 and 1864, men of the Western Gulf squadron, of the Eastern Gulf squadron, of the South Atlantic squadron, of the North Atlantic squadron, of the Mississippi squadron, of the Pacific squadron, of the West India squadron, and of the Potomac flotilla, hear our thanks! Take the benediction of our churches. Accept the hospitalities of the nation. If we had our way, we would get you not only a pension, but a home, and a princely wardrobe and an equipage and a banquet while you live, and after your departure a catafalque and a mausoleum of sculptured marble, with a model of the ship in which you won the day. It is considered a gallant thing when in a naval fight the flag-ship with its blue ensign goes ahead up a river or into a bay, its admiral standing in the shrouds watching and giving orders. But I have to tell you, O veterans of the American navy! if you are as loyal to Christ as you were to the government, there is a flag-ship sailing ahead of you, of which Christ is the admiral, and he watches from the shrouds, and the heavens are the blue ensign, and he leads you toward the harbor, and all the broadsides of earth and hell cannot damage you, and ye whose garments were once red with your own blood shall have a robe washed and made white in the blood of the Lamb. Then strike eight bells! High noon in heaven!

While we are heartily greeting and banqueting the sailor-patriots just now returned, we must not forget the veterans of the navy now in marine hospitals, or spending their old days in their own or their children's homesteads. Oh, ye veterans! I charge you bear up under the aches and weaknesses that you still carry from the war times. You are not as stalwart as you would have been but for that nervous strain and for that terrific exposure. Let every ache and pain, instead of depressing, remind you of your fidelity. The sinking of the *Weehawken* off Morris Island, December 6th, 1863, was a mystery. She was not under fire. The sea was not rough. But Admiral Dahlgren, from the deck of the flag steamer *Philadelphia*, saw her gradually sinking, and finally she struck the ground; but the flag still floated above the wave in the sight of the shipping. It was afterward found that she sank from weakness through injuries in previous service. Her plates had been knocked loose in previous times. So you have in nerve, and muscle, and bone, and dimmed eyesight, and difficult hearing, and shortness of breath, many intimations that you are gradually going down. It is the service of many years ago that is telling on you. Be of good cheer. We owe you just as much as though your life blood had gurgled through the scuppers of the ship in the Red River expedition, or as though you had gone down with the *Melville* off Hatteras. Only keep your flag flying as did the illustrious *Weehawken*. Good cheer, my boys! The memory of man is poor, and all that talk about the country never forgetting those who fought for it is an untruth. It does forget. Witness how the veterans sometimes had to turn the hand organs on the street to get their families a living. Witness how ruthlessly some of them were turned out of office that some bloat of a politician might take their place. Witness the fact that there is not a man or woman now under forty-five years of age who has any full appreciation of the four years' martyrdom of 1861 to 1865, inclusive. But while men may forget,

God never forgets. He remembers the swinging hammock. He remembers the forecastle. He remembers the frozen ropes of that January tempest. He remembers the amputation without sufficient ether. He remembers the horrors of that deafening night when forts from both sides belched on you their fury, and the heavens glowed with ascending and descending missiles of death, and your ship quaked under the recoil of the one hundred pounder, while all the gunners, according to command, stood on tiptoe with mouth wide open, lest the concussion shatter hearing or brain. He remembers it all better than you remember it, and in some shape reward will be given. God is the best of all paymasters, and for those who do their whole duty to him and the world, the pension awarded is an everlasting heaven.

Sometimes off the coast of England the royal family have inspected the British navy, manoeuvred before them for that purpose. In the Baltic Sea the Czar and Czarina have reviewed the Russian navy. To bring before the American people the debt they owe to the navy, I go out with you on the Atlantic ocean, where there is plenty of room, and in imagination review the war shipping of our four great conflicts — 1776, 1812, 1865 and 1898. Swing into line all ye frigates, ironclads, fire-rafts, gun-boats and men-of-war! There they come, all sail set, and all furnaces in full blast, sheaves of crystal tossing from their cutting prows. That is the *Delaware*, an old revolutionary craft, commanded by Commodore Decatur. Yonder goes the *Constitution*, Commodore Hull commanding. There is the *Chesapeake*, commanded by Captain Lawrence, whose dying words were: " Don't give up the ship;" and the *Niagara*, of 1812, commanded by Commodore Perry, who wrote on the back of an old letter, resting on his navy cap: " We have met the enemy, and they are ours." Yonder is the flag-ship *Wabash*, Admiral Dupont commanding; yonder, the flag-ship *Minnesota*, Admiral Goldsborough commanding; yonder, the flag-ship *Philadelphia*, Admiral Dahlgren commanding; yonder, the flag-ship *San Jacinto*, Admiral Bailey commanding; yonder, the flag-ship *Black Hawk*, Admiral Porter commanding; yonder, the flag steamer *Benton*, Admiral Foote, commanding; yonder, the flag-ship *Hartford*, David G. Farragut commanding; yonder, the *Brooklyn*, Rear-Admiral Schley commanding; yonder, the *Olympia*, Admiral Dewey commanding; yonder, the *Oregon*, Capt. Clark commanding; yonder, the *Texas*, Capt. Phillip commanding; yonder, the *New York*, Rear-Admiral Sampson commanding; yonder, the *Iowa*, Capt. Robley D. Evans, commanding.

And now all the squadrons of all departments, from smallest tug-boat to mightiest man-of-war, are in procession, decks and rigging filled with men who on the sea fought for the old flag ever since we were a nation. Grandest fleet the world ever saw! Sail on before all ages! Run up all the colors! Ring all the bells! Yea, open all the port-holes! Unlimber the guns and load, and fire one great broadside that shall shake the continents in honor of peace and the eternity of the American Union! But I lift my hand, and the scene has vanished. Many of the ships have dropped under the crystal pavement of the deep, sea-monsters swimming in and out the forsaken cabin, and other old craft have swung into the navy yards, and many of the brave spirits who trod their decks are gone up to the Eternal Fortress, from whose casements and embrasures may we not hope they look down to-day with joy upon a nation in reunited brotherhood?

All those of you who were in naval service during

the war of 1865 are now in the afternoon or evening of life. With some of you it is two o'clock, three o'clock, four o'clock, six o'clock, and it will soon be sundown. If you were of age when the war broke out, you are now at least sixty. Many of you have passed into the seventies. While in our Cuban war there were more Christian commanders on sea and land than in any previous conflict, I would revive in your minds the fact that at least two great Admirals of the civil war were Christians, Foote and Farragut. Had the Christian religion been a cowardly thing they would have had nothing to do with it. In its faith they lived and died. In Brooklyn navy yard Admiral Foote held prayer-meetings and conducted a revival on the receiving ship *North Carolina,* and on Sabbaths, far out at sea, followed the chaplain with religious exhortation. In early life, aboard the sloop-of-war *Natchez,* impressed by the words of a Christian sailor, he gave his spare time for two weeks to the Bible, and at the end of that declared openly, " Henceforth, under all circumstances, I will act for God." His last words, while dying at the Astor House, New York, were: " I thank God for His goodness to me. He has been very good to me." When he entered heaven he did not have to run a blockade, for it was amid the cheers of a great welcome. The other Christian admiral will be honored on earth until the day when the fires from above shall lick up the waters from beneath, and there shall be no more sea.

> Oh, while old ocean's breast
> Bears a white sail,
> And God's soft stars to rest
> Guide through the gale,
> Men will him ne'er forget,
> Old heart of oak —
> Farragut, Farragut —
> Thunderbolt stroke!

According to his own statement, Farragut was very loose in his morals in early manhood, and practiced all kinds of sin. One day he was called into the cabin of his father, who was a ship master. His father said, " David, what are you going to be, anyhow?" He answered, " I am going to follow the sea." " Follow the sea," said the father, " and be kicked about the world and die in a foreign hospital?" " No," said David: " I am going to command like you." " No," said the father; " a boy of your habits will never command anything," and his father burst into tears and left the cabin. From that day David Farragut started on a new life.

Captain Pennington, an honored elder of my Brooklyn church, was with him in most of his battles and had his intimate friendship, and he confirmed what I had heard elsewhere, that Farragut was good and Christian. In every great crisis of life he asked and obtained the Divine direction. When in Mobile Bay the monitor *Tecumseh* sank from a torpedo, and the great warship *Brooklyn*, that was to lead the squadron, turned back, he said he was at a loss to know whether to advance or retreat, and he says, " I prayed, ' O God, who created man and gave him reason, direct me what to do. Shall I go on?' And a voice commanded me, ' Go on,' and I went on." Was there ever a more touching Christian letter than that which he wrote to his wife from his flag-ship *Hartford?* " My dearest wife, I write and leave this letter for you. I am going into Mobile Bay in the morning, if God is my leader, and I hope He is, and in Him I place my trust. If He thinks it is the proper place for me to die, I am ready to submit to His will in that as all other things. God bless and preserve you, my darling, and my dear boy, if anything should happen to me. May His blessings rest upon you and your dear mother."

Cheerful to the end, he said on board the *Tallapoosa* in the last voyage he ever took, "It would be well if I died now in harness." The sublime Episcopal service for the dead was never more appropriately rendered than over his casket, and well did all the forts of New York harbor thunder as his body was brought to the wharf, and well did the minute guns sound and the bells toll as in a procession having in its ranks the President of the United States and his cabinet, and the mighty men of land and sea, the old admiral was carried amid hundreds of thousands of uncovered heads on Broadway, and laid on his pillow of dust in beautiful Woodlawn, September 30th, amid the pomp of our autumnal forests.

But just as much am I stirred at the scene on warship's deck before Santiago last summer, when the victory gained for our American flag over Spanish oppression, the captain took off his hat, and all the sailors and soldiers did the same, and silently they offered thanks to Almighty God for what had been accomplished, and when on another ship the soldiers and sailors were cheering as a Spanish vessel sank, and its officers and crew were struggling in the waters, and the captain of our war-ship cried out, "Don't cheer! The poor fellows are drowning." Prayers on deck! Prayers in the forecastle! Prayers in the cabin! Prayers in the hammocks! Prayers on the look-out at midnight! The battles of that war opened with prayer, were pushed on with prayer, and closed with prayer, and to-day the American nation recalls them with prayer.

We hail with thanks the new generation of naval heroes, those of the year 1898. We are too near their marvelous deeds to fully appreciate them. A century from now poetry, and sculpture and painting and history will do them better justice than we can do them now. A defeat at Manila would have been an infinite disaster. Foreign nations not overfond of our American institutions would have joined the other side, and the war so many months past would have been raging still, and perhaps a hundred thousand graves would have opened to take down our slain soldiers and sailors. It took this country four years to get over the disaster at Bull Run at the opening of the civil war. How many years it would have required to recover from a defeat at Manila in the opening of the Spanish war I cannot say. God averted the calamity by giving triumph to our navy under Admiral Dewey, whose coming up through the Narrows of New York harbor day before yesterday was greeted by the nation whose welcoming cheers will not cease to resound until tomorrow; and next day in the Capitol of the nation the jeweled sword voted by Congress shall be presented amid booming cannonade, and embannered hosts, and our autumnal nights shall become a conflagration of splendor, but the tramp of these processions, and the flash of that sword, and the huzza of that greeting, and the roar of those guns, and the illumination of those nights will be seen and heard as long as a page of American history remains inviolate.

Especially let the country boys of America join in these greetings to the returned heroes of Manila. It is their work. The chief character in all the scene is the once country lad, George Dewey. Let the Vermonters come down, and find him older, but the same modest, unassuming, almost bashful person that they went to school with and with whom they sported on the playground. The honors of all the world cannot spoil him. A few weeks ago at a banquet in England, some of the titled noblemen were affronted because our American minister-plenipotentiary associated the name of Dewey with that of Lord Nelson. As well might we be affronted because the name of Nelson is associated with that of our most renowned admiral. The one name in all the coming ages will stand as high as the other. So this day, sympathizing with all the festivities and celebrations of the past week, and with all the festivities and celebrations to come this week, let us anew thank God and those heroes of the American navy who have done such great things for our beloved land. Come aboard the old ship Zion, ye sailors and soldiers, whether still in the active service or honorably discharged and at home, having resumed citizenship. And ye men of the past, your last battle on the seas fought, take from me, in God's name, salutation and good cheer. For the few remaining fights with sin and death and hell make ready. Strip your vessel for the fray; hang the sheet chains over the side. Send down the topgallant masts. Barricade the wheel. Rig in the flying jib-boom. Steer straight for the shining shore, and hear the shout of the great Commander of earth and heaven as he cries from the shrouds, "To him that overcometh will I give to eat of the tree of life which is in the midst of the Paradise of God." Hosanna! Hosanna!

MUST THE CHINESE GO

Luke, 10: 29: "Who is my neighbor."

MUST THE CHINESE GO?*

Luke, 10: 29: "Who is my neighbor."

A keen lawyer had Christ under the fire of cross-examination, and this was one of the questions. The answer which Christ gave, enlarged the world's idea of neighborhood, and that idea of neighborhood has ever since been enlarging. It seemed a figure of speech to say that people living on the other side of the world were our neighbors; but steam from Southampton to New York, and from China to San Francisco, and rail-tracks across all the continents, and cables under all the seas, have literally made the whole earth one neighborhood.

Is the Chinaman a neighbor? Does he belong to the race of which God is the Father? Is he a brute, or an immortal? Will he help us, or will he hurt us? Must he be welcomed, or driven back? These are tremendous questions which press upon the nation, and answer them we must, and answer them we will. The subject will yet be as much of an agitation on the Atlantic coast as it is on the Pacific coast. I wish that what I say on this subject might be received in silence, for though neither your approval nor disapproval would disturb me, it might disturb others.

I want you, to start right in your opinions, and therefore, I shall give you the result of one summer's observation in California, where the Chinese populations have become an important factor. Arriving in San Francisco Saturday afternoon, August 7th, I

---

* Delivered at the time this question was being fiercely discussed.

had been but a few moments in my hotel when the highest officers of the city called upon me in the interest of the anti-Chinese sentiment, and from morning until night, and for many days, I do not think there was half an hour in which I was not brought into the presence of this subject by committee, or letter, or document; so that if any man ever had a good opportunity of seeing the whole subject from both sides, I had that opportunity.

It is the habit to take people from the East to see the Chinese quarters, or what they call Chinatown. The newspapers say President Hayes once visited Chinatown, but that they covered up the worst parts of the place, that he might be deceived in regard to the true character of Chinatown. No such imposition was practiced upon me, for the five gentlemen with whom I went were openly and above-board always antagonistic to Chinese immigration, and it was their one desire to have me see the worst side of it.

Dr. Mears, a most obliging gentleman, the President of the Board of Health of San Francisco, went with me, and if there is a man on the continent antagonistic to Chinese immigration it is Dr. Mears. So I saw the worst, and it is bad enough and filthy enough and dreadful enough; but I tell you, as I told the people of San Francisco in their Grand Opera House, that underground New York life is fifty per cent. worse than Chinatown. The white iniquity of our Atlantic coast cities is more brazen than the yellow iniquity of San Francisco, and as to malodors, it is the difference between the malodors of whisky and the malodors of opium; and the malodors of whisky are to me a thousandfold more offensive than the malodors of opium. The crowded tenement-houses of New York are more crowded and more abominable than the crowded Chinese quarters.

Must the Chinese Go

I told the people of San Francisco, standing face to face, " If you will let your three hundred policemen be augmented by five hundred special policemen sworn in for the duty, men from your banking-houses and your churches — if they will go out in the name of God and the strength of the law, they will in one night extirpate the last iniquity of Chinatown." Do you tell me that two hundred and eighty thousand good San Franciscans cannot put down twenty thousand bad people?

From what I saw that summer in San Francisco, and from my observation in California in other years, I give it to you as my opinion, corroborated by the opinion of tens of thousands of people in California, that, of all the foreign populations which have come to the United States during the last forty years, none are more industrious, more sober, more harmless, more honest, more genial, more courteous, more oblig- ing than the Chinese. I have in my possession affi- davits from all classes of people in California, in which they present the truthfulness, the integrity, the love of order, the industry of the Chinese people. They have no equal as laundrymen; they are unrivalled as house help. I was told in many of the homes of San Francisco that one Chinese servant will do the work of three servants of any other kind.

It is objected to the Chinese that they underbid other labor, since they can live so much cheaper than other nationalities, and so they injure American labor and every other style of labor. I reply to that, in many departments the Chinese receive higher wages than any other class of persons. There are no such wages paid in Brooklyn or New York for domestic service as are paid to the Chinese in San Francisco to-day. Besides that, suppose they did underbid other labor, would you cast them out on that account?

Then, to be consistent, you must drive out all those who work sewing-machines and reapers and hay-rakes, because these different styles of machinery are under-bidding other styles of work, and injuring those who toil with the bare hand.

As to this absurd notion that is going through the country about the Chinese injuring American labor, I have to tell you this fact, that wages are higher in California, have been higher in California, than in any other State of the American Union. When we shall have in every great city, twenty or thirty or forty thousand Chinese workmen, wages will be larger than they are now, and we will have greater prosperity.

Again, it is objected to the Chinese that they do not spend all their money where they make it, but send it all back to China. False again. The Chinese pay in the city of San Francisco rent for residences and for wash-houses, and so on, yearly two million four hundred thousand dollars. Would not the people of any city think it was a grand addition to its municipal condition if it had two million four hundred thousand dollars added every year? Further, as taxes to the State government the Chinese in California pay over four million dollars a year. It all stays in California. Moreover, they pay in customs to the United States government annually nine million four hundred thousand dollars. That all stays in this country. Now, away with the falsehood that the Chinese spend none of their money in this country? Besides that, if they did send it all away, could you blame them much? How much money would you invest in a country where you were denied the rights of citizenship, and where you might any hour suffer outrage and expatriation?

The Chinese are blamed because they demand that after death their bones be sent home to China. If you and I were as badly treated as the Chinese have been treated in San Francisco, we would not want to be buried within three thousand miles of where the indignity had been enacted. We would argue, "If they treat us so badly while we have our arms to strike back, how will they treat us when we are powerless?" Besides that, it comes very poorly from us, the charge that the Chinese send home their money. There are hundreds and thousands of American and English merchants in China; where do they send their money to? Besides that, we have been applauding and complimenting for the last thirty years the German and Irish serving-maids who have been denying themselves all luxuries and sending their money back to the old folks at home. We have admired that self-denial and that generosity, and we have had no words to express our admiration for their willingness to send their money to Germany and Ireland; and I think what is good for one nation is good for another.

Besides that, O men of the Atlantic coast! do you know in what direction and for what purpose much of the money goes that is sent back to China? The parents of many of these Chinese in America are serfs, the subject of a base feudal system, and much of the money that is sent back to China is for the liberation of their parents. I have that from a mandarin high in authority. If your parents were in bondage, would not you send some money home to purchase their liberation? Would you not send all you have? Instead of caricaturing the Chinese for sending their money back to China, let us admire their self-denial — for they love luxuries as much as we do — let us applaud their self-denial.

But it is said they have such severe economies. Well, that is bad! That is a crime you cannot charge much upon the American people! The fact is, these people come in with a lower order of civilization, and they are industrious, and they pay all their debts and save something for a rainy day; and such a style of civilization we cannot abide in this country! We do not want our higher style of civilization interfered with — that style which allows a man to spend four times more money than he makes, and to steal the rest! Away with this barbarism, which works all the time and pays all its debts!

Again, it is objected that the Chinese are pagans, and that they have peculiar dress. What, now, do you refer to — the Chinese queue? George Washington wore a queue, Benjamin Franklin wore a queue, John Hancock wore a queue, your great-grandfathers wore queues; and anything that Washington and Franklin and John Hancock and your ancestry did must have been eminently respectable.

Besides that, Chinese apparel is often more than eclipsed by American apparel. Have you forgotten crinoline monstrosities of twenty years ago? the coal-scuttle bonnets of your grandmothers, the silver knee-buckles of your grandfathers, and how at different times in this country there has been an elaboration and an overtopping and appalling mystery of womanly head attire that ought to make us lenient in our criticism of Mongolian conspicuities?

We see in this (for their dress is a part of their religion) and in other things that a man's religious belief is not to be interfered with. Do you think the Huguenots and the Pilgrim Fathers and the patriots of the Revolution would have contended as they did for civil and religious liberty in this country, if they had known that their descendants would make religious belief a test of residence and citizenship? If this government continues to stand, it will be because alike defended are the joss-houses of the Chinese, the cathedrals of the Roman Catholics, the meeting-houses of the Quakers, and the churches of the Presbyterians.

Do you want me to make a choice between a religion which insults and stones a man because of the color of his skin or the length of his hair or the economy of his habits, on the one hand, and a paganism which patiently endures all this, working right on until death comes — if you want to have me make a choice between such a religion and such a paganism, I say, "Give me paganism." If you have a superior civilization, a superior Christianity, present them to these people in a courteous and Christian way. And this brings me to say that the first Sabbath forenoon I spent in a Chinese church in San Francisco, and I had the privilege, through an interpreter, of telling those Mongolians of that Christ who was not an American Christ, nor a Chinese Christ, nor a German Christ, nor an Italian Christ, nor a Spanish Christ, but the round world's Christ; and I think it was the greatest joy of the summer to me that I heard afterward that through the services salvation was brought to some of their souls. There they are to-day, renowned in heaven and little appreciated on earth, the Presbyterian mission under Dr. Loomis, the Methodist mission on Washington street, the Congregational mission near the park, the Episcopalian mission and other great charities, and while I stood in their Grand Opera House, face to face with the San Franciscans, I said: " The man that gives one penny for the support of these Christian missions does more for the settlement of the Chinese question than could be accomplished by ten thousand orators haranguing for ten thousand years about the evils of Chinatown."

These Chinese make grand Christians; and there are going to be more of them — five hundred millions of them — if the Bible be true when it says the land of Sinim is to surrender to God. Oh, how insignificant and contemptible will seem many of the Christians of this generation when in the future it shall be demonstrated that these Chinese were brought to our country, not so much by the stigmatized Six Emigration Companies, but by the God of the Bible, to have them Christianized, and multitudes of them sent home again for the redemption of China.

Now, my friends, these Chinese are either inferior, or they are our equals, or they are our superiors. If they are our inferiors, flat skulls will never dominate high foreheads; stupidity will never overcome large brain. If they are inferior, you have nothing to dread. If they are your equals, does not your sense of justice say then they ought to have equal rights? If they are our superiors, then we cannot afford to maltreat them. Who are these men? Some of them were descended from men who have forgotten more than we ever knew. Education is more widely spread in China than in America. You cannot find a Chinese who cannot read and write. You can find hundreds of thousands of Americans who, when they are compelled to put their names to a legal document, sign it, "his mark." This Chinese nation invented the art of printing, invented the mariner's compass, invented the manufacture of porcelain, invented paper-making, and other important things ages before any other nation could even guess them out. Five hundred years before Christ came, Confucius, a Chinaman, anticipated the Golden Rule, and when some one asked him to compress into one sentence a directory for human life, he answered, "Do not do to others what you would not have them to do you." I think the Chinese are God's favored nation from the fact that he has made

more of that nation than any other nation on earth —
a vast multitude of them.

China is the richest country in all the earth. Think
of the ruby, and the amethyst, and the porphyry, and
the agate, and the lapis lazuli, and the turquoise, and
the emerald, and the crystal — enough precious stones
to build the four walls of heaven! Think of the gold,
and the silver, and the iron, and the lead, and the copper waiting for the cellar-door of her mountains to
be thrown open! Think of the rosewood, and the
camphor, and the cedar, and the cypress, and the var-
nish trees, and the ebony, and the ivory — enough
to make the cabinet-ware of all nations. Think of the
wheat, and the barley, and the mango, and the pine-
apple, and the persimmon, and the cocoanut, and the
rice — enough to make puddings for all the earth,
and tea enough to refresh all nations!

Do you not understand that their right to come here
implies our right to go there? It will not be many
years before there will be as many Americans in China
as there are Chinese in America; and the question all
over China will be, "Must the Americans go?" If,
when a man had to ride in an emigrant-wagon six
months to cross the Pacific coast, many went, do you
not think New Yorkers and Long Islanders will go
to China when they can go there in five weeks, when
they are fully persuaded of all the treasures of that
great land? It is the will of Providence that the whole
world should be on wheels, and the nations are going
to move north, move south, move east, and move
west.

The nations will intermarry, and far down in the
future men will have the blood of fifty nationalities
in their arteries, and there will be in all the earth only
one great nation — one nation on five continents — a
grand homogeneous, great-hearted, all-climated, five-

zoned, world-encircling Christian nation. They broke
to pieces at the foot of Babel; they will come together
at the foot of the Cross. Under the shadow of the
one they were confounded; under the light of the other
they will be harmonized; and when all nations and
kingdoms and people become one empire, can you
doubt who will be king? "Hallelujah! for the Lord
God Omnipotent reigneth."

Again, it is objected that these Chinese are merely
the slaves of the six Chinese emigration companies —
that they are the slaves of the Sam Yup Company, the
Kong Chow Company, the Yung Wo Company, the
Wing Yung Company, the Hop Wo Company, the
Yan Wo Company. Now, say the political parties,
"We don't want any more slavery in this country; we
had black slavery, and got rid of it; now don't give us
any yellow slavery." But what are the facts? The
facts are these: That these six Chinese emigration
companies pay the fare of the Chinese crossing the
Pacific ocean, the Chinese contracting that they will
work it out after they get here, and there is no more
honorable bargain made in any American city than
that. These six Chinese companies say to the Chinese,
"You are poor; now here is clothing and here is
passage-money, and here is money to get food
crossing the ocean, and we will take charge of you a
little while after you get there, and you will, when you
get in America, by your own hands, toil to pay for
this passage-money." That is all there is of it.
Those Chinese are no more slaves in America than you
lawyers are the slaves of the clients that give you a
retaining fee; no more slaves than you builders are
the slaves of the capitalist who prepays you something
before you begin the job. The six Chinese companies
prepay the Chinese, and then the Chinese here work
it out, and the two planks of the two political parties

Must the Chinese Go

which imply the opposite are lying swindles on the American people. I tell you, men of the Atlantic coast, that this Chinese scare is the most unfounded, absurd, and unmitigated humbug that was ever enacted.

For twenty-five years, the Chinese have been coming to America and there are no more than two hundred thousand Chinese in America, whereas of other nationalities that have been coming there are millions, and millions and millions. All the Chinese immigration for the last twenty-five years, as compared with the immigration from other countries, is as a drop of rain on the summer sea; and if they increase no faster for the next hundred years than they have in the last twenty-five, the immigration will be completely insignificant as compared with those people who come from other nations. And, moreover, there are fewer Chinese in America to-day than last year — fewer now than two years ago, while the whole spirit of the Chinese government is against any people going away from their borders. What a pitiable thing it is that the two political parties in order to get the electoral vote of California in the Presidential election, should put these anti-Chinese planks in their platforms! I was not surprised at the Democratic party, because they always have considered the question of color and race a reasonable question; but when I saw the Republican party, after fighting a four years' horrible war to establish the principle that all colors and all races are equal before God and the law; when I remembered that five hundred thousand human lives had been paid as the purchase for the establishment of that principle, and then I saw the Republican party withholding from the yellow man what they had demanded for the black man, I was amazed beyond all expression, and I wondered if the sceptre was not departing.

Sermons by T. DeWitt Talmage

Now, what are the circumstances in the case? Nearly a century ago, in the year 1784, the first American flag was seen in Chinese waters. Ever since then we have been begging and coaxing the Chinese to come out and be neighborly. In 1844 the government of the United States practically said, " Oh, you dear Chinese, do come over and see us; come and bring your work with you; come and stay; come by hundreds and by thousands; do come."

In 1867 the government of the United States sent out Mr. Burlingame, a skillful ambassador, and the United States government said through him to the Chinese nation, " Oh, you dear Chinese, when will you come? We wait, we long, we expect; do come, do come." Mr. Burlingame presented the case in so genial a way that when he died the emperor deified him, and he is one of the gods of China to-day.

" Well," said the coy and shy Chinese, " will you treat us well if we come? " " Oh, yes," we said; " we will not only defend you, but we will welcome you; you can wear your hair as you please; you can worship the gods you please; only do come, and we'll be so happy! " Overpersuaded, and against all the prejudices of the Chinese nation, they came.

Well, how have the Chinese been treated in this country? Brickbatted and slain; taxed before they could get ashore, for the privilege of landing; taxed for street-sweeping, when not one dollar of the money raised went for the cleansing of the Chinese quarters; taxed for the United States government, which gave them no defense; the way from the steamboat wharf to their stopping place in the Chinese quarters one long scene of blasphemy and bloodshed, and no police. In other words, the United States government broke its treaty. Eight hundred thousand dollars by the Chi-

366

nese government cheerfully paid as indemnity for Americans that had been abused in China. The United States government refuses to pay for the wrongs done the Chinese in America. In the name of Almighty God, the Maker of nations, He who hath made of one blood all people, I impeach the United States government for its perfidy toward the Chinese.

Now, I do not want you to join in this crusade against the Chinese. There have been outrages already committed in New York. I understand some have been committed in Brooklyn. When you greet those from European nations who come through the Barge office, and pray for them all prosperity, use the same supplication for the children of Asia, who by the Central Pacific and Union Pacific railways are handed over the mountains. There is no Gospel in brickbats. No room in this land for violence. The meanest and most insignificant and leprous Chinese that ever lay in a hospital will live as long as God lives. That foreigner is immortal — immortal. And that nation is to be evangelized; whether her people are trans-Pacific or cis-Pacific, they are to be evangelized, and in the millennial glory side by side will stand Europe and Africa, America and Asia, and the Sierra Nevadas and the Himalayas will answer each other, with salvation echo and re-echo.

I rejoice to know that this whole question of Chinese immigration and every other style of immigration God is going to settle. Every little while in this country we get in great excitement, and fly around as though everything is going to pieces; but God never gets excited. What a time we had with the slavery question. For half a century the North proposed one thing and the South proposed another thing. Matters grew worse and worse. Then God rose up. He said, "Here is a question higher than human wisdom, and I will settle it;" and He settled it at Shiloh, at South Mountain, and Atlanta, and Gettysburg — settled it by the graves of a million Northern and Southern people. So, this Chinese question is complicate and tremendous. It is a question higher than your city halls, higher than the heathen goddess on the top of your Capitol at Washington, higher than your highest church steeples. It is a question so high that it is on a level with the throne of God, and the same great power that decides the tides of the Atlantic and Pacific oceans, swinging them this way or that, will decide these tides of human migration whichever way He will. If He says "Come," they will come. If He says "Go," they will go.

Do not in your nervousness try to build up a high, stout wall to keep the Chinese out while you let others in. Such a wall as that, God's earthquakes would shake from beneath, and God's thunderbolts of wrath would smite from above, and that wall would heave and rock and fall on the demagogues who built it, and on the nation who favors it, and on the Christianity that is too cowardly to denounce it. God will say, "That American temple I built for civil and religious liberty, and for a Gospel that would have all men saved; I founded that temple in the blood of the Revolutionary fathers. The arches of that temple went up on the shoulders of men who died for their principles; the baptismal fonts of that temple were filled with the tears of exiled nations who came here for refuge; the sword of your patriot ancestry was the trowel that mortared the foundation; and lo! on these sacred altars you have sacrificed the swine of passion and hate, and these columns have been defiled with unholy hands; now let the temple perish. Down it must come

— column and capital, arch and dome — and I will in some other land and among a more generous people, and in a brighter age of the world, demonstrate before earth and heaven how that I would have all men equal and free!"

TWO DECADES—1864 AND 1884

I Chron., 21: 27: "And the Lord commanded the angel; and he put up his sword again into the sheath thereof."

TWO DECADES—1864 AND 1884[*]

I Chron., 21: 27: " And the Lord commanded the angel; and he put up his sword again into the sheath thereof."

One day in Davidic times the people looked up and saw against the sky something which made the blood curdle and the cheek blanch and the breath stop — an angel of overtowering stature, and armed with a sword long and bright as summer lightning when it cleaves the sky from zenith to horizon. The broad blade with curved edge pointed toward doomed Jerusalem. The sheath hung dangling at the side of the great supernatural being, the sheath, of course, of such vast proportion as to have held the sword before it was brandished. As long as that uncovered sword was pointed toward Jerusalem havoc and massacre and bloodshed went on; but after a while, in answer to the prayers of the people and the sacrifices on the threshing-floor of Ornan, the angel drew back the sword with the right hand, and seizing the sheath with the left he inserted the sharp point into the mouth of the scabbard, and flung the sword down deep, until the haft of it struck the rim of the scabbard with resound that made the mountains about Jerusalem tremble. Then the havoc stopped, and the wounds healed, and the former glories of the city were eclipsed by the splendors subsequent. Hear you not the clang of sabre and scabbard as they come together in the words of my text? " And the Lord commanded the angel; and He put up His sword again into the sheath thereof."

---

[*] A sermon preached on Sunday before Decoration Day, 1884.

Sermons by T. DeWitt Talmage

Soldiers of the Grand Army of the Republic! And soldiers who fought on the other side! All one now in kindly brotherhood, whether you wore the color that suggested the gray of the morning sky or the blue of the full noon! And let no man who, by word or deed, tries to open the old wounds, ever offer, either in this world or the next, to take my hand! Hear me while I draw out the contrast betwen the time when the angel of war stood in the American sky, pointing his long, keen sword toward this, our beloved land, plunging the nation for four years in awful hemorrhage, and now, when, in answer to the prayers and sacrifices on ten thousand altars, that angel of war that stood above us hath hurled the bloody scimetar into the scabbard with a clang that made everything from the Canadas to the Gulf vibrate with gladness.

At this season of decoration of the soldiers' graves, both at the North and South, it is appropriate that I rouse your patriotism, and revive your reminiscence, and stir your gratitude by putting 1864 beside 1884. I shall make two circles around these two dates. Around 1864 I shall put a garland of red dahlias for the carnage. Around 1884 I shall put a garland of white lilies for the peace. The first date I shall crown with a chaplet of cypress. The second date I shall crown with a sheaf of wheat. The one date a dead march, and the other a wedding anthem. Twelve o'clock at night compared with twelve o'clock at noon.

Contrast, first of all, the feelings of sectional bitterness in 1864 with the feeling of sectional amity in 1884. At the first date the South had banished the national air, "The Star Spangled Banner," and the North had banished the popular air of "'Way Down South in Dixie." The Northern people were "mudsills," and the Southern people were "white trash." The more Southern people were killed in battle the better the North liked it. The more Northern people were killed in battle the better the South liked it. For four years the head of Abraham Lincoln or Jefferson Davis would have been worth a million dollars if delivered on the other side of the line. No need now, standing in our pulpits and platforms, of saying that the North and South did not hate each other. The hatred was as long and terrible as the sword in the hand of the angel of war, who, standing mid-heaven, gripped it, and pointing toward this nation, swung closer down till it gashed a grave trench clear through the quivering heart of the continent. To estimate how very dearly we loved each other, count up the bombshells that were hurled, and the carbines that were loaded, and the cavalry horses that were mounted. North and South facing each other, all armed in the attempt to kill.

The two sections not only marshaled all their earthly hostilities, but tried to reach up and get hold of the sword spoken of. in the text — the sword of heaven — and the prayer of Northern and Southern pulpits gave more information to the heavens about the best mode of settling this trouble than was ever used. For four years both sides tried to get hold of the Lord's thunderbolts, but could not quite reach them. At the breaking out of the war we had not for months heard of my dear uncle, Samuel K. Talmage, President of Oglethorpe University in Georgia. He was about the mildest man I ever knew, and as good as could be. The first we heard of him was his opening prayer in the Confederate Congress in Richmond, which was reported in the New York Herald, which prayer, if answered, would, to say the least, have left all his Northern relatives in very uncomfortable circumstances. The ministry at the North prayed one way, and the ministry at the South prayed another way. No use in hiding the fact that the North and South cursed each other with a withering and all-consuming curse.

Beside that antipathy of 1864 I place the complete accord of 1884. Meeting in New York to raise money to build a home at Richmond for crippled Confederate soldiers, the meeting presided over by a man who lost an arm and a leg in fighting on the Northern side, and, having the other leg, which was not lost, so hurt that it does not amount to much. Cotton exhibition two years ago at Atlanta attended by tens of thousands of Northern people and by General Sherman, who was greeted with kindness, as though they had never seen him before. United States government soon afterwards voting a million dollars toward a New Orleans exhibition, to be held next December, in which every Northern State will be represented. A thousand-fold kindlier feeling after the war than before the war.

No more use of gunpowder in this country, except for Fourth of July pyrotechnics or a shot at a roebuck in the Adirondacks. Brigadier generals in the Southern Confederacy making their fortunes as lawyers in our northern cities. Rivers of Georgia, Alabama, and North Carolina turning the mills of New England capitalists. The old lions of war — Forts Sumter, and Moultry, and Lafayette, and Pickens, and Hamilton — sound asleep on their iron paws, and instead of our raising money to keep enemies out of our harbor, raising money for the Bartholdi statue on Bedloe's Island, the figure of Liberty with uplifted torch to light the way of all who want to come in. Instead of 1864, when you could not cross the line between the contestants without fighting your way with keen steel, or going through by passes carefully scrutinized at every step by bayonets, you need only

Two Decades — 1864 and 1884

a railroad ticket from New York to Charleston or New Orleans to go clear through, and there is no use for any weapon sharper or stronger than a steel pen. Since the years of time began their roll, has there ever been in two decades such an overmastering antithesis as between 1864, of complete bitterness, and 1884, of complete sympathy? It is the difference between the archangel of war mid-sky with sword brandished, and the archangel of war mid-sky with sword scabbarded.

Contrast also the domestic life of 1864 with the domestic life of 1884. You were either leaving home or far away from it, communicating by uncertain letter. What a morning that was when you left home! Father and mother crying, sisters crying, you smiling outside, but crying inside. Everybody nervous and excited. Boys of the blue and gray! Whether you started from the banks of the Hudson, or the Androscoggin, or the Savannah, don't you remember the scenes at the front door, at the rail car window, or the steamboat landing? The huzza could not drown out the suppressed sadness. Do you not remember those charges to write home often, and take good care of yourself, and be good boys, and the good-bye kiss which they thought, and you thought might be forever?

Then the homesickness as you paced the river bank on a starlight night on picket duty, and the sly tears that you wiped off when you heard a group by a camp-fire singing the plantation song about the " Old Folks at Home." The dinner of hard-tack on Thanksgiving day, and the Christmas without any presents, and the long nights in the hospital, so different from the sickness when you were at home, with mother and sisters at the bedside, and the clock in the hall giving the exact moment for the medicine. And that forced march when your legs ached, and your head ached, and your wounds ached, and more than all, your heart ached — homesickness which had in it a suffocation and a pang worse than death. You never got hardened as did the guardsman in the Crimean war, who heartlessly wrote home to his mother: "I don't want to see any more crying letters come to the Crimea from you. Those I have received I put into my rifle, after loading it, and have fired them at the Russians, because you appear to have a strong dislike to them. If you had seen as many killed as I have, you would not have as many weak ideas as you now have." You never felt like that. When a soldier's knapsack was found after his death in our American war, there was generally a careful package containing a Bible, a few photographs, and letters from home.

On the other hand, tens of thousands of homes waiting for news. Parents saying: "Twenty-thousand killed! I wonder if our boy was among them?" Fainting dead away in post-offices and telegraph stations. Both the ears of God filled with the sobs and agonies of kindred waiting for news, or dropping under the announcement of bad news. Speak, swamps of Chickahominy, and midnight lagoons, and fire-rafts on the Mississippi, and gunboats before Vicksburg, and woods of Antietam, and tell to all the mountains, and valleys, and rivers, and lakes of North and South, the jeremiads of 1864 that have never been syllabled!

Beside that domestic perturbation and homesickness of twenty years ago put the sweet domesticity of 1884. Where do you come from to-night? From home. The only camp-fire you now sit at is at the one kindled in stove, or furnace, or hearth. Instead of a half ration of salt pork, a repast luxurious, because partaken of by loving family circle and in sacred confidences. Oh, now I see who those letters were for, the letters you, the young soldier, took so long in your tent to write, and that you were so particular to put in the mail without anyone seeing — iest you be teased by your comrades. God spared you to come back, and though the old people have gone, you have a home of your own construction, and you are here to-night, contrasting those awful absences and filial, and brotherly, and loverly heart-breaks with your present residence, which is the dearest place you will find this side of heaven ——the place where your children were born, and the place where you want to die. To write the figures 1864 I set up four crystals — crystals of tears; to write the figures 1884 I stand up four members of your household — figures of rosy cheeks and flaxen hair, if I can get them to stand still long enough.

Contrast also the religious opportunities of twenty years ago with now. Often on the march from Sunday morn till night, or commanded by officers who considered the names of God and Christ of no use except to swear by. Sometimes the drum-head the pulpit; and you standing in heat or cold; all the surroundings of military life having a tendency to make you reckless; no privacy for prayer or Bible reading; no sound of church bells; Sabbaths spent far away from the places where you were brought up. To-day the choice of sanctuaries; easy pew; all Christian surroundings; the air full of God, and Christ, and heaven, and doxology; three mountains lifting themselves into the holy light — Mount Sinai thundering its law, Mount Calvary pleading the sacrifice, Mount Pisgah displaying the promised land.

Contrast of national condition. 1864 — Spending money by the millions in devastation of property and life. 1884 — With finances so reconstructed that all the stock gamblers of Wall street have now failed to make a national panic.

1864 — The surgeons of the land setting broken bones, and amputating gangrened limbs, and studying gunshot fractures, and inventing easy ambulances for the wounded and dying. 1884 — Surgeons giving their attention to those in casualty of agriculture, or commerce, or mechanical life. The rushing of the ambulance through our streets not suggesting battle, but quick relief to some one fallen in peaceful industries.

1864 — Thirty-five million inhabitants in this land. 1884 — Fifty-five million.

1864 — Wheat about eighty million bushels. 1884 — The wheat about five hundred million bushels.

In 1864 — Cotton less than three million bales; in 1884 cotton more than seven million bales.

In 1864 — Pacific coast five weeks from the Atlantic; in 1884, for three reasons, Union Pacific, Southern Pacific, and Northern Pacific, only seven days across.

Look at the long line of churches, universities, asylums, and houses with which, during the last two decades, this land has been decorated. Oh, was not this a country worth fighting for? Do not the magnificent prosperities of 1884 compensate for the hardships of 1864? Soldiers! Praise God that He has spared you to see this day, and as you risked your bodies in battle give your souls in peace to God and your country.

Living soldiers of the North and South! Take new and especial ordination at this season of the year to garland the sepulchres of your fallen comrades. Nothing is too good for their memories. Turn all the private tombs and the national cemeteries into gardens.

Two Decades — 1864 and 1884

Ye dead of Malvern Hill, and Cold Harbor, and Murfreesboro, and Manassas Junction, and Cumberland Gap, and field hospital, receive these floral offerings of the living soldiery.

But they shall come back again, all the dead troops. We sometimes talk about earthly military reviews, such as took place in Paris in the time of Marshal Ney, and in London in the time of Wellington, and in our own land. But what tame things compared with the final review, when all the armies of the ages shall pass for divine and angelic inspection! St. John says the armies of heaven ride on white horses, and I do not know why many of the old cavalry horses of earthly battle that were wounded and worn out in the service may not have resurrection. It would be only fair that, raised up and ennobled, they should appear in the grand review of the Judgment Day. It would not take any more power to reconstruct their poor bodies than to reconstruct ours, and I should be very glad to see them among the white horses of apocalyptic vision.

Hark to the trumpet blast, the reveille of the last judgment! They come up, all the armies of all lands and all centuries, on whichever side they fought, whether for freedom or despotism, for the right or the wrong. They come! they come! Darius, and Cyrus, and Sennacherib, and Joshua, and David, leading forth the armies of scriptural times. Hannibal and Hamilcar leading forth the armies of the Carthaginians. Victor Emanuel and Garibaldi leading on the armies of the Italians. Tamerlane and Genghis Khan followed by the armies of Asia. Gustavus Adolphus and Ptolemy Philopater, and Xerxes, and Alexander, and Semiramis, and Washington leading battalion after battalion. The dead American armies of 1776 and 1812, and the one million of Northern and

Southern dead in our civil war. They come up. They pass on in review. The six million fallen in Napoleonic battles. The twelve million Germans fallen in the thirty years' war. The fifteen million fallen in the war under Sesostris. The twenty million fallen in wars of Justinian. The twenty-five million fallen in Jewish wars. The eighty million fallen in the crusades. The one hundred and eighty million fallen in Roman wars with Saracens and Turks. The thirty-five billion men estimated to have fallen in battle, enough, according to one statistician, if they stood four abreast, to reach clear around the earth four hundred and forty-two times.

But we shall have time to see them pass in review before the throne of judgment — the cavalrymen, the spearsmen, the artillerymen, the infantry, the sharpshooters, the gunners, the sappers, the miners, the archers, the skirmishers, men of all colors, of all epaulettes, of all standards, of all weaponry, of all countries. Let the earth be specially balanced to bear their tread. Forward! Forward! Let the orchestra of the heavenly galleries play the grand march, joined by all the fifers, drummers, and military bands that ever sounded victory or defeat at Eylau or Borodino, Marathon or Thermopylae, Bunker Hill or Yorktown, Solferino or Balaclava, Sedan or Gettysburg, from the time that Joshua halted astronomy above Gibeon and Ajalon till the last man surrendered to Garnet Wolseley at Tel-el-Kebir. Attention! companies, battalions, ages, centuries, and the universe. Forward in the grand review of the judgment! Forward!

Gracious and eternal God! On that day may it be found that we were all marching in the right regiment, and that we carried the right standard, and that we fought under the right commander; all heaven, some on amethystine battlement and others standing in shining gates, some on pearly shore and others in turreted heights, giving us the resounding million-voiced cheer: " To him that overcometh." And our Commander and King, having reviewed the troops, all nations of heaven and earth will salute Him as the One who, standing so long in the sky with the sword of conquest stretched toward the earth, hath at last put it back with a mighty thrust and echoing clang into the sheath of universal victory.

SETTLED IN HEAVEN

Psalms, 119: 89: " Forever, O Lord, thy word is settled in heaven."

SETTLED IN HEAVEN

Psalms, 119: 89: " Forever, O Lord, thy word is settled in
heaven."

This world has been in process of change ever since
it was created. Mountains born, mountains dying,
and they have both cradle and grave. Once this planet
was all fluid, and no being, such as you or I have ever
seen, could have lived on it a minute. Our hemisphere turns its face to the sun, and then turns its back.
The axis of the earth's revolution has shifted. The
earth's center of gravity is changed. Once flowers
grew in the Arctic and there was snow in the Tropic.
There has been a re-distribution of land and sea, the
land crumbling into the sea, the sea swallowing the
land. Ice and fire have fought for the possession of
this planet. The chemical composition of the air is
different now from what it once was. Volcanoes once
terribly alive are dead, not one throb of fiery pulse,
not one breath of vapor. The ocean changing its
amount of saline qualities. The internal fires of the
earth are gradually eating their way to the surface.
Upheaval and subsidence of vast realms of continent.

Moravians in Greenland have removed their boat
poles because the advancing sea submerged them.
Linnæus records that eighty-seven years before a
rock was one hundred feet nearer the water than
when he wrote. Forests have been buried by the sea,
and land that was cultured by farmer's hoe can be
touched only by sailor's anchor. Loch Nevis of Scotland, and Dingle Bay of Ireland, and the fjords of
Norway, where pleasure boats now float, were once
valleys and glens. Many of the islands of the sea are

the tops of sunken mountains. Six thousand miles of the Pacific Ocean are sinking. The diameter of the earth, according to scientific announcement, is one hundred and eighty-nine miles less than it was. The entire configuration of the earth is altered. Hills are denuded of their forests. The frosts and the waters and the air bombard the earth till it surrenders to the assault. The so-called "everlasting hills" do not last. Many railroad companies cease to build iron bridges because the iron has a life of its own, not a vegetable life or an animal life, but a metallic life, and when that life dies the bridge goes down. Oxidation of minerals is only another term for describing their death. Mosses and seaweeds help destroy the rocks they decorate.

The changes of the inanimate earth only symbolize the moral changes. Society ever becomes different for better or worse. Boundary lines between nations are settled until the next war unsettles them. Uncertainty strikes through laws and customs and legislation. The characteristic of this world is that nothing in it is settled. At a time when we hoped that the arbitration planned last summer at The Hague, Holland, would forever sheathe the sword and spike the gun and dismantle the fortress, the world has on hand two wars which are digging graves for the flower of English and American soldiery. From the presence of such geological and social and national and international unrest, we turn with thanksgiving and exultation to my text, and find that there are things forever settled, but in higher latitudes than we have ever trod. "Forever, O Lord, thy word is settled in heaven."

High up in the palace of the sun at least five things are settled — that nations which go continuously and persistently wrong, perish; that happiness is the result of spiritual condition and not of earthly environment; that this world is a schoolhouse for splendid or disgraceful graduation; that with or without us the world is to be made over into a scene of arborescence and purity; that all who are adjoined to the unparalleled One of Bethlehem and Nazareth and Golgotha will be the subjects of a supernal felicity without any taking off.

Do you doubt my first proposition, that nations which go wrong perish? We have in this American nation all the elements of permanence and destruction. We need not borrow from others any trowels for upbuilding or torches for demolition. Elements of ruin; Nihilism, infidelity, agnosticism, Sabbath desecration, inebriety, sensuality, extravagance, fraud. They are all here. Elements of safety: God-worshiping men and women by scores of millions, honesty, benevolence, truthfulness, self-sacrifice, industry, sobriety, and more religion than has characterized any nation that has ever existed. They are all here. The only question is as to which of the forces will gain dominancy. The one class ascendant, and this United States government, I think, will continue as long as the world exists. The other class ascendant, and the United States goes into such small pieces that other governments would hardly think them worth picking up.

Have you ever noticed the size of the Cemetery of Dead Nations, the vast Greenwood and Pere le Chaise, where mighty kingdoms were buried? Open the gate and walk through this cemetery and read the epitaphs. Here lies Carthage, born one hundred years before Rome, great commercial metropolis on the bay of Tunis, a part of an empire that gave the alphabet to the Greeks and their great language to the Hebrews; her arms the terror of nations, commanding at one time sixteen thousand miles of coast; her Hamilcar leading forth thirty myriads, or three hundred thousand troops; her Hannibal carrying out in manhood the oath he had taken in boyhood to preserve eternal enmity to Rome, leaving costly and imposing monuments at Agrigentum a ghastly heap of ruins. Carthage! Her colonies on every coast, her ships plowing every sea. Carthage! Where are her splendors now? All extinguished. Where are her swords? The last one broken. Where are her towers and long ranges of magnificent architecture? Buried under the sands of the Bagradas. As ballast of foreign ships much of her radiant marble has been carried away to build the walls of trans-Mediterranean cathedrals, while other blocks have been blasted in modern times by the makers of the Tunis railway. And all of that great and mighty city and kingdom that the tourist finds to-day is here and there a broken arch of what was once a fifty-mile aqueduct. Our talented and genial friend, Henry M. Field, in one of his matchless books of travel, labors hard to prove that the slight ruins of that city are really worth visiting. Carthage buried in the Cemetery of Dead Nations. Not one altar to the true God did she rear. Not one of the Ten Commandments but she conspicuously violated. Her doom was settled in heaven when it was decided far back in the eternities that the nation and kingdom that will not serve God shall perish.

Walk on in the Cemetery of Nations and see the long lines of tombs: Thebes and Tyre and Egypt and Babylon and Medo-Persian and Macedonian and Saxon heptarchy — great nations, small nations, nations that lived a year, and nations that lived five hundred years.

Our own nations will be judged by the same moral

Settled in Heaven

laws by which all other nations have been judged. The judgment day for individuals will probably come far on in the future. Judgment day for nations is every day. Every day weighed, every day approved, or every day condemned. Never before in the history of this country has the American nation been more surely in the balances than it is this minute. Do right and we go up. Do wrong and we go down. I am not so anxious to know what this statesman or that warrior thinks we had better do with Cuba and Porto Rico and the Philippines, as I am anxious to know what God thinks we had better do. The destiny of this nation will not be decided on yonder Capitoline hill or at Manila, or at the presidential ballot-box, for it will be settled in heaven.

Another thing decided in the same high place is that happiness is the result of spiritual condition and not of earthly environment. If we who may sometimes have a thousand dollars to invest find it such a perplexity to know what to do with it, and soon after find that we invested it where principal and interest have gone down through roguery or panic, what must be the worriment of those having millions to invest, and whose losses correspond in magnitude with their resources! People who have their three or four dollars a day wages are just as happy as those who have an income of five hundred thousand dollars a year. Sometimes happiness is seated on a footstool, and sometimes misery on the throne. All the gold of earth in one chunk cannot purchase five minutes of complete satisfaction. Worldly success is an atmosphere that breeds the maggots of envy and jealousy and hate. There are those who will never forgive you if you have more emoluments or honor or ease than they have. To take you down is the dominant wish of most of those who are not as high as you are.

They will spend hours and days and years to entrap you. They will hover around newspaper offices to get one mean line printed depreciating you. Your heaven is their hell.

A dying president of the United States said many years ago, in regard to his lifetime of experience, "It don't pay." The leading statesmen of America, in letters of advice, warn young men to keep out of politics. Many of the most successful have tried in vain to down their troubles in strong drink. On the other hand, there are millions of people who on departing this life will have nothing to leave but a good name and a life insurance, whose illumined faces are indices of illumined souls. They wish everybody well. When the fire-bell rings they do not go to the window at midnight to see if it is their store that is on fire, for they never owned a store; and when the September equinox is abroad they do not worry lest their ships founder in a gale, for they never owned a ship; and when the nominations are made for high political office they are not fearful that their name will be overlooked, for they never applied for office. There is so much heartiness and freedom from care in their laughter that when you hear it you are compelled to laugh in sympathy, although you know not what they are laughing about.

When the children of that family assemble in the sitting-room of the old homestead to hear the father's will read, they are not fearful of being cut off with a million and a half dollars, for the old man never owned anything more than the farm of seventy-five acres, which yielded only enough plainly to support the household. They have more happiness in one month than many have in a whole lifetime. Would to God I had the capacity to explain to you on how little a man can be happy, and on how much he may

Settled in Heaven

be wretched! Get your heart right, and all is right. Keep you heart wrong, and all is wrong. That is a principle settled in heaven.

Another thing decided in that high place is that this world is a schoolhouse or college for splendid or disgraceful graduation. We begin in the freshman class of good or evil, and then pass into the sophomore, and then into the junior, and then into the senior, and from that we graduate angels or devils. In many colleges there is an " elective course," where the student selects what he will study — mathematics, or the languages, or chemistry, or philosophy; and it is an elective course we all take in the schoolhouse or university of this world.

We may study sin until we are saturated with it, or righteousness until we are exemplifications of it. Graduate we all must, but we decide for ourselves the style of graduation. It is an elective course. We can study generosity until our every word and every act and every contribution of money or time will make the world better, or we may study meanness until our soul shall shrink up to a smallness unimaginable. We may, under God, educate ourselves into a self-control that nothing can anger, or into an irascibility that will ever and anon keep our face flushed with wrath and every nerve aquiver. Great old schoolhouse of a world, in which we are all being educated for glory or perdition!

Some have wondered why graduation day in college is called " commencement day," when it is the last day of college exercises, but graduation days are properly called commencement days. To all the graduates it is the commencement of active life, and our graduation day from earth will be to us commencement of our chief life, our larger life, our more tremendous life, our eternal life. But what a day commencement day on earth is! The student never sees any day like it — at any rate, I never did. Old Niblo's theatre in New York comes back to me. The gowned and tassel-hatted professors behind us, and our kindred and friends before us and above us, and the air redolent with garlands to be thrown us. What a commencement day it was for all of us about to graduate! But mightier day will it be when we graduate from this world. Will it be hisses of condemnation or handclapping of approval? Will there be flung to us nettles or wreaths? Will it be a resounding " Come," or a reverberating " Depart " ?

In the real college, before graduation and commencement comes examination day, and before our graduation and commencement will come examination. It will be asked what we have been doing, what we have learned under the tutelage of years of joy and sorrow, and under the teaching of the Holy Ghost are we educated for heaven. Have we done our best with the curriculum of study put before every mortal and immortal? Oh! this world is not the terminus of a journey. It is not a theatre on whose stage we are enacting the tragic or comic. It is a schoolhouse for splendid or disgraceful graduation, and death is commencement. All that is settled in heaven.

Another thing decided in the high places of the universe is that this world, with or without us, will be made over into a scene of aborescence and purity. Do not think that such a consummation depends upon our personal fidelity. It will be done anyhow. God's cause does not go a-begging. If all the soldiers of Jesus Christ now living should become deserters and go over to the enemy, that would not defeat the cause. A large part of the Bible is taken up with telling us what the world will be. There is a large army, human and angelic, now in the field, but God's reserve forces are more numerous and more mighty than those now at the front. And if he could in Gideon's time rout the Midianites with a crash of crockery, and if he could in Shamgar's time overcome a host with an ox-goad, and if in Samson's time he could defeat an army with a bleached jawbone, and if the walls of Jericho went down under a blast of perforated ram's horn, and if in Christ's day blind eyes were cured by ointment of spittle, then God can do anything he says he will do. As yet, he has taken only one sword, out of a whole army of weapons. Do not get nervous, as if the Lord were going to be defeated. The redemption of these hemispheres was settled in heaven, and Isaiah and Ezekiel and Habakkuk and Malachi and St. John only reported what the Lord God Almighty had decided upon. My only fear is that our regiment will not get into the fight to do something worthy of the Christ who redeemed us, and we be left in lazy encampment at Tampa, when we ought to have been at Santiago.

Oh, that coming day of the world's perfection! The earth will be so changed that the sermonology will be changed. There will be no more calls to repentance, for all will have repented. No more gathering of alms for the poor, for the poor will have been enriched. No hospital Sunday, for disjointed bones will have been set and the wounds all healed, and the incurable diseases of other times will have been overcome by a materia medica, and a pharmacy, and a dentistry, and a therapeutics that have conquered everything that afflicted nerve, or lung, or tooth, or eye, or limb. Healthology complete and universal. The poultice, and the ointment, and the panacea, and the catholicon, and the surgeon's knife, and the dentist's forceps, and the scientist's X-ray will have fulfilled their mission. The social life of the world will be perfected. In that millennial age, I imagine ourselves standing in front of a house lighted for levee. We enter among groups filled with gladness, and talking good sense, and rallying each other in pleasantries, and in every possible way forwarding good neighborhood. No looking askance; no whispered backbiting; no strut of pretension; no oblivion of some one's presence because you do not want to know him. Each one happy, determined on making some one else happy. Words of honest appreciation instead of hollow flattery. Suavities and genialities, instead of inflations and pomposities. Equipage and upholstery and sculpture and painting paid for. Two hours of mental and moral improvement. All the guests able to walk as steadily down the steps of that mansion as when they ascended them. No awakening the next morning with aching head and bloodshot eye, and incompetent for the day's duties. The social life as prefect as refinement and common sense, and culture, and prosperity, and religion can make it. The earth made better than it was at the start. And all through gospelizing influences, directly or indirectly.

I suppose the greatest tidal wave that ever rolled the seas was that which in 1868 was started by the Peruvian earthquake. At Arica, Peru, the wave was fifty feet high, and swung warships a mile forward on the land. At San Pedro, California, the wave was sixty feet high. It moved on to the Sandwich Islands and submerged some of them, and beat against the shores of New Zealand, and rolled up the beach of Japan, and stopped not until it had encircled the entire globe. Oh, what a wave! But the earthquake that shook the mountain where our Lord died started a higher and swifter and mightier tidal wave that will roll round and round the earth until all its rebellions and abominations have gone under.

Settled in Heaven

That was an exciting scene after the battle of Bos-
worth, which was fought between Richard III and
the Earl of Richmond, the King falling and the Earl
triumphing, when Lord Stanley brought the crown
and handed it to the Earl, seated on horseback, while
the dying and the dead of the battle were lying all
around. But it is a more thrilling spectacle as we
look forward through the centuries and see the last
armed and imperial iniquity of the world slain and
the crown of universal victory put upon the conqueror
on the white horse of the apocalypse, and all nations
"hail the power of Jesus' name." That the whole
earth will be redeemed is one of the things long ago
settled in heaven.

Another thing decided in that high place is that all
who are adjoined to the unparalleled One of Bethlehem and Nazareth and Golgotha will be the subjects
of a supernal felicity without any taking off. The old
adage says that "Beggars must not be choosers," and
the human race in its depleted state had better not be
critical of the mode by which God would empalace
all of us. I could easily think of a plan more complimentary to our fallen humanity than that which is
called the "plan of salvation." If God had allowed
us to do part of the work of recovery, and he to do the
rest; if we could do three-quarters of it and he do the
last quarter; if we could accomplish most of it and he
just put on the finishing touches, many could look
with more complacency upon the projected reinstate-
ment of the human family. No, no! We must have
our pride subjugated, our stubborn will made flexible
and a supernatural power demonstrated in us at every
step. A pretty plan of salvation that would be, of
human draughting and manufacturing! It would be
a doxology sung to ourselves. God must have all
the glory. Not one step of our heavenly throne made

by earthly carpentry. Not one string could we twist of the harp of our eternal rejoicing. Accept all as an unmerited donation from the skies, or we will never have it at all.

"Now," says some one, "if Christ is the only way what about the heathen, who had never heard of him?" But you are not heathen, and why divert us from the question of our personal salvation? Satan is always introducing something irrelevant. He wants to take it out of a personality into an abstraction. Get our own salvation settled, and then we will discuss the salvation of other people. "But," says some one, "what percentage of the human race will be saved?" What will be the comparative number saved and lost?" There Satan thrusts in the mathematics of redemption. He suggests that you find out the mathematical proportion of the redeemed. But be not deceived. I am now discussing the eternal welfare of only two persons, yourself and myself. Get ourselves right, before we bother ourselves about getting others right. O, Christ, come hither and master our case! Here are our sins — pardon them; our wounds — heal them; our burdens — lift them; our sorrows — comfort them. We want the Christ of Bartimeus to open our blind eyes, the Christ of Martha to help us in our domestic cares, the Christ of Olivet to help us to preach our sermons, the Christ of Lake Galilee to still our tempests, the Christ of Lazarus to raise our dead. Not too tired is He to come, though He has on His whipped shoulders so long carried the world's woe, and on His lacerated feet walked this way to accept our salutation.

By the bloody throes of the mountain on which Jesus died, and by the sepulchre where His mutilated body was enclosed in darkened crypt, and by the Olivet from which He arose, while astonished disciples clutched for His robes to detain Him in their com-

Settled in Heaven

panionship, and by the radiant and omnipotent throne on which He sits, waiting for the coming of all those whose redemption was settled in heaven, I implore you to bow your head in immediate and final submission. Once exercise sorrow for what you have done, and exercise trust in Him for what He is willing to do, and all is well for both worlds. Then you can swing out defiance to all opposition, human and diabolic. In conquering His foes he conquered yours. And have you noticed that passage in Colossians that represents Him " having despoiled principalities and powers, he made a show of them, openly triumphing," so bringing before us that overwhelming spectacle of a Roman triumph?

When Pompey landed at Brindisi, Italy, returned from his victories, he disbanded the brave men who had fought under him and sent them rejoicing to their homes, and entering Rome his emblazoned chariot was followed by princes in chains from kingdoms he had conquered, and flowers, such as only grew under those Italian skies, strewed the way, and he came under arches inscribed with the names of battlefields on which he had triumphed, and rode by columns which told of the fifteen hundred cities he had destroyed, and the twelve million people he had conquered or slain. Then the banquet was spread, and out of the chalices filled to the brim they drank to the health of the conqueror. Belisarius, the great soldier, returned from his military achievements, and was robed in purple, and in the procession were brought golden thrones and pillars of precious stones, and the furniture of royal feasts, and amid the splendors of kingdoms overcome he was hailed to the hippodrome by shouts such as had seldom rung through the capital. Then also came the convivialities. In the year 274 Aurelian made his entrance to Rome in triumphal car, in which he stood, while a winged figure of victory held a wreath above his head. Zenobia, captive queen of Palmyra, walked behind his chariot, her person encircled with fetters of gold, under the weight of which she nearly fainted, but still a captive. And there were in the procession two hundred lions and tigers and beasts of many lands, and sixteen hundred gladiators excused from the cruel amphitheatre that they might decorate the day, and Persian and Arabian and Ethiopian ambassadors were in the procession, and the long lines of captives — Egyptians, Syrians, Gauls, Goths, and Vandals.

It was to such scenes as that the New Testament refers when it speaks of Christ "having despoiled principalities and powers, he made a show of them, openly triumphing." But, Oh, the difference in those triumphs! The Roman triumph represented arrogance, cruelty, oppression, and wrong, but Christ's triumph meant emancipation and holiness and joy. The former was a procession of groans accompanied by a clank of chains, the other a procession of hosannas by millions set forever free. The only shackled ones of Christ's triumph will be Satan and his cohorts tied to our Lord's chariot wheel, with all the abominations of all the earth bound for an eternal captivity. Then will come a feast, in which the chalices will be filled "with the new wine of the kingdom." Under arches commemorative of all the battles in which the bannered armies of the church militant through thousands of years of struggle have at last won the day, Jesus will ride, Conqueror of earth and hell and heaven. Those armies, disbanded, will take palaces and thrones. "And they shall come from the East, and the West, and the North, and the South, and sit down in the kingdom of God," and may you and I, through the pardoning and sanctifying grace of Christ, be guests at that royal banquet!